Anderson Guide to

ENJOYING GREENWICH

Connecticut

An insider's favorite places

This guide is indispensable whether you are new to Greenwich or have lived here all your life. We turn to it as a constant resource.
—Katherine & Albert Kim

It has been said "you can never be too rich or too thin" and "you will never know all about Greenwich until you get the Anderson guide!" It's better than an Oprah read! You just can't put down! All kinds of must-know details. Pick up a few, great for gift giving! When customers come in looking for something that says "Greenwich" for their exchange student to take with them or take home, I steer them right over to the Anderson Guide! It's all Greenwich and more!
—Helen Odell
  Gift Shop, Greenwich Hospital

The Anderson Guide was a lifeline for us when we were new to Greenwich and first-time parents. It is an invaluable reference for everything from playgrounds to shopping to community organizations and restaurants. Now that we have lived here for years we still find the guide helpful as the needs and interests of our family change. Thank you for the updated editions, which provide a wonderful tool to help navigate through the ever-changing local retail and dining landscape. The perfect gift to welcome anyone to town!
—Sid and Susan Khanna

The Guide just keeps getting better and better. I keep all of the editions.
—Livvy Floren

When my family and I moved to Greenwich from Tokyo eight years ago, The Anderson Guide *was my "bible and dictionary" to settle into this town and has continued to be an asset and personal guide for me throughout the years as a mother of three children as well as a founder of a business here in town.* The Anderson Guide *is a "must have" resource for all.*
—Yumi M Kuwana
    Founding Partner, Cook Pine Capital

The Anderson Guide is a treasure trove of information about Greenwich. Solid Gold and five stars!!!!!! Hats off to Anderson Associates.
— Joan Roome

No household should be without one! As I read it, I am learning new things about our town. It is a great gift for new neighbors and friends.
— Betty Deming

The Guide just keeps getting better and better. I keep all of the editions.
- Livvy Floren

Your Guide is so informative, that within the first few minutes of perusing it, we came upon the perfect Christmas gift idea for our son.
— Lou & Barbara Hardvall

I am thrilled with the new edition of the Guide. It is the book I reach for instead of the telephone directory. I truly appreciate all of the effort that goes into it.
— Linda Taylor

Your restaurant reviews are accurate and we rely on them.
— Kathleen and Steven Gray

Your book is so helpful in every way. We have found all kinds of fun activities and trips in the children's section.
— Susan Schuller

Anderson Guide to
ENJOYING GREENWICH

Connecticut
An insider's favorite places

Eighth Edition

Anderson Associates
Greenwich Real Estate Specialists

with illustrations and maps
by Vanessa Y. Chow

Avocet Press

Anderson Guide to
Enjoying Greenwich, Connecticut
An insider's favorite places

Written by
Carolyn Anderson &
Anderson Associates, Ltd.
www.greenwichliving.com
164 Mason Street, Greenwich, CT 06830
203.629.4519

Illustrations and maps by Vanessa Y. Chow

Published by
Ickus Guides, Avocet Press Inc
19 Paul Court, Pearl River, NY 10965
www.avocetpress.com

Find updates at www.greenwichguide.com

ISBN 978-0-9677346-5-1

Cover Photo Credits:
Hamilton Avenue School, Kids Playing Cello – by Bob Luckey Jr., Greenwich Time
Charlie Zeeve, Maverick Football – by Christine Kraninger
Wedding Celebration, Terry Rogers, Philip Matthews – by Bob Capazzo
Kathy and John Augustin – by Philip Kuperberg

Printed in the United States of America

Anderson Guide to
ENJOYING GREENWICH

Connecticut

An insider's favorite places

WHAT KIND OF
GUIDE IS THIS?

The Guide is a list of our favorites...simply that. It is not a book of advertisements. No place mentioned in the Guide had any idea that it would be included. We never accept favors as a result of including someone. Establishments and programs are listed because we like them. Although the Guide is about Enjoying Greenwich, you will note many selections are outside of Greenwich's town limits. These easy-to-reach places complement our many in-town resources .

Initially, many years ago, our first Guide was prepared for our real estate clients. Then the calls came in—their friends needed a copy. The owner of a local book store saw it and said we must publish it. That is where it started. Our initial reason for writing it has not changed. We know finding favorite spots takes awhile. We have lived in Greenwich for many years and we hope the resources in the Guide will help everyone moving into town feel right at home.

The new edition has 238 restaurant reviews. Jerry and Carolyn anonymously visit each one at least twice before writing the review. We are looking at the whole experience—food, ambience and service. If the restaurant is disappointing in too many ways, we do not include it. Restaurant reviewing is a professional responsibility. We have a great deal to do with a restaurant's success or failure. We have extensive food and restaurant experience. Carolyn is the author of the Complete Book of Homemade Ice Cream and several other cookbooks. For a number of years we owned and operated a small vineyard. Tasting foods and wines and knowing how they are prepared is greatly helpful in reviewing. Carolyn is a professional member of the American Society of Interior Designers. Before devoting full time to real estate, she designed restaurants. Many people remember the popular restaurant, Morgan, open for many years in Greenwich, which she designed. Knowing the requirements of good restaurant design is helpful in reviewing. We love discovering new "finds." We hope our readers of the Guide will enjoy them, too.

We are grateful to so many residents for their support and enthusiastic appreciation of the Guide. We hope you will find this 8th edition useful, too! The Greenwich Library keeps copies at their information desk to help people with questions. The Historical Society has copies of our past editions in their archives. We are pleased to be documenting our town's many events, restaurants, shops and tips about the Greenwich way of life.

Please let us know what you think of this Guide or of the restaurants, stores or services we reviewed. We love your comments and suggestions! Please send your comments to Carolyn@GreenwichLiving.net or call Carolyn at 203.629.4519 x 118.

Sincerely,

Carolyn Jerry Amy

Carolyn and Jerry Anderson
Amy Zeeve
and all of us at Anderson Associates.

With a special thanks to Laura Davis and Philip Kuperberg for tireless editing.

Greenwich Guide Website

The Guide website, www.GreenwichGuide.com has the index of Restaurants and Stores together with mapping to out-of-town locations. We hope this will make it easier for Guide owners to find their favorite restaurant or store.

Because stores and restaurants change so frequently, we will post changes and new reviews on the Guide website.

Disclaimer

The purpose of this Guide is to educate and entertain. Every effort has been made to make this guide accurate; however, it should not be relied upon as the ultimate source of information about Greenwich or about any resource mentioned in the Guide.

There may be mistakes both typographical and in content. We have done our best to lead you to spots we hope you will like. This is by no means a complete guide to every resource in Greenwich. Unfortunately, even the best are not always perfect. If you have tried one of our favorites and are disappointed, if we have missed your favorite, or if we have made a mistake in a description, please let us know: fill out the feedback form in the back of the book and send it to us.

A note about "Hours"

The hours and days of operation are intended as a guide, but they should not be considered definitive. Establishments change their hours as business dictates. In addition, many change their hours for winter and summer and during holidays. Finally, just about every establishment takes a vacation.

CONTENTS

CONTENTS

CONTENTS

CONTENTS

CONTENTS

CONTENTS

CONTENTS

CONTENTS – TIPS

CONTENTS – TIPS

- Median age: 43 (2008)
- Median household income: $127,930
- Average residential sales price: $2.74 million
- Median residential sales price: $1.95 million
- Average condominium sales price: $929,000
- Assessed value of all residences: $28 billion
- Assessed value of all real estate: $34 billion
- Highest assessed value of a home: $25 million
- Population 2009: 61,937 (2000 census 61,101)
- Number of households: 22,848 (2000 census)
- 48 square miles
- 1,500 acres of public parks
- 31 miles of shoreline
- 150 miles of riding trails
- 37 houses of worship (34 churches, 3 synagogues)
- 9 yacht clubs, 8 country clubs and 1 tennis club
- 98 special interest organizations
- 11 garden clubs
- 38 languages spoken
- 17% of public school students come from non-English speaking homes
- 11 elementary schools, 3 middle schools, 1 high school 1 alternate HS
- Public School Budget $125 million (2009/10)
- Per pupil expenditure $17,728 (average class size 20)
- 91% of faculty have a masters degree or higher
- Surveys show Greenwich as one the top High Schools in the US
- 10 private schools
- Greenwich Library ranked #2 in New England
- Bruce Museum ranked in the top 5% of US Museums
- Rated safest community in Connecticut
- Town of Greenwich budget: $355,766,400 (2009)
- Town of Greenwich capital budget: $38,826,000 (2009)
- Town of Greenwich Mill Rate: 8.596 (2010, with septic)

Information based on data from the CERC Town Profile, Greenwich Multiple Listing Service, United Way and the Town's Budget presentation to the RTM. For more information on Greenwich check:
- Census bureau www.census.gov
- Town web site www.GreenwichCT.org
- Connecticut Economic Research Center www.cerc.com
- Community Answers www.greenwichlibrary.org/commanswers.htm
- Greenwich Chamber of Commerce www.greenwichchamber.com/greenwichave.asp

GREENWICH

rated best place to live

Time and again, Greenwich is rated as Connecticut's number one place to live. Greenwich is the premier town along what is called the Connecticut Gold Coast. The town's unique beauty has been preserved by very careful town planning and zoning. Like Beverly Hills, Greenwich has the rare distinction of being one of those recognizable names. But unlike Beverly Hills, which is a 5.7 square mile enclave, Greenwich extends over forty-eight square miles with rolling hills, woodlands, meadows and 31 miles of gorgeous shoreline bordering the Long Island Sound. Greenwich is not isolated—it is a real community and a wonderful place to raise a family.

Although Greenwich conjures up thoughts of stately country homes and waterfront estates reserved for the select few, Greenwich is much, much more. As you will discover, Greenwich offers diversity, not only in real estate and architecture, but also in residents. Greenwich is home not only to a cosmopolitan group of executives, but to a great variety of professionals, artists, writers, diplomats, actors, and sports figures.

In addition to being rated tops by Connecticut Magazine, Robb Reports rated Greenwich one of the 10-best places to live in the USA. Greenwich has a vast array of attractions. Whether you look at the picturesque shopping areas, the personal service provided by its mix of elegant shops, its fantastic library (the most used in Connecticut), its ultra modern hospital or its fifty fabulous restaurants, Greenwich has it all. The New York Times declared that Greenwich has more Very Good and Excellent restaurants per capita than any other community in Connecticut. One of the many unique things about Greenwich can be found on Greenwich Avenue every day between the hours of 8 am and 6:30 pm: the police officers at the street corners directing traffic. These officers help to preserve the feeling of a small town and, of course, also help keep the town's crime rate low.

GREENWICH

quality of life

Greenwich is still 25% green. It has 31 miles of coastline, with its main beaches at Greenwich Point (147 acres), Byram Beach and the two city-owned islands (Captain's Island & Island Beach). Greenwich has 8,000 acres of protected land, over 1,000 acres of town parks, 35 town tennis courts (not including the YWCA Courts), an indoor ice rink (open only to residents), 14 public marinas and a 158-acre, 18-hole golf course (open only to residents). Music lovers enjoy the Greenwich Symphony, while the Bruce Museum appeals to everyone and is rated one of the best museums in Connecticut. *See PARKS and CULTURE for more information.*

education

Greenwich public schools (eleven elementary, three middle and one high school) are rated number two in Connecticut (behind West Hartford): 40% of the graduates go to the "Most Competitive Colleges." The school budget is approximately 125 million dollars. The average class size is 20 and 91% of the teachers have masters degrees. In addition, Greenwich has thirty independent pre-schools and nine excellent private and parochial day schools. *For details, see section SCHOOLS.*

TIP: LEAF BLOWER RULES

A blower can be operated weekdays, 8 am - 6 pm; weekends & holidays, 9 am - 3 pm.

GREENWICH

fire department

15 Havemeyer Place
Non-emergency phone: 203.622.3950, To report a fire dial 911
www.GreenwichCT.org/FireDept/FireDept.asp
The Greenwich Fire Department is a combination fire department that consists of uniformed career firefighters and professional volunteer fire fighters who work together to preserve life and protect property in Greenwich.

Our fire department responds to over 4,000 emergency calls per year, ranging from minor fire alarm activations to structure fires, motor vehicle accidents, and even hazardous materials incidents. Equipment consists of 14 Engine Companies, 3 Ladder Companies, and 2 Rescue Companies. The Fire Department operates this equipment out of 8 fire houses within Greenwich (and Banksville, New York) with the help of nearly 100 uniformed career firefighters, and over 150 well-trained and dedicated volunteers. *See NUMBERS YOU SHOULD KNOW for a complete list of fire stations and their telephone numbers.*

police department

11 Bruce Place
Non-emergency phone: 203.622.8000, emergency number: 911
www.GreenwichCT.org/PoliceDept/PoliceDept.asp

The Greenwich Police Department is a group of helpful, kind and competent professionals. They are charged with the protection of life and property, the preservation of public peace, the prevention and detection of crime, the apprehension of offenders and the enforcement of state and local laws and ordinances, as well as the countless calls for service that the Police Department handles on a daily basis. In a typical year they respond to over 40,000 calls. The department offers a ten-week Citizen Police Academy program, allowing residents the opportunity to get a behind the scenes look at police operations.
www.GreenwichCT.org/PoliceDept/pdCitizensPoliceAcademy.asp

GREENWICH

crime

Greenwich is rated the safest community in Connecticut and one of the safest in the country—and it's no wonder: with 14 police cars on the road at all times, traffic downtown directed by police officers, and with a force of 156 dedicated police officers, the average response time to a call is less than 4 minutes.

library — Greenwich

www.greenwichlibrary.org

The Greenwich Library is a special treasure used by young and old alike. In a typical year the library loans 675,000 customers an average of 4.5 books per minute. It is no wonder the library has been rated the best in the country. The library received a $25,000,000 bequest from Clementine Peterson. Based on this bequest and funds raised by the Friends of Greenwich Library, Architect Cesar Pelli designed the 31,000 square foot addition as well as renovations to the original building. In addition to the Main Branch, the library has marvelous branches in Cos Cob and Byram. Old Greenwich has its own superb independent library, Perrot. *For more information on our wonderful libraries see LIBRARIES AND BOOKS.*

hospital

5 Perryridge Road, 203.863.3000

www.greenhosp.org

The 160-bed Greenwich hospital is an affiliate of Yale University School of Medicine. It is a world-class hospital, providing the town with excellent health care. Patients from all over Fairfield and Westchester seek treatment at Greenwich Hospital. The hospital has a state of the art cancer center (Bendheim) as well as a $129,000,000 expansion to make it a high tech diagnostic and healing center without the austere look, normal delays and "red tape" often associated with hospitals. With the $98,000,000 expansion, "The Watson Pavillion", Greenwich residents have a completely new hospital with the best of services and amenities. *For more information on the Hospital and other medical services, see HEALTH.*

GREENWICH

town information

Greenwich Town Hall
101 Field Point Road, 622.7700
Call this number for any town department or go to www.greenwichct.org
See GOVERNMENT for a complete list of departments, their hours of
operation and meeting rooms.
Post Offices and Zip Codes are listed under their own heading.

location

Greenwich is in the southwest corner of Connecticut, providing residents
with the convenience of being close to a big city, while living in the
comfort and security of the country. Greenwich has an excellent transportation system and is just minutes from Westchester Airport, which makes
trips to nearby cities such as Boston or Washington convenient. Greenwich is only 29 miles from Times Square (43 minutes by one of the 78
trains that operate daily between New York City and Greenwich). There
are 4 train stations conveniently located throughout the town. U.S. Route
1, the historic Post Road, is the main commercial artery. Locally, it is
named Putnam Avenue. In addition, Interstate 95 and the Merritt Parkway traverse Greenwich, giving it excellent regional accessibility. It takes
about 10 minutes to drive to Stamford, about 60 minutes to Danbury and
approximately 15 minutes to White Plains. Limousines provide easy and
quick access to New York City's international airports: La Guardia Airport is about a 45-minute drive, Kennedy Airport is about a 60-minute
drive. The Merritt Parkway, built in 1935 for cars only, was placed on the
National Register of Historic Places in 1993. *For more information, see
TRAVEL and AUTOMOBILES.*

TIP: TOWN PERMITS AND PASSES

Permits and passes for many Greenwich activities can be
applied for on the Town's website:
www.GreenwichCT.org/ParksAndRec/ParksAndRec.asp
www.GreenwichCT.org/Parking/Parking.asp

GREENWICH

population

The population of Greenwich grew until about 1970. Since 1970, the resident population has been more or less stable. This has been accompanied by the construction or conversion of more dwellings to house the same number of people. In 1950, the population of 40,835 lived in 10,524 households, with an average of 3.9 persons in each. In 1990, the population of 58,441 persons lived in 23,515 households, with an average of 2.5 persons. In 2000 the population was 61,101. Presently the population is 61,937 living in 22,848 households with an average of 2.7 persons. Two-thirds of Greenwich homes are for single families, mostly detached, one to a lot. The town's residential zones provide a wide variety of housing types, from small condominiums to single family homes of more than 10,000 square feet on 4 acres or more. Greenwich is divided into several strictly enforced zoning areas. In or near town, the density is high as a result of condominiums and apartments. Further from the center of town, the zoning changes to 1 acre per family, then to 2 acres per family and north of the Merritt Parkway it is a minimum of 4 acres per family. The population of the town continues to be diverse. One sixth of all public school students, with 38 different first languages, are learning English as a second language.

jobs and income

Greenwich is a job center where 35,278 people are employed. More people now come to work in Greenwich than go to work elsewhere. As a result of the many offices moving to the suburbs, Greenwich has become a net provider of jobs during the past twenty-five years. At the same time the median household income in Greenwich has been growing steadily. In 1979 it was $30,278. Ten years later, in 1989, it was $65,072. Today it is over $127,000.

taxes

The Town of Greenwich operates on a "pay as you go" basis and does not carry long term debt (except for sewer bonds). This allows Greenwich to keep property taxes low while maintaining a budget of over $355,000,000. Real estate taxes are based on assessments limited by statute to 70% of market value, at present 8.596 (up from 7.449 in 1998) per thousand of assessed value (mill rate). There are no separate school taxes. There are no separate County taxes. There is a personal property tax on cars equal to the mill rate. There is no town income tax. The state has an income tax of 5%.

trends

Greenwich is in the largest metropolitan area of the United States, and is fortunate in its location, natural features, and historic development. Within the New York metropolitan area, Greenwich is the most desirable place to live. The migration of business and jobs from New York City to White Plains, Greenwich and Stamford has increased the demand for housing here. Greenwich intends to keep its place as the premier town to live in. To maintain control of its future, Greenwich has developed a Plan of Conservation and Development. This plan, filled with maps and information on the town, is very influential in preserving the town's goals. It can be purchased from the Planning & Zoning Commission at Town Hall, 203.622.7700. Greenwich has a Geographic Information System (GIS) which allows the town and residents to access information such as property boundaries, assessments and building lines. The GIS map request form is online at www.GreenwichCT.org/GRAllFormsList.asp

TIP: MAKING YOUR VOICE HEARD IN GREENWICH

If you feel strongly about an issue in Town which you feel is not being addressed, gather 20 signatures of Greenwich registered voters and deliver it with your petition to the Town Clerk's office in Town Hall. Your petition will be put on the RTM's next call. Be sure to carefully define in your petition what action you want and to bring a few articulate, concise speakers to support your cause. When you deliver the petition, it would be best to tell the Town Clerk who wants to speak. You might also want to make a presentation to the members of your district before the RTM meets. District meetings are open to everyone. You can find your district members at
www.GreenwichCT.org/RTM/RTM.asp

GREENWICH

government

www.GreenwichCT.org

Unlike many towns and cities, there is a great feeling of community here. Greenwich is run primarily by volunteers, not politicians. The town is governed by a Board of Selectmen (one full-time and two part-time) who are elected every two years. Although town departments are staffed by paid professionals, except for the Selectmen, all town boards (such as the Board of Estimate and Taxation, which serves as the town's comptroller) and the Representative Town Meeting, are made up of unpaid citizen volunteers. In addition to the volunteers in government offices, Greenwich depends on many residents who serve in unofficial capacities. The volunteer network supports and supplements the work of town departments and gives the town its unparalleled cultural and social values. *See GOVERNMENT for details.*

representative town meeting

www.GreenwichCT.org/RTM

Greenwich still retains the traditional New England Representative Town Meeting (RTM). The RTM consists of 230 members selected by the voters in the town's 12 districts. It is larger than the State's House and Senate combined. Candidates run on a non-partisan basis and serve without compensation. As a result, the composition of the RTM is very egalitarian.

The RTM serves as the town's legislative body and most issues of importance, including appointments, labor contracts, town expenditures over $5,000, town ordinances and the town budget, must be approved by the RTM. Any town issue may be brought before the RTM by a petition of twenty registered voters. Because many of the RTM members are quite successful in business and other careers, the town is run efficiently, honestly, conservatively and in the interest of its citizens. RTM meetings are held at night about once every month. RTM meetings are open to everyone and are a good source of information about the town.

The League of Women Voters (203.352.4700) is very active and is a great way to get involved in the electoral process. They publish an informative guide on Greenwich Government, "People Make it Happen."

GREENWICH

history

Greenwich is the tenth-oldest town in Connecticut. Named after Greenwich, England, the town began as a temporary trading post founded by Captain Adrian Block in 1614. Greenwich was settled in 1640 when it was purchased from the Native Americans as part of the New Haven Colony, with allegiance to England. The settlers grew restless under the Puritan influence and, in 1642, withdrew their allegiance to England and transferred it to the more liberal Dutch. At this time, the Cos Cob section of Greenwich was occupied by the Siwanoy Indians and a toll gate was set up between them and the central part of Greenwich, called Horseneck. In 4 years the town was forced back under the domination of the New Haven Colony. Greenwich supported the British during the French and Indian War, but during the Revolution the town was sacked several times by the King's troops. The advent of the New Haven Railroad in 1848 began the transformation of Greenwich into a residential community. This period saw many wealthy New Yorkers, including Boss Tweed, building summer homes. In the twenties, the town began to grow rapidly and land values began to soar. By 1928, Greenwich led the nation in per capita wealth. In 1933 the town had grown so large that it had to abandon open town meetings and adopted the Representative Town Meeting (RTM). Although the population growth has abated (because of the scarcity of buildable land) the property values have continued to climb.

TIP: CONCOURS OF ELEGANCE

To exhibit a concours quality car, call Bruce and Genia Wennerstrom, 203.618.0460 (Cochairs)
www.GreenwichConcours.com
The Concours takes place in the Roger Sherman Baldwin Park the weekend after Memorial Day. This exciting event for all ages features an exhibit of outstanding motorcars from the last decade of the nineteenth-century through the late 1970's. Car lovers in Greenwich have enjoyed this event for over 10 years. It is one of the most prestigious Concours events in the country, attracting over 10,000 spectators. Hours: 10 am - 5 pm.

GREENWICH

areas and villages

Greenwich is made up of a number of small villages and neighborhoods, each with its own character and charm. The largest of these are Byram, Banksville, Back Country, Central, Cos Cob, Mianus, Old Greenwich, Glenville, and Riverside. All parts of Greenwich share the same government, school system, property tax rate and access to public facilities.

main streets

The central street connecting the main part of Greenwich with the Riverside, Cos Cob, and Old Greenwich sections is Putnam Avenue (a.k.a. Post Road, US 1). It runs essentially east to west through the town (of course out-of-town maps show US-1 running North/South from Stamford to Port Chester). Greenwich Avenue, the main shopping street, is the dividing line between East and West Putnam Avenue. Sound Beach Avenue on the eastern end of Putnam Avenue is the main shopping street for Old Greenwich and runs to Greenwich Point Beach (Tod's Point).

TIP: GREENWICH PUBLIC DOCUMENTS

http://greenwichct.virtualtownhall.net/public_documents
This is where you find the "Call" (Agenda) for the Representative Town Meeting and many other fascinating town documents and calendars.

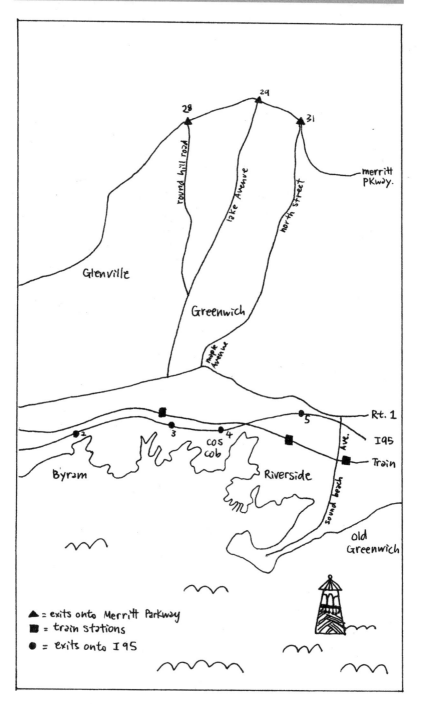

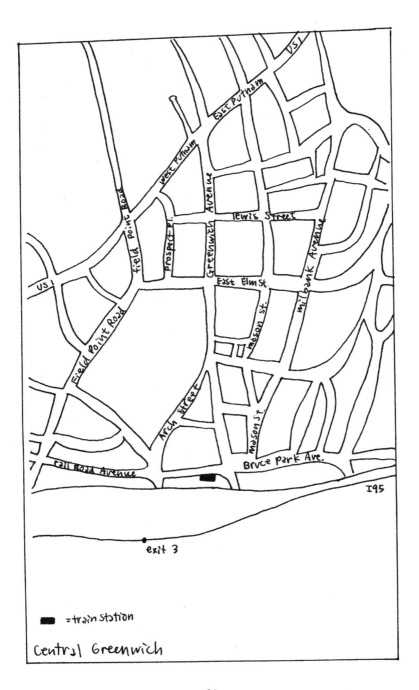

ORGANIZATIONS PRESERVING GREENWICH HISTORY

Children of the American Revolution
Mary Bush Society, Putnam Cottage, 243 East Putnam Avenue
Contact: Lauren Bacon, President, 203.637.6789

Daughters of the American Revolution
Putnam Hill Chapter, 243 East Putnam Avenue, 203.869.9697
www.ctdar.org/Chapters/Putnam_Hill.htm

Historic District Commission
www.GreenwichCT.org/HistoricDistComm/HistoricDistComm.asp

Historical Society of the Town of Greenwich
39 Strickland Road, Cos Cob, 203.869.6899
www.HSTG.org
Debra Mecky, Executive Director

TIP: PUTNAM'S RIDE RE-ENACTED
In February, the Putnam Hill Chapter of the DAR re-enacts General Putnam's 1779 ride. Men are in official revolutionary attire, with muskets and conduct Revolutionary War drills and skirmishes. General Putnam's ride is featured on the seal of the Town. What better way to learn history. The location is Putnam Cottage, 243 East Putnam Avenue. For details call 203.869.9697 or visit www.PutnamCottage.org

AUTOMOBILES

general car information

AAA / CT Motor Club

623 Newfield Avenue, Stamford CT, 203.765.4222
www.aaa.com
The place to get your international driver's license or other help for a trip.
Hours: Weekdays 8:30 am - 5:30 pm, Saturday 8:30 am - Noon.

Commuting Information

Local commuters can untangle their morning commutes by consulting News
12 on Cable or by the following commuter transportation websites:
MetroPool: www.metropool.com
The site offers news and information on commuting in and around Fairfield
and Westchester counties.
Greenwich Traffic Cams: www.ct.gov/dot (click on traffic cams)
Commuters can search for car pool partners on www.nuride.com
For Parking Permits at the Greenwich Station see
http://www.greenwichct.org/Parking/psParkingPermits.asp

Police Directing Traffic

We still have the privilege of having police direct traffic on Greenwich
Avenue. They are always helpful and friendly. When you can't find
something, they are a great source of information. However, be warned,
pedestrians and drivers alike are expected to pay attention. Follow their
crossing instructions or face humiliation. Street crossings are allowed only
when traffic is stopped in all directions.

Performance Outfitters (Custom Alarm Radio Sunroof)

20 Crescent Street, Stamford CT, 203.637.5584, 203.975.1188
If you are envious of your friends' GPS, Satellite Radio, back-up camera and
sensors, you don't have to trade in your car. Instead, take it to Ray Garst
who has been upgrading cars since 1988.
Hours: Weekdays 8:30 am - 4:30 pm.

AUTOMOBILES

automobile dealers

Acura
343 West Putnam Ave
203.625.8200

Aston Martin
273 West Putnam Ave
203.629.4726

Audi
181 West Putnam Ave
203.661.1800

BMW
355 West Putnam Ave
203.413.1900

Bugatti (Miller Motor Cars)
342 West Putnam Ave
203.629.3890

Cadillac
144 Railroad Ave, 203.625.6300

Chevrolet-Hummer
261 Elm Street, New Canaan CT
203.920.4770

Ferrari (Miller Motor Cars)
342 West Putnam Ave
 203.629.3890

Ford- Lincoln-Mercury
212 Magee Ave, Stamford CT
877.705.5417

Honda
289 Mason Street, 203.622.0600

Infiniti
217 West Putnam Ave
203.869.0255

Jeep-Chrysler-Dodge
631 West Putnam Ave
203.531.0505

Lexus
19 Railroad Ave
800.969.5398 or 203.869.6700

Maserati (Miller Motor Cars)
342 West Putnam Ave
203.629.3890

Mercedes-Benz
261 West Putnam Ave
203.869.2850

Nissan
225 Post Road, Port Chester NY
914.937.1777

Porsche
241 West Putnam Ave
203.869.8900

Rolls Royce-Bentley
275 West Putnam Ave
203.661.4430

Saab
144 Railroad Ave
203.227.7287

Subaru
198 Baxter Ave, Stamford CT
203.252.2222

Toyota
75 East Putnam Ave
203.661.5055

Volkswagen
200 West Putnam Ave
203.869.4600

Volvo
107 Myrtle Ave, Stamford, CT
203.359.2632

AUTOMOBILES
bus rentals

Fjord Bus & Yacht Rentals
143 River Rd, Cos Cob, 203.622.4020 www.fjordcatering.com

J&R Tours
Mount Vernon NY, 800.444.5786, www.Buses.com

car rentals

Enterprise Rent a Car
15 Edgewood Ave
(Just off West Putnam Avenue, next to McDonalds)
203.622.1611, www.Enterprise.com
They often have the lowest rates, but charge for mileage.
Hours: Weekdays, 7:30 am - 6 pm; Saturday, 9 am - noon.

Hertz Rent a Car
www.Hertz.com
- 465 West Main Street, Stamford, CT
  203.406.0203
Hours: Weekdays, 7:30 am - 6 pm; Saturday, 9 am - noon;
- 11 Hillside Avenue, Port Chester, NY
  203.622.4044
Hours: Weekdays, 7:30 am - 6 pm; Saturday, 9 am - 1 pm

AUTOMOBILES

truck rentals

Budget Truck Rentals
195 Greenwich Avenue at Greenwich Hardware, 203.661.5548
www.BudgetTruck.com
Hours: Monday - Saturday, 8 am- 5 pm; Sunday, 9 am - 4 pm.

City Truck Rentals (Penske)
860 Canal Street, Stamford, 203.359.2181, 800.467.3675
www.GoPenske.com
When you need a large, well maintained truck, call them first.
Hours: weekdays, 7 am - 6 pm; Saturday, 7 am - 4 pm;
Sunday, 7:30 am - 4:30 pm.

U Haul
25 Jefferson Street, Stamford, 203.324.3869
www.UHaul.com
U Haul rents everything from a van to a large truck. They also have a large stock of boxes and other moving supplies. Their vans are well kept and are great for local moves. Their best trucks are saved for long distance runs, so for local runs you might be better using a truck from Budget. Don't expect customer service to be a high priority.

car detailing

Classic Shine Auto Fitness Center
67 Church Street, 203.629.8077
www.ClassicShine.com
This car detailing firm does not often advertise, but has been in business for many, many years. They operate primarily on the strength of recommendations.
Hours: Monday - Saturday by appointment.

AUTOMOBILES

car wash

Old Greenwich Car Wash and Lube
1429 East Putnam Avenue, Old Greenwich, 203.698.9531
When you are in a hurry and just want a quick $5 wash (at the Mobil station).

Splash Car Wash
- 73 Post Road, Cos Cob, 203.625.0809
- 625 West Putnam Avenue, Byram, 203.531.4497
www.SplashCarWashes.com
Both locations do hand washes and interior cleaning. The Byram location also has an express (machine) lane. Mark Curtis and Chris Fisher, both lifelong Greenwich residents, developed the concept of washing cars on a conveyor by hand. In 1994, they opened their first hand wash in Greenwich and called it Splash. Now with 15 locations, they wash more than 1,000,000 cars a year. They know that good car care means good business.
Hours: Monday - Saturday, 8 am - 6 pm; Friday, until 7 pm; Sunday, 9 am - 5 pm.

TIP: ONLY GEESE HONK IN GREENWICH
Residents know that Greenwich is a place to relax, unwind and enjoy life. Yes, we still need to get to places on time, but we drive with consideration. Honking–except in dangerous situations–is taboo. If someone is honking inappropriately, it is probably a car with an out-of-town license plate. We like to say "in Greenwich only the geese honk."

AUTOMOBILES

drivers licence & car registration

International Drivers's License

AA /CT Motor Club, 623 Newfield Avenue, Stamford CT, 203.765.4222

www.AAA.com

Hours: Weekdays 8:30 am - 5:30 pm, Saturday 8:30 am - Noon.

Department of Motor Vehicles Bureau

540 Main Avenue (Route 7), Norwalk, CT,

800.842.8222, 860.263.5700

www.CT.gov/DMV

New residents must obtain a Connecticut driver's license within sixty days, even if they hold a valid license from another state. Vehicles must also be registered within sixty days after the owner has established residency. The car must pass an inspection before being registered.

Hours: Tuesday, Wednesday & Friday, 8 am - 4 pm (Thursday, until 6:30 pm, Saturday, until 12:30 pm); Closed Sunday, Monday and holidays.

Directions: I 95 N to exit 15, Rte 7 N; follow Rte 7 expressway to end, R and straight into the DMV.

Driver's License Renewals

Licenses can be renewed at the DMV in Norwalk.

driving instruction

Tom's Driving School

1212 East Putnam Avenue, Riverside, 203.869.7240

www.TomsAutoDrivingSchool.com

The drivers education program chosen by most teenagers. Car and motorcycle instruction.

Hours: Monday - Thursday, 9 am to 7 pm,

Friday & Saturday 9 am - 1 pm.

AUTOMOBILES
parking

www.GreenwichCT.org/Parking/Parking.asp

Parking Meters

Parking meters in Greenwich are not expensive, but parking tickets are. Parking meters are a must Monday - Saturday, 9 am - 5 pm. Meters are being converted from coins to credit card payment booths. In the meantime, meters only accept quarters. On Sundays and holidays, parking is free. Old Greenwich is still free of parking meters. The following Town web site www.GreenwichCT.org/Parking/psMunicipalParkingLots.asp gives parking details including a map of municipal parking lots and how to pay your ticket on-line.

Parking Permits

*   Train Station Parking

    Call 203.622.7730, for details about train station parking permits and the location of municipal lots, or go to:
    www.GreenwichCT.org/Parking/psParkingPermits.asp

*   Senior Center Parking

    Call the Senior Center, 203.862.6720, for parking permits in front of the Center.

TIP: PARKING TICKETS

Parking tickets cost between $25 and $90. But, if by chance you get a parking ticket, you can pay by phone 1-800-956-1263, request a hearing or pay online at the Town's website:
www.GreenwichCT.org/Parking/psParkingTickets.asp

AUTOMOBILES

vehicle emission inspection

Car Inspections
888.828.8399
www.ctemissions.com
Cars must be inspected every two years. The following local stations are certified. These stations do inspections on a first-come, first-serve basis.

Mobile Lube Express
1429 East Putnam Avenue, Old Greenwich, 203.698.9531
Hours: weekdays, 8 am - 5 pm; Saturday, until 1 pm.
Gas is available 24 hours.

Shell of Greenwich
83 East Putnam Avenue, 203.661.8871
Hours: weekdays, 8 am - 5 pm; Saturday until 1 pm. Call 800.842.8222 for directions and times.

Soundview Service Center
35 Arcadia Road, Old Greenwich, 203.637.2033
www.SoundviewService.com
Hours: weekdays, 8 am - 5 pm; Saturday until 1 pm.

TIP: RENTING A BUS
Have you ever wanted to take a large group on a trip, but wondered how? Our own, local Fjord has the answer. They have luxury motor coaches for charter at competitive rates. Call 800.925.2622 for prices.
www.FjordCatering.com/Bus_Charters.php
Another choice is J&R Tours in Mount Vernon, NY, 800.444.5786, www.Buses.com

BOOKS and LIBRARIES
book sales & donations

Book Exchange
At the Greenwich Recycling Center, Holly Hill Lane, 203.622.0550
This is fun you cannot miss. Residents drop off unwanted books. A volunteer librarian organizes the books by topic and author. Free books are available on all subjects. Just follow the rules: keep the shelves neat, 10 books per family, enjoy your reading!
Donation hours: weekdays, 7 am - noon.
Exchange open: weekdays, 7:30 am - 3 pm, Saturday, 7 am - noon.

Byram Shubert Book Sale
The Friends of the Byram Schubert Library conduct a not-to-be-missed sale twice a year. Last year over 200 people donated books, CDs, DVDs, and artwork. Proceeds help support the expansion and programs of the library. For more information or to schedule a pickup of your donation, call Lisa Johnson, Sale Chair, 203.570.8527 or the Library at 203.531.0426.

Darien Book Aid Plan
1926 Post Road, 203.655.2777
http://DBA.Darien.org
This worthy group has been sorting and shipping donated books to countries around the world since 1949. They are particularly interested in children's story books, books in braille, grammar texts, teenage literature and books on medicine, agriculture and gardening. They are open for donations 24-hours a day. Check the website for the types of books they are seeking. Workshop hours: Tuesday, 2 - 4 pm, Wednesday & Thursday 9:30 - noon.

Ferguson Library Used Books
Corner of Broad & Bedford Streets, Stamford CT, 203.964.1000
www.FergusonLibrary.org
We discovered this source for used books over a cup of Starbucks Coffee (Starbucks is next door). The library receives books and book collections from a wide area. They receive so many that there is a whole department devoted to selling used books.

Smith College Book Sale

Waveny House, South Avenue, New Canaan, CT, 203.966.0502
For sale or donation information:
203.323.8990, 203.655.8553, 203.323.0017
E-Mail smithdonations@yahoo.com

This annual event (now in its 48th year) is sponsored by the Smith College Club of Darien/New Canaan, benefits the Smith College Scholarship Fund and has more than 80,000 well-priced, quality used books including cookbooks, art histories and bound sets to decorate your home. Just a visit to Waveny House is worth the trip. Dealers descend early on the first morning, grabbing books which they later resell at a substantial profit. It's fun to arrive early with them, but be prepared for pushy, overzealous types. The first day there is an admission charge. On the last day books are free. Don't forget to bring a big book bag.
Look for it at the beginning of April.
Directions: Merritt Parkway N to exit 37, Left on South Avenue.

TIP: GREENWICH LIBRARY ORAL HISTORY

If you want to learn about the town, from the first hand experiences of residents, you will love the oral history series available in the Library. Volunteers have compiled 700 interviews into 131 books. Books are also for sale at the Oral History office. www.GLOHistory.org

BOOKS and LIBRARIES

book stores

Barnes & Noble (Books)
Stamford Town Center, 100 Greyrock Place & Tresser Blvd
203.323.1248
www.BN.com
B&N has 798 stores, this 40,000 sf. store is the largest in Connecticut. It also sells magazines, newspapers, DVDs, CDs, graphic novels, gifts, games, and music. Barnes & Noble began to publish books during the 1980s by re-issuing out-of-print titles.
Hours: Monday - Saturday 9 am - 10 pm (Friday & Saturday to 11 pm); Sunday 9 am - 9 pm.

Borders Books
1041 High Ridge Road, Stamford CT, 203.968.9700
www.Borders.com
With 517 stores, Borders is the second largest book retailer in the US. Sometimes it just feels good to be surrounded by thousands of books. Even when we stop by for one book, we seem to always leave with several. This mega-bookstore has a nice coffee shop with good treats.
Hours: Monday - Thursday 9 am - 9 pm,
Friday & Saturday 9 am - 11 pm, Sunday 10 am - 8 pm.

Diane's Books
8A Grigg Street, 203.869.1515
www.DianesBooks.com
A family-owned independent book store specializing in family books for all ages. You will find a huge selection, including a wealth of children's books, an excellent travel book section and, best of all, a knowledgeable, resourceful sales staff. This is a must-visit bookstore.
Hours: Monday - Saturday 9 am - 5 pm.

Carol Davenport (Antiquarian Bookseller)
5 Oval Avenue, Riverside, 203.637.4160
www.DavenportBooks.com
E-mail: info@davenportbooks.com
She emphasizes modern first editions, art & photography, signed books, and scarce non-fiction titles. She issues catalogs in her areas of specialty. She offers bibliographic services, including appraisals, and collection development services for individuals and institutions.

BOOKS and LIBRARIES

book stores

Gift Shop at Christ Church
254 East Putnam Avenue, 203.869.9030
This is the "in" place to go when you need a special gift with meaning. Marijane Marks and her helpful staff have a fine selection of books, gifts, jewelry and greeting cards. During holidays, gifts cascade out of the shop, making the store a joy to visit.
Hours: Tuesday - Saturday 10 am - 5 pm; Sunday 10 am - 1 pm.

Just Books
28 Arcadia Road, Old Greenwich, 637.0707
www.justbooks.org
Just Books, owned by Marion Holmes, is a haven for the sophisticated reader or someone looking for personal service. Just Books hosts many events to meet important authors, poetry readings, book signings and story hours for children. Check their website for upcoming events and interesting book reviews which will keep you up-to-date with the literary world. Be sure to frequent this charming, locally-owned, independent bookstore. They have something for everyone.
Hours: Monday - Saturday, 9 am - 5 pm; Sunday noon - 4 pm.

TIP: DOWNLOAD BOOKS FROM THE GREENWICH LIBRARY
The Library provides downloadable audio books to Library card holders. To download a book, go to http://Overdrive.GreenwichLibrary.org. You will need to install the free media software and have your Library card number handy.

BOOKS and LIBRARIES

libraries

Armstrong Court Library

Family Center and Books for Kids Foundation joint venture.

Book Clubs

The Libraries often sponsor book clubs, such as the Brown Bag Book Club which meets on the third Wednesday of each month at the Cos Cob Library. All are welcome. Bring your own lunch and have a good time. For information on the Brown Bag Book Club, call 203.622.6883.

Greenwich Library Card Guidelines

Library cards are free to Greenwich residents and are valid for 3 years. Greenwich Residents must show a photo ID with a current Greenwich address or 2 items that include your name and current Greenwich address.

Greenwich Library

www.greenwichlibrary.org

The Greenwich Library is a special treasure used by young and old alike. In a typical year the Library loans 675,000 customers an average of 4.5 books per minute. It is no wonder the library has been rated the best in the country. The library received a $25,000,000 bequest from Clementine Peterson. Based on this bequest and funds raised by the Friends of Greenwich Library, Architect Cesar Pelli designed the 31,000 square-foot addition as well as renovations to the original building. The Byram Shubert branch is beautifully renovated and doubled in size. We have a wonderful new Cos Cob Library. These branches provide convenient neighborhood locations and serve as community centers. The library provides a large number of programs which are noted in other sections of this guide. Use the website to check a book's availability or phone 203.622.7910 to reserve items, and ask to have your reserved materials sent to one of the branches. Membership in the Library is free. There is no limit to the number of books you can check out. In addition to books, the library has over 30 data bases which can be used free of charge. If you use your library number, most can be accessed from you home computer.

BOOKS and LIBRARIES

libraries

- **Greenwich Library (Main Library)**
  101 West Putnam Avenue, 203.622.7900
  Hours: weekdays, 9 am - 9 pm (June & August 5 pm);
  Saturday, 9 am - 5 pm; Sunday, 1 pm 5 pm (September - June).

- **Byram Shubert Library (Branch)**
  21 Mead Avenue, Byram, 203.531.0426
  Hours: Monday, Wednesday & Friday 9 am - 5 pm,
  Tuesday 10 am - 6 pm, Thursday noon - 8 pm, Closed Sunday.
  The recent renovation doubled the Library's space to 10,000 sq. ft.

- **Cos Cob Library (Branch)**
  5 Sinawoy Road, Cos Cob, 203.622.6883
  Cos Cob is a new library, perfect for family enjoyment. While the young-est ones enjoy playing or reading in the children's corner, older ones can read favorite books or search the Internet. The dynamic staff organizes events for both children and adults. It is an important part of Cos Cob community life.
  Hours: Monday Noon - 8 pm, Tuesday - Saturday 9 am - 5 pm,
  Thursday until 6 pm; Closed Sunday.

Perrot Library of Old Greenwich (Independent Library)
90 Sound Beach Avenue, 203.637.1066
Children's Library, 203.637.8802
www.errotlibrary.org
The Perrot Memorial Library is a non-profit institution independent of the Greenwich Library. It is open to all residents of Greenwich, although it principally serves the residents of Old Greenwich, Riverside and North Mianus. Perrot has a new, beautiful $3.3 million, 7,000 square foot Children's Library.
Hours: Monday, Wednesday, Friday, 9 am - 6 pm; Tuesday & Thursday, 9 am - 8 pm; Saturday, 9 am - 5 pm; Sunday, 1 pm - 5 pm (closed Sundays in the Summer).

BOOKS and LIBRARIES

literary organizations

American Pen Women (Greenwich Branch)
www.PenWomen.org
Greenwich Pen Women is a non-profit organization of professional artists, writers, and composers.

Friends of Byram Schubert Library
A volunteer organization founded in 1953 to support the Byram Shubert Library. They sponsor cultural programs and events for children and adults. With a $25 membership, a large tote bag is available as a thank you, and with a $10 membership, a smaller kids bag. To join please see the staff at the library or e-mail byramshubertlibraryfriends@gmail.com

Friends of Cos Cob Library
CosCobFriends@GreenwichLibrary.org
A volunteer organization founded in 1972 to support the Cos Cob library. They sponsor cultural programs, art shows, and special events for children and adults.

Friends of Greenwich Library
The Library is maintained by the Town but all capital improvements are funded by contributions from the Friends. Joining is inexpensive. If you join at the level of $40 you receive a Friends Book Bag, a very "in" bag to be carrying around Greenwich. In addition you will receive the Keep Posted newsletter with book reviews and program events. A great way to be a part of the Town.

Literary Matters
16 Highmeadow Road, Old Greenwich
www.LiteraryMatters.net
Esther Bushell recommends great books to read and holds events to meet the author. Her recommendations and insights are great. Be sure to subscribe to her email newsletter.

CHARITABLE & SERVICE ORGANIZATIONS

AmeriCares
88 Hamilton Avenue, Stamford CT 203.658.9500
www.Americares.org

American Legion (Greenwich)
Greenwich Post 29
248 Glenville Road, 203.531.0109
www.Legion.org
Emile Smeriglio, Commander

Greenwich Jaycees
PO Box 232, Greenwich 06836
www.GreenwichJaycees.org

Greenwich Kiwanis Club
PO Box 183, Greenwich CT 06836
www.GreenwichKiwanis.org

Greenwich Women's Civic Club
PO Box 26, Greenwich 06836
Jackie Cannon, President, 203.353.9100

Greenwich World Hunger
PO Box 7444, Greenwich, CT 06836
www.GreenwichWorldHunger.com
Sarah Boyle, President, 203.661.9771

Junior League of Greenwich
231 East Putnam Avenue, 203.869.1979
www.jlgreenwich.org
All women living or working in Greenwich with an interest in community service are invited to join the league.

Knights of Columbus
37 West Putnam Avenue, Greenwich, 203.622.1939
www.kofc.org/un/eb/en/officers/fac.html

CHARITABLE & SERVICE ORGANIZATIONS

Lions Club of Greenwich
PO Box 1044 Greenwich CT 06836-1044
www.LionsClubs.org
Alan Gunzburg, President, 203.661.2540

Lions Club of Old Greenwich
PO Box 215, Old Greenwich CT 06870
www.LionsClubs.org
C. Jean Dana, President, 203.869.0866

Lions Club of Western Greenwich
www.LionsClubs.org
Jack Nearing, President, 203.531.9668

P.E.O. Sisterhood, Greenwich Chapter
www.PEOInternational.org
Carol Scott, President, 203.968.1974

Red Cross Greenwich Chapter
99 Indian Field Road, 203.869.8444
www.greenwichredcross.org
Joan Irish, CEO
Bina Pate Pierce, Board Chair

Rotary Club of Greenwich
PO Box 1375, Greenwich CT 06836
www.GreenwichRotary.org
Dr. Josefina Van der Poll 203.637.4581

United Way of Greenwich
1 Lafayette Court, 203.869.2221
www.UnitedWay-Greenwich.com
Stuart Adelberg, President

Veterans of Foreign Wars
Cos Cob Post 10112
PO Box 8, Cos Cob 06807
www.VFW.org
Joseph Gregory, Commander, 203.536.5107

CHARITABLE & SERVICE ORGANIZATIONS

Veterans of Foreign Wars
Greenwich Post 1792
PO Box 128, Greenwich
www.VFW.org
James Clifford, Quartermaster, 203.326.0773

Volunteers on Call
P.O. Box 4434 Greenwich CT 06830, 203.550.2222
29 Sachem Lane, Greenwich CT 06830
www.VolunteersOnCall.org
Roxana Bowgen, President

Woman's Club of Greenwich
89 Maple Avenue, 203.869.2046
Valerie Anderson, President

TIP: HOW TO GET ON A TOWN BOARD OR COMMISSION
www.GreenwichCT.org/Town_Hall.asp#Agencies
There are a number of independent boards and commissions that are completely volunteer and yet have great power in how the Town runs. The Board of Selectmen interviews candidates and recommends their appointment to the Representative Town Meeting (RTM). The Appointments Committee of the RTM and one or more of the other RTM standing committees will interview the candidate. The nomination is then brought to the RTM for a vote. If you are interested in serving on one of these boards, you can nominate yourself or talk to a member of the Selectman's Nomination Advisory Committee (SNAC) by going to:
http://greenwichct.virtualtownhall.net/Public_Documents/GreenwichCT_FirstSelect/committees/nominations/index.

CHILD ENRICHMENT

For other Children related activities see the sections CHILDREN or BOOKS & LIBRARIES
For nursery, pre-schools and other public/private schools see SCHOOLS
For children and adult sports see SPORTS

art

Bruce Museum
1 Museum Drive, 203.869.0376 x 325
www.BruceMuseum.org
Art classes offered throughout the year, including during school holidays.

Lakeside Pottery
543 Newfield Avenue, Stamford CT, 203.323.2222
www.LakesidePottery.com
Children's pottery program for ages 8 - 12. They also offer summer and winter camps and birthday parties. Many adult classes offered, too.

Little Rembrandt
Rye Ridge Shopping Center
12a Rye Ridge Plaza, Rye Brook, NY 914.939.1400
www.LittleRembrandt.info
In addition to birthday parties, art classes and art workshops, they have a good selection of unique gift ideas.

Signature Art
YWCA, 259 East Putnam Avenue, 203.869.6501
www.YWCAGreenwich.org
Multi-media art projects for young artists ages 5 - 9.

(The) Greenwich Arts Council
299 Greenwich Avenue, 203.622.3998
www.GreenwichArts.org
Children's after-school art programs.

(The) Greenwich Art Society
299 Greenwich Avenue, 203.629.1533
www.GreenwichArtSociety.com
Junior Art Workshop with Elaine Huyer is a lively course for 7 -10 year old students. They work with pastels, clay, paper collage and sculpture after school. Adult art classes also available.

CHILD ENRICHMENT

chess

National Scholastic Chess Foundation (NSCF)
171 East Post Road, White Plains, NY, 914.683.5322
www.NSCFChess.org
If your child enjoys games and problem-solving, chess lessons from these experts will open up a wonderful world. Classes are held in Scarsdale and Chappaqua.

cooking

Aux Délices
23 Acosta Street, Stamford CT, 203.326.4540 x 108
www.AuxDelicesFoods.com
This wonderful gourmet food shop offers a variety of cooking classes for children and adults at their Stamford location. Birthday parties are offered at home or in their shop.

Kids 'r' Cookin
203.660.4433, 914.937.2012
www.KidsRcookin.com
Restauranteur Bandy Acciavatti offers cooking courses and birthday parties for kids.

computers

Cyber Discoveries
877.376.0048
Greenwich, CT — call for location.
www.CyberDiscoveries.com
Computer classes for ages 3 - 6.

See also computer camps in CHILDREN, Summer Camps.

dance & etiquette

Allegra Dance Studio

37 West Putnam Avenue, 203.629.9162

www.AllegraDanceStudio.com

Claudia Devita, a popular Greenwich dance teacher. Ages 3 to adult; classes in jazz, ballet, tap, hip-hop and ballroom dancing.

Ballet Des Enfances

Shop Rite Center

2000 West Main Street, Stamford CT, 203.973.0144

www.balletdesenfants.net

Ballet studio offering classes for 2 - 6 year olds and up.

Barclay Ballroom Dancing for Young Children

397 Round Hill Road

Lois Thomson, Director, 908.232.8370

Friday evening classes, starting in September, are held at the Round Hill Community Center. The one-hour classes teach ballroom dancing and social etiquette to children in grades 4, 5, & 6.

(The) Chinese Language School Folk Dancing

P.O. Box 515, Riverside CT , 866.301.4906

www.ChineseLanguageSchool.org

Chinese Folk Dance classes. This is the only full-time professional school of Chinese dance in the country. Classes are held at Eastern Middle School. They have an extensive program teaching Mandarin Chinese.

Come Dance with Me

110 Willet Avenue, Port Chester, NY 10573, 914.933.0877

www.ComeDanceWithMe.net

This new studio offers a variety of dance styles and classes for children, beginners, and professional levels. Jazz, Ballet, Youth Latin, and an especially fun Hip-Hop class.

Dance Adventure

36 Sherwood Place, Greenwich, 203.625.0930

www.DanceAdventure.com

Programs for parent and child, 4 months to 2 years; pre-ballet for ages 3 - 5; ballet, tap & jazz for 1st graders to teens.

CHILD ENRICHMENT
dance & etiquette

Greenwich Ballet Academy
203.856.7953
www.GreenwichBalletacademy.org
They hold classes at the Greenwich Arts Council and Western Greenwich Civic Center. Their mission is to nurture young dancers ages 9-21 toward a career in classical ballet and contemporary dance.

Greenwich Ballet Workshop
Felicity Foote, 339 Round Hill Road, 203.869.9373
www.GreenwichBalletWorkshop.com
Dedicated children (up to age 18) coached to look their very best on stage.

Greenwich Dance Studio
YWCA, 259 East Putnam Avenue, 203.536.3990
Kate Truesdell, Director
www.GreenwichDanceStudio.com
Ballet, jazz, hip hop, creative movement classes for children ages 3 years and up.

Lynn Academy of Irish Dance
42 Magee Ave 2nd Floor (2 Studios), Stamford CT, 203.323.0550
www.LynnAcademy.com
Irish dance instruction for children and adults.

Mayfair Ballroom Dancing for Young Children
Call the Brunswick School 203.625.5800
www.BrunswickSchool.org
Mayfair is sponsored by the Brunswick Parents Association, but is open to all children in Greenwich. Like Barclay, they teach ballroom dancing and etiquette to children in grades 5 and 6. Friday classes start in September, 5th grade 4:30 - 5:30; 6th grade 6:00 - 7:00, and are usually taught at Brunswick. For girls, there may be a waiting list. There's always room for boys.

New Dance
11 Rye Ridge Plaza, Rye Brook NY, 914.690.9300
www.NewDance.net
This studio offers a variety of classes to boys and girls including ballet, tap, hip hop, jazz and cheerleading.

CHILD ENRICHMENT

dance & etiquette

YWCA Children's Ballet
259 East Putnam Avenue, 203.661.7175, 203.869.6501 ext. 131.
Kendall Moran Director
www.YWCAGreenwich.org
Pre Ballet for ages 3-4, Beginning ballet ages 5-6, Ballet l ages 7-9,
Ballet ll ages 10-15, Beginning Pointe ages 11-13.

College for Kids
Norwalk Community College
Richards Avenue, Norwalk CT, 203.857.3337
www.NCC.CommNet.edu
Unique courses for children grades K - 8, such as spooky science, web
design, under sea art, manners and chess.

extracurricular kids programs

Greenwich Science Center
7 Granite Ridge Road, Redding CT, 203.605.8334
www.GreenwichScienceCenter.org
Their mission is to provide exceptional educational opportunities to
elementary, junior high and high school students in the areas of science,
math and technology.

languages

Alliance Française
299 Greenwich Avenue, 203.629.1340
www.AFGreenwich.org
Classes for beginners, intermediate and advanced are given in the French Center for children ages 3 - 13 years and teens. "Mommy and Me" lets 2 year olds learn with their mothers. On Tuesdays, French classes are offered for native French-speaking children who are enrolled in English-speaking schools.

(The) Chinese Language School of Connecticut
Eastern Middle School
51 Hendrie Avenue, Riverside, 866.301.4906
www.ChineseLanguageSchool.org
This school operates from September to June. Classes are held Sundays at Eastern Middle School, 51 Hendrie Avenue, Riverside, CT and weekdays at the Greenwich Family Y, 50 East Putnam Avenue, Greenwich, CT. This non-profit organization is dedicated to teaching Mandarin Chinese as a second language to children. They also teach dance.

Evrika Learning Center
Stamford CT, 203.975.1134
www.EvrikaCenter.com
Saturday and summer Russian language school. Russian classes for ages 2 to 15 incorporate games, poems and puzzles.

French-American School
914.250.0451, 203.834.3002 x 253
Larchmont, Mamaroneck 914.250.0504
Scarsdale Campuses 914.250.0522
www.Fasny.org
Adult and children classes in French, Mandarin Chinese, Russian, Spanish, Arabic and Italian. With a knowledge of basic French, children grades 1 - 3 can enjoy cooking, juggling and circus arts, as well as model airplane making and a variety of sports.

CHILD ENRICHMENT

languages

German School
(Rippowam Middle School)
381 High Ridge Road, Stamford CT, 203.792.2795
www.GermanSchoolCT.org, www.dsny.org
Monday and Saturday morning German language and cultural instruction for novice to native speakers. Available for children pre-school through high school. They also have an adult program. Closed during the summer. Classes begin in September.

Linguakids
2 East Avenue, Larchmont NY, 914.833.0781, 914.525.0328
www.LinguaKids.com
Classes in French and Spanish for children ages 2 and up.

(The) Language Exchange
Cos Cob, 203.422.2024
www.ForeignLanguageExchange.com
Adult and children's classes in Spanish, French, Dutch, German, Mandarin Chinese, Italian and Russian. Children's classes for ages 3 to 13. They offer total immersion camps for students in Elementary, Middle and High School.

Little Language League
Western Greenwich Civic Center
449 Pemberwick Road, 914.921.9075
info@languageleague.com
Little Language League offers foreign language courses at the Civic Center on Monday afternoons.

Mencius Mandarin Chinese Preschool
First United Methodist Church
2nd Floor, 59 East Putnam Avenue, 203.540.5770
www.MenciusMandarin.com
English-Mandarin Chinese bilingual preschool for children ages 2 to 5 years old. No prior knowledge of Mandarin Chinese is required.

CHILD ENRICHMENT
music & acting

Be Mused Productions
508 Warburton Avenue, Suite #3, Yonkers NY, 10701
www.BemusedProductions.com
Weekend workshops, 2 hour rehearsals for children ages 4 through teens, culminating with a show. The director is great with kids and BeMused is priced fairly.

Connecticut School of Music
299 Greenwich Avenue, 203.226.0805
www.CTSchoolOfMusic.com
Private lessons for piano, violin/viola, cello, guitar, flute, bass, music theory & composition, voice, ear training as well as ensemble programs. They rent instruments.

Curtain Call, Inc.
1349 Newfield Avenue, Stamford CT 06905, 203.329.8207
www.CurtainCallInc.com
Acting workshops and camps for kids, teens, and adults of all abilities.

Greenwich Music & Fraioli School of Music
1200 East Putnam Avenue, Riverside,
203.637.1119, 203.869.3615
www.GreenwichMusic.com
This is a music store and a school. They offer instruction in voice and many instruments. They even have a class about how to be a rock star.

Greenwich Performing Arts Studio
261 East Putnam Avenue, Cos Cob, 203.327.7666, 203.273.7827
www.GreenwichPerformingArts.com
Private lessons and group classes teach children to act, sing & dance. Under adult supervision, students can write and perform their own original musicals and standard shows. Classes include acting, tap and creative drama, musical theater, ballet, jazz, improv, on camera classes and voice classes.

CHILD ENRICHMENT

music & acting

Greenwich Suzuki Academy
Lessons: Christ Church, 254 East Putnam Avenue, 203.561.6176
Mailing address: 15 E. Putnam Ave #176 Greenwich CT, 06830
www.GreenwichSuzukiAcademy.org
The Suzuki method of teaching violin, viola, flute and cello is available for children ages 3 - 18. It is taught in private and group classes. Parent training is available as well as instruction in beginning orchestra, jazz theory, improvisation, and chamber music.

Kinder Musik
Old Greenwich Music Studio
23 Clark Street, Old Greenwich, 203.637.0461
261 East Putnam Avenue, Cos Cob, 203.637.0461
www.OGMstudio.KinderMusik.net
Pre-instrumental programs for infants to 8 years. A delightful way to encourage a child's love of music.

Mary Ann Hall's Music For Children
YWCA, 259 East Putnam Avenue, 203.854.9797
www.MusicForChildren.net
A song, dance, and instrument program for children birth to 10.

Music Conservatory of Westchester
216 Central Avenue, White Plains NY, 914.761.3900
www.MusicConservatory.org
High quality, individual instrumental instruction for children in violin, Suzuki violin, piano, guitar and woodwinds, provided by the Music Conservatory of Westchester. Music theory lessons also available.

(The) Music Source
1345 East Putnam Avenue, 203.698.0444
www.TheMusicSource.org
A great resource for sheet music, including every Broadway Play in print. A large selection of music, supplies and gifts for all instruments.

music & acting

Music Together of Fairfield County
76 Walbin Court, Fairfield CT, 203.256.1656
www.CTMusicToGether.com
Fun, informal family music-making classes for babies to 5 year olds.
They hold classes in Greenwich.

Riverside School of Music
401 East Putnam Ave, Cos Cob, 203.661.9501
www.AtelierConstantinPopescu.com
They sell instruments and give private lessons for violin, viola, cello,
piano, guitar & voice for children 2 and up. They are great with kids.
Open just about every day.

Studio of Victoria Baker
15 Putnam Green, 203.531.7499
Victoria Baker, an opera singer and columnist for the Greenwich Post,
gives private voice and piano lessons.

Vinny Nobile
24 Grand Street, 914.980.3082
www.linkedin.com/in/VinnyNobie
Vinny will come to your home for private lessons in trumpet, trombone
or piano.

Young Artists Philharmonic
PO Box 3301, Ridgeway Station, Stamford CT, 203.532.1278
www.syap.org
For over 40 years, this highly sophisticated regional youth symphony
orchestra has inspired youth and entertained adults.

TIP: SCULPTURES IN GREENWICH
Greenwich has 30 outdoor sculptures. Some are tucked
away in parks, some are in public buildings. Have fun
on a sculpture hunt. Stop in the Greenwich Arts Council
(second floor of 299 Greenwich Avenue) and ask for the
map of sculpture locations.

CHILD ENRICHMENT
reading

Pre-school Stories

Stories are read to pre-schoolers in the mornings most weekdays. During the summer, stories may be read in a nearby park.
www.GreenwichLibrary.org

- Byram Shubert Library, 21 Mead Avenue, Byram
  203.531.0426
- Cos Cob Library, 5 Sinoway Road, Cos Cob,
  203.622.6883
- Weewalkers at Greenwich Library,
  203.622.7900
  12 - 24 months, Tuesday, Thursday and
  Friday mornings 11 am.
- Perrot Library, 90 Sound Beach Avenue, Old Greenwich,
  203.637.1066

Young Critics Club

Perrot Library
90 Sound Beach Avenue, Old Greenwich, 203.637.8802
www.PerrotLibrary.org
Children in grades 6 - 8 who love to read and talk about books, gather on Friday afternoons with Kate McClelland and Mary Clark for a guided discussion. By application only. It is often over-booked.

TIP: KIDS SAFETY TRAINING

The Greenwich Safety Town is sponsored by the Greenwich Red Cross. www.greenwichredcross.org This full-day program teaches kids (who are ready for kindergarten) about such matters as safety around strangers, household safety and how to cross the street. The program is conducted during the summer, but because it's so popular, register your child before March. Call the Red Cross at 203.869.8444 for details.

CHILD ENRICHMENT

Community Answers Tutors Notebook

Community Answers at the Greenwich Library
101 West Putnam Avenue, 203.622.7979
www.CommunityAnswers.org
They maintain a notebook of resumes and flyers of local tutors, as well as the current tutors from the Greenwich Public Schools.

Gemm Learning

1380 East Putnam Avenue, Old Greenwich
203.292.5410, 877.292.4366
www.GemmLearning.com/ct_learning_center.php
Gemm works predominantly with elementary school-aged children (although the program is available to kids from K-12th grade), who are experiencing stumbling blocks with their reading skills. They also offer math help, SAT prep.

Greenwich Professional Academics

203.559.6284, after hours 203.559.5633
www.GreenwichGPA.com
Tutors and coaches in math, English, other languages, SAT preparation and study skills.

Kumon Learning Center

CVS Building
132 East Putnam Avenue, Cos Cob, 914.433.1116
www.Kumon.com, http://Center.ikumon.com/showpage.aspx?url=91381
Kumon concentrates on math and reading skills for grades K through 12.

Stand By Me

Greenwich High School, 10 Hillside Road, 203.625.8007
www.GreenwichSchools.org/page.cfm?p=5524
A program designed to give underachieving ninth grade students a chance to have a senior stand by them.

CHILD ENRICHMENT

tutors

Sylvan Learning Centers

180 South Broadway, White Plains NY, 914.948.4116
www.tutoring.sylvanlearning.com/centers/whiteplains-tutoring/index.cfm
www.tutoring.sylvanlearning.com
Their tutors tailor individualized learning plans to improve skills, habits and attitudes. Instruction is available in math, reading, writing, study skills, homework help and test preparation.

Tutoring Club

69 High Ridge Road, Stamford CT, 203.323.1929
http://stamfordct.tutoringclub.com/localinfo.asp
www.TutoringClub.com
Individualized instruction from professional tutors to bring each student to the desired academic level as quickly as possible.

Tutoring Match

Director: Henry Lane, 205 Sunset Ave, Fairfield CT, 203.366.3396
www.TutoringMatch.com
Tutoring assistance in just about any subject for students of all ages. Tutors come to your home.

TIP: KIDS' PROGRAMS AT PURCHASE COLLEGE

The Performing Arts Center www.artscenter.org at Purchase College, in addition to their superb adult concert series, has a series of sensational performances designed for children. For pre-k to grade 12. For more information about Arts-in-Education, call 914-251-6232.

CHILDREN

introduction

Greenwich is an ideal place to raise children. We have the top-rated school system in Connecticut, ranked among the best in the country. Children nurtured in Greenwich have unique opportunities to develop their skills and to grow into happy, healthy, mature individuals.
For an excellent book on Children, go to:
   www.cga.ct.gov/coc/playbook_home.htm
A Greenwich-based resource which includes a guide to summer camps, kids' classes and fun events, party places and upcoming local events:
   www.KidsEvents.com

For nursery, pre-schools and other public/private schools see SCHOOLS
For more information on beaches and Greenwich parks see PARKS
Child Safety providers are in SERVICES
See SPORTS for year-around activities
See section TEENS for more ideas.
CHILD ENRICHMENT is a separate Section

babysitting

Babysitting Training
*   Red Cross, 99 Indian Field Road, 203.869.8444
    www.greenwichredcross.org
    The Red Cross sponsors a comprehensive all-day babysitting course which is open to 11 - 15 year olds and offered 2 to 3 times a month.
*   Greenwich Hospital "Tender Beginnings" 203.863.3655
    A babysitting course for students 11 - 13.

Child Care and Parenting Services
Greenwich Library, 101 Putnam Avenue, 203.522.7940.
A wonderful pamphlet compiled by Community Answers and Greenwich Early Childhood Council. Available at the Community Answers desk.

Child Care Infoline
800.505.1000
www.ChildCareInfoLine.org
They provide information on licensed daycare, summer camps and nursery school programs throughout Connecticut.

CHILDREN

Kid's Night Out
YMCA, 50 East Putnam Avenue, 203.869.1630
www.GWYMCA.org
A few evenings a month, parents of children in grades K - 6 can enjoy an evening out, while their children enjoy an inexpensive, fun, safe night of activities, including gym games, swimming, movies, popcorn and board games.

(The) Sitting Service
Kristen Calve, owner.
1031 Post Road, Darien CT, 203.655.9783
www.TheSittingService.com
Office hours are 9am - 1pm, weekdays. This state-registered babysitting, pet-sitting and house-sitting referral service has been in Fairfield County for over 20 years. Yearly membership is $265 + tax per family plus an hourly rate.

Student Employment Service
Greenwich High School, 203.625.8008
www.GHS-SES.org
Hours during the school year are weekdays, 11:45 am - 2:00 pm. During the summer, the service is run through Community Answers, 203.622.7979.

Utilize Senior Energy (USE)
Senior Center, 299 Greenwich Avenue, 203.629.8032
Hours: weekdays 9:30 am - 12:30 pm. Employment referral service for people 50 years and over.

TIP: CHILDCARE RESOURCES
Community Answers gathers information about programs and places of interest to children and parents in the Children's Notebook. Community Answers also publishes an excellent leaflet on Child Care and Parenting Services. Be sure to ask for these informative pamphlets at the Community Answers desk in the Greenwich Library.

For nursery, pre-schools and other public/private schools see SCHOOLS.

Elementary School Programs

The following elementary schools have on-site, before and after-school childcare programs for students enrolled in that school.

- Cos Cob School, 203.869.4670
- Glenville School, 203.531.9287
- Hamilton Avenue School, 203.869.1685 (2nd grade scholars)
- International School at Dundee 203.637.3800
- Julian Curtiss School, 203.869.1896
- New Lebanon School, 203.531.9139
- North Mianus School, 203.637.9730
- North Street School, 203.869.6756
- Old Greenwich School, 203.637.0150
- Parkway School, 203.869.7466
- Riverside School, 203.637.1440

BANC

Byram Archibald Neighborhood Center After School Program
289 Delavan Avenue, 203.531.1522
Ages: 5 - 13 yrs. Four days per week. Follows public school calendar.

Girls Inc.

PO Box 793, Greenwich CT, 203.536.3322
www.girlsincswct.org, www.girlsinc.org
Girls, ages 6 - 18. Hours: 3:15 pm - 5:45 pm. An excellent five day-a-week, informal education program for girls. The focus is on science, math and technology.

Greenwich Boys and Girls Club

4 Horseneck Lane, 203.869.3224
www.bgcg.org
Co-ed, Ages: 6 and up, Hours: 3 pm - 6:30 pm. On school holidays, the program starts at 8 am. Summer hours are 8 am - 6 pm.

before & after-school programs

Kaleidoscope   YWCA
259 East Putnam Avenue, 203.869.6501, x 251
www.ywcaGreenwich.org
Co-ed, Ages: K - grade 5, Hours: 2:30 pm to 6 pm. Follows the public
school schedule, including early release days. Social, educational and
recreational enrichment. Transportation is provided from all Greenwich
schools. Kaleidoscope also provides childcare services during school
closings for holidays and vacations.

Sundial at the Mead School
1095 Riverbank Road, Stamford CT, 203.595.9500
www.MeadSchool.org
An after-school program for ages 1 - 4. Activities include chess, yoga,
Chinese and playground fun.

YMCA After School Program
203.869.3381
www.GWYmca.org
They run after-school childcare programs at Hamilton Avenue, New Lebanon, and North Mianus Schools.

TIP: TOUCH A TRUCK
The Junior League of Greenwich www.jlgreenwich.org
holds an annual spring fundraiser, usually in early June,
called Touch A Truck. This is lots of fun for children (and
adults) who love to climb on interesting equipment such
as construction vehicles, public safety equipment,
Humvees and other assorted vehicles. For information
call the Touch A Truck hotline at 203.977.0770 or the
Junior League office at 203.869.1979.

CHILDREN
childcare

Children's Day School
449 Pemberwick Road, 203.532.1196
8 Riverside Avenue, 203.637.1122
www.ChildrensDaySchool.net
All day daycare and pre-school for children ages 6 weeks - 6 years,
Hours:7:30 am - 6 pm.
Director: Sara Champion

Family Centers
Joan Warburg Early Childhood Center
• 20 Bridge Street, 203.629.2822
• 40 Arch Street, 203.869.4848
www.FamilyCenters.org
Director: Danielle Bridey, 203.869.4848
Children ages 6 weeks - 2 years, Hours: 7:30 - 6 pm.

Gateway School
Director: Danielle Bridey, 203.869.4848
2 Chapel Street, 203.531.8430
www.FamilyCenters.org
Children ages 3 - 4. Full-day, year-round childcare; need-based tuition.
Hours: 7:30 am - 6 pm.

Little Angels Play Group
Greenwich Catholic School, 471 North Street,
203.869.4000 x 109
www.GreenwichCatholicSchool.org
• Children ages 3 - 4; hours: weekdays, 8:30 pm - 11:30 pm;
Tuesday - Thursday, noon - 3 pm.
• Pre-K program, ages 4 - 5, hours: 8:30 am - noon; extended day options.

Little Friends
25 Valley Drive, 203.861.6549
Year-round child care for up to 150 children, ages 6 weeks - 5 years;
hours: 6:30am - 6:30 pm. Early drop off, 6:30 am; late pick up, 6:30 pm.
Also 2, 3 and 5 day programs, either half or full day.

CHILDREN

childcare

YMCA Child Care

2 Saint Roch Avenue, 203.869.3381

Children ages 6 weeks - 5 years. All day, year round childcare. Hours: 7:30 am - 5:30 pm.

YWCA Playroom and Playroom Plus

259 East Putnam Avenue, 203.869.6501 x 221

Children ages 15 months - 3 years. Professional on site childcare services, either for parents attending Y classes or pursuing off site activities. Morning or afternoon sessions available.

TIP: BREAKFAST WITH SANTA

Fortunately our Department of Parks and Recreation has a good relationship with Santa. As a result, for the last 20 years Santa has been coming to the Greenwich Civic Center (90 Harding Road, Old Greenwich) in late November. Mrs. Claus, her friends Frosty, Rudolph and Santa's elves are normally on hand to greet children. Breakfast is usually 9:30 am - 11:30 am. Tickets cost $18 and must be purchased in advance at the Parks and Recreation office on the second floor of Town Hall. Call 203.622.6478 for details.

CHILDREN

fairs, festivals & carnivals

Many of the town's elementary schools and churches hold fairs as fundraisers:

- **Cos Cob School Fair (early May)**
  300 East Putnam Avenue, 203.869.4670
- **North Mianus School Pow Wow (early May)**
  309 Palmer Hill Road, 203.637.9730
- **Renaissance Festival (early June)**
  International School of Dundee
  55 Florence Road, Riverside, 203.637.3800
  Sword fights, horseback jousting and live chess.
- **St. Catherine's Carnival (middle August)**
  4 Riverside Avenue, 203.637.3661
- **St. Paul's Episcopal Church Fair (late May)**
  200 Riverside Avenue, 203.637.2447
- **St. Roch's Bazaar (early August)**
  10 Saint Roch Avenue, Byram, 203.869.4176

United Way September Fest
(middle September) Roger Sherman Baldwin Park at Arch Street
203.869.2221
www.UnitedWay-Greenwich.com

Scarecrow Festival
Mill Pond Park. Strickland Road, Cos Cob
Hosted by the Greenwich Chamber of Commerce (203.869.3500) and the Historical Society (203.869.6899), this fun-filled October day includes live entertainment, lots of food vendors, scarecrow contests, horse-drawn wagon rides, hay maze, art projects, three-legged races and much more.

The Junior League of Greenwich
203.869.1979
www.jlgreenwich.org
The Junior League hosts several popular fund-raising events throughout the year including:

- **Touch a Truck (early June)**
  Held at the Greenwich High School field. Children have a chance to climb onto backhoes, dump trucks, and emergency vehicles. Tattoo artists and musicians make it festive, too.

- **The Enchanted Forest (November)**
  Held at The Hyatt in Old Greenwich, The Enchanted Forest is a two-day event which features over 100 decorated trees, wreaths and ginger bread houses and photos with Santa.

TIP: SEPTEMBERFEST AND SOAPBOX DERBY
Be sure this festival, sponsored by the United Way, is marked on your calendar. You and your family will have a wonderful time. You will find rides, kids' activities, food and live entertainment. Call 203.869.2221 or visit www.unitedway-greenwich.com for details.

Although there is some duplication, adult oriented museums are listed in CULTURE under Museums.

American Museum of Natural History

Central Park West at 79th Street, New York NY, 212.769.5100
www.AMNH.org
This museum is terrific for kids, with lots of special exhibits, programs and workshops.
Hours: Sunday - Thursday, 10 am - 5:45 pm;
Fridays and Saturdays, 10 am - 8:45 pm.

Audubon Center Greenwich

613 Riversville Road, 203.869.5272
www.Greenwich.Audubon.org
Founded in 1942, this 686-acre sanctuary has 15 miles of trails and a superb learning and exhibit center, with a terrific nature store. You will want to stay.
Hours: Open year round except for major holidays, 9 am - 5 pm.

Bridgeport Bluefish

Harbor Yard, 500 Main Street, Bridgeport CT, 203.345.4800
www.BridgeportBluefish.com
Professional Minor League Baseball in the Atlantic League. Verify hours and ticket availability before you go.
Hours: May - September, Monday - Saturday, 7 pm; Sunday, 1 pm.

Bridgeport Sound Tigers

600 Main Street, Arena at Harbor Yard, Bridgeport CT, 203.345.2300
www.soundtigers.com
Ice Hockey, New York Islanders "farm" team. They begin playing their 40 home game season in October.

Bronx Zoo

Fordham Road at Bronx River Parkway, Bronx NY, 718.367.1010
www.BronxZoo.com
World class zoo with terrific rides and exhibits. Easy to find. Free admission every Wednesday. You can purchase tickets online.
Hours: Weekdays 10 am - 5 pm, weekends and holidays 10 am - 5:30 pm, November - March, 10 am - 4:30 pm.

CHILDREN
family outings

Bruce Museum
1 Museum Drive, 203.869.0376
www.brucemuseum.org
Impressive rotating exhibits and many programs for adults and children. They have a terrific gift shop with a large selection of books. The Museum has been accredited by the American Association of Museums as being in the top 10 percent of US museums. The Museum sponsors 2 fairs in Bruce Park every year; the mid-May Craft Fair and the Columbus Day Arts Festival have juried artists from around the country and draw visitors from all over the area.
Hours: Tuesday - Saturday, 10 am - 5 pm; Sunday, 1 pm - 5 pm. Closed on major holidays.

Bush Holley House Museum
39 Strickland Road, Cos Cob, 203.869.6899
www.hstg.org
Home of the Historical Society, this is the place to learn about Greenwich history. They also have a good library and a shop with books on Greenwich history, as well as reproductions of 19th-century children's toys and books. While you are there, pick up a list of their informative programs.
Hours: March - December, Tuesday - Sunday, noon - 4 pm; January - February, weekends, noon - 4 pm.

Dinosaur State Park
400 West Street, Rocky Hill CT, 860.529.8423
www.DinosaurStatePark.org
Dinosaurs fascinate us all. With over 2,000 tracks, this is one of the best sites in North America. Make your own castings right on the site.

Discovery Museum
4450 Park Avenue, Bridgeport CT, 203.372.3521
www.DiscoveryMuseum.org
Hands-on art and science exhibits for children of all ages and their parents. A special section for pre-schoolers with dozens of attractions based on principles of early childhood development. Families who know about the Discovery Museum go there regularly.
Hours: Tuesday - Saturday, 10 am - 5 pm; Sunday, noon - 5 pm. Open Monday in summer.

Essex Steam Train & Riverboat

One Railroad Avenue, Essex CT, 860.767.0103, 800.377.3987
www.EssexSteamTrain.com
Take a trip back in history through the scenic Connecticut River Valley. Passengers board the 1920 steam train at the Essex station for a one-hour ride. At Deep River Landing the train meets the river boat for a one-hour cruise. The North Cove Express offers brunch, lunch and dinner during a two-hour excursion. Call for reservations on the Dinner Train. Pre-schoolers won't want to miss the Thomas the Tank Engine ride, a 25-minute ride with Thomas held in November.
Note: See Connecticut River Valley Inns in the section HOTELS & INNS.

Flanders Nature Center - Maple Sugaring

5 Church Hill (at Flanders Road), Woodbury CT, 203.263.3711
www.flandersnaturecenter.org, www.WoodburyCT.org
Spend an afternoon at a sugarhouse and learn how to make pure maple syrup and then taste it. During a good season, there is sugaring in Connecticut for six or seven weeks. In an off year, the season could be only a couple of weekends, so be sure to call before you go. The Flanders Nature Center is 1½ to 2 hours from Greenwich. Woodbury is a well-preserved colonial town with a number of antique shops and some top restaurants. The syrup operation is open to the public. Demonstrations are given on weekends from 3 pm to 5 pm from late February through March.

Franklin Mineral Museum

Sterling Hill Mine
30 Plant Street, Ogdensburg NJ, 973.209.7212
www.SterlingHill.org, www.SterlingHillMiningMuseum.org
About 2.5 hours from Greenwich, is a world-famous collection of fluorescent rocks, many from the Sterling Mine. The Sterling Hill mine operated from about 1761 to 1986. For the tour of the mine wear sturdy boots and bring a jacket (it's 56° even in the summer). Tours take about 3 hours. Not appropriate for children under six.
Museum Hours: Open everyday, April - November
Tour Hours: 1 pm; everyday, July and August, weekends April - June and September - November.

CHILDREN

family outings

IMAX Theater

At the Maritime Aquarium, 10 North Water Street, Norwalk CT,
203.852.0700
www.MaritimeAquarium.org
With a screen that is six stories high and eight stories wide, and a
24,000 watt sound system, the experience is truly amazing.
Hours: Open daily at 10 am;
September - June until 5 pm; July - Labor Day, until 6 pm.

Lake Compounce Family Theme Park

822 Lake Avenue, Bristol CT, 860.583.3300
www.LakeCompounce.com, www.HauntedGraveyard.com
The best wooden roller coaster in the world is about 1½ hours north of
Greenwich built on the side of a mountain. It is simply "awesome." All
rides in the Circus World Children's Area and some rides in Splash Harbor are designed for young children. Children must be under 54" tall to
ride, but adults may accompany children on some rides. In October, the
"Haunted Graveyard" can be lots of fun.

Maritime Aquarium

10 North Water Street, Norwalk CT, 203.852.0700
www.MaritimeAquarium.org
Interactive exhibits often including a Shark Touch Pool. Cited as one of
the 10 Great Aquariums to visit.
Hours: Open daily, September - June, 10 am - 5 pm; July - Labor Day 10
am - 6 pm.

Mystic Seaport and Museum

Mystic CT, Visitor Information: 888.973.2767
www.MysticSeaport.org
Mystic is a two-hour drive. The Mystic Seaport Museum has a world-
renowned waterfront collection of ships and crafts telling the story of
America and the sea. Mystic also has a good aquarium, with exciting
special exhibits. While in the Mystic area, stop by Stonington, which is
about five miles east on US-1. Stonington is a nineteenth century fishing
village which has kept its charm and has become a center for antique
shops. Don't forget Mystic Pizza, which inspired the movie. There is one
in Mystic, 860.536.3700, and one in North Stonington, 860.599.5126.
Hours: Open every day except December 25th;
Ships & exhibits 9 am - 5 pm, Museum grounds 9 am - 6 pm.

CHILDREN

family outings

TIP: THE ENCHANTED FOREST

Each year in early November, the Junior League organizes a magical display of beautifully decorated Christmas trees and gingerbread houses, all donated by Greenwich organizations and individuals. The auction of these
items helps support the good works of the Junior League.
www.jlgreenwich.org This is a fun event for the whole
family. Call 203.869.1979 for details.

Philipsburg Manor

Sleepy Hollow NY, 914.631.8200, 914.631.3992
www.HudsonValley.org
An 18th-century working farm, with water-powered grist mill and live-
stock. Tours are conducted by interpreters in period costumes.
Hours: April - December, open every day (except Tuesday), 10 am - 5 pm;
Open on weekends in March; closed January & February.

Pick Your Own Fruit & Vegetables

Picking your own fruit and vegetables has become a popular pastime in
Connecticut. There are nine farms in Fairfield County offering urbanites
the opportunity to pick their own produce.
For more detailed information call 860.713.2569 or 800.861.9939
www.state.ct.us/doag
Some you might consider are:

• Bishop's Orchards

1355 Boston Post Road (I-95, exit 57), Guilford CT
203.458.7425, 203.453.2338
www.BishopsOrchards.com
They have a great many varieties of fruit to pick, including over twenty
varieties of apples, nine kinds of blueberries, twelve kinds of peaches,
three kinds of pears, eight kinds of strawberries and two varieties of
raspberries. This orchard is definitely worth the trip.
Market hours: June - October, Monday - Saturday, 8 am to 6 pm,
Sunday 9 am to 6 pm.

family outings

- **Eden Farms**
  947 Stillwater Road, Stamford, 203.325.3445
  A nursery and greenhouse open 7 days a week, just minutes from Greenwich. Eden Farms has seasonal celebrations: Easter Bunnies, Halloween Hayrides, Pumpkin Patch, Haunted House and Santa visits. Call to check events and times before going.

- **Jones Family Farm**
  606 Walnut Tree Hill Road & Route 110, Shelton CT, 203.929.8425
  www.JonesFamilyFarms.com
  This pick-your-own farm began in the 1940s. They have strawberries in June, followed by blueberries in July and August, and pumpkins in the autumn. Hayrides are offered in October, and in December you can cut your own Christmas tree. Hours: Best to call, hours change sea sonally. Closed Sunday & Monday.

- **Silverman's Farm**
  451 Sport Hill Road (exit 46 off Merritt Parkway), Easton CT, 203.262.3306, 203.268.0321
  www.SilvermansFarm.com
  Peaches in July, apples in August. Three-acre animal farm for young sters.
  Hours: Weekdays, 9 am - 5 pm. Closed on major holidays. Call for hours in January or in case of bad weather.

- **White Silo Farm**
  32 Route 37 East, Sherman CT, 860.355.0271
  www.whitesilowinery.com
  Strawberries, asparagus, raspberries, blackberries and rhubarb.

Playland Park
Playland Parkway, Rye NY, 914.813.7010
www.RyePlayland.org
Recently renovated amusement park, just 15 minutes away. A wide variety of rides for older kids from Go Karts to Zombie Castle and Old Mill. Kiddyland has 20 of Playland's 50 rides. Playland also has a beach, swimming pool, lake cruises, ice casino, miniature golf and sightseeing cruises on Long Island Sound and firework shows during the summer. Hours: Open May - mid-September. The ice rink is open October - April. Call for hours.

CHILDREN

Revolutionary War Battle
Putnam Cottage, 243 East Putnam Avenue, 203.869.9697
www.PutnamCottage.org
Originally a tavern serving travelers along the Post Road, it is now a
museum owned by the Daughters of the American Revolution. Each year
on the last Sunday in February (1 pm - 3 pm), the Putnam Hill Revolutionary War battle is recreated. A definite must-see for adults and children alike.
Hours: Wednesday, Friday, Sunday, 1 pm - 4 pm.

Renaissance Faire
Route 17A, Sterling Forest, Tuxedo NY, 845.351.5174
www.RenFair.com
Over 300 actors, in costume, mingle with the visitors (who can also don
costumes) in a mock sixteenth century village. A wonderful way to enjoy
a day of improvisation and learning.
Hours: August - mid-September, weekends only, 10 am - 7 pm.

Six Flags Great Adventure
Route 537, Jackson NJ, 732.928.1821
www.SixFlags.com/Parks/GreatAdventure
The park is a 2½ hour drive from Greenwich. But if you like roller coasters, it is worth a trip. Their large amusement park has rides for every
age. The Nitro and Medusa roller coasters (2 of their 13) are well known
by coaster aficionados. Six Flags Wild Safari is the world's largest drive
thru Safari outside Africa. Hurricane Harbor has water rides. Be sure to
call for hours of operation before you go.

Stamford Museum & Nature Center
39 Scofieldtown Road (corner of High Ridge Rd), Stamford CT,
203.322.1646
www.StamfordMuseum.org
118-acres, with a 10-acre working farm, pond life exhibit, boardwalks,
natural history exhibits, planetarium and observatory. If your child hasn't
grown up on a farm, this is the perfect place to learn about farming and
farm animals.
Hours: Open year round except for major holidays,
Monday - Saturday, 9 am - 5 pm; Sunday 11 am - 5 pm;
Planetarium shows Sunday at 3 pm;
Observatory, Friday, 8:30 pm - 10:30 pm.

CHILDREN

family outings

Stepping Stones Museum for Children

303 West Avenue (Mathews Park), Norwalk CT, 203.899.0606
www.SteppingStonesMuseum.org
Excellent interactive museum for kids under 10.
Hours: Tuesday - Saturday, 10 am - 5 pm, Sunday noon - 5 pm, open
Mondays in the summer.

United States Military Academy

West Point, NY, 845.938.2638
www.USMA.edu
Visitors now need a military ID to enter the grounds of the academy,
except for the visitor's center and military museum. One-hour guided
tours are available but photo IDs are required.
Hours: Guided tours: Daily 9 am - 4:45 pm.
Closed Thanksgiving, Christmas and New Years Day.

CHILDREN

Open Greenwich photo albums and you'll see pictures of fabulous parties. Many of the best parties are hosted by imaginative parents at home. *See ENTERTAINING for tents, caterers, party supply shops and other useful party information. A useful resource for party information is www.KidsEvents.com, developed by local residents, they cover a wide area of children's events.*

Arcade-2-Go

81 Bungay Road, Seymour CT, 203.881.8111, 866.362.6873
www.MobileAmusements.info
A trailer load of video games. 15 kids can play at once.

Aux Délices

23 Acosta Street, Stamford CT, 203.326.4540 x 108
www.AuxDelicesFoods.com
Fun, hands-on cooking parties can be held in their Stamford location or at your home.

Dave's Cast of Characters

914.235.7100
www.DavesCast.com
They specialize in professional entertainment, from full-costumed characters to carnival rides and inflatables.

Franc-O-Fun

807 Ridgefield Road, Wilton CT, 203.762.5645
www.Franc-o-Fun.com
A unique, fun, delicious, French party with a Madeline doll theme. Children learn to make two French tarts (apple and chocolate), play with dolls (and bears for the boys) while having a song time and lesson in French. Each child will receive a chef hat and un sac de surprises which will include Belgian chocolate, French stickers, pencil and coloring sheet.

Fire Trucks

Check with your local firehouse. Many will bring a truck over to your house in exchange for a donation. The fire department's non-emergency phone is 203.622.3950. The non-emergency numbers for all of the local fire companies are in NUMBERS YOU SHOULD KNOW.

parties at home

Gofer's Ice Cream Stand
522 East Putnam Avenue, 203.661.9080
www.GoferIceCream.com, www.IceCreamPartyBox.com
You can order a order a box of ice cream and toppings or you can have a complete catered party with staff and a deluxe cart.

Graham Clarke
43 Butler Hill Road, Somers NY, 914.669.5843
www.GrahamClarke.com
Graham is well known by many a Greenwich child. He sings silly songs with his guitars and the kids go crazy!

Greenwich 1-on-1 Sports Parties
Riverside CT, 203.344.9277
www.Greenwich1on1.com
Parties with a sports theme are always fun. This group provides the equipment and coaches.

Mad Science of Fairfield County
1122 Broadbridge Ave, Stratford CT, 888.381.9754
www.MadScience.org/Connecticut
Interactive experiments for children ages 5 to 12, combining science with entertainment. Party programs are tailored to the age group and can include chemical magic, vortex generators, indoor fireworks, or model rocket launchings.

Pied Piper Pony Rides
203.431.8322, 914.763.6925
www.piedpiperponyrides.com
You may want to invite one of their gentle ponies and friendly staff members to your party. The children will have a good time and the pony droppings will be removed. Closes for the winter.

CHILDREN

parties at home

Princess Tea Parties by Eileen
203.532.0547
Dress-up parties with tea sandwiches and entertainment to charm little girls in your home.

Science Parties
11 Tubbs Spring Court, Weston CT, 203.227.8112, 800.311.9993
www.ScienceMadeFunCT.net
Hands-on interactive parties where each child is involved with every experiment. Children ages 5 - 11 have lots of science fun making edible gummy drops or volcanoes and launching rockets. Parties are age appropriate. They also do after-school programs in elementary schools.

TIP: SIDEWALK SALES
Greenwich residents eagerly await summer sidewalk sales. Expect a good time with bargains galore. Don't forget to go inside the stores. They are also full of incredible buys during these sales. Mid-July (on a Thursday, Friday and Saturday) in Central Greenwich and Old Greenwich. Call the Chamber of Commerce, 203.869.3500. www.GreenwichChamber.com and www.OldGreenwich.org

CHILDREN

AMF Bowling Centers

701 Connecticut Avenue, Norwalk CT, 203.838.7501

47 Tarrytown Road, White Plains NY, 914.948.2677

www.AMFCenters.com

Bowling parties have been a hit for generations.

Audubon Center

613 Riversville Road, Greenwich, 203.869.5272

www.greenwich.center.audobon.org

Holding a party at the Audubon is a wonderful way to foster a love of nature. Highly trained guides will lead nature walks. You can rent space in the gorgeous center for a party.

Boys and Girls Club of Greenwich

4 Horseneck Lane, 203.869.3224

www.BCGC.org

This newly renovated building has a large gym for multi-sport activities led by friendly staff and a party room nearby for the kids to do arts/ crafts, bouncy castle, etc. Another option is to have an ice skating party. Charlie really enjoyed his party here.

Chocopologie Birthday Parties

12 South Main Street, Norwalk CT, 203.838.3131

www.Kinpschildt.com

What could be better than wearing a chef's hat, watching chocolate being made and then eating super sundaes and chocolate treats? Children get all the fun.

Darlene's Heavenly Desires Ice Cream Parties

185 Sound Beach Avenue, Old Greenwich, 203.698.9441

www.DarlenesHeavenlyDesires.com

Children ages 4 and up love ice cream sundaes, decorating Cone People and all of the fun games.

Dance Adventure

36 Sherwood Place, 203.625.0930

www.DanceAdventure.com

They offer sweet theme parties for young girls.

CHILDREN

Dorothy Hamill Skating Rink

Sherman Avenue, Greenwich, 203.531.8560
Call about renting the facility for a fun party.

Dynamic Martial Arts

202 Field Point Road, 203.629.4666
www.GreenwichKarate.com
A party where children can learn karate. Ages 4 and above.
Hours: Saturday parties, noon - 1:30 pm.

Fun for Kids (Laser Tag)

370 West Main Street, Stamford CT, 203.326.5656
www.Fun4KidsArcade.com
Though the location seems a bit seedy, once inside this arcade makes for a super party. Choose a soft play theme for young kids under 8 or go for the laser tag for the older ones.

Great Play

2000 W. Main Street (Shop Rite Center), Stamford CT, 203.978.1333
www.GreatPlay.com
Customized 90-minute parties right on the border of Greenwich. Choose from Field Day (age 3 -10), Fun and Games (ages 1 - 6) and Multi Sport (ages 4 - 10).

Eastern and Western Greenwich Civic Center Gymnasiums

Call Frank Gabriele at Parks & Recreation for details, 203.622.7821.

Greenwich Skatepark

100 Arch Street, Roger Sherman Baldwin Park
203.618.7649, 203.496.9876
www.GreenwichCT.org/ParksAndRec/prSkatePark.asp
The Greenwich Skate Park offers birthday parties on Saturday and Sunday mornings 10 am - noon. The fee is $100 which includes 10 children. Lessons are available for $25 per instructor. Bring a cake and pizza and have fun!

CHILDREN

parties away from home

Kids U

633 Hope Street, Stamford, 203.358.9500
www.KidsU.com
The gym parties include an hour of soft free play then the kids march into the gym for supervised activities and pizza.

My Gym

225 Atlantic Street, Stamford, 203.327.3496
www.My-Gym.com, www.My-Gym.com/Franchisee_schedule.aspx?id=181
2 hours of non-stop fun. Games, gymnastics, puppets, rides, songs you can customize to your child's liking.

My Three Sons (Laser Tag)

62 Wall Street, Norwalk CT, 203.838.3013
www.MyThreeSonsFun.com
Like Fun For Kids, a popular place for laser tag parties.

Nimble Thimble

21 Putnam Avenue, Port Chester NY, 914.934.2934
Choose a project for your age group; for instance, make a fabric covered bulletin board or a vest. Parents can bring cake and ice cream. Ages: 5 and up. Call to schedule a party.

Norwalk Aquarium

10 North Water Street, Norwalk, 203.852.0700 x 2206
www.MaritimeAquarium.org
Everyone loves this aquarium and having a party here combines fun and education.

Route 22 Restaurant

1980 West Main Street, Stamford, 203.323.2229
www.Rt22Restaurant.com
Donut machines, video games, movies, and kid friendly food.

Shaolin Studios

397 Putnam Avenue, Cos Cob, 203.661.5501, 203.844.0960
www.SDSSKungFu.com
A karate studio where Alex had a great birthday party.

CHILDREN

Sharkey's Cuts For Kids
220 East Putnam Avenue, Cos Cob, 203.629.kids
www.SharkeysCutsforKids.com
Glamour Girl parties are bound to make young girls smile. They make-up, dress-up and put on a fashion show.

Slot Car Raceways
344 Sawmill River Road, Elmsford NY, 914.592.5375
www.FlatOutFun.com
For 38 years the del Rosario family has entertained children and their parents with 62" slot car racing. Ages: 4 to 99.

Sports Center of Connecticut (laser tag)
784 River Road (Route 110), Shelton CT, 203.929.6500
About 50 minutes north of Greenwich, they have a Golf Driving Range, 18-Hole Mini-Golf course, Jungle themed Lazer Tag arena, Bowling, Game Zone arcade, Baseball/Softball Batting Cages.

Stepping Stones Museum
Matthews Park, 303 West Avenue, Norwalk CT
203.899.0606 x 228
www.SteppingStonesMuseum.org
Parties for up to 20 children ages 4 and up. After the guided tour, they have a special party room with cake and crafts.

Tumblebugs
6 Riverside Avenue, Riverside, 203.637.3303
www.TumblebugsNY.com/Greenwich.html
Great party for the 3 to 4 year old set. Friendly staff leads the kids in games around the gym and then they go into a party room for pizza and cake.

CHILDREN

parties away from home

YMCA

50 East Putnam Avenue, 203.869.1630

www.gwYMCA.org

Rent the gym or pool for your party with cake and presents in the party room. The Y can even provide a clown or magician. All ages.

Hours: weekdays, 5 am - 10 pm; Saturday, 6:30 am - 7 pm; Sunday, 8 am - 5 pm (summer hours may be shorter).

Yoga Party

Greenwich Yoga, 328 Pemberwick Road (at the Mill)

203.532.0660

www.GreenwichYoga.com

Party includes yoga class, games, henna tattoos and party bags.

YWCA

259 East Putnam Avenue, 203.869.6501 x 235

www.YWCAGreenwich.org

Rent a party room and/or hire one of their special instructors to teach the children activities such as soccer, swimming, gymnastics or climbing their rock wall. Parents provide the refreshments. Parties for all ages.

Hours: Parties are held during regular Y hours:

weekdays, 6:30 am - 10 pm;

Saturday, 7:30 am to 5 pm (summer Saturday hours are shorter).

TIPS: THE BEST CHOCOLATE TRUFFLES AND VANILLA ICE CREAM

We held a tasting contest to choose the best chocolate truffles and vanilla ice cream. Over a hundred people participated. The winner of the chocolate category was: Bridgewater Chocolate, Brookfield, CT, 203.775.2286, Cold Stone Creamery came in first for their ice cream. For all the ratings of the truffles and ice cream go to www.GreenwichGuide.com.

CHILDREN

playgrounds

Town playgrounds are open from 9 am to 4 pm. From late June through early August, the Greenwich Department of Parks and Recreation conducts supervised activities at the playgrounds for children ages 7 to 15. There are a number of small playgrounds scattered throughout the town (Binney Park, Bible Street Park, Christiano Park, Eastern and Western Greenwich Civic Centers, Island Beach and Loughlin Avenue Park), some are worth a trip even if you don't live in that area. Here are our favorites.

See also the section PARKS for more information.

Bruce Park

60 acres, across from the Bruce Museum on Museum Drive. One of Greenwich's prettiest parks, with excellent play equipment.

Byram Park

30 acres, located on Ritch Avenue and Byram Shore Road in Byram. The park has an attractive beach area and the town's only public fresh water pool. How can you go wrong? (The playground is tucked behind the Byram Shore Boat Club.)

Greenwich Common

16 acres, located adjacent to Greenwich Avenue, with an entrance on Greenwich Avenue next to the Havemeyer Building (Board of Education). This is a wonderful place to rest during a busy shopping day and let your children play. The Common has a small but attractive playground area.

Island Beach

See PARKS for information on ferry operation and beach passes.

Public Elementary Schools

These playgrounds are well kept and extensive. They are available to residents during the weekends and summer when school is not in session. For more information on the location of the elementary schools, see the Public Elementary School section under SCHOOLS.

Western Greenwich Civic Center

10 acres, located on the corner of Glenville Road and Pemberwick Road. This playground is a favorite with kids.

CHILDREN

Adventure Guides

YMCA, 50 East Putnam Avenue, 203.869.1630

www.gwymca.org

Outings and camp-outs for fathers and their five to ten year old children.

Boy Scouts of America

Greenwich Council #67, 63 Mason Street, 203.869.8424

www.GreenwichScouting.org or www.GreenwichBSA.com

This is the headquarters of the local chapter of the non-profit organization dedicated to instilling ethical values in young people. The Scouts are fortunate to own the Seton Reservation, a large preserve located at 363 Riversville Road. It serves as the site for the Cub Scout day camp as well as many other scouting outdoor programs. Call to check on a troop near you. The chapter sponsors the following programs: Programs open to boys: Tiger Cubs, age 6; Cub Scouts, ages 7 - 10; Boy Scouts, ages 11 - 18. Programs open to boys and girls: Explorers, ages 14 - 20 (specialties: aviation, scuba, emergency rescue.)

The Greenwich office has a small store for uniforms. A larger selection is available at the Darien Sports Shop (1127 Post Road, Darien CT, 203.655.2575), and the Connecticut Yankee Council #72, Boy Scouts of America (in Norwalk CT, exit 40A on the Merritt Parkway, 362 Main Avenue, 203.847.2445).

Hours: Greenwich Scouts office: weekdays 8:30 am - 4:30 pm.

Girl Scout Council of Southwestern Connecticut

529 Danbury Road, Wilton CT, 800.882.5561, 203.762.5557

www.gscswct.org

This is the headquarters of the local chapter of the non-profit organization dedicated to addressing girls' interests and their future contemporary roles as women.

Programs: Daisies, kindergarten; Brownies, grades 1 - 3;
Junior Girl Scouts, grades 4 - 6; Cadettes, grades 7 - 9;
Seniors, grades 9 - 12.

Uniforms are available from the Darien Sports Shop, 1127 Post Road, Darien CT, 203.655.2575.

Hours: weekdays, 9 am - 5:30 pm, Thursday until 8:30 pm.

CHILDREN

summer camp

No need to travel to New Hampshire or Maine, the Greenwich area has all sorts of camps. For a more complete list:

American Camping Association
New England Section, 781.541.6080
www.ACANewEngland.org
A national non-profit educational organization that accredits children's summer camps. Call to get a copy of their directory.

Community Answers
203.622.7979
www.GreenwichLibrary.org/commanswers.htm
Call for a copy of their Summer Resource Guide.

Summer Camp Website
www.MySummerCamps.com
877.777.7738
Used by many Greenwich Residents. It lists over 15,000 camps.

Summer Camp Fair
Greenwich High School, 203.625.8000
www.Greenwich.K12.ct.us/ghs/ghs.htm
Known as "Summerfare," this event is sponsored by the Greenwich High School PTA and draws hundreds of camps from around the USA. The fair is usually held in February.

Summer Camp Expo
Greenwich Academy, 203.625.8900
www.greenwichacademy.org
Their Summer Opportunity Fair is usually held at the end of January.

TIP: CAMP CARE PACKAGES
Packages Plus-N-More, 215 East Putnam Avenue (Mill Pond Shopping Center), Cos Cob, 203.625.8130, They will pack and ship your child's camping gear.

CHILDREN

summer camp programs

Check SPORTS for summer camp ideas. Many, such as Mead Farm and Getner Farm or Downunder Kayaking, have summer camps.

Allegra Summer Stock Performing Arts Camps
37 West Putnam Avenue, 203.629.9162
www.AllegraDanceStudio.com
Drama, theater, jazz, tap and other fantastic art programs.

All Stars Basketball Clinic
203.513.9583, 914.498.3004
www.AllStarsClinic.com
Summer co-ed day camp for ages 7 - 15 and co-ed specialized skills clinic for ages 8 - 12.

Arch Street Teen Center
100 Arch Street, Greenwich, 203.629.5744
www.ArchStreet.org
Hands-on arts and crafts, graphic design, film and radio production for kids entering grades 7 - 9.

Art Scampers
www.fpcg.org
First Presbyterian Church, 37 Lafayette Place, 203.869.7782
Summer day camp for ages 3 - 6. They Focus on art, music & drama.

Audubon Summer Children's Programs
Audubon Center, 613 Riversville Road, 203.869.5272
http://Greenwich.Audubon.org
The Audubon Summer Nature Day Camp offers themes for children entering K - 5 and for older children. Outstanding Teens Training in Ecological Research for grades 6 - 8.

Banksville Community House Summer Camp
12 Banksville Road, 203.622.9597
www.BanksvilleCommunityhouse.org
A perfect camp for those living in the Banksville area, featuring summer fun activities such as archery and swimming.

CHILDREN

Bible Camps
- St. Paul Evangelical Lutheran Church, 203.531.8466
- Greenwich Baptist Church, 203.869.2437
- Stanwich Congregational Church, 203.661.4420

Boy Scouts of America
Greenwich Council, 63 Mason Street, 203.869.8424
www.GreenwichBSA.com
The Seton Reservation at 363 Riversville Road is a great treasure. Day camp is available for boys in grades 1 - 4 with no prior Scouting experience. The camp does a good job of teaching outdoor sports such as swimming, archery, canoeing and fishing.

Bruce Museum
One Museum Drive, 203.869.0376
www.brucemuseum.org
Week long summer workshops held at Tod's Point. Co-ed ages 6 - 9 years.
For older children Palette, Brushes and Paint at the Bruce Museum; Co-ed, ages 7 - 13. Explores the basics of painting.

Brunswick School Baseball Camp
100 Maher Avenue, 203.625.5800, 203.625.5822
www.BrunswickSchool.org
Six one-week summer baseball camps for boys ages 7 - 13, as well as co-ed summer play camps for ages 3 - 5.

Bush Holley Camps
39 Strickland Road, Cos Cob, 203.552.5329, 203.869.6899
www.Hstg.org
- Summer History Camp: 2-week sessions focusing on history and art. Co-ed, grades 2 - 4.
- Young Artists Camp, grades 5 - 7.

CHILDREN

Camp Pelican

471 North Street, Greenwich

winter: 203.622.6654, summer: 203.869.4243

www.PelicanDayCamp.com

Established in 1965, this day camp provides instruction in a variety of outdoor and indoor activities. The camp begins in June and ends in August.

Sessions are four to seven weeks. Co-ed ages 3 - 13. Capacity 500. The camp is located on the campus of Greenwich Catholic School.

Camp Simmons

744 Lake Avenue, 203.869.0176, 203.869.3224

www.BGCG.org

Run by the Boys and Girls Club of Greenwich. Two-month session includes canoeing, swimming, field sports, archery, and nature hikes. Camp for ages 6 - 12.

Cardinal Baseball Camp

Directed by Greenwich High Varsity Coach, Mike Mora
 203.869.3736

www.CardinalBaseballCamp.com

For players ages 7 - 13, from 9 am - noon. 4-week and 2-week sessions begin in July at Greenwich High School field.

Children's Day School

449 Pemberwick Road, 203.532.1190

8 Riverside Avenue, 203.637.1122

Ages 3 - 7. Art, cooking, creative movement and music.

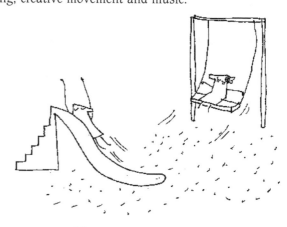

Computer Camps
- **Imagination Computer Camps**

  877.248.0206

  www.computercamps.com

  Email: camp@computercamps.com

  For the kid who can think of nothing but computers. Like-minded children come from all over the world to learn programming, computer graphics and rocketry. The closest camp is just outside Boston.

- **iD tech Camps**

  888.709.8324

  www.internalDrive.com

  Princeton, Columbia, Vassar and Sacred Heart all have programs for children ages 7 - 17 from beginner to advanced.

Creative Summer Camp at The Mead School
1095 Riverbank Road, Stamford 203.595.9500 x 63

www.MeadSchool.org

For boys and girls ages 6½ to 16 interested in dance, painting, design, drawing and more. Emphasis is on creativity, under the guidance of professional artists.

Department of Parks and Recreation
203.622.7830

http://greenwichct.virtualtownhall.net/public_documents/FOV1-00010F03/GreenwichCT_Recreation/programs/summer

There is a great variety of town-sponsored co-ed camps, such as Kamp Kairphree (ages 5 to 12), the Music and Art Program (children ages 8 - 15 who have had at least one year of study with an instrument) and Future Stars Tennis Camp (ages 6 - 14). Don't forget to ask for their program bulletin.
- Baseball programs
- Co-ed T Ball for 5 & 6 year olds.
- Small Fry Baseball 7 to 9 year olds.

CHILDREN

ESF Sports Camp
Held at the Greenwich Academy, 200 North Maple Avenue, 203.869.4444
www.esfcamps.com
Open to boys and girls.
- Day Camp (Crafts, Sports, Music) ages 4 - 8
- Sports Camp (8 sports), ages 7 - 14
- Senior Camp (Sports, Arts & Adventures), ages 9 - 15
- Tennis Camp (full or half-day), ages 6 to 15. Full or 2-day for beginner, intermediate and advanced players.

Field Club Squash Camp
276 Lake Avenue, 203.869.1309
A private club that offers a weekly Junior Summer Squash Camp, sometimes open to the public. The camp instructors are some of the best players in the world.

First Church Day Camp
First Congregational Church
108 Sound Beach Avenue, 203.637.5430
www.FCCOG.org
Co-ed day camp for ages 3 - 9. Beach activities, games, music and sports.

Future Stars Sports Camps
Armonk Tennis Club
546 Bedford Rd, Armonk NY, 914.273.8124, 914.273.8500
www.FSCamps.com
In its 30th year, this camp allows boys and girls, ages 6-16, to focus on a sport of their choice: tennis, soccer, lacrosse, basketball, baseball, softball, even computer, circus arts and magic. Programs run 9 am - 4 pm at SUNY Purchase College and some Greenwich locations.

Gan Israel Camp
270 Lake Avenue 203.869.5486
www.CampGan.com
Run by Chabad Lubavitch of Greenwich, provides traditional camp activities for ages 20 months - 3 years, and 4 to 11 years. Co-ed. July.

CHILDREN

Gilman Lacrosse Camps
Greenwich camp taught at Greenwich Middle School
800.944.7112
www.GilmanLacrosse.com
Summer day camps for boys and girls, grades 1 - 11.

Goatgear Summer Camps
Based at the Westchester Fairfield Hebrew Academy, 201.652.4477
www.GreenwichBasketball.com
www.GreenwichLacrosse.com
www.GreenwichBaseball.com
Run by energetic young men, these camps are offered from June through
August.

Greenwich Academy Squash Training Camp
200 North Maple Avenue, 203.625.8900
www.greenwichacademy.org/podium/default.aspx?t=116113
During the summer, the Academy uses their five international squash
courts to provide training for children in grades 5 and above.

Greenwich Country Day School Summer Camps
Old Church Road, 203.863.5600 x 5504
www.GCDS.net
Summer day camps for ages 4 - 12. Now in its 50th year, they have many
programs for each age group, including swimming, tennis, arts, crafts,
computers, woodworking and sailing.

Greenwich Public Schools Summer Program
Western Middle School, 203.531.7977
www.greenwichschools.org
Enrichment and review courses for all students from pre-K to grade 12.

Greenwich Racquet Club
Wire Mill Racquet Club
1 River Road, Cos Cob, contact: Ricardo Leon 203.661.0606,
www.GreenwichRacquetClub.com
Tennis and sports camp for children ages 4 - 7 and 8-16.

CHILDREN

Greenwich Crew
49 River Road, Cos Cob, 203.661.4033
www.GreenwichWaterClub.com
Rowing for ages 12 to 18.

Greenwich Skate Park Summer Ramp Camp
100 South Arch Street
203.622.7821, 203.622.7830, 203.496.9876
www.GreenwichCT.org/ParksAndRec/prRecPrograms.asp
Ages 6 - 12.

Kamp Kairphree
Greenwich Department of Parks and Recreation, 203.622.7814
www.GreenwichCT.org/ParksAndRec/ParksandRec.asp
A happy camp for 5-12 year olds.

Mad Science Summer Camp
888.381.9754
www.MadScience.org/Connecticut
Sponsored by Mad Science and the Greenwich Department of Parks and
Recreation. Programs for children ages 6 to 12.

Manhattanville College
2900 Purchase Street, Purchase, NY, 914.323.5214
www.Mville.edu
The college (914.694.2200) provides a summer writing workshop for
young people in grades 4 - 11, and hosts a number of sports camps,
including soccer, basketball and tennis.

Nike Camps
800.645.3226
www.US-SportsCamps.com
Nike runs a number of swim, volleyball, golf and tennis camps for boys
and girls ages 10 to 18.

Pre-School Summer Camp
Second Congregational Church
139 East Putnam Avenue, 203.869.8388
www.ThePreSchoolGreenwich.com
An independent, non-sectarian preschool camp for children ages 2 - 6.
Activities center around arts and crafts, music and drama, water play,
gardening and sports.

summer camp programs

Purchase College

735 Anderson Hill Road, Purchase NY, 914.251.6500

www.Purchase.edu

The State University of New York (SUNY) at Purchase offers a number of Summer Youth Programs in the Arts (art, music, and acting) for ages 6 - 17. They have early drop-off and extended-day options.

Robin Hood Camp

Herrick Road, Brooksville ME, 831.659.9143 (winter)

207.359.8313 (summer)

www.RobinHoodCamp.com

One of the best all around camps in the US. It has a strong Greenwich connection. Jerry is proud to count himself as an alumnus.

Saint Paul's Summer Camp

200 Riverside Avenue, Riverside, 203.637.3503

Camp for children 3 - 6; art, dance, sports, music, water play & nature.

Sandpiper's Beach Camp

203.637.3659

www.OGRCC.com

Sponsored by the Old Greenwich Riverside Community Center for children ages 3 - 10.

Silvermine School of Art

New Canaan CT, 203.966.6668

www.SilverMineArt.org

Creative summer camp for the artistically inclined, ages 5 - 17. Learn painting, drawing, photography and sculpture on an attractive 4-acre campus.

Sound Waters Camp

Cove Island Park, 1281 Cove Road, Stamford CT, 203.323.1978

www.SoundWaters.org/camp

Nature Discovery Grades K-5, Sea Stars Grades K-2, Bluefish Grades 3-5, Small Boat Sailing Grades 4-8, Opti Sailing Grades 4-6, Pixel Sailing Grades 5-8, Schooner Adventure Grades 6-9.

CHILDREN

Sunpiper Camp at the Mead School

1095 Riverbank Road, Stamford, 203.595.9500

www.MeadSchool.org

In its 27th year, this four-week camp for children combines art, drama, music, nature, science and story making with outdoor play.

A four-day program is for children 2½ years and a five day program for children 3-7.

U.S. Academy of Gymnastics

6 Riverside Avenue, 203.637.3303

Tumble Bugs Day Camp.

Whitby School Summer Camp

www.WhitbySchool.org

969 Lake Avenue, 203.869.8464

• Co-ed, ages 4 - 6. Montessori staff teaches gardening, cooking, arts, crafts and nature study; as well as math and science enrichment.

• Co-ed, ages 7-14. Multi-sports camp.

Windswept Farm (aka Mead Farm)

107 June Road, Stamford CT, 203.322.4984

www.MeadFarm.com

Co-ed ages 5 - 17. Weekly horseback riding, horse care, grooming, show prep and games. No previous riding experience necessary.

YMCA

50 East Putnam Avenue, 203.869.1630

www.gwYMCA.org

Summer Fun Clubs - 2-week co-ed sessions begin at the end of June. They include field trips, sports, and environmental education.

YWCA

259 East Putnam Avenue, 203.869.6501 x 225

www.YWCAGreenwich.org

• Camp Ta Yi To is a co-ed camp for grades K - 5; includes swimming and tennis.

• Pre-school Camp, ages 15 months - 2 years; songs, stories, play.

• Pre-school Camp, ages 3 - 5; gymnastics, swimming, cooking.

• Dance Camp, ages 10 - 16; Ballet, jazz, choreography, hip hop.

CHILDREN

support services

ABILIS Greenwich
50 Glenville Street, 203.531.1880
www.Abilis.us
Family support services and after-school programs for families of children with special needs.

Child Guidance Center of Southern Connecticut
196 Greyrock Place, Stamford CT, 203.324.6127, 983.5294;
Greenwich 203.983.5294, 24/hour crisis line 203.323.9797
www.ChildGuidanceCT.org
Professionally staffed mental health center for children and adolescents. Individual, group and family therapy, parent guidance, 24-hour crisis services, and community education programs.

Community Answers
203.622.7979
www.CommunityAnswers.org
Information on parent education programs, support groups, crisis programs, counseling services, nannies, au pair and babysitting services.

Family Centers
40 Arch Street, 203.869.4848
20 Bridge Street, 203.629.2822
www.FamilyCenters.org
This United Way human service agency offers a multitude of helpful programs such as the Den for Grieving Kids and individual or family counseling.

Family Health
Greenwich Department of Health, 203.622.7854, 203.622.3782
www.greenwichct.org/HealthDept/HealthDept.asp
Prenatal and postpartum home visits, well child clinics (birth to age 5), immunization and hypertension screening clinic (5 years to adult); school health services; early childhood/daycare licenses.

Kids in Crisis
1 Salem Street, Cos Cob, 203.327.5437
www.KidsinCrisis.org
Crisis intervention counseling and short term shelter. Ages Newborn to 17 years.

CHILDREN

La Leche League

89 Sherwood Place, 203.869.5344

www.LLLUsa.org/CT/WebGreenwichCT.html

Support groups and information on breast feeding.

Parents' Exchange

25 Valley Drive, Greenwich Health at Greenwich Hospital

203.863.3780, 203.863.4444

www.GreenHosp.org/programs_tb.asp#infant_group

Weekly discussion groups led by child development specialists. A good environment to stimulate and provide parents with opportunities to exchange ideas. Parents are grouped by their children's age from infants to adolescents. Babysitting is available.

Parents Together

PO Box 4843, Greenwich CT, 06831

203.698.0158, 273.1767, 203.329.2234

www.ParentsTogetherCT.org

An independent, non-profit organization working in cooperation with the PTA Council and public and independent schools in Greenwich. They publish two good newsletters, one for parents of children from birth - fifth grade and another for grades 6 - 12. For an annual subscription, send a check for $10 and indicate the newsletter you want to receive.

Parent to Parent Network

50 Glenville Street, 203.629.1880 x 300

Information network for families with children who have special needs.

Tender Beginnings

At Greenwich Hospital, 203.863.3655

www.GreenHosp.org/programs_tb.asp

Expectant parent classes, Lamaze classes, baby care and breastfeeding classes, nutrition, prenatal exercise, newborn parenting groups, grand-parenting, baby food preparation, babysitting, sibling classes.

CLUBS

Garden Clubs are listed in the section FLOWERS & GARDENS
Volunteer Organizations are described on
www.GreenwichVolunteerGuide.com. This site organizes them by interest.
Information about clubs and organizations is also available from
Community Answers www.GreenwichLibrary.org/commanswers.htm
See separate section for CHARITABLE AND SERVICE ORGANIZATIONS.

country clubs

Greenwich has a number of yacht and country clubs. Costs to join a club vary from about $12,000 to $40,000 for the initiation fee with annual dues ranging from approximately $6,000 to more than $10,000. Country clubs with golf courses are typically the most expensive. Clubs with dining rooms usually require a quarterly food minimum. In addition, clubs may have assessments for capital improvements. Membership in most private clubs requires a proposer and several seconders or sponsors. Proposers are usually required to have no business connection with the proposed member. The more members you know, the easier it is to join. Clubs which serve a particular area, such as Belle Haven or Milbrook, often give preference to area residents. The waiting period to join a club can be several years.

Bailiwick Club of Greenwich
(Swimming and tennis)
12 Duncan Drive, 203.531.7591 (summer)
www.BailiwickClub.com
Marc Hattem, Manager

Burning Tree Country Club
(Dining, golf, swimming, tennis, paddle tennis)
120 Perkins Road, 203.869.9004, 203.869.9010
Robert Bacon, Manager

Fairview Country Club
(Dining, golf, tennis, paddle tennis, swimming)
1241 King Street, 203.531.6200
www.FairviewCountryClub.org
Timothy Clinton, Manager

CLUBS

country clubs

Field Club

(Dining, tennis (grass & indoor), squash, paddle tennis, swimming)
276 Lake Avenue, 203.869.1300
www.FCofGreenwich.com
Martina Halsey, Manager

Greenwich Country Club

(Dining, golf, tennis, squash, paddle tennis, swimming, skeet)
19 Doubling Road, 203.869.1000
www.GreenwichCountryClub.org
Guy D'Ambrosio, Manager

Innis Arden Golf Club

(Dining, golf, tennis, paddle tennis, swimming)
120 Tomac Avenue, Old Greenwich, 203.637.6900
www.InnisArdenGolfClub.com
Dan Farreil, Manager

Italian Center of Stamford

(indoor and outdoor pools, gym, tennis, paddle tennis, miniature golf)
1620 Newfield Avenue, Stamford CT, 203.322.6941
www.ItalianCenter.org
Situated on 28 acres in a country club setting, the center is a unique type
of club with membership open to everyone.

Milbrook Club

(Dining, golf, swimming, paddle tennis, tennis)
61 Woodside Drive, 203.869.4540
www.MilbrookClub.com
Scott Kloster, Manager

Round Hill Club

(Dining, golf, swimming, tennis, skeet)
33 Round Hill Club Road, 203.869.2350
www.RhClub.org
Dennis Meermans, Manager

CLUBS

country clubs

Stanwich Club
(Dining, golf, swimming, tennis, paddle tennis)
888 North Street, 203.869.0555
www.Stanwich.com
Peter Tunley, Manager

Tamarack Country Club
(Dining, golf, swimming, tennis)
55 Locust Road, 203.531.7300
www.tamarackcountryclub.com
Brian Gillespie, Manager

TIP: HOW TO PRICE YOUR GREENWICH HOME

How much your home is worth is determined not by Realtors, but by supply and demand at the time you list. Buyers are comparison shoppers. They look at what has sold and what is for sale. Then they decide value. It is the job of your Realtor to educate you about the local real estate market and how your home fits into it. It is your job to set an informed price for your home. When you list your home it will be competing with similar homes on the market—as well as those that have recently sold. Your Realtor should provide you with a complete analysis of the real estate market, the sales in your neighborhood and comparable homes presently for sale. You should consider driving by these homes and let your Realtor explain how they compare, and why they sold or were priced the way they were. Don't confuse pricing your property with choosing your Realtor. Choose the Realtor you like and trust first. Then work with them to price your home.

CLUBS

newcomers clubs

Greenwich Newcomers Society

Contact Greg Kraut 917.355.8479

www.GreenwichNewcomersSociety.com

GNS has monthly programs and activities to help new residents forge friendships and become acquainted with Greenwich.

Old Greenwich-Riverside Newcomers' Club

PO Box 256, Old Greenwich, CT 06870

www.greenwichnewcomers.com

Ingrid Winn, President, 203.637.0483

Jane Kikham, Membership Chairman, 203.588.9461

The Club is 48 years old and hosts a great variety of functions, from wine tastings to museum trips. There are events for everyone, and they welcome new and established residents of Greenwich and surrounding areas. Be sure to ask for their excellent newsletter.

skating clubs

Greenwich Skating Club

Cardinal Road, Greenwich, 863.5602

www.GreenwichSkatingClub.org

An always popular club, apply early. You must be proposed by a member. Your children must be interested in actively participating in their hockey or figure skating programs.

CLUBS

As one might expect for a town on the water, Greenwich has a number of excellent yacht and boating clubs. Many yacht clubs have long waiting lists (some as long as 12 years). Like the country clubs, most are private.

Belle Haven Club
(Dining, boating, tennis, swimming)
100 Harbor Drive, 203.861.5353
www.BelleHavenClub.com
Neil P. MacKenzie, Manager

Byram Shore Boat Club
Byram Park, 203.531.9858 (clubhouse)
www.ByramShore.org
Eric Johnson, Commodore
Mooring/docking adjacent to town park and beach.

Cos Cob Yacht Club
PO Box 155, Riverside CT, 06878
Walter X. Burns, Jr, Commodore, 203.661.5946
Social club for people interested in boating. Membership is by invitation.

Greenwich Boat & Yacht Club
(Club House, Mooring/docking and picnic areas)
Grass Island, 203.622.9558
PO Box 40 Greenwich CT, 06830
www.GBYC.org
Michael Curley, Commodore, 203.637.1151
Membership is open to all interested residents of the town.

Greenwich Water Club
River Road, Cos Cob, 203.661.4033
www.GreenwichWaterClub.com
Dining, swimming, aquatics, fitness, boating and rowing.
There is currently a 6 months to one year wait list.
Carla Catanzaro, General Manager.

CLUBS

yacht clubs

Indian Harbor Yacht Club
(Dining and boating facilities including mooring/docking)
710 Steamboat Road, 203.869.2484
www.indianharboryc.com
Samuel B. Fortenbaugh, Commodore
David Foster, Manager

Mianus River Boat & Yacht Club
98 Strickland Road, Cos Cob, 203.869.4689
www.mrbyc.com
Richard Mould, Commodore, 203.531.8042
Boat and yacht club open to any Greenwich resident. Meets the first Monday of the month at 7:30 pm at the clubhouse.

Old Greenwich Yacht Club
Tods Point
PO Box 162, Old Greenwich, 637.3074
www.ogyc.org
Mary Rappa, Commodore
Membership is open to all Greenwich residents. Clubhouse, launch and moorings are handled through the town hall.

Riverside Yacht Club
(Dining, swimming, beach, tennis and boating)
102 Club Road, Riverside, 203.637.1706
www.riversideyc.org
Walter Alder, Commodore
Courtney Wetzel, Manager

Rocky Point Club
(Clubhouse, mooring, salt water pool)
Rocky Point Road, Old Greenwich, 203.637.2397 (summer only)
PO Box 359
www.RockyPointClub.com
Alex Fraser, Commodore

There are many language schools and other continuing education resources in and around the town. The following are some of our favorites.

For additional information on art, dance or music instruction, see the appropriate section under CULTURE.

For Sports Instruction, see FITNESS & SPORTS.

For Children's Education see CHILDREN

For reading and research see BOOKS & LIBRARIES

TIP: THE JOB SEARCH

If you are looking for a job or an employee, check out the Job Board. This free public bulletin board is run by Community Answers for people from the ages 17 - 55. It can be viewed in the window of Community Answers during Library hours. Postings can be phoned in at 203.622.7979 or posted in person weekdays, 9 am - 5 pm at the central Greenwich Library. For older job seekers, check out USE (Utilizing Senior Energy) at the Greenwich Senior Center, 203.629.8032. Younger job seekers should go to The Student Employment Service at the Greenwich High School, 203.625.8008 until June and to Community Answers during the summer.

CONTINUING ED - ADULTS
index

Art Training
Greenwich Arts Council
Greenwich Art Society Art Classes
Silvermine Guild Art Center
Westchester Art Workshop
    Westchester Community College

Computer Training
Diane McKeever
Greenwich Continuing Education
Norwalk Community College
Find computer courses designed for
    seniors in the SENIORS section.
For computer repairs see SERVICES.

Cooking Courses
Aux Delices Cooking School
Chocopologie Cooking School
Cucina Casalinga
Greenwich Continuing Education
Institute of Culinary Education
Lauren Groveman's Kitchen
Ronnie Fein School of Creative
    Cooking
Shaw Guides
Time to Eat
Williams-Sonoma Cooking Classes

Dancing Skills
Arthur Murray
Dick Conseur's Ballroom Dancing
Round Hill Country Dances

Gardening Education
For Gardening Clubs see
    FLOWERS AND GARDENS
Garden Education Center
Loretta Stagen Floral Designs

General Adult Education
Archaeological Associates of
    Greenwich
Astronomical Society of Greenwich
Fairfield University
Greenwich Continuing Education
Lifetime Learners Institute
Manhattanville College
Norwalk Community College
Shaw Guides
Stamford Adult Education
SUNY Purchase
UCONN Stamford
Westchester Community College
World Affairs Forum

Language Training
Alliance Française
French-American School
Language Exchange

Music Training
Greenwich Arts Council
Fraioli School of Music
    (Greenwich Music)
Riverside School of Music
Robert Marullo

Woodworking Skills
Wood Workers Club

Alliance Française
299 Greenwich Avenue (2nd floor Greenwich Arts Center), 203.629.2301,1340
www.AFGreenwich.org
An ideal way to learn or refresh your French.

Archaeological Associates of Greenwich
33 Byram Drive, 203.661.4654
www.ArchaeologyBriefs.Blogspot.com
They have lectures by distinguished archaeological speakers at the Bruce Museum and act as a clearinghouse for archaeological education programs in the Greenwich area. They publish a newsletter eight times a year. Membership is open to all.

Arthur Murray
6 Lewis Street, 203.485.9422, 203.983.5546
www.TryDancing.com
Learn the latest dances with experienced instructors.

Astronomical Society of Greenwich
Bowman Observatory at Julian Curtiss Elementary
203.869.6786 x 338
www.seocom.com/asg
Meetings cover general astronomical, discussions and related information, and usually include a special speaker. Weather permitting, observatory public nights are the 2nd & 4th Tuesdays.

Aux Délices Cooking School
23 Acosta Street, Stamford, 203.326.4540 x 108
Debra Ponzek, well known for her delicious Aux Delices foods, chef-instructor Lynn Manheim, and pastry chef Cyril Chaminade, have a series of hard-to-resist cooking classes, such as: Easy Asian Cooking, Tapas, Cooking with Kids, Cooking for the Jewish Holidays, Spa Cooking and For Chocolate Lovers Only. Usually, classes are for up to 20 people and cost $75 per person.

Chocopologie Cooking School
12 South Main Street, Norwalk, CT, 203.854.4754
Fritz Knipschildt, named one of the best chocolatiers in the world by Gourmet Magazine, shares his secrets for making chocolate truffles.

Cucina Casalinga

Wilton, CT, 203.762.0768

www.cucinacasalinga.com

Sally Maraventano has been teaching homestyle Italian cooking for over 15 years. She has daytime and evening classes and can accommodate groups as large as 15 students. Classes cost about $85 per person (which includes dinner).

Diane McKeever, CPP

www.DianeMcKeever.com

If you want to learn a Microsoft program, you should enroll in one of Diane's Continuing Education classes at the Greenwich High School. But if you don't have the time, she gives private lessons for students of all levels. She is a CPP (Certified Patient Person).

Dick Conseur's Ballroom Dancing

596 Stillwater Road, Stamford, 203.325.1332

For confidence on the dance floor, give Dick Conseur a call. Discreet private lessons for ballroom or country and western dancing. He also teaches social and Latin dance at Greenwich Adult and Continuing Education.

Fairfield University

Fairfield, CT, 203.254.4220, 203.254. 4000

www.fairfield.edu

Fairfield is a major university with a 200-acre campus and great offerings in almost every conceivable subject. Definitely worth a call to get their catalog. They have over 1,000 continuing education students.

Fraioli School of Music @ Greenwich Music

1200 East Putnam Avenue, Riverside, 203.869.3615

www.GreenwichMusic.com

Their store is filled with sheet music and instruments. They have a large selection of guitars & drums and a helpful staff. A full line of instruments are available for rent; a great way to discover if that instrument is right for you or your child. They have a music school (Fraioli School of Music) next door where they give lessons for the instruments they carry. Hours: Monday - Thursday, 10 am - 7 pm;

Friday & Saturday, 10 am - 6 pm; Sunday, noon - 4 pm.

CONTINUING ED - ADULTS

French-American School
Larchmont, Mamaroneck and Scarsdale Campuses
914.834.3002 x 253
www.Fasny.org
Adult and children classes in French, Mandarin Chinese, Russian, Spanish, Arabic and Italian. They also teach adult classes in creative writing, Shakespeare, sculpture and watercolors. They do tours of Manhattan museums to help practice skills in conversation.

Garden Education Center
Montgomery Pinetum, Bible Street, Cos Cob, 203.869.9242
www.gecgreenwich.org
The Center's new horticulture buildings provide classrooms and workrooms for a variety of excellent programs and lectures. Founded in 1957, the center is not only a strong educational facility, but also provides a good framework for new residents to make friends. They are closed during the summer.

Greenwich Arts Council
299 Greenwich Avenue, 203.622.3998
www.greenwicharts.org
The GAC maintains a talent bank of all types of music, theater, dance and art teachers and publishes an informative newsletter three times a year. It is a good resource for classes as disparate as O-Tatsu Taiko Japanese drumming, classical ballet or acting.

Greenwich Art Society Art Classes
299 Greenwich Avenue, 203.629.1533
www.GreenwichArtSociety.org
A delightful place to study painting, drawing, botanical illustration, sculpture or monotype.

Greenwich Continuing Education
Greenwich High School, 203.625.7474, 203.625.7475
http://greenwichschools.org/gce
This amazing program offers a wide range of courses taught at the high school by interesting teachers. It is always priced right. Registration is in January and August/September. Be sure to call for a catalog; you are bound to see several courses you can't resist.

CONTINUING ED - ADULTS

Institute of Culinary Education

50 West 23rd Street, New York NY, 800.522.4610, 212.847.0700
www.iceculinary.com
Although this school is in New York City, it has from time to time conducted courses in the Greenwich area. Founded by Peter Kump in 1975, it has established a large Greenwich following. Hands-on courses and workshops from 5 to 25 hours. The emphasis is on techniques of fine cooking. The average class size is 12 for hands-on instruction and 30 for demonstrations. The school has a staff of 45 who operate from a large facility with 9 kitchens. Hands-on classes range from $85 to $525.

(The) Language Exchange

Mill Pond Shopping Center (203 East Putnam Avenue) Cos Cob, 203.422.2024
www.ForeignLanguageExchange.com
Instruction in 18 languages including ESL. Adult courses as well as children's classes for ages 3 to 13. They offer total immersion camps for students in elementary, middle and high school.

Lauren Groveman's Kitchen

55 Prospect Avenue, Larchmont NY, 914.834.1372
www.LaurenGroveman.com
Established in 1990, the school provides 5-session participation courses as well as individual classes for adults and young people. The emphasis is on techniques and the preparation of comfort foods, breads and appetizers. The average class size is 6. Cost is $450 for a five-session course and $100 for a specialty course.

Lifetime Learners Institute

Norwalk Community College, 188 Richards Avenue, 203.857.3330
office: Room W013, West Campus, Lower Level
www.LifeTimeLearners.org
A fabulous organization, affiliated with the Elderhostel Institute Network. It is an independent continuing education program within NCC. To join you must be over 50 and want to continue learning. Members can choose from over 40 courses.

CONTINUING ED - ADULTS

Loretta Stagen Floral Designs
203.323.3544
www.LorettaStagen.com
She provides innovative flower arrangements and party decorations for corporate events and weddings. She also offers classes and workshops in flower arranging. For five or more students, she will create a special class in their area of interest.

Manhattanville College
Purchase NY, 914.694.2200, 800.328.4553
www.mville.edu
A local college with an attractive campus and good course offerings.

Norwalk Community College
Norwalk CT, 203.857.7080
www.ncc.commnet.edu (Click on Extended Studies)
A surprisingly large selection (more than 300 courses) of adult education courses on a variety of subjects. Nice, modern facilities. They also offer courses at satellite locations in Stamford, Greenwich and Darien. Directions: Exit 13 off I-95 N.

(The) Riverside School of Music
401 East Putnam Avenue, Riverside, 203.661.9501.
www.atelierconstantinpopescu.com
Excellent instructors in a variety of string instruments.

Robert Marullo
203.869.4943
This popular, talented piano teacher at Greenwich Academy,also gives private lessons. We strongly recommend him for lessons as well as piano repairs and tuning.

Ronnie Fein School of Creative Cooking
32 Heming Way, Stamford, 203.322.7114
Year-round cooking workshops with an emphasis on ingredients, techniques and menus for American, baking/pastry, children, French, healthy/vegetarian & Italian. She also has children's classes or will tailor a course to fit your needs. Workshops are usually 4 people and cost $250 per session. She has been teaching cooking and writing food stories for *Greenwich Time* for over 20 years.

Round Hill Country Dances

Round Hill Community House

www.roundhill.net

For information call 914.262.0653 or 203.762.5370

They host callers and bands from around Connecticut. Dances are on the second Saturday every month, as well as the Saturday after Thanksgiving. Their average dance attendance is between 100 and 120 people. First timers are welcomed.

Shaw Guides

www.ShawGuides.com

A database of career and recreational cooking schools, wine courses, golf & tennis schools & camps, high performance programs, writers conferences,photography, film & video workshops & schools, art & craft workshops, language vacations, cultural travel programs, and artists' and writers' residencies & retreats.

Silvermine Guild Art Center

New Canaan, CT, 203.966.9700, 203.966.6668

www.SilvermineArt.org

Excellent art instruction for adults and youngsters alike at a famous art site. They have more than 100 courses to choose from.

Stamford Adult Education

Adult Learning Center, 369 Washington Blvd., 203.977.4209

www.StamfordAdultEd.com

Check their website for their large number of enrichment classes.

SUNY Purchase

735 Anderson Hill Road, Purchase, NY, 914.251.6500

www.Purchase.edu

Purchase College is a part of the State University of New York. It has beautiful grounds and striking modern buildings. Check out their adult education offerings.

Time To Eat

Christopher Peacock, 2 Dearfield Drive, Greenwich

Contact: Nicole Straight, 203.221.8306

www.Time-to-Eat.com

Ninety-minute classes designed to teach busy moms to prepare healthy meals in 15 minutes. $85 to $95 per person.

CONTINUING ED - ADULTS

UCONN Stamford
Connecticut Information Technology Institute
One University Place, Stamford, 203.251.8400
www.stamford.uconn.edu
Close by, in Stamford, is an exciting new facility where the University of Connecticut offers undergraduate programs plus professional and technical continuing education courses.

Westchester Community College
Main campus: 75 Grasslands Road, Valhalla NY, 914.606.6600
Art workshop: 196 Central Avenue (Westchester County Center), White Plains
NY, 914.606.7500
www.Sunywcc.edu
The White Plains location has classes in fine arts, photography, and visual arts. The main campus in Valhalla offers a wide variety of continuing education courses.

Williams-Sonoma Cooking Classes
Stamford Town Center, Stamford, CT, 203.961.0977
The Westchester Mall,125 Westchester Avenue,
White Plains, NY 914.644.8360
www.WilliamsSonoma.com
Classes in this popular store are held on Wednesday evenings from 6 pm to 9 pm. Be sure to call for a reservation. Classes are demonstration only, for 12 - 15 people and cost $50 per person. They teach courses such as: Elegant Holiday Dinners Made Easy, The Antipasto Table, Hors d'oeuvres and First Courses.

Woodworkers Club
215 Westport Avenue, Norwalk CT, 203.847.9663, 203.567.4691
www.WoodworkersClubNorwalk.com
Classes are in their 5,000 square foot shop, next to their store. They teach beginner and intermediate levels. Learn to build bookshelves, build a mortise and tenon bench or turn a spindle.

World Affairs Forum
800 Summer Street, Suite 340, Stamford CT, 203.356.0340
www.WorldAffairsForum.org
A non-profit, non-partisan organization whose mission is to expand understanding of global affairs and America's role in the world. Join this group and get the inside views from experts at their breakfast or dinner meetings.

CULTURE

Greenwich has a rare and full appreciation of the arts. Note the peaceful expressions on the faces in the audience of the Greenwich Symphony, or the joyful chatter of a family in the Bruce Museum, or the smiles surrounding the Grace Notes, and you may discover how many of our high-powered, busiest residents relax and refresh themselves.

Libraries are described under BOOKS & LIBRARIES
See also Family Outings in CHILDREN

art

Art galleries and framers are listed under STORES
For art education see CONTINUING EDUCATION or CHILDREN

Art Society of Old Greenwich
PO Box 103, Greenwich
Gretchen Tatge, President, 203.637.9949
An organization of amateur and professional artists with membership open to everyone. We always enjoy their Sound Beach Avenue sidewalk art show in September.

Brant Foundation Art Study Center
941 North Street, Greenwich CT, 06830
thebrantfoundation@gmail.com
An appointment-only gallery in Conyers Farm. The 1902 stone barn houses Peter Brant's collection of 94 works by 25 artists from Andy Warhol and Jeff Koons to Cindy Sherman and Keith Haring. The gallery is open from late May through February. Reservations may be made by email.

Greenwich Arts Council

Bendheim Gallery
299 Greenwich Avenue, 203.862.6750
www.GreenwichArts.org
The Executive Director in combination with a tiny staff and an outstanding board, is keeping this non-profit organization dynamic. Established in 1973, the GAC provides year-round, high-quality arts programs, educational outreach programs and gallery exhibits. Housed in the lovely landmark Greenwich Arts Center building in downtown Greenwich's shopping district, the GAC is home to The Bendheim Gallery, and offers affordable performance, meeting, exhibition and office space, art studios and a large dance studio. It is also home to the Choral Society, Symphony and the Art Society, as well as the Alliance Francaise and Friendship Ambassadors Foundation (a United Nations-affiliated cultural organization). The GAC maintains a talent bank of all types of music, theater, dance and art teachers and publishes an informative newsletter three times a year. It is a good resource for classes as disparate as O-Tatsu Taiko Japanese drumming, classical ballet or acting. The Bendheim Gallery is available to rent for private functions. Every April at Tod's Point they sponsor Go Fly A Kite!

Flinn Gallery

Greenwich Library, Second Floor
101 W Putnam Avenue, 203.622.7947
www.FlinnGallery.com
The Flinn Gallery of the Greenwich Library is run by volunteers, who select, curate and install exhibitions and hold receptions, They put on six exhibitions a year. These exhibits generally run for six weeks and are scheduled between September and June.

Greenwich Art Society

299 Greenwich Avenue, 203.629.1533

www.GreenwichArtSociety.org

The Art Society founded in 1912 by the Cos Cob Colony of Artists. Today it has more than 350 artists from Fairfield and Westchester counties. Many of these talented artists are from Greenwich. The society has art classes for adults and children. It holds 3 juried exhibitions and one non-juried members exhibition every year. While walking along Greenwich Avenue, stop in the Greenwich Art Center to see the latest show. Hours: Monday, Wednesday, Friday and Saturday 10 am - 5 pm.

TIP: KITE FLYING FESTIVAL (Go Fly A Kite!)

www.greenwicharts.org

Every April, at Tod's Point, children of all ages have fun at the Kite Flying Festival. It is sponsored by the Greenwich Arts Council and the Town of Greenwich Department of Parks and Recreation. Participants are encouraged to bring kites of all shapes and sizes, made of paper, plastic or fabric.

film & movie theaters in greenwich

Criterion Cinemas at Greenwich Plaza 3

2 Railroad Avenue, 203.869.4030

http://www.Bowtiecinemas.com/plaza-3.html

Greenwich's remaining commercial movie house. Use it or lose it. General Admission $10.50, Children (11 and under) $7.50, Seniors (62 & over) $9.00.

Focus on French Cinema

203.698.2742 or Renee Ketcham, 203.629.3644

www.FocusOnFrenchCinema.org

Held at Pepsico Theater, Performing Arts Center, Purchase College, this annual 3-day event is organized by Alliance Francaise of Greenwich. Last year over 2,000 people attended. All films are in French with English subtitles. This exciting film festival, held at the end of March or early April, includes films not usually available in the US and gives a unique insight into the French film industry. Not only do you get to see great films, but the audience has the opportunity to meet actors and directors.

Greenwich Classic Film Series

914.725.0999

www.GreenwichClassicFilmSeries.com

Now in its 36th season and with over 700 members, it has two 6-film series. Movies from the 30s through the 70s with lectures by guest film critics are shown at the Bow Tie Movie Theater, Saturday mornings at 10 am and Monday evenings at 7 pm. Membership is $125 for a 6-film series. Join their mailing list by sending your e-mail address.

Greenwich Library Friday Films

101 West Putnam Avenue, 203.622.7910

www.greenwichlibrary.org/About%20the%20Library/ Greenwich%20Library%20Friends/FriendsFridayFilms.aspx

On most Friday nights at 8 pm (doors open at 7:40) in the Cole Auditorium, the Library shows award-winning US and foreign films. Admission is free. Call or use the web site to get a schedule and verify that a film is being shown.

CULTURE

film & movie theaters nearby

Out of town theaters are mapped on the Greenwich Guide Website www.greenwichguide.com/theaters.htm

AMC Loews 14

40 Westchester Avenue, (Waterfront Place) Port Chester NY, 914.510.1000 www.amcentertainment.com/PortChester/

Lots of free parking and 14 screens in the new Waterfront complex.

Avon Art Films

272 Bedford Street, Stamford, 203.967.3660
www.AvonTheater.org
The Avon Theater is a fully restored classic movie theater. Built in 1939, the Avon was run by Crown Theaters until it closed in 1998. In 2001 it was purchased by a private investor from Greenwich. The theater was fully restored and reopened January, 2004 and shows independent, art and foreign films as well as Hollywood classics.

Bow Tie Cinemas Landmark 9

5 Landmark Square, Stamford, 203.324.3100
www.bowtiecinemas.com/landmark-9.html

Bow Tie Cinemas Majestic 6

118 Summer Street, Stamford, 203,323.1690
www.bowtiecinemas.com/majestic-6.html
The newest theater in Stamford and right in the heart of the restaurant district.

Garden Cinemas

26 Isaac Street, Norwalk CT, 203.838.4504
www.ghcinemas.com
Great movie theater for foreign movies you won't find in local multiplexes. The theater has lots of leg room.

film & movie theaters nearby

IMAX Theater

At the Norwalk Aquarium, 10 North Water Street, SoNo, 203.852.0700
www.MaritimeAquarium.org
The screen is six stories high and eight stories wide and the visual effects are stunning. *See full description under CHILDREN, FAMILY OUT-INGS. Hours: Open daily, 10 am - 5 pm.*

State Cinema

990 Hope Street, Stamford, 203.325.0250
www.GHCinemas.com
One of the least expensive theaters in the area. A good place to take a group of children and your best bet for avoiding long lines.

movie rentals

Greenwich Library

www.GreenwichLibrary.org
The Library has an extensive collection of CDs, Video Tapes and DVDs. Use the website to reserve availability or phone 203.622.7910 to reserve items. Ask to have your reserved materials sent to one of the branches.

Netflix

www.NetFlix.com
Netflix is an internet based movie (and TV show) rental store. For a fixed monthly fee (based on how many films you'd like on hand at any given time) you can rent and/or download for instant viewing any film or show that is available on DVD. The selection is staggering, including thousands of foreign films, and their customer service is excellent. They let you keep a movie for a long as you like—it is all covered in the monthly fee. The DVDs you order arrive by mail very quickly and you return them in red prepaid envelopes. Instant viewing works well if you have a strong, fast internet connection.

CULTURE

museums

Children oriented museums are listed in CHILDREN under Family Outings.

Bruce Museum

1 Museum Drive, 203.869.0376, 203.869.6786
www.BruceMuseum.org
This year the Bruce attracted over 100,000 visitors to their exciting exhibitions making the Bruce one of the most popular museums in Connecticut. In addition, the Bruce sponsored over 50 lectures and gave educational programs to over 18,000 children. Under the leadership of Peter Sutton, the Museum has been able to attract major art exhibits. No wonder the Bruce is placed in the top 10% of US museums. The Museum sponsors two fairs in Bruce Park every year. The mid-May Craft Fair and the Columbus Day Arts Festival have juried artists from around the country and draw visitors from all over the area. When you become a member (which you should), you will be informed about their wonderful events. There are a number of organizations affiliated with the Bruce.
• Astronomical Society of Greenwich, 203.869.6786 x 338
• Connecticut Ceramics Study Circle, 203.869.9478
• Greenwich Antiques Society, 203.869.9531 or 203.661.7988
• Forum for World Affairs, 203.356.0340
• Seaside Center at Greenwich Point, open in July and August, Wednesday - Sunday, 10 am - 4 pm.
Museum Hours: Tuesday - Saturday, 10 am - 5 pm; Sunday, 1 am - 5 pm; Seaside Beach Museum Hours: Wednesday - Sunday, 10am - 4pm.

Bush-Holley House Museum

39 Strickland Road, Cos Cob, 203.869.6899
www.hstg.org
Home of the Historical Society, this is the place to learn about Greenwich history. They have a good library and a shop with books on Greenwich history, as well as reproductions of 19th century children's toys and books. The museum showcases eight period rooms from the late 1890's when it was a boarding house for the Cos Cob art colony. Be sure to take the guided tour. While you are there, pick up a list of the wonderful programs and events sponsored by the Greenwich Historical Society.
Hours: Tuesday - Sunday, noon - 4 pm.

museums

Donald M. Kendall Sculpture Gardens

At Pepsico, 700 Anderson Hill Road, Purchase NY, 914.253.2000
www.SirPepsi.com/pepsi1.htm
One of the world's finest sculpture gardens is located right next to
Greenwich. The collection includes forty pieces by such 20th century artists as Noguchi, Moore, Nevelson, and Calder. The sculptures are set on
168 carefully landscaped acres. Pick up a map at the visitors' parking
lot. There are some picnic tables. Hours: Open every day from dawn to
dusk, except for Saturdays in August.

Historical Society of the Town of Greenwich

39 Strickland Road, Cos Cob, 203.869.6899; Archives x 23
www.hstg.org
Their mission is to collect, preserve and disseminate the history of
Greenwich. The society conducts a wide variety of adult and children's
educational programs, exhibitions and workshops. Their extensive archives are open to anyone wanting to research town history. We sincerely
appreciate this organization's dedication to preserving our community's
historical roots. Hours: weekdays, 9 am - 5 pm.

Katonah Museum of Art

Route 22 at Jay Street, Katonah NY, 914.232.9555
www.KatonahMuseum.org
The Museum offers an extensive range of activities to engage visitors of
all ages. Exhibitions present art from the past to the present. The Museum's
Learning Center is an interactive exhibition space in which children can
experience the fun of artistic exploration.
Hours: Tuesday - Saturday, 10 am - 5 pm. Sunday, noon - 5 pm.

CULTURE

Kykuit

381 North Broadway, Sleepy Hollow NY

914.631.8200 weekdays, 914.631.3992 on weekends.

www.HudsonValley.org

John D. Rockefeller's home, Kykuit, has remarkable architecture, gardens and art as well as spectacular scenery. Home to four generations of Rockefellers, this is the Hudson Valley's most exceptional house and gardens. Tours include Nelson A. Rockefeller's extraordinary collection of 20th-century sculpture as well as the Coach Barn with its antique carriages and autos. A garden and sculpture tour is offered most weekdays. Hours: Open early May - early November. Call before going.

Lyndhurst

Lyndhurst is located ½ mile south of the Tappan Zee Bridge on Route 9 in Tarrytown NY, 914.631.4481

www.Lyndhurst.org

The home of Jay Gould, it is one of the great domestic landmarks of America. A visit to this Gothic Revival mansion and its 67-acre park is a must for all who are interested in 19th-century architecture, decorative arts, and landscape design.

Hours: Mid-April to October, open Tuesday - Sunday 10am - 5pm: November to mid-april, open weekends 10 am - 4 pm.

Neuberger Museum

735 Anderson Hill Road, Purchase NY, 914.251.6100

www.Neuberger.org

The museum is located on the 500-acre campus of the State University of New York (SUNY) at Purchase. It has 25,000 sq. ft. of gallery space, a café, a store and an interactive learning center. It houses a notable collection of modern art.

Hours: Closed Monday, Tuesday - Sunday, noon - 5 pm. Their hours seem to change frequently, call before you go.

CULTURE

NY Botanical Gardens

Bronx River Parkway at Fordham Road, Bronx NY, 718.817.8700
www.NYBG.org
They have recently undergone a $25 million renovation and are considered the best in the country.
Hours: Open year round, Tuesday - Sunday, 10 am - 6 pm. Free admissions on Wednesdays. November - March, 10 am - 4 pm.

Philip Johnson Glass House

Visitor Center, 199 Elm Street, New Canaan CT, 866.811.4111
www.PhilipJohnsonGlassHouse.org
Tickets may be purchased online to view the Glass House and other structures on the 47-acre campus run by the National Trust for Historic Preservation. The tour is limited to ten people and includes a half mile waking tour across the site. Children ages 10 and up are welcomed.
Hours: May 1st - October 1st

Putnam Cottage

243 East Putnam Avenue, 869.9697
www.putnamcottage.org
Originally a tavern serving travelers along the Post Road, it is now a museum owned by the DAR. Each year on the last Sunday in February (1-3 pm) the Putnam Hill Revolutionary War battle is recreated. A definite must-see for adults and children alike.
Hours: April to November, Sundays 1 pm - 4 pm.

Storm King Art Center

Old Pleasant Hill Road, Mountainville NY, 845.534.3115
www.stormking.org
Take a walk or picnic in this leading outdoor sculpture museum with 120 masterworks set in a stunning 400-acre landscaped park. Great place to take the kids for a picnic.
Hours: April 1 to November 15th, Wednesday - Sunday 11 am - 5 pm.

Union Church of Pocantico Hills

555 Bedford Road, North Tarrytown NY, 914.631.8200, 2069
www.HudsonValley.org
Stained glass windows created by Henri Matisse (1869-1954) and Marc Chagall (1887-1985).
Hours: April - October, open daily (except Tuesday), 11 am - 5 pm;
Saturdays, 10 am - 5 pm; Sundays, 2 pm -5 pm.

CULTURE

music

Palladium Musicum

For information contact Marie Williams, President, 203.661.6856
www.PalladiumMusicum.org
They offer several classical music events (vocal and instrumental) each season. Performances often combine music and lectures.

Caramoor Center for Music and Arts

149 Girdle Ridge Road, Katonah NY, 914.232.1252
www.Caramoor.com
About 20-minutes North of Greenwich, Caramoor has wonderful music programs in a very intriguing setting. It should be on everyone's "must do" list. For evening performances, it is fashionable to bring a fancy picnic supper and eat on one of the lawns before the show. Caramoor has 100 acres of parklands and formal gardens. Most performances are under a tent and so go on even if it rains. Mosquitoes are sparse but bringing some bug spray in the summer can't hurt. The main season is June through August although Caramoor provides fall, winter and spring indoor programs on a more limited schedule.

Chamber Players

For more information call 203.622-6611 or 203.869-2664
www.GreenwichSym.org/content-html/chamberplayers.htm
Musicians selected from the Greenwich Symphony Orchestra present concerts each year; usually 4 pm on Sunday afternoons at Round Hill Community Church and 8 pm Monday evenings at the Bruce Museum. A wine and cheese reception at each concert is a wonderful way for the audience to become acquainted with the musicians.

Connecticut Grand Opera

307 Atlantic Street, box office 203.327.2867 or 203.325.4466
www.CTGrandOpera.org
A not-for-profit, professional opera company founded in 1993, it performs at the Palace Theater in Stamford.

CULTURE

Fairfield County Chorale

61 Unquowa Road, Fairfield CT, 203.254.1333

www.FairfieldCountyChorale.org

Founded in 1963, the Chorale's repertoire consists of more than 100 classic works by composers from the 16th through the 20th century. Most performances are held at the Norwalk Concert Hall.

Grace Notes

Contact them by email through their website.

www.TheGraceNotes.com

A women's "a cappella" singing group that has been entertaining Greenwich audiences for over thirty years. Whether you are listening to or singing with this group, it is always a rewarding experience.

Greenwich Choral Society

299 Greenwich Avenue, 3rd floor, 203.622.5136

www.GreenwichChoralSociety.org

Founded in 1925, the Society's 30 singers perform throughout the area primarily during the winter months. Their annual Christmas concert held at Christ Church is a very popular event.

Greenwich Symphony Orchestra

203.869.2664

www.GreenwichSym.org

This 90-member professional orchestra is in its 53rd season. They play consistently excellent music at low ticket prices. Ask for a CD of their music highlights. Concerts are Saturday evenings and Sunday afternoons at Greenwich High School. Be sure to attend pre-concert lectures. Patricia Handy's 30-minute free informative explanation of the music is terrific.

Stamford Symphony Orchestra

Palace Theatre, 61 Atlantic Street, Stamford CT

203.325.4466 or 203.325.1047

www.StamfordSymphony.org

A typical concert lasts about two hours, usually with a 20-minute intermission. An hour before the beginning of each concert, the conductor discusses the program and the music in a Behind the Baton talk from the stage. Very worthwhile.

CULTURE

music

Town Concerts and other summer events

Greenwich Department of Parks and Recreation, 203.622.7830

www.GreenwichCT.org/ParksandRec/ParksAndRec.asp

During July and August the Department of Parks and Recreation arranges free Tuesday afternoon and Wednesday evening concerts. Call or visit the website for locations and times.

1. Wednesday Night Concerts take place at 7:30 at Roger Sherman Baldwin Park
2. Jazz on the Sound concerts are on Island Beach one Sunday in each of June, July and August.
3. Sound Beach Community band plays in Binney Park the last Sunday in July and August at 7 pm.
4. The Silver Shield Concert is at Roger Sherman Baldwin Park.

TIP: GREENWICH POPS CONCERT

For a lovely evening, pack a picnic and head to the Roger Sherman Baldwin Park for one of the Pops concerts sponsored by the Greenwich Arts Council:

www.GreenwichArts.org

and the Department of Parks & Recreation. The park opens for picnics at 6 pm and the concerts start at 7:30 pm. Call the Arts Council at 203.862.6750 for details.

CULTURE

Acting Company of Greenwich

Call 203.629.2094 for information, 203.863.1919 for reservations
www.Tacog.org www.ActGreenwich.org
This local amateur theater group, with good acting and good fun, welcomes actors and audiences for its annual series of plays held in the auditorium of the First Congregational Church in Old Greenwich. They also teach improvisation classes.

Connecticut Playmakers

First Congregational Church
108 Sound Beach Avenue, Old Greenwich
Contact: Peggi de la Cruz, 203.977.8627
www.CTPlaymakers.org
Sponsored by the Greenwich Center for the Arts and the First Congregational Church, Old Greenwich, they provide free, live theater open to adult participants from age 16. In addition to their major productions, the monthly meetings include dramatic presentations. The Playmakers Young People's Theater puts on a musical each summer. This is an enjoyable way for young people to meet each other and learn about the theater.

Curtain Call Theaters

Sterling Farms Theater Complex
1349 Newfield Ave, Stamford, 203.329.8207
www.CurtainCallInc.com
Curtain Call uses two theaters at this location., "The Kweskin Theater" presents full run productions such as "The Odd Couple" and "Arsenic and Old Lace." "The Dressing Room" has cabaret-style seating. Bring your own food and enjoy charming dramas and musicals, such as "The Fantastics". Evening performances start at 8 pm, Matinees at 2 pm. For the aspiring actor, Curtain Call offers a full line of educational workshops in the performing arts, ages 5 through adult.
Performance Times: Fridays and Saturdays 1 pm - 9 pm;
Sundays, 11 am - 3 pm.

CULTURE

Emelin Theater

153 Library Lane, Mamaroneck NY, 914.698.0098

www.Emelin.org

Emelin is the oldest continuously operating performing arts theater in Westchester County. The Emelin holds a variety of terrific events: speakers, cabaret, jazz, classical music, musical theater, children's theater and more. Call for a catalog or get on their mailing list.

Fairfield Theater Company

70 Sanford Street, Fairfield CT

(directly in front of the Metro-North train station)

Box office: 203.259.1036

www.FairfieldTheatre.org

The Fairfield Theater Company was founded in 2000. Their mission is "to bring the best of New York's Off and Off-Off Broadway directly to Fairfield." This is professional theater from NYC, brought intact and delivered to our backyard.

Festival Theater

1850 Elm Street, Stratford CT

www.StratfordFestival.com

This Connecticut Shakespeare theater is hoping to re-open. Check their website for information.

Goodspeed Opera House

6 Main Street, East Haddam CT, 860.873.8668, 860.873.8377

www.Goodspeed.org

The restored 19th century Goodspeed Opera House is now devoted to musicals. April through December season, Goodspeed produces three musicals. At the nearby Norma Terris Theatre in Chester, Connecticut, Goodspeed develops new musicals. *The Connecticut River Valley is less than two hours away and has a great variety of family attractions. See FAMILY OUTINGS for ideas.*

theater

Long Wharf Theater

222 Sargent Drive, New Haven CT
Box office: 203.787.4282, 800.782.8497
www.LongWharf.org
Professional theater which produces traditional plays as well as plays by new playwrights. Over the last 40 years, Long Wharf has presented numerous world premieres, dozens of American premieres and transfers to Broadway. Directions: I-95 N to exit 46.

Off-Beat Players

Arch Street Teen Center
www.OffBeatPlayers.org
A Summer theater company of teens and young adults, with and without disabilities. They welcome any enthusiastic actor who wants to grow professionally and personally. Check the website for show schedule and ticket information.

Palace Theater

61 Atlantic Street, Stamford, 203.358.2305, Box Office 203.325.4466
www.StamfordCenterfortheArts.org
The Palace, along with the Rich Forum, is part of the Stamford Center for the Arts. The Palace is a 1,584-seat vaudeville theater that was acclaimed as "Connecticut's most magnificent" when it opened in 1927.
Box office hours: weekdays 10 am - 5 pm.

Play with Your Food

299 Greenwich Avenue (Greenwich Arts Council), 203.293.8831
www.PlayWithYourFood.org
A winter series of noon-time theater. All shows are noon to 1:30 and include lunch and professional readings of one-act plays for $35. Can there be a better way to spend your lunch time? Call well in advance to reserve.
Box Office Hours: January - March, weekdays, 10 am - 3 pm.

Pound Ridge Theater Group

Conant Hall, 255 Westchester Avenue (Rt 137), Pound Ridge NY, 914.764.1902, www.prtc01.org
Off Broadway-style productions of dramas, musicals and comedies. Play-goers should try our favorite local restaurant, North Star. See its review in the Restaurant Section.

Rich Forum

307 Atlantic Street, Stamford CT, 203.358.2305,
Box office 203.325.4466
www.StamfordCenterfortheArts.org
This theater has excellent facilities and an eclectic program of high quality events. Rich Forum, like the Palace, is committed to presenting the best of live theater, concerts, comedy and dance entertainment.
Box office hours: weekdays 10 am - 5 pm.

Shakespeare on the Sound

Roger Sherman Baldwin Park, 100 Arch Street, Greenwich CT, 203.299.1300
www.ShakespeareOnTheSound.org
In June and July, Shakespeare on the Sound produces an annual free outdoor Shakespeare festival in Connecticut, with performances in public parks in Rowayton and Greenwich. Don't miss this event! Although the performances are free, for a small fee you can reserve seats in the first rows. They also offer free lectures for adults or children before the performances. See their website for details.

Shubert Theater

247 College Street, New Haven CT
Box Office: 203.624.1825, 888.736.2663
For tickets contact you can also call tickets.com at 800.228.6622
www.capa.com/newhaven
This not-for-profit theater is considered the crown jewel of downtown New Haven. Some shows come directly from Broadway.
Box office hours: weekdays 9 am - 9 pm, Saturday 9 am - 7 pm, Sundays Noon - 6 pm.

Summer Theater of New Canaan

Box office: 203.966.4634
www.stonc.org
What fun to have this regional theater so near by! It produces professionally staged family musicals and Shakespearian productions during the summer. Shakespeare is performed in the outdoor walled garden at Waveny Park in New Canaan, CT. Musicals and other performances are held in the Saxe Middle School Theater, South Avenue, New Canaan.

CULTURE

theater

SUNY Performing Arts Center

745 Anderson Hill Road, Purchase NY, 914.251.6200
www.ArtsCenter.org
The Performing Arts Center at the State University of New York at Purchase, just a few minutes from Greenwich, has wonderful music and dance performances, as well as plays. They have a number of summer offerings although the main season is September to May.

Westport Country Playhouse

25 Powers Court, Westport CT, 203.227.4177, 888.927.7529
www.WestportPlayhouse.com
A 6-play summer season starting in June. Very professional. The theater recently underwent $17 million renovation. Only a 20-minute trip. While there, have dinner at Paul Newman's restaurant, The Dressing Room, at 27 Powers Court (adjacent to the Westport Country Playhouse), 203.226.1114; See the review in the restaurant section of the Guide.

Yale University Repertory Theater

1120 Chapel St., PO Box 1257, New Haven, CT, 203.432.1234
www.yale.edu/yalerep
It is an hour's drive, but it's well worth it. Often as good as Broadway, but with much less hassle, better seats and lower prices. You can park right next to the theater for free. Subscribers can get front row seats.

TIP: TOUR GREENWICH HOMES

Each year in December, Antiquarius (The Greenwich Historical Society, www.hstg.org) organizes a fabulous tour of some of Greenwich's most beautiful homes. The annual fund raiser costs about $100. You can also buy a ticket for lunch, held at one of the Country Clubs. Call 203.869.6899 for details.

CULTURE

tickets

All Shows (Formerly the Concert Connection)
22 Elm Place, Rye NY, 203.869.0060, 800.255.7469
www.AllShows.com
Ticket broker to major sports, music, theater and family entertainment events. They can get you those high demand tickets you want, but often at a steep markup. If you can wait to the last minute you will often get a deal, sometimes even below cost. A good place to sell tickets you can't use.

Golden Ticket Events
Mill Pond Shopping Center, 261 East Putnam Avenue, Cos Cob, 203.629.1300
www.GoldenTicketEvents.com
Sporting events, concerts, Broadway plays. Tickets sold at face value + a mark-up depending on scarcity.

Movie Fone
203.323.3456
www.MovieFone.com
On Friday and Saturday nights, the demand for tickets is high and the lines can be very long. They often run out of tickets before you can get in. Call to hear previews and to buy your tickets in advance with your credit card. Still arrive early for the best seating, but when you arrive, you don't wait in the line. Just show your credit card and get your tickets. When calling Movie Phone, their advertisements can sometimes be a nuisance. To get around this: press "*" to repeat or change your previous selection; "***" to start over; if you already know the theater you want, "#" plus the Theater Express Code will get you there immediately. The theaters usually have their Theater Code in their ads.

Movie Tickets & Theater Showtimes
www.fandango.com
Another online resource to purchase movie tickets.

(The) Seat Up Front
15 E Putnam Avenue, Suite 102, 203.661.7111
www.SeatsUpFront.com
They provide tickets to all major events at cost plus a mark-up depending on demand. Hours: weekdays, 9:30 am - 5 pm.

CULTURE

tours & special events

Calendars of Events

- The *Greenwich Time* on Thursdays has a Week End supplement with a calendar of events, shows and reviews. They also have a good on-line Entertainment Guide www.greenwichtime.com/entertainment
- Community Answers has a good on-line Events Calendar. www.greenwichlibrary.org/commanswers.htm

Art to the Avenue

www.greenwicharts.org/arttotheavenue.asp

If you want to enjoy Greenwich Avenue at its best, do not miss a stroll down the Avenue on the opening night of this festival. The Greenwich Arts Council sponsors this event in early May. Over 150 artists and retailers take part. Call the Council 203.622.3998 for details.

Bruce Museum Outdoor Crafts Festival

www.brucemuseum.org/events

This show of exceptionally fine crafts is held annually one week prior to Memorial Day weekend in May.

Bruce Museum Outdoor Arts Festival

www.brucemuseum.org/events

Held annually on Columbus Day weekend in October. This show features fine arts only, no crafts.

Connecticut Art Trail

www.ArtTrail.org

Visit fifteen world-class museums and historic sites throughout Connecticut and explore interesting towns.

Connecticut Wine Trail

www.ctwine.com

Visit 28 wineries. See details in FOOD AND BEVERAGES

Greenwich Grand Tour

Cheryl Dunson, The League of Women Voters' Land Use Specialist, conducts a very special bus tour of Greenwich every year, usually in early May. Whether you are new to Greenwich or have lived here a while, you are sure to learn something new and to have a good time. Call Greenwich Continuing Education at 203.625.7477 for details.

CULTURE

Historic Greenwich Harbor Cruise

Annually, in late September, the Friends of the Greenwich Library and the Department of Parks and Recreation sponsor a two-hour cruise of the Greenwich waterfront on the Island Beach Boat. The tour is narrated by Captain Henry Marx of Landfall Navigation.

Old Greenwich Sidewalk Art Show

www.sidewalkartshow.com
We always enjoy the Sound Beach Avenue sidewalk art show held on a Saturday and Sunday in September by the Old Greenwich Art Society.

Putnam Hill Revolutionary Battle

Putnam Cottage, 243 East Putnam Avenue, 203.869.9697
www.PutnamCottage.org
Each year on the last Sunday in February (1-3 pm) the Putnam Hill Revolutionary War battle is re-enacted outside of the Putnam Cottage.

TIP: SoNo ARTS CELEBRATION

In early August South Norwalk has an exciting art festival with over 150 juried artists as well as an interesting mix of performances on five stages. The festival runs from 10 am - midnight and is appropriate for children as well as adults. Visit www.SonoArts.org

ENTERTAINING

Party information specific to Children is listed in CHILDREN
For wine, see FOOD AND BEVERAGES
To practice your dancing, see Adult CONTINUING EDUCATION
Cakes are listed under Bakeries in FOOD AND BEVERAGES
Florists and Nurseries are listed in FLOWERS AND GARDENS.

caterers

These caterers have delicious food, they usually arrive on time and are dependable. As a result, they are often in high demand. Reserve early. However, remember, no one person or group is always perfect.

Abigail Kirsch Culinary Productions
914.631.3030
www.AbigailKirsch.com
Caterer of choice for many Greenwich residents when they are having a large party. Dear friends used Abigail for both daughters' weddings. Their website has a number of exclusive and non-exclusive locations to host larger events.

Aux Délices Gourmet Food Shop & Catering
1075 East Putnam Avenue, Riverside
203.326.4540 x 101
www.AuxDelicesFoods.com
Debra Ponzek and Aux Delices are well known for excellent food. They will cater or plan events of all types and sizes. In our Tasting Contest, Aux Delices received the highest overall score.

Fjord Fisheries
143 River Road, Cos Cob, 203.622.4020
www.FjordCatering.com
If you are invited to a clambake or lobster party, chances are Fjord is the provider. They are a full-service caterer. You must try their salmon. From May through September, Fjord can cater a party of 40 to 120 on one of their four ships. Breakfast, lunch and dinner cruises lasting two to three hours are available. Their website has a number of suggested menus.

ENTERTAINING

caterers

Garelick and Herbs
48 West Putnam Avenue, Greenwich
203.972.4497, 203.661.7373
www.GarelickandHerbsCatering.com
This gourmet delicatessen caters everything from a light lunch to fancy
dinners. They will also provide staff for your events.

Great Performances
304 Hudson Street, New York NY, 212.727.2424
www.GreatPerformances.com
We recently went to a Greenwich party where they were serving fabulous
hors d'oeuvres, entrees and desserts. Like Abigail Kirsch, they are good
at large functions and have their own list of exclusive locations.

LexZee Gourmet
197 Sound Beach Avenue, Old Greenwich, 203.698.9277
www.LexZeeCatering.com, www.LexZeeGourmet.com
LexZee scored at the top during our Catering Contest. To taste their
delicious food, try one of their daily take-out specials. We have found
them to be a pleasure to work with.

Libby Coverly Cooke Catering
49 Brownhouse Road (Sportsplex Health Club), Stamford CT
203.406.9664
www.LibbyCookeCatering.com
Known for her fabulous presentations, she is equally competent with an
intimate dinner party or a grand affair. If you want to try her food, order
a take-out (48-hours in advance).

Marybeth's Catering
136 Hamilton Avenue, 203.661.8833
www.MarybethsCaterers.com
Marybeth Boller, called one of the top ten rising star chefs by *Food and
Wine* magazine has purchased the Susan Morton Catering company. This
chef with great credentials is making party-goers happy.

ENTERTAINING

caterers

On The Marc Events
Research Park, Stamford CT, 203.858.8570
www.OnTheMarcEvents.com
Chef Marc Weber started in 2007 as a personal chef doing parties for 12 to 20 people. Since then he has expanded to handle an event completely. He also offers cooking classes.

Patricia Blake Catering
7 Tokeneke Road, Darien CT, 203.655.1221
www.PatriciaBlake.com
Many choices on her catering menu from comfort foods to exotic delicacies. She has an impressive repertoire of hors d'oeuvres. She especially enjoys customizing the menu to meet your needs. Whether your party is for 25 or 500, she can do it.

Plum Pure Foods
236 East Putnam Avenue, Cos Cob, 203.869.7586
www.PlumPureFoods.com
Plum provides delicious takeout foods made primarily from natural products grown locally. They are exceptional caterers. Plum scored at the top during our 2005 Catering Contest.

Le Potager Catering
1127 High Ridge Road, Suite 291, Stamford CT, 203.975.2546
www.LePotagerCatering.com
Joseph Jenkins, one of New York City's upscale caterers, has moved to our area. He is receiving rave reviews for his tasteful, elegant parties. He was one of the winners in our Catering Contest.

Royal Tea Company
Trumbull CT, 203.452.1006
www.RoyalTeaCompany.net
Listed in *Connecticut Magazine*'s Best of Connecticut, their teas are perfect for bridal and baby showers, birthdays and Christmas parties. Every one loves their tea sandwiches and scones.

caterers

Victorian Teas

Eileen Grossman, 203.406.9820

www.VictorianTeasCuisine.com

For an elegant event, with a creative presentation, a Victorian tea party will make your party memorable. Eileen caters weddings, corporate functions and home events, including tea parties for children.

Watson's on Pemberwick

87 Pemberwick Road, 203.532.0132

www.WatsonsCatering.com

You will want to have a cocktail or dinner party just to have Sue Scully's delicious food. Although large parties are her forte, she handles intimate parties equally well.

TIP: HOR D'OEUVRE CONTEST

Carolyn & Jerry Anderson hosted a "blind" tasting party to evaluate hot and cold hors d'oeuvres from 10 local Greenwich caterers. Over 200 present and former Anderson Associates' clients evaluated the hors d'oeuvres. Details of the hors d'oeuvres that won are on www.GreenwichGuide.com.

The winners were:

- Aux Delices, 203.326.4540 x 101
- Gourmet Galley, 203.629.8889
- Le Potager Catering, 203.975.2546
- LexZee Gourmet, 203.698.9277
- Libby Cook, 203.406.9664
- Plum Pure Foods, 203.869.7586

ENTERTAINING

entertainment

For musicians see CULTURE.

David Ferst
914.649.4246
www.Magicdave.net
Slight of Hand artist for private parties, corporate events and even magic lessons. We love him.

Gig Masters
www.GigMasters.com
A good source for bands, DJs, and just about every form of entertainment. Most listings have reviews, but it is always a good idea to get a couple of local references.

James Daniel
125 Bedford Street, Stamford CT, 203.969.2400
www.JamesDaniel.com
A reliable source for music, entertainment or event lighting.

PM Amusements
36 Bush Avenue, Port Chester NY, 914.937.1188, 800.336.5853
www.PMAmusements.com
This is the ultimate party fun source. If you want to turn your backyard into an amusement park or just rent a cotton candy machine, they have it all. Ask about sumo wrestling, a velcro wall, miniature golf, karaoke, clowns, inflatable rides, or perhaps an Abe Lincoln or Mick Jagger look-a-like/impersonator. They have a great catalog.
Hours: weekdays, 8 am - 5 pm; sometimes on Saturday.
Call before going.

TIP: ROUND HILL COUNTRY DANCING
www.roundhill.net
The Round Hill Country Dancers meet on the second Saturday of every month at the Round Hill Community House, 397 Round Hill Road, from 8 pm - 11 pm. This multi-generational group welcomes singles and couples, beginners and advanced. There is a lesson before the program begins. Call 914.244.7248.

ENTERTAINING

invitations

The following invitation sources are described in STORES.

- j papers, 100 Bruce Park Avenue, 203.769.5104
- Kate's Paperie, 125 Greenwich Avenue, 203.861.0025
- Letter Perfect, 231 East Putnam Avenue, 203.869.1979
- Papyrus, 268 Greenwich Avenue, 203.869.1888
- Saint Clair, 23 Lewis Street, 203.661.2927

parking services

Advanced Parking Concepts
Verona NJ, 203.353.1415, 973.857.2008
www.AdvancedParkingConcepts.com
They are totally professional, impeccably groomed and knowledgeable about Greenwich.

Greenwich Town Traffic Division
203.622.8015
If you are having a large party, consider hiring an off-duty policeman to help your guests know where to park safely. Be sure to call well in advance and to confirm back that someone has signed up to help you.

Parking Productions
Clark NJ, 203.629.0003
www.ParkingProductions.com
We are impressed by their ability to effortlessly take care of a large number of cars in a short period of time. Valet parking at its best.

ENTERTAINING

party goods

The following Party Goods sources are reviewed in STORES
- East Putnam Variety, 88 East Putnam Avenue, 203.869.8789
- Packages PlusNMore, 215 East Putnam Ave, Cos Cob, 203.625.8130
- Party City
  Kohl's Shopping Center, 535 Boston Post Road, Port Chester 914.939.6900
  Ridgway Shopping Center, 2255 Summer Street, Stamford 203.964.4961
- Party Paper and Things, 403 East Putnam Avenue, 203.661.1355
- Strauss Warehouse, 140 Horton Avenue, Port Chester, 914.939.3544

party planners

Frank and Julio
945 Summer Street, Stamford CT, 203.353.9250
www.FrankAndJulio.com
If you are thinking of a wedding or large event, this is a resource to explore.

Hollywood Pop Gallery
24 Field Point Road, 203.622.4057
www.HollywoodPop.com
A global event production company. They will create and coordinate every element of your event from amazing decorations to cutting edge entertainment. If you want your party to be remembered decades later, just give them a call. They put together about 200 adult and 1,000 children's parties a year.
Hours: weekdays, 10 am - 5 pm.

party rentals

Northeast Tent Productions
55 Poplar Street, Stamford, 203.961.8100
www.NorthEastTent.com
You will be impressed with the variety of tent styles and lighting possibilities.

Party Fixins
327 West Avenue, Stamford CT 203.352.3718
www.PartyFixins.com
Ice cream carts to pretzel machines, they have everything you might wish to rent for a party.
Showroom Hours: weekdays 9 am - 5 pm, Saturday 9 am - 4 pm.
See website for winter hours.

Prestige Party Rental
Prospect Park NJ, 973.942.5300
www.PrestigePartyRental.com
For a large tented affair, they have nice service, great tents and usually the best prices. Because they aren't in Greenwich, you will need to go to Town Hall for the tent permit. Of course, they rent all the equipment, plates, table cloths, podiums, etc.

Smith Party Rentals
133 Mason Street, 203.869.9315
www.SmithPartyRentals.com
For years this has been the leading party rental source in town. They are still the source for just about everything possible for adult and children's parties. If they don't have it, you probably don't need it.

Stamford Tent and Party Rental
84 Lenox Avenue, Stamford CT, 203.324.6222
www.StamfordTent.com
A good local resource for almost any type of tented party. Check the website for helpful tent sizing advice.

party services

Arctic Glacier (aka East Coast Ice)
179 Hamilton Avenue, Byram, 203.622.2969
Tom will deliver the regular or dry ice you need just before your party. If you need a refrigerated box, he has those to rent as well.
Hours: weekdays, 8 am - 5 pm.

Round Hill Tree Service
1 Armonk Street, Greenwich, 203.531.5759
www.RoundHillTreeService.com
Rick Masi will make sure your limbs are trimmed back and your yard sprayed for mosquitos just before your party.

TIP: CHOWDER COOKOFF
Want to find the best bowl of New England clam chowder? Every year, in early June, chefs in Norwalk, CT compete in the annual "Splash! Clam Chowder Cook-Off." Check their website www.norwalk.ws or www.seaport.org for the annual winner and their recipe. Better yet, for a $5 donation you can attend the festival, taste the soups and place a vote for the best. Call the Norwalk Seaport Association 203.838.9444 for details.

FITNESS

index

This Section covers improving your strength or flexibility.
For all other activities including walking, climbing and running see the sections SPORTS or PARKS. If you need a chiropractor or physical therapy to recover from an excess of activity see HEALTH. For child focused activities see CHILDREN. To exercise your mind see CONTINUING EDUCATION, CULTURE or BOOKS AND LIBRARIES.

Exercise Class
Bodd
Dynamic Martial Arts Family Center
Go Figure Exercise Studio
Kneaded Touch
Thompson Exercise
YMCA
YWCA (many programs including Boutelle Method and Liftime Fitness)

Gym
Fitness Edge
Greenwich Fitness Center
New York Sports Club
Peak Physique
Bruce Park Fitness
Sportsplex
Western Greenwich Civic Center
YMCA
YWCA

Kick Boxing
Fitness Edge

Personal Trainers
Bruce Park Fitness
Greenwich Fitness Center
Kneaded Touch
New York Sports Club
Peak Physique
YMCA
YWCA

Pilates
Greenwich Pilates Center
MeJo Wiggin Pilates
YMCA
YWCA

Spinning
Fitness Edge
New York Sports Club
YMCA
YWCA

Tai Chi
Greenwich Continuing Education
Wudang Tai Chi of Stamford
YWCA

Yoga
Glow Yoga
Greenwich Continuing Education
Greenwich Yoga
Yoga Center
Yoga Samadhi
YMCA
YWCA

Zumba Fitness
www.zumba.com
Fitness Edge
Sportsplex
YMCA
YWCA

FITNESS

Bodd
181 Greenwich Avenue (upstairs), 203.983.5470
www.BoddFitness.com
The Bodd technique class is an intense 60-minute workout. The movements are rigorous but gentle and are designed to help you improve your posture, strength, stamina and flexibility. Babysitting is available. They also sell exercise clothing.

Bruce Park Fitness
209 Bruce Park Avenue, 203.661.5017
www.BruceParkFitness.com
They have their own personal trainers, but a lot of independent personal trainers use this gym.
Hours: Monday - Thursday, 5:30 am - 9 pm; Friday, 5:30 am - 8 pm; Saturday, 7 am - 3 pm; Sunday, 8 am - 1 pm.

Dynamic Martial Arts Family Center
202 Field Point Road, 203.629.4666
www.GreenwichKarate.com
See more complete description in SPORTS.

Fitness Edge
1333 East Putnam Avenue, Riverside, 203.637.3906
www.TheEdgeFitnessClubs.com
A popular place to work out. Lots of machines and classes, including one-on-one personal training. Dozens of classes per week including Zumba, spinning, yoga and kickboxing. The Kidz program is a plus, children exercise while you are working out. The cost to join is $30 month.
Hours: Monday - Thursday, 5 am - 10 pm; Friday, 5 am - 9 pm; Saturday, 5 am - 6 pm; Sunday, 7am - 5 pm

Glow Yoga
1345 East Post Road, Old Greenwich (2nd floor), 203.326.0470
www.GlowYourWay.com
Vinyasa and light Vinyasa yoga with low heat as well as well as gentle yoga for beginners. Classes 60 or 75 minutes.

FITNESS

Go Figure Exercise Studio
141 West Putnam Avenue, 203.625.7616
www.GoFigureStudio.com
This method combines the principles of ballet, yoga, Pilates and ortho-pedic exercises to give you great posture, flexibility and lean muscles. This studio believes in using a holistic approach to exercise to create a method that is gentle, yet challenging. In addition to the Figure Method classes, which are held for different levels, they also offer a half hour abdominal class and a 75-minute cycling class. Their website is very informative.

Greenwich Continuing Education
Havemeyer Building, 290 Greenwich Avenue, 203.625.7474, 7475
www.GreenwichAce.org
Most classes are held at the Greenwich High School, they usually offer beginning and advanced yoga courses as well as tai chi ch'uan classes.

Greenwich Fitness Center
5 Oak Street, 203.869.6189
Well-equipped fitness center with weight rooms. They have a staff of 10 personal trainers, but they also allow members to bring in their own personal trainer. Summer members welcome.
Hours: Monday - Thursday, 6 am - 8 pm; Friday, 6 am - 6:30 pm; Saturday, 8 am - 2 pm.

Greenwich Pilates Center
309 Greenwich Avenue # 204, 203.869.3900
With over ten years teaching experience, Edvins Puris personalizes every client's workout, ranging from elite athletes to post physical therapy rehabilitation. Located above Starbucks in downtown Greenwich it It is an exclusive one-on-one studio experience. Pilates and Gyrotonics les-sons are $95 a session; $65 each for duets.

Greenwich Yoga
328 Pemberwick Road @ The Mill, 203.532.0660
Greenwich Water Club
www.KaiaYoga.com
They practice a variety of styles for asanas (postures), pranayama (breath exercises), meditation and yoga nidre (deep relaxation). At the Green-wich Water Club, they offer "HOT" vinyasa yoga classes as well. You don't have to be a member of the Water Club to come.

FITNESS

Kneaded Touch

83 Harvard Avenue, Stamford, 203.967.1121

www.KTHealthAndFitness.com

For 9 years Anthony Mirabel and William Asher have, as the name implies, encouraged optimal fitness for many Greenwich residents. The very helpful, friendly staff will help you evaluate your needs. They are well-known for their sports massage therapies.

MeJo Wiggin Pilates

203.550.6592 (private lessons in the Greenwich area)

www.MeJoWiggin.com

Certified and trained by master teacher Romana Kryzanowska. They are recognized by the Pilates Studio of New York and Romana's Pilates, LLC. Pilates is a methodology of movement based on carefully developed principles that teach you to use your buttocks, abdominal and lower back muscles. Fully equipped with all 16 pieces of equipment, they give private lessons only. Lessons range from $100 to $130 per hour.

New York Sports Club

6 Liberty Way, 203.869.1253

www.MySportsClubs.com

There are over 150 NYSC clubs in New York, New Jersey and Connecticut. In addition to a 6,000 sq. ft. state-of-the-art fitness center, the aerobics and spinning studios offer classes seven days-a-week. Medically based health and wellness programs include nutrition, massage, personal training and a Medicare certified physical therapy department. Childcare available. Initiation fee approximately $80 plus $70 to $80.

Hours: weekdays, 5:30 am - 9:30 pm; Saturday, 7 am - 5 pm; Sunday, 8 am - 5 pm.

Optimal Fitness

1171 East Putnam Avenue, Riverside, 203.637.0622

Greenwich Physical Therapy's one-on-one personal training. About a $100 hour.

FITNESS

Peak Physique
50 Holly Hill Lane, 203.625.9595
www.PeakPhysique.biz
If you are not down to the weight you want for your beach vacation, sign up for their bikini boot camp. In one month (5-day a week program of diet and exercise) they promise to have you ready for the beach. Dom Novak, the owner of Peak Physique, is a well regarded trainer keeping many Greenwich residents fit year round.

Sportsplex (fitness, squash, swimming, racquetball)
49 Brownhouse Road, Stamford, 203.358.0066
www.Sportsplex-CT.com
On the border of Stamford and Old Greenwich is a complete training facility for adults and children. Morning programs for pre-schoolers and after school programs for ages 6 - 8. Supervised nursery for children. In addition to machines and spinning, they have an Olympic-length pool, four squash courts and one racquetball court. Swimming and squash lessons are available. The aerobics center has a specially designed exercise floor and, of course, they have Zumba. Call for an enthusiastic tour. Hours: Monday - Thursday, 5:30 am - 10 pm; Friday, 5:30 am - 9 pm; Saturday, 7 am - 8 pm; Sunday, 7 am - 8 pm. (Different summer hours.)

Thompson Exercise
at Grand Slam Tennis Center, Bedford NY, 914.234.9206
www.GrandSlamTennisClub.com
Thompson Method classes work on stretching, strength and stamina (including combinations). Associates who attend the school love it. Classes are held at the Ivan Lendl Grand Slam Tennis Club. Bill believes that anyone, no matter what age or ability has the potential to achieve a high level of fitness and well being.

Western Greenwich Civic Center
a.k.a. Bendheim Greenwich Civic Center
449 Pemberwick Road, Glenville, 203.532.1259
Director: Frank Gabriele
www.GreenwichCT.org/ParksAndRec/prFacilityPrograms.asp
See a more complete description in SPORTS.

Wudang Tai Chi of Stamford
414 West Main Street, Stamford CT, 203.570.1752
www.TaiChiStamford.com
Luis teaches Tai Chi, Qi Gong and Nei Kung in Stamford and at several locations in Greenwich. He offers group and private classes.

Yoga Center
125 Greenwich Avenue, 203.661.0092
www.YogaCenterGreenwich.com
In the heart of Greenwich, this popular studio for yoga is run by a mother and daughter team, Toni Goodrich and Heather Trzuskowski. You will find a variety of classes at this center, including hot yoga. Call for more information.

Yoga Samadhi
328 Pemberwick Road at The Mill, 203.532.0660
www.GreenwichYoga.com
The key to a happy and healthy life is balance, and this yoga studio is a wonderful place to start. With views of the Byram River, this studio offers a wide variety of classes designed for all levels. Classes range from "Foundations" and "Restorative," which are gentle and great for beginners, to "Vinyasa" and "Astanga" classes, which are more vigorous and powerful. They also hold invigorating classes such as "Contempo Yoga," set to modern music. This studio has a variety of specialty classes (held regularly) for pregnant women, women with newborns, teens and seniors. The studio is committed to enriching the yoga practice of their students, so you will often find well-known national and international teachers who have been recruited for workshops. Their website is very informative.

YMCA (a.k.a. Greenwich Family Y)
50 East Putnam Avenue, 203.869.1630
Rebecca B. Fretty, President & Chief Executive Officer
www.gwymca.org, www.greenwichymca.org
See a more complete description in SPORTS

YWCA
259 East Putnam Avenue, Greenwich, 203.869.6501
Adrianne Singer, President and CEO
www.YWCAGreenwich.org
See a more complete description in SPORTS

FLOWERS & GARDENS

The Greenwich Department of Parks has a green thumb and together with the talents of garden club volunteers (who you will see gardening on many of the town's intersections) make Greenwich so beautiful.
See PARKS for more information.
Florists and Nurseries are described in the STORES.

gardening education

Garden Education Center
Montgomery Pinetum, 130 Bible Street, Cos Cob, 203.869.9242
www.GECGreenwich.org
The Center's horticulture buildings provide classrooms and workrooms for a variety of programs and lectures. Founded in 1957, the center is not only a strong educational facility, but also provides a good framework for new residents to make friends. The quality of their programs is amazing. Each month they have speakers who have written books and are experts in their fields. If you are interested in gardening, these programs should not be missed. Call and get on the list for their newsletter.
Hours: Closed during the summer. Open September 1 to Memorial Day; weekdays, 9 am - 3:30 pm; In October and December, also Saturday 10 am - 3 pm.

New York Botanical Gardens
Bronx NY, 718.817.8700
www.NYBG.org
Greenwich garden enthusiasts know their way to the NY Botanical Gardens. The gardens have recently undergone a $25 million renovation and are considered the best in the country.
Hours: Tuesday - Sunday, 10 am - 6 pm. Wednesdays are free.

Loretta Stagen Floral Designs
Stamford, 203.323.3544
www.LorettaStagen.com
Innovative flower arrangements and party decorations for corporate events and weddings. She also offers classes and workshops in flower arranging. For five or more students, she will create a special class in their area of interest.

FLOWERS & GARDENS

florists & nurseries

The following Florists and Nurseries are described in STORES:

- Colony Florist, 315 Greenwich Avenue, 203.227.7836
- Cos Cob Farms, 61 East Putnam Avenue, Cos Cob, 629.2267
- Flowers By George, 7 Strickland Road, Cos Cob, 203.661.0850
- Greenwich Hospital Gift Shop Flowers, 203.863.3371
- Greenwich Orchids, 106 Mason Street, 203.661.5544
- Loretta Stagen Floral Designs, 203.203.323.3544
- Mark Mariani's Garden Center, 45 Bedford Rd, Armonk, 914.273.3083
- McArdle-MacMillen, 48 Arch Street, 203.661.5600
- Sam Bridge Nursery, 437 North Street, 203.869.3418
- Shanti Bithi Nursery, 3047 High Ridge Road, Stamford, 203.329.0768
- Tulips Greenwich, 91 Lake Avenue, 203.661.3154

TIP: OX RIDGE HORSE SHOW

Enjoy the nationally acclaimed hunter-jumper competition in June at the Ox Ridge Hunt Club in Darien CT. Olympic as well as local riders compete in this Grand Prix event. Call 203.655.2559 for details or visit www.OxRidge.com.

FLOWERS & GARDENS

garden clubs

Byram Garden Club
Byram Shubert Library
21 Mead Avenue, Byram
Contact: Lynn Elise Friend, President, 203.531.7978
This friendly group is dedicated to preservation and beautification.
Membership is open to anyone in Western Greenwich.

Garden Club of Old Greenwich
PO Box 448, Old Greenwich CT, 06870
Contact: Lorese McQuinn, 203.637.0430
They care about keeping the Old Greenwich area beautiful and work on
many civic projects. They share their talents and knowledge through
horticulture programs designed for the young and the elderly. Membership is by invitation.

Garden Education Center
130 Bible Street, Cos Cob, 203.869.9242
www.GECGreenwich.org
Contact: Adrienne Parker, Managing Director
This is a gardener's heaven. Started in 1957, this volunteer organization
is dedicated to the appreciation of horticulture and nature through educational programs and special events. All kinds of classes in gardening,
flower arranging, and landscape design are happening all the time. Volunteers are needed to work in the greenhouse, gift shop, and also to help
with workshops, trips and special events.

Green Fingers Garden Club
PO Box 4655, Greenwich 06830
Contact: Betsy Mulcare, President, 203.661.3295
An active club, responsible for the biennial "Preview of Spring", a major
flower show usually held at Christ Church in early March. The club recently gave the Town $30,000 for renovation of the area around the ferry
boat landing. Membership is by invitation.

Greenwich Daffodil Society
40 Bruce Park Drive,
Contact: Lyn Hurlock, President, 203.861.4130
In the Spring, daffodils burst into bloom all over town. If you love daffodils you will love membership in this group. The group sponsors the
annual Connecticut Daffodil Show at Christ Church.

FLOWERS & GARDENS

garden clubs

Greenwich Garden Club

PO Box 4896, Greenwich, CT 06831
www.GreenwichGardenClub.org
Contact: Urling Searle, President, 203.869.4805
Founded in 1914, they promote interest in horticulture, flower arranging, and conservation. Membership is by invitation.

Greenwich Green & Clean

Yantoro Community Center, 113 Pemberwick Road, 203.531.0006
Contact: Mary G. Hull, Executive Director
When someone says, "Wow, Greenwich is so beautiful!" tell them about this dedicated group of volunteers, working hard to keep it that way. Founded in 1986, when the town was going through some drastic budget cutting, this group formed and took action. Now working in partnership with the town, they are the inspiration for the pretty flowering baskets along the Avenue and the flowers on many of the traffic islands. Join this group and take part in the fall and spring Town Clean Up. Take a bag, join your neighbors and have fun in this well organized effort to clean our streets and parks.

Greenwich Woman's Club Gardeners

89 Maple Avenue, 203.869.2046
Contact: Mary Ann Moore, Chair
The Woman's Club, a greatly enjoyed, highly respected philanthropic service organization in our town has a special branch of women devoted to gardening, horticultural education and projects to enhance the beauty of our town. New members to the Woman's Club and to this special branch of Gardeners are welcomed.

Hortulus

PO Box 4666
Contact: Linda Bishop, President, 203.629.2670
This garden club, founded in 1930, is dedicated to furthering a knowledge and love of gardening. Membership is by invitation.

FLOWERS & GARDENS

garden clubs

Knollwood Garden Club

PO Box 1666, Greenwich 06836

Contact: Lorna Tompkins 203.629.2386 or Jane Hoffman, 203.661.6060

This garden club, founded in 1955, maintains and supports the Seaside Garden at Greenwich Point and they provide garden therapy at Nathaniel Witherell. Membership is by invitation.

Riverside Garden Club

PO Box 108, Old Greenwich

Contact: Barbara Butler 203.637.3730 or Janet Thomas, 203.259.3652

This local club is a member of the National Council of State Garden Clubs and is a charter member of the Federated Garden Clubs of America. Members have a wonderful time together as they work on horticultural education programs and on projects to enhance the beauty of Greenwich. New members are heartily welcomed.

TIP: TOUR GREENWICH GARDENS

Each year in June, the Garden Education Center www.GECGreenwich.org organizes a tour of some of Greenwich's most special, private gardens. Call 203.869-9242 for details.

FOOD & BEVERAGE

index

Bakeries
Black Forest
Di Mare Pastry Shop
Dunkin Donuts
Kneaded Bread
Le Pain Quotidien
Neri Bakery
St. Moritz
Sweet Lisa's Exquisite Cakes
Upper Crust Bagel Co.
Versailles
Whole Foods

Caterers
Reviewed in ENTERTAINING

Cheese & Milk
Balducci's
Marcus Dairy
Plum Cheese Shop
Whole Foods

Chocolates & Candy
Ada's Candy Store
Bridgewater Chocolates
Chocopologie by Knipschildt
Darlene's Heavenly Desires
Deborah Ann's Homemade
    Chocolates
Godiva Chocolates
Lindt Chocolates
(The) Little Chocolate Company
Munson's Chocolates
Schakolad Chocolate Factory

Coffee Shops
Reviewed in RESTAURANTS
  Arcadia Coffee Co.
  Dunkin Donuts
  (The) Drawing Room
  Starbucks

Delicatessens
Alpen Pantry
Aux Délices (French)
Balducci's
Fjord Fisheries
Food Mart
Garelick & Herbs
North Mianus Country Store
Pasta Vera
Plum Pure Foods
SAKie's (Thai)
Villarina's (Italian)

Ethnic Groceries
Asia Bazaar (Indian)
Bella Cucina (Italian)
Bukovina (Russian)
Fuji Mart (Japanese)
Scandia Food and Gift
    (Scandanavian)
Villarina's (Italian)

Fruit & Vegetables
Augustine's Farm
Balducci's
Bishop's Orchards (Pick Your Own)
Cos Cob Farms
Edible Arrangements
Farmer's Market
Jones Family Farm (Pick Your Own)
White Silo Farm (Pick Your Own)

FOOD & BEVERAGE

index

Grocery
(Ethnic Groceries are listed separately)
A & P Fresh (Food Emporium)
Balducci's
Costco
Food Mart (Porricelli's)
Round Hill Store (The)
Stew Leonard's
Stop & Shop
(Super) Stop & Shop
Trader Joe's
Whole Foods

Home Delivery
Fresh Direct
Marcus Dairy
Stop & Shop (Peapod)

Ice Cream
Baskin-Robbins
Carvel
Cold Stone Creamery
Daniella's Gelateria
Darlene's Heavenly Desires
Gelatissimo (Gelato)
Gofer Ice Cream
HäagenDazs
Longford's
Meli Melo (Sorbet)
Sweet Ashley's

Meat
Food Mart
Greenwich Prime Meats
Scarpelli's Market
Village Prime Meats

Seafood
Bon Ton
Fjord Fisheries Market
June & Ho
Lobster Bin
Whole Foods

Spices
Penzey's Spices
Asia Bazaar (Indian)

Vitamins
Reviewed in HEALTH

Wine
Connecticut Vineyards
Greenwich Wine Society
Horseneck Liquors
Horse Ridge Cellars *(Wine Storage reviewed in Services)*
Le Wine Shop
Make Your Own Wine
Var Max Liquor Pantry
Wine Wise

FOOD & BEVERAGE

A & P Fresh (Grocery)
160 West Putnam Avenue, 203.622.0374
www.APFreshOnline.com
A good general purpose grocery, A&P had gone from about 10,000 stores in1955 to 500 stores in 2002. The former Food Emporium has been restructured to compete with Whole Foods.
Hours: Monday - Saturday, 7 am - midnight; Sunday, 7 am - 9 pm.

Ada's Variety Shop (Candy)
112 Riverside Avenue (Corner of Chapel Lane & Riverside Ave) 203.637.0305
An old-fashioned candy store loved by children and their children.
Hours: weekdays, 7:30 am - 5 pm; weekends, 7:30 am - 2 pm.

Alpen Pantry (Delicatessen)
23 Arcadia Road, Old Greenwich, 203.637.3818
Nice take-out sandwich selection.
Hours: Monday - Saturday, 9 am - 5 pm.
Size: takeout only.

Asia Bazaar (Indian Grocery)
131 Cove Road, Stamford CT, 203.961.1514
A little market, stocked floor to ceiling with just about anything you might need for your Indian pantry. It's not fancy, but you will want to stock up at the bargain prices.
Hours: Monday - Sunday, 10 am - 9 pm.

Augustine's Farm (Fruit & Vegetables)
1332 King Street, 203.532.9611
For more than 50 years Kathy and John Augustin (pictured on the cover) have been providing Greenwich residents with fresh corn, tomatoes, apples, pumpkins, honey and cider. In the Fall, many youngsters have enjoyed hay rides. The town proclaimed August 15th as Farmer John Day in Greenwich. Great fun to stop here, load up on fresh vegetables and buy one of Grandma Ann's homemade pies. This is the perfect place to buy your Christmas tree, holiday wreath and firewood.
Hours: Open every day, 9 am - 5 pm during the season.
Call farm for hours during the winter.

FOOD & BEVERAGE

Aux Délices (Delicatessen, French-American)

- 1075 East Putnam Avenue, Riverside, 203.698.1066
- 3 West Elm, Greenwich, 203.622.6644

For delivery orders call 203.326.4540 x 115 or 101
www.auxdelicesFoods.com

Provencal-style food with an American twist prepared under the direction of talented Chef Debra Ponzek. Delicious gourmet take-away food. Both locations have a few tables - grab one for a quick breakfast or late lunch. They also have excellent hors d'oeuvres. In our 2005 Hors D'Oeuvres Tasting Contest they received top scores. They have a weekday home delivery service and will deliver your order even when you are not home, packaged to keep the food at the proper temperature.

Greenwich Hours: weekdays 7 am - 6:30 pm; Saturday, 8 am - 6:30 pm; Sunday, 9 am - 4 pm.

Riverside Hours: Monday - Saturday, 7 am - 6:30 pm; Sunday, 7:30 am - 5 pm.

Balducci's (Grocery)

1050 East Putnam Avenue, Riverside, 203.637.7600
www.Balduccis.com

One of a large chain of sophisticated gourmet delis and country shops for fruits, vegetables and unique foods. Balducci's carries imported and American cheeses and a nice selection of highly spiced soups. We are not fans of their deli bistro meals.

Hours: every day, 8 am - 8 pm; Sunday 8 am - 7 pm.

Baskin-Robbins (Ice Cream)

at Dunkin Donuts, 375 Putnam Avenue, Cos Cob, 203.869.7454
www.BaskinRobbins.com

Hours: open every day, 5 am - 11 pm.

Bella Cucina (Italian Grocery/Delicatessen)

160 Hamilton Avenue, 203.622.1693
www.GrecosBellaCucina.com

In a wing of one of our favorite Pizza places (Express Pizza) is a friendly Italian Deli.

Hours: everyday, 9 am - 10 pm.

FOOD & BEVERAGE

Bishop's Orchards (Pick-Your-Own)
1355 Boston Post Road (I-95, exit 57), Guilford CT, 203.458.7425, 203.453.2338
www.BishopsOrchards.com
They have many fruits to pick, including over twenty varieties of apples, nine kinds of blueberries, twelve of peaches, three of pears, eight of strawberries and two varieties of raspberries. This orchard is definitely worth a family trip.
Hours: From June through October, Monday - Saturday, 8 am to 7 pm; Sunday, 9 am to 6 pm. Their Winery and Bakery is open year around.

Black Forest (Bakery)
52 Lewis Street, 203.629.9330
www.BlackForestPastryShop.com
German-style bakery. Don't miss the black forest cake and chocolate mousse bombe, summer fruit tarts, delicious wedding cakes. We love their melt-away pastry.
Hours: Monday - Saturday, 7:30 am - 6 pm; Sunday 8 am - 1 pm.

Bon Ton (Seafood)
100 Bruce Park Avenue, 203.869.0462
www.BonTonFishMarket.com
In Greenwich since 1902, this is a reliable fish store. They have high quality fish as well as prepared seafood specialties, including poached and smoked salmon platters, and a full line of Russian caviar. Ample parking and right next to a Greenwich Prime Meats, another quality supplier.
Hours: Monday - Saturday, 8 am - 6 pm.

Bridgewater Chocolates (Chocolates)
559 Federal Road, Brookfield CT, 203.775.2286, 800.888.8742
www.BridgeWaterChocolate.com
Bridgewater won the chocolate truffle contest. Their factory store is only an hour away - a short drive for chocolate addicts.
Hours: Weekdays 9 am - 5 pm; Saturday 10 am - 4 pm.

Bukovina (Russian Grocery)
301 Hope Street, Stamford CT, 203.978.0408
The local source for Russian and Ukrainian food.
Hours: Monday - Saturday, 10 am - 8 pm.

FOOD & BEVERAGE

Carvel (Ice Cream)

604 North Main Street, Port Chester NY, 914.939.1487

www.Carvel.com

Located just on the border of Greenwich and Port Chester on US-1, this standby is open seven days a week. If you like hot fudge sundaes the way we do, Wednesday is your day. You can get two for the price of one.

Hours: Sunday - Thursday, 10 am - 10 pm;

Friday & Saturday, 10 am - 11 pm.

Prices: Medium Hot Fudge Sundae, $4.25; cash only, no credit cards.

Chocopologie by Knipschildt Chocolatier (Chocolates)

12 South Main Street, South Norwalk CT, 203.838.3131

www.Knipschildt.com www.Chocopologie.com

Some of the world's best chocolates are made nearby. These chocolates can often be found at Whole Foods and Aux Délices, but it is more fun to visit the restaurant & factory. Enjoy a chocolate crepe while placing your order. Reviewed under RESTAURANTS.

Hours: Closed Monday; Wednesday, 11 am - 9 pm;

Thursday, 11 am - 10 pm;

Friday & Saturday, 11 am - midnight; Sunday, 11:30 am - 5 pm.

Cold Stone Creamery (Ice Cream)

1109 High Ridge Road (High Ridge Center), Stamford CT, 203.487.7400

www.ColdStoneCreamery.com

Who doesn't have fun while eating ice cream? This franchise has a formula for success: stores are popping up all over the United States. You choose all your favorite sweet treats (from nuts to gummy bears) and they mix them in the ice cream, and if you tip, they'll burst into song. Their vanilla took first place in our 2004 Ice Cream Tasting Party.

Hours: Sunday- Thursday 12 pm - 10 pm ;Friday & Saturday to 11 pm.

Connecticut Vineyards

There are 28 vineyards in two viticultural areas: southeastern New England and the Western CT Highlands. To tour the vineyards try the CT Wine Trail, however, more than 3 wineries a day may be a stretch. The trail starts in Litchfield.

- CT wine Trail, 860.267.1399, www.CTWine.com
- For a list of the vineyards, with addresses and web sites go to
    www.GreenwichGuide.com/Vineyards.htm
- Our Favorite CT winery, Chamard Vineyards
    115 Cow Hill Road, Clinton CT, 860.664.0299
    www.Chamard.com

FOOD & BEVERAGE

Cos Cob Farms (Fruit & Vegetables)
6163 East Putnam Avenue, Cos Cob, 203.629.2267
Fresh fruit, vegetables and flowers at reasonable prices.
Hours: Monday - Saturday 8 am -7 pm, Sunday 9 am - 6 pm.

Costco (Grocery & Department Store)
1 Westchester Avenue, Port Chester, NY 914.935.3103
www.Costco.com
You have to buy a membership to shop at this international chain, but
that hasn't kept this megastore from being a Greenwich hit. From pesto
in their grocery section to a refrigerator, this huge store tries to give
good value. Don't miss the flower section.
Hours: weekdays 10 am - 8:30 pm, Saturday 9:30 am - 6 pm,
Sunday 10 am - 6 pm.

Daniella's Gelateria (Gelato, Sorbet)
315 Greenwich Avenue, 203.992.1030
It is easy to support our local shops when they are making gelato as
good as this. There are so many flavors to try, you will need to visit
frequently. Named after the owner's 8 year old - what a lucky daughter.
Daniellas has a sleek appearance and just a few seats.
Hours: weekdays, 11 am - 10 pm; weekends, noon - 11 pm.

Darlene's Heavenly Desires
(Ice Cream, Gelato, Chocolates)
185 Sound Beach Avenue, Old Greenwich, 203.698.9441
In summer, you will see happy people licking cones outside this shop
which has 34 flavors of Sedutto ice cream, delicious Belgian chocolates,
Bindi gelato, Coney Island custard and Weight Watchers ice cream. In our
Tasting Contest, the Sedutto ice cream scored at the top. You'll want to
take some home. Darlene imports her Gelato and Sedutto Ice cream di-
rectly from Italy. Ask Darlene about parties.
Hours: Every day; Winter, Monday - Saturday 9 am to 7 pm,
Sunday - 10 am - 6 pm; Summer hours are longer, sometimes to 10 pm.

Deborah Ann's Homemade Chocolates
381 Main Street, Ridgefield, CT 203.438.0065
www.DeborahAnns.com
These truffles are a wonderful reason for visiting this pretty town which
is 45 minutes away..
Hours: everyday 10 am - 7 pm. Their hours change frequently, check
before going.

FOOD & BEVERAGE

Di Mare Pastry Shop

Riverside Commons Shopping Center (1263 East Putnam), 203.637.4781

www.DimarePastry.com

A hot spot to order your child's birthday cake with a large selection of themes & characters for decoration (computerized and handmade). Selected as the best bakery in Fairfield County.

Hours: Monday - Saturday, 8 am - 6:30 pm;

Sunday, 8 am - 3 pm (10 pm in the summer); holidays, 8 am - 1 pm.

Prices: Cheesecakes $6 a pound, croissants $1.50 each.

Dunkin' Donuts (Bakery)

* 375 East Putnam, Cos Cob, 203.869.7454
  This location also sells Baskin Robbins, ice cream.
* 271 West Putnam Avenue, Greenwich, 203.869.5791

www.DunkinDonuts.com

We are addicted to their coffee. But who can resist their donuts?

Hours: Open every day, 5 am - 11 pm.

Edible Arrangements (Fruit)

456 Main Avenue, Norwalk CT, 203.229.0895, 877.363.7848

www.EdibleArrangements.com

The first Edible Arrangements store opened 1999 in Hamden, Connecticut and has grown to over 900 locations. The business specializes in fresh fruit arrangements, designed to look like a basket of flowers.

Hours: Weekdays 8 am - 5 pm, Saturday 8 am - 3 pm.

Farmer's Market (Fruits & Vegetables)

Horseneck Parking Lot (across from the Boys & Girls Club)

www.LocalHarvest.org

www.BuyCTgrown.com

www.WholesomeWave.org

www.CitySeed.org

From mid-May to mid-October, farmers come to our local area, set up stands and sell their produce. It is usually sold the day it is picked and couldn't be fresher. At some of the stalls you can also find homemade items such as breads, jellies and cheese.

Hours: Mid-May to Mid-October, Saturday 9:30 am - 1 pm.

FOOD & BEVERAGE

Fjord Fisheries (Seafood)

158 East Putnam Avenue, Cos Cob, 203.661.5006

www.FjordFisheries.com

This market has an abundance of fresh fish plus a delicatessen and sandwich shop. If you were to ask "Where can I find the best fish and chips?" you would probably be directed here. We also think their Crab Cake Po' boy, Salmon Club and Tuna sandwiches are outstanding. Fjord is a great place for sliced smoked salmon or salmon tartare. If you are in a hurry, place your order in advance.

Hours: Every day, Fish market 8 am to 7 pm;

Cooked take-out 11:30 am to 6:45 (Sunday to 6 pm.)

Prices: sandwich prices: $9 - $13.

(Porricelli's) Food Mart (Grocery)

26 Arcadia Rd, Old Greenwich, 203.637.4412

www.Porricellis.com

Full-service supermarket which has been family-owned and operated for the past 56 years. We really like it. It's a neighborhood meeting spot where regulars highly praise their family service and excellent meat, fish and produce departments. Their deli makes some of the best sandwiches in town.

Hours: Monday - Thursday 7 am - 7 pm; Friday 7 am - 8 pm;

Saturday 7 am - 6 pm; Sunday 8 am - 6 pm. Closed most holidays.

Fresh Direct (Home Delivery)

www.FreshDirect.com, 212.796.8002

An online grocer, Fresh Direct provides next day delivery of fresh food from local farms and fisheries. They also have over 600 choices of ready-to-heat meals.

Fuji Mart (Japanese Grocery)

1212 East Putnam Avenue, Riverside, 203.698.2107

An authentic Japanese grocery, very well stocked with most everything you will need, all in a very small space. Buy a bag of frozen gyoza.

Hours: Tuesday - Friday, 10:30 am - 7 pm;

Saturday & Sunday, 10am - 6:30pm.

FOOD & BEVERAGE

Garelick & Herbs (Delicatessen)

48 West Putnam Avenue, 203.661.7373

www.GarelickandHerbs.com

A sophisticated deli. It has a wide selection of first-rate, ready-to-serve dishes. There is a very small seating area.

Hours: weekdays, 7 am - 7 pm; Saturday, 8 am - 6 pm;
Sunday 9 am - 5 pm.

Size: Seats 16 inside and 10 outside in the summer. Primarily a takeout store, except for the lucky few who get there first.

Gelatissimo (Gelato)

26 Forest Street, New Canaan CT, 203.966.5000

www.Gelatissimo.net

They sell only Gelato, which they make fresh every day starting about 9 am, so not every flavor is available until later in the day. Cash only, so be prepared because you will find every flavor is terrific and you will want to take some home.

Hours: Summer, open every day 11 am - 10 pm;
Winter, Closed Monday, open the rest of the week 11 am - 9 pm.

Size: A few tables, but mostly take-out.

Godiva (Chocolate)

www.Godiva.com

J. Papers, 100 Bruce Park Avenue, 203.769.5104

Godiva, a Turkish-owned company, operates more than 450 shops world-wide and is available in over 10,000 specialty retailers. In the Fall and Winter, we buy our Godiva Chocolates from J. Papers. During the Summer, we go to the Stamford Town Center (100 Greyrock Place) 203.357.8110.

Hours: Every day 9am - 5 pm

(Cosed Sunday & Monday during the summer).

Gofer Ice Cream (Ice Cream)

522 East Putnam Avenue, Cos Cob, 203.661.9080

www.GoferIceCream.com   www.IceCreamPartyBox.com

Good hard and soft ice cream. We are fans of their Razzles. For a party, they will bring an ice cream cart to you.

Summer Hours: Monday - Thursday, 12:30 pm - 10:30 pm,
Friday & Saturday 12:30 pm - 11 pm, Sunday, 11:30 pm - 9:30 pm.
Winter/Fall Hours: Monday - Saturday, 12:30 pm - 9:30
(Friday & Saturday to 10 pm), Sunday, 1:30 - 9:30 pm.

Size: Seats 16

FOOD & BEVERAGE

Greenwich Prime Meats (Meat)
100 Bruce Park Avenue, 203.861.6328
A shop run by former members of famed Manero's butcher shop, they are located next to the Bon Ton Fish store. Same terrific meats (even Kobe steaks) and friendly advice along with Manero's special take-out treats: Gorgonzola salad, garlic bread, fried onions, steak fries and steak sandwiches. Easy parking behind the store. Free delivery in the local area.
Hours: Every day 9 am - 6 pm.

Greenwich Wine Society (Wine)
Dean Gamanos, Director, 203.629.1261
www.GreenwichWineSociety.com
Taste wine, visit wineries and meet once a month for tastings at a local restaurant. There are no age parameters. Married couples and singles are welcome.

HäagenDazs (Ice Cream)
374 Greenwich Avenue, 203.629.8000
It's a toss up between a hot fudge sundae or a chocolate-laced cone filled with creamy dulce de leche.
Hours: During the Summer, open everyday 11:30 am - 9 pm (Friday & Saturday to 10 pm.) During the winter hours, or during bad weather, the hours vary.

Horseneck Liquors (Wine)
25 East Putnam Avenue, 203.869.8944
www.Horseneck.com
Established in 1934, it was purchased by Terry Rogers in 1989 (Terry is pictured on the cover). Always known as the premier wine store in Greenwich, Terry has continued to make it the favorite destination for wine lovers. Horseneck has the largest inventory of Bordeaux, Burgundy and Italian wines in Connecticut, plus an excellent selection of wines from California and all over the world. You can count on their friendly, good advice. They will deliver and, if needed, gift wrap for you. You will enjoy her blog: Off the Vine, www.MofflyMedia.com/Off-the-Vine
Hours: Monday - Saturday 9 am - 7 pm.

FOOD & BEVERAGE

Jones Family Farm (Pick-your-own)
266 Israel Hill Road & Route 110, Shelton CT, 203.929.8425
www.JonesFamilyFarms.com
This pick-your-own farm began in the 1940s. They have strawberries in
June, followed by blueberries in July and August, and pumpkins in the
autumn. In December, come and cut your own Christmas tree. They even
have hay rides in October.
Hours: Best to call, hours change seasonally. Closed Sunday & Monday.
The Winery tasting room is open Friday - Sunday 11 am - 5 pm.

June & Ho (Salmon)
70 Purchase Street, Rye NY, 914.967.1900
A small, upscale food store owned by June and Ho Park. June is a graduate of the French Culinary Institute. Lots of gourmet take- outs, including
what is reputed to be the best smoked salmon in Westchester. The prices
are high, the store is almost always crowded and the staff seems too
busy to be polite.
Hours: Monday - Saturday, 8 am - 6 pm.

(The) Kneaded Bread (Bakery)
181 North Main Street, Port Chester NY, 914.937.9489
www.KneadedBread.com
A first-rate bread bakery. Every day they bake over 17 varieties of crusty,
European-style breads. Be sure to try their chocolate or raisin walnut
bread. They also have croissants, danishes, scones, cookies, pies, muffins, salads, soups, focaccia and sandwiches. Make their fresh donuts or
croissants a Sunday morning treat. There are a few seats, so stop in for
a good coffee and sandwich. Be sure to order holiday breads in advance.
Hours: weekdays 7 am - 5 pm; Saturday 8 am - 4 pm;
Sunday, 8 am - 1 pm.
Prices: Breads $5 - $6; Size: Seats 15.

Lindt (Chocolates)
5th level Stamford Town Center, 100 Greyrock Place, Stamford
CT, 203.359.1781
www.LindtUSA.com
Lindt & Sprüngli, a Swiss company that owns Ghirardelli Chocolates,
knows how to make a truffle that melts in your mouth. The US factory is
in Stratham New Hampshire. The company store in Stamford has a large
selection, their Lindor chocolates are usually available at the A & P
Fresh.
Hours: Monday - Saturday 10 am - 9 pm, Sunday 11 am - 6 pm.

(The) Little Chocolate Company (chocolates)

99 Mill Street, Byram CT, 203.531.6190
www.TheLittleChocolateCompany.com
Martine Coscia, a Greenwich resident and mother of four children, launched The Little Chocolate Company in 2008 as a wholesale and web retail operation. In 2010 she opened a retail store. She makes all of her chocolates and they are great.
Hours: Monday - Thursday 9:30 am - 4:30 pm,
Friday & Saturday 9:30 am - 8 pm.

Longford's (Ice Cream)

146 Sound Beach Avenue, Old Greenwich, 203.637.0480
www.LongfordsIceCream.com
Oh yummy, one of our favorite ice creams is now available in Old Greenwich! This high quality ice cream is made daily at their factory in Port Chester. For 18 years, Tom Banca, was dipping up Baskin Robbins ice cream in this same location. He recently switched to Longford's. Their Tahitian Vanilla was one of the top two ice creams in our Ice Cream Tasting Competition. If you ask, you will discover many fine restaurants and country clubs get their ice cream from Longford's.
Summer Hours: Monday - Saturday 10:30 am - 11 pm,
Sunday 11 am - 11 pm.
During the winter, or during bad, weather the hours may be shorter.

Le Pain Quotidien Bakery (Bakery, Restaurant)

382 Greenwich Avenue
www.LePainQuotidien.com
The restaurant is reviewed in RESTAURANTS. If you are in a hurry and can't sit down, you can get good coffee, muffins, pastries and bread to take out. They also have good quiche ready to go.
Hours: Open every day 7 am - 7:30 pm (Saturday & Sunday open at 7:30).

Le Wine Shop

39 East Elm Street, 203.869.6008
www.leWineShop.com
A small shop, run by Etienne Touzot, with a good selection of French wines.
Hours: Monday - Saturday 10 am - 7 pm (Friday & Saturday to 8 pm).

FOOD & BEVERAGE

Lobster Bin (Seafood)
204 Field Point Road, 203.661.6559
Just off Railroad Avenue. Plenty of fresh, sushi-quality fish as well as parking. We like their helpful advice when we not sure which fish to select.
Hours: Monday - Saturday 8 am - 6 pm, Sunday 9 am - 1 pm.

Make Your Own Wine
105 Fairview Park Drive, Elmsford NY, 914.741.5425
www.MYOWine.com
Hands-on wine making instruction, personalized labeling and tastings.

Marcus Dairy (Home Delivery Milk)
Danbury, CT, 800.243.2511
www.MarcusDairy.com
Get milk delivered? Apparently 6,000 customers do. Isn't it wonderful that we still have milk boxes and milk delivery? In addition, they deliver products such as juices, eggs, yogurt, cottage cheese, sour cream, butter and ice cream.

Meli-Melo (Sorbet, Ice Cream)
362 Greenwich Avenue, 203.629.6153
Catering: 374 Greenwich Avenue, 203.422.5001
www.MeliMeloGreenwich.com
A tiny, always popular, always crowded, restaurant with French casual foods and fresh fruit sorbets to die for. See our full review in the restaurant section.
Hours: every day 10 am - 10 pm.

Munson's Chocolates
(Green Farms Plaza) 1460 Post Road East, Westport CT, 203.259.6991
www.MunsonsChocolates.com
This store, with lots of CT locations, came in third in our Truffle Tasting.
Hours: weekdays 9 am - 8 pm, Saturday & Sunday 10am - 6 pm.

Neri Bakery
31 Pearl Street, Port Chester NY, 914.939.3311, 914.939.3235
At a beautiful wedding, we discovered this resource for delicious wedding cakes at reasonable prices. Check out their great frosted donuts.
Hours: Monday - Saturday 7 am - 7:30 pm, Sunday 7 am - 4:30 pm.

North Mianus Country Store (Deli)
322 Palmer Hill Road, Riverside, 637.2835
Operated by the Cozzolino family, expect a warm greeting and a variety of home-made treats. Havemeyer Park and Palmer Hill Road residents are delighted to have this local deli and grocery.
Hours: Monday - Saturday 7 am -6 pm, Sunday 9 am - 3 pm.

Pasta Vera Delicatessen
48 Greenwich Avenue, 203.661.9705
www.Pastavera.com
This popular, casual restaurant is noted for its homemade pastas. See our full review in the restaurant section. In the front of the restaurant is a deli area with a variety of fresh, scrumptious, ready-to-go selections.
Hours: Lunch, Monday - Saturday 11:30 - 3 pm;
Dinner, Monday - Saturday, 5 pm - 10 pm,
Sunday, 3 pm - 9 pm; Open most holidays.
Prices: Lunch entrees, $9 - $13; Dinner entrees, $15 - $28.
Size: Seats 58; reservations are accepted for parties of six or more.

Penzey's Spices
197 Westport Avenue, Norwalk, CT, 203.849.9085
www.Penzeys.com
Fresh spices make all the difference, and Penzey's has them in abundance. This store, one of over 40 in the US, is near Stew Leonards. Their large selection of spices, their blends and extracts—as well as pretty wooden boxed sets—make appreciated hostess gifts.
Hours: Monday - Saturday 9:30 am - 5 pm, Sunday 11 am - 5 pm.

Plum Pure Foods (Delicatessen)
236 East Putnam Avenue, Cos Cob, 203.869.7586
www.PlumPureFoods.com
Plum provides delicious takeout foods made primarily from natural products grown locally. They have something for everyone: soups, sandwiches, hot entrees and a nice selection of cheese. The owners aim to please with their food and their service. They are exceptional caterers. Plum scored at the top during our 2005 Catering Contest.
Hours: Closed Sunday; weekdays 7:30 am - 6 pm,
Saturday 9 am - 5 pm.

FOOD & BEVERAGE

(The) Round Hill Store (Grocery)

Corner of Old Mill and Round Hill Road, 203.869.5144

This small country store, which opened in 1801, still provides milk, eggs and staples for the surrounding area. Try one of their delicious turkey sandwiches. About half of their customers are people who work in the backcountry and half live nearby. The owners are working hard to restore it, while keeping its old-fashioned appeal.

Hours: weekdays 7 am - 7 pm, Saturday 7 am - 5 pm.

St. Moritz (Bakery)

383 Greenwich Avenue, 203.869.2818

www.StMoritzPastryShop.com

Luscious, rich pastries, chocolate mousse and cakes. Be sure to try the Sarah Bernhardt cookies.

Hours: Monday - Saturday, 7 am - 6 pm; Sunday ,8 am - 1 pm.

SAKie's (Thai Deli)

65 East Putnam Avenue, Cos Cob, 203.622.1184, 203.622.1187

If you grew up in Greenwich you will remember the delicious food at the Mai-Thai restaurant on Railroad Avenue. The Sak family has come out of retirement to open this winning deli. The days' choices are printed on a chalk board and more than Thai choices are offered. They serve breakfast, lunch and dinner.

Hours: Everyday 7 am - 7 pm.

Size: Seats 12

Scandia Food and Gifts (Scandinavian foods)

30 High Street (off US1), Norwalk CT, 203.838.2087

www.ScandiaFood.com

The area source for Scandinavian food and gifts.

Hours: Wednesday - Saturday 10 am - 5 pm.

Scarpelli's Market (Sausage)

Bible Street, Cos Cob, 203.869.2771

Mac Scarpelli is still making the same wonderful sausage his parents, Maria & Peter, made when they opened the store in 1920. Mac makes amazingly delicious sausage every morning. Stop in here and you will have one more reason why you love living in Greenwich. Many local restaurants pick-up their sausage here.

Hours: Closed Monday & Wednesday;
Tuesday, Thursday - Sunday 9 am - 1 pm.

Schakolad Chocolate Factory (chocolate)

172 Bedford Street, Stamford CT, 203.359.1886

www.Schakolad.com

A very fun place to shop for chocolate gifts. They mold chocolate into an amazing variety of shapes.

Hours: Monday - Saturday, 11 am - 6 pm.

Stew Leonard's (Grocery)

100 Westport Avenue, Norwalk CT, 203.847.7214

www.StewLeonards.com

Famous throughout the metropolitan area and worth the trip. This huge food store has been called the Disneyland of grocery stores by the New York Times. Bring your children.

Hours: every day 7 am - 11 pm.

Stop and Shop (Grocery)

- Super Stop & Shop, 15 Waterfront Place, Port Chester NY 914.937.7318
- 161 West Putnam Avenue, 203.625.0622
- 11 Glenville Road, Glenville, 203.531.0541

www.StopAndShop.com

With 360 stores, Stop & Shop is the largest New England food retailer. You can order food delivered by placing your order through www.StopAndShop.com or www.PeaPod.com. Call 800.573.2763 for delivery information.

Hours: Monday - Saturday 7 am - 11 pm, Sunday 7 am - 10 pm.

Sweet Ashley's (Ice Cream)

248 East Avenue, Norwalk CT, 203.866.7740

www.Sweet-Ashleys.com

An independent ice cream shop in East Norwalk with many kudos. It is known for its unusual ice cream flavors. If you are in South Norwalk, it is just across the bridge at end of Washington Street on route 136.

Hours: March through about December, open 7 days 11 am - 10 pm.

Sweet Lisa's Exquisite Cakes (Bakery)

3 Field Road, Cos Cob, 869.9545

www.SweetLisas.com

Wonderful cakes, party pastries and designer cookies by special order only. They usually require seven days' notice. Their website has lots of pictures of their creations.

Hours: Tuesday - Friday 9 am - 5 pm, Saturday 9 am - 3 pm.

FOOD & BEVERAGE

Trader Joe's (Grocery)

436 Boston Post Road (US-1), Darien CT, 203.656.1414

www.TraderJoes.com

Trader Joe fans will be glad to know there is a store not far from Greenwich. A grocery store selling healthy food at good prices. Try one of their soups or frozen dinners.

Hours: every day, 9 am - 9 pm.

Upper Crust Bagel Company (Bakery/Deli)

197 Sound Beach Avenue, Old Greenwich, 203.698.0079

www.UpperCrustBagel.com

Our favorite bagels! They have tasty old-fashioned kettle-boiled and hearth-baked bagels, as well as gourmet spreads, sandwiches and coffees. They accept checks but no credit cards.

Hours: weekdays, 6 am - 4 pm; Saturday, 7 am - 4 pm;
Sunday, 7 am - 3 pm.

Var Max Liquor Pantry (Wine)

16 Putnam Avenue, Port Chester, NY, 914.937.4930

www.VarMax.com

They have a very large selection of well-priced wines. Nice descriptions on their wine specials. Because they are not subject to CT Blue Laws they are open Sundays.

Hours: Monday - Thursday 9 am - 9pm, Friday - Saturday 9 am - 10 pm, Sunday Noon- 6 pm.

Villarina's (Italian Deli)

551 East Putnam Avenue, Cos Cob, 203.422.0174

On your way home, grab a dinner like eggplant rollatini or lasagna for your family or guests. They also sell pasta sheets. Everyone will think you are a great cook! Free local delivery for orders over $20.

Hours: weekdays 8:30 am - 6 pm, Saturday 8:30 am - 5 pm,
Sunday 10 am - 3pm.

Versailles Bakery (Bakery & Restaurant)

339 Greenwich Avenue, 203.661.6634

A very French bistro with a front counter full of pastries and croissants that will make your day worth living. Try their operas and éclairs. Just the right place to order a takeout quiche. The good food and atmosphere are reminiscent of our Paris favorites.

Hours: every day 7:30 am - 3 pm.

Village Prime Meats (Meat)

475 Main Street, Armonk NY, 914.273.5222

An old-fashioned butcher shop. It is worth the trip when you want something special. Where else can you get rabbit, game birds, Peking or Muscovy duck or just that special cut of meat you need? They also have a number of unique food products, such as white or black truffle oil and a large number of fresh pates.

Hours: weekdays, 8 am - 6 pm; Saturday, 8 am - 5:30 pm.

White Silo Farm (Winery & Pick-your-Own)

Sherman, CT, 860.355.0271

www.WhiteSiloWinery.com

Pick your own strawberries, asparagus, raspberries, blackberries and rhubarb.

Hours: Winery, May - Dec, Friday - Sunday & Holidays 11 am - 6 pm; Pick-Your-Own farm is in season Sept & Oct, everyday 10 am - 6 pm.

Whole Foods (Grocery, Cheese, Bakery, Seafood)

90 East Putnam Avenue, 203.661.0631

www.WholeFoods.com

www.GenjiWeb.com

This organic grocery store has a first class deli. When you shop here you are bound to meet your friends buying their Sunday bagels, fresh fish, vitamins, deli foods, cheese, flowers, fruits and vegetables. It is great to have an expert available in each food area to happily give you advice about selections. In addition to its amazing assortment of natural foods, the store has many strong departments including seafood, produce, meat and cheese. On a recent evening, we served their lemon pepper rotisserie chicken, sesame green beans, mixed green salad and corn bread. Everyone loved it! Don't miss their authentic Indian dishes. Serve with their whole wheat Tandoori Naan. Their fresh sushi is prepared by Genj's sushi chefs. Large platters should be ordered 24-hours in advance.

Hours: Everyday 8 am - 10 pm.

Wine Wise

122 East Putnam Avenue, 203.340.2440

www.WineWiseShop.com

This unusual wine store stocks wines from many smaller vineyards. If you don't know the wine, you can taste almost any wine in the shop, free of charge.

Hours: Monday - Saturday 10 am - 7 pm.

GAMBLING

Gambling has come to Connecticut and our two casinos are closer and more attractive than those in Atlantic City, NJ. The casinos are very close to each other. For bus transportation call Dattco, 888.770.0140. *For more information on the area see HOTELS & INNS.*

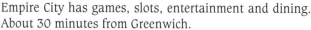
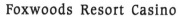

Empire City at Yonkers Raceway
810 Yonkers Avenue, Yonkers NY, 914.
968.4200
Reservations: 914.457.2457
www.YonkersRaceway.com
Yonkers Raceway has live harness racing year-round. The racing schedule is five nights per week, with the first post at 7:10 pm on Monday, Tuesday, Thursday, Friday and Saturday.
Empire City has games, slots, entertainment and dining.
About 30 minutes from Greenwich.

Foxwoods Resort Casino
800.369.9663
www.Foxwoods.com
Just seven miles from Mystic, CT, this resort is owned by the Mashantucket Pequot Tribal Nations. It is the largest hotel complex in the Northeast. The 312 room Grand Pequot Tower is very comfortable, and in addition to an array of restaurants, entertainment and, of course, gaming tables, there is a 36 hole golf course, www.LakeOfIsles.com.
Directions: I-95 N to exit 92, about 2 hours from Greenwich.

Mohegan Sun
General Info: 888.226.7711; Hotel Reservations: 888.777.7922
www.MoheganSun.com
Somewhat smaller than Foxwoods, this casino still has over 192 gaming tables and 3,000 slot machines. The casino is owned by the Mohegan Nation and Sun International. The Mohegan Sun complex reflects the culture and history of the Mohegan Nation. Many people prefer its Native American theme decoration.
Directions: I-95 N to exit 76, about 2 hours from Greenwich.

GROOMING INDEX

Barbers

Benford Barber at the Palm
Classic Barber
Generations Barber
Graham's Kids Cuts
(The) Hair Cut Place
Palm Barber Shop
Sharkey's Cuts for Kids

Day Spas

Celia B. Skin Care
Halcyon Spa & Boutique
Empy's Day Spa
Noelle Spa for Beauty and Wellness
Serenity Spa

Hairdressers

Becker Salon
Carlo and Company
Empy's Day Spa
Enzo Ricco Bene Salon
Frederic Fekkai
Greenwich Salon and Day Spa
Hopscotch
Noelle Spa for Beauty and Wellness
Partners Salon and Spa
Salon 221
Salon Moda Enzo
Spa-zzano's
Visible Changes
Warren Tricomi Salon

Nail Salons

Coco Nail Spa
Dream Nails
Empy's Day Spa
Hilltop Nails
Nail Boutique
Tiffany Nails
Tip Top Nails

TIP: MAKING FRIENDS

Whether you are new to town or a long-term resident and
want to have an easy, fun way to meet others, join one of
the two newcomers' clubs. For details see
www.greenwichnewcomers.com.

GROOMING

Becker Salon

268 Mason Street 203.340.9550

www.BeckerSalon.com

A must try salon—great cuts and color by a staff that knows how to make hairdressing fun.

Hours: Monday-Saturday 8:00 am-7:00 pm

Prices: Women's Haircut $60-$95; Men's Haircut $35-$50; Children's Haircut $25-$50

Benford Barber Shop at The Palm

20 Church Street, 203.661.7383

This out-of-the way barber tucked in the back of the Palm Barber Shop is used by many of Greenwich's prominent residents.

Haircuts are by appointment.

Hours: Wednesday - Saturday 8 am - 5 pm.

Prices: Haircut $25

Carlo and Company

70 East Putnam Avenue (Whole Foods shopping center) 203.869.2300

Long established in Greenwich, you will enjoy the friendly, attentive atmosphere as well as their expert haircuts, coloring and styling. Thank you, Alison!

Hours: Monday - Saturday, 8:30 am - 5 pm.

Prices: Women's Haircut $85

Celia B. Skin Care

24 Greenwich Avenue (2nd Floor), 203.861.6850

Celia offers a wonderful menu of facials. A very nice experience. She shares space with the Jose Henrique Salon.

Hours: By appointment.

Prices: Women's Facial $132

Classic Barber

396 Greenwich Avenue (upstairs), 203.869.3600

www.ClassicBarberGreenwich.com

The Merollas have relocated from the longtime Subway barbershop to start their own shop. A modern, atmosphere with flat-screen TVs and an airplane chair for children.

Hours: Tuesday - Saturday 8 am - 5 pm (Thursday to 7 pm) & by appointment.

Prices: Haircut $20

GROOMING

Coco Nail Spa

1263 E. Putnam Avenue, Riverside, 203.698.2220
www.CocoSpa.com
They offer everything from manicures/pedicures, waxing to wonderful
Spa packages that range from $125 - $420.
Hours: Monday - Saturday 9:30 am - 7 pm.
Prices: Manicure $12; Pedicure $25; Facial $125

Dream Nails

280 Railroad Avenue, 203.629.6888 / 6398
Reasonably priced nail salon.
Hours: weekdays 9:30 am - 7:30 pm, Saturday 9:30 am - 7 pm,
Sunday 10 am - 6 pm.
Prices: Manicure $9; Pedicure $23.

Empy's Day Spa

143 West Putnam Avenue, 203.661.6625
Excellent facials, waxing, manicures and pedicures by a friendly staff in
a low key atmosphere. Empy and her staff do great haircuts.
Hours: weekdays 9:30 am - 6 pm (Thursdays until 8),
Saturday 9 am- 4 pm. By appointment or walk-in.
Prices: Women's haircuts $45 and up, Facials $125,
one hour massage $100; Manicure $18; Pedicure $38.

Enzo Ricco Bene Salon

1800 East Putnam Avenue(at the Hyatt), Old Greenwich
203.698.4141
This attractive salon located off the lobby of the Hyatt Regency Hotel
offers a pleasant and talented staff of colorists and stylists. For the
easiest access use the free valet parking.
Hours: Monday 9 am - 5 pm, Tuesday, Wednesday & Friday 8 am - 6 pm,
Thursday 8 am - 8 pm, Saturday 8 am - 5 pm.
Prices: Women's Haircut $90-$119; Facials $95-$105.

Frederic Fekkai

2 Lewis Court, 203.861.6700
www.Fekkai.com
Highly trained stylists offering luxury pampering services.
Hours: Monday, Tuesday & Wednesday 8:30 am -6 pm,
Thursday 8:30 am -8 pm, Friday 8:30 am - 7 pm,
Saturday 8:30 am - 6 pm.
Prices: Women's Haircut from $125-$190;
Haircut with Frederic Fekkai $750.

GROOMING

Generations Barber Parlor
- 138 Hamilton Avenue, Greenwich, 203.413.2344
- 3 Boulder Avenue, Old Greenwich, 203.637.8266

www.GenerationsParlor.com

The High School generation is finding this a favorite spot. They are open 7 days a week, setting them apart from traditional barber hours.
Hours: Monday 10:30 am - 8 pm, Tuesday-Friday 8 am 8 pm, Saturday 8 am - 5 pm, Sunday 9 am - 3 pm.
Prices: Men's Haircut $23; Boys $23; Women $65; Girls $30

Graham's Kids Cuts of Greenwich
60 Greenwich Avenue, 203.983.6800

Unique children's hair salon in the back of a toy store. Appointments for haircuts are recommended.
Hours: Tuesday - Saturday 10 am - 5:30 pm.
Prices: Haircut $32

Greenwich Salon and Day Spa
120 Post Road, Cos Cob (above Food Mart), 203.661.4093

Popular full service salon:styling, cuts, manicures, pedicures, facials and waxing. Free parking.
Hours: Tuesday - Saturday 8:30 am - 5 pm.
Prices: Women's Haircut $50; Women's Facial $80 and up.

(The) Hair Cut Place
259 Sound Beach Avenue, Old Greenwich, 203.637.1313
www.TheHairCutPlace.com

An Old Greenwich institution formerly called Off Center Barber Shop. Kids love haircuts in the Jeep. Appointments are available, walk-ins welcomed.
Hours: Monday 8 am-6:30 pm, Tuesday-Saturday 8 am - 5 pm (Thursdays until 7).
Prices: Haircut for Men & Children $24; Women $30

Halcyon Spa & Boutique
151 Greenwich Avenue (above Talbots), 203.622.0300
www.PremierSpaCollection.com

Professional treatments and products for your specific needs. Services include: facials, massage therapies, body treatments, pedicure, manicure, waxing, make-up, eyebrow and lash tinting. Spa for men.
Hours: Monday - Saturday, 9 am - 6 pm; Sunday, 10 am - 4:30 pm.
Prices: Facials $55 - $130

GROOMING

Hilltop Nails
235 Old Mill Road, Glenville, 203.532.8000
Several of our associates treat themselves to the services here, including the manicure/pedicure combination package. Walk-ins are accepted.
Hours: weekdays, 9:30 am - 7 pm; Saturday, 9 am - 6:30 pm; Sunday, 10 am - 5:30 pm.
Prices: Manicure $12 +, Pedicure $25 +.

Hopscotch
10 Railroad Ave, 203.661.0107
www.HopscotchSalon.com
A cutting-edge high-tech salon with very nice owners catering to a fashionable clientele. People come from New York City to go here.
Hours: Monday - Saturday 8:30 am - 6 pm (Tuesday & Thursday to 8 pm), Sunday 10 am - 5 pm.
Prices: Women's Haircut $70 - $150; Men's Haircut $40 - $90; Children's Haircut $40 - $75; Facials $85 - $170.

Nail Boutique
522 East Putnam Avenue, 203.422.5512
Centrally located salon near I-95 exit 4, next to the Pizza Post. This salon is staffed by friendly, capable women.
Hours: weekdays 9:30 am - 7 pm, Saturday 9:30 am - 6:30 pm.
Prices: Manicure $12; Pedicure $20.

Noelle Spa for Beauty and Wellness
1100 High Ridge Road, Stamford, 203.322.3445
www.Noelle.com
Complete day spa with talented hair colorists and stylists. They have a great variety of services from make-up, bridal, hand & foot, massages, body treatment, esthetic, teeth whitening, healing therapies & yoga. Spa for men.
Hours: Monday & Wednesday 9 am - 5:30 pm, Tuesday & Thursday 8 am - 8 pm; Friday 8 am - 8 pm, Saturday 8 am - 6 pm.
Prices: Women's Haircut-Stylist $60; Lead Stylist $90; Men's Haircut $55 to $65; Women's Facials $100-$120; one hour massage $100.

GROOMING

Palm Barber Shop
20 Church Street, 203.869.0292
Tony gives good cuts for youth and adults.
Hours: Monday-Saturday 7:30 am - 6:00 pm.
Prices: Haircut $20

Partners Salon and Spa
1200 East Putnam Avenue, Riverside, 203.637.0478
Full salon and spa services with excellent staff. Valet Parking.
Hours: Tuesday & Thursday 9 am - 7 pm,
Wednesday & Friday 9 am - 5 pm, Saturday 8 am - 5 pm.
Prices: Women's Haircut $95-$135; Women's Facial $85-$95

Salon 221
221 East Putnam Avenue
(2nd floor, Mill Pond Shopping Center), Cos Cob, 203.661.8838
Full service salon with custom hair color and precision cuts. Lynn, a
client for a decade, would follow Joe anywhere.
Hours: Tuesday & Wednesday 9:30 am - 5 pm,
Thursday & Friday 9:30 am - 7 pm, Saturday 9 am - 5 pm.
Prices: Women's Haircut $75 and up.

Salon Moda Enzo
522 East Putnam Avenue, 203.552.0680
www.Modaenzo.com
This relaxed full-service hair salon is conveniently located next to the
Pizza Post. Stephanie, age 6, loves Katie's cuts.
Hours: Tuesday - Friday 9 am - 5 pm, Saturday 8 am - 4 pm.
Prices: Haircuts Men's $35+, Women's $65+, Boy's $35+, Girl's $45+.

Serenity Spa
116 East Putnam Avenue, 203.629.9000
www.SerenitySpaNow.com
Experience the essential indulgence of nurturing skin care services and
all-natural facial products in a serene environment.
Hours: Monday 9 am-5 pm, Tuesday & Thursday 9 am-7 pm, Wednesday
& Friday 9 am - 6 pm, Saturday 9 am - 5 pm.
Prices: Women's Facials $85 - $150

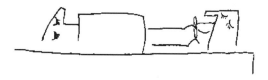

GROOMING

Sharkey's Cuts for Kids
220 East Putnam Avenue, Cos Cob, 203.629.5437
www.SharkeysCutsForKids.com
This is all about kids having fun while their hair is being cut.
Hours: weekdays 10 am - 6 pm, Saturday 9 am - 5 pm,
Sunday 10 am - 4 pm.
Prices: Men & Children Haircut $28; Women $45

Spa-zzano's
80 Valley Road, Cos Cob, 203.769-5147
Charming new hair salon in Cos Cob. Featuring cutting edge services.
Owner, Michael Spezzano III, has been a Greenwich stylist for 30+ years.
Michael, formerly with Claude Maxine in Paris France, has returned to
Greenwich. Treat yourself to a new look.
Hours: Monday - Saturday 9 am - 5 pm.
Prices: Women's Haircut $75; Men's Haircut $40; Children's $35

Tiffany Nails
349 Greenwich Avenue, 203.661.3838
Walk-ins only.
Hours: Monday - Saturday 9:30 am - 7 pm, Sunday 10 am - 5:30 pm.

Tip Top Nails
1 Havemeyer Lane, Old Greenwich, 203.698.3320
By appointment or walk in.
Hours: weekdays 9:30 am - 7 pm, Saturday 9 am - 7 pm,
Sunday 10 am - 5:30 pm.

Visible Changes
204 Sound Beach Avenue, Old Greenwich, 203.637.9154
If you've seen a great haircut, it's likely to have been cut here.
Hours: Monday 9 am - 5 pm, Tuesday - Friday 9 am - 7 pm,
Saturday 8:30 am - 5:30 pm.   Prices: Haircut $75-$85.

Warren Tricomi Salon
1 East Putnam Avenue, 203.863.9300
www.WarrenTricomi.com
Popular, NYC-style salon, but friendlier. Excellent talent, particularly the
colorist. Tamara is one of the best, and perhaps most expensive, make-
up artists and eyebrow shapers in the area. Great stop for bridal parties.
Free parking.
Hours: Mon-Wed & Saturday 8 am - 6 pm, Thurs & Friday 8 am - 8 pm.
Prices: Women's Haircut $136 - $300 (by owner).

HEALTH INDEX

See FITNESS for Yoga, Pilates, Trainers and Exercise Classes
See SENIORS for Senior Housing and Home Care
See SHOPPING for Glasses and Contact Lens

Addiction Recovery

Greenwich Al-Anon
  888.825.2666
Greenwich Alcoholics Anonymous,
  203.869.522
  800.530.9511(national)
Greenwich Hospital Addiction Recovery Program
  203.863.4673
Silver Hill Hospital,
  203.966.3561, 866.542.4455

Domestic Abuse

211 Infoline
YWCA Domestic Abuse Service
  203.869.6501 ext 175

Drugstores (Pharmacies)

CVS 24-Hr Pharmacy & Minute Clinic
Finch Pharmacy
Grannick's Pharmacy
North Street Pharmacy
Walgreens 24-Hr Pharmacy

Emergencies

Dial 911
Access Ambulance
CVS Minute Clinic
Fire Fly (after hours Pediatrics)
Greenwich Convenient Medical
  Center (Walk-in-clinic)
Greenwich Emergency Medical
  Service (GEMS)
Greenwich Hospital Emergency
  Room

Exercise Equipment

(The) Fitness Store
Gym Source
Relax the Back

TIP: OPTOMETRISTS and OPHTHALMOLOGISTS

Upon completion of optometry school, candidates graduate from accredited college of optometry and hold the Doctor of Optometry (O.D.) degree.

Optometrists are considered the general practitioners of eye healthcare. They prescribe eyeglasses and contact lenses to correct nearsightedness, farsightedness and astigmatism. This doctor also identifies various eye conditions, such as retinal diseases, glaucoma and cataracts, and treats these disorders with non-surgical methods.

Ophthalmologists are medical doctors (M.D.) or Doctors of Osteopathic Medicine (D.O.). who have completed a college degree, medical school, and an additional four years of post-graduate training in ophthalmology in many countries.

HEALTH INDEX

Eyeglasses and Contact Lenses
See SHOPPING

Hair Replacement
Mega HairSystems

Health Information
211 Infoline
Angie's List
Castle Connolly Top Doctors
Connecticut Magazine Survey of
    Top Doctors and Hospitals
Greenwich Hospital Consumer
    Health Reference Center
Greenwich Library Health
    Information Center
Greenwich Magazine Survey of
    Top Doctors in Fairfield County
Health Extensions
Physician Referral Service
Planned Parenthood
Tick Testing Laboratory

Health and Wellness Organizations
American Red Cross
Breast Cancer Alliance
Greenwich Hospital Auxiliary

Hearing Aids
Solomon-Shotland Audiology

Hospitals
Advanced Radiology Consultants
(mammogram walk-in Clinic)
Burke Rehabilitation Hospital
Greenwich Convenient Medical Center (walk-in Clinic)
Greenwich Hospital
Physician Referral Service
Silver Hill Hospital
Westchester Medical Center
Yale New Haven Hospital

Medical Insurance Assistance
National Medical Claims

Medical Supplies & Equipment
Care Center
Grannick's Pharmacy
Liberty Rehab and Patient Aid
    Center
Relax the Back

Physical Therapy & Chiropractors
Burke Rehabilitation Hospital
Greenwich Healing Hands
Greenwich Physical Therapy
Greenwich Rolfing
Greenwich Sports Medicine
Oetting-Stebbins Physical Therapy
Peak Wellness
Performance Physical Therapy
Physical Therapy & Sports
    Rehabilitation
Sam Schwartz
Tully Health Center

Senior Housing
See SENIORS for Senior Housing and Home Care

Shoe Orthotics
Stride Custom Orthotics

Vitamins
GNC
Greenwich Health Mart
Vitamin Shoppe
Whole Body

211 Infoline

Dial 211 or 800.505.2000 or www.infoline.org

United Way's free, confidential, 24-hour information on subjects such as pre-natal care, legal assistance, AIDS testing and emergency assistance provided by trained call specialists.

Access Ambulance

1111 East Putnam Avenue, Riverside, 203.637.2351

Private, for-profit, emergency and non-emergency ambulance service owned by Nelson Ambulance Service. They provide transportation between patients' homes and medical facilities.

Advanced Radiology Consultants

1325 Washington Boulevard, Stamford CT, 203.356.9729

www.AdRad.com

They will schedule appointments, but also accept walk-in mammograms. Hours: weekdays 8:30 am - 5:30 pm, Saturday 8 - 12 pm.

American Red Cross

Greenwich Chapter, 99 Indian Field Road, 203.869.8444

www.GreenwichRedCross.org

They are staffed with trained and caring volunteers. Their mission is to prevent, prepare for and respond to emergencies. They offer many programs such as CPR, transportation services and baby sitting training.

Angie's List

www.AngiesList.com

Besides rating service providers, they have also started rating doctors.

Breast Cancer Alliance

48 Maple Avenue, 203.861.0014

www.BreastCancerAlliance.org

Burke Rehabilitation Hospital (Hospital)

785 Mamaroneck Avenue, White Plains NY, 914.597.2500

www.Burke.org

A nearby 60-acre private, not-for-profit, facility specializing in inpatient and outpatient multi-disciplinary physical rehabilitation and research.

HEALTH

(The) Care Center (Equipment)
29 Arcadia Road, Old Greenwich, 203.637.3599
www.TheCareCenter.com
A home medical equipment company with just about everything you need to recover from a short illness or long term care. They specialize in scooters, power wheelchairs, seat lift chairs and courteous service.
Hours: weekdays 8:30 am - 5:00 pm, Saturday 9 am - 12 pm.

Castle Connolly Top Doctors
42 West 24th Street, New York NY, 212.367.8400
www.CastleConnolly.com
The source of information used by Greenwich and Connecticut Magazines' survey of Top Doctors.

Connecticut Magazine Survey of Top Doctors and Hospitals
www.ConnecticutMag.com (Click on the Top Doctors icon on the right side)

CVS (Pharmacy)
www.CVS.com
• 99 Greenwich Avenue, 203.862.9341, pharmacy 203.862.9320
Pharmacy Hours: weekdays, 7 am - 10 pm; Saturday, 8 am - 6 pm; Sunday, 9 am - 6 pm.
• 225 Sound Beach Avenue, Old Greenwich, 203.698.2428, Pharmacy 203.698.1457. Pharmacy Hours: weekdays, 8 am - 9 pm; Saturday & Sunday, 8 am - 6 pm.
• 1239 East Putnam Ave (Thru Way Shopping Center), Riverside 203.698.4006. This location is open 24-hours and has a Minute Clinic.

CVS Minute Clinic
1239 East Putnam Avenue, Riverside, 866.389.2727
www.MinuteClinic.com
Clinic hours: weekdays 8:30 - 7:30 (lunch break 2 pm - 3 pm), Saturday & Sunday 10 am - 5:30 pm (lunch break 1 pm - 1:30 pm).

Finch Pharmacy
3 Riversville Road, Glenville, 203.531.8494
Friendly pharmacy in the heart of Glenville, where people know you and care about your needs.
Hours: weekdays 8 am - 6 pm, Saturday, 9 am - 6 pm.

Fire Fly (after hours Pediatrics Urgent Care)

1011 High Ridge Road, Stamford CT, 203.968.1900

www.FireFlyPediatrics.com

Board certified pediatricians will help you with no appointment necessary. The visit records will be faxed to your pediatrician. Most medical coverage is accepted.

Hours: Open 365 days a year, weekdays 4 pm - 11 pm,
Weekends & Holidays 12 pm - 11 pm.

(The) Fitness Store (Exercise)

65 Harvard Avenue, Stamford CT, 203.359.9702

A variety of home gym equipments such as cycles, treadmills, stair climbers and ellipticals. This store is jointly located with Creative Playthings www.Creativeplaythings.com, reviewed in Stores.

Hours: Monday - Saturday 10 am - 6 pm, Sunday noon - 5 pm.

GNC (General Nutrition Centers)

1237 East Putnam Avenue (Riverside Commons), Riverside
203.637.4262

www.GNC.com

They typically stock a wide range of weight loss, bodybuilding and nutritional supplements as well as health and fitness books, magazines, vitamins, natural remedies, and health and beauty products. GNC has over 6,000 stores in the US and is the largest US retailer of nutritional supplements.

Hours: weekdays 9 am - 8 pm, Saturday 9 am - 7 pm,
Sunday 10 am - 5 pm.

Grannick's Pharmacy

277 Greenwich Avenue, 203.869.3492

www.GrannicksPharmacy.com

A family business that has been helping its customers since 1942. Like the chain stores you can call in your subscription for refill. Unlike the chain stores they deliver. They sell and rent some medical equipment. Why be just a number when you can deal with someone who knows and cares about you?

Hours: Monday - Saturday 9 am - 6 pm.

HEALTH

Greenwich Convenient Medical Center

1200 East Putnam Avenue, Riverside, CT 203.698.1419
www.GreenwichConvenientMedicalCareCenter.com
Walk-in clinic run by Dr. Robert Gabriel; no appointment is required.
Quick and efficient service for immunizations, minor injuries and routine
illnesses. Dr. Gabriel takes the time to understand and explain.
Hours: weekdays 8 am - 8 pm,
Saturday 8 am - 6 pm, Sunday 10 am - 5 pm.

Greenwich Emergency Medical Service (GEMS)

111 East Putnam Avenue, 203.637.7505 (general information)
www.GreenwichEMS.org
GEMS has six ambulances, 11 paramedics and 12 full-time EMTs. GEMS
also provides programs in CPR and basic first aid. GEMS ambulances
have the latest equipment and well-trained Emergency Medical Techni-
cians and paramedics. Once you call 911, their computer-aided dispatch
system allows them to reach 75% of patients within 5 minutes and 95%
with 8 minutes. Greenwich is lucky to have such a coordinated ambulance organization. They also give CPR and First Aid Classes.

Greenwich Healing Hands

Bob Jensen, 203.253.5576
www.GreenwichHealingHands.com
Bob is well liked in Greenwich, he offers a variety of massage therapies
including pregnancy and sports massage.
Hours: by appointment Monday - Saturday.

Greenwich Health Mart (Vitamins)

30 Greenwich Avenue, 203.869.9658
A well-stocked health product store, including some foods and a great
variety of vitamins and homeopathic remedies. Their cheerful service
makes everyone feel well. Be sure to ask for their excellent newsletter.
Hours: Monday - Wednesday 8:30 am - 5:30 pm,
Thursday 8:30 am - 7:30 pm, Friday 8:30 am - 5:30 pm,
Saturday 8 am - 5 pm; Sunday 11 am - 3 pm.

HEALTH

Greenwich Hospital
5 Perryridge Road, 203.863.3000
Greenwich Hospital Emergency Room: 203.863.3637
www.GreenHosp.org
Greenwich Hospital is a 160-bed, non-profit, community teaching hospital, affiliated with Yale-New Haven Hospital. Since 1996, the Hospital has been completely rebuilt and it is a model for health care. The cost of the entire project (including the Helmsley Building and the Watson Pavilion) was $220,000,000, of which $138,000,000 came from private community donations. The rooms have been carefully designed to make the patient feel comfortable. As a result, many feel it's more like staying at a fine hotel than a hospital. Even the intensive care unit has woodland views and amazing amenities. Word is spreading fast that this is the most comfortable place to have your baby. Greenwich Hospital is ranked first in Connecticut in patient satisfaction and was named in the "Top 100 Most Wired Hospitals."

Greenwich Hospital Auxiliary
Greenwich Hospital, 5 Perryridge Road,
Auxiliary office: 203.863.3220, Volunteer Office: 203.863.3222
Mimi Grady, President

Greenwich Hospital Consumer Health Reference Center
5 Perryridge Road, 203.863.3285
Hours: weekdays, 8:30 am - 4:45 pm.

Greenwich Library Health Information Center
www.GreenwichLibrary.org/Health.asp
Everyone in Greenwich can be a well-informed healthcare consumer. Greenwich Library has an extensive health information center with 18 subscription databases. Most databases are available through the library's website by entering your library card number. In addition the Center has over 100 authoritative reference materials, 40 journals, 5,000 circulating books, more than 300 videos and a large collection of audio books. A specially trained librarian is on duty to assist with healthcare research. The library also has speakers on current health topics. If you give them your email address, they will keep you posted.

Greenwich Magazine Survey of Top Doctors
in Fairfield County
www.mofflymedia.com/Moffly-Publications/Greenwich-Magazine/January-2010/Top-Doctors/

Greenwich Physical Therapy Center (Physical Therapy)

1171 East Putnam Avenue, Riverside, 203.637.1700
An independent (non-physician owned) physical therapy center specializing in orthopedic and sports-related injuries. Everyone raves about Scott Gelbs and his team.
Hours: Monday, Wednesday, Friday, 7 am - 4 pm;
Tuesday & Thursday 9 am - 7 pm.

Greenwich Rolfing (Chiropractor)

296 Sound Beach Avenue, Old Greenwich, 203.698.2965
www.GreenwichRolfing.com/craigswanonrolfingvideo.html
Rolfing is the commonly used name for the system of Structural Integration soft tissue manipulation (originally called Postural Release) developed by Dr. Ida Rolf. Rolfing is system of soft tissue manipulation that claims to make clients stand straighter, gain height, and move better. Some clients find rolfing painful.
Hours: weekdays 7 am - 8 pm, Saturday & Sunday 7 am - 5 pm.

Greenwich Sports Medicine (Chiropractor)

7 Riversville Road, 531.3131
www.GreenwichSportsMedicine.com
www.FitAndFunctional.com
Dr. Gil Chimes is a sports chiropractor who specializes in Active Release Techniques (ART) to help athletes recover from injuries. ART breaks up scar tissue, eliminates pain and increases range of motion. Their treatments can incorporate acupuncture, chiropractic, exercise therapy, weight loss and nutritional counseling.
Hours: Monday & Wednesday, 8 am - 7 pm (break 1:45 to 3),
Tuesday 8 am - 7 pm, Thursday, 2 pm - 7 pm,
Friday 8 am - 5:45 pm (break 1:45 - 3).

Gym Source (Exercise Equipment)

1008 High Ridge Road, Stamford CT, 203.329.9233
www.GymSource.com
New and pre-owned exercise equipment to meet just about any need.
Hours: weekdays 10 am - 7 pm, Saturday noon - 5 pm.

HEALTH

Health Extensions (Health Information)
Community Wellness Programs @ Greenwich Hospital
203.863.3126
www.greenhosp.org
The Greenwich Hospital publishes an amazingly extensive schedule and description of the community's many wellness programs. To get your copy, contact the Public Relations office at 863.3126.

Liberty Rehab and Patient Aid Center
(Home Medical Equipment)
65 Stillwater Avenue, Stamford CT, 203.327.5250
www.libertyrehab.net
This nearby medical equipment shop has items to rent as well as buy. You will appreciate their prices.
Hours: weekdays 8:30 - 5 pm, Saturday 9 am - 1 pm.

Mega Hair Systems (Hair Replacement)
49 Greenwich Avenue, 203.861.4134
Susan Parent is the person to contact when you are facing the prospect of hair loss. She is absolutely wonderful in helping you look completely natural. Her hair extensions and wigs are so natural and well fitted, no one will know.
Hours: By Appointment.

National Medical Claims Service (Insurance Assistance)
3 Thorndal Circle, Darien, CT 06820, 203.655.1800, 800.862.9374
www.MedicalBillAdvocate.com
If you or someone you know is overwhelmed with the task of understanding and obtaining insurance benefits, call this Greenwich family business. They are caring, reliable and greatly helpful.
Hours: weekdays, 9 am - 5 pm.

North Street Pharmacy
1061 North Street, 869.2130
www.NorthStreetPharmacy.com
In a world where change is the norm, it is wonderful to be greeted by Paul Fiscella and his wife who have been running this neighborhood pharmacy for more than 20 years.
Hours: weekdays, 9 am - 6 pm; Saturday, 9 am - 5 pm.

Oetting-Stebbins Physical Therapy (Physical Therapy)
25 Valley Drive, Greenwich, 203.302.3570
Doctor Oetting, a doctor of physical therapy, has done a miraculous job of helping my 97-year old father. He is consistent, kind and encouraging. He and his group work with sports injuries, post-opts and general rehabilitation as well as seniors.

Peak Wellness
195 Field Point Road, Greenwich, 203.625.9608
www.PeakWellness.com
They provide a combination of traditional and alternative approaches to medical care. Their services include dietary guidance, including weight loss, sports medicine, physical therapy. They offer private, VIP medical services.

Performance Physical Therapy and Hand Therapy
35 River Road, Cos Cob, 203.422.0679
www.CtPerformancePT.com
Todd Wilkowski has been the rehabilitation consultant for the New York Rangers. His specialty is working with adolescent sports injuries.

Physical Therapy and Sports Rehabilitation
6 Greenwich Office Park, 203.869.3470
Owned and supervised by ONS (the Orthopaedic & Neurological Surgery Specialists). The therapists in this group are positive, encouraging and friendly.

Physician Referral Service (Health Information)
203.863.3627 or 888.357.2409
Sponsored by Greenwich Hospital, this service is available 24 / 7. They will find the doctor with the qualifications you are looking for and will even make your first appointment.

Planned Parenthood
1039 East Main Street, Stamford CT 203.327.2722,
Emergency 800.820.2488
www.PPCT.org

HEALTH

Relax the Back (Equipment, Furniture)
367 Greenwich Avenue, 203.629.2225, 800.421.2225
www.RelaxTheBack.com
For people seeking relief and prevention of back and neck pain, they offer attractive posture and back support products and self-care solutions.
Hours: Monday - Wednesday 10am - 5:30pm,
Thursday - Saturday, 10am - 6pm.

Dr. Sam Schwartz (Chiropractor)
492 Northridge, Rye Brook NY, 914.939.0558
Dr. Sam has boundless energy and great comprehension of each individual's needs. In addition to his years in Chiropractic, he has a 14-year background as a Registered Respiratory Therapist. He spends every minute of each visit personally with each patient. We will be forever grateful for his rehabilitation of my father, which saved him from surgery.

Silver Hill Hospital (Substance Abuse)
208 Valley Road, New Canaan, CT 866.542.4455, 203.966.3561
www.silverhillhospital.com
A private, not-for-profit, full-service psychiatric and substance abuse hospital, providing inpatient, outpatient, partial hospital programs and transitional care. Their DBT program provides treatment for people with a history of impulsive behaviors, including suicide attempts. Anonymity is important. Many celebrities have quietly restored their health here.

Solomon-Shotland Audiology (Hearing aids)
Julie O'Shea, Au.D, FAAA
Debra Skorney, MS, FAA, Patricia Martucci, MS, FAA
at the Burke Rehabilitation Hospital
785 Mamaroneck Avenue, White Plains, NY, 914.949.0034
www.Hearing-Care.org
If you or someone you know is having some difficulty with their hearing, head straight to this audiologist. They are very competent and caring. They provide comprehensive diagnostic hearing testing for all ages. They work with the latest technologies from a number of the best hearing aid companies, including the Lyric's invisible, non-surgical hearing aid.

HEALTH

Stride Custom Orthotics

80 Turnpike Drive, Middlebury, CT 203.758.8307, 800.787.7879
www.StrideOrthotics.com
Their only business is orthotics. You can make an appointment at the factory (Middlebury is about 1 hr.) or arrange a local fitting with one of their certified representatives.

Tick Testing Laboratory

Greenwich Department of Health
101 Field Point Rd, 203.622.7843
www.GreenwichCT.org
Place the tick dead or alive in a small plastic bag and bring to the lab in Town Hall. They will test it for Lyme disease bacteria.
Laboratory Hours: weekdays 8 am - 3 pm.

Tully Health Center (Physical Therapy)

32 Strawberry Hill Court, Stamford, 355.4567, 353.2000
www.StamHealth.org
A modern 250,000 sq. ft. healing facility for those who have suffered from illness or injury. The Tully Center is part of the Stamford Health System. They offer, among many other programs, a number of sophisticated massage therapies and water therapies.

(The) Vitamin Shoppe (Health)

• 535 Post Road, Port Chester, NY, 914.939.5189
• 1003 High Ridge Road, Stamford, 609.0147
www.VitaminShoppe.com
A national chain with a good website and large selection of products.
Hours: Monday - Saturday 9 am - 9 pm, Sunday, 11 am - 6 pm.

Walgreen's (Pharmacy)

1333 East Putnam Avenue, Old Greenwich, 203.637.1496
www.Walgreens.com
In addition to normal drugstore items, they carry a large variety of general grocery foods, staples and snacks.
Hours: Open 24-hours, every day.

HEALTH

Westchester Medical Center (Hospital)

Valhalla, NY, 914.493.7000

www.WCMC.com

Connected with the New York Medical College, their Trauma Center and Children's Hospital are renowned.

Whole Body at Whole Foods

90 East Putnam Avenue, 203.661.0631

www.WholeFoodsMarket.com/Stores/Greenwich

Products to promote health and wellness, such as: vitamins, herbal teas, cosmetics, hair care and homeopathic remedies.

Hours: Open daily 8 am - 10 pm.

Yale-New Haven Hospital

20 York Street, New Haven, CT, 203.688.2000, 4242

www.YNHH.org

This private, not-for-profit hospital, is the teaching hospital for Yale University School of Medicine. It is considered one of the premier hospitals in the area. Greenwich Hospital is affiliated with this hospital.

YWCA Domestic Abuse Service

YWCA, 259 East Putnam Avenue, 203.869.6501 ext 175

National YWCA Abuse Hotline: 800.799.7233

www.ywca.org

Free, professional and confidential crisis intervention for anyone experiencing violence in their life. They provide counseling & emergency shelter. When you call or see them, you can count on it being private.

Hours: Monday - Thursday 9 am -5 pm,

Friday 9 am - 4 pm & by appointment.

TIP: LYME DISEASE

Ticks, unfortunately, also live in Greenwich—even some carrying Lyme Disease. If you remove a tick you might want to take it "Dead or Alive" to the Department of Health in Town Hall. They will test it for the Lyme Disease bacteria. For information on Lyme disease, call the Greenwich Lyme Disease Task Force at 203.969.1333 www.timeforlyme.org or www.cdc.gov/ncidod/diseases/submenus/sub_lyme.htm

HOTELS & INNS

greenwich area

For other Travel Information see TRAVEL
For Connecticut Vacation Information see NUMBERS YOU SHOULD KNOW

Cos Cob Inn
50 River Road, Cos Cob, 203.661.5845
www.CosCobInn.com
Charmingly redecorated, 1870 Federal bed-and-breakfast. Many of the fourteen rooms have scenic views of the Mianus River; each has its own bath. There are data ports in every room. Continental breakfast, no restaurant.
Rates: $119 - $219 per night, Suites $159 - $219 per night.

Delamar Greenwich Harbor
500 Steamboat Road, 203.661.9800, 866.335.2627
www.TheDelamar.com
Greenwich's newest hotel. An 83-room Mediterranean-style luxury hotel with wonderful harbor views, just minutes from the Greenwich train station and Greenwich Avenue. Yachts can safely dock at their 600-foot private dock. This is a pet-friendly hotel.
High-speed internet is available.
Rates: $399 to $1,700.

Doral Arrowwood
975 Anderson Hill Road, Rye Brook, NY, 914.939.5500
www.DoralArrowwood.com
Just on the border of Greenwich is a 373-room resort hotel, with golf, tennis, squash and swimming. A great place for a conference.
Rates: $149 -$229. Weekend packages with golf are $299 per night.

Harbor House Inn
165 Shore Road, Old Greenwich, 203.637.0145
www.HHInn.com
This 100-year-old Victorian mansion has always served as an inn. Guests are corporate clients, people relocating and out-of-town visitors. The twenty-three room bed-and-breakfast is within walking distance of the beach. There isn't a restaurant but continental breakfast is included. The atmosphere is very informal. If you need the latest amenities, this may not be your place.
Rates: $99 - $179

HOTELS & INNS

Holiday Inn Select

700 East Main Street, Stamford CT, 203.358.8400, 800.465.4329
www.HiStamford.com
Recently renovated for $20,000,000. This 380-room hotel is a top level
Holiday Inn with a health club, indoor lap pool and lots of meeting
rooms.
Rates: $189-$264, suites $400.

Homestead Inn

420 Field Point Road, 203.869.7500
www.HomesteadInn.com
Exceptionally attractive country inn, with 22 lovely rooms/suites and
superb food. See the restaurant review under Thomas Henkelmann in
RESTAURANTS. Some rooms have wireless internet connections. A great
choice.
Rates: $250 - $495

Hyatt Regency

1800 East Putnam Avenue, Old Greenwich, 637.1234
www.Greenwich.Hyatt.com
This 374-room luxury hotel has an elegant interior with excellent food.
Greenwich residents often check into this hotel for a weekend of pamper-
ing. The hotel also has a very nice health club.
High speed internet access.
Rates: $149 - $1,000

Rye Town Hilton

699 Westchester Avenue, Rye Brook, NY, 914.939.6300
www.Hilton.com
Situated on 45 acres just next to Greenwich this large hotel with a pleasant restaurant hosts many conventions. Pets allowed.
Rates: $149 - $650

HOTELS & INNS

greenwich area

Stanton House Inn
76 North Maple Avenue, 869.2110
www.ShinnGreenwich.com
Located in Central Greenwich, within walking distance of the shops and restaurants, this turn-of-the-century home, converted into a 24-room bed-and-breakfast, is a welcoming first stop for many new residents. Internet access in some rooms. No restaurant.
Rates: $159 - $239

Stamford Suites
720 Bedford Street, Stamford, 359.7300, 866.394.4365
www.StamfordSuites.com
An extended-stay hotel with 45 furnished suites for nightly or longer term residence. Each unit contains a bedroom, living room, bathroom and a full-size kitchen. Dial-up internet access. Renovated in 1998.
Rates: Daily $169 - $229, Seven-day rate: $139, 30-day rate: $119

TIP: GREENWICH GRAND TOUR
Cheryl Dunson, The League of Women Voters' Land Use Specialist, conducts a very special bus tour of Greenwich every year, usually in early May. Whether you are new to Greenwich or have lived here a while, you are sure to learn something new and to have a good time. Call Greenwich Continuing Education at 203-625-7477 for details.

HOTELS & INNS
worth a trip

Bedford Post (American)
954 Old Post Road, Bedford, NY, 914.234.7800
www.BedfordPostInn.com
Richard Gere's Post has two terrific restaurants and 8 lovely guest rooms.
A great place for a quiet, romantic weekend. See their review in
RESTAURANTS.
Rates: $395 to $550

Roger Sherman Inn
195 Oenoke Ridge, New Canaan CT, 203.966.4541
www.RogerShermanInn.com
Built in the 1700s, this 17-room inn is one of the oldest and prettiest in
Fairfield County. With its gracious service, the Inn is just right for elegant parties or romantic evenings. See their review in RESTAURANTS.
Rates: Singles $135-$200, Doubles $175-$240, Suite $350

Woodstock Inn
14 The Green, Woodstock Vermont, 800.448.7900, 802.457.1100
www.woodstockinn.com
www.suicide6.com
www.woodstockvt.com
The Woodstock Inn is a lovely, historic Inn in a beautiful, charming town.
The Inn, owned by the Rockefellers, has 142 guest rooms, a golf course,
Suicide Six Ski Area, and a health spa. It has indoor and outdoor pools
and tennis courts. You can't go wrong here whether you come in the
winter or summer.
Rates: Doubles $149-$434, Suites $360-$664 suite. Off-season rates lower.
Packages available. 2-night minimum.

TIP: STAMFORD PARADE
A spectacular parade is put on every November in Stamford; huge balloons and fun for everyone. For information call 203.348.5285 or visit
www.Stamford-downtown.com

HOTELS & INNS

connecticut river valley

The Connecticut River Valley (Middlesex County), has outstanding inns in interesting, quaint New England towns, particularly: Chester, Clinton, Deep River, Essex, Old Lyme and Hadden. They are loaded with antique shops, art galleries and interesting activities such as the Essex Steam Train (described under Family Outings), the beach in Old Lyme and the Camelot dinner, Long Island or Murder Mystery dinner cruises, Rte.9, exit 7 in Hadden, 860.345.8591 or the Goodspeed Opera House in East Hadden, 860-873-8668, www.Goodspeed.org. Excellent restaurants also abound in the area. The Restaurant Du Village is located in Chester at 59 Main Street, 860.526.5301. This restaurant is one of the fine French restaurants in the state. You should also try what many consider the best pizza in Connecticut, served at Alforno, 654 Boston Post Road, Brian Alden Shopping Plaza, Old Saybrook, open daily from 4:30 pm to 10 pm, 860.399.4166. Another great place for lunch or Sunday brunch is the Water's Edge at 1525 Post Road (I-95 exit 65) in Westbrook, 860.399.5901. Ask for a table on the water. You will also want to try these two Old Lyme Inns for a meal: the Old Lyme Inn, 85 Lyme Street, Old Lyme, 800.434.5352, and the Bee and Thistle Inn, 100 Lyme Street, (Rte.1, I-95 exit 70), Old Lyme, 860.434.1667. Both inns, particularly the Bee and Thistle, have received many awards for excellent dining. *In the area, there is a large shopping mall (Clinton Crossing - see Outlets in SHOPPING at I-95 exit 63 and another large mall in Westbrook at exit 65.*
The state's two casinos, Foxwoods (I-95 exit 92) and Mohegan Sun (I-95 exit 76) are within easy driving distance, see GAMBLING.
See also Essex Steam Trains and Riverboat under CHILDREN, FAMILY OUTINGS.

Bee and Thistle Inn (New London County)
100 Lyme Street, Old Lyme, CT, 800.622.4946
www.BeeAndThistleInn.com
About an hour from Greenwich (close to the Clinton Crossing clothing outlets and the Connecticut casinos) is one of the great old inns in Connecticut. Often written up as the most romantic. As an added plus, it has good, artfully simple American food. At a recent party, one of our guests arrived very late. The staff cheerfully allowed us to enjoy the evening with no hint of the inconvenience of the late hour.
Rates: $140 - $260.
Directions: I-95N to exit 70 CT-156, L on Ferry, L on Lyme.

connecticut river valley

Copper Beach Inn (Middlesex County)

46 Main Street, Ivoryton, CT
www.CopperBeechInn.com
860.767.0330, 888.809.2056
Gracious inn with 13 guest rooms and excellent food in a charming New England town, about an hour from Greenwich. High on our list, this inn fits the perfect image of what a New England inn should be. The inn is best suited for adults unless the children have very nice manners.
Rates: $150- $375 per night. January through March, the dining room is closed Tuesday as well as Monday evenings.
Directions: I-95 N to Exit 69, Rte 9 N to exit 3, L (west) 1.75 miles.

Mayflower Inn & Spa (Litchfield County)

118 Woodbury Road, Route 47, Washington, CT 860.868.9466
www.MayFlowerInn.com
Set on 58 acres of lovely grounds, this 30-room Inn is a perfect place to rest and refresh. Enjoy fine dining, walks in the garden, and antiquing in nearby shops and, of course, the spa. The Inn is about an hour from Greenwich.
Rates: $400 to $1,300.

(The) Water's Edge (Middlesex County)

1525 Boston Post Road, Westbrook, CT, 860.399.5901
www.WatersEdgeResortAndSpa.com
Not a charming old inn, but a highly rated 169 room resort hotel with excellent food. It is often used for upscale meetings.
Rates: $140 - $240.

TIP: TOUR THE CONNECTICUT STATE CAPITOL

The Connecticut League of Women Voters conducts tours of our State Capitol. When the House and Senate are in session it is especially interesting to watch their proceedings. To find out details call 860.240.0222 or visit www.cga.ct.gov/capitoltours

atHome Magazine

203.222.0600

www.atHomefc.com

www.mofflymedia.com/Moffly-Publications/atHome

Published semi-annually in April and October. This magazine is filled with inspiration, information and decorating trends in Fairfield County.

Connecticut Cottages & Gardens

203.227.1400

www.CTCandG.com

A free, very high quality magazine with pretty photos and good articles. Even if you just use it for a coffee table book, you will enjoy it.

Connecticut Magazine

203.380.6600, 800.974.2001

www.ConnecticutMag.com

This comprehensive, attractive magazine always has well-researched articles on the best of Connecticut. Subscribe! You will love this magazine. They do a great job of rating everything from golf courses to towns to the top doctors.

Fairfield County Weddings Magazine

203.222.0600

www.MofflyMedia.com

Published semi-annually in June and December. Plan your wedding with this magazine. Available at local newsstands.

Greenwich Magazine

203.222.0600, 869.0009

www.GreenwichMag.com

Sophisticated articles on topics of interest for everyone. A valuable source of information about Greenwich and Greenwich residents. A subscription to *Greenwich Magazine* is essential. The Mofflys also publish the leading magazines for Westport, Stamford and New Caanan/Darien.

NEWS MEDIA

magazines

Serendipity
203.588.1363
www.SerendipityGreenwich.com
Launched in January of 2010, it covers the Greenwich lifestyle. It is geared toward family living: residents starting their families, juggling jobs, kids and home.

Westchester Magazine
914.345.0601, 800.254.2213
www.WestchesterMagazine.com
This magazine focuses on Westchester and Fairfield counties. It often has articles on Greenwich. It is an excellent resource for discovering events and resources you will want to take advantage of in our neighboring towns.

local news online

www.thedailygreenwich.com
Many residents rely on this online site for their news about Greenwich. The website is easy to navigate. The articles, written by local respected reporters cover Greenwich news, events, styles and opinions. Bookmark this one. It's a fun way to keep in touch with what's going on in our town.

www.fairfieldcountylook.com
If you want a glimpse of beautiful and fashionable events happening in and around Greenwich, you will enjoy this site. Elaine and ChiChi Urina, photographers are taking pictures of beautiful weddings, parties and benefits and posting them on this site.

TIP: OLD GREENWICH MEMORIAL DAY PARADE
This annual event began in 1923. It draws thousands of people to the parade down Sound Beach Avenue and to the ceremony afterwards in Binney Park. Attending this wonderful town event, organized by the Sound Beach Volunteer Fire Department, will make you glad to be part of the community.

NEWS MEDIA

newspapers

See SERVICES for newspaper delivery information.

Fairfield County Business Journal
914.694.3600
www.fairfieldcountybusinessjournal.com
www.westfaironline.com/fairfield-county-business-journal.html
This weekly newspaper tracks trends and developments that impact local businesses. If you are thinking of opening a business or simply want to know the commercial news, this paper is just the ticket.

Greenwich Citizen
1455 East Putnam Avenue, Suite 102, Old Greenwich
203.625.4460
www.greenwichcitizen.com
This free weekly newspaper is focused on local news. It is a must read for anyone living in Greenwich. If you miss any of the Town events, this paper with its articles and many pictures will keep you in the know. Every month you will enjoy reading their supplement - Inside Fairfield County.

Greenwich Post
124 West Putnam Avenue, 861.9191
www.acorn-online.com/joomla15/greenwich-post/news.html
The *Greenwich Post* is a lively weekly newspaper covering the Town. Each week they publish a comprehensive Real Estate section, with real estate news you won't want to miss. Each paper is filled with excellent articles, updates, editorials and summaries of what is happening in Greenwich. They have extensive calendars of local and regional activities, and many special publications, including Home Magazine and 100 Things to Do. This is a free newspaper, so be sure to give them a call if you are not on their list. Check their website for "Things to Do."

NEWS MEDIA

newspapers

Greenwich Time

1455 East Elm Street, Old Greenwich, 203.625.4400
www.GreenwichTime.com
Greenwich is lucky to have a daily newspaper. If we were judging a national competition for the best daily local newspaper, *Greenwich Time* would win the top award. The Letters from Readers section is a good barometer of town concerns. To understand what is happening in Greenwich, you must read this paper.

Voices (formerly Teen Speak)

www.VoicesofTomorrow.org
This internet newspaper by and for tomorrow's leaders was founded by Greenwich resident Debra Mamorsky. It is a weekly international publication written solely by 17 to 25-year-olds for their peers around the world. The publication tackles important domestic, international and youth-related issues.

TIP: THE BEST HAMBURGERS IN TOWN

Anderson Associates held a tasting of 18 local restaurants serving hamburgers. 226 clients of the firm took part in the tasting. The winners were:
* Burgers, Shakes, and Fries, 302 Delavan Ave, Byram 203.531.7433
* Sundown Saloon, 403 Greenwich Avenue, 203.629.8212
* Thataway Café, 409 Greenwich Avenue, 203.622.0947
* Katzenberg Kafé, 342 Greenwich Avenue, 203.625.0103
See www.GreenwichGuide.com for details and articles on the tasting.

NEWS MEDIA

radio & television

Bloomberg News AM 1130
xm Channel 129 / Sirius Chanel 130 www.Bloomberg.com
Good national and international news. Best for financial news.

Cablevision Channel Lineup
www.Optimum.com/lineup.jsp?regionId=30

Connecticut Television
www.cpbi.org
Connecticut Public Television has Connecticut-based documentaries as well as sports coverage of Connecticut teams.

Channel 79 is our local community access station. It broadcasts "Greenwich Weekly Video Magazine" Wednesdays at 10:30 pm and Fridays at 9:30 am. RTM meetings are shown live. The meeting calendar is shown between broadcasts or go to www.greenwichct.org/channel79

Channel 78 is the Greenwich Educational Access Channel.

Channel 79 - Connecticut Government Access.

Cable Channel 12 - Connecticut News www.news12.com/CT

Continuous news, weather and traffic reports.
CBS AM 880, www.NewsRadio88.com
WINS AM 1010, www.1010wins.com

Greenwich Radio
71 Lewis Street, Greenwich, 203.869.1490
AM 1490   www.WGCH.com
Tune in between 6 am and 10 am for an update on Greenwich happenings, including school closings. Their interviews with Greenwich people making the news are essential to understanding town issues. "Ask the First Selectman" airs Fridays at 9 am. A fun Greenwich program, "A Fashionable Life" with Jayne Chase and Jennifer Goodkind, airs Wednesdays at 9:30. Darby Cartun's Darby and Friends airs weekdays at 5 PM.

Public Radio
Great in depth coverage of national and international events without (much) commercial interruption.

Connecticut Public Radio FM 88.5, www.cpbi.org/radio

National Public Radio AM 820 & FM 93.9, www.npr.org

NUMBERS & WEBSITES YOU SHOULD KNOW

See GOVERNMENT for Local, State and Federal Numbers.
For a complete list of useful Greenwich numbers, see:
www.GreenwichLiving.com/contacts_relocation.htm

Anderson Associates
Greenwich Real Estate Specialists
203.629.4519
www.greenwichliving.com
If you don't know where to turn, call us.

Ambulance - Greenwich Police
911 Emergency, 203.622.8000 (non-emergency), 203.637.7505 (office)
See GEMS below.

Aquarion
(formerly The ConnecticutAmerican Water Company)
203.869.5200 (office)
203.445.7310, 800.732.9678 (emergency)
800.732.9678 (customer service)
www.aquarion.com

AT&T/SNET/SBC (Old Greenwich exchanges 637 & 698)
From AT&T coverage area, dial 811 for repairs; from out-of-state,
800.331.0500, 800.453.7638; Customer Service, 800.274.3131,
203.420.3131 or 611 from cell phone.
www.snet.com, www.sbc.com, www.att.com

Cablevision of Connecticut
203.348.9211, 203.846.4700, 203.750.5600
www.cablevision.com www.optimum.com

NUMBERS & WEBSITES YOU SHOULD KNOW

Community Answers

101 West Putnam Avenue, 203.622.7979
www.greenwichlibrary.org/commanswers.htm
Funded by the United Way and private donations, this volunteer group is located in the Greenwich Library. Ask them anything about Greenwich (all calls are confidential). Their website is a storehouse of valuable information.

Community Calendar

Community Answers provides a Community Calendar of all Greenwich events. It comes out every three months. Be sure to call and ask for it.

Useful Article Reprints

Stop by Community Answers and pick up articles which might be helpful, such as: Childcare and Parenting Services, Summer Camp and Programs in Greenwich.
Hours: weekdays, 9 am - 3 pm.

Connecticut Natural Gas

203.869.6900 (customer service)
203. 869.6913 (repair & emergency)
www.cng.com

Connecticut Vacation Planning

888.288.4748, 800.282.6863
Coastal Fairfield County Tourist Information
at 800.866.7925 or 203.853.7770
www.CTVisit.com, www.visitfairfieldcountyct.com

Domestic Abuse

211 Infoline
YWCA Domestic Abuse Service, 203.869.6501 ext 175

Federal Express

800.238.5355, 800.GO.FEDEX
www.fedex.com

FedEx/Kinkos

48 West Putnam Avenue, 203.863.0099

GEMS (Greenwich Emergency Medical Service)

911 for emergency ambulance
203.637.7505 (office)

NUMBERS & WEBSITES YOU SHOULD KNOW

Greenwich Fire Department
911 Emergency
203.622.3950 (non-emergency)
   Amogerone Fire Company(Havemeyer Place),
      203.249.2421 or 203.622.3959 www.amogerone.com
   Byram Fire Company, 203.532.9752 or 203.622.3973
   Cos Cob Fire Company, 203.622.3972 or 203.622.1506
   Glenville Fire Company, 203.532.9606 or 622.3974, www.911fire.org
   Old Greenwich Fire Company,
      203.637.1806 or 203.622.3975, www.sbvfd.com
   Round Hill Vol. Fire Company, 203.869.7185
   Banksville Independent Fire Company, 914.234.7104
   Back Country Fire Company, 203.661.2452

Greenwich Hospital
203.863.3000
www.GreenwichHosp.org
See complete description in HEALTH.

Greenwich Police
911 Emergency, 203.622.8000 (complaints and information)
www.GreenwichCT.org/PoliceDept/PoliceDept.asp

Greenwich Public Schools
203.625.7400
www.GreenwichSchools.org, www.Greenwich.K12.ct.us
See complete description and other numbers in SCHOOLS.

Modern Gas (propane)
18 Old Track Road, Greenwich, 203.869.4226
www.ModernGasCT.com

Northeast Utilities/Connecticut Light & Power
800.286.2000, 800.286.5000
www.NU.com
Residents whose power has been turned off by CL&P should call the Town of Greenwich Building Inspection Division at 203.622.7755.

Post Offices
For Post Office numbers & hours and Zip Codes see POST OFFICES.

NUMBERS & WEBSITES YOU SHOULD KNOW

Poison Control Center
800.222.1222
http://PoisonControl.uchc.edu

Telemarketing (NO CALL List)
CT Department of Consumer Protection
800.842.2649
www.DoNotCall.gov/default.aspx
www.CT.gov/dcp/cwp/view.asp?a=1629&q=285064
Call the following number from your cell phone to avoid telemarketer calls to your cell, 888.382.1222.

UPS Store
• Greenwich: 15 East Putnam Avenue, 203.622.1114
• Stamford: 65 High Ridge Road, Stamford, 203.356.0022
www.UPS.com/Tracking/Tracking.html

USE (Senior Center Job Placement Service)
203.629.8031
Utilize Senior Energy, run by volunteers, is a good resource for everything from office help to painters to babysitters.
Hours: weekdays, 9:30 am - 12:30 pm

Verizon Land Line Help
203.869.5222, 800.837.4966 (new phone service)
203.661.5444 (repairs), 611 from Cell phone.
203.625.9800 (customer service)
www22.verizon.com, www.Verizon.com

Verizon Internet and TV (FIOS)
888.881.8161, 888.625.8111
www.VerizonFios.com
Verizon is offering, FIOS, a fiberoptic service competing with Cablevision.

24-Hour Pharmacies
See HEALTH for details.
• Walgreen's, 1333 East Putnam Avenue, Old Greenwich
   203.637.1496
• CVS, 1239 East Putnam Ave, Riverside, 203.698.4006

The Town's Website
www.GreenwichCT.org

Old Greenwich Association website
www.OldGreenwich.org

Community Answers
www.CommunityAnswers.org
A good source for information on Greenwich.
Be sure to sign up for their quarterly Community Calendar.
Call 203.622.7979 or email:
    CommunityAnswers@greenwichlibrary.org

Greenwich Guide
www.GreenwichGuide.com
Keep up with the changes and latest information.

Greenwich Real Estate
www.GreenwichLiving.com
Check out real estate in Greenwich.

Volunteer opportunities in Greenwich
www.GreenwichVolunteerGuide.com

Newcomers
www.GreenwichNewcomers.com
Join if you are new in town.

Greenwich Chamber of Commerce
www.GreenwichChamber.com

Better Business Bureau of CT
http://CT.BBB.org/

PARKS & BEACHES

Greenwich extends over 47 square miles with rolling hills, woodlands, meadows and 32 miles of gorgeous shoreline bordering the Long Island Sound. Greenwich's main beaches are at Greenwich Point (147 acres), Byram Beach and the 2 town-owned islands (Captain's Island & Island Beach). Greenwich has 8,000 acres of protected land, over 1,000 acres of town parks, 35 town tennis courts (not including the YWCA Courts), an indoor ice rink (open only to residents), 4 public marinas and a 158-acre, 18-hole golf course (open only to residents).

The Parks and Recreation office is on the second floor of Town Hall. Hours are weekdays, 8 am to 4 pm. Outside their door are good handouts on upcoming opportunities. For information call 203.622.7814 or visit www.GreenwichCT.org/ParksAndRec/ParksandRec.asp. The website has a complete list of Greenwich Parks.

For Playgrounds see CHILDREN

TIP: SAND SCULPTURE
www.GreenwichArts.org
Every year in July at Tod's Point Beach, The Greenwich Arts Council and the Town of Greenwich Department of Parks and Recreation sponsor a Sand Blast! There is no specific theme for sand sculptures beyond the enjoyment of creating art in the sand.

PARKS & BEACHES
beaches

Greenwich beaches are open to residents and non-residents. You must have a beach pass before entering the beach. Passes are strictly enforced. Apply early and be sure to have it when you enter. Passes are required from May 26th to September 17th. Dogs are allowed on a leash from December 1st to March 31st. No charge is required from the middle of November to the middle of April.

Beach Cards and Passes

The Beach Card Office (203.622.7817) is located on First Floor of Town Hall. It is open weekdays, 8 am to 3:45 pm from March to December. Proof of residency is required for a Beach Card. The Town will accept: moving documents, lease papers, a drivers license, phone or electric bills. Beach cards cost $27 for adults, $5 for children ages 5 to 13, and are free for seniors and toddlers. Daily admission passes for non-residents cost $10 per person and $20 per vehicle per day. Passes can be purchased at Eastern Civic Center or Town Hall. The Town also requires residents to obtain a seasonal parking sticker for each car or pay $20 for daily parking. Parking stickers can be obtained free with a copy of a current vehicle registration indicating that the car is on the Greenwich tax rolls. If the car is not on the tax rolls, the sticker costs Greenwich Residents $100 per season.

Byram Beach

203.531.4040, 203.531.8938
This beach on Byram Shore Road has a swimming pool, 3 tennis courts, a picnic area and playground.

Cruise to Nowhere

Department of Parks and Recreation, 203.622.7814
The cruise is popular and had 11 of its 12 cruises sold out for the last two years in a row. For $7 a person you can cruise around the Islands of Greenwich.

Ferry Information

Ticket office, 203.661.5957; Ferry schedule, 203.618.7672, 203.622.7814
The ferry service from the Arch Street dock to Great Captain's Island or Island Beach varies according to the tides and time of the year. Service begins in the middle of June and lasts until the middle of September. For fees & schedule go to:
www.GreenwichCT.org/ParksAndRec/prFerryService.asp

PARKS & BEACHES

beaches

Captain's Island

It is rustic with no concession stand, so bring a picnic lunch. Camp sites available with permits. For camping reservations, call 203.622.7824. Take a ferry from the Arch Street dock to this 17-acre island with beach and picnic area. Several morning and afternoon ferries are available depending upon the day and date.

Greenwich Point (Tod's Point)

Entrance at the south end of Shore Road in Old Greenwich. This 147-acre beach, with concession stand, has jogging, hiking and biking trails, lots of picnic facilities and wind surfing. Dogs on a leash are normally allowed in the winter.

Island Beach (Little Captain's Island)

203.661.5957

Take a ferry from the Arch Street dock to this 4-acre island with beaches, picnic area and concession stand.

Hours: weekdays, every hour, 10 am - 7 pm through mid-August; 10 am - 6 pm through mid-September, weekends every half-hour.

Calf Island

A 28-acre island off Byram Shore, purchased from the YMCA for $6 million by the Stewart B. McKinney National Wildlife Refuge. It has beaches, trails, woods and wetlands. A fun place to explore, but you will need a boat to get there.

TIP: PLAN OF CONSERVATION AND DEVELOPMENT

The Greenwich Plan of Conservation and Development (POCD) took several years to develop and will be the Town's governing document for the next ten years.
www.greenwichct.org/PlanningZoning/
PlanningZoning.asp.
It is well worth reading. While doing so you might also want to look at the South West Regional Planning Agency's (SWRPA) plan for lower Fairfield County transportation. www.swrpa.org

civic centers

The Civic centers are the sites for many sporting events and public events such as antique shows. Call for their latest catalog of events.

Eastern Greenwich Civic Center

(aka: Greenwich Civic Center or Old Greenwich-Riverside Civic Center)
90 Harding Road, Old Greenwich, 203.637.4583
www.GreenwichCT.org/ParksAndRec/prFacilityPrograms.asp
The center is on 14 acres and operates weekdays from 8 am - 10 pm, weekends as scheduled. The center has a basketball court, 2-tennis courts with lights, a baseball diamond and playground. The center is used extensively for a wide variety of activities such as roller skating, men's basketball, soccer, tennis for tots, Old Greenwich Art society painters and Halloween Happenings.

Western Greenwich Civic Center

(Aka Bendheim Western Civic Center)
449 Pemberwick Road, Glenville, 203.532.1259
www.GreenwichCT.org/ParksAndRec/prFacilityPrograms.asp
The newly renovated center on 9.97 acres, is the pride of the Town. In 1997 the Glenville Community led by the 9th district of the RTM and other concerned citizens started a fund raising campaign to refurbish the Civic Center. After the group raised approximately 3.5 million dollars, the Town of Greenwich matched the gift and work began in June of 2005. The new building features a state of the art Daycare Center, a new gym/auditorium, a dance, exercise studio, weight room and meeting rooms. Call for a program guide.

TIP: ANSWER BOOK

The Greenwich Post publishes an excellent guide called The Answer Book. The guide is available online at www.acorn-online.com/joomla15/greenwich-post/community/answerbook.html

PARKS & BEACHES
parks & nature preserves

Greenwich, in addition to its beaches and 32 miles of coastline, has 8,000 acres of protected land, with over 1,000 acres of Town parks. The parks and nature preserves listed below are some of the more popular of the twenty parks in Greenwich. For a complete list of Greenwich parks, see http://www.GreenwichCT.org/ParksAndRec/prFacilitiesIndex.asp

Audubon Center
613 Riversville Road, 203.869.5272
http://Greenwich.Audubon.org
285 acres with well-kept trails, a great place to walk.

Babcock Preserve
North Street, 203.622.7814, 203.622.7700
297 acres located two miles north of the Merritt Parkway. Well-marked running, hiking, and cross country ski trails.

Binney Park
Sound Beach Avenue, Old Greenwich, 203.622.7824
The park is 22 landscaped acres with a beautiful pond, 4 tennis courts, a playground, baseball diamond and pond skating. A favorite place for wedding photos. The park is the site of a variety of community activities including band concerts, July 3rd fireworks and the model sailboat regatta.

Bruce Park
Bruce Park Drive and Indian Field Road, 203.622.7824
Athletic fields, bowling green, fitness trail, picnic area, tennis courts and a new exciting, playground.

Mianus River Park
Cognewaugh Road, 203.622.7824
215 acres owned by Greenwich and Stamford. Trout fishing, wooded hills and steep cliffs with miles of hiking trails. Take Valley Road to Cognewaugh; the entrance is on Cognewaugh Road about three miles on the right. (There is no sign.)

Montgomery Pinetum

Bible Street, Cos Cob

Armed with a map and tree guide from the Garden Center, you will have fun exploring this beautiful 91-acre wilderness. To reach Montgomery Park and Pinetum, go north on Orchard Street from the Post Road in Cos Cob. Bear right onto Bible Street and continue .7 mile. The entrance is on the west side directly opposite Clover Place.

Sabine Farm Field

A field along Round Hill Road was purchased in 2001 for $2.9 million by the Greenwich Land Trust. However, all of the money came from private donations, raised primarily through the efforts of a local resident, Edward Bragg.

Pomerance-Tuchman Preserve

This 118-acre tract adjacent to the Montgomery Pinetum lies between Orchard and Bible Streets in Cos Cob. The Town has undertaken to purchase the property for $35 million. Along with the Pinetum and Bible Street playing fields, this tract gives the Town a corridor of 227 acres of pristine woodlands.

Treetops

In 2002 the Town of Greenwich and 3 land trusts raised $11.5 million dollars to purchase 110 acres bordering the Mianus River. This tract forms the southern boundary of the 220 acre Mianus River Park. Inspired by David Ogilvy, residents (from Town officials to school children) united to make this possible.

TIP: SHAKESPEARE ON THE SOUND

www.ShakespeareOnTheSound.org

Don't miss this event held at Roger Sherman Baldwin Park in June and July. Shakespeare on the Sound produces an annual free outdoor Shakespeare festival in Connecticut, with performances in public parks in Rowayton and Greenwich. Although the performances are free, for a fee you can reserve seats in the first rows. They also offer free lectures for adults or children before the performances. See their web site for details.

public marinas

Four marinas are available to town residents, from April 15th through November 15th each year. Launching ramps are available at all Marinas. Winter storage is available at all marinas from September 1st - June 1st. A mooring requires 2 permits, a use facilities permit issued by the Department of Parks and Recreation (2nd Floor Town Hall) 203.618-7651 and a mooring permit issued by the Harbormaster, Jonathan Asch.

Harbormaster, Jonathan Asch

203.861.3118, Harbormasterasch@aol.com
Harbor masters are charged with the general care and supervision of the harbors and navigable waterways over which they have jurisdiction, subject to the transportation commissioner's direction and control. They are responsible for the safe and efficient operation of such harbors and navigable waterways.

Town Boating Information

www.GreenwichCT.org/ParksAndRec/prBoating.asp

Town's mooring and anchoring rules at

http://greenwichct.virtualtownhall.net/public_documents/FOV1-0000E248/
committees/coastal/docs/index

TIP: HAVING A TAG SALE

No Town permit is required. The best days for sales are Saturday and Sunday 9 am - 4 pm. The best seasons are Fall and Spring. Avoid sales on or near a holiday. Advertise one week before and the weekend of the sale in The Greenwich Time (203.629.2204) in the Friday Tag Sale section. If you are planning a large sale, off-duty Greenwich Police can help you manage crowds. Call the traffic division (203.622.8016). Professional Tag Sale managers typically charge from 20% to 30% commission, depending on the services rendered. *For more information on tag sale companies see SERVICES.*

(The) Byram Marina in Byram Park

It has 300 slips for vessels up to 23' overall in length with beam widths up to 9'. The marina has outwater mooring space for approximately 100 vessels up to 36' overall length and drafts up to 7'. There is some rack storage for kayaks and canoes. The Byram Dockmaster's office is 203.532.9019.

Located in Byram Park just south of exit 2 of I-95 on Ritch Avenue

(The) Cos Cob Marina

River Road, Cos Cob

The Cos Cob Marina has approximately 300 slips for vessels up to 23' overall length with beam widths up to 9'. There is also limited rack storage for kayaks and canoes.

The Dockmaster's office can be reached at (203) 618-9698.

Located on River Road just south of the I-95 overpass.

(The) Grass Island Marina

Shore Road

Grass Island has 150 slips for boats up to 23' in length with beam widths of up to 9' (a few can accommodate boats up to 36' in length). There is out-water mooring space for approximately 75 vessels up to 36' overall length and drafts up to 5'. Grass Island has some rack storage for kayaks and canoes. Grass Island has tie-up space for visitors. There is no charge during the day and an overnight charge based upon vessel size. The Grass Island Dockmaster, 203.618.9695, is located off Shore Road in central Greenwich just south of I-95.

The Greenwich Point Marina

Greenwich Point Park. There are out-water moorings for about 250 boats up to 36 feet long and up to 7' drafts. There is rack storage for about 250 canoes, kayaks, and other small boats. Greenwich Point Dockmaster's office, 203.698.7792, is located at Greenwich Point Park in Old Greenwich.

PARKS & BEACHES
specialized parks

Dog Park
The Greenwich Dog Park is located on 3/4 acre at Grass Island.
The park is open from sunrise to sunset. For your dog to have a good experience go during a quiet time on your first visit. We recommend a weekday from 9 am to 11 am. The rules are posted on the fence. Children under 10 are not permitted and the owners must remain in the fenced area with their dog while the dog is off leash. Aggressive dogs are not allowed and owners are responsible for the behavior of their dog.

Dorthy Hamill Skating Rink
Skating Rink Road off Sherman Avenue in Byram, 203.531.8560
www.GreenwichCT.org/ParksAndRec/prFacilityPrograms.asp
Set on 18 acres, this large skating facility has been a joy to Greenwich skaters for over 34 years. All kinds of programs are available, such as: hockey clinics, Town-wide figure skating competition and general skating. Normal hours of operation are 6 am to 12 am, from September to Mid-March. Sessions are open to Greenwich residents. Guests are admitted when accompanied by a Greenwich resident and proof of residency is required. During the off season the rink is covered with indoor turf for lacrosse and soccer.

Griffith E Harris Golf Course
1300 King Street, General Information: 203.531.7200
Reservations: 203.531.8253, Pro Shop: 203.531.7261
www.GreenwichCT.org/ParksAndRec/prGolfCourse.asp
This 18-hole, Robert Trent Jones-designed course, is the town's only municipal golf course and the only non-private golf course in the Town. Use of the course is open to all Town of Greenwich residents who become members. Members are permitted to bring guests with them to play at the course. All guests are required to be accompanied by a member to play.

Skate Park

Roger Sherman Baldwin Park, Arch Street, 203.618.7649, 203.496.9876
www.greenwichct.org/ParksAndRec/prSkatePark.asp
http://greenwichct.virtualtownhall.net/Public_Documents/
GreenwichCT_ParkRec/GreenwichCT_Recreation/skatepark/programs
The Greenwich Skate Park is a supervised facility for youths 6 years of
age and over to skateboard and inline skate. The area is supervised
whenever the park is open. Full protective gear is required. Children 6 to
9 years of age must be accompanied by an adult (18 years or older)
during the time they are in the park. The facility provides a friendly and
supportive environment for beginners to experts. Private and semi-private lessons are offered during regular skate park hours. They offer
beginning techniques as well as tricks. The park is open 3:30 pm to 6
pm on weekdays from April 2th to October 28th. Weekends and holidays
noon to 4 pm. Off-peak hours are between October 29th and March 31st,
check the schedule. It is closed December to February.

Tennis and Paddle Courts

For information, call Frank Gabriele at 203.622.7821
www.GreenwichCT.org/ParksAndRec/prTennis.asp
Tennis courts are located all over Town. There are also two Paddle Courts.
Tennis passes are required from May through August. Applications for
tennis passes are available at Town Hall or on line with proof of Greenwich residency required. The Town offers instruction and holds an annual town-wide tournament.

PARKS & BEACHES

organizations devoted to our parks, water & green space

We are all grateful to the Garden Clubs. They give generously of their time and money to keep Greenwich beautiful.
Garden Clubs are listed in the section FLOWERS AND GARDENS.

Audubon Society of Greenwich
613 Riversville Road, 203.869.5272
www.Greenwich.Audubon.org
Karen Dixon, Center Director

Board of Parks and Recreation
www.GreenwichCT.org/ParksAndRec/prBoardofParksandRec.asp
The nine member board is nominated by the Board of Selectmen and appointed by the Representative Town Meeting (RTM). They advise the First Selectman and help coordinate department activity.

Bruce Park Association
Tom Cahill, President, 203.622.9177
A homeowners group focusing on maintaining the integrity of Bruce Park.

Calf Island Conservancy
www.CalfIsland.org
Calf Island Conservancy works in partnership with the U.S. Fish and Wildlife Service to promote beneficial public uses and habitat enhancement on Calf Island.

Friends of Grass Island
Sylvester Pecora, Sr., Chairman
Jo Conboy, Secretary, 203.661.6343

Friends of Greenwich Point
PO Box 711, Old Greenwich, 06870
www.FriendsofGreenwichPoint.org

Greenwich Conservation Commission
Denise Savageau, Director, 203.622.6461
www.greenwichct.org/ConservationCommission/ConservationCommission.asp
The Commission is an advisory board to assist the Town with planning and management of its natural resources.

organizations

Greenwich Green & Clean

113 Pemberwick Road, Greenwich, 203.531.0006

www.GreenwichGreenandClean.org

Since their founding in 1986, they have been committed to developing partnerships with companies and volunteers to beautify the public spaces we all share. We love Mary Hull! She makes it happen.

Greenwich Land Trust

132 East Putnam Avenue, 2 East, Suite D, Cos Cob, 203.629.2151

PO Box 1152, Greenwich 06836-1152

www.GLTrust.org

Greenwich and its residents are committed to expanding the Town's large amount of green space. Funding comes from a variety of sources, including the Town, the State, the Federal Government (www.tpl.org), the Greenwich Land Trust and private donations.

Greenwich Point Conservancy

www.GreenwichPoint.org

Chris Franco, President, 203.637.4851, 203.637.6806

The conservancy has raised over $1,000,000 to renovate the Queen Anne Building at Greenwich Point.

Greenwich Recycling Advisory Board (GRAB) Services

Greenwich Town Hall, Department of Public Works

Sally Davies, Chair, 203.531.0006

Greenwich Tree Conservancy

www.GreenwichTreeConservancy.org

They preserve and add to the tree and forest resources in Greenwich. One tree will absorb the CO_2 from four cars every year.

Plan of Conservation and Development (POCD)

http://greenwichct.virtualtownhall.net/public_documents/FOV1-00010EFC/POCD/index

This is the Town's 10-year plan.

Planning and Zoning Department (P&Z)

www.greenwichct.org/PlanningZoning/PlanningZoning.asp

The Town Department responsible for developing and enforcing Greenwich zoning regulations.

PARKS & BEACHES

organizations

Planning and Zoning Commission
www.GreenwichCT.org/PlanningZoning/pzCommission.asp
The Commission is composed of five regular members and three alternates who are nominated by the Board of Selectmen and appointed by the Representative Town Meeting (RTM). They prepare long-range plans, based on the POCD, for future development and make recommendations for the most desirable use of the land within the Town. They also regulate and review municipal improvement projects and subdivisions of land.

RTM Parks and Recreation Committee
www.GreenwichCT.org/ParksAndRec/prRTMParksandRec.asp
The twelve-member Representative Town Meeting (RTM) committee is made up of one representative of each of the Town's voting districts. They advise the RTM on issues involving our parks.

RTM Land Use Committee
The twelve-member Representative Town Meeting (RTM) committee is made up of one representative of each of the Town's voting districts. They advise the RTM on issues involving land use.

Selectman's Coastal Resources Advisory Committee
They advise the First Selectman regarding the development and implementation of the Town's Waterways Management Plan.

Shellfish Commission
www.GreenwichCT.org/Shellfish/Shellfish.asp
The Commission provides recreational shell fishing for the inhabitants of Greenwich by overseeing the shell fish beds.

Trout Unlimited (Mianus Chapter)
PO Box 663, Riverside, 06878
www.MianusTU.org
703.522.0200 National Headquarters (Arlington VA)
Mike Law, President, 203.966.3364
The Mianus Chapter is comprised of more than 500 anglers from Greenwich to Ridgefield CT, dedicated to preserving and protecting the rivers and streams of lower Fairfield County.

PETS

index

Pets, popular in Greenwich, bring great cheer to their owners and often assume the role of "Head of the Household." Over 3,000 dogs are masters of homes in Greenwich. If you hear someone calling Maggie, Max, Sabrina, Buddy, Sam, Solan, Molly or Jake, chances are it isn't a child being summoned.

Adoption of Dogs and Cats
Adopt-A-Dog
Adopt a Seeing Eye Dog
Animal Shelter (aka Dog Pound)
Connecticut Humane Society
Greyhound Adoption
Puttin' On The Dog Show

Dog Breeders
Greenwich Kennel Club
CT Pet Guide

Lost Pets
Paw Prints and Purrs
Sherlock Bones

Pet Grooming
Barks and Bubbles Grooming
Bow Wow Barber Mobile Dog
   Groomers

Pet Information
Connecticut Pet Guide
Dog License & Connecticut Canine
   Laws
Dog Park
Friends of Animals
Paw Prints and Purrs

Pet Care
(Pet Walkers, Sitters and Kennels)
Best Friends Pet Resort & Salon
Camp Bow Wow
Canine Athletic Club
Doggie Grandparents
North Wind Kennels
Pet Sitters
Poop Patrol

Pet Photographers
Amanda Jones

Pet Stores
The following pet stores are described in the SHOPPING Section:
- Canine Corner
  177 Sound Beach Avenue
  Old Greenwich, 637.8819
- House of Fins
  99 Bruce Park Avenue
  203.661.8131
- Pet Pantry
  290 Railroad Avenue
  203.869.6444
- Choice Pet Supply
  44 Amogerone Xway
  203.869.4999

PETS
index

Pet Training
Dog Training by Ken Berenson
Dog Training by Simply Sarah
Good Dog Foundation
Invisible Fencing (Canine Fence
& E-Fence)

Stray Cats
- Project SaveACat
  203.661.6855
- PAWS
  (Pet Animal Welfare Society)
  Norwalk CT, 203.854.1798
- SCAT
(Southern Connecticut Animal Trust)
  Stamford CT, 203.968.9385

Veterinarians
Animal Eye Clinic
Animal Hospital of
    Greenwich - Stamford
Blue Cross Animal Hospital
Greenwich Veterinary Hospital
Just Cats Hospital
Veterinary Oncology & Hematology
    Center
Veterinarian Referral & Emergency
    Center (24 Hr)

Wildlife Rescue
All about Bats
Wild Wings
Wildlife in Crisis

TIP: DOG VOLUNTEERS NEEDED
Adopt-a-Dog shelters and places abandoned dogs and cats
in loving homes. They need volunteers to help with functions such as fundraising, dog walking, public relations
and animal care. If you have a warm place in your heart
for these sweet creatures, call 203.629.9494 for information or www.AdoptaDog.org.

PETS

Adopt-A-Dog

Corporate Office: 849 Lake Avenue, Greenwich.

Shelter: 23 Cox Avenue, Armonk NY

   203.629.9494 or 914.273.1674

www.AdoptaDog.org

Since 1981, this unique, local, not-for-profit animal agency has helped over 7,000 homeless dogs find loving families. If you have a soft spot in your heart for animals, consider adopting or becoming a foster "parent." You are always welcome to call or visit their kennels. They hold the annual October show, "Puttin' on the Dog."

Shelter Hours: Weekdays 11 am - 4 pm, by appointment only.

Adopt a Seeing Eye Dog

www.SeeingEye.org/aboutUs/?M_ID=129

Adopt a well trained dog. Some dogs are just too friendly to make the grade as a seeing eye dog.

Amanda Jones (Pet Photographer)

North Adams MA, 877.251.2390

www.AmandaJones.com

One of our nation's top animal photographers grew up in Greenwich. Mention Amanda Jones to a dog enthusiast and you will hear how beautiful her work is. Amanda books shooting tours in advance. Check her website for a schedule. Greenwich is on most of her tours.

Animal Eye Clinic

at the Veterinarian Referral & Emergency Center

123 West Cedar Street, Norwalk, CT, 203.855.1533

www.AnimalEyeClinic.net

People from all over the area bring their pets here for eye problems.

Hours: Monday & Tuesday 8 am - 5 pm,

Wednesday & Thursday 1 am - 8 pm, Friday 8 am - noon.

Animal Hospital of Greenwich - Stamford

2061 West Main Street, Stamford CT, 203.967.8008

Our favorite pug, Honey, loves to be boarded here.

PETS

Animal Shelter (aka Dog Pound)
Museum Drive, 622.8299, 622.8081
North Street (next to North Street Elementary)
Greenwich is looking forward to the new North Street 3,400 sf. animal shelter being built with $900,000 of private donations for the $1,000,000 project. There will be 12 kennels, a separate space for cats and an adoption room for people to meet pets. The Shelter is a Town of Greenwich Police Department service that handles dead or sick animals as well as stray dogs or cats. Clearly, animals lost in Greenwich receive tender loving care.
Hours: weekdays, 8 am - 3 pm; weekends, until 2 pm.

Barks and Bubbles Grooming
80 Pemberwick Road, Greenwich, 203.531.7787
Chip likes to be groomed here. We think it is especially kind that owner Patricia Gabriele gives a discount for adopted dogs.

Best Friends Pet Resort & Salon
528 Main Avenue, Norwalk CT, 203.849.1010
www.BestFriendsPetCare.com
Doggy day camp with 4-legged playmates (assuming your pet can pass the interview process). Longer stays are available. Joya loves their grooming salon.
Hours: weekdays, 7 am - 6 pm; Saturday, 8 am - 5 pm;
Sunday, 3 pm - 6 pm.

Blue Cross Animal Hospital
530 East Putnam Avenue, 203.869.7755
The ladies behind the desk are very kind and caring. Dr. Wolff provides holistic pet care, including acupuncture and homeopathy as well as conventional care.
Hours: Weekdays 8 am - 6 pm; open one Saturday a month, 9 am - 1 pm.

Bow Wow Barber Mobile Dog Groomers
149 Cedar Heights Rd, Stamford CT, 203.968.6214
Calls will be returned in the evening because they are on the road during the day.

Camp Bow Wow
581 Hope Street, Stamford CT, 203.504.2288
www.CampBowWow.com/US/CT/Stamford
Assuming your dog can pass the 20-minute interview, this camp could be just the ticket for a day or overnight camp.

PETS

Canine Athletic Club

40 Decatur Street, First Floor, Cos Cob, 203.587.1155

Kristin's Mobile: 203.561.9541

www.K9Athletic.com

Perhaps your dog would like to belong to the Lunch Bunch. According to one of our pet friends, he is picked up every day, lunches with several of his dog buddies, and then returns home, ready for his afternoon nap. Kristin Leggio and Keith Fernim provide dog walking, exercise, and socialization service as well as in-home pet care services. If you are too busy to take your dog to the vet, they'll do that, too.

Connecticut Humane Society

455 Post Road East, Westport CT, 203.227.4137

www.CTHumane.org

Although the Greenwich Animal Shelter and adopt a dog have pets to adopt, the Humane Society is the major area resource. They have many hopeful dogs, cats and even rabbits and fish waiting to meet you. They maintain a lost and found file and will come to your home to remove injured or sick wild animals or birds.

Hours: Monday - Saturday, 10:30 am - 5:30 pm; Sunday, 10 am - 4 pm.

Connecticut Pet Guide

http://www.ctpetguide.com/

Pet resources from around Connecticut.

Dog License & Connecticut Canine Laws

All dogs six months or over must be licensed and wear collar and tag at all times. Licenses are issued by the Town Clerk's office (203.622.7897) in Town Hall (8 am - 4 pm). Make checks payable to: Town of Greenwich Dog License. All dogs must be vaccinated against rabies and owners must submit a certificate to the Town Clerk when licensing their dog. Dog licenses expire on June 30th each year. To get a license request and information on licensing go to:

www.GreenwichCT.org/TownClerk/TownClerk.asp or directly to:

http://GreenwichCT.VirtualTownhall.net/Public_Documents/
GreenwichCT_TownClerk/tcDogLicense.pdf

Dog Parks

Dogs are allowed in all town parks with a leash except for Byram Beach and Greenwich Point. From December 1st until March 31st dogs are allowed at Greenwich Point. Call Parks and Recreation 203.622.7830.

The first (and only) Greenwich Dog Park is located on 3/4 acre at Grass Island. The park is open from sunrise to sunset. For your dog to have a good experience go during a quiet time on the first visit. We recommend a weekday between 9 am and 11 am. The rules are posted on the fence. Children under 10 are not permitted and the owners must remain in the fenced area with their dog while the dog is off leash. Aggressive dogs are not allowed and owners are responsible for the behavior of their dog.

Dog Training by Ken Berenson

914.699.4982

www.KenBerenson.com

Ken holds dog (and owner) training sessions at the Round Hill Community House, 397 Round Hill Road. These are excellent classes, conducted by Ken Berenson's Canine Services. For more information call Ken. Ken is a highly qualified educator of humans and, for that reason, an effective educator of dogs. Ken also gives private lessons.

Dog Training by Simply Sarah

Sarah Hodgson, 914.241.1111

www.DogPerfect.com

Author of several dog training books, Sarah gives group and private lessons.

Doggie Grandparents

47 Wake Robin Lane, Stamford, 203.595.0176

If you hate to put your dog in a kennel while you are away, Francine Garb has the answer. Her Stamford home is the perfect place to keep your dog happy in your absence. Dogs can wander around her home. The door to the fenced back yard is always open. She usually boards 4-5 dogs at a time. An interview with your dog is required. Our dog, Daisy, has a good time here.

Friends of Animals

77 Post Road Suite 205 Darien CT, 203.656.1522

Priscilla Feral, President

www.FriendsOfAnimals.org

An international, non-profit, organization founded in 1957 which is dedicated to increasing awareness of animal rights and to preventing abuse of animals. It provides the names of local veterinarians who do low cost spaying and neutering.

Hours: weekdays, 9 am - 5 pm.

(The) Good Dog Foundation

607 6th Street, Brooklyn NY, 718.788.2988

www.TheGoodDogFoundation.org

This foundation, part of a nationwide group, operates training sessions in Greenwich for people willing to bring their animals to visit local patients. The dogs ease depression in the elderly and calm hyperactivity in children.

Greenwich Kennel Club

Community Center, 54 Bible Street, Cos Cob

203.426.1173, 426.2881

www.GreenwichKC.org

The GKC is a non-profit organization whose membership is comprised of area dog enthusiasts with interests in conformation, obedience and performance events. The GKC holds an annual all breed dog show every June. If you are not sure whether you want to bring a beagle or vizsla into your home, attend this show. It is a wonderful way to meet them all, as well as to find a suitable breeder.

Greenwich Veterinary Hospital

358 West Putnam Avenue, 203.661.1437

He can be expensive, but many of our knowledgeable friends take their pets to Dr. Sean Bell.

Hours: weekdays, 8am - 6 pm; Saturday, 8 am - 2 pm; Closed Sunday.

Greyhound Adoption

If these listings save one of these dogs, we will be so grateful.

- Pups Without Partners, Penny Zwart adoption coordinator
  West Haven CT, 203.933.3607. www.PupsWithoutPartners.org
- Greyhound Protection League, Melani Nardone
  212.580.0283. Summer, 203.869.8484
  www.greyhounds.org

PETS

Invisible Fencing

If you see small white flags around the perimeter of a Greenwich yard, most likely it is one of the "Invisible Fences." This is a safe way to keep your dog in your yard. Also works to keep your pet out of designated rooms in your home. Moose and Tipsy like their E-Fence.

- Canine Fence
  493 Danbury Road, Wilton CT, 800.628.2264
  www.caninefence.com
  Hours: Monday - Saturday, 7 am - 8 pm.
- E-Fence
  329 Longmeadow Road, Orange CT 203.795.3283
  www.EFence1.com

Just Cats Hospital

1110 East Main Street, Stamford, 203.327.7220
They provide excellent medical services, boarding, grooming and TLC, just for cats.
Hours: weekdays, 7:30 am - 8 pm (Friday 6 pm); Saturday, 8 am - 5 pm.

North Wind Kennels

Route 22, Bedford NY, 914.234.3771
www.NorthWindKennelsNY.com
If you would like to leave your dog or cat where Glenn Close and Chevy Chase are said to leave theirs, go no further. Jake Feinberg's kennel has four "doggie suites" and can house 225 dogs and 45 cats. Unfortunately, our experience was less than satisfactory.
Hours: Monday - Saturday, 9:30 am - 5:30 pm; On Sunday or off-hours, their machine doesn't take messages.

Paw Prints and Purrs

800.666.5678
http://www.SnikSnak.com/hotlines.html
A great resource for information on lost animals.

Pet Sitters

When in need, try www.PetSitters.org or www.PetSit.com. These are national organizations that usually have reliable sitters. However, it is wise to ask for references and to make sure they are insured and bonded.

PETS

Pet Stores
The following pet stores are described in the SHOPPING Section:
- Canine Corner, 177 Sound Beach Avenue, Old Greenwich, 637.8819
- House of Fins, 99 Bruce Park Avenue, 203.661.8131
- Pet Pantry, 290 Railroad Avenue, 203.869.6444
- Choice Pet Supply, 44 Amogerone Xway, 203.869.4999

Poop Patrol
Stamford CT, 203.531.6661
www.PoopPatrolCT.com
Got poop? Sally Cimino, a graduate of Connecticut College, will scoop! Poop Patrol scoops and removes dog waste from yards, commercial properties and kennels.

Puttin' On The Dog (Annual Dog Show)
Roger Sherman Baldwin Park, Late September to the middle of October
Run by Adopt-a-Dog, 849 Lake Avenue, 203.629.9494 www.adoptadog.org
This show is a great place to show off your dog, learn about dogs, or adopt a new friend. Always a hit with children of all ages.

Sherlock Bones
800.942.6637
www.SherlockBones.com
Since 1975 this California pet detective has helped recover missing pets around the USA.

Stray Cats
If you know of a stray cat that needs to be captured or you would like to adopt a cat, call these volunteer organizations:
- Project SaveACat, 203.661.6855
- PAWS (Pet Animal Welfare Society) Norwalk CT, 203.750.9572
- SCAT (Southern Connecticut Animal Trust) Stamford CT
  203.359.1439
  www.adoptatscat.org

Veterinary Oncology & Hematology Center
178 Connecticut, Avenue, Norwalk CT, 203.838.6626
www.OnCoVet.com
Specialists in the diagnosis and treatment of cancer in animals. They don't make you wait and are particularly nice to you and your pet.

Veterinarian Referral & Emergency Center

123 West Cedar Street, Norwalk, CT, 203.854.9960
www.VCAVREC.com
If your vet is not available, this is a wonderful emergency room for your pet. During normal hours, appointments must be made for specialists.
Hours: 24 hours a day, 7 days a week.

Wild Wings

Old Greenwich CT, 203.637.9822, 203.967.2121
Wildlife Hotline: 203.389.4411
Alison Taintor and Meredith Sampson are state and federally licensed wildlife rehabilitators who operate a wildlife rescue and rehabilitation center in Old Greenwich and Stamford. They will respond to oil spill emergencies that affect wildlife.
Hours: They are on call 24 hours a day, 7 days a week for emergencies.
          For general information, call weekdays, 9 am - 5 pm.

Wildlife in Crisis

Weston CT, 203.544.9913
www.WildlifeInCrisis.com
If you happen to have an injured cormorant (as the Greenwich Police Department did recently) and perhaps any other wild animal who needs help, this group is willing to rehabilitate and save the animal or bird.

PHOTOGRAPHY

Framers are described in STORES
Passport photos are described in TRAVEL
The following camera stores are described in STORES
- *Camera Wholesalers, 1034 High Ridge Road, Stamford, 203.357.0467*
- *Images, 202 Sound Beach Avenue, Old Greenwich, 203.637.4193*
- *Ritz Camera, 82 Greenwich Avenue, Greenwich, 203.869.0673*

photographers

All photographers require an appointment.

Amanda Jones
North Adams, MA, 877.251.2390
www.AmandaJones.com
One of our nation's top animal photographers grew up in Greenwich. Mention Amanda Jones to a dog enthusiast and you will hear how beautiful her work is. Amanda books shooting tours in advance. Check her website for a schedule. Greenwich is on most of her tours.

Annie Watson
125 Spencer Place, Mamaroneck, NY 914.777.7505
www.AnnieWatson.com
A photographer with an artist's eye.

Ben Larrabee
26 Fairview Avenue, Darien, CT 203.656.3807
www.BenLarrabee.com
Ben is a graduate of RISD and Yale University. His pictures are in museums in New York and Boston.

Bob Capazzo
31 East Elm Street, Greenwich, 203.273.0139, 203.358.3402
http://www.pagedezigner.com/capazzo/0-contact.htm
Bob is the senior photographer for Greenwich Magazine. He likes to photograph people and events and he has a wonderful way of helping people relax and look their best. It is easy to see his work, just pick up an issue of Greenwich Magazine.

PHOTOGRAPHY

photographers

Sarah Forman
845.248.0447
www.SarahSnaps.com
Sarah is a young photographer just starting out. She comes with a love of children, babies and animals. Her prices are very reasonable and she's easy to work with. She'll meet you, your children and/or animals at a park or garden and get great candid photos.

Classic Kids
54 Greenwich Avenue, 203.622.2358
www.ClassicKidsPhotography.com
Charlie and Stephanie had a wonderful time having Kathleen Miller take their photographs here. They are very popular with Greenwich residents.

Jeffery Shaw Portrait Photography
601 West 26th Street, NYC, 203.622.4838
www.jeffreyShaw.com
He moved his studio from Greenwich to Manhattan, but he still does a lot of well-loved Greenwich work. You will treasure his photographs of your family.

Karen Reyes
85 Greenwich Avenue, 917.861.9052, 212.799.0855
www.korenreyes.com
She specializes in taking pictures of pregant women and newborns in artistic poses. She shares her space with Ella Vickers (reviewed in Stores).

Venture Portraits
48 West Putnam Avenue, 203.861.9100
www.ventureportraits.us.com
They specialize in unique family action photos. The pictures are processed and framed in England. Check the prices before you have a session.

POST OFFICES & ZIP CODES

For shipping services other than the Post office see Delivery Services in SERVICES

Premium Forwarding Service

www.USPS.com/PremiumForwarding

If you want all of your mail (including magazines) forwarded to you at a temporary address (two weeks to one year), for $14 a week plus an enrollment fee of $15, the post office will package your mail and send it to you once a week.

Greenwich Post Offices

www.USPS.com

There are six post offices and five zip codes in Town. The window service hours are different for each office. Mail for Greenwich zip codes is usually sent to Stamford to be sorted. The only post office with bins for all Greenwich zip codes is in Old Greenwich. Post Office hours are continuing to shrink, don't expect them to stay open late on April 15th.

TIP: VOTER REGISTRATION

622.7889, 7890, vote@greenwichct.org

www.greenwichct.org/VoterRegistration/VoterRegistration.asp

You must be registered at least 14 days before a regular election and by noon of the last business day before a party primary. You must be registered by the day before a special election or referendum. Register in person at the Town Clerk's Office or Registrar of Voter's Office at Town Hall, at any office of the State Motor Vehicles, or at libraries throughout the state. Proof of residency and age 18 or over on election day are required.

POST OFFICES & ZIP CODES

Greenwich Avenue Post Office [Zip: 06830]
310 Greenwich Avenue, 203.869.3737
Hours: weekdays, 9 am - 5 pm;
Saturday, 9:30 am - 12:30 pm.

Greenwich Post Office [Zip: 06831]
29 Valley Drive, 203.625.3168
Hours: weekdays, 9 am - 5:30 pm;
Saturday, 9 am - 2 pm.

Glenville Post Office [Zip: 06831]
25 Glen Ridge Plaza, 203.531.8744
Hours: weekdays, 8:30 am - 4 pm;
Saturday, 8:30 am - noon.

Cos Cob Post Office [Zip: 06807]
152 East Putnam Avenue, 869.0128
Hours: weekdays, 9 am - 4:30 pm;
Saturday, 9:30 am - 12:30 pm.

Riverside Post Office [Zip: 06878]
1273 East Putnam Avenue, 203.637.9332
Hours: weekdays, 8:30 am - 5 pm;
Saturday, 9 am - 12:30 pm.

Old Greenwich Post Office [Zip: 06870]
36 Arcadia Road, 203.637.1405
Hours: weekdays, 9 am - 5 pm;
Saturday, 9 am - noon.

REAL ESTATE

Buyer Agency

On June 1st, 1997, Connecticut mandated that Realtors represent either the buyer or the seller, but not both (unless dual or designated agency is disclosed and agreed to by both parties) in the same transaction.

Buyers like being represented by their own Realtor because their Realtor can now tell them what they think a house is worth and provide excellent guidance through the real estate process. This extra protection costs the buyer nothing because the buyer's Realtor is still paid by the seller. In the first meeting, the buyer signs a representation agreement with their Realtor much the way a seller signs a listing agreement with their Realtor. For more information on Buyer Agency see:
www.GreenwichLiving.com/buyeragency.htm

Greenwich Multiple Listing Service

Greenwich has an outstanding organization devoted to local real estate. This service is funded by the Realtors in town and is extremely helpful to homeowners, buyers and Realtors. Member Realtors follow a strict code of ethics. Greenwich properties are valuable and unique. It is important to understand how Greenwich real estate works.

For more information on the home buying process in Greenwich, see www.GreenwichLiving.com/salesprocess.htm
When many other towns gave up their local boards, Greenwich did not. In Greenwich all properties, with rare exceptions, are multiple-listed with the Greenwich MLS. To buy property in Greenwich, you need to select a Realtor you like and trust and you will have access through your Realtor to the entire market.

REAL ESTATE

Anderson Associates

164 Mason Street, 203.629.4519, 800.223.4519
www.GreenwichLiving.com

Anderson Associates are Greenwich real estate specialists. We have been helping Greenwich Buyers and Sellers for over 20-years. We all live, as well as work, in Greenwich. We spend our full time on Greenwich real estate. You can depend on us to represent your best interests. Our knowledge of Greenwich and our real estate expertise will make your real estate transaction rewarding and stress-free. As we mentioned in the introduction, we wrote the book you are reading to help our buyers feel at home in this wonderful community.

"With special thanks for all you do; for knowing what we wanted better than we did; for giving us that extra push when we needed it, but never pushing us hard; for your expertise; for much more, but especially for just being you."
- Naomi & Steve Myers

"Whether you are buying or selling, you will love working with Anderson Associates. Their website is filled with information—just what you'd expect from a company as customer-driven as they are. I found information on renovating my house, my children found statistics for school projects, and there are pictures of lots of Greenwich houses for sale. Highly recommended."
- Melanie Kuperberg

For more comments by Anderson Associates' clients, see:
www.GreenwichLiving.com/recommend.htm

For more information and comments about Carolyn Anderson, see:
www.GreenwichLiving.com/meetcarolyn.htm

Strategy Mortgage Corporation

222 Railroad Avenue, 203.618.4444
www.StrategyMortgage.com

Strategy is located in Greenwich. They started in 1994 and originated over $42 million in their first year. Strategy now represents fifty-eight of the most aggressive national and regional lenders and generates over $400 million a year in mortgage loans. They work hard to find the best loans for their clients, and best of all, they are available from 8 am - 10 pm every day.

RELIGION

Each week the Greenwich Time publishes Sabbath services in the Thursday issue and church services in the Saturday issue. This is the best place to find updated information and times of services.

Albertson Memorial Church of Spiritualism
293 Sound Beach Avenue, Old Greenwich, 203.637.4615
www.AlbertsonChurch.org

Anglican Church of the Advent
(Anglican-Episcopal)
Meeting at North Congregational Church, 606 Riversville Road
Rectory, 17 Salem Street, 203.861.2432
www.ChurchOfTheAdvent.org

Annunciation Greek Orthodox Church
1230 Newfield Avenue, Stamford, 203.322.2093
www.AnnunciationofStamford.org

Bethel AME Church
42 Lake Avenue, 203.661.3099

Christ Church of Greenwich
254 East Putnam Avenue, 203.869.6600
www.ChristChurchGreenwich.com

Church of Jesus Christ of Latter Day Saints
800 Stillwater Road, Stamford, 203.662.0867
www.morman.org,www.lds.org

Diamond Hill United Methodist Church
521 East Putnam Avenue, 203.869.2395
www.DiamondHillUMC.org

Dingletown Community Church
(Nondenominational Protestant)
Stanwich Road and Barnstable Lane, 203.629.5923
www.Dingletown.org

First Baptist Church
10 Northfield Street, 203.869.7988

RELIGION

houses of worship

First Church of Christ, Scientist
Church: 11 Park Place, 203.869.2503
Reading Room: 333 Greenwich Avenue, 203.869.2503
www.ChristianScienceCT.org/greenwich

First Church of Round Hill
(interdenominational)
464 Round Hill Road, 203.629.3876
www.FirstChurchOfRoundhill.org

First Congregational Church
108 Sound Beach Avenue, Old Greenwich, 203.637.1791
www.FCCoG.org

First Lutheran Church
38 Field Point Road, 203.869.0032
www.1stLutheranGCT.org

First Presbyterian Church
One West Putnam Avenue, 203.869.8686
www.FPCG.org

First United Methodist Church
59 East Putnam Avenue, 203.629.9584
www.FUMCGreenwich.org

Grace Church of Greenwich
(Presbyterian Church in America)
Meets at Woman's Club of Greenwich
89 Maple Avenue, 203.861.7555
www.GraceChurchGreenwich.com

Greek Orthodox Church of the Archangels
1527 Bedford Street, Stamford, 203.348.4216
www.archangels.ct.goarch.org

Greenwich Baptist Church
10 Indian Rock Lane, 203.869.2437
www.GreenwichBaptist.org

RELIGION

Greenwich Congregation of Jehovah's Witnesses
471 Stanwich Road, 203.661.1244
www.Watchtower.org

Greenwich Reform Synagogue
257 Stanwich Road, 203.629.0018
www.grs.org

Harvest Time Assembly of God
1338 Kings Street, 203.531.7778
www.HTChurch.com

Japanese Gospel Church
(Protestant Evangelical Christian Church for Japanese speakers)
Meeting at St. Paul Evangelical Lutheran Church
286 Delavan Avenue, 203.531.6450
www.jgclmi.com

North Greenwich Congregational Church
606 Riversville Road, 203.869.7763
www.NorthGreenwichChurch.org

Presbyterian Church of Old Greenwich
38 West End Avenue, Old Greenwich, 203.637.3669
www.PCOGOnline.org

Quaker Religious Society of Friends
317 New Canaan Road, Wilton, CT, 203.762.5669
www.WiltonFriends.org

Round Hill Community Church
(independent & nondenominational Christian)
395 Round Hill Road, 203.869.1091
www.RoundHillCommunityChurch.org

Sacred Heart Roman Catholic Church
95 Henry Street, Byram, 203.531.8730 (Rectory)

St. Agnes Roman Catholic Church
247 Stanwich Road, 203.869.5396 (Rectory)
www.StAgnesRC.org

RELIGION

St. Barnabas Episcopal Church
954 Lake Avenue, 203.661.5526
www.StBarnabasGreenwich.org

St. Catherine of Siena Roman Catholic Church
4 Riverside Avenue, 203.637.3661
www.StCath.org

St Mary's Holy Assumption
(Russian Orthodox)
141 Den Road, Stamford, 203.329.9933
www.StMaryofStamford.org

St. Mary Roman Catholic Church
178 Greenwich Avenue, 203.869.9393 (Rectory)
www.StMaryParishGreenwich.org

St. Michael the Archangel Roman Catholic Church
469 North Street, 203.869.5421 (Rectory)
www.stmichaelgreenwich.org

St. Paul Evangelical Lutheran Church
286 Delavan Avenue, 203.531.8466
www.stpaulsbyram.org

St. Paul Roman Catholic Church
84 Sherwood Avenue, 203.531.8741
www.StPaulGreenwich.org

St. Paul's Episcopal Church
200 Riverside Avenue, 637.2447
www.stpaulsriverside.org

St. Roch Roman Catholic Church
10 St. Roch Avenue, 203.869.4176

St. Saviour's Episcopal Church
350 Sound Beach Avenue, Old Greenwich, 203.637.2262
www.SaintSaviours.org

St. Timothy Chapel
1034 North Street, Banksville NY, 203.869.5421

RELIGION

houses of worship

Second Congregational Church
139 East Putnam Avenue, 203.869.9311
www.2cc.org

Stanwich Congregational Church
202 Taconic Road, 203.661.4420
www.stanwichchurch.org

Temple Sholom
300 East Putnam Avenue, 203.869.7191
www.TempleSholom.com

Trinity Church
15 Sherwood Place, 618.0808
www.TrinityChurchOnline.org

Unitarian Universalist Society
20 Forest Street, Stamford, 348.0708
www.uusis.org

TIP: BEACH SERVICES
www.FCCoG.org
The First Congregational Church in Greenwich conducts
Sunday services on the beach at Tod's Point during the
summer months at 8:00 am. Visitors are welcome. A beach
pass is not required for these services. The Saturday Greenwich Time lists all of the religious services in the area.

RELIGION

religious organizations

Chabad Lubavitch of Greenwich
75 Mason Street, 203.629.9059
www.ChabadGreenwich.org

Chavurat Deevray Torah
49 Arcadia Road, 203.637.9478
Reform/Conservative Jewish Study Group

Greenwich Center for Hope and Renewal
237 Taconic Road, Greenwich CT, 203.340.9816
www.HopeAndRenewal.org
Private and confidential services such as: counseling, interventions, renewal groups, seminars, and professional training.

Greenwich Chaplaincy Services
70 Parsonage Road, Greenwich, 203.618.4236
www.GreenwichChaplaincy.org
A non-profit supported by local churches and synagogues. They provide pastoral and spiritual care to the residents of nursing homes and assisted living facilities.

Greenwich Leadership Forum
www.GreenwichLeadershipForum.org
Lectures on faith and ethics in the workplace.

Hadassah, Greenwich Chapter
Temple Sholom, 300 East Putnam Avenue, 203.869.7191
www.Westchester.Hadassah.org

Interfaith Council of Southwestern Connecticut
(formerly the Council of Churches and Synagogues)
1 Canterbury Green, Stamford, 203.348.2800
www.InterfaithCouncil.org

Philoptochos
www.Philoptochos.org
Despina Fassuliotis, 203.661.5991

Soto Zen Buddhism
@ First Congregational Church, Old Greenwich, 914.772.1974
www.TwiningVines.org

RELIGION

religious organizations

UJA Federation of Greenwich
1 Holly Hill Lane, 203.622.1434
Pamela Ehrenkranz, Executive Director
www.UJAFedGreenwich.org

Young Life of Greenwich
(nondenominational Christian organization for teenagers)
203.340.2123
www.Greenwich.Younglife.org

TIP: COMMUNITY CALENDARS
- **Community Events Calendar**
If you want to know the coming Town events, you will love the Community Answers "Planning Ahead Community Calendar." Call Community Answers, 203.622.7979 and ask to be on their list or check out their calendar (click on Events Calendar):
www.GreenwichLibrary.org/CommAnswers.htm
- **Greenwich Citizen Calendar**
www.GreenwichCitizen.com
On Fridays the Citizen runs a calendar of area events organized into sections such as: children, exhibits, theater, music, dance, lectures & meetings. Send calendar listings to Calendar@bcnnew.com
- **Social Calendar**
Greenwich Magazine publishes a Social Calendar. It can be found on-line at www.FairfieldEvents.com
- **Town Committee Meeting Calendar**
The Town committee and department calendar can be found at:
http://greenwichct.virtualtownhall.net/Public_Documents/
GreenwichCT_Calendar/?formid=158

RESTAURANTS - THE BEST

The Best Restaurants in Greenwich
Jean-Louis (French)
Nuage (Asian Fusion)
Rebecca's (New American)
Thomas Henkelmann (French)
Valbella (Italian)

The Best Area Restaurants in each Category (in alphabetical order)
Our ratings reflect our reaction primarily to food, with ambiance and
service taken into consideration.

American
American Bounty
   (Culinary Institute of America)
Bedford Post
Blue Hill at Stone Barns
Harvest Supper
Match
Napa & Company
Rebecca's
School House
Xaviar's
X20

Asian
Asiana Cafe
Ching's Table
Nuage

Barbeque
Q
Smokey Joe's Bar-B-Que

Breakfast
City Limits Diner
Hyatt

Brunch on Sunday
Hyatt/Winfields (buffet)
Hunan Café (dim sum)

Chinese
Hunan Café
Ching's Table

Delicatessens
(reviewed in FOOD)
Aux Délices
Garelick & Herbs

Diner
City Limits Diner

Fast Food
Boston Market
Bruckner's
Burger Shakes & Fries
Chicken Joe's
Garden Catering
Panera
Rotisserie
Subway Sandwiches

French
(La) Pantiere
Bernard's
Crémaillère
Escoffier
   (Culinary Institute of America)
Jean-Louis
L'Escale
Thomas Henkelmann

RESTAURANTS - THE BEST

Greek
Eos

Hamburgers
Burgers, Shakes & Fries
Sundown Saloon
Thataway Cafe

Ice Cream
(reviewed in FOOD)
Carvel (soft ice cream)
Cold Stone Creamery (ice cream)
Daniella's Gelateria
Darlene's Heavenly Desires
    (Sedutto ice cream)
Gelatissimo (Gelato)
Longford's (ice cream)
Meli-Melo

Indian
Coromandel
Rasa
Thali

Italian
Pasta Nostra
Pierangelo
Polpo
Tarry Lodge
Valbella

Japanese
Kira Sushi
Sushi Nanase

Latin American
Sonora
Valencia Luncheria

Mexican
Lolita Cocina
Ole Mole

Middle Eastern
Laya's Falafel (Main Street location)

Pizza
Express Pizza
Glenville Pizza
Pizza Post

Portugese
Douro

Pub
Brewhouse

Seafood
Elm Street Oyster House
Osetra
Rowayton Seafood Company

Smoothie
Robeks

South Western
Ash Creek Saloon
Boxcar Cantina
Telluride

Spanish
Barcelona
Meigas

Steak
Also see Barbeque
Steak au poivre at MacKenzies
Steak at Rye Bar and Grill
Hibachi Steak at Abis

Tea
(The) Drawing Room

Thai
Kit's Thai Kitchen
Little Thai Kitchen

RESTAURANTS by CUISINE

American
(Also see Pubs and American, New)
Applebee's
Beach House
Bedford Post
Beehive
Buffalo Wild Wings
Cafeteria at Greenwich Hospital
(The) Cheesecake Factory
Chocopologie
Cobble Stone Creek
Dressing Room
Elms Restaurant & Tavern
Favorite Place
Garden Café at Greenwich Hospital
Gates
Ginger Man
Greenwich Tavern
I-HOP
Joey B's Chili Hub
Katzenberg's Kafe
Kona Grill
Long Ridge Tavern
MacKenzie's Grill
Meetinghouse
Putnam Restaurant
Q
Rotisserie
Rouge
Route 22
Rye Grill
Smokey Joe's
Sundown Saloon
Ten Twenty Post
Thataway Café
Upper Crust Bagel Co.
Winfield's at the Hyatt

American, New
American Bounty
   (Culinary Institute of America)
Blue Hill at Stone Barns
Crew
Harvest Supper
Market
Match
Mirage Café
Napa
North Star
School House Restaurant
Rebecca's
Xaviar's
X2O

Asian
(Indian, Chinese & Japanese are listed separately)
Asiana Café
Bambou Asian Restaurant
Duo
Euro Asian
Penang Grill
Republic Grill Asian Bistro
Tengda Asian Bistro

Asian Fusion
Baang
Ching's Table
Nuage
Thai Chi
Wasabi Chi

Bakeries
(Bakeries are listed under FOOD)

Barbecue
Q
Smokey Joe's
Rotisserie

RESTAURANTS by CUISINE

Catering
(Caterers are listed under ENTER-TAINING)

Chinese
Chilichicken
China Pavillion
Ching's Table
Hunan Café
Hunan Gourmet
Oriental Gourmet
Panda Pavilion 3
PF Chang's China Bistro
Wild Ginger Dumpling House

Coffee, Tea and Smoothies
Arcadia Coffee Co.
Dunkin' Donuts
(The) Drawing Room
Robeks
SoNo Caffeine
Starbucks

Cuban
Habana

Delicatessens
(Delicatessens are listed under FOOD)

Fast Food
Boston Market
Bruckner's
Burgers, Shakes and Fries
Chicken Joe's
Cosi
Dougie's
Frank's Franks Lunch Wagon
Greenwich Health Mart
McDonald's
Panera
Rodney's Roadhouse Lunch Wagon
Rotisserie
SoNo Baking Company & Café

(FAST FOOD continued...)
Sophia's Café
Standing Room Only Lunch Wagon
Subway Sandwich
Taco Bell
Upper Crust Bagel Company
Village Bagels
Wendy's

Diners
City Limits
Glory Days

French
Aux Délices
Bernards
Bistro Bonne Nuit
(La) Bretagne
(Le) Château
Chez Jean-Pierre
(La) Crémaillère
Escoffier
    (Culinary Institute of America)
(Le) Figaro
Jean-Louis
L'Escale
Le Pain Quotidien Restaurant
Meli-Melo
(La) Pantiere
Roger Sherman Inn
Thomas Henkelmann
Versailles Restaurant

German
Brew House

Greek
Eos

Ice Cream
(Ice Cream Shops are reviewed under FOOD)

RESTAURANTS by CUISINE

Indian
Coromandel
Rasa
Tandoori
Tawa
Thali

Irish
Tigin

Italian
(also see PIZZA)
Albas
Applausi Osteria
Aria
Café Silvium
Capriccio
Caterina de' Medici
   (Culinary Institute of America)
Cava Wine Bar and Restaurant
Centro Ristorante
Columbus Park Trattoria
Eclisse
Ferrante
Frank's
Goccia
Il Sogno Ristorante
Marianacci's
Matteo's
Mediteraneo
Morello Bistro
Nessa
Pasquale
Pasta Nostra
Pasta Vera
Pellicci's
Pierangelo
Piero's

(ITALIAN continued...)
Polpo
Pomodoro
Siena
Spazzio
Tarry Lodge
Terra
Valbella
Villa Italia

Jamaican
(K & S) Top of the Hill

Japanese
Abis
Edo
Kato -Chan Ramen Stand
Kazu
Kira Sushi
Saito
Sushi Nanase
Tengda
Tsuru

Latin American
Mexican Restaurants are listed separately
Acuario
Brasitas
Café Brazil
Copacabana
Habana
Sonora
Valencia Luncheria

Mexican
Fonda La Paloma
Lolita Cocina
Ole Mole
Rio Border
Tequila Mockingbird

RESTAURANTS by CUISINE

Middle Eastern
Laya's Falafel
Myrna's Mediterranean Bistro
Tabouli Grill

Pizza
Arcuri's
California Pizza Kitchen
Mediterraneo
Express Pizza
Pizza Factory
Glenville Pizza
Pizza Post
Planet Pizza
Sound Beach Pizza Grill

Portugese
Douro

Pubs
Brewhouse
Ginger Man
MacDuffs Public House
MacKenzie's Grill Room
SBC
Tigin

Seafood
Crabshell
Elm Street Oyster House
F.I.S.H.
Greenwich Lobster House
Morgan's Fish House
Osetra
Paradise Bar & Grill
Rowayton Seafood
Saltwater Grill
SoNo Seaport Seafood

South American
See Latin American

Southwestern
Ash Creek Salon
Boxcar Cantina
Q
Smokey Joe's Bar-B-Q
Telluride

Spanish
Barcelona
Meigas
(La) Paella

Steak
Abis
(The) Capital Grille
Copacabana
Edo
Morton's The Steak House
Outback
Q
Smokey Joe's Bar-B-Q
Willett House

Swiss
Melting Pot

Thai
Kit's Thai Kitchen
Little Buddha
Little Thai Kitchen
Thai Basil

Vegetarian
(also most Indian Restaurants)
Bruckner's
Greenwich Healthmart
Juice Bar Café
Layla's Falafel
Le Pain Quotidien Restaurant
Lime
Rasa

RESTAURANTS by CATEGORY

Afternoon Tea
The Drawing Room

Breakfast
Aux Délices (Riverside)
City Limits Diner
Glory Days
I-HOP
L'Escale
Putnam Restaurant
Versailles

Brunch on Sunday
Abis (buffet)
Doral Arrowwood Atrium (buffet)
Fjord Sunday Brunch Cruise
Hunan Café (Dim Sum)
Long Ridge Tavern (buffet)
Roger Sherman Inn
Saltwater Grill (buffet)
Versailles
Winfield's at the Hyatt (buffet)

Dinner, Late Night
Barcelona
Beach House
Buffalo Wild Wings
Capriccio
Cheesecake Factory
City Limits
Cobble Stone
Cosi
Crabshell @ the Crab Shell
Glory Days
Kona Grill
Lolita Cocina
Louie's
MacDuffs Public House
MacKenzie's
McDonald's

(DINNER, LATE NIGHT continued...)
Mirage Café
P.F. Chang's China Bistro
Pellicci's
Planet Pizza
Route 22
Sundown Saloon
Taco Bell (Drive Thru)
Thataway Café
Wendy's (Drive Thru)

Family Restaurants
(In addition to Fast Food and Pizza restaurants)
Abis
Applebee's
Ash Creek Saloon
Beach House
Boxcar Cantina
Centro
Chocopologie
(The) Cheesecake Factory
City Limits
Cobble Stone
Edo
Favorite Place
Frank's
Gates
Glory Days
Goccia
Hunan Gourmet
I-HOP
Joey B's Chili Hub
MacKenzie's Grill
Melting Pot
Oriental Gourmet
Outback
(le) Pain Quotidien
Panda Pavilion 3

RESTAURANTS by CATEGORY

(FAMILY RESTAURANTS continued...)
Pasquale
Pellicci's
P.F. Chang's China Bistro
Pomodoro
Putnam Restaurant
Q
Rotisserie
Route 22
Rowayton Seafood
Rye Grill and Bar
Smokey Joe's Bar-B-Q
SoNo Seaport Seafood
Sundown Saloon
Tequilla Mockingbird
Thataway Cafe
Upper Crust Bagel Company

Hot Spots
Baang
Barcelona
Beach House
Crab Shell / Crab Shack
L'Escale
Gingerman
Greenwich Tavern
Lolita Cocina
MacDuffs
MacKenzie's Grill
Rye Grill and Bar
Route 22
Sundown Saloon

Inns Worth a Trip
(see their descriptions in HOTELS & INNS)
Bee and Thistle Inn
Copper Beach
Mayflower

Lunch, For Ladies Who...
Asiana
Cremaillere
Jean-Louis
L'Escale
Elm Street Oyster House
Figaro
Morello Bistro
Mediterraneo
Rebecca's
Terra
The Drawing Room
Thomas Hinkelmann
Valbella
Versailles
Winfield's at the Hyatt

Lunch, Late (after 3 pm)
Asiana
Aux Délices Café (Riverside)
Beach House
Centro
City Limits
Cobble Stone
Douro
(the) Drawing Room
Elm Street Oyster
Ginger Man
Glory Days
Hunan Café
Katzenberg's Kafe
Kira Sushi
Le Pain Quotidien

RESTAURANTS by CATEGORY

(LUNCH, LATE continued...)
Little Thai Kitchen
Louie's
MacDuffs
MacKenzie's Grill
Meli-Melo
Mirage Café
Oriental Gourmet
Panda Pavillion 3
Penang
Polpo
Pomodoro
Putnam Restaurant
Rotisserie
Sundown Saloon
Terra
Thataway Café

Romantic
Bedford Post
Bernard's
Bistro Bonne Nuit
Elm's Restaurant
(Le) Château
(La) Crémaillère
Jean-Louis
L'Escale's terrace in the summer
(La) Pantiere
Polpo
Roger Sherman Inn
Thomas Henkelman
Valbella
Xavier's

TIP: GREENWICH CHAMBER OF COMMERCE

Residents of Greenwich have discovered that even if you are not the owner of an in-town business, membership in the Greenwich Chamber of Commerce is a wonderful way to be involved in our town. The Chamber has many interesting events such as the Business Roundtable, Lunch and Learn programs, and monthly fun get-togethers at local businesses. 45 East Putnam Avenue, Suite 121. 203.869.3500, www.greenwichchamber.com
Mary Ann Morrison, President

RESTAURANTS by NEIGHBORHOOD

Armonk, NY
Beehive
Mark Mariani's Garden Center Café

Banksville, NY
(La) Crémaillère

Bedford
Bedford Post
Meetinghouse

Byram
Burgers, Shakes & Fries
Garden Catering
Greenwich Lobster House
Little Thai Kitchen
Lolita Cocina

Cos Cob
Arcuri's
Chicken Joe's
Drawing Room
Dunkin' Donuts
Favorite Place
Fjord Sunday Brunch
Fonda La Paloma
Joey B's Chili Hub
Kato-Chan Ramen Stand
Nuage
Pizza Post
Robek's Smoothies
Starbucks

Darien
Melting Pot
Ole Mole
Ten Twenty Post
Wild Ginger Dumpling House

Glenville
Bambou Asian Restaurant
Centro Ristorante
Juice Bar Cafe
Pizza, Glenville
Rebecca's
Rodney's Roadhouse Lunch Wagon

Greenwich (Central)
Abis
Asiana Café
Aux Délices
Barcelona
Boxcar Cantina
Bruckner's
Cafeteria at Greenwich Hospital
China Pavillion
Cosi
Crew
Douro
Dunkin' Donuts
Elm Street Oyster House
Favorite Place
Figaro
Frank's Franks Lunch Wagon
Garden Café at Greenwich Hospital
Ginger Man
Glory Days
Greenwich Bagels
Hunan Gourmet
Jean-Louis
Katzenberg's Kafe
Kira Sushi
L'Escale
Le Pain Quotidien Restaurant
MacDuffs Public House
Mary & Martha's Café at the YWCA
McDonald's
Mediterraneo
Meli-Melo
Morello Bistro
Panda Pavilion 3
Pasta Vera

RESTAURANTS by NEIGHBORHOOD

(GREENWICH CENTRAL cont...)
Penang Grill
Pierangelo
Pizza Express
Pizza Factory
Planet Pizza
Polpo
Putnam Restaurant
Rasa
Rotisserie
Saito
Standing Room Only Lunch Wagon
Starbucks
Subway Sandwich
Sundown Saloon
Tengda Asian Bistro
Terra
Thai Basil
Thataway Café
Thomas Henkelmann
Versailles
Village Bagels
Wendy's

Hartsdale
Tsuru

Hyde Park, NY
Culinary Institute Restaurants:
  American Bounty
  Caterina de' Medici
  Escoffier

New Canaan, CT
Bistro Bonne Nuit
Cava Wine Bar and Restaurant
Ching's Table
Gates
Harvest Supper
Roger Sherman Inn
Tequilla Mockingbird
Thali

Norwalk, CT
Ash Creek Saloon
Barcelona
Brasitas
Brewhouse
Chocopologie
Coromandel
Goccia
Kazu
Lime
Match
Meigas
Ostera
Pasta Nostra
(la) Paella
Rio Border
Rouge
SoNo Caffeine
SoNo Baking Company & Cafe
SoNo Seaport Seafood
Valencia Luncheria
Wasabi Chi

Old Greenwich
Applausi Osteria
Arcadia Coffee Co
Beach House Café
Boston Market
Garden Catering
Greenwich Tavern
MacKenzie's Grill
Oriental Gourmet
Sophia's
Sound Beach Pizza Grill
Taco Bell
Upper Crust Bagel Co
Winfields at the Hyatt

Piermont, NY
Xaviar's

RESTAURANTS by NEIGHBORHOOD

Port Chester, NY
Albas
Applebee's
Buffalo Wild Wings
Café Brazil
Copacabana
Dougie's
Edo
Euro Asian
F.I.S.H
Frank's
Garden Caterering
Il Sogno Ristorante
Marinacci's
Mirage Café
Nessa
Panera
Pasquale
Patrias
Piero's
Q
Sonora
Tandoori
Tarry Lodge
Willett House

Pound Ridge
North Star

Purchase, NY
Cobble Stone
Creek

Riverside
Aux Délices
Baang
Hunan Café
McDonald's
Pomodoro
Starbucks
Valbella

Ridgefield
Bernard's
Elm's Restaurant

Rowayton, CT
Rowayton Seafood

Rye, NY
Morgan's Fish House
(La) Panetiere
Rye Grille and Bar

Rye Brook, NY
Doral Arrowwood Atrium

South Salem, NY
(Le) Château

Stamford, CT
Aria
Brasitas
(la) Bretagne
Café Silvium
California Pizza Kitchen
Capital Grille
Capriccio
Chez Jean Pierre
ChiliChicken
City Limits
Columbus Park Trattoria
Coromandel
Crab Shell

(STAMFORD continued...)
Duo
Eclisse
Eos
Ferrante
Habana
I-Hop
Kit's Thai Kitchen
Kona Grill
Layla's Falafel
Little Buddha
Long Ridge Tavern
Market Restaurant
Matteo's
Michell's Fish Market
Morton's The Steak House
Myrna's Mediterranean Bistro
Napa
Ole Mole
Paradise Bar & Grill
Pellicci's
P.F. Chang's China Bistro
Route 22
Salt Water Grill
SBC Pub
Siena
Smokey Joe's Bar-B-Q
Spazzio
Tabouli Grill
Tawa
Telluride
Thai Chi
Tigin
Top of the Hill
Villa Italia

Tarrytown, NY
Blue Hill at Stone Barns

White Plains, NY
(The) Cheesecake Factory
Outback
P.F. Chang's China Bistro
Sushi Nanase

Westport, CT
Dressing Room

Wilton, CT
School House Restaurant

Yonkers, NY
X20

RESTAURANT NOTES

Wine, Restaurant Economics and Corkage Fees

Corkage fees can run as high as $38 a bottle, so check the restaurant before you decide to bring your own bottle. Restaurant owners often depend on income from wine sales and those with an extensive wine selection want to discourage BYOB clients. Some restaurants reward servers with the highest beverage total per month. Software, like Avero (www.AveroInc.com), allows restaurants to track how often servers sell particular items like wine, dessert and specials (where they make more profit). The average restaurant charges 2.5 to 3 times the retail price of a bottle of wine in a wine store. Then they charge a quarter of the bottle price for a glass of that wine. There are about 5 glasses of wine in a 750ml bottle, depending upon the pour. The average pour is 5-6 ounces. Check www.Gobyo.com for the latest prices on corkage and wine by the glass (just enter the zip code).

Food Stores

Grocery stores, bakeries, delicatessens, ice cream, fruit & vegetables, butchers, seafood, spices, wine shops, chocolates, sweets and ethnic food markets are reviewed under FOOD & BEVERAGES.

TIP: WHERE TO FIND THE BEST PIZZA IN TOWN

Anderson Associates had a blind tasting of regular pizzas from twelve of our local pizza places. The winners of the best pizza in town were:

- Arcuri's, 226 East Putnam Avenue, Cos Cob, 203.869.6999
- Express Pizza, 160 Hamilton Avenue, 203.622.1693.
- Glenville Pizza, 243 Glenville Road, 203.531.9852 (no delivery)
- Pizza Post, 522 East Putnam Avenue, 203.661.0909 (no delivery).
- Sound Beach Pizza, 178 Sound Beach Avenue, 203.637.1085

See www.GreenwichGuide.com for details and articles on the tasting.

Abis (Japanese)

381 Greenwich Avenue, 203.862.9100

www.AbisJapanese.com

A restaurant with two personalities—one side traditional Japanese cuisine, the other an Hibachi steakhouse. In the steakhouse, youngsters have a wonderful time watching their hibachi meals being prepared. The other side offers more relaxed dining with a menu full of familiar choices, including a sushi bar, with a large selection. We are fans of their Japanese noodle dishes such as Udon or Soba. For lunch be sure to try their box lunch. If you like to indulge yourself with sushi and other Japanese delicacies, you will love the all-you-can-eat Sunday Brunch buffet.

Hours: Lunch, weekdays, 11:30 am - 2:30 pm; Saturday, noon - 2:30 pm; Sunday, 11:30 am - 2:30 pm; Dinner, weekdays, 5:30 pm - 9:30 pm (Friday until 10:30 pm); Saturday, 5 pm - 10:30 pm; Sunday, Brunch 11:30 am - 2:30 pm, Dinner 5 pm - 9:30 pm. Open most holidays, including Christmas and New Year's for dinner.

Prices: Sunday Brunch $23 per adult, $12 for children under 12; Lunch, Donburi & Noodle entrees $8 - $11, Lunch box $10 - $14, Hibachi $10 - $11; Dinner, Donburi & Noodle entrees $12 - $18, Habachi, $14 - $19; Hibachi children's menu, $13 - $15.

Size: Hibachi side has 10 cook tables, each seating 8; the traditional side seats 36.

Acuario (Latin American, Peruvian)

163 North Main Street, Port Chester NY, 914.937.2338

www.acuariorestaurant.com

If you like ceviche, this is a must-dine spot. Their large sign "Cevicheria Y Mas" makes this clear. As might be expected with the name Acuario, aquariums with pretty little fish, are the restaurant's main decorations. Not dressy, but certainly not your local dive. Even though there is a wide selection of Peruvian seafood and other entrees, we prefer to skip the entrees, and order the generous sized Ceviche, followed by their good flan. We especially like the Pescado Ceviche. If you order an entree, try the Pescado Saltado. The Peruvian soft drinks must be an acquired taste.

Hours: Open every day, noon - 10 pm

Prices: Ceviche $15 - $26; entrees $8 - $22.

Size: Seats 45.

RESTAURANTS

Albas (Italian)

400 North Main Street, Port Chester NY, 914.937.2236
www.AlbasRestaurant.com
The parking lot is always filled (we presume) with "regulars" who enjoy dining here. Our best experience was at a wine-tasting dinner party hosted by a regular. On our other visits we left un-impressed. Of all the dishes we tried, our favorite was the Ceasar salad for two, prepared at our table. The restaurant is being renovated now and we look forward to visiting again.
Hours: Lunch, weekdays, noon - 3 pm;
Dinner, weekdays, 5:30 pm - 10 pm; Saturday, 5:30 pm - 11 pm.
Prices: Lunch, pastas $18 - $21, other entrees $19 - $33; Dinner, pastas $19 - $22, other entrees, $20 - $34 (Caesar salad for two $20); Wine by the glass, $7 - $9, special wines start at $13 per glass.
Size: Seats 150.

Applausi Osteria (Italian)

199 Sound Beach Avenue, Old Greenwich, 203.637.4447
www.OsteriaApplausi.com
One of the three successful Marchetti-Tarantino family restaurants is located right in the heart of Old Greenwich. They own Columbus Park in Stamford and Tarantino's in Westport. Perfect for diners wishing to have a leisurely conversation and very good meal in a refined atmosphere. You will find lots of interesting choices, but with Maria still making most of the pastas, be sure to order a pasta like the one we had with artichokes and truffles.
Hours: Lunch, weekdays, noon - 2:30 pm;
Dinner, Monday - Saturday, 5:30 pm - 10 pm
(Friday & Saturday until 10:30 pm.)
Prices: Lunch entrees, $19 - $26;
Dinner pasta entrees $22 - $26, specialties $22 - $35.
Size: Seats up to 55.

266

RESTAURANTS

Applebee's (American)

42 Westchester Avenue (The Water Front), Port Chester NY
914.253.5358

www.Applebees.com

The franchise chain is owned by IHOP and has 1,900 locations. This casual restaurant has a "weight watchers" menu section, but for most people, dining healthy is not why they come here. Kids love the mini cheeseburgers or chicken fingers. Adults like the Cowboy burger with great onion rings and shakes or the Cajun Lime Tilapia. Applebee's is struggling to distinguish itself from the other "apostrophe-s" restaurants like Chili's or T.G.I. Friday's.

Hours: Every day, 11 am - midnight (Sunday to 11 pm.)
Prices: Burgers & sandwiches, $9 - $11, steaks $13 - $18;
kids menu, $5 -$6. Wine by the glass, $6 - $8.
Size: Seats 250.

Arcadia Coffee Company (Coffee Shop)

20 Arcadia Road, Old Greenwich, 203.637.8766

www.ArcadiaCoffee.com

"Let's meet at Arcadia." This is the local friendly coffee house where you can take your newspaper and relax with a good cup of coffee. Stop by early for a Croque Monsieur or Croissant for breakfast. Arcadia is the ideal place for a lite late lunch. The walls are decorated with works for sale by local artists. Arcadia is a venue for many author book discussions. Teenagers enjoy meeting here to listen to music performed by young-adult bands. Check the website for upcoming events. Arcadia is a popular place to rent for a private party.

Hours: Weekdays, 6:30 am - 4 pm; weekends, 7 am - 5 pm.
Prices: Breakfast $2 - $12; Lunch sandwiches $8 - $9, salads, $6 - $9.
Size: Seats about 50.

Arcuri's (Pizza)

226 East Putnam Avenue, Cos Cob, 203.869.6999

www.arcurispizza.com

Extensive selection of specialty pizzas. In the Anderson Pizza Contest, they came in only 7 votes behind the winner. They are well-known for their bountiful, hard-to-beat salads. We would skip the burgers.

Hours: Open every day from 11 am - 9:30 pm.
Prices: Specialty Pizzas (16") $14 - $18; large salads, $6 - $10.
Size: Seats about 20.

RESTAURANTS

Aria (Italian)
1033 Washington Blvd, Stamford CT, 203.324.2742
With a flower on each table and white cloths, the decor is stylish and sets the right mood for a pleasant meal. You will not be disappointed. Even the ordinary menu items, such as lentil soup, can be quite special. One flaw - some portions are piccolo. Aria is a relatively new restaurant, their hours and prices may change.
Hours: Lunch, weekdays noon - 3 pm;
Dinner, every night, 5 pm - 10 pm (Saturday to 11:30 pm.)
Prices: Lunch, salads $8 - $14, sandwiches & wraps $15 - $17, pasta $14 - $20, other entrees $19 - $30; Dinner, pasta $15 - $21, risotto $18 - $21, other entrees $24 - $35.
Size: Seats 60, party area seats 10.

Ash Creek Saloon (South Western)
2 Wilton Avenue, Norwalk CT, 203.847.7500
www.AshCreekSaloon.com
We are willing to travel a distance from Greenwich for a fun experience. When we went to Ash Creek Saloon, we were certainly glad we had made a reservation. This very large restaurant was packed with families and folks of all ages. Ash Creek has transformed what was formerly a hat factory into an informal, nostalgic, cowboy-style restaurant. Even with the large number of tables, the service was quick and friendly. The portions were large. The food may not be completely authentic Texas, or even Oklahoma, but it was still delicious. Where else can you find Chicken Fried Steak? The BBQ beef brisket and ribs are also winners.
Hours: Open everyday, Sunday - Thursday, 11:30 am - 10 pm; Friday and Saturday until 10:30 pm.
Prices: Sandwiches $8 - $15, Barbecues $16 - $28,
Other Entrees $17-$28, Buckaroos menu (12 and under) all selections $8.
Size: Seats 180.

RESTAURANTS

Asiana Cafe (Asian)

130 East Putnam Avenue, Greenwich, 203.622.6833

www.AsianaCafe.com

Ready for a savory twist on Pan Asian food? Like their cousin, Penang Grill, don't expect their dishes (Vietnamese, Chinese, Thai and Japanese) to be like you have had in other restaurants. The Szechuan spicy beef is oh-so-good. They also make great satay, tempura shrimp and papaya salad. The helpings are generous and the service attentive. The atmosphere is minimalist modern. In the summer you can dine outside.

Hours: Monday - Thursday, 10:30 am - 10 pm; Friday & Saturday, 1:30 am - 11 pm; Sunday, 11:30 am - 10 pm. Lunch served to 3:30 pm, except on Sunday when the dinner menu is served all day.

Closed most major holidays.

Prices: Lunch, Classic Maki lunch $10, sushi rolls $12 - $14, classic rolls $9 - $10; Dinner, contempo and classic entrees $15 - $23, sushi $17 - $30. Take-out menu slightly less expensive.

Size: Seats 140 inside, about 32 outside.

Aux Délices (Delicatessen, French-American)

- 1075 East Putnam Avenue, Riverside, 203.698.1066
- 3 West Elm, Greenwich, 203.622.6644

For delivery orders call 203.326.4540 x 115 or 101

www.AuxDelicesFoods.com

Provençal-style food with an American twist prepared under the direction of talented Chef Debra Ponzek. Delicious gourmet take-away food. Both locations have a few tables, so grab one for a quick breakfast or late lunch. They also have excellent hors d'oeuvres. In our 2005 Hors D'Oeuvres Tasting Contest they received top scores. They have a weekday home delivery service and will deliver your order even when you are not home, properly packaged to keep the food at the correct temperature.

Greenwich Hours: weekdays, 7 am - 6:30 pm; Saturday, 8 am - 6:30 pm; Sunday, 9 am - 4 pm.

Riverside Hours: Monday - Saturday, 7 am - 6:30 pm;
Sunday, 7:30 am - 5 pm.

Prices: Lunch, salads $7 - $10, entrees $6 - $12;
Dinner, entrees $9.50 - $30.

Size: Greenwich location seats 8, mostly take-out; Riverside seats 13+.

RESTAURANTS

Baang Café (Asian Fusion)

1191 East Putnam Avenue, Riverside, 203.637.2114
www.DecaroRestaurantGroup.com

Just because they can't hear you when you call in for a reservation and the wait staff has learned to lip read, doesn't keep this noisy, lively, starkly modern restaurant from continuing to be popular. It is less noisy around 6:30, but the volume turns up steadily through the evening as the younger crowd arrives. The rare tuna, crispy spinach and grilled Shanghai beef are all very good and beautifully presented. Appetizers & entrees are generous and meant to be shared.

Hours: Lunch, weekdays noon 2:30 pm;
Dinner, Monday - Thursday 6 pm - 10 pm,
Friday & Saturday 6 pm - 11 pm, Sunday 5:30 pm - 9 pm.
Prices: Lunch Bento boxes $20, Light Bites $10 - $16;
Dinner entrees $23 - $33; Sunday prix fix menu, $35;
Wine by the glass $11 - $14.
Size: Inside seats 76, outside seats about 12.

Bambou Asian Restaurant (Asian, Japanese)

328 Pemberwick Road (@ the Mill in Glenville), 203.531.3322
www.BambouRestaurant.com

Tucked inside the Mill, is a unique Japanese restaurant—a treat for the eye and the pallet. The entrees are presented with artistic flair. The decor is sophisticated. The service is attentive. We recommend the mango jicama salad and sweet potato tempura roll.

Hours: Lunch, weekdays, Noon - 3 pm;
Dinner, Monday - Thursday, 5 pm - 10 pm,
Friday and Saturday until 11 pm, Sunday 5 pm to 9:30 pm.
Prices: Lunch, entrees $8 - $16, sushi, 2 rolls for $11, 3 for $15;
Dinner, entrees $16 - $30, sushi, special rolls $13 - $20,
regular & vegetable rolls $4 - $14; Wine by the glass $8 - $12.
Size: Seats 36 in front room, 28 in back room.

RESTAURANTS

Barcelona (Spanish)
- 63 North Main Street, South Norwalk, CT, 203.899.0088
- 222 Summer Street, Stamford CT, 203.348.4800
- 18 West Putnam Avenue, Greenwich, 203.983.6400

www.BarcelonaWinebar.com

We first enjoyed this authentic tapas restaurant near the SoNo theaters in Norwalk. It's still there, so you can have fun in Norwalk, Stamford or in Greenwich. The Greenwich bar is lively. There is an excellent wine list, with over 30 wines by the glass. We love the tapas and the service. Try the mouth-watering gambas, the empanadas, scallops, asparagus and potato tortilla.

Greenwich Hours: Lunch, weekdays, noon - 3 pm;
Dinner, Sunday -Thursday, 5 pm -10 pm (Friday & Saturday, to 11 pm.)
Bar may stay open later. Closed on major holidays.
Greenwich Prices: Lunch, sandwiches $7 - $9, tapas $4-$10, Salads $9-$14, entrees, $15 - $23; Dinner, entrees, $20 - $26; tapas $4 - $12;
Wine by the glass, $7 - $21.
Greenwich Size: Seats 110, private room seats 50.

Beach House Café (American)

220 Sound Beach Avenue, Old Greenwich, 203.637.0367
www.BeachHouseCafe.com

The decor is light, bright, cheerful and comfortable. A large portion of the restaurant is devoted to a bar populated by a sophisticated, youthful crowd. Food is served continuously from noon on, making it a good choice for a late lunch or early dinner. The service is friendly. Live music on Friday and Saturday evenings after 10 pm.

Hours: Monday - Saturday, 11 am - 10 pm (bar open till about midnight);
Sunday, 11 am - 9 pm.
Prices: Lunch, entrees $13 - $17, sandwiches $11 - $17; Dinner, entrees $19 - $32, sandwiches $13 - $19; Wine by the glass, $7 - $10.
Size: Seats 80.

RESTAURANTS

Bedford Post (American)

954 Old Post Road, Bedford NY, 914.234.7800
www.BedfordPostInn.com

If celebrity sightings delight you, have fun and a fine meal in Richard Gere's Post restaurants. In a beautiful country setting, with first-class rustic design, the Post is divided into two restaurants. The Barn serves casual food in a casual atmosphere from a limited menu. Excellent service and toothsome food. It even has a yoga studio. The Farmhouse is simple but elegant. The service is attentive and very gracious. The food is good to excellent, depending upon the dish—the variation may be the result of changing the menu so often. Ask for a table near the window. The Post has eight lovely guest rooms ranging from $400 to $550 a night.

Hours for The Barn Café; Breakfast, weekdays 8:30 am - 10:30 pm;
Lunch, Monday - Saturday, 11:30 am - 2:30 pm;
Supper, Sunday - Tuesday, 5:30 pm - 8:30 pm.
Hours for the Farmhouse Restaurant: Sunday Brunch, 9 am - 3 pm;
Dinner, Wednesday - Saturday, 5:30 pm - 10 pm.
Barn Prices: Brunch & Breakfast, $9 - $15, kids $8; Lunch Pre-fixe, $19, casual entrees, $12 - $20; supper entrees, $13 - $26, sides, $6, kids, $6
Farmhouse prices: Dinner, Pastas $15 - $17, main courses $32 - $45, tasting menus $95 or $150 with wine; Wine by the glass, $11 - $15.
Size: Barn seats 48; Farmhouse seats 60 plus a private room for 20-40.

Beehive (American)

30 Old Route 22 (Kaysal Court), Armonk NY, 914.765.0688

For those in northwest Greenwich, Armonk is only 15 minutes away. The large menu with large servings of American, Greek & Italian dishes makes this casual place popular. Their pastry chef turns out creative concoctions, like baklava sundaes. Though slightly worn on the edges, this does not seem to matter to the loyal following.

Hours: Open every day for lunch and dinner;
Monday - Saturday, 11 am - 9 pm (Friday and Saturday to 10 pm);
Sunday, Brunch 9 am - 2 pm, Lunch and dinner to 9 pm.
Prices: Sunday brunch $9 - $17, children $5; same menu for lunch & dinner: Small plates $9 - $14, sandwiches, wraps & burgers $9 - $15, entrees $18 - $30; Children's menu $7 - $14; Wine by the glass $8.
Size: Seats 24 in the front, 32 in the back.

RESTAURANTS

Bernard's (French)

20 West Lane, Ridgefield CT, 203.438.8282

www.BernardsRidgefield.com

We wish it were closer. While Chef/Owner Bernard Bouissou works his magic culinary skills, his wife, Sarah, greets and charms their guests. The menu varies with the season. On one occasion there was a large selection of truffle dishes and game meats - elk, buffalo, antelope. It is certainly worth a trip for special occasions or a romantic dinner. Piano music, fresh flowers, and the attractive inn-style dining room set the mood. The service is sweet, but not as polished as one would expect.

Hours: Sunday Brunch, noon - 2:30 pm;

Lunch, Tuesday - Saturday, noon - 2:30;

Dinner, Tuesday - Saturday, 6 pm - 9 pm (Friday & Saturday to 10 pm);

Sunday, 5 pm - 8 pm.

Prices: Brunch $35; Lunch, salads $17 - $29, entrees $14 - $24;

Dinner entrees $26 - $38; children's menu entrees $10 - $15;

Wine by the glass $9 - $10.

Size: Seats 80.

Bistro Bonne Nuit (French)

12 Forest Street, New Canaan CT, 203.966.5303

http://www.culinarymenus.com/bistrobonnenuit.htm

White tablecloths and fresh flowers give a dressy flair to this intimate bistro, where you feel like you are having a happy night out in France. The unpretentious, caring service plus the good food would make Julia Child smile. She would have loved their cassoulet, as well as many of their typical French dishes. We do, too.

Hours: Monday - Thursday, 5:30 pm - 9 pm;

Friday & Saturday, 5:30 - 10 pm; Sunday, 5:30 pm - 8 pm.

Prices: Monday - Thursday pre-fixe $40; Dinner entrees $28 - $46;

Wine by the glass, $9 - $25.

Size: Seats 60.

Blue Hill at Stone Barns (New American)

630 Bedford Road, Pocantico Hills, Tarrytown NY, 914.366.9600
www.BlueHillStoneBarns.com; www.BlueHillFarm.com
By all means worth the trip. This unique restaurant was converted from a stone barn once owned by the Rockefellers. It is surrounded by a working farm which provides many of the ingredients, which are picked fresh each day. Top chefs are in the kitchen creating innovative cuisine. You need to make a reservation. Arrive early so you can take a walk around the pretty grounds. The dress code is business casual.
Hours: Closed Monday & Tuesday; Lunch, Sunday, 11:30 am - 2 pm; Dinner Sunday, Wednesday & Thursday 5 pm to 10 pm, Friday & Saturday until 11 pm.
Prices: Dinner, 5 course tasting $105, Farmers feast $135; Sunday lunch four course tasting $68; Wine by the glass $10 - $24.
Size: Seats 75 in the main dining room, 64 in the private dining room.

Boston Market (Fast Food)

1345 East Putnam Avenue, Old Greenwich, 203.637.4088
www.BostonMarket.com
Homestyle cooking in a fast-food setting.
Hours: every day 11 am - 9 pm.

Boxcar Cantina (Southwestern)

44 Old Field Point Road, 203.661.4774
www.BoxcarCantina.com
Popular, informal, and child friendly, this restaurant is an incredible hit in town. It was conceived as an homage to all of the Route 66 Cantinas of the Southwest, serving a mix of high quality, ultra-fresh Mexican and Southwestern food. We are hooked on their posole soup and Mexican pizza. Choose one of the festive margaritas.
Hours: Lunch, weekdays 11:30 am - 3 pm;
Dinner, weekdays 5:30 pm - 9:30 pm;
Friday and Saturday, 5:30 pm - 10:30 pm; Sunday, 4:30 pm - 9 pm.
Reservations are accepted only for large parties.
On Friday and Saturday nights, be sure to arrive early.
Prices: Lunch entrees (salads, quesadillas, tacos, burritos, burgers) $5 - $15; Dinner entrees $12- $22; Wine by the glass $8 - $10.
Size: Seats 94.

RESTAURANTS

Brasitas (Latin American)

- 954 East Main Street, Stamford CT, 323.3176
- 430 Main Avenue, Norwalk CT, 203.354.7329

www.Brasitas.com

Without Linda and Don saying we must meet under the plastic palms, we would never have discovered this funky, fun, thriving Stamford restaurant. It is the kind of place you would pass if you didn't know. We are not the first to discover it. Their valet parking lot is full of sports cars. *Connecticut Magazine* "Readers Choice" awarded both Brasitas locations The Best Latin American in Fairfield County. You must make a reservation. Whether you order the coconut shrimp or fried red snapper, you are sure to be delighted. As you sip your Mojitos and Margaritas you will forget you are on the Post Road.

Prices: Lunch entrees, $12 - $18; Dinner entrees, $19 - $27.

Wine by the glass, $8 - $12. 20% gratuity added to tables of 6 or more.

Hours: Monday - Thursday, 11 am - 10 pm;

Friday & Saturday, 11 am - 11 pm; Sunday, 12:30 pm - 10 pm.

Dinner begins at 4 pm.

Size: Stamford location seats 55 - 60

       Norwalk seats 50 and has a private room for 20.

(La) Bretagne (French)

2010 West Main Street (US-1 just across the Greenwich border) Stamford, CT, 203.324.9539

For a restaurant to stay in business for more than 30 years, they have to offer consistently good food and pleasant hospitality. The interior is dimly lit and eating here is like taking a step back in time. The dishes are traditional French. The staff is attentive and formally attired. This may be a good choice for entertaining aunts, uncles and parents.

Hours: Lunch, Monday - Saturday, noon - 2:30 pm;

Dinner, Monday - Saturday, 6 pm - 9:30 pm; Closed Sunday.

Prices: Lunch, salad $12 - $14, entrees $17 - $22;

Dinner entrees $22 - $40, wine by the glass $9 - $10.

Size: Main area seats 60, adjoining room also seats 60.

Bruckner's (Fast-Food, Vegetarian)

1 Grigg Street, 203.422.6300   www.Bruckners.com

Just off the Avenue, this friendly, small restaurant has quick service and tasty, healthy wraps and soups. It is the "in" place for a good takeout . We dash in here all the time. A few tables are also available. The owner/chef Richard Fertig has an impressive ability to spice his food just right. They have excellent vegetarian/vegan food.

Hours: Monday - Thursday 8 am - 4 pm; Friday 8 - 3 pm;
Saturday 10 am - 3 pm.
Prices: sandwiches, $7 - $9. Size: Seats 12.

Brewhouse (Pub -German/American)

13 Marshall Street, South Norwalk CT, 203.853.9110
www.SoNoBrewHouse.com

When you feel like a casual evening in a friendly, informal restaurant, this is the place. Reminiscent of an upscale German beer hall, this large, comfortable restaurant attracts the young and the young at heart. There is a nice selection of casual foods on the menu, and a large selection of beers. Try the beer burger or wiener schnitzel. The seafood chowder is a winner as is the apple strudel (order in advance as it takes 20 minutes).

Hours: Sunday Brunch, 11 am - 3 pm; Lunch, Monday - Saturday 11:30 am - 5 pm; Dinner, Monday 5 pm - 9 pm, Tuesday - Thursday, 5 pm - 10 pm; Friday & Saturday, 5 pm - 11 pm; Sunday, 4 pm - 9 pm.
Prices: Lunch, quick combos $9 - $14, salads $9 - $15, sandwiches $9 - $19, entrees $10 - $14;
Dinner, salads & sandwiches $12 - $15, entrees, $16 - $24;
Wine by the glass $7 - $10, draft beer $5 - $7; children's menu $5 - $7.
Size: 250 downstairs, 250 upstairs (usually for a party) & 22 outside.

Buffalo Wild Wings (American)

44 Westchester Avenue (The Water Front), Port Chester NY, 914.690.9453 www.BuffaloWildWings.com

A sports bar chain located at the movie theater complex. Buffalo Wild Wings (commonly referred to as B-Dubs, BWW, B2W or BW3) has 550 locations. Best-known for buffalo-style chicken wings and its 14 signature sauces.

Hours: Everyday noon - 11 pm; Maybe later on Friday & Saturday.
Prices: 12 wings $9.
Size: Seats 200.

Burgers, Shakes & Fries (Hamburgers)

302 Delavan Avenue, Byram, 203.531.7433
www.BurgersShakesnFries.com
Winner of the Anderson competition for the best burger in town, this small, corner burger place, will bring back happy childhood memories. In the tasting contest everyone felt the burger was cooked just right. They liked it being served on toast. Many felt "the french fries and onion rings are divine" and " It is worth the crazy wait". Reasonable prices, too.
Hours: Lunch, Monday - Saturday, 11:30 am - 3 pm
(Friday & Saturday to 4:30 pm);
Dinner, Monday - Saturday, 4:30 - 8 pm (Friday & Saturday to 9:30)
Prices: burger $3.77, toppings $ 0.57 to $1.50, fries $2.50.
No credit or debit cards.
Size: Seats 20, mostly take-out.

Cafe Brazil (Latin American - Brazilian Food)

37-39 North Main Street, Port Chester NY, 914.939.1139
A small, informal help-yourself buffet. You pay by the pound, but count on exceptionally good value. Have fun discovering Brazilian dishes. Don't miss the barbecued meat or Brazil's national dish (Feijoada) a black bean stew of beans and pork. The flan and coconut balls are yummy. If you don't know what to choose ask the staff. They are sweet and helpful.
Hours: Monday - Saturday, 7 am - 8 pm; Sunday, 7 am - 6 pm.
Size: Seats 20 inside and about the same outside.

Café Silvium (Italian)

371 Shippan Avenue, Stamford CT, 203.324.1651
www.cafeSilvium.com
This is one of those modest restaurants easy to pass by. But once inside, the waiters are accommodating and the southern Italian food is good and servings generous. Our favorite is Scaloppine al Gorgonzola. They accept reservations on the weekend for parties of 5 or more.
Hours: Lunch, weekdays noon - 2:30 pm;
Dinner, Monday - Thursday, 5 pm - 10 pm
(Friday and Saturday to 11 pm).
Prices: Dinner entrees $15 - $22, wine by the glass $7.
Size: seats 60.

Cafeteria at Greenwich Hospital (American)

5 Perryridge Rd (ground floor of the Helmsley Pavillion), 203.863.3000

The food is simple, freshly-prepared and satisfying. The portions are generous and well-priced. It is a real find for someone on a limited budget.

Hours: Open everyday, Breakfast, 6:30 am - 10:45 am;
Lunch, 11:30am - 2:30pm; Dinner, 3:30 pm - midnight.

Prices: Entree with two vegetables, $7 (30% off for seniors).

California Pizza Kitchen (Pizza)

230 Tresser Blvd at The Stamford Town Center, Stamford CT, 203.406.0530

www.CPK.com, www.CPKtakeout.com

One of five featured restaurants at the Town Center. Started in Beverly Hills CA in 1985, the chain has over 230 locations. The chain is known for its innovative pizzas, such as BBQ Chicken, BLT, Thai Chicken, and Jamaican Jerk Chicken. Bigger and more stylish than the normal pizza parlor, it is our choice when we are shopping at the Mall with kids and need to relax. The Children's menu - an activity book - has lots of kid friendly foods to keep them happy while we enjoy a salad or Neapolitan (thin crust) pizza. Skip the desserts.

Hours: Monday - Saturday, 11:30 am - 10 pm
(Friday & Saturday to 11 pm); Sunday, 11:30 am - 9 pm.

Prices: Pizzas $11 - $14, Salads $9 - $15; Children's Menu $5.50.

Size: Seats 50 plus.

(The) Capital Grille (Steak)

Stamford Town Center, 230 Tresser Blvd., Stamford CT
203.967.0000

www.TheCapitalGrille.com

We appreciate good service, but the staff here is so attentive—constantly asking how you like it, describing food in detail and sharing little stories—it borders on intrusive. The tender, cooked just right steak, the mahogany clubby atmosphere and valet parking make this an easy place to entertain. It has a huge wine list, as well as wine lockers for frequent visitors to rent for their private supply.

Hours: Lunch, weekdays, 11:30 am - 3 pm, bar is open to 5 pm;
Dinner, Monday - Saturday, 5 pm - 10 pm, Friday & Saturday, to 11 pm, Sunday, 4 pm - 9 pm.

Prices: Lunch, Entree Salads $13 - $17, Sandwiches $13 - $17; Dinner, Appetizers $15 - $96, Entrees $31 - $45, Sides $8 - $14. Half Bottle of wine, $25 - $175. Captains wine list, bottle $55 - $795. Free valet parking. Size: Seats 200, including three private dining rooms.

Capriccio (Italian)

189 Bedford Street, Stamford CT, 203.356.9819

www.Capriccio-Cafe.com

A popular, casual café. Terrific desserts including gelato, to die for. Our favorite is the hazelnut. Unfortunately they are not well equipped for gelato takeout.

Hours: Every day, 11 am - 11 pm, (Friday & Saturday until midnight.)

Prices: Panini & Piadine $7 - $8, Pizza $7 - $11, Pasta, $11 - $15, Entrees $13 - $18; Gelato $5; Wine by the glass $7 - $9.

Size: Seats 24 on each side, plus outside seating for 120 in the summer.

Cava Wine Bar & Restaurant (Italian)

2 Forest Street, New Canaan CT, 203.966.6946

www.CavaWineBar.com

Entering this just-below street level, brick-faced space you have the feeling of dining in a private wine cellar (albeit a large one.) This is the place to go when you want to relax, unwind, have a good glass of wine and a pleasant meal.

Hours: Lunch, Monday - Saturday, 11:30 pm to 3 pm;
Dinner, Monday - Saturday 5 pm - 10 pm, Sunday 5 pm - 9 pm;

Prices: Lunch, salads $7 - $14, pasta $11 - $18, Panini $10 - $14, entrees $13 - $16; Dinner, pizza $13 - $16; pasta $18 - $28; entrees $23 - $33; Wine by the glass $7 - $16. Size: Seats 60.

Centro Ristorante (Italian)

323 Pemberwick Road (at The Mill), Glenville, 203.531.5514
www.CentroRistorante.com

Bright, cheery, and popular with an unpretentious atmosphere. Just right when you hunger for pizzas or homemade pastas and a glass of wine from their extensive list. We wouldn't recommend their burgers. Request the outdoor patio overlooking the waterfall and order their Ravioli Centro. Some of our friends go just for the desserts. Child-friendly with crayons and a kid's menu.

Hours: Lunch, Monday - Saturday 11:30 am - 3 pm; pizzas & light fare, Monday - Saturday 3 pm - 5 pm; Dinner, Monday - Saturday 5 pm - 10 pm, Sunday 5 pm - 9:30 pm.

Prices: Lunch salads $10 - $14, sandwiches $8 - $13, pasta and pizzas $10 - $13; Dinner entrees $16 - $24; Kids menu $4 - $9;
Wine by the glass $8 - $9.

Size: Seats 120 inside & 50 on the patio.

(Le) Château (French)

Junction of Routes 35 and 123, South Salem NY, 914.533.6631
www.LeChateauNY.com

A spacious, elaborate restaurant about thirty minutes from Greenwich, on the grounds of the 32-acre, 1907 J.P. Morgan estate. It is perfect if you are wishing for a romantic setting for a large party, wedding reception or just a night out with a close friend. The food is classic French. Be sure to order the soufflé early.

Hours: Closed Monday and some holidays including New Year's Day; Sunday brunch, noon - 3 pm; Dinner, Tuesday - Friday 5:30 pm - 9 pm, Saturday 6 pm - 9:30 pm, Sunday, 4 pm - 9 pm. Reservations in advance are a must, as is a jacket and tie.

Prices: Sunday Brunch $38 ($17 for children);
Dinner, prefix menu $46 - $95 (not available on holidays);
entrees $32 - $41; Wine by the glass $11.

Size: Main dining room seats 175; private party rooms: JP Morgan room seats 50, Rainsford room seats 50, Salem room seats 20.

(The) Cheesecake Factory (American)

One Maple Avenue

(at The Westchester Mall), White Plains, NY,

914.683.5253 www.TheCheesecakeFactory.com

With over 160 restaurants across the US, you've likely had the experience and know that a 20-40 minute wait to be seated is standard (beepers are assigned.) With a 14-page menu, expect to find something to please everyone. Plan to share because the portions are big. Appetizers are large enough for a meal. We like the avocado eggrolls and the sweet corn tamale cakes. The decor is elaborate Cleopatra. The service is quick and attentive. You can buy one of their 30 cheesecakes in the bakery. I wish we liked them. Amazingly, there is no children's menu.

Hours: Sunday Brunch 10 am - 2 pm;

Lunch, Monday - Saturday, 11:30 am - 4pm;

Dinner, Monday - Saturday 4pm - 11pm

(Friday and Saturday to 12:30 am,) Sunday 2pm - 11pm.

Prices: Sunday Brunch $8 - $16;Lunch specials, $9 - $14;

Dinner, appetizers $8 - $12, burgers $9 - $14,

entrees (specialties) $11 - $32; Wine by the glass $7 - $13;

cheesecakes from the bakery 6" (serves 4 - 6) $16 - $19,

7" (serves 6 - 8) $20 - $28, 10" (serves 12 - 15) $43 - $50.

Size: Seats 390.

Chez Jean-Pierre (French)

188 Bedford Street, Stamford CT, 203.357.9526

www.ChezJeanPierre.com

Classic French dishes are still the mode in this slightly dowdy Paris-style restaurant. In warm weather, dine on the sidewalk or choose a seat in the main dining room. The rear room has no ambiance. Unfortunately, the food is inconsistent. The escargots are often an excellent choice as is the duck l'orange. We recommend skipping the desserts. They have a wide selection of wines by the glass.

Hours: Lunch, Monday - Thursday, noon - 2:30 pm;

Dinner, Monday - Thursday, 6 pm 10 pm

(Friday, Saturday to 10:30 pm, Sunday to 9:30 pm);

Closed Memorial Day, Christmas & New Year's & Labor Day.

Prices: Lunch entrees $12 - $28; Dinner entrees $25 - $30;

Wine by the glass $8 - $15.

Size: Seats 42 in the main dining room & 25 in the rear private room.

RESTAURANTS

ChiliChicken (Chinese)
19 High Ridge Road, Stamford CT, 203.977.0400/0450
www.ChiliChickenCT.com
This small, attractive, out-of-the way restaurant is named for its signature Hakka dish Chili Chicken. They serve Chinese (primarily Hakka) dishes adapted to Indian tastes. Not all dishes are spicy, but most are, and we like them.
Hours: Lunch weekdays, noon - 3 pm. Dinner, weekdays, 5 pm - 10 pm; Weekends, noon - 10 pm.
Prices: $9 - $14; kids menu $3 - $4; wine by the glass $7.
Size: seats 36

Ching's Table (Asian Fusion)
64 Main Street, New Canaan CT, 203.972.2830
www.ChingsRestaurant.com
This is a popular New Canaan restaurant. The service is attentive and the food equally good. It was rated the best Chinese restaurant in the country by Chinese Restaurant News. We like the wonton seaweed soup, Vietnamese salad, Pad Thai with shrimp, lemon grass chicken, glazed ginger duck and wok beef tenderloin. On busy nights, consider takeout if you can't get a reservation.
Hours: Open every day for lunch and dinner except major holidays; Sunday noon - 10 pm;
Lunch, Monday - Saturday, 11:30 am - 3 pm; Dinner,
Monday-Thursday 3 pm - 10 pm, Friday & Saturday, 3 pm - 11 pm.
Prices: Lunch entrees, $10 - $14; Dinner entrees, $15 - $24; on Sunday the dinner menu is served all day; Wine by the glass $8 - $13.
Size: Seats 60.

Chicken Joe's (Fast Food)
231 East Putnam Avenue, Cos Cob, 203.861.0075, 203.861.0099.
www.OriginalChickenJoes.com
Great fried chicken, chicken bits, french fries, potato cones and onion rings. When you are hankering for grandma's fried chicken, head here. Toddlers, teens and adults love it. They have a huge selection of wraps, salads and specialty sandwiches, too.
Hours: Weekdays 6 am - 6 pm; Saturday 6 am - 4:30 pm;
Sunday 8 am - 2:30 pm.
Prices: 2 piece fried chicken platter (w/french fries) $5.50, 2 piece breast platter $8, pound chicken nuggets, $5.50,
Size: Strictly takeout, although there are four stools.

RESTAURANTS

(The) China Pavillion (Chinese)
374 Greenwich Avenue, 203.629.3332, 203.629.9333
This low-cost, Chinese fast food has been a fixture on Greenwich Avenue since the 1980s.
Hours: Monday - Saturday, Lunch 11 am - 4 pm,
Dinner 4 pm - 10:30 pm; Sunday Noon - 10:30 pm.
Prices: Lunch combination plates $6.25;
Dinner, combination plates $7 - $9, Chef's specials $10 - $11.
Size: Seats 26, but most the business is take-out.

Chocopologie (American)
12 South Main Street, South Norwalk CT, 203.838.3131
www.Chocopologie.com
If chocolate is your passion, go to this small restaurant in the front of the Knipschildt's chocolate factory. When our tasting experts, Matthew and Cameron, gave it thumbs up, we knew Chocopoligie would be a hit. The menu includes soups, salads, quiches, omelets, as well as a variety of savory crepes and great hot chocolate and devine chocolate desserts. Try their crepe with strawberries in green peppercorn jus and "chocolate love" for dessert or stop by to bring home some luscious chocolates.
Hours: Wednesday, 11 am - 9 pm; Thursday 11 am - 10 pm,
Friday & Saturday, 11 am - midnight; Sunday, 11:30 am - 5 pm.
Closed Monday & Tuesday.
Prices: entrees $5 - $20, desserts $6 - $15.
Size: Seats 20 in front+14 bar stools to see the factory while you eat.

City Limits Diner (American Diner, Bakery)
135 Harvard Avenue (at La Quinta), Stamford CT, 203.348.7000
www.citylimitsdiner.com   www.livanosrestaurantgroup.com
"A restaurant, disguised as a diner." This large restaurant, with its whimsical decor, serves upscale casual and comfort food. Their bread, pasteries and ice cream are made in-house. Try their chicken-corn quesadilla, corned beef hash, shrimp or curry chicken wrap and Valrhona chocolate pudding. For a good early morning breakfast (orange-lemon waffles or country breakfast) or a late-night meal head here. They are rated one of the best breakfasts in Fairfield County.
Hours: Open every day, Breakfast menu starts at 7am and runs all day;
Lunch menu from 11 am - 4 pm; Dinner, Sunday - Thursday 5pm - 11pm;
Friday & Saturday until midnight.
Prices: Breakfast $8 - $17; Lunch and dinner, wraps, sandwiches and burgers, $7 - $16; entrees, $14 - $26; Children's menu $4 - $13; Wine by the glass $7 - $10.
Size: Seats 160 in the main area; private room seats 100.

Cobble Stone (American)

620 Anderson Hill Road, Purchase NY, 914.253.9678
www.Cobblestone-TheCreek.com
Open since 1933, this informal, pub-style restaurant is more than just a
college hang-out. It's a good choice before a SUNY event. It has been
owned and run by five generations of the same family. Try the onion
soup or one of their many hamburgers. For dessert, have their Oreo
cookie madness. On SUNY performance evenings, be sure to reserve.
Hours: Sunday brunch 11:30 am - 3 pm;
Lunch, Monday - Saturday 11:30 am - 5 pm, Sunday, 3pm - 5pm;
Dinner, Sunday - Wednesday 5 pm - 8 pm,
Thursday - Saturday, 5 pm - 9 pm; Late night menu until midnight.
Prices: Brunch, $8 - $12; Lunch Salad $5 - $10,
sandwiches & burgers $8 - $10, entrees $11 - $13;
Dinner burgers and sandwiches $8 - $10, entrees $14 - $19;
children's menu $6; Wine by the glass $5 - $6.
Size: Seats 80.

Columbus Park Trattoria (Italian)

205 Main Street (Washington Blvd), Stamford CT, 203.967.9191
www.ColumbusParkTrattoria.com
The owners of this restaurant (Marchetti-Tarantino) own the Osteria
Applausi in Old Greenwich. As you might expect, they have perfected
good service and good pasta. A fall specialty, Pumpkin Ravioli, is to-
tally terrific! Though the restaurant is attractive, the tables are close so
you may be rubbing shoulders with your neighbor. Parking may be a
challenge. The Columbus Park area is a mecca for restaurants.
Ask about their summer Young Chef's Cooking camp.
Hours: Lunch, weekdays, Noon - 2:30 pm;
Dinner, Monday - Thursday, 5 pm - 10 pm
(Friday & Saturday until 11 pm.)
Prices: Lunch entrees $18 - $35, Dinner entrees $19 - $35;
Wine by the glass $9 - $20.
Size: Downstairs seats 50; private dining room upstairs seats 65.

RESTAURANTS

Cosi (Fast Food)

129 West Putnam Road, 203.861.2373, Catering: 203.861.2674
www.GetCosi.com
Pronounced Cozy, a restaurant popular in Manhattan, has found its niche
in Greenwich. Kids love the S'mores desserts. Lots of room to sit down,
good pizzas, soup, salad and sandwiches. There are more than 140
restaurants in the US. The name comes from the opera Cosi Fan Tutte
which was a favorite of the original owner.
Hours: Monday - Saturday, 7 am 11 pm; Sunday 7 am -9 pm.
Prices: sandwiches & melts $6 - $7, pizza (7.5 ") $7 - $8,
children's menu $5.
Size: Seats 58.

Copacabana (Latin American/Brazilian Steak House)

29 North Main Street, Port Chester NY, 914.939.6894
www.CopacabanaPortChester.com
This steak house - called a churrascaria - is all about meat. You can
choose from 12 cuts of meat. It is based on a Brazilian tradition of
serving meat right off the cooking skewer and carving it individually at
each table (Rodizio.) The salad bar has lots of choices to accompany the
meat. Upscale in appearance with a helpful staff, this makes a fun night
out with carnivore friends. Copacabana has live jazz on Friday nights
and live Bossa Nova on Saturday nights.
Hours: Tuesday - Thursday, noon - 10 pm; Friday and Saturday noon -
11 pm; Sunday, noon - 9:30 pm.
Prices: Lunch $17 per person; Dinner $35 per person;
Wine by the glass $7 - $8.
Size: Seats up to 200.

Coromandel (Indian)

- 68 Broad Street (corner of Summer), Stamford CT
  203.964.1010
- 25-11 Old Kings Hwy N (Good Wives Shopping Cntr),
  Darien CT, 203.662.1213
- 86 Washington Street, South Norwalk CT, 203.852.1213

www.CoromandelCuisine.com

Hungry for Indian cuisine? Want to know where connoisseurs of fine Indian food dine? Want to be able to have a conversation? This restaurant, with its delicious specialities from many regions and its attentive staff will capture you. The Stamford location is one of six restaurants named after "Coromandel", the southeast coast of the Indian Peninsula. Many consider it the best.

Stamford Hours: Lunch, every day, noon - 2:30 pm;

Dinner every day, 5 pm - 10 pm (Friday & Saturday to 10:30 pm.)

Stamford Prices: Lunch buffet week days $11 & weekends $14, lunch boxes to go $7 - $9; Dinner entrees, Tandoor $15 - $24, Vegetarian $14 - $15, other entrees $18 - $23; Wine by the glass $8 - $10.

Stamford Size: Seats 80, party room for 120 upstairs.

Crab Shell (Seafood)

46 Southfield Avenue, Stamford CT, 203.967.7229

www.CrabShell.com

Good casual seafood in a nautical setting. During the summer evenings, especially the weekends, it is a meeting ground for the 30 to 50 something crowd. From May to September the restaurant expands onto a huge outdoor deck—The Crab Shack—which can accommodate 200. The Crab Shack has its own late night menu and a live band most weekends. The band schedule is on the website.

Hours: Open every day: Lunch, 11 am to 3 pm;

Dinner, Sunday - Thursday, 5 pm - 9:30 pm, Friday -Saturday, 5 -10pm. During the summer the bar is open to 1:30 am or later and the kitchen often stays open until they run out of food.

Prices: Lunch salads $13 - $19, sandwiches $10 - $17, casual entrees $13 - $25, children (under 12) $9; Dinner Burger & stir fry $14 - $16, entrees $20 - $29, crab and lobster at market; children $9;

Wine by the glass $6 - $10.

Size: Cocktail lounge will accommodate 40, center dining room seats 70, East Dining room seats 30, Riverboat room seats 40, entire restaurant seats 125.

Directions: At Stamford Landing, near Dolphin Cove. I-95 N to exit 7, R on Southfield.

(La) Crémaillère (French)

46 Bedford/Banksville Road, Banksville NY, 914.234.9647

www.Cremaillere.com

A restaurant for celebrations since 1947. Many Greenwich couples have become engaged in this restaurant. Fine wines with refined French food in a dressy, romantic setting. Pleasant, semi-attentive service. Jackets and ties are expected. They make all of the stocks from scratch so their sauces are superb. Mussel soup is a must.

Hours: Closed Monday; Lunch, Thursday - Saturday noon - 2:30 pm ; Dinner, Tuesday - Saturday, 6 pm - 9:30 pm; Sunday, 1 pm - 8 pm.

Prices: Lunch is prix-fixed at $36; Dinner entrees, $32 - $42;

Wine by the glass $10. Size: Seats 70+.

(The) Creek (American)

578 Anderson Hill Road, Purchase NY, 914.761.0050

www.Cobblestone-TheCreek.com

Just minutes away from the SUNY Performing Arts Center is a local up-scale choice for SUNY performance nights. Be sure to reserve. On non-performance nights, this restaurant is not crowded.

Hours: Lunch, weekdays 11:30 am - 2:30 pm;

Dinner, everyday 5 pm - 9 pm (Friday & Saturday to 10 pm.)

Reservations needed on SUNY performance nights.

Prices: Lunch, sandwiches $9 - $11, pasta $15 - $19, entrees $18 - $20; Dinner, pasta $15 - $19, entrees $19 - $27; Wine by the glass $7 - $8.

Size: Seats 46.

Crew Restaurant (New American)

280 Railroad Avenue, 203.340.9433

www.Crew280.com

This restaurant is like one you love to discover following a day of skiing - wood paneling, a large bar and 18 small tables covered in white cloths. Yummy pita and dips arrive with the menu. Every item on the menu is available in a small plate or entree size. It is fun to share small plates. Three small plates are ample for a party of two. The menu, which changes with the season, is a mix of nationalities, which they call "global American". They are better at some dishes than others.

Hours: Lunch, Wednesday, Thursday & Friday Noon - 2:30 pm; Dinner, Tuesday - Friday 5 pm - 10 pm, Saturday 5 pm - 11 pm.

Closed Sunday and Monday;

Prices: Entrees, $18 - $32 as a large plate and $12 - $18 as a small plate; Wine by the glass $8 - $15. Size: Seats 36.

Culinary Institute of America Restaurants

1946 Campus Drive, Hyde Park NY, 845.471.6608
www.Ciachef.edu

- American Bounty (New American)
- Ristorante Caterina de Medici (Italian)
- Escoffier (French)

Superb dining, illustrating the quality of this renowned cooking school. Food, ambiance and service are all top notch. The Craig Claiborne Bookstore is located on the first floor of Roth Hall. We hope a lot of these chefs are attracted to the Greenwich area. Reservations well in advance are a must, even if you are going for lunch. The dress code is business casual. No jeans or sneakers.

Hours: Bounty & Escoffier open Tuesday - Saturday, Medici & St. Andrews Cafe are open weekdays; Lunch 11:30 am - 1 pm; Dinner 6 pm - 8:30 pm.
Prices:
Lunch: Bounty, Lunch, entrees, $12 - $21, pre-fixe (Tue, Wed, Friday) $20; Escoffier, entrees $16 - $18, pre-fixe $20;Medici, entrees $19 - $22; Prefix (Monday - Thurs) Lunch $20
Dinner: Bounty, entrees $24 - $29, pre-fixe $30. Medici entrees $20 - $27; Prefix (Monday - Thurs) Dinner $30. Escoffier, Dinner, entrees $25 - $33, pre-fixe $30;
Wine by the glass (oz) $6 - $12, some restaurants also provide 3 oz wine servings.
Directions: About 1.5 hours north on I-684 & Route 9 N.

Doral Arrowwood Atrium (Sunday Brunch)

975 Anderson Hill Road, Rye Brook NY
914.935.6600 (914.939.5500)
www.DoralArrowWood.com

The Atrium is a large restaurant in a resort hotel. One side is all windows looking over the lovely golf course. The other side, for Sunday brunch, is a banquet of foods. With such great variety, there is something for all tastes. Live music plays in the background, as a magician tours the tables showing young and old a good time. Large groups are easily accommodated.

Hours: Sunday Brunch seatings, 11:45 am & 1:45 pm
Prices: Brunch: Adults $38, Children $19.
Size: Seats 300.

RESTAURANTS

Dougie's (Fast Food)

604 North Main Street, Port Chester NY, 914.939.0022
We might have expected Barbara Zaccagnini's son Doug would have a first-rate burger shop, and he does. This old fashioned shop is located just on the border of Greenwich and Port Chester on US-1, next door to Carvel. Everyone is talking about it because it is well priced and served up with a smile. When we crave a steak wedge with chili, this is where we go. On Wednesday, you can get two hot dogs for the price of one, then for dessert go next door to Carvel and get two hot fudge sundaes for the price of one.
Hours: weekdays 5 am - 6pm, Saturday 6 am - 4 pm,
Sunday 7 am - 1pm. Hours may be longer during the summer.
Prices: burgers $3 - $5, steak wedge $8 - 9; chili to go $5.
Size: Seats 20 inside and about 8 outside.

Douro (Portugese)

28 West Putnam Avenue, Greenwich, 203.869.7622
www.DouroRestaurantBar.com
Greenwich's first Portugese restaurant. Dimly lit, simple decor. Delicately flavored food. Their signature dish is Frango (chicken on the bone). It's good, but we prefer one the many fish dishes. Be sure to try their rosé sangria. Excellent, kind service.
Hours: Lunch, Monday - Saturday 11:30 am - 3 pm,
Dinner: Monday - Wednesday 5 pm - 10 pm;
Thursday - Saturday, 5 pm - 11 pm.
Closed Sundays from July until Labor Day.
Prices: Lunch, entrees $15-$18, Sandwiches $9;
Dinner, entrees $19-$24, Paelhas $19-$26.
Size: Seats 40

TIP: CALL BEFORE YOU DIG

Never dig around your home without first calling "Call Before You Dig" (CBYD) www.cbyd.com 800.922.4455. This clearing house will arrange free-of-charge to locate and mark the underground utilities on your property.

RESTAURANTS

(The) Drawing Room (Tea)

5 Suburban Avenue, Cos Cob, 203.661.3737

www.thedrawingroomcc.com

Tucked around the corner from the Post Road, near the Cos Cob Library is the perfect place for light lunch and/or afternoon tea. This small, cheerfully decorated tea room serves tea, hot chocolate, finger sandwiches, scones and desserts. The staff are tea experts who can help you make delightful tea choices. Having tea and browsing through the adjoining antique store, make this a fun and civilized break in the day.

Hours: Café Monday - Saturday 8 am - 5 pm; (Official tea time is considered to be 11 am - 4 pm); Boutique open from 10 am - 5 pm.

Prices: Lunch entrees, $8 - $13, Grand Afternoon Tea, $26.

Size: Seats 15 inside and 16 outside. No reservations.

Dressing Room (American)

27 Powers Court, Westport CT, 203.226.1114

(located next to the Westport County Playhouse)

www.DressingRoomHomeGrown.com

This "Newman's Own" sponsored restaurant, specializes in cooking American heritage recipes with locally grown, organic food.

The $25 P. L. Newman Burger is a favorite, as are the fish entrees.

Hours: Brunch Saturday & Sunday 11 am - 3 pm; Lunch, Wednesday - Sunday, 11:30 am - 2 pm; Dinner (non-show season), Tuesday - Saturday 6 pm - 10:30 pm, Sunday 5 pm - 9 pm; Dinner (Show Season) Tuesday - Thursday, 6 am - 9 pm, Friday-Sunday, 5 pm - 10:30 pm.

Prices: Lunch, entrees (salads, sandwiches, burgers) $17 - $24; Dinner, entrees $18 - $26; Wine by the glass $8 - $12.

Size: seats 140 in the winter and 170 in the summer.

Dunkin' Donuts (Coffee, Ice Cream)

- 375 East Putnam, Cos Cob, 203.869.7454
  (This location also sells Baskin-Robbins, ice cream)
- 271 West Putnam Avenue, 203.869.5791

www.DunkinDonuts.com

We are addicted to their coffee and who can resist their donuts. Be sure to try their summer coffees.

Hours:Open every day, 5 am - 11 pm.

RESTAURANTS

duo (Asian Fusion)
25 Bank Street, Stamford CT, 203.252.2233
www.DuoEuroJapanese.com
Tokyo chic, with high ceilings, nicely spaced tables, white walls & cloths, steel chopsticks and unique white plates—the euro-Japanese food, artistically prepared, is the focus. Duo takes its name from their theme of doing each sushi roll in two ways, often using unusual ingredients, like yuzu or burdock. To begin, try the rock shrimp, crispy tofu or lobster soup. For a main course, the bayou duo roll, is a good choice. Desserts, like the coconut crepe, are delicious.
Hours: Lunch, Monday to Saturday 11:30 am - 3 pm;
Dinner, Everyday 5 pm - 10 pm (Friday & Saturday to 11 pm.)
Prices: Dinner, entrees $18 - $24, Duo rolls, $11 - $14,
Wine by the glass, $5 - $11.
Size: Seats 36

Eclisse (Italian)
700 Canal Street, Stamford CT 203.325.3773
www.EclisseStamford.com
Situated in a Stamford renovation area, this upscale old-world-style restaurant is attracting a crowd with its four course fixed-price menu (available Sunday through Friday). The servings are generous and good. The service, which is well intentioned but slightly incompetent, can be funny.
Hours: Lunch every day 12 pm - 4 pm,
Dinner: Sunday - Thursday 4 pm - 10 pm,
(Friday & Saturday until 11:30 pm).
Prices: Lunch, fixed price $17, pizzas $10-$23, Panini $7-$9, entrees $15- $26; Dinner, 4-course fixed price menu $25, pizza $12-$13, entrees $16- $27; wine by the glass $6 - $10.
Size: seats 250.

RESTAURANTS

Edo (Japanese Steak House)

140 Midland Avenue (shopping center next to Home Depot)
Port Chester NY, 914.937.3333
www.EdoHibachi.com

Just across from Home Depot, in a nondescript shopping strip, is a surprisingly attractive hibachi steak house. The cooking process, done in front of you, is very dramatic—perhaps too theatrical. If you are thinking of hosting a children's party around a hibachi table, you will have plenty of room and accommodating service. You and the children will enjoy the food and the show.

Hours: Dinner, Monday - Thursday 5:30 pm - 10 pm,
Friday & Saturday 5:30 pm - 11 pm, Sunday 4 pm - 9 pm.
Prices: Complete dinners $16 - $31, children's menu $11 - $15.
Size: 11 hibachi tables each seating 8.

Elm Street Oyster House (Seafood)

11 West Elm Street, 203.629.5795
www.ElmStreetOysterHouse.com

Their raw bar and chowders are hard to beat. We have yet to be disappointed. You will like the creative recipes and yummy desserts. Try their wasabi sesame-crusted tuna or the Lobster Paella. The pan fried oysters are top-rate for an appetizer. This small, lively restaurant is a great place to meet after work and to stay for dinner.

Hours: weekdays, 11:30 am - 10 pm; Saturday, 11:30 am - 11 pm;
Sunday, 11:30 am- 9 pm. Closed on major holidays.
They now accept reservations by phone or over the internet.
Prices: Same menu lunch & dinner, small entrees $16 - $22;
larger entrees $26 - $32; salads & sandwiches $11 - $19;
Wine by the glass $9 - $16.
Size: Seats 42.

RESTAURANTS

Elms Restaurant & Tavern (American)

500 Main Street (Route 35), Ridgefield CT, 203.438.9206
Overnight Accommodations at the Elms Inn 203.438.2541
www.elmsInn.com
Steve and Kathleen treated us to a happy evening at the Elms. The food is yummy and plentiful, the vintage dining room in the 200-year-old house is charming and cozy. The service is friendly and attentive. No background music, no noise, just sounds of conversation and laughter. The menu has American heritage favorites, such as veal in sherry cream sauce and potted brisket of beef. Reserve a table on the porch in warm weather. For a romantic weekend, request one of 23 charming rooms (including 6 suites), some with poster beds at the Elms Inn next door.
Hours: Lunch, Wednesday - Sunday, 11:30 am - 2:30 pm;
Dinner, Wednesday - Sunday, 5:30 pm - 8:30 pm
(Friday & Saturday until 10 pm.)
Prices: Dinner: Starters, $8 - $14; Tavern Favorites, $14 - $21;
Entrees, $24 - $33.

Eos (Greek)

490 Summer Street, Stamford CT, 203.569.6250
www.eosgreekcuisine.com
Our dear Greek friends, Roula and Evans, discovered this bright white, small restaurant. "You must try it, their moussaka is better than mine". We have eaten their home cooking, so this restaurant had to be good. We recommend skipping the main courses and sharing plates of appetizers, such as Moussaka, Pastitsio and Kolokythakia. Top this off with Baklava. While our Greek friends complemented the authenticity, we complemented the tastiness.
Hours: Monday - Thursday, 11:30 am - 10 pm;
Friday and Saturday, until 11 pm; Sunday, noon to 9 pm.
Prices: Lunch Entrees, $ 10 - $26, Wraps, $ 9 - $10;
Dinner Entrees, $18 - $29, Mezedes (appetizers), $5 to $17;
Wine by the glass, $6 - $11.
Size: seats 40.

RESTAURANTS

Euro Asian (Asian)

30 Westchester Avenue (@ The Water Front), Port Chester NY
914.937.3680

www.EuroAsianRestaurant.com

Very handy to the movies, but not our favorite choice.

Hours: Lunch, Monday - Saturday 11:30 am - 3 pm;

Dinner, Every day 5 pm - 10 pm (Friday & Saturday to 11 pm.)

Prices: Lunch, wide choice of set lunches for $9, sushi specials $12 - $15

Dinner, sushi entrees $10 - $48, other entrees, $12 - $28;

Children's menu, $9; Wine by the glass $7.

Size: Seats 140.

Express Pizza (Pizza)

160 Hamilton Avenue, 203.622.1693

www.ExpressPizzaOnline.com

www.Grecosbellacucina.com

We discovered this friendly, small neighborhood pizzeria when it won
the 2003 Town competition for the best pizza. We still love their pizza.
Try their homemade soup or ravioli. They also have a deli next door
(Greco's Bella Cucina).

Hours: Monday - Saturday, 9 am - 10 pm; Sunday, 10 am - 10 pm.

Prices: Pizzas (10", 14", 16") 14 "speciality pizzas $15 - $20.

Size: Seats for 14.

Ferrante (Italian)

191 Summer Street, Stamford CT, 203.323.2000

www.FerranteRestaurant.com

Gracious service and appealing, sophisticated decor—a mix of bright
white and dark wood tones. A good choice for a leisurely night out. Their
pastas are our favorites.

Hours: Lunch, everyday noon - 2:30 pm;

Dinner, everyday 5 pm - 10:30 pm (Friday & Saturday until 11 pm.)

Prices: Lunch, pre fixe menu $25, risotto & pasta $11 - $15, pizza $12,
entrees $17 - $20; Dinner, risotto & pasta $19 - $27, pizza $15 - $19,
entrees $21 - $48; Wine by the glass $10 - $14.

Size: Seats 80 in the dining room, private room for 80.

RESTAURANTS

(Le) Figaro (French)

327 Greenwich Avenue, 203.622.0018
www.figarogreenwich.com
Le Figaro calls itself a Paris bistro and nothing could be more descriptive. From the moment you enter you feel like you are in France, albeit in a rather elegant bistro. The food is upscale casual French and quite good. The service is friendly and at the pace you would expect in France.
Hours: Sunday Brunch 11 am - 3 pm;
Lunch, Monday - Thursday 11:30 - 2:30 pm;
Dinner, Monday - Thursday 5:30 pm - 9:30 pm; (Friday & Saturday until 10:30 pm); Sunday, 5:30 pm - 9 pm.
Prices: Lunch, pizza $13 - $19, entrees & sandwiches $12 - $23;
Dinner entrees, $22 - $38. Size: Seats 92.

F.I.S.H. Fox Island Seafood House (Seafood)

102 Fox Island Rd, Port Chester NY, 914.939.4227
www.FishFoxIsland.com
Finding this waterfront restaurant is part of the fun. You will discover a casual restaurant serving fresh seafood (including a variety of mussels, clams and oysters) served by a friendly staff.
Fall-Winter Hours: closed Monday; Sunday Brunch noon - 3 pm; Lunch, Tuesday -Saturday noon - 3 pm; Dinner, Tuesday - Thursday 5:30 pm - 10pm, Friday & Saturday 5:30 pm - 11 pm, Sunday 5 pm - 9 pm. In the summer, they may be open longer, be sure to call before going.
Prices: Lunch, pizza $11 - $14, sandwiches $10 - $15, entrees $19 - $30; Dinner entrees, $12 - $27 (most in the range of $23 - $26); Wine by the glass $8 - $12; Order by 6:30 and you might get a free bottle of wine.
Size: Seats 70 inside, 14 tables outside.
Directions: Route 1 South through Main street in Port Chester to Grace Church Street, L on Fox Island, continue to the waterfront.

Fjord Sunday Brunch and Evening Cruises (American)

143 River Road, Cos Cob, 203.622.4020 or 203.325.0248
www.FjordCatering.com
Cruises sail from Cos Cob harbor. This is an especially nice way to experience the Greenwich waterfront. Of course, you need a reservation. Fjord also charters buses and caters large events.
Hours: Sunday Brunch, board 11:15, sail 1:30 am - 2 pm;
Friday evening dinner cruise, board at 7 pm, sail 7:30 pm - 10:30 pm.
Prices: Brunch, $64 adult, $25 child; Evening $79 adult, $35 child.
Size: Both yachts can seat 100.

Fonda La Paloma (Mexican)

531 Post Road, Cos Cob, 203.661.9395

www.FondaLaPaloma.com

Rarely do restaurants survive a decade. This one has been here for over thirty years! Our waiter had been working there for twenty-six years. They have a loyal following despite the dated decor and average food.

Hours: Lunch, weekdays noon - 3 pm;
Dinner, Monday - Thursday 5 pm - 9:45 pm;
Friday & Saturday, 5 pm - 10:30 pm; Sunday, 4 pm - 9 pm.
Prices: Lunch, salads $9 - $15, wraps & burgers $7 - $11,
entrees, $9 - $15; Dinner entrees $18 - $25. Size: Seats 70.

Frank's (Italian)

23 Putnam Avenue (just across the CT border), Port Chester NY 914.939.8299

This popular pizza take-out is also a popular dining spot. Your food is served with cloth napkins and on stylish plates. The service is friendly. We were wowed by the quality and variety of their freshly prepared entrees. We especially like the garlic balls, eggplant parmigiana and the fettuccine Alfredo.

Hours: Closed Sunday; Monday - Thursday, 10:30 am to 10 pm;
Friday & Saturday to 10:30 pm. Lunch served until 3 pm.
Prices: Pasta $11 - $17, speciality salads $10 - $14, wraps & sandwiches $9 - $10, Pizzas (10") $10 - $13, Lunch entrees $12 - $15,
Dinner entrees $15 - $25. Size: Seats 60.

Frank's Franks (Lunch Wagon Fast Food)

Town Hall Parking Lot

Whether you are having a bacon, egg and cheese sandwich or a chili dogs, this is a good place for a quick bite. Open for breakfast and lunch.

RESTAURANTS

Garden Café at Greenwich Hospital (American)

5 Perryridge Road, 1st Floor, Watson Pavilion, 203.863.3228
The hospital's garden café is a good place to lunch, whether you are visiting someone or not. Diners can enjoy a surprisingly good salad or sandwich as well as garden views through floor-to-ceiling windows, and in good weather, from the trellised bluestone terrace. This welcoming addition was donated by the Victor Borge family.
Hours: weekdays, Breakfast 8 am - 11 pm; Lunch, 11:15 am - 3 pm.
Prices: Lunch sandwiches $6 - $7, salads $7 - $8, pasta & other entrees $6 - $8. Size: Seats 75.

Garden Catering (Fast Food)

www.GardenCatering.net
Retail locations:

- 185 Sound Beach Avenue, Old Greenwich, 203.698.2900
- 177 Hamilton Avenue, Byram, 203.422.2555
- 140 Midland Avenue, Port Chester, NY, 914.934.7810 or 7852
  Catering office: 203.637.7966

Now one of eight locations, their fried chicken and chicken nuggets have made them famous. If you like fried chicken, don't miss this takeout.
Sound Beach Hours: weekdays 6 am - 7 pm, Saturday 6 am - 6 pm; Sunday 7 am - 5 pm.
Prices: Fried chicken platter $5, Breast platter $8, Nuggets $6.

Gates (American)

10 Forest Street, New Canaan CT, 203.966.8666
www.CulinaryMenus.com/gates.htm
An informal standby for over thirty years. On a back street, this large, gaily decorated, cheerful restaurant, is a popular place to have lunch if you are shopping in New Canaan. Service is good humored and youthful. The menu is strong on burgers, salads and wraps as well as some more sophisticated entrees.
Hours: Lunch, every day 11:30 am - 3:30 pm (Brunch on Sunday); Bar menu 3:30 pm - 5 pm; Dinner, Monday Thursday, 5:30 pm - 10 pm; Friday & Saturday to 10:30 or 11 pm; Sunday 4:30 pm - 9:30 pm.
Prices: Brunch, $11 - $18; Lunch, salads $10 - $18; burgers & sandwiches $9 - $15, entrees, $11 - $18; Dinner, burgers and sandwiches $10 - $17, entrees $20 - $26; children's menu $6 - $8.
Size: 120+

RESTAURANTS

Ginger Man (Pub)

64 Greenwich Avenue, 203.861.6400

www.GingerManGreenwich.com

A lively burger / beer place in a classic, upscale tavern atmosphere, with dimly lit rooms and vintage Greenwich photos. Twenty-three beers on tap and sixty bottled beers. The oversize burgers on English muffins, require a large bite. If you stop here and you are not in the mood for a burger or fish and chips, have the delicious pear salad.

Hours: Monday - Thursday, 11:45 am - 10 pm; Friday & Saturday until 11 pm, Sunday until 9 pm.

Prices: Sandwiches and burgers $10 - $15; entrees $17 - $33; Wine by the glass $6 - $10; Drafts $6 - $8.

Size: Downstairs 100, upstairs 55 (upstairs is available only Thursday, Friday & Saturday nights.)

Glenville Pizza (Pizza)

243 Glenville Road, 203.532.1691

Glenville residents, as well as people all over town (including our son), love Glenville Pizza. It is one of the few places serving by the slice. They were one point from winning the town pizza contest. No deliveries. Only large pizzas.

No credit cards, but they will accept a local check.

Hours: Monday - Saturday 11 am - 11 pm; Sunday noon - 10 pm.

Prices: Slice $3 - $4, Large (16") regular $15 - $20, Sicilian $18 - $20.

Size: Seats 26.

Glory Days (American)

69 East Putnam Avenue, 203.661.9067

A welcoming diner, with a celebrity-studded clientele, that has been open since 1923. It was completely rebuilt in 2002 with a sleek new look. Nick, the friendly owner, has operated the restaurant for over 17 years. He keeps prices low and serves hearty portions. This is what a diner is supposed to be. Everyone has their favorites here; we particularly like their Greek salad and baklava. It is a popular late-night meeting place for students.

Hours: Sunday - Thursday, 6 am - 1 pm; Friday & Saturday open 24 hours. Lunch hours, 11 am - 3 pm. No reservations.

Prices: Breakfast $2 - $5; Lunch, burgers $5 - $9, sandwiches $8 - 14; Complete dinner entrees $13 - $18.

Size: Seats 35.

RESTAURANTS

Goccia (Italian)

19 North Main Street, Norwalk CT, 203.642.3345

www.GocciaRestaurant.com

A welcoming place for families and children to relax after a visit to the Aquarium next door (validated parking at the Maritime Garage.) You will discover 20 different styles of pizza and a children's menu. Goccia means a drop of water and is pronounced "got.cha".

Hours: Closed Monday; Tuesday-Sunday noon-close (about 10 pm.)

Prices: Personal pizzas $9 - $13, signature salads $10 - $13, entrees $17 - $19; Wine by the glass $8 - $10; Children's menu $6 - $7.

Size: Seats 80.

Greenwich Health Mart (Vegetarian Fast Food)

30 Greenwich Avenue, 203.869.9658

In the back of this health product store, is a very small vegetarian & vegan food bar, serving soups, salads, wraps and sandwiches. They have good tofu chili and organic fruit smoothies. You will like going here. It is a charming old-fashioned store with wonderful service. They have a few seats. *Their vitamins and other health products are reviewed in HEALTH.*

Hours: weekdays, 8:30 am - 5:30 pm; Saturday 8:30 am - 5 pm;
Sunday, 11 am - 3 pm (not all food choices are available on Sundays.)

Prices: Sandwiches & Wraps $7 - $10.

Greenwich Lobster House (Seafood)

2 Water Street, Byram, 203.531.6400

www.GreenwichLobsterHouse.com

If you decide to try this restaurant, stick to the lobster dishes—lobster bisque or steamed lobster. The kind servers are not professional, but they mean well. The atmosphere is old-fashioned. A table by the fireplace is pleasant in the winter.

Hours: Open every day, Lunch, Noon - 4 pm;
Dinner 5 pm - Close (usually 9 or 10 pm.)

Prices: Lunch, burgers and sandwiches $9 - $19,
entrees $13 - $20, lobster, $26 - $52;
Dinner, entrees $17 - $36, Lobster $26 - $52; sides are extra;
Wine by the glass $6 - $12.

Size: 100 upstairs (including upstairs party room for 25), 80 downstairs.

Greenwich Tavern (American)

1392 East Putnam Avenue, Old Greenwich, 698.9033

www.GreenwichTavern.net

Designed to be informal and fun, the menu has sophisticated, casual food. Not exactly tavern fare. They have a yummy beet and goat cheese salad. Whatever you order, be sure to ask for Rosemary Parmesan Fries. The flag murals are bright and cheerful and that is how a night out at Chef Palomino's Tavern makes us feel.

Hours: Brunch, Saturday & Sunday 11:30 am - 3 pm; Lunch, Monday - Friday Noon - 3 pm; Dinner, Sunday-Wednesday 5 pm - 10 pm (Thursday, Friday, Saturday to 11pm).

Prices: Brunch price fix $20;

Lunch & Dinner Menu, salads $10 - $16, sandwiches $13 - $17, pasta $17 - $23, steak $24 - $32, entrees $16 -$26;

Wine by the glass, $10 - $19.

Size: main room seats 78, party rooms for 40 and 26.

Habana (Cuban)

245 Hope Street, Stamford CT, 203.964.1801

We like it. The good humored service and interesting food, like Tuna Con Miel, make for a fun evening. The restaurant is not fancy and it can be crowded and noisy.

Hours: Lunch, weekdays 11 am - 3 pm;

Dinner, Monday - Saturday 5 pm - 10 pm, Sunday 5 pm - 9 pm.

Prices: Lunch, sandwiches $9-$11, entrees $15 - $22;

Dinner entrees $19 -$28. Size: Seats 36 upstairs and 14 downstairs.

Harvest Supper (New American)

15 Elm Street, New Canaan CT, 203.966.5595

With a family room ambiance (plaid wallpaper, brick and wood) and despite a hamburger on the menu, you will be surprised by the unique and high level of the cuisine. This is not really a farm menu. On the small plate side of the menu you might find crispy quail or roasted cottechino. On the entree side you might find Lobster macaroni and cheese or spiced tuna. The service is very caring and professional. But we find them sightly understaffed.

Hours: Lunch, Wednesday - Friday noon - 2 pm;

Dinner, Tuesday - Saturday 5:30 pm - 10 pm.

Prices: Lunch, small plates $8-$14, entrees $13-$19; Dinner, small plates $11-$8, entrees $23-$29 (Burger $18), sides $7.

Wine by the glass $8 - $14. Size: seats 38.

RESTAURANTS

Hunan Café (Chinese)

1233 East Putnam Avenue, Riverside, 203.637.4341

Well-prepared, authentic Chinese cuisine. If you are planning a multi-course feast with entrees such as Peking duck, place this meal in their hands and you will have a first-rate experience. On Saturday and Sunday, they have a habit-forming dim sum brunch— highly recommended.
Hours: Dim Sum, Saturday & Sunday, 11:30 am - 3 pm;
Lunch, weekdays 11:30 am - 3 pm;
Dinner, every day 3 pm - 9:30 or 10 pm.
Prices: Lunch entrees, $6 - $7; Dinner entrees, $13 - $18.
Size: Seats 64.

Hunan Gourmet (Chinese)

68 East Putnam Avenue, 203.869.1940

A Chinese restaurant with white tablecloths and an elegant flair. Just thinking about their shredded pork with dried bean curd or sea bass with ginger makes us hungry. The staff is especially nice to children, making it a popular family place.
Hours: Everyday, Lunch, noon - 3 pm; Dinner, 5 pm - 10 pm
(often to 11 pm Friday & Saturday.)
Prices: Lunch specials $8 - $9; Dinner entrees, $12 - $17, chef's specials, $16 - $32; Free delivery with a minimum purchase of $20.
Size: Seats about 100.

Hyatt/Winfields (American)

Hyatt Regency, 1800 East Putnam Avenue, Old Greenwich
203.637.1234 / dining reservations, 203.409.4400
www.Greenwich.Hyatt.com

Set in a beautifully converted publishing building, this is not a typical hotel with typical hotel fare. This is what good hotel dining can be. Located in the atrium's indoor garden with water, flowers and very high ceilings, it feels like outdoor dining even in the middle of the winter. The buffet lunches and Sunday brunches are first rate. Make reservations.
Hours: Open everyday and all holidays:
Breakfast buffet 6:30 am - 10:30 am (a la carte until 11 pm);
Lunch buffet, Monday - Saturday, 11:30 am - 2:30 pm (a la carte until 5 pm); Dinner, 5 pm - 10 pm; Sunday brunch, seating 11:30 & 2:30.
Prices: Breakfast buffet $27, al la carte $15 - $22; Lunch buffet $24, children between 4 & 12 are half price, children under 4 free, a la carte sandwiches and salads $16 - $25;
Dinner entrees $21 - $35; Brunch price fixed - Adults $55, children ages 4 - 12, $30, children under 4 are free.
Children's menu for lunch and dinner $6 - $11. Size: Seats 120.

Joey B's Chili Hub (American)

118 River Road Extension, Cos Cob, 203.661.0573

When Joey B opened, we were not surprised at the instant popularity of this diner-style restaurant with its counter and stools. It's a magnet for children (adults like the clam chowder with corn fritters.) For years Joey B had been serving Greenwich residents hot dogs, hamburgers and casual food from his mobile van. At his restaurant he is determined to continue serving tasty foods at moderate prices. His overwhelming success shows he has a winning formula. Joey B does a lot of takeout.
Prices: Lunch & Dinner, $2 - $10.
Hours: weekdays, 6 am 8 pm; Saturday & Sunday, 8 am - 4 pm; (Breakfast served until 11 am.) Size: 14 seats.

Juice Bar Café (Vegan)

328 Pemberwick Rd @ The Mill, Glenville, 203.532.0660

If you are taking one of the yoga classes, you already know about this small café. Before entering class, students place orders for one of their organic drinks or smoothies. Orders are ready when class is over. Even if you are not taking yoga, you will like the smoothies, coffee, wraps or salads for a light, healthy, refreshing lunch. Vegans will like their raw foods. They have a delivery service for local organic foods run by Erica's Kitchen, 914.906.6892.
Prices: Smoothies $4 - $10 (depending size); wraps $6.
Hours: Every day 8 am - 6 pm. Size: Seats about 8.

Kato-Chan Ramen Stand (Japanese)

137 River Road, Cos Cob

If you are feeling in a casual mood and want to eat in one of Greenwich's most unique spots, pull in behind the former Fjord Fishery market on River Road, sit at picnic table outdoors and order one of their seven kinds of Ramen. Prices: Bowl of Ramen noodles $7 - $10.
Hours: Wednesday - Sunday 5 pm - 9 pm (mid-June to mid-October)
Size: Seats 16 at outside tables.

Katzenberg's Kafé (American)

342 Greenwich Avenue, 203.625.0103 www.katzenbergKafe.com
A New York-style eatery with a wide selection of sandwiches. Primarily takeout, but there are a few places to sit. This conveniently located spot has thirteen hamburger choices. No wonder they did so well in the "Hamburger Tasting Competition." Be sure to order sweet potato fries.
Hours:weekdays, 8 am-5 pm; Saturday,9 am-5 pm;Sunday, 10 am-4 pm.
Prices: Wraps, $8 - $9, Hamburgers, $5 - $8. Size: Seats 15.

RESTAURANTS

Kazu (Japanese)

64 North Main Street, South Norwalk CT, 203.866.7492

www.KazuSoNo.com

Very near the Norwalk movies. Order the movie box, it has a tasty sampling of their Japanese specialties. The sushi and teriyaki are good choices. We like the mix of traditional Japanese and creative Asian dishes.

Hours: Lunch, weekdays noon - 2 pm; Dinner, weekdays 5:30 pm - 10 pm, Friday & Saturday 5:30 pm - 11 pm, Sunday 5 pm - 9:30 pm.

Prices: Lunch, sushi entrees, $12 - $16, Bento boxes $10 - $12, entrees $9 - $12; Dinner, sushi entrees $19 - $15, Bento $19, entrees $17 - $20; Wine by the glass $8 - $10; children's menu $11. Size: Seats 100.

Kira Sushi (Japanese)

4 Lewis Court, 203.422.2990

This hidden restaurant, just off Greenwich Avenue, is worth finding. The decor with its remarkable rock-water wall, is attractive and soothing. The seafood miso soup and avocado salad are superb, as are the beef teriyaki and chicken tempura. As you might expect, the sushi and their special rolls, such as the iridescent Kira Wasabi roll, get high marks.

Hours: Monday-Thursday, 11:30 am to 10 pm; Friday until 11 pm; Saturday, noon to 11 pm; Sunday, noon to 10 pm.

Prices: Lunch, specials $10 - $18, Bento $10 - $16; Dinner, sushi entrees $15 - $28; special rolls $14 - $17, entrees, $13 - $26; Wine by the glass $8. Size: Seats 40.

Kit's Thai Kitchen (Thai)

927 High Ridge Road (Turn of River Shopping Cntr)

Stamford CT, 203.329.7800

www.KitsThaiKitchen.com

A find! Tiny spot in a shopping center with mouth-watering curries and chicken. They use organic products and are not afraid to make spicy dishes. We suggest you say medium spicy even if you like spicy. Pleasant seating outside and tables inside. There is nothing better than their Chicken Satay or Sum Tum (Papaya Salad) or Tom Ka Gai (coconut based soup). You can't go wrong with their curries or Pad Thai.

Hours: Monday - Thursday, 11 am - 10 pm; Friday & Saturday until 10:30 pm; Sunday, 11 am - 9 pm.

Prices: Lunch special $11; Dinner, noodles $12 - $20, curry $13 - $20, stir-fried $13 - $20, other entrees, $13 - $20.

Size: Seats 40.

Kona Grill (American)

230 Tresser Blvd. (Stamford Town Center)

Stamford CT, 203.324.5700

www.KonaGrill.com

18 Kona Grills are located in 12 states. Sushi was their original specialty. Now the menu has sandwiches, pizzas and traditional American fare while still maintaining a strong sushi bar. The large bar area is popular with the twenty-something crowd during happy hour. The restaurant lighting is so low, you might think it is closed. If you are not going for happy hour appetizers, we recommend the macadamia nut chicken and the chili glazed salmon.

Hours: Sunday - Thursday, 11 am - 11 pm,

Friday & Saturday until midnight.

Happy hour: weekdays, 3 pm - 7 pm; Monday - Thursday, 10 pm- 12 pm; Friday & Saturday, 11 pm - 1 pm.

Prices: Entrees, $18 - $23; Pizza, $10 - $11; Children's menu $3 - $5; Glass of wine, $7 - $12. During happy hour, drinks are generally, $4 - $7 & appetizer, pizzas and sushi are half price.

Size: Seats 305.

Layla's Falafel (Middle Eastern)

- 245 Main Street, Stamford CT, 203.316.9041
- 926 High Ridge Road, Stamford, CT, 203.461.8004

www.LaylasFalafel.com

Repeatedly voted the best Middle Eastern restaurant in Fairfield County, these two small, clean, neat eateries are creating delicious ethnic foods you might not have had a chance to taste. Many vegetarian dishes are available. Have a falafel sandwich, chicken shawafal or a middle eastern salad and you will become a regular.

Hours: Open every day: Main Street, 11 am - 10 pm

(Friday & Saturday to 2 am); High Ridge, 11 am - 9 pm.

Prices: Salads $6 - $9, falafel platters $11 - $12,

grilled entrees $11 - $17.

Size: Main Street seats 30; High Ridge seats 20.

RESTAURANTS

L'Escale (French / Mediterranean)

500 Steamboat Road, 203.661.4600

http://www.LEscaleRestaurant.com

L'Escale, French for "port of call," evokes good memories of dining along the French Riviera. What better style restaurant to be on our Greenwich waterfront! In the summer the terrace is the perfect spot to dine. This bright, airy restaurant has nicely spaced tables and attentive service allowing diners to have good conversations and a good time. The Chef, Francois Kwaku-Dongo, is not only a celebrity chef, but an active Greenwich volunteer.

Hours: Breakfast, everyday, 7 am - 10 am;

Lunch, Monday - Saturday 11:30 am - 2:30 pm,

Sunday Brunch 11:30 am - 3 pm;

Dinner, Sunday - Thursday 5 pm - 10 pm (Friday & Saturday to 11 pm.)

Prices: Brunch entrees $14 - $24; Lunch entrees $16 - $42;

Dinner entrees $27 - $42; Wine by the glass $9 - $18

Size: Seats 100 inside; terrace seats 40.

Le Pain Quotidien (Bakery, Restaurant)

382 Greenwich Avenue, 203.404.7533

www.LePainQuotidien.com

Le Pain Quotidien (often called LPQ) has 114 locations, of which 28 are in the USA. The restaurant is decorated in rustic, farmhouse style with large wooden communal tables. The company encourages customers to sit together and converse with strangers at these table. Fortunately, there are also a large number of individual tables for the less gregarious. Fresh food and good service are priorities as are the desserts and breads, like their famous Challah bread. They have a good selection vegan dishes.

Hours: Open every day 7 am - 8 pm (Saturday & Sunday open at 7:30 am)

Prices: quiche $12 - $13, tartines $9 - $14, specials $13 - $15, salads $8-$16.

Size: Seats 100 (2 large tables, each seats 24; 26 tables for 2).

RESTAURANTS

Lime (Vegetarian)

168 Main Avenue, Norwalk CT, 203.846.9240

www.LimeRestaurant.com

A neo-hippie restaurant in an out-of-the-way section of Norwalk with vegetarian dishes as well as fish and meat. Despite being named the best vegetarian restaurant for the last 15 years, we find the food inconsistent. Dishes we like are the tofu in orange sauce and salmon burger.

Hours: Open everyday, Lunch, Monday - Saturday 11 am - 4 pm;
Dinner Monday - Saturday, 5 pm - 10 pm, Sunday, 4:30 pm - 9:30 pm
Prices: Lunch, Roll-ups & sandwiches $8 - $9, salads $8 - $9; Dinner, entrees $17 - $24, salads $13 - $14; Wine by the glass $7 - $9.
Size: Seats 40.

Little Buddha (Thai)

2270 Summer Street, Stamford CT 203.356.9166

www.littlethaikitchen.com/littlebuddha.htm

A small restaurant that serves excellent Thai & some Hakka Chinese dishes. Lots of delicious wok-tossed vegetable dishes. Try the Vegetable Manchurian Balls and the Pumpkin Thai custard dessert. Little Buddha is owned by Shiva Natarajan's Little Thai Kitchen, but only some of its dishes are the same.

Hours: Lunch, Every day 11:30 am - 4 pm,
Dinner every day 4 pm - 10 pm.
Prices: Lunch, most dishes $8 - $9; Dinner, most dishes $12 - $15; No alcohol is served, so bring your own, no corkage fee. Size: Seats 16.

Little Thai Kitchen (Thai)

21 St. Rochs Avenue, Byram, 203.622.2972

www.LittleThaiKitchen.com

A tiny jewel of a place, serving some of the best Thai cuisine outside of Bangkok, is tucked away on St. Rochs. If you don't like your food spicy, you will have to tell them. We love their Nau Nam tok (beef salad), Mee Grob (Thai crispy noodles), Pad Thai noodles as well as their curries, particularly the Thai Massaman and Thai green curry. The Thai iced tea must be an acquired taste.

Hours: Lunch, weekdays 11 am - 3 pm, Saturday noon - 2:30 pm;
Dinner, Monday - Thursday, 3 pm - 9:30 pm;
Friday & Saturday, 3 pm - 10 pm; Sunday, noon pm - 9 pm.
Prices: Lunch entrees, $8 - $13, Thai bib bowl noodle soup $10 - $15;
Dinner entrees, $12 - $21; Dinner menu is served all day Sunday;
No alcohol is served, so bring your own, corkage fee is $3.
Size: Seats 26.

RESTAURANTS

Lolita Cocina and Tequila Bar (Mexican)

228 Mill Street, Byram, 203.813.3555

www.LolitaMexican.com

Oh yes, this is fun. With a large bucket of chips, three yummy salsas, a myriad of margaritas (or over 100 varieties of tequila) and nueva Mexican food, you will enjoy the winning combo created by Jody Pennette, cb5 restaurant group founder. You have a choice of an inside table in their hip black and red dining room or in summer outside on their small terrace. By all means, try their lobster enchilada appetizer. The bill comes with good cotton candy.

Hours: Sunday, Brunch 11 am - 3 pm;

Dinner, Tuesday - Sunday 6 pm - midnight (until 2 am on weekends).

Prices: Appetizers $9-$15, tacos $13-$14, quesdaillas $9-$12; Entrees chicken $16-$18, fish $24-$25, carne $18-$29; Tequila $9-$100, Margaritas $12-$14, wine by glass $8-$17.

Size: 14 seat bar, seats 68 inside, 18 outside.

Long Ridge Tavern (American)

2635 Long Ridge Road, Stamford CT, 203.329.7818

www.LongRidgeTavern.com

Dating from the 1880s, this charming country restaurant gives you a sense of stepping back into history. If you are looking for tavern fare such as Chicken Pot Pie, Yankee Pot Roast or Bread Pudding, you won't be disappointed. They have live entertainment on Friday & Saturday evenings. Check their website for details.

Hours: Sunday Brunch Buffet 11 am - 2:30 pm;

Lunch, every day noon - 3 pm;

Dinner, Monday - Thursday 3 pm - 9 pm (Friday & Saturday, to 10 pm.)

Prices: Brunch Buffet $25; Lunch entrees, $12 - $16;

Dinner, tavern fare $14 - $20, entrees $18 - $28; children menu $11;

Wine by the glass $8 - $9.

Size: Main dining room seats 80, private rooms seat 16, 40 and 65.

RESTAURANTS

Louie's (Italian)

136 River Road Extension, Cos Cob, 203.422.2177

www.LouiesRestaurantBar.com

For years this spot has been a casual restaurant serving comfort food at modest prices. Many remember it as the Mianus River Tavern, then Augies, then Bull dog. Now Ron Rosa, owner of Polpo, has transformed it into a southern Italian restaurant with white tablecloths and valet parking. We gravitate to the more rustic dishes such as the tasty Rigatoni Nonna and applaud having specials with prices on a blackboard.

Hours: Monday - Thursday, 11:45 am - 11 pm;

Friday & Saturday, to 11:30 pm, Sunday to 10 pm.

Prices: Lunch sandwiches $12; Dinner entrees $17 - $28, sides $6 - $7; Wine by the glass $7 - $11. Size: Seats 80.

MacDuffs Public House (Pub - British/Scottish)

99 Railroad Avenue, 203.422.0563

www.MacDuffsPub.com

When you are yearning for scotch eggs, bangers and mash, or fish and chips, this pub-style restaurant, across from the movie theater and train station, is your best bet. The service is pleasant. Expect it to be dimly lit —even at noon you may need a flashlight to read the menu. It is especially full of cheers during world cup soccer matches.

Hours: Sunday - Wednesday 11:30 am - 9 pm, Thursday - Saturday 11:30 am - 11 pm; Late night menu until midnight or 1 am.

Prices: Pub fare 10 - $14; entrees $12 - $27; Wine by the glass $9.

Size: Seats 26.

MacKenzie's Grill Room (Pub -American)

148 Sound Beach Avenue, Old Greenwich, 203.698.0223

www.MacKenziesGrillRoom.com

"Wear your best sweat shirt and jeans (loose fitting)" to enjoy this casual, friendly restaurant and bar, with good food, celebrating its 15th year. The perfect place to watch a game. Sit at the bar or a table and try the nachos, skins or wings, or choose a booth and have a tasty meal. Try their steak au poivre—we love it. For dessert have the Lava cake or Mac's mud pie. A "hot spot" on weekends—crowded and lively. Starting at 9 pm on Thursdays they have live entertainment.

Hours: Sunday - Thursday, 11:30 am - 1 am; Friday and Saturday until 2 am. Open most holidays. Reservations accepted for 6 or more.

Prices: Lunch entrees $8 - $20; Dinner entrees $14 - $28; Wine by the glass $5 - $8; Kid's menu $6.

Size: Seats 58, plus 25 on high stools.

RESTAURANTS

Marianacci's (Italian)

24 Sherman Street, Port Chester NY, 914.939.3450

www.Marianaccis.com

For over 50 years, this family owned restaurant has been serving southern Italian dishes in a refined and quiet atmosphere. Here, except on Friday's when there is live music, you can easily have a conversation while enjoying terrific dishes such as red snapper in orange sauce. You are not likely to pass this restaurant while driving through Port Chester, so knowing about it is part of the fun.

Hours: Lunch, weekdays 11:30 am - 2 pm;

Dinner, weekdays 5pm - 9:30 pm,

Saturday 5 pm - 10 pm, Closed Sunday.

Prices: Lunch, pasta $14-$16, other entrees $18-$20;

Dinner, pasta $18- $22, other entrees $20-$32, wine by the glass $8.

Size: seats 120

McDonald's (Fast Food)

- 268 West Putnam Avenue, 203.629.9068
- 1207 East Putnam Avenue, Riverside, 637.8598

Hours: Dining room open every day; Monday-Thursday 5 am - 1 pm, Friday & Saturday to 2 am, Sunday to midnight.

Size: Seats 50 (Greenwich location.)

Mark Mariani's Garden Center Café (American)

45 Bedford Road, Armonk NY, 914.273.3083

www.MarianiGardens.com

This stylish greenhouse garden center with rare trees, shrubs, and decorative pottery for sale has a café open for breakfast and lunch. I loved my fresh fig salad and lemonade. I can't wait to return.

Hours: The café is open 7 days a week, everyday 8:30 am - 4 pm; Breakfast and lunch are served all day.

Prices: Breakfast $7 - $10; Lunch $11 - $17.

Size: Seats about 28.

RESTAURANTS

Market Restaurant (New American/Italian)

249 Main Street, Stamford CT, 203.348.8000

www.MarketStamford.com

Stylish, hip, swift moving waiters, open kitchen, good food, make this a popular place. Market is located in the Columbus Park area, among a number of new and old restaurants. It has the same ownership, and therefore excellent customer attention, as Match in South Norwalk.

Hours: Lunch, weekdays, 11:30 am - 3 pm;

Dinner, Sunday - Thursday 5 pm - 10 pm

(Friday and Saturday until 11 pm)

Prices: Dinner, burger $19, pasta $22 - $28, other entrees $17 - $36; sides $8; Wine by the glass $9 - $13.

Size: Seats 100.

Mary & Martha's Café (Fast Food)

Skylight Café at YWCA, 259 East Putnam Avenue, 203.869.6501

www.MaryMarthasCatering.com

For 12 years this well-priced, bright and sunny eatery run by Diane Russo has been putting smiles on people's faces. From her small counter, you can select a continental breakfast, a healthy sandwich or salad for lunch or just grab a freshly baked muffin. She makes the best chicken-salad sandwich in town. Children are always welcome! Don't expect to meet Mary or Martha, they are biblical ladies.

Hours: Monday - Thursday 9 am - 6 pm, Friday 9 am - 3pm,

Saturday & Sunday private catering only.

Prices: $5 - $8. No credit cards.

Size: Nearby tables seat up to 24.

Match (New American)

98 Washington Street, South Norwalk CT, 203.852.1088

www.MatchSono.com

Connecticut Magazine readers have voted Match the Best Restaurant in Fairfield County. As a result of Chef Matthew Storch's innovative creations, which change with the season, this restaurant continues to grow in popularity. Be sure to reserve. Match has a trendy, happy atmosphere with helpful, efficient service and very good food.

Hours: Dinner everyday, 5 pm - 10 pm (Friday & Saturday, until 11 pm.)

Prices: Dinner entrees, $22 - $38;

Wine by the glass $8 - $14. Size: Seats 40.

Matteo's (Italian)

299 Long Ridge Road, Stamford CT, 203.964.9802

www.MatteosRestaurants.com

This place is usually packed with hungry families. Their "family style entrees" are designed to be shared. Most dishes have a choice between full and half portions. Portions are generous, so two full portions should be enough for four. This location is one of 10 restaurants in the Matteo's chain. Although the restaurant is upscale with its white tablecloths, the service is a bit homey. Because they don't take reservations for small parties, it is best to arrive early.

Hours: Monday - Thursday 5 pm - 10 pm,

Friday and Saturday 4:30 pm - 11 pm; Sunday 4 pm - 9 pm.

No reservations for parties under 10.

Prices: Pastas, full portion $20 - $26, ½ portion $17;

Chicken, full portion $22 - $30, ½ portion $15 - $19;

Veal, full portion $23 - $27, ½ portion $18 - $20;

Seafood, full portion $22 - $30, ½ portion $16 - $20;

Glass of wine $8. Size: Seats 70 at 16 tables.

Mediterraneo Restaurant (Italian)

366 Greenwich Avenue, 203.629.4747

www.MediterraneoOfGreenwich.com

Lively, bustling, welcoming. Lots of people seem to order their pizzas and spaghetti, but the kitchen can turn out really good seafood dishes. Try the halibut. The terrace provides an interesting perspective on life along Greenwich Avenue and also allows you to have a conversation. Inside, the tables in the back are the quieter ones. Popular Terra, has the same ownership.

Hours: Lunch, weekdays noon - 2:30 pm (Saturday until 3 pm);

Dinner, weekdays, 5:30 pm - 10 pm; weekends 5:30 pm - 10:30 pm;

Sunday brunch, 11:30 am - 3 pm

Reservations are usually required.

Prices: Lunch, pizza & pasta $14 - $24, entrees $16 - $26;

Dinner, pizza and pasta, $14 - $21, entrees $24 - $36.

Size: Seats 40 in the front and about 30 in the back; some tables on the outside terrace in the summer.

Meetinghouse (American)

Route 22 (next to the Bedford Playhouse) Bedford Village NY
914.234.5656 www.BedfordMeetingHouse.com
With sweet service and cheerfully simple decor, this is a casual spot for
a meal timed to the movie next door (Clearview Cinema: 914.234.3315.)
Burgers and salads are popular. If you want a more elaborate entree, try
the cumin crusted salmon.
Hours: Closed Monday; Tuesday, 5:30 pm - 10pm;
Wednesday - Saturday, Lunch: 11:30 am - 3pm; Dinner: 5 pm - 10 pm
Sunday, 11:30 am - 9 pm;
Prices: Lunch $8 - $14; Brunch $10 - $15; Dinner, burgers $12 - $14,
entrees $19 - $33; Wine by the glass, $7 - $12; splitting charge $4.
Size: Seats 40, reservations only for parties of 5 or more.
Directions: North Street to Rt. 22. Turn right. Left at the fork.

Meigas (Spanish)

10 Wall Street, Norwalk CT, 203.866.8800
www.meigasrestaurant.com
Count on a pleasant evening. The decor is simple, but dressy. The service
is attentive and the food artfully prepared and totally delightful. The
tapas are awesome.
Hours: Closed most major holidays; Sunday brunch 11:30 am - 3 pm;
Lunch, weekdays 11:30 am - 3 pm;
Dinner Monday - Thursday 5 pm - 9:30 pm,
(Friday and Saturday to 10:30 pm.)
Prices: Lunch entrees, tapas $5 - $11, salads $7 - $10, wraps $11 - $14,
entees $15 - $17; Dinner, tapas $10 - $14, entrees, $29 - $34;
Wine by the glass $8 - $14.
Size: Seats 72, plus 20 outside. Private rooms for 10 - 100.
Directions: For the Parking lot, set your GPS to 15 High Street.

RESTAURANTS

Meli-Melo (French, Ice Cream)

362 Greenwich Avenue, 203.629.6153
(catering 374 Greenwich Avenue, 203.422.5001)
www.MelimeloGreenwich.com

A tiny, always popular, always crowded restaurant with French casual foods such as yummy onion soup and a large variety of crepes. They also have an amazing variety of fresh squeezed juices. Our favorite is their croque monsieur. The fresh fruit sorbets are to die for. The owner, Chef Marc Penvenne, is very gracious as well as talented. The weekend breakfast menu features delicious omelets. This is where Holly met Tod. Rosanna and Clifford rave about it.

Hours: every day, 10 am - 10 pm. No reservations.

Prices: Buckwheat crepes $8 - $17, salads $6 - $14, sandwiches $6 - $11, dessert crepes $3 - $11.

Size: Seats 20.

(The) Melting Pot (Swiss, Fondue)

14 Grove Street, Darien CT, 203.656.4774
www.MeltingPot.com

Don't expect to dash in and have a quick fondue. This restaurant chain, with its 138 locations scattered across the US, is for "an experience", a date or a party. The "experience" will take, at least, two hours. The menu offers an extensive array of choices, great for some, daunting for others. A long dark hall leads to a variety of private alcoves. Our friends in Switzerland surely could not imagine what has happened to the traditional fondues we savored in the Alps. A whole new genre of fondues is on the menu in this entertaining, if not traditional, restaurant. After trying some of the unusual combinations we settled on the traditional Emmenthaler cheese fondue and one of the chocolate fondues (original or pure chocolate or flaming turtle) as our favorites.

Hours: Dinner, Monday - Thursday 5 pm - 10 pm,
Friday & Saturday 5 pm - 11 pm, Sunday 4 pm - 10 pm.

Prices: Cheese fondue $19 (included salad serves 1 - 2); Entree $20 - $30, Chocolate Fondues, small - $19, regular - $35;
Four-course dinner for two (The Big Night Out) $92 per couple;
Wine by the glass $6 - $16.

Size: Seats 136; two private rooms, seats 12 - 16 and 26 - 36.

RESTAURANTS

Mirage Café (New American)

531 North Main Street, Port Chester NY, 914.937.3497

www.CafeMirageNY.com

A relaxed restaurant, with funky decor and excellent dishes. We love it. The chef-owner, calls his menu a melting pot of Caribbean, French, Asian, Cajun and American cuisines. Especially popular for late night dining, you will have fun at this restaurant. Try the wonderful steak au poivre or steak diablo (available only for dinner). Their lemon grass shrimp is also a good choice. For salads, it's a toss up between the chopped and the Greek. It can be noisy inside. In the summer, escape the noise and dine on the terrace.

Hours: Monday - Thursday noon - 11 pm; Friday noon - midnight, Saturday 6 pm - midnight; Sunday 5 pm - 9:30 pm.

It is a small restaurant, advance reservations are recommended - especially for weekends.

Prices: Lunch sandwiches $7 - $9, entrees $11 - $16; Dinner sandwiches $9 - $14, entrees $19 - $24; Wine by the glass $8 - $10.

Size: Seats 36 inside and 30 on the terrace.

Mitchell's Fish Market (fish)

230 Tresser Blvd at The Stamford Town Center

Stamford CT, 203.323.3474

www.MitchellsFishMarket.com

One of five featured restaurants at the Town Center. Started 10 years ago in Columbus Ohio by Cameron Mitchell, the Fish Market with its 19 locations, was sold in 2008 to the Ruth Chris chain. The interior of the restaurant, with it dark wood paneling is intended to resemble dining on a cruise ship. The fish is fresh, but the taste is uninspired.

Hours: Monday - Thursday, 11:30 am - 10 pm; Friday and Saturday until 11 pm; Sunday until 9 pm.

Prices: Lunch, Sandwiches, $10 - $15, Salads, $11 - $14, entrees, $13 - $22; Dinner entrees, $19 - $30;

Wine by the glass, $7 - $17, micro brews, $5 - $10.

Size: Seats 280 - 300.

RESTAURANTS

Morello Bistro (Italian)

253 Greenwich Avenue, 203.661.3443

www.MorelloBistro.com

Bernard's, Dome, Gaia—this architectural gem of a restaurant has given us many happy memories. Now Morello, with Chef Townsend Wentz's interpretation of classic Italian favorites, we are in for more good times. Expect the same exciting domed interior, a meeting place style bar and refined cuisine. Portions are not too generous, but maybe this is a good thing, it leaves room for tiramisu.

Hours: Saturday brunch, noon - 3 pm; Sunday brunch, 11:30 am - 3 pm; Lunch, weekdays, noon - 2:30 pm;

Dinner, Monday - Wednesday, 5 pm - 9:30 pm; Thursday 5 pm - 10 pm; Friday and Saturday, 5 pm - 10:30 pm, Sunday dinner 5 pm - 9 pm.

Closed Mondays from July 5 - September 6.

Prices: Sunday, prix fixe Brunch $22; Lunch, Pasta entrees $18 - $20, Meat & Fish entrees $23 - $34, prix fixe lunch $20;

Dinner, Pasta entrees $19 - $22, Meat and Fish entrees $23 - $34;

Wine by the glass $6 - $18.

Size: Seats 120, plus second-floor private dining rooms.

Morgans Fish House (seafood)

22 Elm Place (bet. Purchase & Theodore Fremd)

Rye NY, 914.921.8190

www.MorgansFishHouse.net

Morgans is part of the Pearl Restaurant group which also owns the Rye Grill,1020 Post and Elm Street Oyster House. They know what dining is all about: cheerful, knowledgeable service and expertly prepared food in a pretty setting. Morgans is ultra-modern with the chefs preparing the food clearly on view.

Hours: Sunday brunch, 11:30 am - 3 pm.

Monday - Thursday, noon - 10 pm,

Friday and Saturday, noon - 11pm, Sunday noon - 10 pm.

Prices: Sunday Brunch $12 - $25; one menu for Lunch & Dinner: salads and casual entrees $11 - $25, entrees $21 - $34, sides $5 - 9;

Wine by the glass $8 - $15.

Size: Seats 150 plus a private room which seats 50.

RESTAURANTS

Morton's The Steakhouse (formerly Morton's of Chicago)

377 North State Street (Swiss Bank Center)
Stamford CT, 203.324.3939, www.Mortons.com
A carnivore's paradise with excellent service. This upscale chain, with
79 locations, was founded in 1978. Their business seems to be based on
business expense accounts, with the average bill running $90 - $100 per
person. If the menu presentation doesn't turn you into a vegetarian, you
will find the steak quality as good as it gets. Forget the seafood and the
sauces, this restaurant is all about the cuts and quality of their beef.
Choose creamed spinach as a side and the hot chocolate cake (not the
souffles) for dessert.
Hours: No Lunch; Dinner, Monday - Saturday, 5 pm - 11 pm;
Sunday, until 10 pm.
Prices: Entrees $25 - $84. All side dishes are a la carte;
Wine by the glass $9 - $23 Size: Seats 200

My Favorite Place (American)

1 Strickland Avenue, Cos Cob, 203.869.1500
343 Greenwich Avenue
Order from the counter and take it home or sit down at one of the few
tables. They even have curbside pickup. This is a home-town, casual
restaurant at its best. Besides the good salads and popular hamburgers
(our favorite is "white heat"), we like the homemade potato chips, and
the chicken chili. This is a kid-friendly place.
Hours: weekdays 10 am - 9 pm; Saturday 11 am - 4 pm.
Prices: Burgers and Sandwiches $6 - $11; Salads $10 - $12;
Kids menu $2 - $6. Size: Seats 16.

Myrna's Mediterranean Bistro
(Middle Eastern/Lebanese)

866 East Main Street, Stamford CT, 203.869.2007,203.325.8736
www.Myrnas.com
Myrna Yanni, has created a restaurant serving her favorite foods—aro-
matic, healthy and colorful—in an informal setting. We like the spinach
pie, cheese samboussek and the fava beans as appetizers. Our favorite
entree is the chicken kebab. Try the combination plate, it's a good way to
find your favorite. Save room for the Katayey Ashta dessert.
Hours: Monday - Saturday, 10 am - 9:30 pm; Sunday noon - 9 pm
Prices: Lunch & Dinner Entrees $117 - $23, pita wraps $10, Salads $10 -
$12, price fixed menu $38; Limited Children's menu $9;
Wine by the glass $7-$9. Size: Seats 50.

Napa & Company (New American)

75 Broad Street, Stamford CT, 203.353.3319

(located in the Courtyard By Marriott)

www.NapaAndCompany.com

This restaurant is not only about good food, but fun. When you see the menu, you will realize this is a "tasting party". All kinds of wines by the glass (with your choice of a three-ounce or seven- ounce size), 20 different cheeses, interesting small plate servings and a short list of unusual main course entrees. Whimsical descriptions of the wines and cheeses, for instance "award winner, barnyard, hay", make choosing fun. The menu changes often to allow the use of local seasonal organic produce. The ambiance is chic modern, with bottle lined walls. The happy bar crowd can make table conversation challenging.

Hours: Breakfast weekdays, 6:30 am - 10 am; weekends, 7:30 am - 10: 30 am; Lunch, weekdays, 11:30 am - 2:30 pm;

Dinner, Monday - Saturday, 5:30 - 10 pm.

Prices: Lunch, salads $14 - $21, sandwiches $16 - $19, entrees $17 - $25; Dinner, artisan cheeses 3 for $15 or 6 for $23, small plates, $15 - $20, entrees, $28 - $45, a Napa Wagyu (kobe-style beef) Burger for $24; Wine by the glass, (3 oz) $3 - $12, (7 oz) $ $6 - $24.

Size: Seats 30 in one section and 45 in another.

Nessa (Italian)

325 North Main Street, Port Chester NY, 914.939.0119

www.NessaRestaurant.com

When you are ready for a perky twist to Italian cuisine, try this charming enotecca, named after co-owner Marc Tessitore's wife, Vanessa. Intimate, with glowing candles and low light. The main part of the restaurant is lively and noisy. A quieter, romantic space, with seating for 10, is at the back of the restaurant. We were delighted to find the service swift and attentive. Bruschettas and panini are featured, you can even have a panini with Nutella and bananas for dessert. We are fond of starting with the prosciutto (ricotta and figs) bruschetta followed by the linguine con vongole. Be sure to reserve on weekends.

Hours: Dinner, Sunday - Thursday, 5:30 pm - 10 pm;

Friday and Saturday, 5:30 pm - 11 pm; Sunday, 11 am - 3 pm.

Prices: Beginning courses, bruschetta $3 each, Panini $8 each,

salads, $12 - $15, main courses, $17 - $38;

Wine by the quartino (about 1/3 bottle) $11 - $19.

Size: Seats 76.

RESTAURANTS

North Star (New American)

85 Westchester Ave, (Scotts Corners) Pound Ridge NY
914.764.0200
www.NorthStarNY.com
Next to New Canaan, in quaint Scotts Corners, is a cozy country restaurant with a menu filled with savory selections. The Halibut and sea bass are their signature dishes. We also like the steak with peppercorn sauce. The service is welcoming. Always make a reservation—even on weekdays.
Hours: Dinner, Monday - Saturday 5:30 pm - 9:30 pm;
Sunday, 5 pm - 9 pm, live music Sunday and Thursday evenings.
Prices: Entrees $19 - $36; Wine by the glass $8 - $12.
Size: Seats 42 inside, 20 seats outside in the summer.

Nuage (Asian Fusion, Japanese-French)

203 East Putnam Avenue (Mill Pond Plaza), Cos Cob, 203.869.2339
www.NuageRestaurant.com
This small restaurant, with its unpretentious decor, has a menu of sophisticated and artistically presented dishes that diners with discriminating taste rave about. The noise level is relatively low, making it a pleasant place to have a conversation. We always choose one of the tasting menus and the delicious chocolate pyramid for dessert. A favorite of ours!
Hours: Lunch, weekdays 11:45 am to 2:30 pm; Dinner every night, 5:30 pm - 9:45 (Friday & Saturday to 10:30, Sunday to 9:30)
Prices: Lunch, entrees $15 - $25 (Kobe beef $60); Dinner, entrees, $22 - $38 (Kobe beef $78); tasting menus: five course $70 and up, six course (w/Kobe) $110, seven course $85 and up; wine by the bottle $25-$52, wine by the glass $9-$23.
Size: seats 46.

TIP: PAUL TUDOR JONES CHRISTMAS LIGHTS

The unbelievable display of Christmas lights by Paul Tudor Jones at his waterfront home on Harbor Drive in Belle Haven, has become so popular that the Greenwich Police are assigned to direct traffic. Public viewing is usually from 5 to 9 pm daily through December 20.

Ole Mole (Mexican)

- 130 High Ridge Road, (shopping center), Stamford CT
  203.461.9962
- 1020 Boston Post Road (behind 1020), Darien CT,
  203.202.7051

www.OleMole.net

When you are in the mood for fresh, healthy Mexican cuisine, Ole Mole is your best bet. The Darien restaurant is the place to go when you want to sit down and enjoy a meal. The unimposing Stamford location is bare bones and primarily for take-out. Both places have quick friendly service and the same great food. Be sure to try the Sopa de Tortilla, Ole Mole salad, enchiladas suizas or the mole poblano.

Hours: Monday - Thursday 11:30 am - 9:30 pm;

Friday & Saturday until 10 pm; Sunday Noon - 9 pm.

Prices: Entrees $14 - $17; Wine by the glass in Darien $7 - $11.

Size: Stamford seats about 12, Darien seats 42.

Oriental Gourmet (Chinese)

214 Sound Beach Avenue, Old Greenwich, 203.637.1010

For years Olivia and her family have been traveling across town to eat in their favorite Chinese restaurant, where they always order Szechuan Dumplings and Sesame Chicken. Old Greenwich residents have long been in the know about the very good food in this modest restaurant. Eat-in or takeout, this is a real find. This restaurant was the launching place for the owners of Penang and Asiana.

Hours: Monday - Saturday 11 am - 10 pm (Friday & Saturday to 11pm), Sunday (dinner menu all day) noon -10 pm; lunch menu until 3 pm.

Prices: Lunch specials, $6 - $7; Dinner entrees $9 - $14, gourmet specialties $11 - $15. Size: Seats 27.

RESTAURANTS

Osetra Restaurant (Seafood)

124 South Washington street, South Norwalk, 203.354.4488
www.OsetraSono.com

We were fifteen minutes late and they had given our 7 o'clock table away
—but they might have one available for us at 10 pm. Its popularity can't
be the simple, unobtrusive, beige decor or the friendly, but slightly incompetent service. It certainly is not a dress-up restaurant, the staff wears
"frayed" Madewell jeans. So it must be the food—and we love it. Nouvelle
fish dishes dominate the menu. Sides must be purchased separately and
are equally nouvelle and delicious, such as our favorite "roasted hearts
of palm".

Hours: Lunch, Thursday - Sunday 12 pm - 3 pm;
Dinner, Tuesday - Thursday 5 pm - 10 pm (Friday & Saturday to 11 pm),
Sunday 12 pm - 8 pm.
Prices: Dinner, burgers and sandwiches $12 - $22, entrees $15 - $32,
sides $4 - $10; wine by the glass $7 - $16.
Size: seats 46 inside (plus stools for 12), seats for 8 outside (summer).

Outback (Steak)

60 S. Broadway, White Plains NY, 914.684.1397
www.Outback.com

Outback is a casual chain based in Florida. It was founded in 1988 and
has 900 locations. Despite its Australian theme, Outback serves American cuisine, with Creole influences. The Bloomin' Onion is the signature
Outback item. Most Outbacks serve Foster's Lager, an Australian brand
of beer largely sold outside of Australia.

Hours: Dinner only, Monday - Thursday, 4 pm - 10 pm,
Friday 4 pm - 11 pm, Saturday 3 pm - 11 pm, Sunday 3 pm - 10 pm.
Prices: Burgers & Sandwiches $9 - $14, Steak $15 - $24,
other entrees $11 - $28.
Size: Seats 60, 30 on each side.

RESTAURANTS

P. F. Chang's China Bistro (Chinese)

* Stamford Town Center, 230 Tresser Blvd, Stamford CT
  203.363.0434
* Westchester Mall, 125 Westchester Avenue, White Plains NY
  914.997.6100

www.PFChangs.com

Without a reservation the wait for a table in this elaborately decorated restaurant can often be 45 minutes. This chain of 133 restaurants manages to keep their large dining rooms filled with adults and children, clearly having a good time. If you have enjoyed delicacies from the different regions of China, you will discover this is not fine Chinese food, but it is not bad. It comes from that mystical Chinese region "PF Chang", where the cuisine is intended to please the American pallet. (Actually the initials stand for the founder Paul Fleming.) Enjoy it for what it is, try their orange peel chicken and lettuce wraps. This is family fare for mall shoppers. Ask for a pager, then shop until your table is ready.

Hours: Every day, 11 am - 11 pm (Friday & Saturday to midnight.)
Lunch menu ends at 4 pm.
Prices: Lunch bowls $8 - $10, Chicken/Duck entrees $12 - $20,
Beef/Pork/Lamb $12 - $15, grilled $15 - $23, seafood $13 - $18,
noodles $7 - $12.
Size: Seats 360.

(La) Paella (Spanish)

44 Main Street, Norwalk CT, 203.831.8636

www.LapaellaTapasWineBarRestaurant.com

On a mostly commercial street with an unpretentious facade, you will discover a cheerful, attractive restaurant. There is something about this restaurant that makes you expect the kitchen to turn out top quality paellas and tapas. You won't be disappointed. Don't forget the sangria.

Hours: Closed Monday; Lunch, Tuesday - Friday, noon - 2:30 pm;
Dinner Tuesday - Sunday, 5:30 pm - 10 pm.
Prices: Lunch, Paellas $11 - $15, tapas $6 - $25, platos $12 - $16;
Dinner, Paellas $19 - $25, tapas $10 - $25, platos $20 - $27;
Wine by the glass $7 -$9.
Size: Seats 48.

RESTAURANTS

Panda Pavilion 3 (Chinese)

420 West Putnam Avenue, 203.869.111
203.869.1931, 203.869.1209
www.Panda3gw.com
We always feel relaxed at this Chinese restaurant and sushi bar. This is a good place for little ones to learn to use chop sticks. Try one of our favorites: General Tao's chicken, orange beef or ginger beef. Free delivery for orders of $20 and over. Check the website under "special" for coupons.
Hours: Lunch everyday, 11:30 am - 3 pm;
Dinner, Sunday & Monday - Thursday, 3 pm - 9:30 pm,
Friday & Saturday, until 10:30 pm.
Prices: Lunch specials $7 - $9; Dinner entrees, $10 - $18, sushi $5 - $12;
Wine by the glass, $4 - $5; Size: Seats about 60.

Panera (Fast Food)

10 Westchester Avenue, Port Chester NY, 914.939.0079
www.Panerabread.com
Located at the movie complex in Port Chester, their soups and sandwiches are a delight. Order at the counter, then have a seat in the large airy dining space and wait for your name to be called. We wish they had shorter lines, although the wait does afford time to decide what to order.
Hours: Sunday - Wednesday, 7 am - 8 pm; Thursday, 7 am - 9 pm;
Friday & Saturday 7 am - 10 pm.
Prices: Panini & sandwiches $7, salads $6; Size: Seats 100.

(La) Pantiere (French)

530 Milton Road, Rye NY, 914.967.8140
www.LaPanetiere.com
For 21 years, one of Westchester County's best, only fifteen minutes away, serving classic French food in an attractive Provenal-style dining room. Relatively quiet, you can have a conversation. For that special evening, the decor, attentive service and delightful food make this restaurant a perfect choice. We recommend the July 14 (Bastille Day) tasting menu. Jackets required, ties preferred.
Hours: Lunch, Tuesday - Friday & Sunday, noon - 2:30 pm; Dinner, Monday to Saturday, 6 pm - 9:30 pm; Sunday, 5 pm - 8:30 pm.
Advance reservations strongly recommended, no minimum.
Prices: Lunch entrees $10 - $19 (rather small portions), Lunch Pre Fix menu $15, Sunday Lunch Pre Fix $45; Dinner entrees $33 - $41, Pre Fix menu 3 course $45 or $63 with wine, 5 course $68 or $101 with wine; wine by the glass $9-14. Size: Seats 80, downstairs and upstairs.

RESTAURANTS

I-HOP (American)
2410 Summer Street, Stamford CT, 203.324.9819
www.ihop.com
As you probably know, IHOP, a.k.a. International House of Pancakes, is the place for chocolate pancakes and every imaginable breakfast treat.
Hours: Open every day, 7 am - 10 pm.

Il Sogno Ristorante (Italian)
316 Boston Post Road, Port Chester NY, 914.937.7200
www.IlSognoNY.com
Not where you would expect - in the midst of tire stores and fast foods - there is a sophisticated, NYC style Italian restaurant run by a Manhattan chef. The decor is stylish and the wait staff is professional. The Risotto with white truffles is a speciality, as is the baked bronzino. While waiting, we were given a delicious potato croquette. The bread comes with a wonderful vegetable dip. We like the ravioli stuffed with goat cheese, but whatever you order, save room for the zabaglione for dessert.
Hours: Open 7 days a week, Lunch noon - 3 pm; Dinner, 5 pm - 10 pm (Friday & Saturday to 11 pm.)
Prices: Lunch & Dinner, pasta $14 - $18, other entrees, $19 - $28 (bronzino at market price.)
Size: Seats 85 in the main dining room and 45 upstairs.

Jean-Louis (French)
61 Lewis Street, 203.622.8450
www.RestaurantJeanLouis.com
Still our favorite French restaurant. This is an elegant, intimate, refined restaurant; not a large, grandiose one. You will be delighted with Jean-Louis Gerin's new French cuisine. He was named by the James Beard Foundation as the best chef in the Northeast. He won the Toque D'Argent which is awarded to the top French chef in North America. His skillfully prepared dishes are made from ingredients as fresh as spring. The service makes you feel special and comfortable, due in large part to Linda Gerin's gracious hospitality. The prix fixe menu is always a great choice.
Hours: Lunch, weekdays, noon - 2 pm (no lunch in August);
Dinner, weekdays, seating starts at 5:45 pm; Saturday, seatings at 6:15 & 8:45 pm. Be sure to make reservations.
Prices: Lunch entrees $20 - $22, (prix fixe menu $29); Dinner entrees, $38 - $41, (Prix fixe menus $59 & $69.)
Size: Seats 45, private room for 8 - 20 guests.

RESTAURANTS

Paradise Bar & Grill (Seafood)

78 Southfield Avenue (Stamford Landing), Stamford CT, 203.323.1116
www.ParadiseBarAndGrille.com
Located on the water at the Stamford Landing, near Dolphin Cove. Eating here is like stepping into a tropical sea-side restaurant. In summer, dine open-air on the boardwalk. Try the charcoal-broiled fish entrees. The pizzas are another good choice. Children are welcome.
Hours can change, check before going.
Summer Hours: Lunch, everyday, noon - 3pm; Dinner, every day, 5 pm - 10 pm (Sunday, until 9:30 pm.) Summer reservations may only be accepted for eight or more.
Winter Hours: Monday - Wednesday, 11:30 am - 9 pm;
Thursday - Sunday, 11:30 am - 10 pm.
Winter reservations are accepted for two or more.
Prices: Sunday Brunch $12 - $17; Lunch, salads & sandwiches $12 - $15, Pizza $10 - $12, casual entrees, $14 - $16; Dinner, salads & sandwiches $12 - $15, pizza $10 - $12, fajitas $16 - $17, entrees $20 - $35; Wine by the glass $7 - $10. Size: 160 winter, 200 summer.

Pasquale Ristorante (Italian)

2 Putnam Avenue (border of Greenwich), Port Chester NY
914.934.7770
www.pasqualeristorante.com
This family-style restaurant serves traditional southern Italian food in a friendly, homespun atmosphere. The setting is unpretentious—specials are presented on a blackboard with prices. The menu offers a large selection of good food. We recommend the the Pollo alla Francese and the Salmone ala Dijonese.
Hours: Closed Monday; Tuesday - Thursday noon - 10 pm,
Friday noon - 11 pm; Saturday 3 pm - 11 pm, Sunday 1 pm - 9 pm.
Prices: Lunch, pasta $11 - $13, other entrees, $11 - $19; Dinner, pasta $14 - $21, other entrees $20 - $27; Wine by the glass $8.
Size: Main dining room seats 58, party room for 60.

RESTAURANTS

Pasta Nostra (Italian)
116 Washington Street, Norwalk CT, 203.854.9700
www.PastaNostra.com
You must dine at this restaurant. The Spartan, simple decor sends a clear message, this place is about food and service. Its inventive, continually changing menu is brilliant. If it says the best stuffed pepper you will ever eat, it is. If they have seafood on the menu, devour it. Beware: reservations are usually necessary but owner, Chef Bruno often requires a $25 credit card deposit in case you don't show or don't cancel by 3 pm. American Express cards are not accepted.
Hours: Dinner only, Wednesday - Saturday, 6 pm - closing (about 10 pm.)
Prices: Entrees, $23 - $40; Wine by 1/4 bottle $8 - $17.
Size: Seats about 40.

Pasta Vera (Italian)
48 Greenwich Avenue, 203.661.9705
www.PastaVera.com
This popular, casual restaurant is noted for its homemade pastas. But that doesn't mean pasta is the only tasty choice. We like their other dishes too. First-time visitors should try their homemade ravioli or seafood special. It's a great place for a late lunch. For takeouts, they have a variety of fresh, ready-to-go selections.
Hours: Lunch, Monday - Saturday 11:30 am - 3 pm; Dinner, Monday - Saturday, 5 pm - 10 pm, Sunday, 3 pm - 9 pm; Open most holidays.
Prices: Lunch entrees, $9 - $13; Dinner entrees, $15 - $28.
Size: Seats 58; reservations are accepted for parties of six or more.

Patrias (Spanish)
35 North Main Street, Port Chester NY, 914.937.0177
When you are looking for something interesting, this small, attractive restaurant with its friendly service is just the spot. Begin with tapas or the shrimp chowder, then try one of the fish dishes or the skirt steak. Finish with fried ice cream.
Hours: Breakfast, weekdays, 10am-noon; Lunch, weekdays,noon - 3 pm; Dinner, every day 5 pm - 10 pm.
Prices: same menu for lunch & dinner, tapas $7 - $10, Paellas $22 - $45, Fish $13 - $19, meat, $12 - $20; children's menu $6 - $7.
Wine by the glass $8 - $9, pitcher of sangria $30;
Size: Seats 40.

Pellicci's (Italian)

96 Stillwater Avenue, Stamford CT, 203.323.2542
www.pelliccis.com

After almost 60 years serving bountiful family-style meals, Pellicci's knows how to do it. Tucked away on a side street where you might not expect to find a bustling large restaurant, you will be greeted by helpful valet parking in a secure parking lot. Expect good food in this informal, friendly place. First time visitors should try their "Family Style Dinner". A great place to go with a group.

Hours: Monday - Thursday, 11 am - 11 pm;
Friday and Saturday, 11 am - midnight; Sunday, 11 am - 10 pm.
Prices: One menu all day: Family style menu $18,
Italian specialties $11 - $14, Beef & pork entrees $19 - $27,
Chicken & veal $15 - $20, Seafood $16 - Market, Pizzas $10 - $23.
Wine by the glass $8; Children's menu $9 - $10.
Size: Seats 200 upstairs, 90 downstairs.

Penang Grill (Asian)

55 Lewis Street, 203.861.1988

Casual dining with very good Pan-Asian food. When you want something flavorful and unique, head to this small, established restaurant. The service is friendly and attentive. The refreshing mango chicken is our favorite. Popular for takeout.

Hours: Monday - Thursday, 11 am - 10 pm;
Friday & Saturday, 11 am - 11 pm; Sunday, noon - 10 pm.
Lunch menu until 3 pm except Sunday with dinner menu all day.
Prices: Lunch specials $8 - $11; Dinner entrees, $12 - $20.
Take-out menu is slightly less expensive.
Size: Seats 24. No reservations accepted. Bring your own wine.

Pierangelo (Italian)

355 Greenwich Avenue, 203.869.3411
www.pierangeloonline.com

The decor in this 10-table restaurant is sophisticated and puts you in the mood for a nice experience. We like dining here. Usually it is quiet enough to have a conversation. We especially like the tuna, salmon & fettuccini. Good wine list with many choices by the glass. This warmly lit restaurant is busy, be sure to reserve.

Hours: Lunch, weekdays, noon - 3 pm;
Dinner, Monday - Saturday 5:30 - 10 pm, Sunday, 5 pm - 9 pm.
Prices: Lunch, salads $9 - $18, Pastas $15 - $18, other entrees $20 - $25;
Dinner, Pastas $22 - $29, other entrees, $30 - $45;
Wine by the glass $11 - $25. Size: Seats 40.

RESTAURANTS

Piero's (Italian)
44 South Regent Street, Port Chester NY, 914.937.2904
Casual, off-the-beaten-path Italian. This little restaurant, with decor that doesn't seem to change, has a loyal following. Diners like being greeted by the owner and treated like family by the waiters.
Hours: Lunch, Tuesday - Friday, noon - 2:30 pm; Dinner, Tuesday - Thursday & Sunday 5 pm - 9:30 pm; Friday & Saturday 5 pm - 10:30 pm.
Prices: Lunch, $12 - $17; Dinner, $15 - $25; Wine by the glass $5 - $7. Visa and Master Card only. Size: Seats 45 - 55.

Pizza Factory (Pizza)
380 Greenwich Avenue, 203.661.5188
Not everyone can agree on the best pizza place, but Pizza Factory's pizza is always competing for the top of the list. In the 2003 Pizza Contest held by Anderson Associates, they were voted one of the top four. Be sure to try their gorgonzola salad and four cheese thin crust pizza. They have table service, carry out and delivery. They accept credit cards or a Greenwich check.
Hours: Monday - Thursday & Sunday, 11 am - 10 pm; Friday and Saturday, until 11 pm.
Prices: Specialty Pizzas(10", 14" & 16"), the 14" size is $15 - $19. Size: Seats about 25.

Pizza Post (Pizza)
522 East Putnam Avenue, Cos Cob, 203.661.0909
A local favorite. Winner of the town wide pizza contest. No deliveries. Credit cards and local checks.
Hours: Monday - Thursday 11 am - 10 pm; Friday & Saturday 11 am - 11 pm; Sunday noon - 10 pm.
Prices: Pizzas (10", 12", 16") 16" special pizzas $13 - $20; Sandwiches, calzones & Panini $7 - $10, pastas $11 - $17, entrees $16 - $18; Sauces by the pint $5 - $9. Size: Seats 34.

Planet Pizza (Pizza)
28 Railroad Avenue, 203.622.0999
www.PlanetPizza.com
A small chain serving traditional New York City-style pizza, calzones, subs, salads, wraps, pasta and entrees right next to the theater and train station. Clean, well-lighted dining area.
Hours: Monday - Thursday, 10 am - 11 pm; Friday & Saturday, 10 am - midnight; Sunday, 11 am - 10:30 pm.
Prices: pizzas (14", 16" & 18"); the 14" size is $14 - $19; entrees $14 - $17. Size: Seats about 30.

Polpo (Italian)

554 Old Post Road #3, 203.629.1999

www.PolpoRestaurant.com

This out-of-the-way Italian restaurant serves delicious Tuscan cuisine. It is a popular Greenwich destination for those in the know. It is located in a charming 100 year-old stone house. The restaurant has good vibes. The ambiance is warm, the service is attentive. Diners always seem to be in a festive, noisy mood. Quieter tables are upstairs. The lively piano music is downstairs. Allow time for making decisions—the menu is filled with appealing choices.

Hours: Monday - Saturday, 11:45 am - 11:30 pm; Sunday, noon - 10 pm.

Prices: pastas $22 - $26, other entrees, $24 - $42; Wine by the glass .

Size: seats 53

Pomodoro (Italian)

1247 East Putnam Avenue (Riverside Shopping Center) 203.698.7779

www.PomodoroRiverside.com

Friendly, casual, family dining. A popular spot with youngsters. If there were a contest for the largest portions, this small, charmingly decorated restaurant might win. Pizzas are popular, but we also like their "Greenwich Avenue" salad and Chicken Francese. They sell sauces by the pint.

Hours: Sunday - Thursday, 11 am - 10 pm;

Friday and Saturday, 11 am - 11 pm.

Prices: Lunch specials (sandwiches, panino & wraps,) $8 - $11; Dinner, medium gourmet Pizzas, $18 - $21; pastas $10 - $16, dinner entrees, $16 - $20; children's menu is $8; Wine by the glass $10 - $12.

Size: Seats 40.

Putnam Restaurant (American)

373 Greenwich Avenue, 203.869.4683

www.putnamrestaurant.com

This inexpensive, informal hometown restaurant, with clouds painted on the ceiling, has been in business since 1955. We hope it stays. Their menu is like a diner's with a large number of selections. The menu has a vegetarian section. Their specials are always a good choice. We like the Gorgonzola salad and Fettuccine Alfredo. Stop here for a traditional breakfast, morning, noon & night.

Hours: Every day, even most holidays, 7 am - 10 pm.

Prices: Burgers & sandwiches, $5 - $7; Dinners, $10 - $17.

Size: Seats 32 in the front booths & 32 at tables in the back.

RESTAURANTS

Q (Barbeque)

112 North Main Street, Port Chester NY, 914.933.7427

www.QRestaurantAndBar.com

Jeffrey and Jennifer Kohn, owners of the terrific Kneaded Bread opened another top-notch place. They went on a 25-restaurant barbecue tasting journey before opening Q, a slightly Spartan restaurant (order at the counter and they bring the food to your table.) Thank heavens they took this journey and we can satisfy our cravings for authentic pulled pork and beef brisket. For sides, order collard greens and baked beans.

Hours: weekdays, 11 am - 3 pm, 5 pm - 11 pm;

Saturday, 10 am - 11 pm; Sunday, 10 am - 10 pm.

Prices: Sandwich + 1 side $9 - $12, combo plate (2 meats + 2 sides + cornbread) $17. Size: Seats 75.

Rasa (Indian)

107-109 Greenwich Avenue, 203.869.0700 (1084)

www.FineIndianDining.com

Slightly hidden away, there is an entrance on Greenwich Avenue, but the main entrance is upstairs next to the CVS parking lot. This stylish and brightly decorated restaurant has very tasty Indian food, with many vegetarian and vegan options. The lunch buffet is a great way to enjoy their food and service. Be sure to call ahead to tell them you want to try their dessert Semiya Payasam.

Hours: Open every day, Lunch 12 pm - 3 pm , Dinner 4 pm - 9:45 pm.

Prices: Lunch, buffet $9 ($11 on weekends), entrees $6 - $9;

Dinner entrees $11 - $20. Size: seats 44.

Rebecca's (New American)

265 Glenville Road, 203.532.9270

www.RebeccasGreenwich.com

This Manhattan-chic restaurant is tucked in southwestern Greenwich. It serves modern American cuisine with a French flair. Rebecca Kirhoffer has assembled a sophisticated wine list to match her husband Chef Reza Khorshidi's awesome food. He received *Connecticut Magazine's* best contemporary chef award. The sleek modern restaurant has a large window so you can see the kitchen. It can be noisy.

Hours: Lunch, Tuesday - Friday, 11:30 am - 2:30 pm; Dinner, Tuesday - Thursday 5:30 pm - 9:30 pm; Friday & Saturday, 5:30 pm - 10:30 pm.

Be sure to make a reservation well in advance (a month's notice wouldn't hurt), although you might be able to drop in and eat at the bar.

Prices: Lunch entrees $25 - $40, Dinner entrees $38 - $46 (specials often more); Wine by the glass $12-25. Size: Seats 74.

RESTAURANTS

Republic Grill Asian Bistro (Asian)

235 Bedford Street, Stamford CT, 203.353.8005
www.asianbistrogroup.com
Even if you didn't know it was owned by Tengda, you would notice the similarities between the two. The menu is almost the same and the decor is strange contemporary. The food and service are hit and miss. The patrons are just as eclectic as the food: couples with babies, octogenarians, and singles on a date.
Hours: Monday - Thursday, 11 am - 10 pm; Friday to 11 pm;
Saturday, 11:30 am - 11 pm; Sunday, Noon - 10 pm.
Prices: Lunch, rolls $8, entrees $6 - $8;
Dinner, Rolls $5 - $16, entrees $16 - $24;
Wine by the glass $7 - $11.
Size: Seats 40.

Rio Border (Mexican/Tex Mex)

330 Connecticut Avenue, Norwalk CT, 203.855.9577
www.rioborderrestaurant.com
When *Connecticut Magazine* awarded their best Mexican in Fairfield County to Rio Border we were surprised. Rio is a tacky restaurant in a unpretentious shopping center, serving large portions of mediocre food. Many of the friendly servers have been there since Rio opened 11 years ago.
Hours: Lunch menu, weekdays 11:30 am - 2:30 pm,
Dinner menu weekdays 5 pm - 9:30 pm (Friday to 10 pm),
Saturday 11:30 am - 10:30 pm, Sunday 11:30 am - 9 pm.
Prices: Lunch entrees $8-$11, kids $4-$5, Dinner entrees $13-$18, kids $5- $6. Size: seats 100

Rodney's Roadside (Lunch Wagon Fast Food)

Glenville Road
Nothing beats a tasty hot dog. Do you like yours with chili, mustard, cheese, relish or all of the above? Joe Kralik serves hotdogs, hamburgers, steak sandwiches and more from his roadside lunch stand nestled in the pretty little park on Glenville Road.
Hours: summertime, weekdays, 10 am - 2:30 pm.

RESTAURANTS

Rouge (American - Tapas & Wine Bar)

88 Washington Street, South Norwalk CT, 203.354.4781

www.RougeWineBar-CT.com

A large bar dominates the middle of this mostly red, slightly bordelloesque, fun place for a glass of wine and one or two small plates. We like the "Greek Spreads with Pita Bread". Nice service but slow.

Hours: Dinner: Monday - Thursday & Sunday 5 pm - 10 pm (bar open to 1 am), Friday & Saturday 5 pm - 11 pm (bar open to 2 am).

Prices: tappas & mezze $9 - $14, entrees $19 - $25;

Wine by the glass $7 - $11, Champagne by the glass $10 - $19.

Size: seats 36.

Rowayton Seafood Company (Seafood)

89 Rowayton Avenue, Rowayton CT, 203.866.4488

www.RowaytonSeafood.com

Located in a charming town, this popular, informal and relaxed restaurant is just right for summer dining. A good place to bring landlocked visitors for lobster and a view of the water. Consistently good food and our favorite place for New England clam chowder and fried oysters. The service is kind and accommodating.

Hours: Lunch, every day, 11:30 am - 3 pm; a limited menu is sometimes available from 3 pm - 5 pm;

Dinner Monday - Wednesday, 5 pm - 10 pm; Thursday - Sunday, 5 pm - 11 pm.

On weekends, be sure to make reservations well in advance.

Prices: Lunch, sandwiches $11 - $17, entrees, $16 - $22; Dinner, burger $11, fish entrees, $24 - $29, other entrees, $22 - $45; Lobster @ market;

Wine by the glass, $8 - $12.

Size: Seats 65.

TIP: GREEK FESTIVAL

In October every year, the Church of the Archangels, (Bedford & Third Streets), Stamford CT has a festival with authentic Greek food. To find out the exact date or request a take out, call 203.348.4216 or visit :
www.ArchAngels.CT.GoArch.org

RESTAURANTS

Robeks (Smoothies)

132 East Putnam Avenue, Cos Cob, 203.622.6520

www.Robeks-ctny.com

California smoothies have come to Greenwich. Robeks is a franchise chain started in 1966. It has 140 locations in 16 states (90 of the locations are in California.) They offer a huge assortment of smoothies. Healthy eating is their theme. We like the nutritional information they provide on each product.

Hours: weekdays, 6:30 am - 8 pm; Saturday, 8 am - 8 pm; Sunday, 9 am - 7 pm.

Prices: Junior, $4; Regular, $5; Large, $5.50.

Size: Take-out only.

Roger Sherman Inn (French/American)

195 Oenoke Ridge Road (Route 124), New Canaan CT 203.966.4541

www.RogerShermanInn.com

Built in the 1700s, this is one of the oldest and prettiest inns in Fairfield County. With its gracious service, the Inn is just right for elegant parties or romantic evenings. The menu, which changes with the seasons, is American with a lovely French accent. Remember to order the Arlequin souffle in advance.

Hours: Breakfast for guests only; Sunday brunch noon - 2:30 pm; Lunch, Monday - Saturday noon to 2:30; Dinner, every day, 5:30 pm - 9:30 pm. (not served January March);

Dinner, weekdays, 6 pm - 8 pm; weekends, 6 pm - 9:30 pm; It's wise to make reservations.

Prices: Lunch entrees $12 - $32; dinner entrees $21 - $42; Wine by the glass $9 - $15; Pre-fixe Sunday brunch $28; Double bedrooms $175-$350 a night.

Size: Seats 80 in the main dining room.

RESTAURANTS

Rotisserie (Fast Food)

280 Railroad Avenue, 203.661.0100

www.WillMortonsRotisserie.com

As soon as we tasted the North Carolina-style pulled pork sandwich, we knew we would be returning to this small, quick, casual eatery. Will Morton knows what people want—healthy food, good flavors and reasonable prices. If you are ordering take-out, check your order before you leave to make sure all the items are in the bag.

Hours: Monday - Thursday 11:30 am - 9 pm;

Friday & Saturday 11:30 am - 10 pm.

Prices: Sandwiches $9 - $19; entrees specialities $9 - $17; Wine by the glass, $8 - $12. Size: Seats 26 - 30.

Route 22 (American)

1980 West Main Street (US-1 at Commerce/ShopRite shopping center), Stamford CT, 203.323.2229 www.RT22Restaurant.com

Just across the border from Greenwich, in a shopping center, is a fun restaurant. During the day, all ages enjoy the funky 50's casual booth-style dining. Once in a while, everyone should treat themselves to a root-beer float and a banana split. On Friday evenings, a magician circulates, amazing children. Older kids enjoy the upstairs arcade and pool table. Then about 9:30 it morphs into a 20-something singles hot spot, with all kinds of entertainment.

Hours: Monday - Thursday, 11 am - 10 pm;

Friday and Saturday, 11 am - 11 pm; Sunday, 11 am - 9 pm.

Prices: salads $7 - $14, burgers, $10 - $16, sandwiches $12 - $13, entrees $15 - $26; kids menu $9 - $12.

Wine by the glass $6 - $12; Size: Seats 80.

Rye Grill & Bar (American)

1 Station Plaza, Rye, NY 914.967.0332 www.RyeGrill.com

"Lets meet at the Rye Grill"—this fun, attractive, high energy place is a great location to meet and greet your NY friends. The bar is large, noisy and an evening hot spot. In the main dining area, tables are filled with families. Upstairs is slightly dressier with white cloths. The service is swift and friendly. The un-fussy menu has some awesome food. This place is popular, always reserve.

Hours: Monday - Wednesday 11:30 am - 10 pm, Thursday - Saturday until 11 pm, Sunday brunch, 11: 30 am - 3 pm; Dinner, 3 pm - 9 pm.

Prices: Lunch & Dinner menu, salads $7 - $10, pizza $9 - $12, Sandwiches/sliders $8-$12, entrees $19-$34; children's menu $8-$9; wine by the glass $8-$13. Size: seats 300, party room seats 45.

RESTAURANTS

Saito (Japanese Fusion)

249 Railroad Avenue, Greenwich, 203.557.0880

www.Saito249Railroad.com

A stylish white, stark setting with an open kitchen, gives one the impression that food is the priority—and it is. What kind of cuisine? It is hard to say, although Asian ingredients predominate. Each dish we have tried was prepared to perfection. The portions can be tiny.

Hours: Lunch, Monday - Saturday 11:30 am - 2 pm;

Dinner, Tuesday - Thursday, 5:30 pm - 10 pm;

Friday and Saturday, 5:30 pm - 10:30 pm; Sunday, 5 pm - 9:30 pm. Closed Monday.

Prices: Lunch, Price fix 3-course menu $29, Sushi $16-$27, other entrees $13-$17;

Dinner, entrees $26-$35, Sushi Tasting (ordered in advance) $75; wine by the glass $8-$19. Size: seats 42

Saltwater Grill (Seafood)

183 Harbor Drive, Stamford CT, 203.391.6500

www.SaltwaterGrill.net

Boats in the harbor and evening sunsets (yes, the terrace faces West) make this a very pleasant place to be on a summer evening. This is not our destination for a gourmet meal, but it is perfect for relaxing, having a bloody Mary or a pomegranate martini and having a good time. We especially like the Lobster fritters and calamari starters as well as the nicoise salad. On weekends, the bar can be very active, most Saturday nights they have a DJ from 9 pm - 2 am. Be sure to make a reservation for dining.

Hours: Lunch, weekdays, 11:30 am - 4:30 pm;

Sunday Brunch, 11:30 am - 3:30 pm;

Dinner, Monday - Sunday, 5 pm - 10:30 pm (Friday & Saturday until 11.)

Prices: Lunch, entrees $8 - $21, sandwiches $8 - $9;

Dinner, entrees $17 - $45 (sides are $6), glass of wine $9 - $13.

Size: seats 340 inside and 150 outside.

RESTAURANTS

SBC (Pub)

131 Summer Street, Stamford CT, 203.327.2337
www.SouthPortBrewing.com
Once listed as the best place for beer in Connecticut, this brewery-style
eatery—though still very popular—needs polishing.
Hours: Sunday Brunch, 11:30 am - 2 pm;
Lunch, Monday - Saturday, 11:30 - 2 pm;
Dinner, Sunday, 2 pm - 9:30 pm,
Monday - Thursday, 2 pm - 10 pm, (Friday and Saturday to 11 pm);
Bar open, Sunday 2 pm - 1 am, Monday - Thursday, 11:30 am - 1 am
(Friday and Saturday to 2 am)
Prices: Lunch, salads $10 - $13, sandwiches $6 - $10,
entrees & pasta $8 - $14; Dinner, salads $13 - $17, sandwiches $9 - $11,
specialties $13 - $19; Tier 1, 2 & 3 beers, samplers $6.
Size: Seats 96 downstairs and 48 upstairs.

School House Restaurant (New American)

34 Cannon Road, Cannondale section of Wilton CT, 203.834.9816
www.SchoolHouseAtCannondale.com
It is rated one of the top fifty restaurants in the USA by
www.opentable.com and after eating in this quaint, attractive restaurant
we know why. The menu is limited (usually only five entrees), but you
should expect each one to be superb. The servers want the diners to have
a pleasant evening. Don't even think about going without a reservation.
Hours: Sunday brunch 10 am - 3 pm; Lunch Friday & Saturday 11:30 am
- 2 pm; Dinner Wednesday - Saturday 5:30 pm - 9:30 pm.
Prices: Brunch $12-$23, entrees $28-$30, 4-course prix fixe dinner
Thursday evening $40, wine by the glass $9-$14. Size: seats 36

Siena (Italian)

519 Summer Street, Stamford CT, 203.351.0898
www.sienaristorante.net
We are not sure why this Tuscan style Italian restaurant is so popular.
The setting is attractive, but the tables are close together and it is noisy.
When they are busy, reservations seem to carry only a little weight. We
find the food inconsistent. Your best bets are the duck ragu and the
chicken with sausage.
Hours: Lunch, weekdays noon - 2:30 pm;
Dinner Monday - Saturday 5:30 pm - 10 pm (10:30 Friday & Saturday)
Prices: Lunch entrees $14-$19, Dinner entrees $18-$31
Wine by the glass $10-$13. Size: seats 60.

RESTAURANTS

Smokey Joe's Bar-B-Q (Barbeque)

1308 East Main Street (US 1, exit 9 off I-95.), Stamford CT
203.406.0605 www.SmokeyJoesRibs.com

This is the best Texas Bar-B-Q this side of Fort Worth. Casual and inexpensive, Smokey Joe's offers a great variety of meats, gumbos and side dishes, in a cafeteria-style restaurant setting. The servings (on paper, not porcelain) are large, especially the Texas size. Order their beef brisket and pulled pork, with a side of collard greens and sweet potato fries. For cafeteria dining, enter the side door to the lower level.

Hours: Monday - Thursday 11:30 am - 9:30 pm,
Friday & Saturday 11:30 am - 10:30 pm, Sunday, 11:30 am - 9:30 pm; lunch specials served until 3 pm.
Prices: Lunch specials, 2 meats plus + 2 sides $12; Dinner, sandwiches, Burgers and Quesadillas $8 - $10; two-meat with sides $14 - $15; Wine by the glass $6. Size: seats 40 downstairs, 50 upstairs.

SoNo Baking Company & Café (Fast Food / Bakery)

101 South Water St., South Norwalk CT, 203.847.7666
www.SoNoBaking.com

A dear friend and food writer, first introduced us to this place, saying "its full of delicious pastries and breads." Soups and sandwiches are good here, too. Its not surprising, the owners are John Barricelli, Senior Food Editor for *Martha Stewart Living*, and Margot Olshan, Commissary Chef for Martha Stewart.

Hours: Sunday Brunch, 7 am - 2 pm;
Breakfast, Monday - Saturday, 7 am - 11:30 am;
Lunch, Monday - Saturday 11:30 am - 2 pm;
Bakery hours, Monday 7 am - 3 pm , Tuesday - Saturday 7 am - 5 pm (Sunday to 4 pm.)
Prices: Breakfast, $3 - $8, plus sides;
Lunch, salads & sandwiches $6 - $11.
Size: seats 26.

SoNo Caffeine (Coffee)

133 Washington Street, South Norwalk CT, 203.857.4224

A fun, eclectic place. Sink into a sofa and revive with a light meal and a cup of Joe. Check the website for music events.

Hours: Monday 7 am - 6 pm, Tuesday 7 am - 9 pm,
Wednesday & Thursday 7 am - 10 pm,
Friday & Saturday 8 am - midnight, Sunday 8 am - 9 pm.
Prices: Wraps & Paninis $7 - $8, breakfast sandwiches $6 - $7, desserts $3 - $7, medium teas and coffees $2 - $4.
Size: Seats 26.

RESTAURANTS

SoNo Seaport Seafood (Seafood)

100 Water Street, South Norwalk CT, 203.854.9483

www.sonoseaportseafood.com

A very, very informal, fun spot on the water to have lobster or fish and chips. The service is friendly and equally informal. Nice outside deck with picnic tables. Bring your children.

Hours: Open everyday; November - April, 11 am - 10 pm;
May - October, 11 am - 10 pm; reservations for parties of six or more.
Prices: Sandwiches $8 - $15, entrees $10 - $20, market for lobster, crab & mussels; Wine by the glass $5 - $7; children's menu $4 - $8.
Size: Seats 46 inside and 220 outside.

Sonora (New Latin American)

179 Rectory Street, Port Chester NY, 914.933.0200

www.SonoraRestaurant.net and www.PasionCatering.com

We continue to sing the praises of this popular, out-of-the-way restaurant. The total experience, unique decor, cheerful service, and "Latin American food with a flair"makes us happy. Start with the fresh guacamole (one order is more than enough for two) and it is sooo good. The country of origin is listed by each entree. You are bound to find one that fits your mood. Be sure to save room for passion fruit flan. Chef Palomino teaches cooking classes. Call for times.

Hours: Everyday, 5 pm - 10 pm (Friday & Saturday until 11 pm.); Sunday brunch, 11 am - 3 pm.
Prices: Lunch entrees, tapas $12 - $18, pre-fixed lunches $15 & $20; Dinner entrees, $20 - $30;
Wine by the glass $9 - $10, margaritas & mojitos $10.
Size: Seats 87 downstairs, 60 upstairs.

Sophia's Café (Fast Food)

1 Boulder Avenue, Old Greenwich, 203.344.1688

Featured in the *Greenwich Time* as one of the best places for "cheap eats", this tiny café has surprisingly good food and generous portions. Slightly difficult to find, it is just across the Post Road from Boston Market but totally opposite in concept. Owner and Chef Victor Colachagua prepares new soups and specials every day from scratch. Be sure to try one of his soups.

Hours: Monday - Saturday, 8:30 am - 8 pm. Closed Sunday.
Prices: Lunch, top 10 choices $7 - $8, Wraps $8, Paninis $7 - $8; Dinner entrees, $12 - $15, children's menu $6.95.
Size: stools for 5 inside, outside seating for 8.

RESTAURANTS

Sound Beach Pizza Grill

178 Sound Beach Avenue, Old Greenwich, 203.637.1085
www.sbpizza.com
Bare bones decor and service. Extensive selection of specialty pizzas.
They came in second in the Anderson Pizza Competition, only 4 votes
behind the winner. If you are not ordering pizza, try a chicken dish, but
skip the hamburgers.
Hours: Open every day from 7 am - 9:30 pm.
Prices: Gourmet large pizzas $12 - $18; wraps & sandwiches $6 - $8.
Size: Seats 30.

Starbucks (Coffee)

- 301 Greenwich Avenue, 203.661.3042
- 60 East Putnam Avenue (Whole Foods Shopping Center)
  203.629.0432
- 147 East Putnam Avenue, Cos Cob, 661.1543
- 1253 East Putnam Avenue (Riverside Shopping Cntr)
  203.698.1790

www.Starbucks.com
One of the few places you can get your coffee made with soy milk, or just
about any other way. During the summer, their Vivanos are great.
Greenwich Avenue
Hours: weekdays, 5:30 am - 10 pm, Saturday 6 am - 11 pm,
Sunday 6:30 am - 10 pm; other locations may close earlier.

Standing Room Only (Lunch Wagon Fast Food)

Liberty Way and Lewis Street, 203.613.3470
www.facebook.com/pages/Greenwich-CT/Standing-Room-Only-Gourmet-
Food-Truck/113783261863
This terrific lunch wagon is located on Liberty Way just off Lewis Street
and behind Black Forest Bakery. Their vegetable panini and chicken
quesadillas are very popular as is their chicken chili. They deliver in the
local area.
Hours: Lunch only, weekdays, 11 am - 3:30 pm.

RESTAURANTS

Subway Sandwich (Fast Food)
- (Top of Avenue) 28 Greenwich Avenue, 203.622.1515
- (Bottom of Avenue) 401 Greenwich Avenue, 203.422.2218

www.Subway.com

Here's the take-out place for those famous sandwiches made with bread freshly baked on the premises. Our favorite is the sweet onion chicken teriyaki on honey oat.

Hours:

Top of Avenue: weekdays, 7 am - 9 pm; Saturday, 9 am - 9 pm; Sunday, 9 am - 7 pm.

Bottom of Avenue: everyday, 8 am - 9 pm.

Prices: Footlongs range from $6 - $8.

Sundown Saloon (American)
403 Greenwich Avenue, 203.629.8212

www.SundownSaloon.com

In the Anderson Hamburger Contest, Sundown's slider and saloon burger came in as top choices. The menu has seven different burgers. This restaurant is an interesting combination of an adult bar and an informal, cute restaurant serving casual food with a western theme. There is a special menu for "little dudes." Be sure to order the lemonade. The friendly staff, and crayons for writing on the tablecloths, make this a good choice for the whole family. The bar is a popular after work meeting place.

Hours: Kitchen open every day, 11:30 am 11 pm. They do not accept reservations.

Prices: Entrees, $10 - $20 (burgers $10); Wine by the glass $8 - $9.

Size: Seats 60 in the dining area.

Spazzio (Italian)
401 Shippan Avenue, Stamford CT, 203.324.1515

If you are looking for a comfortable place for your family to have a good meal, you can't beat Spazzio. Despite their rather obscure location and rather ordinary decoration, the service is top notch and their large menu has well prepared choices to please everyone. When in doubt, try one of the pasta bowls like the Fettuccini a la Mitty or the Capellini Poverino. They also own the hip Habana.

Hours: Lunch, weekdays 11 am - 2 pm,

Dinner Monday to Saturday 4 pm - 10 pm, Sunday 4 pm - 9 pm.

Prices: Lunch and Dinner prices: Pasta $15- 20, Pizza (large) $18-22 (small) $12-$15, entrees $17-$28; children's menu $7-$9;

Wine by the glass $6- $7.

Size: seats 140.

RESTAURANTS

Sushi Nanase (Japanese)

522 Mamaroneck (corner of DeKalb Ave), White Plains NY
 914.285.5351

Eating in this minuscule sushi place is a real treat. Step inside and you are in Japan. This unique restaurant serves only sushi and sashimi, but this is served to perfection. If you have never had Omakase, treat yourself here. Be sure to order it in advance. Never expect to eat here without a reservation.

Hours: Closed Wednesday, open every other day from 6 pm - 10 pm.
Prices: Minimum per person is $30; sushi and sashimi combo plates $30 - $45; Omakase starts at $80 and must be ordered a week in advance.
Size: 5 tables for 2, plus 6 seats at the bar.

Tabouli Grill (Middle Eastern)

59 High Ridge Road (Bull's Head Plaza) Stamford CT
 203.504.8888 www.TabouliGrill.com

In middle of a shopping strip, this small, simple but attractive eatery serves Middle Eastern food with an Israeli twist. The food is prepared by the talented chef Judith Roll. The baklava is excellent.

Hours: Monday -Saturday 11:30 am - 9 pm;
Thursday, Friday and Saturday until 10 pm; Sunday noon - 9 pm.
Prices: Entrees $15-$18, Children $4-$6, Wine the glass $6-$9.
Size: Seats 30

Taco Bell (Fast Food)

1371 East Putnam Avenue, Old Greenwich, 203.698.2290
www.TacoBell.com

Hours: Dining room open every day, 10 am - 10 pm;
Drive-thru, Monday - Thursday 8 am - midnight,
Friday & Saturday 8 am - 1 pm, Sunday 10 am - 10 pm.

Tandoori (Indian)

163 North Main Street, Port Chester NY, 914.937.2727
www.TandooriTasteOfIndia.com

It's nice to have good Indian restaurants close by. Try their fixed price buffet lunch on weekdays. Their chicken tikka masala and shrimp malabar are favorites. We always order sweet lassi.

Hours: Lunch buffet, everyday, noon - 2:30 pm;
Dinner, every day, 5 pm - 10 pm.
Prices: Lunch buffet, $11 (Sunday $13); Dinner entrees, $12 - $22;
Wine by the glass, $7.   Size: Seats 50.

RESTAURANTS

Tarry Lodge (Italian)

18 Mill Street, Port Chester NY, 914.939.3111

www.TarryLodge.com

The Tarry Lodge has been here for over 100 years. Once a speakeasy, it is now totally restored. The bold yellow walls and separate dining areas give it a refined old world charm. It is owned by superstars Mario Batali and Joe Bastianich of Babbo in Greenwich Village. Expect very good food, exceptional service and an extensive wine list. The black fettuccini is brilliant. Be sure to make a reservation.

Prices: Pizza, $10 - $14; Pasta, $14 - $24; Entrees, $17 - $60; Specials $24 - $29; Wine by the glass $8 - $24.

Hours: Monday and Tuesday, noon - 9 pm;
Wednesday - Friday, noon - 11 pm; Saturday brunch, noon - 3 pm;
Dinner, 3 pm - 11 pm; Sunday brunch, noon - 3 pm;
Dinner 3 pm - 9 pm; Lunch, weekdays, Noon - 2:30 pm;
Dinner, weekdays, 5 pm - 8:30 pm (Friday to 10:30 pm);
Saturday and Sunday, 11 am - 11 pm. Size: Seats 180.

Tawa (Indian)

211 Summer Street, Stamford CT, 203.359.8977, 8978

www.TawaOnLine.com

Reviews of this upscale Indian restaurant often tout their breads. We certainly agree. Be sure to order the Nan stuffed with dry fruits and nuts. They also have top notch Indian cuisine. We love the Baingan Bharta (eggplant) and chicken Chettinad. We suggest you don't take their challenge to eat Five Chili Phall. Save your taste buds for their other delightful choices.

Prices: breads $3-$5, entrees $16-$28; Bread Bar small plates $6-$12; Wine by the glass $8-$12.

Hours: Buffet lunch every day, noon - 2:30 pm; Monday - Thursday, noon - 10 pm; Friday and Saturday, noon - 11 pm, Sunday, noon - 9:30 pm.
Size: seats 60 (almost all of the seating is upstairs)

RESTAURANTS

Telluride (Southwestern)

245 Bedford St, Stamford CT, 203.357.7679
www.telluriderestaurant.com
Innovative western cuisine in a casual, western mountain ambiance with friendly service. Dip your bread in the salsa and have a good time. Our favorites are the informal foods such as Telluride's crab cakes or empanadas. The extensive wine list offers 18 wines by the glass. We like the wine suggestions listed with each dish.
Hours: Monday - Thursday, 11: 45 am - 10 pm; Friday 11:45 am - 11 pm; Saturday, 5 pm - 11 pm; Sunday, 5 pm - 9 pm. Closed on major holidays.
Prices: Lunch, Greens $10 - $18, pizza $14 - $15, entrees $14 -$20; Dinner, greens & things $10 - $18, pizza $15 - $16, entrees $22 - $39; Wine by the glass (7 oz) $8 - $16. Size: Seats 60.

Ten Twenty Post (American)

1020 Post Road, Darien CT, 203.655.1020
www.TenTwentyPost.com
A fun restaurant featuring oysters, chicken pot pie, french onion soup, sea scallops w/risotto, steak frites and hamburgers.
Hours: Sunday and Monday, 11:30 am - 9 pm;
Tuesday -Thursday, 11:30 am - 10 pm;
Friday and Saturday, 11:30 am - 11 pm.
Prices: Sunday brunch $10 - $18; lunch & dinner menu, appetizers and small plates $7 - $20, entrees (everyday specials) $21 - $30, entree salads, $11 - $20, Sandwiches & burgers $11 - $16, fish $25 - $29; Sides $5 - $7;
Glass of wine $8 - $16. Size: Seats about 100.

Tengda Asian Bistro (Asian/Japanese)

21 Field Point Road, 203.625.5338
www.AsianBistroGroup.com
The decor is hip factory, with lots of metal, noise, and typically filled with chic clientele in a festive mood. The sushi, which includes many special creations such as our favorite, the magical roll, is popular. If you are not having sushi, we recommend skipping the other entrees and having the Tengda Classics—generous servings of tempura, teriyaki or mango chicken. We like the cheerful, fast-paced service.
Hours: Lunch, weekdays, 11:30 to 3 pm, Saturday & Sunday, lunch starts at noon; Dinner, every day 4:30 pm - 10 pm (Saturday to 11 pm.)
The dinner menu is served all day on Sunday.
Prices: Lunch, lunch boxes $9 - $14, sushi rolls $5 - $16,
special rolls, $13 - $20, entrees $12 - $30; Dinner, entrees $20 - $32
Wine by the glass $8 - $16. Size: Seats about 100.

RESTAURANTS

Tequila Mockingbird (Mexican)

8 Forest Street, New Canaan CT, 203.966.2222

www.culinarymenus.com/tequilamockingbird.htm

A fun restaurant with colorful decorations surrounding the booths. A place to go when you are in the mood for chips and salsa or a Margarita. This is not a gourmet's Mexican restaurant, but it is popular with families and adults of all ages. On weekends you will need a reservation.

Hours: daily, 5:30 pm - 10 pm (Sunday to 9) may be open to 11 pm on Friday & Saturday; bar open to midnight or later.

Prices: Fajitas $14 - $22, Entrees $13 - $28; Children's menu $5 - $8; Margaritas $9 - $11.

Size: Seats 100.

Terra Ristorante Italiano (Italian)

156 Greenwich Avenue, 203.629.5222

www.TerraOfGreenwich.com

Walking along Greenwich Avenue, wonderful smells come from their wood-burning ovens serving up Northern Italian food. A popular, lively, hip trattoria. If you want to escape the noise, dine on the terrace.

Hours: Lunch, weekdays, noon - 2:30 pm; Saturday, noon - 3 pm;

Afternoon, Monday - Sunday, 2: 30 - 5 pm;

Dinner, Monday - Saturday, 5:30 pm - 10 pm;

Sunday brunch, 11 am - 3 pm; Sunday dinner, 5 pm - 9:30 pm.

Dinner, Monday - Sunday, 5 pm - 10 pm (Friday & Saturday to 10:30 pm.)

Prices: Lunch & Dinner, pasta & pizza entrees $14 - $22, Fish & meat entrees $26 - $38; Wine by the glass $8 - $10;

18% gratuity added to parties of 6 or more.

Size: Seats 62 inside, small outside terrace.

TIP: CONNECTICUT IS A WINE-DOGGY-BAG-STATE

Public Act No. 03-228 and 04-33 allow a restaurant, café or hotel dining room patron to remove one unsealed bottle of wine for off-premises consumption provided the patron has purchased a full course meal and consumed a portion of the wine with such meal. The bottle that is removed must be securely sealed and placed in a bag by restaurant personnel.www.vinodoggybag.com/statelaws.html New York is also a Wine-Doggy-Bag State.

Thai Chi (Southeast Asian)

25 Bank Street, Stamford CT, 203.961.9877

www.ThaiChiStamford.com

Sophisticated, minimalist decor, friendly service and interesting cuisine make this South Asian restaurant a good choice. The food is a mix from Malaysia, Vietnam and Thailand. We like the sesame tofu and basil shrimp. Don't leave without having fried bananas for dessert.

Hours: Lunch, weekdays 11:30 am - 3 pm;

Saturday and Sunday 12:30 - 3;

Dinner, Monday - Thursday 5 pm - 10 pm, Friday 5 pm - 11:30 pm;

Saturday 3:30 pm - 11:30 pm)

Prices: Lunch, entrees $8 - $12, sushi $12 - $19;

Dinner, stir fried $10 - $15, special entrees, $12 - $25;

Wine by the glass $8 - $9. Size: Seats 80.

Thai Basil (Thai)

95 Railroad Avenue, 203.618.9888

Just across from the train station & movie theater is a simply decorated, "authentic" Thai restaurant that we love. Expect, friendly greetings and good service. If you are not familiar with Thai food, they will be happy to guide you. The drunken noodles we like are not for the faint of heart. Many milder dishes - curries and wok stirred- are on the menu. The coconut sticky rice is listed as a side, but we like it as a dessert. The owner of Penang and Asiana also owns this restaurant.

Hours: Open every day, Lunch 11 am - 3:30 pm (Sunday opens at Noon);

Dinner 5 pm - 10 pm;

Friday & Saturday until 11 pm (kitchen closes at10:45.)

Prices: Lunch, Bangkok Box $9 - $11; Lunch & Dinner, entrees $10 - $20.

Size: Seats 38.

RESTAURANTS

Thali (Indian, Fusion)

87 Main Street, New Canaan CT, 203.972.8332
www.Thali.com
This is not just another Indian restaurant. A waterfall rolls across the ceiling of what was formerly a bank. Expect quirky decor and often quirky service along with delightful and unusual flavors. Many of the dishes seem to be a fusion of French and southern Indian with a touch of whimsy. Our mouth waters at the mention of the ragda patties, jalapeno nan and the Navrattan Korma. Yes, their chicken tikka masala is also very good. David Rosengarten says this is the best Indian restaurant in the U.S. We haven't tried them all, but he could be right.
Hours: Monday - Thursday, noon - 10 pm, Friday and Saturday, noon - 11 pm; Sunday, noon - 9:30 pm
Prices: Lunch, small plates $7 - $11, large plates $9 - $19;
Dinner, small plates $7 - $15, large plates $23 - $33;
Sunday Brunch Buffet $17. Wine by the glass $8 - $11
Size: Seats over 100 + private room for 40.

Thataway Café (American)

409 Greenwich Avenue, 203.622.0947
www.ThatawayCafe.com
Great atmosphere - "just casual enough and just pubby enough, without losing the ability to be a real restaurant." This popular restaurant is located at the end of the Avenue. The large outdoor patio is a delightful place to dine in the summer. Try the Avenue Sandwich or Whichaway Burger. Top the evening off with Appleberry Crumb Pie or Oreo Decadence. Tuesdays and Sundays are Karoke night. Thursday evenings from 9 pm to midnight feature the Songwriters Den which showcases local up-and-coming talent. Lots of fun.
Hours: Lunch, every day 11:30 am - 5 pm; Sunday Brunch 11 am - 3 pm; Dinner, Monday - Thursday 5 pm - 11 pm
(Friday & Saturday until midnight);
Bar is open until 1 am, Monday to Sunday, Saturday until midnight;
Reservations are accepted for parties of 6 or more.
Prices: Lunch, entrees $14 - $19, sandwiches $10 - $17,
salads $13 - $18; Dinner entrees $19 - $26
Wine by the glass $7 - $9.
Size: Seats 92 inside and 66 outside on the patio.

RESTAURANTS

Thomas Henkelmann (French)

420 Field Point Road (at the Homestead Inn), 203.869.7500
www.ThomasHenkelmann.com

Nestled in Belle Haven, in a lovely, formal inn with antiques and a garden setting, there is a restaurant with delicious contemporary French food. We rate this as one of Greenwich's best. The owner and chef, Thomas Henkelmann, is regarded as one of the premier chefs in the US. The wait staff is attentive, polite and informed. Men should wear a jacket and tie.

Hours: Breakfast only for the inn guests; Lunch, weekdays noon - 2:30 pm; Dinner, every day 6 pm - 9 pm; Closed the first two weeks in March. Closed Sundays from mid-July through August.

Make reservations well in advance.

Prices: Lunch entrees, $35 - $55; Dinner entrees, $55 - $75

Wine by the glass $14-$15.

Size: seats 120

Tigin (Irish)

175 Bedford Street, Stamford CT, 203.353.8444
www.TiginIrishPub.com

A pub designed to make you feel you have stepped into Ireland. Hearty food and lots of cozy nooks.

Hours: Sunday - Thursday, 11:30 am - 1 am; Friday, 11:30 am - 2 am; Saturday opens early for sports and closes at 2 am; Sunday opens early for sports and closes at 12:30 am.

Prices: One menu, salads $5 - $10, sandwiches $9 - $11, traditional fare, $12 - $14; Wine by the glass, $7 - $8, beers $6.

Size: Seats 80.

(K & S) Top of the Hill (Jamaican)

114 West Broad Street, Stamford CT, 203.975.8795

When we asked our Jamaican friend what would make him happy on his birthday, he said "Oxtail from Top of the Hill." Finding this dish is rare. It is too rustic for most restaurants. You might also want to try the stew pea soup, jerk chicken and jerk pork. Servings with rice, beans and cabbage are generous.

Hours: Monday - Saturday, 7 am - 9 pm.

Prices: $7 - $13.

Size: Takeout only, no tables.

RESTAURANTS

Tsuru (Japanese)
259 North Central Avenue, Hartsdale NY, 914.761.0057
www.Tsurushushibar.com
About 20 minutes from Greenwich, in a modest restaurant in a rather nondescript shopping mall. Until its new ownership, is was one of the best Japanese restaurants outside of New York City. Let's hope it regains its former standing. $20 minimum for a credit card.
Hours: Closed Tuesday; Every other day, Lunch, noon - 2:30 pm; Dinner 5 pm - 9:30 pm.
Prices: Lunch entrees $10 - $16, sushi $11 - $20;
Dinner entrees $15 - $32;
Size: Seats 44; private tatami room for 4 - 20 people.

Upper Crust Bagel Company (Fast Food)
197 Sound Beach Avenue, Old Greenwich, 203.698.0079
(catering 203.637.2794) www.UpperCrustBagel.com
A good place to sit down and chat while having a deli sandwich and a fruit smoothie. They have tasty old-fashioned kettle-boiled and hearth-baked bagels, as well as gourmet spreads and coffees. We think they make the best bagels in Fairfield County. Since incorporating LexZee Gourmet and Catering, there is no end to the great food you can get here.
Hours: weekdays, 6 am - 4pm, Saturday, 7 am - 4 pm;
Sunday, 7 am - 3 pm.
Prices: Gourmet sandwiches, $6 - $8. Size: Seats 20.

Valencia Luncheria (Latin American - Venezuela)
172 Main Street, Norwalk CT, 203.846.8009
www.ValenciaLuncheria.com
Imagine a small, inexpensively decorated, store front restaurant, with a few metal tables crammed into a tiny dining space. Now imagine every table filled with happy customers and a line of people waiting for tables or take-outs. That is Luncheria; where one patron, on being told he would have to wait an hour, responded "don't worry, I would wait forever to dine here." They take no reservations or credit cards. Cash or check only. Bring your own wine or beer.
Hours: Monday and Tuesday, 6 am - 3 pm;
Wednesday - Friday, 7 am - 9 pm; Saturday, 7 am - 9 pm;
Sunday, 8 am - 8 pm.
Prices: Breakfast Arepas (Venezuelan corn cake fried or roasted with your choice of filling) $4 - $5; Lunch, $8 - $15; Dinner, $14 - $22.
Size: Seats 20.

RESTAURANTS

Valbella (Italian)

1309 East Putnam Avenue, Riverside, 203.637.1155

http://www.ValbellaCT.com

Excellent Italian food in a dressy decor. Everyone gets good service, even the celebrities who dine here frequently. There is something wonderful on the menu for everyone. Top off your meal with a chocolate souffle. They have a spectacular wine cellar with 850 wines to choose from. A Town favorite and our vote as the best Italian restaurant in town. If only it were less noisy. Reservations required.

Hours: Lunch, weekdays, 11:30 am - 3:30 pm;

Dinner, Monday - Saturday, 5 pm - 10 pm (11 pm Friday and Saturday).

Prices: Lunch entrees, $15 - $20; Dinner entrees, $24 - $40

Wine by the glass $12. Size: seats 120

Versailles (French)

339 Greenwich Avenue, 203.661.6634

www.versaillesgreenwich.com

A very French bistro with a front counter full of pastries and croissants that will make your day worth living. The right place to meet a friend for lunch for a quiche and a dessert. We have an excuse for trying the desserts. We hope you can figure one out too.

Hours: Monday - Wednesday, 7 am - 6 pm;

Thursday - Saturday, 7 am - 7 pm; Sunday, 7 am - 6 pm.

Prices: Breakfast entrees $7 - 11; Lunch entrees $14 - $20 (Quiche $12.)

Size: Seats 58.

Villa Italia (Southern Italian)

812 East Main Street, Stamford CT, 203.348.7742

www.VillaItaliaStamford.com

Bob said his favorite is manicotti. George only orders the chicken parmigiana. Carolyn really likes the lasagne. What will your favorite be? This small, bright, attractive restaurant is tucked in a tiny, grey shopping center that is easy to pass by. The service in this family run restaurant is endearing. Reservations for 6 or more, on the weekend arrive before 7 pm or after 8 pm. Despite the tables being close together, it is not noisy. We like having the specials printed with prices.

Hours: Lunch, everyday 11:30 am - 3 or 4 pm; Dinner, Monday - Thursday 4 pm - 9:30 pm, Friday, Saturday & Sunday 4 pm - 10 pm.

Prices: Lunch, sandwiches & wraps$7-$9, personal pizzas $10-$13; Lunch Express (small plates weekdays until 3 pm), pasta $8-$9, Specialties $10-$14; Dinner pasta $13-$15, Specialties $16-$21, seafood $17-$21, personal pizzas $12-$14; wine by the glass $7-$10.

Size: seats 56

RESTAURANTS

Village Bagels (Fast Food)

375 Greenwich Avenue, 203.869.6200 www.villagebagel.com
They have been voted the best bagels in Fairfield County 8 years in a row. The name is bagels, but they offer a variety of breakfast and lunch items, from "make your own salad" to smoothies.
Hours: Monday - Saturday, 6 am - 5 pm; Sunday 7 am - 3 pm.
Prices: Panini $9, specialty egg sandwiches, $5 other sandwiches $7 - $9, bagels $1.25 - $3.50 (depending on spread.) Size: Seats 22.

Wasabi Chi (Asian Fusion, Japanese-French)

2 South Main Street, South Norwalk CT, 203.286.0181
www.WasabiChi.com
When you enter a trendy restaurant, where the bar is prominent and colorful drinks are being served, you don't always expect the food to be inspired. But we like the food. The creative combinations are fresh and fun. By all means have the tuna pizza. We also recommend the wasabi calamari and the scallops.
Hours: Closed Monday; Lunch, Tuesday - Friday ,noon to 2:30 pm;
Dinner, Tuesday - Friday 5 pm - 10 pm, Saturday 1 pm - 11 pm,
Sunday 1pm - 9 pm.
Prices: Lunch entrees, $14 - $17, omakase $11 - $16;
Dinner entrees $21 -$27 ($55 for Kobe steak), small plates $11 - $18, omakase $13 - $15; Wine by the glass $8 - $12. Size: Seats 180

Wendy's (Fast Food)

420 West Putnam Avenue, 203.869.9885 www.Wendys.com
The only fast food burger place with a drive-through in Greenwich.
Hours: Dining room, open every day, 10 am - 10 pm; drive-Thru open every day, 10 am - 12 pm.
Size: Seats 74.

Wild Ginger Dumpling House (Chinese fusion)

971 Post Road, Darien CT, 203.656.2225, 203.656.3468
www.WildGingerDumplingHouse.com
We happily discovered this primarily Chinese restaurant has translated some of our favorite dishes in a fresh and delicious way, such as the Szechuan dumplings or scallops and shrimp Huanan style.
Hours: Sunday - Thursday, 11:30 am - 10 pm,
Friday & Saturday, 11:30 am - 11 pm.
Prices: Lunch specials, $6 - $7; Dinner, Chinese dishes $10 - $14, gourmet selections $11 - $16. Size: Seats 65.

RESTAURANTS

Willett House (Steak)

20 Willett Avenue, Port Chester NY, 914.939.7500

www.TheWillettHouse.com

An old fashioned steak house in a restored turn-of-century granary building. The atmosphere is fun and the steaks are good, but we understand why it is nicknamed the "Wallet House." At lunch everyone seems to order the $12 hamburger with fries and onion rings.

Hours: weekdays, noon- 10 pm; Saturday noon - 10:30 pm;

Sunday, 5 pm - 9 pm.

Prices: Lunch, Luncheon salads $17 - $22, wraps, sandwiches & burgers $12 - $28; Dinner, meat $42 - $50, seafood, $36-$42, other entrees $38 - $60. Sides ($7-$8) not included, 3 course dinner special $55.

Wine by the glass, $10 - $17.

Size: Seats 300, including 3 private party rooms.

Xaviar's (New American)

506 Piermont Avenue, Piermont NY, 845.359.7007

www.Xaviars.com

Rockland County's best. Just twenty-five minutes from Greenwich across the Tappan Zee Bridge. This intimate, romantic restaurant serves contemporary cuisine. It is the Hudson Valley's most celebrated restaurant. Piermont is fun to walk around. Don't even consider going without making reservations well in advance.

Hours: Lunch, Friday & Sunday, noon - 2 pm;

Dinner, Wednesday - Friday 6 pm - 9 pm;

Saturday, seatings at 6 pm or 9 pm, Sunday, 5 pm - 8 pm.

Prices: Lunch, price fixed at $35; Dinner, price fixed $90 or $100, entrees $30 - $39; Wine by the glass $10 - $26. Size: Seats 40.

RESTAURANTS

X20 (New American)

71 Water Grant Street, Yonkers NY, 914.965.1111

www.Xaviars.com/yonkers

About 40 minutes from Greenwich, this is a special occasion restaurant - impeccable food and service right on the Hudson River. As you drive through Yonkers, the city can look pretty scruffy, but the area just by the water is quite nice. Just under the Rail Road bridge is the restaurant with valet parking in front. Although most tables have river views, it wouldn't hurt to ask for a table next to the window.

Hours: Lunch, Tuesday - Friday 12 pm - 2 pm;

Sunday Brunch 12pm - 2 pm; Dinner, Tuesday - Friday 5:30 pm - 10 pm, Saturday 5 pm - 10 pm, Sunday 5 pm - 9 pm.

Prices: Brunch, Price Fix $38; Dinner entrees $26-$32;

Wine by the glass $9- $18.

Size: Seats 100 downstairs and about 80 upstairs. You want to be seated downstairs.

SCHOOLS

preschools

For early childcare and after school programs, see CHILDREN
For enrichment opportunities, including language schools, see CHILD
ENRICHMENT. For local Colleges see CONTINUING EDUCATION.
Pre-school programs are usually very popular. You should contact the
school well in advance to make sure you have reserved a place. Usually
programs are half-day until the child is four years old.

Banksville Nursery School
12 Banksville Road, 203.661.9715
www.BanksvilleNurserySchool.com
Children, ages 3 - 4. Creative movement classes. Morning and afternoon
sessions available. Closed during the summer.

Bridges
296 Valley Road, Cos Cob, 203.637.0204
www.BridgesSchool.org
Children, ages 2 - 4. New theme each month. Morning and afternoon
sessions.

Brunswick Pre-school
100 Maher Avenue, 203.625.5800
www.BrunswickSchool.org
Boys age 4. Admission to pre-K often ensures admission to the school.

Children's Day School
• Glenville Civic Center, 449 Pemberwick Road, 203.532.1190
• 8 Riverside Avenue, 203.637.1122
Children, ages 6 weeks to 6 years. All-day, year-round childcare and
pre-school. Emphasizes cooperation and integration of projects.

Christ Church Nursery School
254 East Putnam Avenue, 203.869.5334
www.ChristChurchNursery.org
Children, ages 2 - 5. Blend of enrichment and free play. Kindergarten
alternative, 9 am - 1:30 pm.

Clover Hill Early Childhood Learning
Office: The Clover Hill School, P.O. Box 206, Riverside CT 06878-0206
Christ Episcopal Church, 2 Emerson Street, East Norwalk CT
    203.661.6484   www.TheCloverHillSchool.org
A Waldorf -based school for children, ages 3 to 6.

SCHOOLS

preschools

Convent of the Sacred Heart Early Learning Program
1177 King Street, 203.532.3510, 203.531.6500
www.CSHGreenwich.org
Girls, ages 3 - 4; Half-day program for 3-year-olds optional; 4-year-olds, full day. Grounded in the Roman Catholic tradition, although 35% of students are not Catholic.

Family Center
40 Arch Street, 203.869.4848
www.familycenters.org
Children, ages 3 - 4. An all-day, year-round childcare and pre-school. 5:30 pm pickup available. Learn-through-discovery approach.

Giant Steps Head Start at Wilbur Peck Court
203.869.2730 Ages: 3 - 4.

Kids Corner Head Start at Armstrong Court
203.869.2730 Ages: 3 - 4.

First Church Pre-school
108 Sound Beach Avenue, Old Greenwich, 203.637.5430
www.FirstChurchPreschool.org
Children, ages 3 - 4. Hours: 9 am - 11:30 am or 12:30 pm - 3 pm. Some preference is given to church members. Summer camp program for ages 3 - 4.

First Presbyterian Church Pre-school
37 Lafayette Place, 203.869.7782
http://www.FPCG.org/Nursery-School-index.html
Children, ages 2 - 4. Morning and afternoon classes.
Also 2 x 2 program, 2 days per week. Enrichment programs change every 6- 8 weeks. Art Scampers summer camp for ages 3 - 6.

Greenwich Academy
200 North Maple Avenue, 203.625.8900
www.GreenwichAcademy.org
Girls, ages 4 - 5. Morning and afternoon sessions.
Admission to pre-K usually ensures admission to the school.

SCHOOLS

Greenwich Catholic School

471 North Street, 203.869.4000
www.GreenwichCatholicSchool.org
Children, ages 4 - pre-K. Pre-K is a structured program with academics
for 4-year-olds. Little Angels is a play group for younger children.
Admission to these programs does not ensure admission to the school.

Greenwich Country Day

401 Old Church Road, 203.863.5600
www.GreenwichCDS.org
Starting at age 3. Admission to pre-K often ensures admission to the
school. Summer camp for children ages 4 - 5.

Greenwich Kokusai Gakuen

Worldwide Children's Corner
521 East Putnam Avenue, 203.629.5567
www.GreenwichKokusai.com
Children, ages 2 - 5 years. Full-day program.

Greenwich Public Pre-Schools

Office: 290 Greenwich Avenue, Greenwich CT, 203-625-7400
www.greenwichschools.org/page.cfm?p=76
Held at a number of locations around the community on a lottery basis.
Their integrated model includes children with special needs.

Just Wee Two

800.404.2204   www.JustWeeTwo.com
Fun-filled programs for children 8 months to 3 years and their mommies
(daddies, nannies or grandparents). Programs are held at Western
Greenwich Civic Center, 449 Pemberwick Road and other locations around
town.

Mead School

1095 Riverbank Road, Stamford CT, 203.595.9500
www.MeadSchool.org
Co-ed ages 2 - 5. Warm learning environment, where families work in
partnership with educators. Children work with specialists in Spanish,
music, drama and movement.

SCHOOLS

pre-school

Mencius Mandarin Preschool
First United Methodist Church,
2nd Floor, 59 East Putnam Avenue, 203.540.5770
www.MenciusMandarin.com
English-Mandarin Chinese bilingual preschool for children ages 2 to 5 years old. No prior knowledge of Mandarin Chinese is required.

North Greenwich Nursery School
606 Riversville Road, 203.869.7945
www.NorthGreenwichNurserySchool.org
Children, ages 2 - 5. Half-day program with optional extended-day available. Computers integrated into program. US Gymnastic Academy is at the same location and can provide afternoon classes.

(The) Pre-School at Second Congregational Church
Second Congregational Church,
139 East Putnam Ave, 203.869.8388
www.ThePreSchoolGreenwich.com
Established in 1996, it is an independent non-sectarian preschool for children ages 2 to 5 years. Flexible 3, 4 or 5 day a week programs.
Half-day programs with extended-day options. Summer camp program.

Putnam Indian Field School
101 Indian Field Road, 203.869.0982, 661.4629
www.pifs.net
Co-ed pre-school, children, ages 2 - 5.
Summer camp program for ages 2 - 6.

Round Hill Nursery School
466 Round Hill Road, 203.869.4910
www.roundhillnurseryschool.com
Children, ages 2 - 4. Fifty years of giving children a love of going to school. Computer training and special teachers for music and art.

St. Paul's Day School
200 Riverside Avenue, Riverside, 203.637.3503
Children, ages 2 - 5. Non-sectarian, with enrichment program for older children. Summer camp program for ages 3 - 6.

SCHOOLS

St. Savior's Nursery School
350 Sound Beach Avenue, Old Greenwich, 203.698.1303
Children, ages 2 yrs 5 mos - 5-years-old. Non-denominational.
Summer camp program for ages 3- 5.

Selma Maisel Nursery School
Temple Sholom, 300 East Putnam Avenue, 203.622.8121
Children, ages 2 - 5. "Mommy & Me" program for 2 and under.
Programs with Judaic content.

Stanwich School Pre-Kindergarten
257 Stanwich Road, 203.542.0035
www.StanwichSchool.org
Character based education.

Tiny Tots
97 Riverside Avenue, Riverside, 203.637.1398
Children, ages 3 - 5. Residential setting. One of the oldest nursery schools
in town. Summer camp program for ages 2 years 9 months - 6.

Whitby School
969 Lake Avenue, 203.869.8464
www.WhitbySchool.org
Children, ages 1 - 5 years. One of the oldest American Montessori schools.
Summer camp program for ages 3 - 5.

YMCA Child Care Center
2 St. Roch's Avenue, Greenwich, 203.869.3381
www.GWYMCA.org/ChildCare.php
Children, ages 2 years 9 months - 5 years, 9 am - 1 pm. Follows public
school calendar. Offers enrichment curriculum.

YWCA 123 Grow/Beginnings
259 East Putnam Avenue, 203.869.6501 x 221
www.YWCAGreenwich.org
Children, ages 15 months - 3 years; toddlers, 9 am - 11:30 am;
age 2, 9 am - 11:30 am or noon - 3 pm.

SCHOOLS

YWCA Tinker Tots

259 East Putnam Avenue, 203.869.6501 x 241
www.YWCAGreenwich.org
Children, ages 3 - 4. Half-day program for age 2; ages 3 - 4, full-day,
7:30 am - 6 pm. Enrichment programs. Summer camp.

SCHOOLS

private/parochial

Greenwich has an abundance of excellent private schools. Typical annual tuition is $20,000 to $55,000, depending upon the grade. Private schools typically have more applicants than they have spaces. It is prudent to apply early. Private schools often have one or more open houses for parents of prospective attendees. Many offer extended-day programs or early dropoff for their pre-schoolers. More details are available on our website: www.greenwichliving.com

Brunswick School
100 Maher Avenue, 203.625.5800
www.BrunswickSchool.org
Boys, pre-K (age 4) through 12th grade.

Hebrew School (Chabad of Greenwich)
75 Mason Street, 203.629.9059, 203.629.9467
www.GanOfGreenwich.org
www.ChabadGreenwich.org
First Taste program for ages 4 - 8. Hebrew School ages 9 - 11. Discovery ages 11-13, Hebrew High ages 13-16.

Convent of the Sacred Heart
1177 King Street, 203.531.6500
www.CSHGreenwich.org
Girls, pre-K (age 4) through 12th grade.

Eagle Hill
45 Glenville Road, 203.622.9240
www.EagleHillSchool.org
Coed, ages 6 - 16. A school for bright children with learning disabilities. Day and 5-day boarding. Student faculty ratio is 4:1.

French-American School
Admissions Office, 914.834.3002 ext. 233
www.FASNY.org
The pre-school is in Scarsdale, the elementary in Larchmont and the secondary in Mamaroneck.

German School

50 Partridge Road, White Plains, 914.948.6513
www.DSNY.org
The German School is an independent bilingual (German/English) international school which teaches classes according to German as well as American standards. The elementary school includes grade K (for five- year-olds) through grade 4 and the secondary school includes grade 5 through 12.

Greenwich Academy

200 North Maple Avenue, 203.625.8900
www.GreenwichAcademy.org
Girls, pre-K (age 4) through 12th grade.

Greenwich Country Day

Old Church Road, 203.863.5600
www.GreenwichCDS.org
Co-ed, pre-K (age 3) through 9th grade.

Greenwich Catholic School

471 North Street, 203.869.4000
www.GreenwichCatholicSchool.org
Co-ed, pre-K (age 4) through 8th grade.

Greenwich Japanese School

15 Ridgeway, 203.629.9039
www.GWJS.org
Co-ed, grades 1 - 9.

Mead School

1095 Riverbank Road, Stamford CT, 203.595.9500
www.MeadSchool.org
An innovative, progressive school founded in 1969. Co-ed, pre-school through 8th grade.

SCHOOLS

private/parochial

Stanwich School

257 Stanwich Road, 203.542.0000, admissions 203.542.0035
www.StanwichSchool.org
A thriving co-educational independent day school, founded in 1998 by the former head of the lower school at Greenwich Academy. It currently serves students in grades Kindergarten through 8. The school intends to add a grade each year through Grade 12.

Westchester Fairfield Hebrew Academy

270 Lake Avenue, 203.863.9663
www.WFHA.org
Co-ed, grades K - 8. Founded in 1997, Westchester Fairfield Hebrew Academy serves 110 students. It is a Jewish community day school with a curriculum in general and Judaic studies. It includes children from all branches of Judaism.

Whitby School

969 Lake Avenue, 203.869.8464
www.WhitbySchool.org
Co-ed, grades pre-K - 8. Founded in 1958, it is one of the oldest Montessori schools in the country. During the summer Whitby conducts a drama day camp for ages 8 - 16.

TIP: TEDDY BEAR CLINIC

Once a year (usually in September), the Greenwich Hospital invites young children and their teddy bears to learn about surgery, ambulances and health check-ups. Each teddy bear is given its own ID bracelet. Call 203.863.3627 or visit www.greenhosp.org/teddybear_intro.asp for more information. Be sure to see:
www.greenhosp.org/flash/bear.html

SCHOOLS

public school information

www.greenwichschools.org
Greenwich public schools rank among the best in the nation and are consistently ranked among the best in Fairfield County. In addition to their other fine programs, Greenwich schools have outstanding ESL (English as a second language) programs for all grades K through 12.

The Greenwich School System
Greenwich has 11 elementary, 3 middle, 1 high school and an alternative high school, Arch School, for students who need special attention. 40% of the graduates go to the "Most Competitive Colleges." The school budget is more than $125 million. The average cost per student is $17,728. The average class size is 20 and 91 percent of the teachers have masters' degrees. There are over 9,000 students in the public school system. To attend you must be a Greenwich resident.

The elementary schools serve students in grades K - 5, the middle schools serve students in grades 6 - 8, Hamilton Avenue, Julian Curtiss, New Lebanon and Dundee are Magnet schools. The high school has 2,745 students and serves grades 9 - 12. Schools open for students around Labor Day and close in the middle of June.

Board of Education
290 Greenwich Avenue, Havemeyer Building
Weekdays, 8am - 4pm 625.7400
www.greenwichct.org/BoardOfEd/BoardOfEd.asp
Call 203.625.7400 for school district information.
Call 203.625.7447/6 for brochures and pamphlets.
Superintendent, Sidney Freund.

Public School Before and After School Child Care Programs
Ten of the elementary schools offer before and after-school programs for enrolled students. These programs are paid for by the parents. Children can usually be dropped off at 7:30 am and must be picked up by 6 pm. There is often a waiting list, so apply early. Some of the schools also offer enrichment programs where children can take computer or other classes. Call your elementary school to see what programs they sponsor.
For other programs, see CHILDREN, Childcare or Pre-schools.

SCHOOLS

Public School Kindergarten

To register for kindergarten, your child must have reached the age of five on or before January 1 of his or her kindergarten year. Parents must provide a birth certificate and proof of residence. Your child must also have a complete physical examination and a record of immunizations.

Public School Closings

www.greenwichschools.org

If schools are closed for snow, or if opening is delayed, listen to Greenwich Radio WGCH (1490). Announcements begin at 6:30 am. You may also find information on cable channel 12.

Public School Bus Information

203.625.7449

Call for information on school bus pickup times and locations. If your child is young and other children are not nearby, you can often get the school bus to stop in front of or near your home. Bus service is provided for students who live beyond these distances:

Grades K - 5, one mile from the school;

Grades 6 - 8, one and a half miles from school;

Grades 9 - 12, two miles from school.

SCHOOLS

Cos Cob Elementary School
300 East Putnam Avenue, Cos Cob, 203.869.4670
Kimberly Beck, Principal (415 students, 8:45 am - 3:15 pm)

Glenville Elementary School
33 Riversville Road, 203.531.9287
Marc D'Amico, Principal (429 students, 8:30 am - 3 pm)

Hamilton Avenue Elementary School
184 Hamilton Avenue, 203.869.1685
Barbara Riccio, Principal (255 students, 8:15 am - 2:45 pm)

International School at Dundee
55 Florence Road, Riverside, 203.637.3800
Teresa Ricci, Principal (345 students, 8:45 am - 3:15 pm)

Julian Curtiss Elementary School
180 East Elm Street, 203.869.1896
Patricia McGuire, Principal (351 students, 8:15 am - 2:45 pm)

New Lebanon Elementary School
25 Mead Avenue, Byram, 203.531.9139
Gene Nyitray, Principal (237 students, 8:15 am - 2:45 pm)

North Mianus Elementary School
309 Palmer Hill Road, Riverside, 203.637.9730
Angela Schmidt Principal (436 students, 8:45 am - 3:15 pm)

North Street Elementary School
381 North Street, 203.869.6756
Charles Smith, Principal (474 students, 8:45 am - 3:15 pm)

Old Greenwich Elementary School
285 Sound Beach Avenue, Old Greenwich, 203.637.0150
Patricia Raneri, Principal (413 students, 8.45 am - 3.15 pm)

Parkway Elementary School
141 Lower Cross Road, 203.869.7466
Paula Bleakley, Principal (354 students, 8:45 am - 3:15 pm)

Riverside Elementary School
90 Hendrie Avenue, Riverside, 203.637.1440
John Grasso, Principal (471 students, 8:45 am - 3:15 pm)

SCHOOLS

public middle schools

Central Middle School
9 Indian Rock Lane, 203.661.8500
Shelley Somers, Principal (730 students, 7:45 am - 2:35 pm)

Eastern Middle School
51 Hendrie Avenue, Riverside, 203.637.1744
Ralph Mayo, Principal (709 students, 7:45 am - 2:35 pm)

Western Middle School
Western Junior Highway, 203.531.5700
Stacy Gross, Principal (594 students, 7:45 am - 2:35 pm)

public high schools

Arch School
289 Delavan Avenue, 203.532.1956
Barbara Varanelli, Program Administrator (8 am - 2 pm)
The Arch School is an alternative high school for students who need special attention.

Greenwich High School
10 Hillside Road, 203.625.8000
Chris Winters, Headmaster (2,745 students, 7:30 am - 2:15 pm)

SENIORS

Seniors in Greenwich typically stay actively involved in the community, often serving on town boards, the RTM, and philanthropic organizations. Many of our volunteer organizations are run by the retired presidents and leaders of major companies. This wealth of talent of our senior leaders is a significant reason Greenwich is America's number one town. Most senior citizens continue living in their own homes by utilizing the many services the town has available.

index

Senior Activities
Friendly Connections
Greenwich Adult Day Care
Senior Center
Weekend Lunch Bunch
YMCA Exercise Programs

Senior Clubs and Organizations
AARP Greenwich, Chapter 1210
Glenville Senior Citizens
Greenwich Old Timers
Greenwich Seniors Club
Red Hat Society
Retired Men's Association

Senior Education
Diane McKeever
    (Computer Training)
Lifetime Learners Institute
Senior Net

Senior Home Services
At Home in Greenwich
Comfort Keepers
Friendly Connections
Greenwich Adult Day Care
Life Alert
Life Line
Meals on Wheels
Premier Home Health Care of CT
Supermarketing for Seniors

Senior Housing (Independent & Assisted Living)
Atria
Brighton Gardens
Edgehill
(The) Greens At Greenwich
Greenwich Woods Rehabilitation
    and Health Care Center
Hill House
Mews
Nathaniel Witherell
Osborn
Parsonage Cottage
Waveny

Senior Information

(For information on medical resources, see the HEALTH section.)
Commission on Aging
Directory of Senior Services
Elder Care Service Locator
Generations
Greenwich Senior Services Information (Community Answers)
Infoline
Medicare Ratings for
    Nursing Homes
Senior Health Fair

Senior Resources

Burke Rehabilitation Center
Friendly Connections
Greenwich Adult Day Care
Greenwich Hospital
    (Healthy Living and Aging)
National Medical Claims Service
Tax Counseling for Seniors
USE Utilize Senior Energy

Senior Transportation

Call-A-Ride
Red Cross Transportation Services
TAG

TIP: THE SAVVY SENIOR

This quarterly publication of the Greenwich Commission on Aging is filled with information on Greenwich programs and topics of interest to seniors. Visit www.greenwichct.org/commissiononaging/ca SeniorCenter.asp or call 203.862.6720.

SENIORS

AARP Greenwich, Chapter 1210
Louise Burns President, 203.531.6387
www.aarp.org
www.benefitscheckup.org

At Home in Greenwich
139 East Putnam Avenue, 203.422.2342
www.AtHomeInGreenwich.org
They help Greenwich Residents 50 and over live in their own home as they grow older. They provide a broad range of services such as problem-solving information, services and social activities. It is a form of assisted living in your own home. The annual fee is $500 per individual.

Atria
Rye Brook, NY 914.939.2900
www.AtriaSeniorliving.com
http://www.atriaseniorliving.com/community.aspx?id=1472
Independent living in an attractive setting, with a dining room that makes your family and friends want to visit. Atria Senior Living Group is a privately-held, for-profit seniors company based in Louisville, Kentucky, It operates 121 facilities in 27 states. Atria is one of the largest assisted living companies in the United States, with the capacity to house and provide services to as many as 14,000 residents. The company serves a moderate-to-upscale assisted living niche, primarily in suburban markets.

Brighton Gardens
59 Roxbury Road, Stamford, CT 203.322.2100
www.sunriseseniorliving.com
Sunrise is a senior living company based in McLean Virginia, which operates over 440 Sunrise locations worldwide. Sunrise Senior Living is a provider of senior care services, including independent and assisted living, short-term stays, Alzheimer's and hospice care, and rehabilitation and nursing services. Suzie's father enjoys living here.

Burke Rehabilitation Center
785 Mamaroneck Avenue, White Plains, 914.948.0050
www.burke.org
Burke is known for its extensive rehabilitation services, it also offers geriatric evaluations, memory evaluations and treatment services.

Call-A-Ride

37 Lafayette Place, Collyer Center, 203.661.6633

Non-profit volunteer organization. Five days a week, residents 60 years or older can call for a ride anywhere in Greenwich for any purpose. Please give them 24 hours notice.

Hours: weekdays, 9 am - noon and 12:30 pm - 3:15 pm.

Comfort Keepers

17 Heronvue Road, Greenwich

203.629.5209, 203.899.0465; cell: 203.461.1013

www.ComfortKeepers.com

A national franchise that offers non-medical services to those who might not otherwise be able to live independently. They provide services such as in-home meal preparation, grocery shopping, transportation, house-keeping and companionship. Dennis and Marian Patouhas decided to buy the franchise for this much-needed business in Greenwich. They maintain a large library of information at www.TheHealthyAgingShow.com.

Commission on Aging

Senior Center, 299 Greenwich Avenue

203.862.6710, 203.622.3992

www.greenwichct.org/CommissionOnAging/CommissionOnAging.asp

Located in the Senior Center, the Commission on Aging provides information, referral services and written materials on a variety of issues of interest to seniors. For instance, the Commission can assist a senior to connect with TAG, Call-A-Ride, a Share-The-Fare Taxi, Red Cross, or other specialized transportation services. Ask to be on the mailing list for "The Savvy Senior."

Office Hours: weekdays, 8 am - 4 pm.

Diane McKeever, CPP (Computer Training)

www.DianeMcKeever.com

www.linkedin.com/pub/diane-mckeever/5/b9/923

If you want to learn a Microsoft program, you should enroll in one of Diane's Continuing Education classes at the Greenwich High School. But if you don't have the time, she gives private lessons for students of all levels - she is a CPP (Certified Patient Person).

Directory of Senior Services

This very thorough, impressive directory, developed by the Junior League and the Commission on Aging, is available on the town's website: http://greenwichct.virtualtownhall.net/Public_Documents/ GreenwichCT_COA/SeniorServicesDir

Edgehill

122 Palmers Hill Road, Stamford CT, 203.323.2323

www.EdgehillCommunity.com

Independent, almost condo-style living, in an attractive setting. Skilled nursing and rehabilitation services in the same facility.

Elder Care Service Locator

800.677.1116

www.eldercare.gov

A public service of the U.S. Administration on Aging. The Eldercare Locator helps you find local agencies to help older persons and their families access home and community-based services like transportation, meals, home care, and care giver support services.

Friendly Connections

20 Bridge Street, 203.629.2822

www.familycenters.org

Family Centers, 40 Arch Street, 203. 869.4848 provides three Friendly Connections programs:

Telephone Groups

This program brings seniors (or those who have difficulty getting out) together on the telephone for a variety of recreational, support and discussion groups. All groups are conducted over the phone and are facilitated by a moderator. There are more than 50 groups scheduled each month. They are a great way to meet new friends and stay connected.

Friendly Callers

Professionally trained volunteers make daily calls to elderly, homebound or isolated individuals. Telephone Reassurance provides an opportunity to have a friendly chat, stay in touch and feel safer at home. They can also provide medication reminders and a "safety check," when requested. Calls are made every day from 9 am - 9 pm.

Friendly Visitors

This program provides volunteers to visit seniors.

Generations

203.863.4375

www.greenhosp.org/programs_ha_generations.asp

A free membership program for people 50 years and older, run by the Greenwich Hospital Healthy Aging department. They provide seminars on various medical and wellness topics.

SENIORS

Glenville Senior Citizens
Western Greenwich Civic Center
Marily Sobeskin, President, 203.531.7033

(The) Greens At Greenwich
1155 King Street, Greenwich, 203.531.5500
www.TheGreensAtGreenwich.com
28 apartments and assistance with daily living for residents with memory impairment. The Greens is affiliated with Greenwich Woods which provides priority admission for its specialized Alzheimer's Unit.

Greenwich Adult Day Care
125 River Road Extension, Cos Cob, 203.622.0079
www.gadc.org
Day programs designed to give home caregivers a day off and participants a day filled with socialization, activity and fun. GADC has completely renovated a wonderful new center at the historic 1927 Railroad Pump House on the Mianus River in Cos Cob. The renovation creates a facility designed specifically for adult day care. With more than 8,000 square feet of space, the facility has capacity for 75 clients a day.

Greenwich Hospital
5 Perryridge Road, Greenwich, 203.863.3000
(Healthy Aging 203.863.4373)
www.greenhosp.org
www.greenhosp.org/programs_hlc.asp
http://www.greenhosp.org/medicalservices_aging.asp
Provides community outreach by offering support groups, health screenings and community health education. They have very strong programs for Healthy Living and Healthy Aging .

Greenwich Old Timers Athletic Association
www.GreenwichOldTimers.org
A large social club for men interested in sports. They provide scholarship help and support youth sports in Greenwich. For information, call John Carlucci @ 203.561.8547.

Greenwich Seniors Club
John Titsworth, President, 203.531.6618
Jean Connaughton, Membership, 203.637.1251
A social club for area residents over 55. Meetings are held once a month at Saint Mary's Parish on Greenwich Avenue.

SENIORS

Greenwich Senior Services Information

Community Answers: 203.622.7979

www.CommunityAnswers.org

A valuable point of contact for all local services for seniors can be found on the Community Answers home page or by calling the numbers above. Gathering this information was the joint initiative of the United Way of Greenwich, Commission on Aging and Community Answers.

Greenwich Woods Rehabilitation and Health Care Center

1165 King Street, Greenwich, 203.531.1335

www.GreenwichWoods.com

A privately owned 217-bed rehabilitation and nursing facility. They have a 33-bed secured dementia unit.

Hill House

10 Riverside Avenue, 203.637.3177

37 one-bedroom apartments for the healthy elderly. Residence is open to any able-bodied person over age 62 who meets income guidelines.

Infoline

In Connecticut dial 211 (outside CT 800.203.1234)

www.InfoLine.org

A 24-hour confidential information, referral, advocacy and crisis help line supported by The United Way and the State of Connecticut. Caseworkers have information about hundreds of services, including health, transportation, housing, safety, employment, support services, counseling, financial/legal services and activities.

Life Alert

New York City Office, 350 5th Ave. Ste 929

800-523-6976, 800.815.5922

www.LifeAlert.com, www.SeniorProtection.com

Life Alert is a nationwide company which provides a service that helps the elderly contact emergency services. The company's system uses a base unit connected to the telephone line and a small wireless help button that is worn by the user at all times. Help buttons can be a pendant or built into a watch.

SENIORS

Life Line Connecticut
9 Mott Avenue, Norwalk CT, 203.855.8765, 203.831.2900
Lifeline Systems,111 Lawrence Street, Framingham MA 877.221.8756
www.LifeLineSystems.com, www.familyandchildrensagency.org
The Life Line help button can be worn as a neckless or a bracelet or on a
Tempo Watch. The button connects wirelessly to a base station connected
to the telephone line. Life Line is available in Greenwich through the
Family and Children's Agency. Maurice uses it and likes it.

Lifetime Learners Institute
Norwalk Community College, 188 Richards Avenue, Norwalk, CT
203.857.7316, 203.857.3330
Office: Room W013, West Campus, Lower Level
www.LifeTimeLearners.org email: info@LifeTimeLearners.org
A fabulous organization, affiliated with the Elderhostel Institute Network. It is an independent continuing education program within NCC. To
join you must be over 50 and want to continue learning. Dues are $30
per academic year. Members can choose from over 40 courses for $20 per
course. Members also have free use of the well-equipped college fitness
center.

Meals on Wheels
89 Maple Avenue, Greenwich, 203.869.1312
www.Mealsonwheelsofgreenwich.org
Non-profit organization prepares, packages and delivers meals to homes
of anyone recovering from illness or an injury, regardless of age. Drivers
deliver meals weekdays, 10:30 - noon.

Medicare Ratings for Nursing Homes
www.Medicare.gov
On Medicare.gov's home page is a link to addresses and ratings for
nursing homes in the USA. There are 23 nursing homes listed within 10-
miles of the Greenwich zip code 06830. The top rating is 5 stars. Nathaniel
Witherell has a five-star rating.

(The Merry-Go Round) Mews
Bolling Place, 203.869.9448
Assisted living for seniors 65 and over. The Mews is a managed-care
residential community in the heart of downtown Greenwich, very close
to the town's Senior Center. 88 rooms and suites are available at affordable rates.

Nathaniel Witherell

70 Parsonage Road, 203.618.4200, 4232, 4227

www.witherell.org

The town is planning to renovate our Town-owned nursing home. Nathaniel Witherell cares for 202 residents both long term and short term rehabilitation. They have a large Alzheimer program. Admission preference is given to Greenwich residents, but because the facility is almost always 100% occupied, it is wise to call for an application well in advance of expected need.

Friends of Nathaniel Witherell

70 Parsonage Road, 203.618.4227

www.friendsofwitherell.org

A nonprofit group supporting the Town-owned nursing and rehabilitation center.

National Medical Claims Service (Insurance Assistance)

3 Thorndal Circle, Darien, CT 06820, 203.655.1800

If you or someone you know is overwhelmed with the task of understanding and obtaining insurance benefits, call this Greenwich family business. They are caring, reliable and greatly helpful.

Hours: weekdays 9 am - 5 pm.

(The) Osborn

101 Theall Road, Rye NY, 914.967.4100, 914.921.2200

www.TheOsborn.org

Independent and assisted living and skilled nursing in a landscaped 56-acre setting in Rye. A luxurious, popular choice.

Parsonage Cottage

88 Parsonage Road, 203.869.6226

www.ParsonageCottage.org

A charming residence for 40 seniors (32 private rooms and 4 semi-private rooms). It is funded by low income tax credits, the Town of Greenwich, CDBG and private donations. It is on land leased from Nathaniel Witherell, but it is a separate operation.

Premier Home Health Care of CT

Stamford CT Office: 777 Summer Street, Suite 401, 203.629.4792

www.PremierHealthCare.com

Live in and hourly home health aids, homemakers and companions to assist the elderly to live in their home. Works well for Maurice.

SENIORS

Red Cross Transportation Services
99 Indian Field Road, 203.637.4345, 203.869.8444, ext. 122
www.GreenwichRedCross.org
The transportation service is one of the many superb Red Cross programs. Volunteers, using Red Cross vehicles, provide transportation for Greenwich residents to and from health care and rehabilitation appointments.
Hours: Monday - Thursday 7:30 am - 4 pm, Friday 7:30 am - noon.

Red Hat Society
Fullerton, CA, 714.738.0001, 866.386.1850
www.RedHatSociety.com
The Red Hat Society began as a result of a few women deciding to greet middle-age with verve, humor and élan. To contact one of the local chapters use the website.
Local Greenwich Chapters:
   All Ahead Reds
   Red Hot Babes of Greenwich
   Scarlot Harlots of Greenwich
   The Chickahominy Chicks

Retired Men's Association of Greenwich
YMCA, 50 East Putnam Avenue, 203.869.1630
www.GreenwichRMA.org
Sponsored by and located at the YMCA, this active group of retirees hold weekly business meetings with interesting speakers. They also have special interest trips. Members volunteer many hours of community service work. Membership is for retired men in the Greenwich area, 55 and older.

Senior Center
299 Greenwich Avenue, 203.622.3990
www.GreenwichCT.org/CommissionOnAging/caSeniorCenter.asp
Stop in to see the monthly bulletin board of activities for Greenwich seniors 55 and older. There are a lot of activities going on! Recent listings included: "Qigong" Chinese exercises, chess and bridge instruction, a luncheon cruise, trips to the opera, ice cream socials, painting, shopping center trips and a brown bag auction. Free classes (in conjunction with Greenwich Continuing Education) were being held in line dancing, writing short stories, writing your memoirs and sewing.
Hours: weekdays, 9 am - 4:00 pm.

SENIORS

Senior Health Fair

Contact Greenwich Commission on Aging, 203.862.6710, for details.
The Commission on Aging, Department of Health and Greenwich Hospital join together once a year in October to provide free tests and helpful information.

Senior Net

Greenwich Senior Center 299 Greenwich Avenue, 203.862.6734
www.GreenwichSeniorNet.Community.OfficeLive.co
frede16@aol.com
The Greenwich chapter of Senior Net is a non-profit organization with the basic goal of teaching seniors to use and to enjoy computers. Classes for seniors, 50 and older, are taught by senior volunteers.

Supermarketing for Seniors

One Holly Hill Lane, 203.622.1881
www.JFSGreenwich.org
A free service of the Jewish Family Services of Greenwich. They provide home-bound Greenwich residents over 60 (any denomination) with grocery shopping; also, carpentry, minor plumbing and snow shoveling. They will come to your home, pick up the list and shop for or with you. They provide services for 220 homebound frail elderly Greenwich residents annually.

TAG (Transportation Association of Greenwich)

13 Riverside Avenue, Riverside CT, 203.637.4345
www.RideTAG.org
Non-profit organization operates a fleet of 15 specially modified vehicles. They drive elderly and disabled people of all ages to health, social and educational organizations in Greenwich and neighboring communities. Operates weekdays 6 am - 7 pm, Saturday 8:30 am - 6 pm.

TIP: SPECIAL NEEDS HELP

The Department of Health has a registry of people with disabilities and special needs. The Office of Emergency Management, The Department of Social Services and the Department of Health use this database and encourage seniors to register. In the event of a storm or other emergency the Town will use the registry to evacuate or help seniors and other people with special needs.

SENIORS

Tax Counseling for Seniors

Commission on Aging 203.862.6710, Senior Center 203.862.6700
Volunteer counselors provide free tax return assistance to Seniors starting in mid-February. Site locations are announced in January. Counselors are required to pass an examination administered by the IRS.

USE Utilize Senior Energy

Greenwich Senior Center, 299 Greenwich Avenue, 203.629.8032
This non-profit "employment agency" is run by volunteers from the basement of the Senior Center. This brilliant organization founded in 1977 by Viola Caldwell allows retired seniors to continue working and provides an excellent resource for the community. It is a good place to find all manner of help: receptionists, business consultants, painters, baby sitters, etc.
Hours: Weekday, 9:30 am to 12:30 pm.

Waveny

3 Farm Road, New Canaan CT, 203.594.5200
www.Waveny.org
Waveny offers several options, independent living at the very attractive New Canaan Inn, Assisted Living for Alzheimer's at the Village and skilled nursing at Waveny Care Center. They also have adult day care and geriatric evaluations.

Weekend Lunch Bunch

Greenwich Hospital, 203.863.3690
Anyone age 55 or older can enjoy a $6, four-course meal in the cafeteria. Call to find out the menu for the weekend.
Hours: Saturday & Sunday noon - 2 pm.

YMCA Exercise Programs

50 East Putnam Avenue, 203.869.1630
www.GWYMCA.org
The Y offers a number of programs tailored to the needs of seniors, including walking, stretching, resistance training and swimming.

SERVICES INDEX

For Wildlife & Animal Rescue see PETS.
For Home Delivery also see FOOD, RESTAURANTS and SENIORS.
For Sports Training see FITNESS.
For Car and Truck Rentals, see AUTOMOBILES.
For Travel Agents, see TRAVEL.
For Ticket Agencies, see CULTURE.
For Baby Sitting and language training see CHILDREN, CHILD ENRICH-MENT.
For Art Shops and Framing see STORES.
For Barbers, Hairdressers, Spas and Nail Salons see GROOMING.
For Senior Services see SENIORS.
For Photographers see PHOTOGRAPHY.

Alarm Systems
See Security

Art
Art Shops and Framers are reviewed in STORES
Lending Art Program of the Greenwich Library, 203.622.7900
Miranda Arts frame repair, 914.935.9362

Audio Visual / Home Theater
See also Contractors below.
See also Television below.
See Computer below for repair and software help
EPI Sytems Integration, 845.855.5785
Everett Hall, 203.325.4328
Performance Imaging, 203.862.9600

The following AV stores are reviewed in STORES
Audiocom, 321 Greenwich Avenue, 203.552.5224
Bang & Olufsen, 365 Greenwich Avenue, 203.769.5500
Best Buy, 330 Connecticut Avenue, Norwalk, CT, 203.857.4543
Computer Super Center, 103 Mason Street, 203.661.1700

SERVICES INDEX

Banking

Greenwich has been invaded by banks, 25 at last count. Many Greenwich residents still prefer to work with in-town banks. Friendly hellos and loans from bankers who know and work in the community are a much more civilized way to bank than dealing anonymously with a big, inflexible institution. Greenwich is fortunate to have two locally owned hometown banks. Drop in and say hello.

First Bank of Greenwich, 203.629.8400
Greenwich Bank & Trust, 203.618.8900

Environmental and Water Remediation Services

Connecticut Basement Systems (Water), 203.381.9633
Connecticut Basement Systems (Radon), 203.381.9633
Enviro Shield, 203.380.5644
Home Guard Environmental, 203.323.8000
Northeast Systems Radon and Water, 203.296.4269
Service Master, 203.327.3477

Child Safety

For Baby Sitting See CHILDREN.
Baby Pro (internet directory)
Children Car Seat Help (Greenwich Fire Department), 203.622.8087
Child Pool Fencing (internet directory)
Safety Mom, 203.594.7452

Chimney Cleaning

You should have your chimneys cleaned every three years. This business seems to attract con men, so be sure you know who is coming into your home. We recommend the following cleaning services:

Bill Ingraham, Cos Cob, 203.869.5242.
Steve Oldham, Chimney Swifts, Cos Cob, 203.661.7243

Cleaning

See Chimney Cleaning above
For Dry Cleaning see p. 380
For Duct Cleaning see p.380
For Carpet Cleaning and repair see Rugs and Carpets p.386
For Trash removal and dumpsters see Refuse Collection p.384
Health First Home Cleaning, 203.531.1766
Personal Touch, 203.531.7431
Superior Home Services, 203.359.3861
Window Genie, 203.363.0783

SERVICES INDEX

Computer (Donations)
Cristina Foundation (under 5 years old) 203.863.9100
Good Will (under 6 years old) 203.363.5228
Salvation Army (under 6 years old) 800.958.7825
Greenwich Hospital Thrift Shop (under 3 years old) 203.869.6124

Computer (Repair, Training and Services)
See also Websites p. 388
Canaan Technology, 203.847.2444
Computing Central, 203.637.8017
Computer Guru, 203.629.5394
Computer Super Center, 203.661.1700
Decaro Associates, 203.943.4705
Diane McKeever, diane@dianemckeever.com
Fast Teks, 203.661.3278
Geek Squad, 800.433.5778
PC Repair and Sales, 203.359.4732
Vernon Computer Rentals, 203.969.0060

Contractors
See also Audio-Visual p. 377
See Repairs p. 385
All American Sewer & Drain Services
Bright Homes (energy solutions) 914.909.5300
Connecticut Closet and Shelf, 203.838.9089
Detail Painting & Repairs, 203.515.8256
EPI Sytems Integration, 845.855.5785
Greenwich Blue Print Company, 203.869.0305
Greenwich Window Doctor, 203.531.4485
Hupal Masonry, 203.531.5245
Hupal Septic and Excavation, 203.532.1401
Jason, The Handyman, 203.625.0411
Joe Piro (tile mason), 203.661.2266
John Calorossi, (carpet / laminate laying) 203.249.1721
Joseph Williamson (wallpapering), 203.629.7911
Longo's Rent-a-Tool, 203.975.0569
Masterpiece Floor refinishing, 203.219.2047
Mr. Mailbox, 203.849.1144 (in SHOPPING)
Mr. Shower Door, 800-663.3667 (in SHOPPING)
New York Steel Window, 914.736.5208
Seekircher Steel Window Repair, 914.734.8004
Service Master, 203.327.3477

(Contractors continued...)
There are many good architects, general contractors and trade contractors. We have opted not to try to list them all. Try these Rating services:

Angies List www.AngiesList.com (888.944.5478) is a website that rates these and other service providers. One annoyance is you have to register to use the site. You should take the ratings with a grain of salt, its hard to know who is making the comments.

Franklin Report www.FranklinReport.com The Franklin Report rates service providers by price and quality. We have found their ratings to be reliable. However, most contractors charge more when they are busy and less when they are not, so be sure to get at least two estimates.

Custom Embroidery and Screen Printing
Chillybear, 203.622.7115
(The) Monogram Studio, 203.428.5700

Deer Control
Deer Tech, 866.319.6530

Delivery Services (including home delivery)
For US Postal Services see POST OFFICES
ASAP Messenger Services, 914.769.2727
Berman Newspaper Delivery, 203.323.5955
Deliver Ease, 203.532.0370
Fresh Direct, 212-796.8002
i-SOLD-it, 203.845.0290
Kinko's / FedEx, 203.863.0099
Mail Boxes Etc, 203.622.1114
Marcus Dairy, 800.243.2511
Packages PlusNMore, 203.625.8130
Stop and Shop/Pea Pod, 800.573.2763
UPS, 800.742.5877

Dry Cleaning and Laundry
Berger Cleaners, 203.869.7650
Brighton Cleaners, 203.531.5679
Commuter Cleaners, 203.861.7121
Thomas Dry Cleaning & Chinese Laundry, 203.869.9420
Triple S Carpet and Drapery Cleaners, 203.327.7471

Duct Cleaning
The National Air Duct Association website is www.nadca.com
Duct-Clean, 203.380.0191
Duct & Vent Cleaning of America, 203.327.5655

SERVICES INDEX

Dumpsters
See Refuse Collectors p. 384

Estate Sales
See Tag Sales p. 386

Exterminators
Aavon Pest Control, 203.329.2600
All County Pest Control, 203.327.0259
All about Bats, 203.323.0468
Honey Bee Removal 203.249.2733

Firewood
A cord is a stack of wood 4 feet high x 4 feet wide x 8 feet long
Augustine's Farm, 203.532.9611
Firewood by Gus, 203.637.5804
Firewood from Buzz and Ray, 203.862.9271
Vermont Good Wood, 203.637.5200

Generators
Cannondale Generators, 203.762.2608

Glass, Mirrors and Acrylic
Anything In Acrylic, 203.324.7179
Associated Glass, 914.937.7300

Handyman
See Contractors p. 379

Home Delivery Services
For Home Delivery see also FOOD or RESTAURANTS.
See also Delivery Services p. 380

Home and Office Services
See also Delivery Services above
See STORES for Office Furniture Rentals
Judith Heft & Associates, 203.978.1858
Kinko's / FedEx, 203.863.0099
Landmark Document Services, 203.325.4300
Words to Go, 203.661.1711

SERVICES INDEX

Information (services)
Angie's List, 888.888.5478
Better Business Bureau, 203.269.2700
Community Answers, 203.622.7979
CT Energy Information, www.CTEnergyInfo.com
Greenwich Chamber of Commerce, 203.869.3500

Installers
Joe Piro (tile mason), 203.661.2266
John Calorossi, (carpet / laminate laying) 203.249.1721

Insurance
Greenwich Independent Insurance (aka Elkanah Mead), 203.869.0302
Rand Insurance, 203.637.1006

Landscaping (lawns, Sprinklers and Tree Services)
County Wide Sprinklers, 914.698.5112
Round Hill Tree Service, 203.531.5759

Locksmiths
Greenwich Lock and Door, 203.622.1095
(Charles) Stuttig, 203.869.6260

Metal Work
Architectural Metals, 203.532.8089
Post Road Iron Works, 203.869.6322

Moving and Storage
Your move depends on the people assigned to your job. We sure hope you get the best. Perhaps it will help if you tell them you will be reporting both good and bad news to us. To check on a moving company and any complaints that have been filed, call the Department of Transportation at 860.594.2870. They are very helpful.
Alexander Services, 203.324.4012
Callahan Brothers, 203.869.2239
Easy Going Home, 212.535-3511
Joe Mancuso. 914.937.2178
Morgan Manhattan Moving & Storage, 203.869.8700
Navis Pack & Ship, 203.335.7447
Packages PlusNMore, 203.625.8130
PODS, 866.229.4120
(the) Settler, 203.858.3054 (cell)
Two Men and A Truck, 203.831.9300
Westy Self Storage, 203.961.8000

SERVICES INDEX

Painting
Detail Painting & Repairs, 203.515.8256
See also Contractors p. 379

Pests
See Exterminators p. 381

Photographic Services
Images, 203.637.4193
PD Photo, 203.637.0340
Ritz Camera, 203.869.0673 (*also reviewed in SHOPPING*)

Piano (lessons and tuning)
Gerhar Feldmann, 212.717.2907
Piano Service, 203.359.2231
Pyrianos Collection, 203.661.2566
Robert Marullo, 203.869.4943

Property Management
GEC Property Management, 203.329.9262

Radon
See environmental services

Rentals
For Car and Truck Rentals, see AUTOMOBILES.
For Furniture Rentals see SHOPPING
Coppola Tailors Tux Rentals, 203.869.2883
Cort Furniture Rental, 203.353.0400
Greenwich Hardware and Home 203.622.2350
Longo's Rent-a-Tool, 203.975.0569
Sophia's Great Dames Costume Rentals, 203.869.5990
Vernon Computer Rentals, 203.969.0060

SERVICES INDEX

Recycling

The Public Works department of the Town has a good description of your options: http://greenwichct.org/PublicWorks/pwWARecycling.asp

Recycling is now mandated by the state, but it is interesting to note that thanks to Mariette Badger and the active Greenwich Recycling Advisory Board of community volunteers, Greenwich recycling has been organized for over twenty-five years. Our recycling program saves the Town money and protects the environment. Each week at a designated day and time, the Town picks up recyclables and brings them to the Holly Hill Transfer Station.

Blue Bins for Recycling, 203.622.0550

City Carting, Dumpsters & Recycling, 203.324.4090

Got-Junk, 800.468.5865

Holly Hill Recycling Facility (aka The Dump), 203.622.0550

i-SOLD-it, 203.845.0290

Junk Luggers, 888.584.5865

Recycling Cell Phones

Recycling Christmas Trees

Recycling Computers

   Cristina Foundation (under 5 years old) 203.863.9100

   Good Will (under 6 years old) 203.363.5228

   Salvation Army (under 6 years old) 800.958.7825

   Greenwich Hospital Thrift Shop (under 3 years old) 203.869.6124

   www.YouRenew.Com

Refuse Collectors

Garbage collection is done by independent contractors. New residents may call the Greenwich Independent Refuse Collectors Association at 203.622.0050 to find out which collector services their home. When you move to a home it helps to ask the former owner or a neighbor who is servicing their home.

Junk Luggers, 888.584.5865

City Carting, Dumpsters & Recycling, 203.324.4090

See also Town Services

SERVICES INDEX

Repairs (Furniture, appliances, etc)

For Painting and other Building Repairs see Contractors p. 379
See also Replace or Repair China or Crystal p. 386
For shoe repair see Shoes p.386
For television and other electronic repairs see Television p.387
For Carpet and Rug repair see Rugs and Carpets p. 386
See Locksmiths p. 382

Action Appliance Services, 203.698.0211
American Typewriter, 860.354.6903
Anything In Acrylic, 203.324.7179
Appliance Service Center of Stamford, 203.322.7656
Associated Glass, 914.937.7300
Atelier Constantin Popescu, 203.661.9500
Betteridge Jewelers, 203.869.0124
David A Sabini Company (large appliance repair), 203.324.6109
Ed's Garage Doors, 203.847.1284 (in SHOPPING)
Gordon Sweeny clock repair, 203.857.0807
Graham Company ceiling fan repair, 800.942.5575
Greenwich Metal Finishing, 203.977.0494
Greenwich Window Doctor, 203.531.4485
Longo's Rent-a-Tool, 203.975.0569
Masterpiece Floor refinishing, 203.219.2047
Miranda Arts frame repair, 914.935.9362
New York Steel Window, 914.736.5208
Nimble Thimble, 914.934.2934
Patti's Portico, 203.869.6227
Raphael's Furniture Restoration, 203.348.3079
Seekircher Steel Window Repair, 914.734.8004
Sears Home Services, 800.349.5075
Sterling Vacuum Center, 203.846.2442
Super Handy Hardware, 203.531.5599
Willett Vacuum Repair, 914.937.5948
Wood Den, 203.324.6957

SERVICES INDEX

Replace or Repair China or Crystal (Oops, I broke it!)
China & Glass Restoration, 800.669.1327
Table Top Designs, 800.801.4084
Thomas Libby, 203.854.0300
If for some reason these resources can't help you, try these out-of-the-area replacement services:
Clintsman International, 800.781.8900
Pattern Finders, 631.928.5158
Replacements Ltd, 800.737.5223

Rugs and Carpets (repair and cleaning)
Carpet Ron, 203.359.4285
Golden Horn, 914.670.6666
John Calorossi, (carpet / laminate laying) 203.249.1721
Personal Touch, 203.531.7431
Triple S Carpet and Drapery Cleaners, 203.327.7471

Security and Safety
Advanced Electronic Systems, 203.846.0700
Dark House Service (Greenwich Police, 203.622.8000)
Executive Services, 914.962.4077
Interstate Fire and Safety, 203.531.1333
Kennedy Security Services, 203.661.6814
Metroguard, 800.495.0400
PI Security, 203.862.9300

Shoe & Leather Repair
Greenwich Shoe Repair, 203.869.2288
Occhicone, 914.937.6327

Snow Plowing
Most landscapers and refuse collectors also plow, but if yours doesn't try Greenwich Hardware

Tag Sales (aka Garage Sales, Estate Sales)
For book sales see LIBRARIES AND BOOKS
Betty's Tag Sales, Betty Shopovick, 203.613.4613
Consign It Tag Sales, 203.869.9836
Good Riddance Girls Tag Sales, Lynn Westmeyer 203.329.0009

SERVICES INDEX

Tailors & Dressmakers

Charles Custom Tailor, 203.531.7640
Coppola Tailors, 203.869.2883
Greenwich Furs, 203.869.1421
Nibia Stezano, Master Seamstress, 203.629.5474
Ted The Tailor, 203.869.5699

Telephone

Greenwich is on the border between Verizon (formerly Bell Atlantic, formerly Nynex) and AT&T (formerly SNET, formerly SBC) coverage areas. Old Greenwich exchanges (637 & 698) are covered by AT&T. The rest of Greenwich is controlled by Verizon. This means that many numbers outside of Greenwich require you to dial 1-203 first. All customers must dial the area code for all calls, including local calls. 911 (emergency), 411 (information), 811 (Call before you Dig) and 611 (phone repair) continue to require only 3 digits. New numbers given out in the 203 area code will have a new area code of 475 or 860.
AT&T/SNET/SBC
Verizon
The stores for these companies are reviewed in the SHOPPING section.

Television

Cablevision of Connecticut, 203.846.4700
Discount TV, Camcorder & VCR Repair, 203.323.2683
EPI Sytems Integration, 845.855.5785
Satellite TV Networks
    Direct TV, 888.777.2454
    Dish Network, 888.825.2557
Ultrawiz Electronics Repair, 203.532.0175

Termites

See Exterminators

Waste (Hazardous)

Whenever you wish to dispose of items such as bug spray, engine oil, old paint cans or other items which are not part of the normal recycling program, call Department of Public Works at 869.6910, 622.7838 or 622.7740.

SERVICES INDEX

Leaf Collection
Town leaf collection is limited to all properties on public streets only in building zones R20 (half-acre) and below. Many residents with one or more acres compost on their own property. For a schedule of leaf collection, call 622.7718, 618.7698 or watch for the schedule printed by the Greenwich Time in the fall.

Christmas Tree Recycling
Residents may begin to bring their Christmas Trees for recycling from December 28th to January 30th. All trees to be recycled must be undecorated (ornaments, tinsel, lights and stands must be removed). Trees may be dropped off at the following locations:
- Byram Park - 8:00 am to 4:00 pm - the parking lot by the Concession.
- Bruce Park - 8:00 am to 4:00 pm - the parking lot by the Children's playground
- Greenwich Point - 6:00am until sunset - first parking lot across from Nature Center.
- Holly Hill Recycling Center 7:00am to 3:00pm weekdays and 7:00am 12:00 noon on Saturdays place trees in the yard waste area.

Tuxedo Rentals
Coppola Tailors, 203.869.2883

Utilities
See also Telephones, Television and Generators
A more complete list is in NUMBERS YOU SHOULD KNOW, or online at
www.GreenwichLiving.com/Contacts_Relocation.htm
Aquarion (water company) 203.869.5200
Connecticut Natural Gas, 203.869.6900
CT Energy Information, www.CTEnergyInfo.com
Modern Gas (propane), 203.869.4226, www.ModernGasCT.com
Northeast Utilities / Connecticut Light & Power, 800.286.2000

Wallpapering
Joseph Williamson, 203.629.7911
See also Contractors above.

Websites
See also computers above
Web Weavers, 203.532.0700

Wine Storage
Horse Ridge Cellars, 860.763.5380

SERVICES

For Wildlife & Animal Rescue see PETS.
For Home Delivery also see FOOD, RESTAURANTS and SENIORS.
For Sports Training see FITNESS AND SPORTS.
For Car and Truck Rentals, see AUTOMOBILES.
For Travel Agents, see TRAVEL.
For Ticket Agencies, see CULTURE.
For Baby Sitting and Language Training see CHILDREN, CHILD ENRICH-MENT.
For Art Shops and Framing see STORES.
For Barbers, Hairdressers, Spas and Nail Salons see GROOMING.
For Senior Services see SENIORS.
For Eyeglasses see STORES.
For Medical Services see HEALTH.

Aavon Pest Control (exterminator)
49 Ryan Street Stamford CT, 866.228.6611, 203.329.2600
www.aavonpestcontrol.com
They will get rid of almost any kind of unwelcome pest: termites, ants and even bats and yellow jackets. Call Dave Curtis and he will be able to help you.

Action Appliance Services (Appliance Repair)
569 Old Stamford Road, New Canaan CT, 203.698.0211
If you have washers, dryers, dishwashers, ranges or refrigerators that aren't working, call Bill Miles. For 16 years Bill has rescued many a homeowner.

Advanced Electronic Systems (Alarm Systems)
16 Brookfield Street, Norwalk CT, 203.846.0700
www.AdvancedElectronicSystems.net
They have been helping Greenwich residents with alarm systems for over 30 years. Howard Friedman can be counted on to help you choose the right system.

Alexander Services (movers)
Call Shawn Alexander at 888.656.6838, 203.324.4012.
They are the mover of choice for many antique shops.

All about Bats (Pest Removal)
203.323.0468
They carefully remove wildlife from your home and relocate it so you won't have unwanted pets. They can also help prevent furry intrusions.

SERVICES

All American Sewer & Drain Services (drain repair)
52 Larkin Street, Stamford, 203.661.6199, 203.357.1322
www.allamericansd.com
They can fix just about any drain problem.

All County Pest Control (exterminator)
9 Kenilworth Drive West, Stamford CT 203-327-0259
888-327-0259
www.allcountypest.com

American Typewriter (repair)
Route 202, New Milford, CT, 860.354.6903
David Morrill repairs typewriters and sells refurbished ones. One of the last places around to do this work.

Angie's List (service providers)
888-888-5478
www.AngiesList.com
A website that rates service providers and has customer comments (good and bad) about their services. One annoyance is you have to register and pay to use the site.

Anything In Acrylic (Acrylic displays)
73-B Maple Tree Avenue, Stamford CT, 203.324.7179
Paul Nardozza crafts anything out of acrylic from sheets cut to size to memorabilia displays.

Appliance Service Center of Stamford (Repair)
15 Cedar Heights Road (off High Ridge Road), Stamford
203.322.7656
If you can carry it, they can probably repair it. In addition they service stoves, refrigerators, washers and dryers in your home.
Hours: weekdays 8:30 am - 5:30 pm, Saturday 8:30 am -1:30 pm.

Aquarion
(formerly Connecticut-American Water Company)
www.Aquarion.com 203.869.5200 (office)
203.445.7310, 800.732.9678 (emergency)
800.292.2928, 800.732.9678 (customer service)
Our local water company.

SERVICES

Architectural Metals (metal work)
31 Buena Vista Drive, Greenwich 203.532.8089
Thanks to Glen Fox we have a very attractive railing in our garden.

ASAP Messenger Services (delivery service)
914.769.2727
www.ASAPMessenger.com
An affiliate of Leros Limousines, they deliver small packages in the tri-state area.

Associated Glass (glass and mirror repair)
71 Cottage Street, Port Chester NY, 914.937.7300
This is a helpful, cost effective resource for glass and mirror replacement. They do a lot of work for contractors. They would prefer you to measure, but will come out if you need them to. They also supply shower doors. Hours: weekdays 9 am - 5 pm, Saturday 9 am - 1 pm.

Atelier Constantin Popescu (musical instrument repair)
403 East Putnam Avenue, Cos Cob, 203.661.9500
www.atelierconstantinpopescu.com
Sells, repairs and rents string instruments. The Riverside School of Music is located next to his store at 401 East Putnam Avenue (203.661-9501). Hours: weekdays 10 am - 6 pm, Saturday 10 am - 2 pm.

AT&T/SNET/SBC: (telephone)
From AT&T coverage area, dial 811 for repairs; from out-of-state, 800.453.7638 (Customer Service); 203.420.3131 (repairs) or 611 from cell phone.
www.snet.com, www.sbc.com, www.att.com
They service Old Greenwich exchanges 637 & 698. Verizon services the rest of Greenwich.

Augustine's Farm (firewood, flowers and vegetables)
1332 King Street, 203.532.9611
Kathy and John Augustin sell firewood at their farm. They will deliver from October to March. One half a cord is $130, delivery is extra (unstacked).

Baby Pro (child safety)
www.BabyPro.com
Child proofing products and a directory of child proofers in CT.

SERVICES

Berger Cleaners (dry cleaners)
282 Mason Street, 203.869.7650
A good choice for your curtains and draperies.
Hours: weekdays 7 am - 6:30 pm, Saturday 7:30 am - 4:30 pm.

Berman Newspaper Delivery (home delivery)
203.323.5955
Depending upon where you live, Berman will deliver to your home between 5 and 6 am, where you want it, all of the major papers including: The New York Times, Financial Times and USA Today. The local papers come out too late for this delivery, so unless you want these papers a day late, you should contact them directly: Greenwich Time, 203.625.4400; Greenwich Post, 203.861.9191; Greenwich Citizen, 203.750.5313.

Better Business Bureau (information)
94 South Turnpike Road, Wallingford, CT 203.269.2700
www.ctbbb.org Office hours: 8:30 am - 4:30 pm

Betteridge Jewelers (jewelry repair and appraisal)
117 Greenwich Avenue, 203.869.0124
www.Betteridge.com
A third-generation family-owned business. Totally trustworthy with excellent service and repair, as well as appraisal services.
Hours: Closed Monday, Tuesday - Saturday 9 am - 5 pm (Call for holiday hours).

Bill Ingraham (chimney cleaning)
105 River Road, Cos Cob, 203.869.5242
Bill is a very reliable chimney/fireplace cleaner. The cost is about $135.

Blue Bins for Recycling
To get your blue bin(s) and recycling details, call 203.622.0550. Blue Bins cost $10. Hours: weekdays, 9 am - 3 pm.

Bright Home (Energy Solutions)
5 Westchester Plaza, Elmsford NY, 914.909.5300
www.BrightHome.com
Energy assessments, air sealing, insulation.

Brighton Cleaners (dry cleaners)
- 25 Glenville Street, Glenville, 203.531.5679
- 146 Sound Beach Avenue, Old Greenwich, 203.698.1135
Reliable dry-cleaning on their premises. They offer same day service.

SERVICES

Cablevision of Connecticut (television)
203.348.9211, 203.846.4700
www.cablevision.com www.optimum.com
Internet, phone service and, of course, cable TV. They are in a price war with Verizon Fios which competes in all three of these areas, www22.verizon.com/Residential/fiostv/ and with Satellite TV networks (www.directTv.com or www.dishnetwork.com)

Callahan Brothers (movers)
133 Post Road, Cos Cob, 203.869.2239
www.CallahanBrothers.net
They are the local agent for Joyce Van Lines and have been a fixture in Greenwich for many years. When you need to move across the country or across the world, give them a call. Hours: weekdays, 8 am - 5 pm.

Canaan Technology (computer help)
194 Main Street, Norwalk CT
203.847.2444, 203.422.6226, 203.613.6112
www.CanaanTechnology.com
Canaan Technology specializes in services to individuals and small e-businesses needing help with technology (design, repair, installation and support). If you are installing or servicing a network be sure to call David Felton.
Hours: weekdays, 9 am - 5 pm. Service is available 24 hours a day, every day of the year.

Cannondale Generators (generators)
390 Danbury Road, Wilton CT, 203.762.2608
www.CannondaleGenerators.com
A distributor of Generac's Guardian natural gas or LP gas powered generators, www.Generac.com. They provide reliable service.

Carpet Ron (rug cleaning)
Ron Laroche, 52 Toms Road, Stamford CT
203.359.4285, cell 203.326.0758
Recommended by our friends as a good rug cleaner. We recommend him too! He also cleans upholstery.

Charles Custom Tailor
Charles Park, 36 Glenville Street, Glenville, 203.531.7640
Recommended by friends as an excellent tailor with reasonable prices.

SERVICES

Children Car Seat Help (child safety)
Children under the age of one need to be in a rear facing car seat. Children between the ages of one and seven need to be in car seats. The Greenwich Fire Department, 622.8087, will help you install or inspect your seat. Call for an appointment.

Child Pool Fencing (child safety)
800.992.2206
www.protectacwww.callahanbrothers.nethild.com
A list of local distributors of "Baby Safe" pool fencing.

Chillybear (custom embroidery)
180 Sound Beach Avenue, Old Greenwich,
203.622.7115 or 888.463.2707
www.chillybear.com
A great resource for custom printing, embroidery and silk screening on shirts, hats, bags and all kinds of clothing, as well a store for the hip young adolescent. Very nice customer service.
Hours: Monday - Saturday 10 am - 6 pm, Sunday noon - 5 pm.

Chimney Swifts (Chimney Cleaning)
Steve Oldham, Cos Cob, 203.661.7243, 761.9823
They will inspect and clean your chimney. The cost is about $145. They have been operating in Greenwich since 1979 and are very reliable and honest.

China & Glass Restoration (repair)
324 Guinevere Ridge, Cheshire, CT, 800.669.1327, 203.271.3659
www.ChinaAndCrystalrepair.com/
Send them a photo of your broken or chipped piece and they will give you an estimate for repair.

City Carting & Recycling (dumpsters and trash Removal)
8 Viaduct Road, Stamford CT, 800.872.7405, 203.324.4090
www.CityCarting.net
Residential waste removal and dumpsters from 2 yards to 30 yards. City Carting will provide weekly curbside trash pickup. City Carting offers residential open-top services for small repair jobs.
Hours: weekdays, 6 am - 6 pm, Saturday to 1 pm.

Commuter Cleaners (dry cleaners)

121 E Putnam Avenue, Cos Cob, 203.861.7121

www.CommuterClearners.net

Same day dry cleaning, shirt laundry, tailoring and alterations, drapery curtain and leather cleaning—even shoe repair. If you want home delivery, they will pick-up on Monday and deliver back to your home on Thursday. Prices are on their website.

Hours: weekdays, 7am-7:30pm, Saturday 8am-5pm.

Computing Central (computer repair)

1128 East Putnam Avenue, Riverside, 203.637.8017

www.hyundailab.com

Guy Kim's English may not be perfect, but his hardware skills are excellent. He works on any type of computer and handles most repairs, including data recovery, in one or two days.

Hours: weekdays 10 am - 6 pm, Saturday 10 am - 5 pm.

Computer Guru (computer help)

93 Richards Avenue, Norwalk CT, 203.899.1926, 203.325.8935

Nicholas Guild repairs, troubleshoots, and solves PC computer problems. Joan, one of our clients, loved the way he set up her computer and got her back into action following her move.

Computer Super Center (computer repair)

103 Mason Street, 203.661.1700

www.ComputerSuperCenter.com

A helpful, friendly store that sells and services computers as well as HDTV and Audio equipment, such as Apple - Sony - BOSE - Shure - HP - Lenovo (IBM) - Fujitsu and OKI.

Community Answers (information)

101 West Putnam Avenue in the Greenwich Library, 203.622.7979

www.CommunityAnswers.org

Such an incredible source of information, they have their own section in our guide - INFORMATION RESOURCES. They maintain an extensive data base on Greenwich activities and resources as well as specialized files on local groups - computer training, tutors and other cottage industries such as dog sitting. If you can't find an answer on their website, call and ask them just about any question about Greenwich.

SERVICES

Connecticut Natural Gas (utility)
203.869.6900 (customer service)
203.869.6913 (repair & emergency)
www.CNGCorp.com

Connecticut Basement Systems
(wet basement mitigation)
60 Silvermine Road, Seymour CT, 800.638.7048
www.ConnecticutBasementSystems.com
They specialize in curing wet basements.

Connecticut Basement Systems Radon (radon mitigation)
720 Woodend Road, Stratford CT, 203.381.9633, 800.319.8867
www.ConnecticutRadon.com
A separate company from the one above, they specialize in mitigating Radon. The EPA recommends that Radon at or above 4.0 pCi/L should be mitigated.

Connecticut Closet and Shelf
26 Fitch Street, Norwalk CT, 203.838.9089
www.CTcloset.com
They design, manufacture and install closets. Ask for Melissa.

County Wide Sprinkler (lawn Sprinklers)
220 Frank Avenue, Mamaroneck NY, 914.698.5112
You can depend on Rudy Amatuzzo, to set up a good sprinkler system and keep it running. Very nice to deal with.

Coppola Tailors (tailor and tux sales / rental)
347 Greenwich Avenue, 203.869.2883
Just the right place for suit alterations. Greenwich residents have been renting and buying their tuxes here for years.

Cort Furniture Rental
417 Shippan Avenue, Stamford, 203.353.0400
www.Cort.com
A Berkshire Hathaway company. They claim to have the world's largest inventory of rental furniture.
Hours: weekdays, 9 am - 6 pm, Saturday 10 am - 5 pm.

SERVICES

Cristina Foundation (recycle computers)
500 West Putnam Avenue, Greenwich, 203.863.9100
www.Cristina.org
Donate your used computers, printers, peripherals and software. National Cristina Foundation (NCF) is a not-for-profit organization that provides computer technology to people with disabilities and economically disadvantaged persons. They only accept more recent computers under 5 years old. Systems must have a hard drive, monitor, keyboard, & mouse.

CT Energy Information
www.CTEnergyInfo.com, 877.947.3873
If you have every wanted to know your options for alternate, clean energy, this is the first place to go. The site was developed by the Connecticut Department of Public Utility Control to help consumers navigate the ever increasing number of energy-related resources.

Dark House Service (home security)
Greenwich Police, 203.622.8000 (main number)
If residents notify the police that they will be away for an extended period of time, Greenwich police will patrol the area with an extra-cautious eye. You can also hire an off-duty police officer to personally check your home when you are away. To hire an off-duty officer for this or to direct traffic at a party, call 203.622.8015

David A Sabini Company (large appliance repair)
Darien CT, 203.324.6109
David specializes in repairing dishwashers, dryers, washers and refrigerators.

Decaro Associates (computer help)
3 Sweet Briar Lane, Cos Cob, 203.943.4705
Fred DeCaro is an expert technology consultant used by the Town and many Greenwich businesses and individual residents.

Deer Tech (deer control)
101 Castleton Street Suite 202, Pleasantville, NY 10570
866.319.6530 www.deertechusa.com
www.NatureTechnologies.com
The company was founded in 2003. They operate throughout the tri-state area and have a number of happy customers, but very few happy deer.

SERVICES

Deliver Ease of Greenwich (delivery)

203.532.0370

www.DeliverEase.com

For $10 for every 15 minutes of travel time, this reliable service will pamper your every need. They promptly deliver to or pick up from your door just about anything you can imagine: aspirin from your drugstore, poster board for a project, food from your favorite restaurant, forgotten dry cleaning, a late video, or just a cup of Dunkin' Donuts' coffee. Why not send a gift to cheer up someone at the hospital?

Hours: Open 7 days a week from 8 am - 9 pm.

Detail Painting & Repairs (painting, handyman)

Norwalk, CT, Marcos Souza, 203.846.1157, Cell: 203.515.8256

If you need an expert interior or exterior paint job, if you need your gutters cleaned or minor carpentry, you will not find a nicer person to work with and you will be pleased with the results.

Diane McKeever, CPP (software training)

www.dianemckeever.com, diane@dianemckeever.com

www.linkedin.com/pub/diane-mckeever/5/b9/923

If you want to learn a Microsoft program, you should enroll in one of Diane's Continuing Education classes at the Greenwich High School. But if you don't have the time, she gives private lessons for students of all levels - she is a CPP (Certified Patient Person) as well as a good teacher.

Discount TV, Camcorder & VCR Repair (repair)

54 Hamilton Street, Stamford, 203.323.2683

Ed Fraioli and Len DiChiara repair Camcorders, VCRs, and TVs (including plasma). Before throwing out your television, give these repairman a call. They charge a flat fee for repairs rather than an hourly rate.

Hours: weekdays, 9 am - 5 pm; Saturday, 9 am - 1 pm.

Be sure to make an appointment.

Duct & Vent Cleaning of America (duct cleaning)

Stamford CT, 203.327.5655

www.ductandvent.com

A large company with 21 offices. All calls go to the national office for scheduling.

Duct-Clean (duct cleaning)

20 Stagg Street, Stratford, CT 203.380.0191

A small local company with a good reputation.

SERVICES

Easy Going Home (movers)
212.535.3511
www.EasyGoingHome.com
Recently a client hired this relocation consultant and moving coordinator to help her move from her Greenwich home to an apartment in a senior residence. As our client said, they were not inexpensive (they charge seniors $95 an hour) but they were enormously helpful. They took care of everything, even the selection of the movers, the careful labeling of her items and when she arrived at her new home, the pictures were hung and the books were in the same order as before.

Ed's Garage Doors (garage door repair)
136 Water Street, Norwalk CT, 203.847.1284
www.EdsGarageDoors.com
Whether you are looking for a new overhead door, a new garage door opener or just a repair, Ed's is very dependable and an excellent resource. Hours: weekdays, 8 am - 5 pm, Saturday 9 am - 3 pm.

Enviro Shield (environmental remediation)
Stratford CT, 203.380.5644 www.Enviroshield.com
A trustworthy group to call if you have any concerns about mold abatement, testing, removal or installation of oil tanks or remediation of areas contaminated by petroleum or other chemicals.

EPI Sytems Integration (home theater/ electricians)
538 Route 22, Pawling, NY, 845.855.5785 www.Episi.com
Pawling may not seem nearby, but they do a lot of high quality work in Greenwich. They are a great resource for system integration and home theaters. They have their own electrician specialists working with them.

Everett Hall (audio/visual equipment)
76 Progress Drive, Stamford, CT 203.325.4328, 800.942.2097
www.EverettHall.com
They rent & sell AV equipment and stage shows.

Executive Services (home security)
7 Adrienne Court, Smithtown NY,
Cell: 203.496.0216, (Office) 914.962.4077 www.VanCoExec.com
Bodyguards, chauffeurs, property management, parties and other special events. Run by ex-law enforcement professionals.

SERVICES

Fast Teks (computer help)
www.FastTeks.com
286 North Ridge Street, Rye Brook NY, 914.935.3278, 203-661-3278
On site computer trouble shooting, virus removal and software training.
Fast Teks is a computer franchise serving over 200 cities. Gus Carmona
is the area director. His cell is 914.393.8783.

Firewood by Gus (firewood)
(also called Connecticut Demolition)
2 Apple Tree Lane, Riverside, 203.637.5804
$220 per cord, stacking costs $40.

Firewood from Buzz and Ray (firewood)
(also called Ray's Lawn Service)
31 St. Rochs Place, 862.9271
$300 a cord, they will stack near your driveway for an extra $20.

(The) First Bank of Greenwich (banking)
www.TheFirstBankOfGreenwich.com
444 East Putnam Avenue, Cos Cob CT, 203.629.8400
This local bank was founded by highly respected local residents, who
care about our community.
Hours: Monday, Tuesday, Wednesday & Friday 8:30 am - 4 pm,
Thursday 8:30 am - 6 pm, Saturday 9 am - Noon.

Franklin Report (information)
www.FranklinReport.com
The Franklin Report rates service providers (aka contractors) by price
and quality. We have found their ratings to be reliable. However, most
contractors charge more when they are busy and less when they are not,
so be sure to get at least two estimates.

GEC Property Management (property management)
97 Sweet Briar Road, Stamford CT, 203.329.9262
www.gecpropertymanagement.com
Beverly Catchpole offers three levels of service: "House Mind": checking
your home while on vacation, including pet service; "White Glove": scheduled maintenance such as window and duct cleaning; and "Butler Silver
Tray": the anything-you-want service.

SERVICES

Geek Squad (computer help)
www.geeksquad.com
A Best Buy Computer Service, that will work on items whether or not they were purchased from Best Buy. For an on-site appointment call 800-433-5778. Besides computers, they handle Audio/Visual equipment, mobile phones, GPS and just about anything electronic.

Gerhar Feldmann (Piano Tuner)
208 East 70th Street, NYC 212.717.2907, Cell: 917.686.5946
Specialist for Bsendorfer pianos, but does all makes. Expensive, good choice for professional pianists who tax their instruments through heavy practicing.

Golden Horn (carpet repair)
464 North Main Street, Port Chester, NY, 914.670.6666
www.RugRestoration.com
They specialize in restoration, cleaning and sale of fine oriental and European carpets. They can repair almost any woven art including tapestries. Hours: Monday - Saturday 8:30 am - 6 pm.

Gordon Sweeny (clock repair)
3 Outlook Drive, Norwalk CT, 203.857.0807
Gordon can repair almost any kind of mechanical clock, including its cabinet. If he can't find the part, he can usually make it. He will make house calls.

Got Junk
Chris Kirk, 456 Seymour Street, Stratford CT
800.468.5865, 203.385.0036
www.1800gotjunk.com/fairfieldcounty
1-800-Got-Junk is a Canadian company with more than 220 franchised locations throughout the United States and Canada. They will remove just about anything from old furniture to used appliances to yard waste to concrete, bricks and electronics.

Graham Company (ceiling fans)
Mark Graham, 800.942.5575
Mark actually lives in Florida, but comes to Greenwich about once a month. His whole business is repairing and installing ceiling fans.

Greenwich Blue Print Company (blueprints)

255 Greenwich Avenue, 869.0305

Friendly quick service. This upstairs blueprint company is known to architects and builders. It is the perfect source for homeowners.

(The) Greenwich Bank & Trust Company (banking)

A Division of Connecticut Community Bank

- 115 East Putnam Avenue, 203.618.8900 (main branch)
- 22 Railroad Avenue, 203.983.3370
- 1103 East Putnam, Riverside, 203.698.4030
- 273 Glenville Road, Glenville 203.532.4784

www.ccbankonline.com

Its great to walk into a bank where everyone knows you and says hello.
Hours: Monday - Thursday, 8:30 am - 4 pm; Friday, 8:30 am - 5 pm;
Saturday 9 am - noon. The Glenville branch is not open on Saturday.

Greenwich Chamber of Commerce (information)

45 East Putnam Avenue, 203.869.3500

www.GreenwichChamber.com

A vibrant group of business leaders and residents. Everyone should join and enjoy their many events.

Greenwich Furs (fur storage)

5 West Putnam Avenue, 203.869.1421

Since 1948 residents have been storing their furs here. On-site storage.

Greenwich Hardware and Home
(snow plowing, rentals and more)

300 West Putnam Avenue, 203.622.2350

www.GreenwichHardwareAndHome.com

www.TaylorRental.com/GreenwichTR

A one stop emergency supply and service center. They seem to rent just about anything. Hours: Monday - Saturday, 7:30 am - 5 pm.

Greenwich Independent Insurance
aka Elkanah Mead (Insurance)

87 Greenwich Avenue, 203.869.0302

www.greenwichinsurance.com

They have been serving Greenwich since 1891. Call them, reach them on face book or do your insurance on-line.
Hours: Monday - Thursday 8:30 am - 5 pm, Friday 8:30 am - 4 pm.

Greenwich Lock and Door (locksmith)
280 Railroad Avenue, 203.622.1095
www.greenwichLockandDoor.com
A reliable local source for architectural hardware, doors, security products and lock-smithing. Good customer service.
Hours: Monday & Wednesday 7 am - 4 pm; Tuesday,
Thursday & Friday 8 am - 4 pm.

Greenwich Metal Finishing (metal polishing)
300 West Main Street, Stamford, 203.977.0494
www.GreenwichMetalFinishing.com
If you have an ailing silver piece or chandelier, you may want to visit these metal artisans. They polish, replate, refinish and even fabricate metal items. They will completely refinish and rewire your chandelier.
Hours: weekdays, 8 am - 4 pm.

Greenwich Shoe Repair (shoe repair)
15 East Elm Street, 203.869.2288
Greenwich's only remaining shoe repair shop is hidden in an alley off of East Elm. George Togridis has been mending Greenwich shoes for over 15 years. He offers free pick-up and delivery.
Hours: Monday - Saturday 8 am - 5 pm.

Greenwich Window Doctor (window repair)
Andrew Coviello, 104 Pemberwick Rd, Greenwich, 203.531.4485
www.GreenwichWindowDoctor.com
Replacement windows are not always necessary or desirable when you can rehabilitate your older windows. Since 1989 Andrew has been repairing broken cords, re-chaining, unsticking and repairing old windows.

Health First Cleaning (house cleaning)
20 Palace Place, Port Chester NY, 203.531.1766, 914.690.9294
www.HealthFirstCleaning.com
George Botticelli uses heap-filters and non-toxic cleaning products to clean homes, including ducts, carpets, upholstery and even post construction.

SERVICES

Holly Hill Recycling Facility (aka The Dump)
Holly Hill Lane, 203.622.0550

Greenwich has one of the world's best dumps. You have to see it to believe it. On any given day, you may see BMWs and Mercedes dropping off items. The "in" decal for your car is a dump permit. Permit applications are available at the Holly Hill entry gate. To get one of these valuable permits, you must show proof of residency, as well as valid vehicle registration and insurance.

Hours: weekdays, 7 am - 3 pm; Saturday, 7 am - noon.

Honey Bees (bee expert)
Ray DuBois, Greenwich, 203.249.2733

www.BeeLove.org

If honey bees have inappropriately chosen your home as their home, Ray will remove and relocate the swarm. The fee for extractions is based on the degree of difficulty. If you are interested in keeping bees you should also contact Ray. He is extraordinarily nice to work with and a great local resource.

Home Guard Environmental
aka Envirotech (environmental services)
48 Union Street, Stamford CT, 203.323.8000

www.environmental.net

Asbestos, lead and mold abatement, decontamination, hazardous waste, oil tank services - removal, soil remediation, and more. For years we have enjoyed working with Gary Stone. They do quality work.

Horse Ridge Cellars (wine storage)
11 South Road, Somers, CT, 860.763.5380

www.HorseRidgeCellars.com

Where serious collectors store their wine. (About a 2 hour drive from Greenwich.)

Hupal Masonry (mason)
242 Weaver Street, Greenwich, 203.531.5245

Tim Hupal is not only an excellent stone mason, he can be very helpful with the project's design.

Hupal Septic and Excavation (septic systems)
244 Weaver Street, Greenwich, 203.532.1401

Problems with your present septic system, need a new one? You will be in good hands with our friend Mike Hupal.

SERVICES

Images (Photographic Services)
202 Sound Beach Avenue, Old Greenwich, 203.637.4193
www.ImagesCenter.com
In addition to framing your photographs, they restore damaged photographs by removing scratches, tears and stains, enhance photographs to reduce red-eye or correct color and brightness, and, of course, enlarge, crop or add a border. No negative is required.
Hours: Monday - Saturday, 10 am - 5 pm.

Interstate Fire and Safety (fire extinguishers)
404 Willett Avenue, Port Chester, NY 203.531.1333, 914.937.6100
www.InterstateFireandSfty.net
If you have ever wondered where to get your fire extinguisher refilled, you can't beat this place. Serving Greenwich residential and commercial needs since 1951, they sell new extinguishers and even kitchen stove hoods. Hours: weekdays, 8 am - 4 pm.

i-SOLD-it (eBay consignment)
607 Main Ave (Rt. 7 across from the DMV), Norwalk, 203.845.0290
www.877isoldit.com
A chain of 180 stores, helping people sell their items on eBay. They photograph, write copy, ship and collect payment for you. The item must sell for at least $75. Their commission is 33% - 25% of the money received, depending upon the value of the item.
Hours: Monday- Saturday 10 am - 6 pm.

Jason, The Handyman, Inc. (handyman)
17 Cognewaugh Rd, Cos Cob 203.625.0411
If you need a mirror hung, gutters installed or cleaned, walls painted, tile re-grouted, or an electrical outlet installed, call Jason Wahlberg. Reasonably priced and offers senior discounts. If he can't do it, he'll recommend someone who can.

John Calarossi (carpet and wood laminate laying)
203.249.1721

Joe Mancuso (Moving)
50 Hawthorne Ave, Port Chester NY, 914.937.2178
An excellent resource when you are making a local move.

SERVICES

Joe Piro (tile and plaster repair)
104 Hamilton Ave, Greenwich 203.661.2266
Joe is reputed to be the best tile mason in the area. We believe it.

Joseph Williamson (wallpapering)
2 Kent place, Cos Cob, 203.629.7911
A graduate of the US School of professional paperhanging in Rutland, VT. He does decorative painting and faux finishes as well.

Judith Heft & Associates (office services)
15 East Putnam Avenue, #122, Greenwich CT, 203-978-1858
www.judithheft.com
A professional financial organizer, bookkeeper, bill payer and personal organizer.

Junk Luggers (Trash Removal)
168 Irving Avenue, Suite 500F, Port Chester NY, 888.584.5865
www.JunkLuggers.com
Call Kevin Phillips. He will take away just about anything from yard waste, to used appliances to electronics and renovation debris. The prices are in writing and include labor and dump fees. They sort for recyclables and give you a tax-deductible receipt.

Kennedy Security Services (Security)
58 East Elm Street, Greenwich, 203.661.6814
www.KennedySecurity.com
For extra security while you are away from home, Kennedy Security has been serving Greenwich residents for over 40 years.

Kinko's / FedEx (Office Services)
- 48 West Putnam Avenue, Greenwich, 203.863.0099
- 980 High Ridge Road, Stamford, CT, 203.968.8100

www.Kinkos.com, www.FedEx.com
FedEx / Kinko's offers a wide variety of production and finishing services, as well as FedEx shipping. Their target clients are small business and home offices. You can place an on-line print order using the FedEx web site.
Greenwich Hours: weekdays, 7:30 am - 9 pm; Saturday, 10 am - 6 pm.
Stamford Hours: weekdays 7 am - 11 pm; weekends, 9 am - 9 pm.

Landmark Document Services (Office Services)

375 Fairfield Avenue, Stamford, 325.4300

www.LandmarkPrint.com

Our favorite place for large volume printing. They are very careful and easy to work with. Their reasonable prices don't hurt, either.

Hours: Weekdays, 8 am - 5:30 pm.

Lending Art Program of the Greenwich Library

203.622.7900

The Lending Art Program of the Library has an extensive collection of artworks acquired by the Friends of the Library. It is available to all patrons and can be checked out on a short-term or long-term basis.

Longo's Rent-a-Tool (tool rentals)

263 Selleck Street, Stamford CT, 203.975.0569

A family-owned company renting just about any power tool. A do-it-yourselfer's paradise.

Hours: weekdays 7:30 am - 5 pm, Saturday 8 am - noon.

Metroguard Inc (home security)

Bridgeport, Connecticut, 800.495.0400

www.MetroGuardInc.com

A CT firm which will watch your house while you are away, hold your key, and perform other private security services.

Miranda Arts (Art)

6 North Pearl Street, Suite 404E, Port Chester, NY

914.935.9362, 318.7178

www.MirandaFineArts.com

Art Gallery featuring local artists. Patricia Miranda teaches painting and gilding techniques to adults and youth. She does museum quality framing and frame repair.

Mail Boxes Etc (packing and shipping)

- 15 East Putnam Avenue, 622.1114
- 1117 East Putnam Avenue, 698.0016

Mail box rentals, packing, crating and shipping, even Notary services. Hours: weekdays, 9 am - 6 pm; Saturday, 10 am - 2 pm.

SERVICES

Marcus Dairy (Dairy Products Delivery)
Danbury, CT, 800.243.2511
www.MarcusDairy.com
Get milk delivered? Apparently 6,000 customers do. Isn't it wonderful that we still have milk boxes and milk delivery. In addition they deliver products such as juices, eggs, yogurt, cottage cheese, sour cream, butter and ice cream.

Masterpiece Floor refinishing
Stamford Cell phone 203.219.2047
Recommended by the Property Group.

Monogram Studio (Custom embroidery)
60 Lewis Street, 203.428.5700
www.WinstonsTuckernuck.com/Monogram-Studio.html
Offers full service monogramming and embroidery to individuals, schools and businesses. Hours: Check the website for hours.

Morgan Manhattan Moving & Storage (moving)
16 Bruce Park Avenue, 203.869.8700
www.MorganManhattan.com
A regional moving company with corporate headquarters in Greenwich.

NAVIS Pack & Ship (moving)
Patrick Ryan, 540 Grant Street, Bridgeport CT
203.335.7447, 800.344.3528
www.Gonavis.com
NAVIS specializes in small shipments, ones that are too big for a mail and parcel center (UPS, Fed Ex), but too small for a traditional mover. They pick up items from your home or business, like a chandelier, a computer, a painting or a dining table, and deliver them to your destination across town or around the world.

New York Steel Window (window repair)
12G White Street, Buchanan NY, 914.736.5208
Denis Rooney makes storm windows for leaded-glass steel windows.
See Seekircher for steel window repair

Nibia Stezano (master seamstress)

203.629.5474

Nibia works out of her attic studio in Cos Cob. She is an extremely skilled dressmaker capable of designs from scratch. She is also willing to do small alterations for both men and women.

Nimble Thimble (sewing machine repair)

19 Putnam Avenue, Port Chester NY, 914.934.2934

www.BretonesFamily.com/NimbleThimble

The resource for home sewing needs. Lots of fabrics, notions, quilting supplies and sewing machines. A good place to have your sewing machine repaired.

Hours: weekdays 10 am - 5 pm, Saturday 10 am - 1 pm.

Northeast Systems Radon and Water (radon)

Stratford, CT 203.296.4269, 203.375.6526

www.SystemsRadon.com

Fernando Alvarado is the owner of this local Radon mitigation company. The EPA recommends that Radon at or above 4.0 pCi/L should be mitigated.

Northeast Utilities/Connecticut Light & Power (utility)

Customer Care Walk-in Center, 107 Selden Street, Berlin, CT

800.286.2000 (main),

800.286.5000 (Customer Service, emergencies)

www.nu.com

Our local power company.

Occhicone (leather repair)

42 North Main Street, Port Chester, NY, 914.937.6327

Expert repairs, by Italian craftsmen, for high quality leather items, such as handbags, briefcases, leather apparel, suitcases and shoes. They can make just about anything look new.

Hours: Monday - Saturday, 8:30 am - 5 pm.

Packages PlusNMore (shipping)

Mill Pond Center, 215 East Putnam Avenue, Cos Cob
203.625.8130

www.PackagesPlusNMore.com

An up-scale packing and shipping company, that will not only ship packages for you, but will pick up a package from your home or office upon request. They are authorized shippers for FedEx, DHL and UPS. Use them to ship your luggage and skis directly to your hotel without having to check and lose them during air travel.

Hours: weekdays, 7 am - 7 pm; Saturday, 9 am - 4 pm,
Sunday (Christmas Season Only).

Patti's Portico (outdoor furniture repair)

140 Highland Street, Port Chester NY, 203.869.6227

www.PattisPortico.com

My garden chair needed re-strapping and Patti did a great job. She repairs just about any outdoor furniture, powder coating, sand blasting, welding, re-strapping and sling repair.

Hours: weekdays, 8 am - 4 pm.

PODS (Portable On Demand Storage)

95 Leggett Street, East Hartford CT, 866.229.4120

www.Pods.com

PODS allow you to load at your own pace. Move local, cross country, or store in their storage center.

Post Road Iron Works (metal work and welding)

345 West Putnam Avenue, 203.869.6322

www.Priw.com

Serving Greenwich since 1927, they do a lot of ordinary iron work, but their specialty is structural and ornamental welding. A good place to find a pair of andirons.

Hours: Weekdays, 8 am - 5:30 pm; Saturday, 8 am - noon.

PC Repair and Sales (computer repair)

502 Glenbrook Road, Stamford CT, 203.359.4732

www.PCRepairAndSales.com

They repair and recover data. They will also build a computer for you to your specifications.

SERVICES

PD Photo (photographic services)
1 Boulder Avenue, Old Greenwich. 203.637.0340
www.PDPhoto.net
Craig Kotover has one of the few remaining stores that develops film and can transfer old video tapes and 8-millimeter movies to DVDs. Customers can upload their digital photos. He also carries a wide variety of frames and can put your photos on over 700 items.

Performance Imaging (home theater)
550 West Avenue, Stamford, 203.862.9600 or 203.504.5200
www.PerformanceImaging.net
They have temporarily given up their showroom, but they are still a terrific source for system integration, home theater design and installation.

Personal Touch Cleaning (Rug cleaning)
124 Pilgrim Drive, Greenwich, 203.531.7431
Scott Nastahowski cleans carpets, rugs, upholstery and draperies. Hopefully you will never need it, but he also does flood restoration and water and septic clean ups. Shayne says "We've seen him work miracles on rugs we were sure would have to be ripped up."

PI Security (home fire & security systems)
81 Ridge Brook Drive, Stamford, CT, 203.862.9300, 203.504.3153
A high-end, completely trustworthy, alarm system distributor/installer that can meet anyone's needs.

Piano Service (piano tuning)
Stamford CT, 203.359.2231
Ken Svec tunes pianos and is a good consultant if you wish to buy or sell a piano.

Pyrianos Collection (Steinway pianos)
90 Linden Street, New Haven CT, 203.661.2566.
www.Pyrianos.com
Maureen Walsh specializes in the acquisition, restoration, and sales of vintage Steinway pianos.

Rand Insurance (insurance)
1100 East Putnam Avenue, Riverside CT, 203.637.1006
www.RandInsurance.com
A local, very knowledgeable insurance agency that handles it all.

SERVICES

Raphael's Furniture Restoration (furniture repair)
655 Atlantic Street, Stamford, 203.348.3079
www.RaphaelsFurniture.com
They will repair and restore just about any piece of furniture, but they specialize in the restoration of eighteenth and nineteenth century antiques.
Hours: Monday - Thursday, 7 am - 5 pm; Friday, 7 am - 3 pm;
Saturday, 7 am - 1 pm. Call for an appointment before you go.

Recycling Cell Phones
Collection boxes are located all over town for old cell phones, PDAs, pagers and chargers. Check the Public Works site
www.GreenwichCT.org/PublicWorks/PublicWorks.asp
for their location or call Sally Davies, Chair of the Greenwich Recycling Advisory Board, at 203.629.2876. This equipment is refurbished and used for 911 phones for women in crisis. Older equipment is sent to countries where the technology is less advanced. Support this program. Collection boxes are available to put in your own work place.

Recycling Christmas Trees
Between December 26th and January 5th, you can bring your un-decorated tree to Bruce Park, Byram Beach or Greenwich Point and the tree will be chipped and transported by the town. Of course, you can bring your tree at any time to the Holly Hill recycling facility. The idea that the tree will be recycled back to nature lifts our spirits.

Ritz Camera (photographic services)
82 Greenwich Avenue, Greenwich, 203.869.0673
www.RitzCamera.com
They do one-hour photo developing. You can e-mail your pics to www.RitzPix.com for prints in one hour and you can pick up at the store. If you buy a camera, they will give you free class lessons. A good place to get your passport photos or convert a video to DVD.
Hours: Weekdays, 8:30 am - 6:30 pm (Friday until 8 pm);
Saturday, 10 am - 6 pm; Sunday, 11 am - 5 pm.

Robert Marullo (Piano lessons, repair and tuning)
203.869.4943
This popular, talented piano teacher at Greenwich Academy, also gives private lessons. We strongly recommend him for lessons as well as piano repairs, tuning and reliable advice about purchases.

SERVICES

Round Hill Tree Service (tree service)
1 Armonk Street, Greenwich, 203.531.5759
www.RoundHillTreeService.com
Rick Masi will make sure your dead trees are cut down, your limbs are trimmed back and your yard sprayed for mosquitos.

Safety Mom (child safety)
267 Thayer Pond Road, Wilton CT, 203.594.7452
Www.SafetyMomSolutions.com
Alison Rhodes or her partner will come out to consult with new parents. Alison is a well known safety expert. Consultations normally cost $95.

Satellite TV Networks (television)
*   Direct TV, 888.777.2454, www.DirectTV.com
*   Dish Network, 888.825.2557,www.DishNetwork.com

Seekircher Steel Window Repair (window repair)
423 Central Avenue, Peekskill, NY 914.734.8004
www.SeekircherSteelWindow.com
John Seekircher repairs leaded-glass steel casement windows. New York Steel Window makes interior storm/screen windows for steel windows.

Service Master (home services)
Steven Wills, Stamford CT,
203.327.3477, 800.325.3261, 800.500.5558
www.ServiceMasterClean.com
Service Master is a privately held Fortune 500 company. The core services of the company include lawn care and landscape maintenance, termite and pest control, home warranties, disaster response and reconstruction, cleaning and disaster restoration, house cleaning, furniture repair, and home inspection. Service Master has more than 5,500 company-owned and franchise locations around the country and employs 32,000 people.

Sears Home Services (appliance repair)
800.349.5075   www.SearsHomeServices.com
A nation-wide network of service people servicing just about anything. Service Live (www.ServiceLive.com) is a Sears auction system which allows users to name their own price for services such as home and appliance repair. The Service Live site also allows consumers to rate and review contractors, as well as forums and guides on home improvement and repair topics. Service live screens contractors for licenses and criminal records.

SERVICES

(The) Settler (moving service)

25-13 Old Kings Highway North, Darien CT, 203.858.3054 (cell),
www.TheSettlersUSA.com
Pinny Randal helps you take the stress out of moving. She helps hire
movers and manage them. Helps you dispose of un-needed furnishings,
helps pack, unpack and organize utilities.

Sophia's Great Dames (costumes women and children)

1 Liberty Way, Greenwich, 203.869.5990
www.SophiasCostumes.com
Wonderful shop for vintage clothing, antiques, collectibles, gifts and
costumes. A large selection of costumes (for all occasions) for sale or
rent. Fun to visit. Hours: Tuesday - Saturday 10 am - 5:30 pm.

Sterling Vacuum Center (vacuum cleaner repair)

454 Main Avenue, Norwalk CT, 203.846.2442
www.sterling-vac.com
Robert Lopez loves fixing vacuum cleaners and installing central vacuum
systems.

Stop and Shop/Pea Pod (Home food delivery)

You can order food delivered by placing your order through
www.StopAndShop.com or www.PeaPod.com. Call 800.573.2763 for delivery information. For orders over $75.00 the delivery fee is $4.95, for
orders less than $75.00 the delivery fee is $9.95. The minimum order is
$50.00.

(Charles) Stuttig (locksmith)

158 Greenwich Avenue, 203.869.6260
A fixture in Greenwich for many years, they provide a wide variety of
locks and safes. Whether you have an emergency or just need a key
replaced, they can be counted on and trusted.
Hours: weekdays, 7:30 am - 5:30 pm.

Super Handy Hardware
(firewood, propane, screen repair)

1 Riversville Road, Glenville Center, 203.531.5599
www.AceRetailer.com/SuperHandy/
A good old-fashioned hardware store with most everything you would
need. They supply firewood and propane for your barbecue. They also
repair screens.
Hours: Monday - Saturday 8 am - 5 pm, Sunday 9 am - 1 pm.

Superior Home Services (Cleaning)

31 Parker Ave, Stamford CT, 203.359.3861

A reliable, very accommodating, residential and commercial cleaning service that can do just about anything, thorough house cleaning, windows and even post construction clean up.

Table Top Designs (replace missing china or silver)

57 Vista Terrace, Cheshire CT, 800.801.4084

www.tabletopdesigns.com

Formerly called Tablescraps, if you are missing a piece of china, crystal or silver from your collection, this is a good place to find a replacement. Call, visit their website or email them.

Tag Sales (aka Garage Sales, Estate Sales)

For book sales see LIBRARIES AND BOOKS

- Betty's Tag Sales, Betty Shopovick, 203.613.4613
- Consign It Tag Sales, 203.869.9836 www.Consignitinc.com
- Good Riddance Girls Tag Sales, Lynn Westmeyer (203) 329-0009 www.GoodRiddanceGirls.com

Ted The Tailor (tailor)

2 Church Street, 203.869.5699

They have been tailoring in Greenwich since 1948. Mr. Puglia and his staff can do everything from alterations to custom suits. They also work on leather. Hours: weekdays 8:30 am - 6 pm, Saturday to 5 pm.

Thomas Dry Cleaning and Chinese Hand Laundry

68 Lewis Street, 203.869.9420

A good choice for fine linens and tablecloths.
Hours: weekdays, 7:30 am - 6 pm; Saturday, 7:30 6 pm.

Thomas Libby (crystal/ceramic repair)

61 North Main Street, South Norwalk CT, 203.854.0300

www.TKLibby.com

An excellent source for ceramic and glass repairs. He also sells Japanese and Chinese 19th & 20th Century Ceramics.
Hours: Tuesday - Saturday, 11 am to 5 pm.

Triple S Carpet and Drapery Cleaners (dry cleaning)

400 West Main Street (Post Road), Stamford, 203.327.7471
www.triplesclean.com
They clean draperies and upholstery and will come to the house to clean rugs and upholstery. They do a great job of cleaning and/or repairing rugs. They will clean and store boat and patio cushions for the winter.
Hours: weekdays, 8 am - 5:30 pm; Saturday, 8 am - 1:30 pm.

Two Men and A Truck (moving)

25 Van Zant St. Suite 1A1, Norwalk CT, 203.831.9300
www.twomenandatruck.com
This is a locally owned mover franchised by a national company located in Lansing MI. We are impressed with their careful and courteous ways.

Ultrawiz Electronics (TV Repair)

20 Henry Street, 203.532.0175
www.UltraWiz.com
Have you ever wondered how to get a plasma or projection television repaired? Greenwich residents are lucky to have Ultrawiz, a factory authorized service center for most plasma TVs. They also repair VCRs, camcorders and hi-fi equipment.
Hours: weekdays, 9 am - 5 pm, Saturday, 9 am - 1 pm.

UPS

www.ups.com/tracking/tracking.html
Self-serve Drop Boxes
• 100 Field Point Rd, Greenwich
• 100 Mason Street, Greenwich
The UPS Store, 65 High Ridge Road, Stamford, 203-356-0022
www.theupsstore.com

Verizon (telephone)

203.869.5222 (new service)
203.661.5444 (repairs), 611 (home and cell phone repairs)
203.625.9800 (customer service)
www.bellatlantic.com www22.verizon.com
They service Greenwich, Byram, Cos Cob, Glenville & Riverside.

Vermont Good Wood (fire wood)

17 Binney Lane, Old Greenwich, 203.637-5200
www.VermontGoodWood.com
Home delivery and stacking of kiln dried oak and white birch, approximately $780 a cord. Of course it is available in smaller amounts.

SERVICES

Vernon Computer Source (computer rentals)
77 Selleck Street, Stamford CT, 800-347-7333, 203.969.0060
www.vernoncomputersource.com
Daily, weekly or monthly computer equipment rentals. Delivery and on-site business installation services are also available.

Westy Self Storage (storage)
- 80 Brownhouse Road, Stamford, CT, 203.961.8000
- 351 North Main Street, Port Chester, NY, 914.937.2222
www.westy.com
Convenient, clean, secure, private storage rooms. They will recommend a mover or loan you a truck for self storage moving.
Stamford Hours: Monday Friday 8 am - 6 pm, Saturday 9 am - 6m, Sunday 11 am - 4 pm.

Webweavers (website design)
203.532.0770, info@webweavers.com
www.webweavers.com
Web weavers was founded in 1998 by a Greenwich mother-daughter team Elizabeth Ross and Barbara Ross. They can work with you from creating a logo to building your site and hosting it.

Willett Vacuum (vacuum repair)
440 Willett Avenue, Port Chester NY, 914.937.5948
www.WillettVacuumNY.com
This helpful family-owned business can repair most any kind of vacuum, including central vacuum systems. They are also Miele vacuum dealers.

Window Genie (window cleaning)
761 Stillwater Road, Stamford CT, 203.363.0783, 866.494.3643
www.WindowGenie.com
A franchise owned by Bob and Staci Zampa, they clean windows, but offer a variety of other services such as window tinting, gutter clean-out, brick cleaning and sealing. These genies have a good reputation.

Wood Den (furniture stripping)
266 Selleck Street, Stamford CT, 203.324.6957
www.TheWoodDen.com
Wood and metal furniture stripping, chair canning and furniture repairs, sand basting and powder coating.
Hours: Tuesday, Wednesday & Friday, 9 am - 5 pm;
Thursday, 8 am - 8 pm; Saturday 9 am - 3:30 pm.

SERVICES

Words to Go (word processing services)
255 Greenwich Avenue, 2nd Floor, 203.661.1711
www.wordstogo.com
Word processing, resumes, school applications, Notary services and more.

www.YouRenew.Com (electronics recycling)
www.YouRenew.com
We are proud of Greenwich resident, David Walker for helping to develop a company where you can be paid to recycle your old electronic devices. You Renew is part of the Yale Entrepreneur Institute.

TIP: SCARECROW FESTIVAL
Every year in October, the Mill Pond Park on Strickland Road is taken over by scarecrows waiting to be judged. Activities include pumpkin painting, scarecrow making, games, crafts and lots of fun for everyone. For information on the event contact the Greenwich Chamber of Commerce, 203.869.3500.

SINGLES

According to the 2000 US Census, Greenwich has an adult population of 54,557 of which 16,533 are singles. If you are single, no matter what your age or life style, there are many ways to meet others. In addition to joining one of the numerous volunteer organizations, there are a variety of organized social events.

Catholic Widows and Widowers Club
St. Michael the Archangel Church, 469 North Street, 203.869.5421
Support and social group for Catholic widows and widowers.

Connecticut Contacts
64 East Grand Avenue, New Haven CT, 203.468.1144
www.ctcontacts.com
For the last 25 years, they have been setting up dance parties on Friday and Saturday nights all over Connecticut for singles in their late 30's, 40's, 50's, & 60's.

Cotton Club
www.CottonClubGreenwich.com
A non-sectarian and non-denominational, primarily Greenwich social club, with approximately 350 members, for singles ages 40 and up. Members participate in a variety of activities, from hiking and tennis to attending the theater and polo matches. Be sure to get their newsletter.

Greenwich Jaycees
PO Box 232, Greenwich, 06836, 203.358.3134
www.GreenwichJaycees.org
Membership is open to young professionals ages 21-39. This group has a good time working together on fund rasing events for worthy charities in Greenwich.

Hiking Group for Singles and Friends
Contact Steve Bailes 203.854.5508 or Al Edly 203. 323.9443
www.TheHikingGroup.com
Established in 1981 as part of the Westport Singles, this group has weekend hikes for various degrees of difficulty and length of time.

Not Alone
Jewish Family Services of Greenwich   www.jfsGreenwich.org
One Holly Hill Lane, Greenwich 203.622.1881
A support and social network for Jewish widows, widowers, and divorced singles. Meetings are once a month.

SINGLES

Parents Without Partners
Fairfield County Chapter, P.O. Box 117 Southport CT, 06890,
203.767.8612
www.ParentsWithoutPartners.org
Begun in New York City in 1957, PWP is for single parents and their
children. This chapter, one of three in state and 200 nationwide has 175
members. Monthly meetings are at various locations throughout the
county. They have weekend events for adults and for children.

Pinnacle Ski and Sports Club
www.pinnacleski.org
Non-profit social and recreational organization founded in 1990 which
sponsors year-round activities: ski and snowboarding trips in the winter
and a variety of other sports, excursions, and events during the rest of
the year. It has around 270 single and family members from the Fairfield
/ Westchester area ranging in age from 21 to 70.

Singles Under Sail
Contact: Kelly Barney 929.6886
www.SinglesUnderSail.org
Social events for singles who love sailing.

Ski Bears of Connecticut
Pastiore Club, 59 Sea view Avenue, Norwalk CT 203.866.5106
www.skibears.org
A ski and social club for singles and married adults. Membership is
open to anyone over 21. Emphasis is on outdoor activities.

Young Friends of the Bruce
For information call Whitney Lucas Rosenberg, Membership Manager,
203.869.6786 ext 366.
A Bruce Museum membership group for singles and couples, ages 20's,
30's, and 40's. Enjoy quarterly get-togethers to mingle in a cultural setting. Members and their guests enjoy exhibition tours, wine tastings,
and cocktail receptions. Events are held on certain Thursdays.

SPORTS INDEX

Fans and players of almost every imaginable sport live in Greenwich. Paddle tennis was even invented in Greenwich. Best of all, whether you are a professional or an amateur, finding a place to fish, skate, golf, sail or play ball is easy in our town.

See FITNESS for exercise classes, yoga, personal trainers and gyms.
Uniforms and Equipment listed in STORES
Children's Summer Camps are listed in CHILDREN
If you need to recover from an excess of activity see HEALTH.
For child focused activities see CHILDREN.
To exercise your mind see CONTINUING EDUCATION, CULTURE or BOOKS AND LIBRARIES.

Archery
Cos Cob Archers

Auto Racing
See also Go Karts
Alpine Motor Sports Club
Lime Rock Park
Overland Experts
Skip Barber Racing School
Sports Car Driving Association

Badminton
YWCA
See also Tennis and Squash

Baseball
(including Softball)
See T-Ball below
Blue Fish Professional Baseball
Blue Fish Professional Baseball is also listed in CHILDREN under FAMILY OUTINGS
Bobby Valentine Sports Academy
(Greenwich) Department of Parks and Recreation Programs
Doyle Baseball Academy
Goat Gear
Greenwich 1-on-1
Greenwich Babe Ruth League
Nike Sports Camps
Sports Center of Connecticut

Basketball
Boys and Girls Club of Greenwich
Eastern Greenwich Civic Center
Goat Gear
Greenwich 1-on-1
Greenwich Basketball Association
Men's basketball League
Nike Sports Camps
Western Greenwich Civic Center
YMCA
YWCA

SPORTS INDEX

Biking

For Spinning see FITNESS
Appalachian Mountain Club
(the) Bicycle Tour Company
Connecticut Bicycle Map
East Coast Greenway
Greenwich Biking
Greenwich Safe Cycling
Sound Cyclists

Boating

(including Sailing, Rowing, Rafting, Canoeing and Kayaking)
Appalachian Mountain Club
Clarke Outdoors
Downunder Kayaking
Greenwich Community Sailing
Greenwich Marine Facilities
Greenwich Sail & Power Squadron
Greenwich Rowing Club
Greenwich Water Club
Indian Harbor Yacht Club Sailing
Kayak Adventure
Kayak/Canoe Guide
Kittatinny Canoes
Longshore Sailing School
Mianus River
New York Sailing School
Norwalk Rowing Association
North American Outdoor Adventure
Old Greenwich Yacht Club
Rex Marine Center
Sound Environmental Associates
   (safe boating & jet ski courses)
Small Boat Shop
   (kayak instruction)
Sound Sailing Center
Stamford Kayak Group
Yachting Magazine

Bowling

(including lawn bowling)
AMF Bowling Centers
Greenwich Lawn Bowls Club
Sports Center of Connecticut

Bridge

Lest you wonder why bridge is in this section, we regard it as fitness for the brain.

Camping

See CHILDREN for summer camps.
Camping on Greenwich Islands
Camping with Rvs

Canoeing

See Boating
The Mianus River in Greenwich is a good place to practice canoeing. There is no need to worry if you fall in because the water is very clean. For the more adventurous, the Housatonic River has class I and II rapids, and is a center for trips and instruction.

Cheerleading

Cos Cob Athletic Club
Greenwich Tumble and Cheer
Greenwich Youth Cheerleading
   League

Chiropractors

For chiropractors and other therapies see HEALTH

Climbing

See also Hiking
Appalachian Mountain Club
(The) Cliffs
Club Get Away
YWCA Climbing Wall

SPORTS INDEX

Croquet
Greenwich Croquet Club

Driving
See Auto Racing

Fencing
Greenwich Fencing

Field Hockey
Academy of Sports
(Greenwich) Department of Parks
   and Recreation Programs
Greenwich 1-on-1
Nike Sports Camps

Fishing
Greenwich is ideally located on the Long Island Sound for excellent salt water fishing from May to December. Going east or west at different times of the year provides a multispecies catch including Striped Bass, Bluefish, Fluke, Porgies and Blackfish. Light spin, fly or bait tackle is the most fun.

Freshwater fishing for Trout and Bass is good in the Mianus River. Fishing in reservoirs is prohibited. Blue ribbon trout streams in CT and NY are within a 90-minute drive. The resources below can help you. Also see Fishing Stores, such as Orvis or the Sportsman's Den, under SHOPS for more than just equipment. The fishing season for trout runs from April to February. Fishermen 16-years and older must have a valid state fishing license. The cost is $20.

Bedford Sportsman
Compleat Angler
Connecticut Angler's Guide
Licenses and Permits
North East Saltwater Fishing publication
Shell Fishing
Trout Unlimited
Also see Sportsman's Den and Rudy's Tackle Barn in SHOPPING
Salt Water Fishing Charters
Bill Fish Charters, 914.967.8246;
   sails from Cos Cob
Devil's Compass, 914.980.5779;
   sails from Byram
Sound Fishing Charters
   (Snow Goose), 203.255.4522;
   sails from Byram
Sparky Charters, 914.747.5825;
   sails from Cos Cob

Flying
(soaring, skydiving *& ballooning)*
Fighter Pilot for a Day
Flight Safety
K & L Soaring
Panorama Flight School
Soaring Adventures of America
Westchester Flying Club
Wings of Eagles Soaring School
Zombi Kite Boarding

Football
Bobby Valentine Sports Academy
Cos Cob Athletic Club
Greenwich Youth Football League
Gateway Youth Football League

SPORTS INDEX

Golf

There are a number of nearby courses open to non-residents. Some of these have limited times for non-residents. Many facilities have discounts for seniors, juniors, early morning or late afternoon play, or for 9-hole rounds. If you like the course, check out their policy on season passes. Be sure to book before you go. Check out the following sites:
www.ctgolfer.com &
www.co.westchester.ny.us/parks
If you need a little practice before playing, use the golf range at Griffith Harris Memorial Golf Course or one of these:

Doral Golf Club
Eastern Greenwich Civic Center
  (indoors)
Gaynor Brennan Municipal Golf
  Course
Greenwich 1-on-1
Griffith Harris Memorial Golf
  Course
Lake of Ilses Golf Course and Golf
  Academy
Maple Moor Golf Course
Nike Golf Schools and Junior Camps
Oak Hills Golf Course
Richter Park Golf Course
Ridgefield Golf Course
Saxon Woods
Sports Center of Connecticut
Sterling Farms
Vails Grove Golf Course
Westchester Golf Range

Go Karts

Checkered Flag Raceway
Grand Prix New York
Norwalk Karting Association
On Track Karting

Gymnastics

Arena Gymnastics
Great Play
Jack Rabbits Gymnastics
My Gym
US Academy of Gymnastics
YMCA Gymnastic Programs
YWCA Gymnastic Programs

Hiking

(including walking)
See also Climbing
See also Running
Appalachian Mountain Club
Audubon Center
Babcock Preserve
Connecticut Walk Book
Mianus River Park
Montgomery Pinetum Park
Outward Bound

Hockey (Ice)

See also Field Hockey
Dorothy Hamill Skating Rink
Greenwich Blues Youth Ice Hockey
Association
Nike Sports Camps
Stamford Twin Rinks

Horseback Riding
(Including Polo)

Picture fall leaves, stone walls and a rider on a handsome horse on a scenic woodland trail. Yes, this is Greenwich with over 150 miles of riding trails which connect to the 100 miles of trails in Stamford. For insurance reasons, most stables will not rent horses for unaccompanied trail rides unless you have been taking a series of lessons and they have determined your skill level.

Back Barn Farm
Coker Farm
Getner Farm
Greenwich Polo Club
Greenwich Riding and Trails
    Association
Lionshare Farm
Mead Farm
On The Go Farms
Ox Ridge Hunt Club
Pegasus Therapeutic Riding
Red Barn Stables
Stratford Stables

Hunting and Shooting
See Shooting, See Archery

Karate
(and other Martial Arts)

Calasanz Physical Arts
Devita Karate
Dynamic Martial Arts Family
    Center
Kang Tae-kwon-do & Hapkido
Old Greenwich School of Karate
Shaolin Studios
Shidogakuin
Tiger Schulmann's Mixed
    Martial Arts
White Tiger Tae Kwon Do

Kayaking
See Boating

Lacrosse
Bridgeport Barrage major League Lacrosse is listed in CHILDREN, FAMILY OUTINGS.

Academy of Sports
(Greenwich) Department of Parks
    and Recreation Programs
Goat Gear
Greenwich Youth Lacrosse
Nike Sports Camps

Laser Tag
See the section CHILDREN, Parties Away from Home

Paddle Ball
See Tennis

Paintball
For equipment try Chili Bears in Old Greenwich
Liberty Paintball

Platform Tennis
See Tennis

SPORTS INDEX

Riding
See Horseback Riding

Rock Climbing
See Climbing

Rowing
See Boating

Running
See also Hiking
For Orthotics see Stride Custom Orthotics or Foot Solutions in HEALTH
Greenwich Kids Triathlon
Greenwich Point
Jim Fixx Memorial Day Race
Running Events in Greenwich

Sailing
See Boating

Skating
(Ice and Roller Skating)
See also Hockey (for Ice Hockey)
See also Skateboarding
Binney Pond
Boys and Girls Club of Greenwich
Dorothy Hamill Skating Rink
Eastern Greenwich Civic Center (roller skating)
Greenwich Skating Club
In-Line Roller Hockey
Mianus River
Western Greenwich Civic Center
Windy Hill Figure Skating Club

Skateboarding
For skate boards and inline skates, try Chili Bears or Rink & Racquet.
Greenwich Skateboard Park

Squash
See Tennis

Soccer
Academy of Sports
(Greenwich) Department of Parks and Recreation Programs
Eastern Greenwich Civic Center
Greenwich 1-on-1
Greenwich Soccer Association
Greenwich Soccer Club
Nike Sports Camps

Shooting
See also Archery
Cos Cob Revolver & Rifle Club
Forest and Field Outdoor
Licenses and Permits
Smith & Wesson Academy
State Forest Camping Areas

Skiing (snow)

LOCAL FAMILY SKI RESORTS
Hunter Mountain
Mohawk Mountain
Mount Southington
Powder Ridge
Windham Mountain
Winding Trails Cross Country Ski Center

LARGE REGIONAL SKI AREAS
These areas have extensive summer family activities. Check their websites
for details.
Killington Resort
Mont Tremblant
Mount Snow Resort
Okemo Mountain
Stowe Mountain Resort
Stratton Mountain Resort
Sugarloaf
Whiteface Mountain

SPORTS INDEX

SPORTS

Uniforms and Equipment listed in STORES
Children's Summer Camps are listed in CHILDREN

(The) Academy of Sports
55 Crescent Street, Stamford, CT, 203.353.1199
Www.TheAcademyOfSports.com
Lacrosse, Soccer and Field Hockey clinics for boys and girls, 4th through 12th grades as well as pre-school sports fun classes.

Alpine Motor Sports Club (auto racing)
Eldred Township, Monroe County, Pennsylvania, 610.954.8174
Contact: Deb Smith, 800.795.2638.
www.AlpineSignature.com
About 90 miles away, Alpine is located on 350 acres. You can put the "pedal to the metal" on their 4 mile straightaways and high speed turns.

AMF Bowling Centers (bowling)
701 Connecticut Avenue, Norwalk CT, 203.838.7501
47 Tarrytown Road, White Plains NY 914.948.2677
www.AMFcenters.com

Appalachian Mountain Club
Fairfield County Group, 7 Vera Drive Bethel CT, 203.762.0216
www.CT-AMC.org
The Fairfield County group sponsors or participates in a variety of outdoor activities, such as hiking, mountain and road biking, rock climbing, canoeing, kayaking and cross country skiing.

Arena Gymnastics
911 Hope Street (Riverbend Center), Stamford, CT, 203.357.8167
www.ArenaGymnastics-CT.com
Coed Preschool Program ages 1 1/2 - 5 yrs, After School Program for Girls ages 5 & up, After School Program for Boys ages 5-10, Competitive Programs for Girls at all Levels. This school has been highly recommended for more serious gymnasts.

Armonk Tennis Club
546 Bedford Road, Armonk NY, 914.273.8124
www.ArmonkTennis.com
Situated on 14-acres, they have 14 courts—10 outdoor (5 red clay & 5 Har-Tru) and 4 Har-Tru indoor courts. Adult and Junior programs, summer camps and tournaments.

SPORTS

Audubon Center

613 Riversville Road, 203.869.5272
Greenwich Audubon Society, PO Box 7487, Greenwich, CT 06831.
www.Greenwich.Center.Audubon.org
A 63-page guide to 26 area walking trails is available.
280 acres of well-kept trails, a delightful place to walk. The entrance is on the corner of Riversville Road and John Street.

Babcock Preserve (running, hiking)

North Street, 203.622.7814, 203.622.7700
Two miles north of the Merritt Parkway, the Preserve has 297 acres of well-marked running trails from 1 to 3.5 miles.

Back Barn Farm aka New England Farm (riding)

203 Greenwich Road, Bedford, NY, 914.234.6692
www.BackBarnFarm.com
Boarding and lessons both indoor and outdoor.

Bedford Sportsman (Fishing equipment & clothing)

25 Adams Street, Bedford Hills, NY, 914.666.8091
www.BedfordSportsman.com
Specializes in freshwater fly and spin fishing equipment. A good resource for New York watershed streams & guide services. They teach fly fishing during the summer.
Hours: Tuesday - Friday, 10 am - 6 pm; Thursday, until 7pm.
Saturday 10 am - 6 pm, Sunday 10 am - 3 pm, closed Monday.

Billfish Fishing Charters (Salt Water fishing)

Palmer Point Marina, Cos Cob
Captain Bill Herold, 914.967.8246
Captain Bill Herold is one of the best saltwater guides in the area.

Binney Pond (ice skating)

Sound Beach Avenue, Old Greenwich
This is the prettiest pond for skating and it is town-tested for safety.

(The) Bicycle Tour Company

9 Bridge Street, Kent, CT, 888.711.5368 www.BicycleTours.com
Bicycle explorations give you a whole new perspective. Tour Greenwich and many other interesting sites on the Eastern Seaboard. Bicycle Tour Company routes are generally 25 - 30 miles per day. They rent bicycles & organize routes for all ability levels. Owner, Sal Lilienthal grew up in Greenwich.

SPORTS

Blue Fish Professional Baseball (baseball)
Harbor Yard, Bridgeport, CT 203.345.4800
www.BridgeportBlueFish.com

Bobby Valentine Sports Academy (baseball, softball, football)
72 Camp Avenue, Stamford, CT, 203.968.2872
www.BobbyVAcademy.com
A state of the art baseball and softball training center. They also conduct run and shoot football camps.

Boys and Girls Club of Greenwich (skating, ice hockey, basketball,football, ping pong, chess)
4 Horseneck Lane, 203.869.3224,
Melissa Hawkins Program Coordinator x 111 www.BGCG.org
They have an extensive hockey program, including co-ed Broomball, girls ice hockey clinics and Mite Development Hockey League. A good place for private lessons: learning to skate & figure skating. They have girls and boys basketball, punt-pass-Kick football.Home of the Barracudas swim team.

Bridge at the YMCA (aka Contract Bridge, Duplicate Bridge)
www. ywca.org   203.869.6501
The Y has courses for beginners (Y membership required), advanced supervised bridge games, and Duplicate Bridge games franchised by the American Contract Bridge League.

Calasanz Physical Arts (karate)
507 Westport Ave (Rt. 1) in Norwalk CT, 203.847.6528
www.Calasanz.com
Self defense using a number of techniques from kick boxing to kung fu.

Camping on Greenwich Islands (camping)
www.greenwichct.org/ParksAndRec/prOverNightCamping.asp
You can camp on Island Beach & Great Captain's Island between June 10th and Sept 16th. Families find this lots of fun. Reservations must be made in person at the Department of Parks and Recreation, 2nd floor, at least two weeks prior to date. Reserve in January. Proof of residency is required. Camping reservations limited to one night per family.

SPORTS

Camping with RVs
www.CampConn.com
This is the site of the Connecticut Camp Ground Owners Association.
They list sites throughout CT.

Checkered Flag Raceway (go-karts)
http://www.gokartrides.com/
1762 Berlin Turnpike, Berlin CT, 860.829-5278 (KART)
Checkered Flag Raceway, offers three different go-karts: two seaters for
an adult and a child up to fast karts for drivers 16 years-old and above.

(The) Cliffs (Climbing)
1 Commerce Park, Valhalla NY, 914.328.7625
www.thecliffsClimbing.com
Indoor climbing practice on over 200 climbs set by a full time professional staff. Climbers can start at age 9. Training programs for beginners and advanced climbers.

Club Get Away (Adventure Weekends)
P.O. Box 737, Kent CT 06757
877.746.7529, 800.643.8292, 860.927.3664
www.ClubGetAway.com
About an hour away, the Club is a 300 acre resort in the foothills of the
Berkshire Mountains, with just about every activity available: trapeze
school, tennis, volleyball, rock climbing, yoga and more.

Coker Farm (riding)
69 Stone Hill Road, Bedford, (North Salem) NY 914.234.3954
Set on 100 acres with indoor and outdoor riding areas, they give lessons
from beginner to advanced.

Clarke Outdoors (canoeing)
163 Rte. 7, West Cornwall, CT, 860.672.6365
www.ClarkeOutdoors.com
Canoeing and kayaking rentals, lessons, and white water rafting on the
Housatonic River.

Compleat Angler (Fishing Equipment & Clothing)
555 Post Road, Darien CT, 203.655.9400
www.Compleat-Angler.com
A large selection of fly fishing and light tackle spin fishing equipment as
well as outdoor clothing. Ask about their lessons and guide service.
Hours: Monday - Saturday, 9:30 am - 5 pm; Sunday, 11 am - 4 pm.

SPORTS

Connecticut Angler's Guide (fishing)
Connecticut Department of Environmental Protection
860.424.3474 (FISH)
www.dep.state.ct.us/burnatr/fishing/fishinfo/angler.htm
This guide should come with your license. It provides a summary of the rules and regulations governing sport fishing in Connecticut, descriptions of places to fish, the kinds of fish found there, and license information.

Connecticut Bicycle Map
Information: 860.594.2000
2800 Berlin Turnpike, PO Box 317564, Newington, CT 06131-7564
The Connecticut Department of Transportation Bicycle Map is published by the State. Write for a copy.

Connecticut Walk Book
For information call 860.346.2372
www.CTWoodlands.org or www.WalkCT.org
The books (Eastern and Western Connecticut) are published by the Connecticut Forest and Park Association. They are available on their website. The Association is a non-profit group of hikers and conservationists. The Walk Books are complete guides to day trips, with fold out maps.

Cos Cob Archers
205 Bible Street, Clubhouse: 203.625.9421
Contact: Dee Fletcher (membership and meetings) 203.322.5492
www.CosCobArchers.com
Twenty-four regular targets. Members must have their own equipment and be over 18. Members have a key to the range and can practice any time. To join, visit the range Saturday or Sunday or attend the meeting on the second Wednesday of each month at 7 pm.

Cos Cob Athletic Club (T-Ball, football, cheerleading)
Contact: Heidi & Tom Pastore, 203.637.7767
A community organization sponsoring spring coed T-Ball for beginners in grades K-2 (T-Ball uses a batting tee) and The Cos Cob Crushers football teams (elementary and middle school football teams for ages 8 -13). The Crushers have cheerleaders in the fall.

SPORTS

Cos Cob Revolver & Rifle Club

451 Steamboat Road, 203.622.9508

www.CCRRC.com

For those looking for a safe way to practice target shooting, this Greenwich club (despite its Cos Cob name), just across from the train station, has terrific facilities and a very helpful membership (including the Greenwich Police, many of whom practice here). To join, call and listen to the recorded announcement. Usually, all you have to do is attend a meeting (the second Wednesday of each month at 8 pm). To transport a gun to and from the club you need a Connecticut handgun license, which they can help you obtain.

Devil's Compass (Fishing)

Byram Dock, Capt. Bill Piciulli, 914.980.5997

www.DevilsCompass.com

Fishing charters and bird hunting on the long Island Sound.

Devita Karate

37 West Putnam Avenue, 629 2467

www.DevitaKarate.com

Tang-soo-do Karate, Tai Chi Classes and kickboxing. Joseph Devita is a 6th degree Black Belt and has been teaching in Greenwich since 1981.

(The) Dolphins (swim team)

YWCA of Greenwich,259 East Putnam Avenue, 203.869.6501

www.GreenwichDolphins.com

In addition to the high school swim team, the town has several superior competition swim teams, like the Dolphins. The Dolphins are for serious swimmers. Kids start early: swim practice is every day, with meets held on most Sundays. All that is required to join is parental consent and the ability not to sink. Some children start as early as four.

Doral Arrowwood (tennis, racquet ball, squash)

975 Anderson Hill Road, Rye Brook NY, 914.935.6688

www.ProformTennis.com

www.DoralArrowwood.com/proform_tennis.asp

www.DoralArrowwood.com/health_racquetballandsquash.asp

4 hard courts (2 indoor and 2 outdoor), with ATP professionals to provide junior and adult programs. Two racquetball courts and one squash court located in their fitness center.

Doral Golf Club

975 Anderson Hill Road, Rye Brook, 914.939.5500

www.DoralArrowwood.com

Nine holes, par 35. 5,689 yards, pro shop, driving range, putting green and restaurant.

Hours: Monday - Thursday, 7 am - 6 pm.

(Greenwich) Department of Parks and Recreation

2nd floor, Town Hall, 101 Field Point Road, 203.622.7830,7814

www.greenwichct.org/ParksAndRec/ParksandRec.asp

The Department sponsors a multitude of sports programs. Always go to their website to see what they are currently sponsoring. Below are some of their programs.

Indoor baseball clinics January - March for children ages 7 to 13
Co-ed spring outdoor clinics for Small Fry age 7 and Midget for age 8
Doyle Baseball School for ages 7 - 12, during school vacation in April
July & August co-ed baseball league for ages 9 - 12
Indoor softball clinics for girls ages 10 to 15
Co-ed baseball clinics, K to 6th grade
Girls' baseball clinics, K to 6th grade
Girls' Middle School baseball clinics, 6th through 8th grade
Indoor Lacrosse Clinics
Co-ed introductory, non-contact Lacrosse clinics (ages 7 & 8, 9 & 10)
Field Hockey Programs
Co-Ed volley ball games from elementary to adult
Co-Ed indoor soccer for children k-6th grade

The department publishes a number of valuable publications such as the Town's Bicycle Master Plan, measured running and walking routes (Created as an Eagle Scout Project). Office Hours: weekdays, 8 am - 4 pm.

Dorothy Hamill Skating Rink (skating, hockey)

Sherman Avenue, 203.531.8560, off season: 203.622.7830.

www.GreenwichCT.org/ParksAndRec/prSkating.asp

An excellent municipal skating facility for Greenwich residents and their guests. You will need proof of residency such as a beach card. The Rink offers a full schedule of skating & figure skating lessons and ice hockey programs for children, teens, and adults.

Directions: US-1 W, L on Western Junior Highway, R on Henry, R on Sherman Avenue.

SPORTS

Downunder Kayaking (kayaking)
157 Rowayton Avenue, Rowayton CT, 203.852.0011
www.DownUnderKayaking.com
Located on the five mile river, they provide instruction and guided tours of Long Island Sound. They even offer yoga Kayak classes.

Doyle Baseball Academy (baseball)
203.622.7830, Rick Siebert: 865.560.8765
www.DoyleBaseball.com/
Rick.Siebert@DoyleBaseball.com
Hosted by Greenwich Department of Parks and Recreation in April at the Eastern Greenwich Civic Center. Groups are divided by age: 6-8, 9-10, 11 & 12.

Dynamic Martial Arts Family Center (karate)
202 Field Point Road, 203.629.4666
www.GreenwichKarate.com
They have fitness programs, many children's classes and Kempo karate and Tai Chi classes for adults.

East Coast Greenway (bicycle)
Headquarters: 27B North Road, Wakefield RI, 401.789.4625
www.Greenway.org
The East Coast Greenway Alliance has created bicycle routes along the East Coast, part of which is between Greenwich and New Haven. A map of this route, championed by local resident Franklin Bloomer, is available by calling the headquarters.

Eastern Greenwich Civic Center
90 Harding Road, Old Greenwich, 203.637.3659
Director: Billie Schock   www.ogrcc.com
www.greenwichct.org/ParksAndRec/prFacilityPrograms.asp#eastern
Home of the Old Greenwich-Riverside Community Center, 203.637.3659
Together they sponsor a variety of basketball, baseball and softball teams as well as instruction programs for girls and boys from kindergarten through 8th grade. Among their activities are indoor golf, indoor soccer, Adult Pick-Up Basketball for 18+, roller skating and yoga. OGRCC sponsors basketball programs for young children through adults: Youth Basketball for boys and girls in the 3rd and 4th grades; Boys' & Girls' Basketball for 5th to 8th graders as well as a number of summer tennis, baseball and soccer camps. The Old Greenwich-Riverside Soccer Association provides a soccer program for over 700 youngsters who just wish to play for fun, as well as for those who wish to compete.

Field Club

276 Lake Avenue, 203.869.1309

A private club which offers a weekly Junior Summer Squash Camp often open to the public. They have international singles and doubles courts.

Fighter Pilot for a Day (flying)

800.522.7590, www.AirCombat.com

Since 1988 they have been giving civilians the experience of being a fighter pilot. Guest pilots fly real military fighters with licensed fighter pilots in the cockpit with them. Aircraft are outfitted with high end digital multi-camera systems to capture your fighter pilot experience. No pilot's license is required. Course begins with pilot training, then real dogfight experience, then a briefing on your performance (or lack thereof). They travel around the country, but fly out of Montgomery, New York in April & October. It is great fun. Carolyn beat Jerry 4 out of 5 times.

Flight Safety (flying)

Vero Beach Florida, 772.564.7600 or 800.800.1411

www.FlightSafetyAcademy.com

The premier flight training school. Started by Greenwich resident Al Ueltschi. It is directed toward teaching people who want to be professional pilots, but there is no better place for a private pilot to begin their training. The weather is great so you will be able to fly every day.

Forest and Field Outdoor (Firearms)

4 New Canaan Ave, Norwalk CT, 203.847.4008

www.ForestAndField.com

A 12,000 square foot firearm store representing a variety of manufacturers of guns, clothing and equipment. They have a 14-point shooting range and offer pistol certification courses.

Hours: Tuesday - Friday, 10 am - 7:30 pm; Saturday, 9 am - 5 pm.

Gaynor Brennan Municipal Golf Course (golf)

451 Stillwater Road, Stamford, 203.324.4185

www.BrennanGolf.com

Par 71. You can reserve seven days in advance.

Getner Farm (riding)

22 Richards Avenue, Norwalk CT, 203.524.3275

www.GetnerBarn.com

Barn is located at 22 Richards Avenue Located on the Darien/Norwalk line English riding in a relaxed atmosphere for ages 6 and up. Blue jeans are the norm.

SPORTS

Grand Prix New York (go-kart)
333 North Bedford Road, Mount Kisco NY, 914.241.3131
www.GPNY.com/
120,000 square foot indoor go-kart racing for 8 years and above. Special adult races.
Hours: Monday, 12 pm - 10 pm, Closed Tuesday, Wednesday & Thursday 3 pm-10 pm, Friday, 12 pm-12 midnight, Saturday, 9 am-12 midnight, Sunday 12 pm-8 pm.

Grand Slam (tennis)
1 Bedford-Banksville Road, Bedford NY, 914.234.9206
www.GrandSlamTennisClub.com
Five HarTru courts, five DecoTurf II (hard surface) courts. During the winter, eight are indoor, during the summer, five are outside. Excellent junior and adult programs including USTA League Play.

Great Play
Shop Rite Cntr, 2000 W Main Street, (Stamford/Old Greenwich border), 203.978.1333
www.GreatPlay.com
A unique gym that offers fun classes to help kids develop motor skills, fitness and coordination.

Greenwich 1-on-1 (training in many sports)
1117 East Putnam Avenue, Suite 374, Riverside CT, 203.344.9277
www.Greenwich1on1.com
Whether you are learning a sport, a musical instrument, or a hobby, it helps to have an instructor who is both accomplished himself/herself in that discipline and who has a passion for teaching. 1 on 1 provides private, semi- private and small group training in baseball, basketball, cheerleading, field hockey, football, golf, lacrosse, running / track, self defense, soccer, softball and yoga.

Greenwich Academy Squash Training Camp
200 North Maple Avenue, 203.625.8900 x 7287
www.GreenwichAcademy.org
During the summer, the Academy uses their five international squash courts to provide training for children in grades 5 and above.

SPORTS

Greenwich Babe Ruth League (baseball)
Hotline: 203.618.7659
Contact: Steve Monick 203.531.4451
www.GreenwichBabeRuth.org
Non-profit organization sponsoring baseball. The Bambino division is for children 10 - 12; Junior division is for ages 13 - 15; Senior division is for ages 16 - 18. Teams play from late May through mid-July at the Greenwich High School and Julian Curtiss Elementary School. Registration starts in February at Town Hall.

Greenwich Basketball Association
Dr. Scott Fisher, 203.869.2929; Bob Haugen, 203.698.0273
www.GreenwichBasketball.org
Now in its 20th season, the Association was founded by a group of Greenwich fathers. It provides a townwide instructional and competitive co-ed basketball program for 5th - 10th graders, designed to encourage and stimulate each child to build basketball skills. All skill levels are welcome and everyone is guaranteed to play at least half of each game. Registration and evaluation start in October.

Greenwich Blues Youth Ice Hockey Association
PO Box 1107, Greenwich, CT 06836
Contact: see website for contacts and telephone numbers.
www.GreenwichBlues.com
Non-profit organization sponsoring competitive travel teams for boys and girls: Mites, under age 9; Squirts, 9 - 11; Peewees, 11 - 13; Bantam, 13 - 15. Dorothy Hamill Rink is their home rink. Season is from September through March, tryouts are in early September.

Greenwich Community Sailing
PO Box 195, Old Greenwich, 203.698.0599
www.GreenwichSailing.com
CT approved safe boating certificate courses. They have a variety of junior and adult programs open only to Greenwich residents. The Junior programs are for ages 9 - 16. Learn to sail, keelboat or kayak in group or private lessons.

Greenwich Croquet Club

www.GreenwichCroquet.com

Founded by Greenwich residents Bill and Marjorie Campbell in 1986, this private club is open to everyone. It plays on the Bruce Park Green. Besides providing instruction, the Club holds the Greenwich Invitational Tournament every July 4th, and in August, hosts the Connecticut State Championship. To join, stop by the lawns at Bruce Park on Thursday evenings in the summer.

Greenwich Fencing

Western Greenwich Civic Center, 449 Pemberwick Road,

203. 532.1259

www.GreenwichFencing.com

Greenwich Goat Gear Basketball

201.652.4477

www.GreenwichBasketball.com, www.CTYouthSports.com

Goatgear Basketball Leagues and camps for grades k-7 are offered at locations such as the Hebrew Academy 270 Lake Avenue and Greenwich Catholic School 471 North Street.

Greenwich Kids Triathlon

www.GreenwichKidsTri.com

The triathlon consists of a swim, bike and run, at the Greenwich High School campus. It is for 7-10 and 11-12 year olds. Founded in 2003 by Fionnuala Mackey, it is run by Bill Bogardus (203.861.6835) , a physical education teacher at North Street School and head of Project Fitness, a personal training company for kids.

Greenwich Lacrosse

201.689.9155

www.GreenwichLacrosse.com, www.CTYouthSports.com

Leagues and camps for grades k-7 are offered at locations such as the Hebrew Academy 270 Lake Avenue and Greenwich Catholic School 471 North Street.

Greenwich Lawn Bowls Club

Contact: Barbara Pollard, 203.869.3918

This 25-member club, welcomes men and women of all ages. The group has fun bowling on the course, built in 1940 in Bruce Park. The club is affiliated with the Northeast Division of the U.S. Lawn Bowl Association.

Greenwich Marine Facilities (boat moorings)

Superintendent: Fred Walters 203.622.7818
Location: Town Hall, Second Floor
Hours: Open from 8:15 am - 3:45 pm
www.GreenwichCT.org/ParksAndRec/prBoating.asp
They assign boat moorings for the town. To apply for a slip (as always, bring in a utility bill as proof of residency and a photo ID) you must own a boat and know the vessel's length, draft and beam. Boats are categorized as sail or power and over or under 20 feet; 20 feet and over receive deepwater moorings. After registering, you are put on a waiting list. The list is never short, but the amount of time varies with the vessel's type and size, as well as the location you request. The town has moorings at Greenwich Point, Cos Cob, Grass Island and Byram. They will also provide storage of kayaks and canoes.

Greenwich Point/Tod's Point
(swimming, bicycling, running)

Shore Road, Old Greenwich
Craig Whitcomb (Operations Manager) 203.622.7814
147 acres at the end of Sound Beach Avenue and Shore Road. Greenwich Point is a popular spot for water sports, as well as walking, bicycle riding, roller blading and running. A network of trails leads along the changing coastline and through the woods. A trail guide is available at the Seaside Center of the Bruce Museum. During the summer a beach pass is required. *See PARKS & BEACHES.*

Greenwich Polo Club

Field Location: Upper North Street at Conyers Farm
Office: 80 Field Point Road, 3rd Floor, Greenwich, CT 06830, 203.863.1202. 203.661.5420
www.GreenwichPolo.com (website has good directions)
Greenwich has a world class polo facility. Most summer Sundays you can watch a good polo match in a beautiful setting. Matches begin at 3 pm, the gates open at 1 pm. General admission is $30 per car. Attire is "Garden Party Chic". The Greenwich Polo Club also offers individual and group polo lessons. Lessons include the use of a polo pony, all tack, polo mallets and balls. Call their office to get a copy of their magazine "Greenwich Polo".

Greenwich Racquet Club (Tennis)
1 River Road, Cos Cob, 661.0606 www.leontennis.net
4 indoor DecoTurf hard-surface courts. They have an excellent junior development program, as well as adult clinics taught by USPTA certified pros to all levels. Play in round robins for men and women or rent a court for the season. During the summer they operate the Wire Mill Racquet Club in Stamford (203.329.9221).

Greenwich Riding and Trails Association
PO Box 1403, Greenwich 06836, 203.661.3062
www.theGRTA.org
Greenwich has an extensive trail network. This nearly 100 year-old organization maintains 150 miles of horse trails in town and devotes its resources to conservation and open space. For information and help, call them. A great organization to join.

Greenwich Rowing Club
The Greenwich Water Club, (Mianus River) at 67 River Road
Cos Cob, 203.661.4033 www.GreenwichWaterClub.com
The Club staff is ready to help you learn, train, and push the limits to meet your every goal, whether you are a competitive crew team or a new trainee. The club has 35 rowing machines and a training staff available to accommodate your needs, whether you are a novice, intermediate, or highly advanced rower. Membership is open to men and women of all ages and juniors 12- 18. Stop by the club to see their facilities and meet the coaches. You don't have to join the club to participate in crewing.

Greenwich Safe Cycling (bicycle)
PO Box 117, Cos Cob CT 06807-0117
Franklin Bloomer, Chairman
The mission of this organization of town residents, both serious cyclists and recreational riders, is to make Greenwich a bicycle- and pedestrian-friendly community. They helped develop the Town's Master Bicycle Plan. They are responsible for the 7.5-mile bicycle trail from Grass Island to Greenwich Point.

Greenwich Sail and Power Squadron (boating)

PO Box 307, Greenwich CT, 06830

For information or to join send a letter, an email through their website or contact Commander Susan P. Ryan @ 203.698.0441

www.CaptainHarbor.org

The Power Squadron is an all-volunteer civic organization with 200 Greenwich members whose primary goal is education and boating safety in both sailing and power boating. The Squadron teaches two Safe Boating courses at the Greenwich High School through the Continuing Education program (203.830.8144) and depending upon demand, runs additional courses throughout the year. All boaters (even jet skiers) must have a Connecticut Boating License. The Power Squadron course qualifies you for your Connecticut license. This course is the first step for anyone who wants to enjoy the miles of coastline available to Greenwich residents.

Greenwich Soccer Association

PO Box 1535, Greenwich CT 06830, 203.558.0739, 203.292.6208

www.GreenwichTravelSoccer.com

Girls' and boys' travel soccer teams for ages 7 to 11. They play travel teams from other Fairfield County towns on Sunday afternoons. Tryouts are required and usually begin in November for the spring season.

Greenwich Soccer Club

PO Box 383, Cos Cob CT 06807, 203.661.2620

www.GreenwichSoccer.com

The Greenwich Soccer Club is a volunteer based, all-inclusive, recreational and instructional program with a firm commitment to safety, fun and fairness. The GSC is a townwide recreational program open to every boy and girl, ages 6 - 14, who either resides in or attends school in town. In the fall, over 1,700 boys and girls participate on Saturdays (coached by some 350 parent volunteers) with mid-week clinics taught by professional instructors. There are separate leagues for the boys and girls. The GSC is a privately funded, non-profit community service organization founded in 1976. Anne Orum is the Executive Director.

SPORTS

Greenwich Skateboard Park

Roger Sherman Baldwin Park, Arch Street,
203.622.7830, 203.496.9876
www.greenwichct.org/ParksAndRec/prSkatePark.asp
The 7,754 sq. ft. skate park was a gift of the Junior League of Greenwich. The maximum number of skaters is 40. Membership is $10 for a day pass. Greenwich residents may apply for a $175 annual membership at the Parks and Recreation office in Town Hall weekdays from 8 am-4 pm. The Department of Parks and Recreation conducts clinics in basic techniques, safety and etiquette for children 6 - 14. Check the town website for information on clinics, camps and birthday parties.
Hours: The usual skate park hours are weekdays 3 pm - 7 pm, weekends noon - 7 pm. Hours vary depending upon when schools are in session.

Greenwich Skating Club (ice skating)

Cardinal Road, 203.622.9583
www.GreenwichSkatingClub.org
The Skating Club, set inconspicuously off Fairfield Road, has an outdoor rink and offers a strong skating program for children. Because of its small membership, it is one of the more difficult clubs to join. See the website for admissions.

Greenwich Tennis Headquarters

54 Bible Street, Cos Cob, 203.661.0182, 203.618.7613
There are 36 all-weather courts available throughout Greenwich, as well as a paddle tennis court location. The town runs junior and adult clinics for all levels (including tots) and provides private lessons. It also sponsors a junior and adult town tennis tournament which attracts some very good players. Call for information, a map of the courts and tennis permit information. For more information call Contact Frank Gabriele at 203.622.7821.

Directions to Town Tennis Courts

www.greenwichct.org/ParksAndRec/prDirectionsTennis.asp
Courts are available at:
Binney Park, Bruce Park, Byram Shore Park, Central Middle School, Christiano Park, Eastern Greenwich Civic Center, Eastern Middle School Greenwich High School, Loughlin Ave. Park, Western Middle School, Pemberwick Park. The lights at the Eastern Greenwich Civic Center are usually on until 10 pm.

SPORTS

Tennis Passes

www.greenwichct.org/ParksAndRec/prTennis.asp

Resident's tennis card is $27 for the season. Guest cards are $45. Cards are available at Town Hall Lobby, Park Pass Office, Monday - Thursday 4:30 - 7:30.

Tennis Court Reservations

Tennis reservations must be by phone. Call 203.622.2210 starting in May.

Platform Tennis

The town has two Platform Tennis courts, located at Loughlin Avenue in Cos Cob. This 6-acre park has the only public paddle tennis courts in Greenwich. The courts are lighted and can be used by Greenwich residents and their guests. Courts are open October to April. Seasonal permits cost $300 for residents. Lights are on Tuesday- Thursday, dusk to 9 pm. When you purchase a permit you should register for two 1-hr time slots per week. For information or cancellations call 203.618.7650 or 203.622.7830.

Greenwich Tumble and Cheer (cheerleaders)

222 Mill Street, 203.532.1223

www.GreenwichTumbleAndCheer.com

Gigi Lombardi runs a year-round cheerleading and tumbling training center located at the Sokol Gymnastic Club in Byram. The school is for children in kindergarten through grade 12, all interest levels and abilities.

Greenwich Water Club (boating)

49 River Road, Cos Cob, 203.601.4033

www.GreenwichWaterClub.com

The Club has a full working marina with a 250-slip capacity, onsite repair service, fueling dock, visiting slip privileges, winter storage facilities, and a ship's store. They teach safe boating as well as other boating classes.

Greenwich Youth Cheerleading League

Greenwichcheer@aol.com

GYCL operates as an entity underneath the GYFL and is open to girls 3rd to 8th grade throughout town. Sign-ups are in May. The season runs from September to November.

Greenwich Youth Football League

Gateway Youth Football League
Contact: Michael Dunster, 203.637.0766   www.gyfl.net
Town wide instructional/competitive tackle football league for children
ages 8- 13. Registration takes place in May. First-timers sign up at Town
Hall Department of Parks and Recreation. Spaces fill quickly. The season
runs from September to November. Practices are held 2 - 3 time a week.
Games are on Sunday mornings. Each team has three levels: Bantam,
3rd & 4th graders; Junior, 5th & 6th graders; Senior, 7th & 8th graders.
See Greenwich Youth Cheerleaders (GYCL) above. The teams are:
   Mavericks (Glenville)
   Banc Raiders (Byram) www.BancGreenwich.org
   Crushers (Cos Cob) www.CrusherFootball.com
   Bulldogs (North Mianus) www.NMBulldogsFootball.com
   Gators (Riverside) www.GatorFootball.ws
   Putnam Generals (Old Greenwich) www.PutnamGeneralsFootball.com

Greenwich Youth Lacrosse

www.GreenwichYouthLacrosse.org
PO Box 4627, Greenwich CT 06831-0412
Patrick Coleman, President: 203.637.7360 Home, 917.744.8379 Cell
A non-profit organization sponsoring lacrosse teams. House League for
boys and girls in grades 1 - 6; Travel teams for boys and girls in grades
3 - 4 and 5 - 6. Boys travel teams for grades 7 - 8. Registration is usually
in March.

Greenwich Youth Water Polo League

P.O. Box 38, Cos Cob, 203.352.3405 (recording)
www.GreenwichWaterPolo.com
Founded by the coaches of the Greenwich High School water polo team,
the GHS has one of the strongest programs on the Eastern seaboard.
This league is for boys and girls ages 9 to 15 who want to learn to play
water polo. See the website for email contacts.

Griffith Harris Memorial Golf Course

13231 King Street, 203.531.7200, for reservations 203.531.8253
www.GreenwichCT.org/ParksAndRec/prGolfCourse.asp
Open only to Greenwich residents (including tenants). This par 71, 18-hole golf course designed by Robert Trent Jones has a club house, pro shop, putting green and driving range. Call about obtaining a membership card. You must complete the application form from the golf course office. You will need to bring proof of Greenwich residency (such as a current phone bill) and a photo ID such as a driver's license. Membership is $140 for an adult permanent resident.

Hunter Mountain (skiing)

Route 23A, Hunter NY, 800.486.8376
www.HunterMtn.com
Difficulty: Beginner, Intermediate, Advanced.
Size: 12 lifts, 53 trails, snowmaking, snowtubing.
Distance: 2.5 hrs, I-87 N exit 20, Rte 32 N, Rte 23A W.

(The) Hunting and Trapping Guide

and Wildlife area maps can be obtained from the Town Clerk's office, 203.622.7894 or on-line at:
http://dep.state.ct.us/burnatr/wildlife/fguide/fgindex.htm

Indian Harbor Yacht Club Sailing

710 Steamboat Road, 203.869.2484
Ask for the Sailing Office
One of the few private clubs with a sailing program open to the public. The program has such a good reputation that it is usually filled by February.

In-Line Roller Hockey

Eastern Greenwich Civic Center
(aka Old Greenwich Riverside Community
Center), 90 Harding Road, Old Greenwich, 203.637.3659
Adult pickup roller hockey as well as spring and summer instruction and games for boys and girls ages 6 - 14. Call for times and details.

Jack Rabbits Gymnastics

Round Hill Community House, 395 Round Hill Road
203.622.0004
www.JackRabbitsGym.com
Jack Rabbits has classes for kids ages 1- 9 years; a great way to wear your children out!

SPORTS

Jim Fixx Memorial Day Race

Greenwich Recreation Office, 203.622.7830 or

Threads and Treads, 17 East Putnam Avenue, Greenwich, 203.661.0142

www.ThreadsandTreads.com

The Jim Fixx Memorial 5-mile race starts and ends on Greenwich Avenue. It is usually in May and begins the running season. If you run in no other event, you should consider it. It is always well attended and attracts a great variety of talented and not-so-talented runners.

K & L Soaring

5996 State Route 224, Cayuta NY, 607. 594.3329

www.KLSoaring.com

A good place to purchase the Schweizer Soaring School Manual before you go for a glider lesson.

Kang Tae-kwon-do & Hapkido (karate)

263 Sound Beach Ave, Old Greenwich, 203.637.7867 or 8253

www.KangMartialArts.com

One of several locations run by Grand Master Ik Jo Kang.

Kayak Adventure

24 Poplar Street, Norwalk CT, 203. 852.7294

www.Kayak-Adventure.net

Instruction & day trips on the Long Island Sound.

Kayak/Canoe Guide

SWRPA (South Western Regional Planning Agency) publishes a fullcolor laminated guide to help you find your way around Norwalk's 23-island archipelago. SWRPA is located at 888 Washington Blvd in Stamford. Call 203.316.5190 for a copy.

Killington Resort (skiing)

4763 Killington Road, Killington, VT

800.621.6867, 802.422.6200

www.Killington.com

One of the areas largest and most popular ski resorts. Spread out over six mountains, it has 141 trails and has a very extensive snow making system.

Kittatinny Canoes (canoeing, kayaking , rafting)

Dingmans Ferry PA, 800.356.2852, 570.828.2338

www.Kittatinny.com

Canoeing, kayaking or rafting the Delaware. Calm water for families or beginners, white water for experts.

Lake of Ilses Golf Course

1 clubhouse Drive, North Stonington CT (Near Foxwoods Casino), 888.475.3746

www.LakeOfIsles.com

36-hole top rated golf course and golf academy.

Liberty Paintball

(Thunder Ridge Ski Area) 1 Thunder Ridge Road, Patterson NY, 845.878.6300

www.LibertyPaintball-NY.com

350 acres of varied terrain just North and West of Danbury, CT. Friends tell us they rate it 5 stars. They suggest the beginner bring their own group of about 20-participants and rent equipment there. Kids parties require a group of 15. Don't forget to wear protective clothing. *Laser Tag locations are described in CHILDREN - Parties At Home.*

Licenses and Permits

See Greenwich Tennis Headquarters above for information on Tennis and Paddle Tennis passes.

• **Fishing Licenses** can be obtained from the Town Clerk's office, 203.622.7897, Fishing licenses are $20 for residents and $40 for non-residents. They are good for the calendar year. There is usually good trout fishing at the Mianus River Park, Merrybrook Road (Cognewaugh Road), 203.622.7814. Be sure you have your license, they do check. *See section on PARKS & BEACHES for directions.*

• **Hunting Licenses** are issued by the Connecticut Department of Environmental Protection, (DEP License and Revenue Unit,79 Elm Street, Hartford, CT 06106-5127). License applications can be obtained from the Town Clerk's office, 203.622.7894 Landowner Deer Permit can be obtained from the Town Clerk's office, 203.622.7894. It is required to hunt deer on your own property.

• **Parking Permits** are available through the Department of Parking Services, contact Christina Gorbal, 203.622.7730.

www.greenwichct.org/Parking/psParkingPermits.asp

- **Park/Beach/Daily Passes:** Day passes are available at Town Hall, 101 Field Point Road. The Park Pass Office is open Monday through Friday, 8:00 am to 3:45 pm or at the Eastern and Western Civic Centers. Passes are required from May 1 through October 31. Leashed dogs are only allowed from December 1 through March 31. New residents can get an application from the Park Pass Office at Town Hall or on line at: http://greenwichct.virtualtownhall.net/Public_Documents/ GreenwichCT_ParkRec/GreenwichCT_Recreation/ParkPasses/index

Lime Rock Park (auto racing)

60 White Hollow Road, Lakeville CT, 800.435.5000
www.LimeRock.com
About two hours north of Greenwich is the Lime Rock Race Track. The track is closed on Sundays, but most Saturdays (from early April to November) there are formula and sports car races. Lime Rock has no grandstands. You can get tickets online or at the gate. Call to find out about the race schedule or to get a copy of their free newspaper, Track Record. The biggest race days are usually Memorial Day and Labor Day.

Lionshare Farm (riding)

404 Taconic Road, 203.869.4649
www.LionshareFarm.com
An excellent riding academy with programs for children and adults. The farm, owned by Peter Leone, an Olympic silver medalist, has two indoor rings and an outdoor ring, as well as access to the Greenwich trails. It is the premier show jumping stable in the Greenwich area. This is the first place to go if you want to buy a jumper.

Longshore Sailing School

260 Compo Road South, Westport, CT, 203.226.4646
www.LongshoreSailingSchool.com
If you or your children (ages 9 - 16) want to learn to sail and can't get in one of the Greenwich programs, try this school in Westport. It provides instruction from basic sailing to racing techniques. Register in February for two-week sessions blending fun and substance.

Maple Moor Golf Course

1128 North Street, White Plains NY, 914.995.9200
automated reservations: 914.995.4653
Par 71, You can reserve seven days in advance.

(The) Marlins (Swim Team)

Contact Nick Baker, Swim Team Coach, 203.869.1630

www.GreenwichMarlins.org

Run at the YMCA, this swim team competes with the Dolphins. The Marlins is a year-round swim club that starts at age 6. They compete in USA sanction swim meets and the Connecticut Summer Swim League.

Mead Farm (aka Wind Swept Farm) (riding)

107 June Road, Stamford, 203.322.4984

www.MeadFarm.com

They give outdoor riding lessons for boys and girls 5 - 17. No previous riding experience is required. Located at the Greenwich/Stamford border, the stable has access to the 150 miles of the Greenwich trail system. Their June through August pony summer camp is extremely popular. Sign up early. Campers have fun riding, learning horse etiquette and how to tack and clean their horses.

Men's Basketball League (basketball)

Call Frank Gabriele, Recreation Supervisor, 203.622.7821 for information. A recreation program from January through March at the Eastern Greenwich Civic Center, Central and Eastern Middle Schools and Greenwich High School. Programs for Town resident teams, B and C corporate teams.

Mianus River (ice skating, canoeing)

Park off of Valley Road, bring your skates and hockey sticks (a snow shovel, too.)

Mianus River Park (walking)

Cognewaugh Road, Cos Cob, 203.622.7814

www.greenwichct.org/ParksAndRec/prFacilitiesIndex.asp

220 acres stretching from Greenwich into Stamford. The entrance is a mile east of Stanwich Road on Cognewaugh Road. The two trails we think are of most interest are the Pond Trail and the Oak Trail.

Mohawk Mountain (Skiing)

46 Great Hollow Road, Cornwall, CT, 860.672.6100, 800.895.5222

www.MohawkMtn.com

Difficulty: Beginner & Intermediate.

Size: 5 lifts, 24 trails, snowmaking, night skiing.

Distance: 1.5 hrs, I-95 N to Rte 8 N to exit 44.

Mont Tremblant (skiing)

Mont Tremblant, Quebec, Canada
www.Tremblant.ca
A European-type ski village with just about every conceivable activity and amenity including very good food and, of course, good snow on its 650 acres of skiable area. It is about an 8-hour drive from Greenwich. Of course, you can fly there directly from Newark. It can be very cold, first timers may want to try it for spring skiing.

Montgomery Pinetum Park (walking)

Bible Street, Cos Cob, 203.622.7814
www.greenwichct.org/ParksAndRec/prFacilitiesIndex.asp
91 acres, just off of Bible Street in Cos Cob. The entrance is on the west side directly opposite Clover Place. Obtain a map and tree guide from the Garden Center office, then enjoy the extraordinary diversity of trees and plantings. One path leads to the 22-acre Greenwich Audubon Society's Mildred Bedard Caldwell Wildlife Sanctuary.

Mount Snow Ski Resort

12 Pisgah Road, West Dover, VT
800.451.4211, 800.245.7669 www.MountSnow.com
A large and very popular ski resort.

Mount Southington (skiing)

396 Mount Vernon Road, Plainsville, CT
860.628.0954, 800.982.6828 www.mountsouthington.com
Difficulty: Beginner & Intermediate.
Size: 7 lifts, 14 trails, snowmaking, night skiing.
Distance: 2 hrs, I-84 N exit 30.

Mount Tom / suicide 6 (skiing)

Woodstock VT, Information: 802-457-6661, Snow Phone: 802-457-6666
www.Suicide6.com
www.WoodstockVT.com/hiking.php
A great place to learn to ski in the winter, wonderful hiking in the summer - all in a town beautified by Laurence Rockefeller. The Woodstock Inn is the place to stay. (www.woodstockinn.com, 800.448.7900)

My Gym

7 Hyde Street, Stamford CT, 203.327.3496
www.My-Gym.com
Gymnastics / movement classes for children ages 3 months to 13 years.

New York Sailing School (sailing)

22 Pelham Road, New Rochelle NY, 914.235.6052

www.NYSS.com

Sailing programs for all skill levels. Take their course and then rent a boat to practice your sailing.

Nike Golf Schools and Junior Camps

800.645.3226

www.USSportsCamps.com

Nike sponsors a great number of adult and junior golf camps. The closest are Williams College, Williamstown, MA; Stowe, VT; and Loomis Chaffee, Windsor, CT.

Nike Adult and Junior Tennis Camps

800.645.3226   www.USSportsCamps.com

Nike sponsors a great number of adult and junior tennis camps. The closest are: Amherst College, Amherst, MA; LoomisChaffee, Windsor, CT; Peddie School, Hightstown, NJ; Lawrenceville School, Lawrenceville, NJ.

Nike sports Camps

800-645-3226 (Nike Camps), 800-433-6060 (All other camps)

800-406-3926 (NBC Camps),

877-308-7325 (Peak Performance Swim

Camps), 888-780-2267 (Vogelsinger Soccer Academy)

www.USSportsCamps.com

Besides Tennis and Golf camps, Nike has camps for Volleyball, Field Hockey, Swimming, Basketball, Lacrosse, Softball, Running, Soccer, Baseball, Hockey and Water polo.

Norwalk Rowing Association (rowing)

Moody's Lane, Norwalk, 203.866.0088

www.NorwalkRiverRowing.org

Adult programs range from learn-to-row to racing. Youth programs starting in the 6th grade.

North American Outdoor Adventure

West Forks ME, 800.727.4379, 207.663.4472

www.NAWhitewater.com

Whitewater rafting from Maine to Connecticut, as well as kayaking, canoeing, snowmobiling and hunting primarily in Maine.

Northeast Saltwater Fishing (fishing)
www.NOREast.com
A publication devoted to Northeast Sportfishing.

Norwalk Karting Association
Voice Mail: 203.319.2981, Contact : 203.246.3386
www.NorwalkKartingAssociation.net
NKA is a go kart racing club located in Norwalk Connecticut. They race at Calf Pasture Beach on the weekend.

Oak Hills Golf Course (golf)
165 Fillow Street, Norwalk, CT, 203.838.0303 www.OakHillSGC.com
Par 71; You can reserve seven days ahead for weekdays only. They have an automated tee time reservation system.

Okemo Mountain (Skiing)
77 Okemo Ridge Road, Ludlow VT, 866-706-5366,
Snow reports 802.228.5222 www.Okemo.com
A family ski place with lodging right on the slopes. Five mountain areas serviced by 19 lifts. Great training programs for younger skiers, starting at age 2.

Old Greenwich School of Karate (Karate)
242 Sound Beach Avenue (action Arts), 203.698.1057, 637.2685
www.GreenwichKidsKarate.com or www.OGKarate.com
Japanese Isshinryu Karate and Filipino Jitsu taught by 6th dan Sensei Rick Zimmerman.

Old Greenwich-Riverside Community Center
See Eastern Greenwich Civic Center above.

Old Greenwich Tennis Academy
151 Sound Beach Avenue, 203.637.3398
www.OldGreenwichTennisacademy.com
5 indoor HarTru courts. Often used by groups who contract for court time. Open September to May, they have Junior and Adult programs for all levels.

Old Greenwich Yacht Club (boating)
Greenwich Point, Old Greenwich, 637.3074
www.OGYC.org
Open to all residents with beach cards. It has deep water moorings as well as Mercury sailboats for member use. The club provides sailing lessons on weekends and trophy races during the summer. *See the section on CLUBS & ORGANIZATIONS for details on other yacht clubs.*

On The Go Farms (riding)
40 Locust Road, Greenwich, 203.532.4727
A friendly stable, focused on safety, with horses that are well cared for. Participants like the camaraderie.

On Track Karting
984 North Colony Road (Rt 5), Wallingford CT, 203.626.0464
www.OnTrackKarting.com
Adult and Junior racing in a 63,000-square-foot indoor karting facility.

Outward Bound
100 Mystery Point Road, Garrison NY
845.424.4000 general inquiries,
866.467.7651 Admissions Advisor
www.Outwardbound.org
It was founded in Greenwich in 1961 and offers adventure-based learning to develop personal growth through experience and challenge. One of its five core programs is climbing.

Overland Experts (auto racing)
112 Hemlock Valley Road, East Haddam CT, 860.873.9640
www.OverlandExperts.com
4WD on and off-road driving instruction and international expeditions.

Ox Ridge Hunt Club (riding)
512 Middlesex Road, Darien, CT, 203.655.2559
www.OxRidge.com
There are many places to learn to ride, but serious riders will like Ox Ridge. This private hunt club offers riding lessons to the public. Ten half-hour private lessons are about $800. You will find good horses, indoor and outdoor facilities and top instructors.

Park Tennis USA

34 East Putnam Ave, Suite 128, Greenwich, 203.340.2160, 2161
www.ParkTennisUSA.com
Rita and Scott Staniar have a terrific idea. Bring high quality tennis instruction to the 70% of players who don't belong to private clubs. These professionals teach on public courts during the summer as well as at Greenwich Catholic School, Eastern Greenwich Civic Center and the YMCA. They also provide private home lessons.

Panorama Flight School (flying)

67 Tower Road, Hangar T, Westchester County Airport
914.328.9800
www.PanoramaFlightService.com
Flight lessons for all levels of pilots. A good place to get experience in the NY air traffic area. Lessons cost about $55/hr for the instructor and $152/hr for the airplane.

Pegasus Therapeutic Riding Inc (riding)

845.669.8235
www.PegasusTr.org
Non-profit organization provides riding as therapy for disabled children and adults.

Personal Pro Services (tennis)

May - October, Greenwich, 203.962.2673;
November - April, Scottsdale Arizona, 480.575.9702.
Tim Richardson is a USPTA Pro 1 tennis instructor. During the playing season, Tim will help you perfect your tennis game in the privacy of your own court and on your own schedule. Tim has been teaching on private Greenwich courts for almost 20 years.

Powder Ridge

99 Powder Hill Road, Middlefield CT, 877.754.7434, 860.349.3454
www.PowderRidgeCT.com
Difficulty: Beginner & Intermediate, snowtubing.
Size: 7 lifts (2 for tubing), 5 wide runs, 14 trails, night skiing.
Distance: 45 minutes, Merritt Pkw N exit 67.

Red Barn Stables (riding)

40 Bangall Road, Stamford CT, 203.223.3358
Family run, affordable facility with 200'x100' lighted indoor riding arena, indoor riding stables, boarding and horses for sale. Full board $900/month. Nearby access to Greenwich trails.

Rex Dive Center (Sporting Equipment-Diving)

144 Water Street, South Norwalk, CT, 203.853.4148
www.RexDiveCenter.com
A good place to go for your scuba equipment. You will be greeted by a friendly, knowledgeable staff. They provide lessons for beginners.
Hours: Tuesday - Friday, 11 am - 7 pm; Saturday, 9 am - 5 pm; Sunday, noon - 5 pm.

Rex Marine Center (Boating)

- 144 Water Street, South Norwalk, CT, 203.866.5555
- 50 Calf Pasture Beach Road, East Norwalk, CT 203.604.1295
www.RexMarine.com
If you are looking for a yacht or a small boat or boating paraphernalia, they are worth a visit. You can even charter a boat with captain. The Rex Boating Club provides training and rental boats. Hours vary - call ahead.

Richter Park Golf Course

100 Aunt Hack Road, Danbury CT, 203.792.2550
www.RichterPark.com
Considered to be the top public course in Connecticut. 18 holes, weekday starting times can be reserved 3 days in advance; slots start at 9 am.

Ridgefield Golf Course

545 Ridgebury Road, Ridgefield CT, 203.748.7008
www.RidgeFieldGC.com
Par 71; You can reserve up to 3 days ahead for weekends.

Running Events in Greenwich

For Information contact: Threads and Treads
17 East Putnam Avenue, Greenwich, 203.661.0142
www.ThreadsandTreads.com
This fine outfitting store has sponsored and created all kinds of running events for our town. Stop in to find out about running events all over Fairfield County. Typical events are the Greenwich Cup Biathilon, Greenwich Cup Triathlon, The Tour De Greenwich, Beach Front Bushwack and Jingle Bell Jog. The Jim Fixx Memorial 5-mile race starts and ends on Greenwich Avenue. It is usually in May and begins the running season. If you run in no other event, you should consider it. It is always well attended and attracts a mix of talented and not-so-talented runners.

Saxon Woods (golf)
315 Mamaroneck Road, Scarsdale NY, 914.231.3461
Automated reservations: 914.995.4653
www.Westchestergov.com/parks/golf/saxonwoods.htm
Par 71

Shaolin Studios (karate)
397 East Putnam Avenue, Cos Cob, 203.661.5501
www.SDSSKungfu.com
Private and group lessons for adults (16+0), teens (12-15) and kids (4-6 & 7 - 11) in martial arts and self defense. A good place to hold a birthday party.

Shell Fishing
Due to the efforts of our wonderful Shellfish Commission (which is working to restore the oyster beds in Greenwich waters), residents can have the fun of digging for shellfish (clams and oysters) in the sand at Greenwich Point. A season permit is required and can be obtained from the Town Clerk's office. The season starts about mid-October, but call 203.622.7777 first to learn which beds are open.

Shidogakuin (Kendo and Iaido)
Office: 38 Mary Lane, Riverside CT,
contact: Shozo Kato, 212.431.1322 or 203.613-1773
Shidogakuni Dojo, 100 Research Drive, Stamford, CT
Western Greenwich Civic Center, 449 Pemberwick Road, Greenwich
www.kendoka.org

Shippan Racquet Club
45 Harbor Drive, Stamford, 203.323.3129
www.ShippanRacquet.com
Junior, adult clinics & ATP program on their 6 hard courts.

(The) Ski & Scuba Connection
26 Saint Roch Avenue, Byram, 203.629.4766
www.SkiAndScubaConnection.com
Scuba lessons and equipment for scuba or snorkeling. Friendly, knowledgeable service.
Hours: weekdays, 11 am - 6 pm, Saturday 10 am - 6 pm.

Skip Barber Racing School (auto racing)

Lime Rock Park, Lakeville CT, 860.435.1300, 800.221.1131
www.SkipBarber.com
Skip Barber is the largest racing school in the country. If you have always wanted to learn to race, this is the place to go. Two basic driving courses are offered, with a lot of variations for each course: Advanced Driving School (one and two-day courses driving three different cars supplied by the school); Racing School (three hours to eight days) The school supplies the formula cars.

Small Boat Shop (Kayak Instruction)

144 Water Street (in Rex Marine), Norwalk, CT 203.854.5223
www.TheSmallBoatShop.com
They carry sea and recreational kayaks, canoes, dinghies, row boats, rowing shells, small sailboats and paddle boats. Their services include tours, instruction, rentals, small boat storage and repair.
Hours: Monday - Saturday, 10 am - 5 pm; Sunday, 10 am - 3 pm.

Smith & Wesson Academy

299 Page Boulevard, Springfield MA, 413.846.6400, 800.331.0852
www.SmithWesson.com
20 shooting lanes open to the public. Private lessons and a number of handgun courses such as defensive shooting and handgun techniques.
Hours: weekdays, 10 am - 9 pm, Saturday 10 am - 6 pm,
Sunday Noon - 5 pm.

Soaring Adventures of America

Wilton CT, 800.762.7464, 203.762.9583
www.800Soaring.com
Hot Air Balloons, Soaring and Skydiving. Call them to arrange for a fun adventure for you or your family.

Sound Cyclists (bicycle)

PO Box 1144, Darien CT
www.SoundCyclists.com
This social cycling club offers, at no cost, rides for all levels of ability led by experienced cyclists. Routes are along scenic coast lines and country roads and vary from 12 miles to 60+ miles. To join contact them by email through their website.

SPORTS

Sound Environmental Associates (boating)

800.510.9995 www.SeaDolphin.com

One day Safe Boating and PWC Jet Ski courses to meet Connecticut requirements. Courses are held around the state and are usually held Saturday or Sunday 9 am - 5 pm.

Sound Fishing Charters

Byram Dock, Capt. Kevin Reynolds, 203.255.4522

www.SnowGoose2.com

Starting in April, they sail 7 days a week. Join a group or rent the boat for a private party.

Sound Sailing Center

54A calf Pasture Beach Road, Norwalk CT, 203.838.1110

After hours, call 203.454.4394

www.SoundSailingCenter.com

US Sailing Certified Instruction as well as sailboat rentals & charters on 23 foot - 44 foot sailboats. Selected to manage the Old Greenwich Yacht Club sailing program, SSC focuses on adult education at its Norwalk Harbor facility.

Sound Shore Tennis

303 Post Road, Port Chester, NY, 914.939.1300

Twelve indoor hard surface courts. Open September to May and rain-only weekends after May. They can give lessons in Japanese.

Sparky Charters (fishing)

Riverscape Marina on the Mianus, Cos Cob

Captain Hank Weis, 914.747.5825

You can't go wrong with him guiding you in his 28-foot boat "Sparky."

Sports Car Driving Association (auto racing)

18 Maple Avenue, Essex, Connecticut, 860.767.1906

www.SCDA1.com

SCDA provides drivers of all skills the opportunity to experience high performance driving. Events are strictly educational and non-competitive.

SPORTS

Sportsman's Den (Fishing)

33 River Road, Cos Cob, 203.869.3234

Supplies and classes on angling and fly fishing. One visit and you will be hooked. Get your fishing license here. They also carry heritage kayaks and kayaking accessories.

Hours: weekdays 9 am - 5 pm (Monday until 2 pm), Saturday 9 am - 5 pm, Sunday 9 am - 2 pm.

Sports Center of Connecticut

784 River Road (Route 110) Shelton CT, 203.929.6500

About 50 minutes north of Greenwich, they have a Golf Driving Range, 18 Hole Mini-Golf course, Jungle themed Lazer Tag arena, Bowling, Game Zone arcade, Baseball/Softball Batting Cages.

Stamford Indoor Tennis Club

23 Radio Place, Stamford, CT 203.359.0601

www.StamfordTennisClub.com

6 courts and excellent instruction. On most Friday nights from 8 pm, Hank Silverston (203.324.3397) runs a terrific late night doubles party for players who love the sport.

Stamford Kayak Group

www.Meetup.com/StamfordKayakGroup

The Stamford Kayak Group is a local group of paddling enthusiasts looking to meet up with others who share the same interest. This group is for people of all skill levels. They meet in the Stamford, Greenwich, Rowayton areas. They were founded in 2007 and have over 500 members. Email them through the website to join.

Sterling Farms (golf)

1349 Newfield Avenue, Stamford, 203. 461.9090

www.SterlingFarmsGC.com

Par 72; On weekends, non-residents can play after 2:30 pm. You can reserve up to seven days in advance.

Sterling Farms Tennis Center

1349 Newfield Avenue, Stamford, CT 461.8329

www.SterlingFarmsGC.com

Located on the grounds of Sterling Farms Golf Course, the tennis facility has 6 outdoor courts. Spring Session Begins May 1st; Summer Session Begins June 26th; Junior Camp Begins June 12th.

Stowe Mountain Resort (Ski)

5781 Mountain Road, Stowe VT, 802.253.3000, 800.253.4754
www.Stowe.com
The premier ski mountain on the East Coast. Every activity from Dog
Sledding to a wellness center. Like all of the major ski resorts they also
have a variety of summer programs, such as: horseback riding, hiking,
tennis, inflatable obstacle course and alpine slides.

Stratford Stables (riding)

120 Cottage Avenue, Purchase NY, 914.939.9294
www.StratfordStables.net
Seven acre boarding and training facility, which includes an 80' X 200'
indoor arena. Lessons for beginners through advanced ages 6 and up,
with a specialty in training for show.

Stratton Mountain Resort (ski & golf)

Stratton Mountain (South Londonderry), VT
802.297.4000, 800.787.2886 www.Stratton.com
Stratton is another major ski destination. During the summer it is the
home of the David Leadbetter Golf Academy.

Stamford Twin Rinks (ice skating and ice hockey)

1063 Hope Street, Stamford 203.968.9000
www.StamfordTwinRinks.com
They have a wide variety of programs for all level and interests

State Forest Camping Areas
(camping, trap shooting, fishing & hunting)

Campsites are usually available May - September.
www.dep.state.ct.us/stateparks/camping
www.ct.gov/dep/cwp/view.asp?a=2716&q=325034&depNav_GID=1621
There are 11 Connecticut State Park camping areas and 2 State Forest
camping areas. The State Forests also have equestrian camp grounds.

Sugarloaf (Skiing)

Carrabassett Valley, Maine   www.Sugarloaf.com
Sugarloaf is the only above-the-timberline ski area in the East. Sugarloaf
has excellent beginner and intermediate trails as well as a Nordic ski
area and even double black diamond trails for the adventurous. Sugarloaf
has 1,400 skiable acres and 138 trails. Like Mont Tremblant it usually
has great snow, but can be very cold. Sugarloaf is about 7-hours from
Greenwich.

SPORTS

Tiger Schulmann's (karate)

2333 Summer Street, Stamford, 203.969.0352
www.tsk.com
The largest Mixed Martial Arts training school in the United States, with over 45 schools in five states. They teach self-defense skills combining karate, Thai kickboxing and submission grappling.

Trout Unlimited, Mianus Chapter (fishing)

Dick O'Neill, President, 203.438.5918
Mike Law, Vice President, 203.966.3364
Mianus TU, P.O. Box 475, Wilton CT, 06897
www.MianusTU.org
Non-profit organization dedicated to preserving water quality. The Mianus Chapter has over 500 members living in the Greenwich, Stamford, Darien, Norwalk, New Canaan, Ridgefield and Wilton communities. Classes in fly fishing and fly tying.

United States Tennis Association

70 West Red Oak Lane, White Plains NY, 914.696.7000
www.USTA.com
National governing body for the sport of tennis. Join and play in a league.

US Academy of Gymnastics

6 Riverside Avenue, Riverside, 203.637.3303
www.TumbleBugsCT.com
Tumble Bugs and Snuggle Bugs for children 18 months to 5 years. Serious gymnastics training for children from 1st grade through high school. They also host great birthday parties.

Vails Grove Golf Course

PO Box 417, Peach Lake, Brewster, NY, 845.669.5721
Par 66 (9-hole, doubletee).
On weekends, non-members can play after 1 pm.

Westchester Flying Club (flying)

Westchester Count Airport
Vice President, Ron Weinstein, 914.909.0546 www.wfc-hpn.org
Westchester Flying Club provides economical flying for its members.

SPORTS

Westchester Golf Range

701 Dobbs Ferry Road, White Plains, NY, 914.592.6553
www.ewgawestchester.com
Seventy-five lighted tees. PGA teaching professionals conduct individual lessons and instruction programs.
Summer hours: open every day 8:30 am - 9 pm.

Westchester Squash

628 Fayette Avenue, Mamaroneck NY 914.698.0095
www.westchestersquash.com
They have four international squash courts with programs for adults and juniors.

Western Greenwich Civic Center

a.k.a. Bendheim Greenwich Civic Center Director: Frank Gabriele
449 Pemberwick Road, Glenville, 203.532.1259
www.greenwichct.org/ParksAndRec/prFacilityPrograms.asp
The Center has programs for a variety of activities such as weight lifting, fitness and exercise, roller skating, basketball, indoor soccer, youth and adult ballet, indoor field hockey, fencing (See Greenwich Fencing), Tennis for tots, kendo, guitar lessons, theater and dance classes, karate classes, coed volley ball, little language league, chess club, boot camp and sports clinics for children. They are also the site of a child care / children's day school.
Hours: weekdays, 7:30 am - 9:30 pm, Saturdays 8:30 am - 8:30 pm, Sunday 9 am - 6 pm.

Whiteface Mountain
(skiing, skating, bobsled, cross country, jumping)

Lake Placid, Route 86, Wilmington NY , 518.946.2223
www.Whiteface.com
Site of the 1980 Winter Olympics, besides great skiing, the Olympic Sports Complex has bobsledding, cross country, ski jumping and skating. The Olympic Center runs a variety of programs for figure skaters training for regional, national and international competitions. For more information on training here, please visit www.lakeplacidskating.com

White Tiger Tae Kwon Do (karate)

181 Greenwich Avenue (second Floor), 203.661.6054
www.WTTKD.com
Master Kwan Ji, 5th Degree Black Belt.

Windham Mountain

Windham NY, 518.734.4300, 800.754.9463
The snow report hotline, 800.729.4766
www.SkiWindham.com
Difficulty: Beginner, Intermediate & Expert.
Size: 33 trails, 7 lifts, snowmaking. Distance: 2.5 hrs

Winding Trails Cross Country Ski Center

50 Winding Trails Drive, Farmington, CT, 860.674.4227
www.WindingTrails.com
Difficulty: Beginner, Intermediate.
Size: 20 Kilometers of trails in 350 acres of woodland, lakes and wildlife. Distance: 2.5 hrs.

Windy Hill Figure Skating Club (ice skating)

Linda Myder, Membership Chair, 203.531.7774
www.WindyhillSC.com
Non-profit skating club affiliated with the US Figure Skating Association. Membership is open to all figure skaters who have progressed beyond "Basic 6". Home ice is the Dorothy Hamill Rink.

Wings of Eagles Soaring School

Elmira Airport, 17 Aviation Drive, Horseheads NY, 607.739.4202
www.WingsOfEagles.com
This glider school is about four hours away. Courses are available for beginners. The training is in classic Schweizer sailplanes. www.sacusa.com See K & L Soaring above for the training manual.

Wire Mill Racquet Club

578 Wire Mill Road, Stamford, 203.329.9221
www.LeonTennis.net
Just off exit 35 of the Merritt Parkway, Wire Mill (four outdoor red clay courts) is owned by the pros who teach in the winter at the Greenwich Racquet Club. Excellent junior and adult programs. Season is May to September. There is no membership fee.

Yachting Magazine

www.yachtingmagazine.com
Published in Norwalk, this is the magazine for sailors. Subscribe from the website.

YMCA (a.k.a. Greenwich Family Y)

50 East Putnam Avenue, 203.869.1630

Rebecca B. Fretty, President & Chief Executive Officer

www.gwymca.org, www.greenwichymca.org

The Y is open to men and women. You should consider joining, but you don't have to be a member to use their facilities. The Y spent $6,000,000 to build an Olympic size pool. As you might expect they have some terrific swimming programs, such as: Skippers (for parents and babies 6 months to 2 years), Perch for ages 2 - 3 (Children, with help of a parent, propel themselves using flotation aids) Progressive youth lessons (for ages 5-12), Polliwog, Guppy, Minnow, Fish, Flying Fish, Shark, water polo, and water aerobics. The YMCA is the home of the Marlins youth swim and diving teams, ages 6-18. The Y has an impressive weight room and they provide programs for a variety of activities such as aerobics, studio cycling (spinning), basketball and yoga, Pilates, Zumba, indoor tennis (provided by Park Tennis), Cardio Dance, Boot Camp and many others. The Y has sessions for boys & girls, ages 4 - 8 to learn the fundamentals of baseball, as well as clinics for children in grades 1 - 5. The Y provides clinics in basketball for children in grades 1 - 5. They also sponsor A and B levels and an Adult Summer Outdoor Basketball League for ages 19 and up. There is a flag football league and informal, co-ed volleyball games for adults. Experienced babysitters are usually available to watch children while you work out.

Hours: weekdays, 5 am - 10 pm, Saturday 6:30 am - 7pm,

Sunday 8 am - 5 pm.

Pool area closes 30 minutes prior to closing. Members must exit the building by closing time.

YMCA Gymnastic Programs

50 East Putnam Avenue, 203.869.1630

www.GWYMCA.org

  Baby Power 12 to 24 months.
  Toddler Gym 24 to 36 months.
  Rockers 3 to 4 years.
  Rollers 4 and 5 years.
  Beginner 6 to 11 years.
  Intermediate 6 to 11years.

Youth Football Cheerleaders (cheerleaders)

www.gyfl.net

Banc Raiders, Cos Cob Crushers, Glenville Mavericks, North Mianus Bulldogs, Old Greenwich Putnam Generals and the Riverside Gators.

Each team has a cheerleading squad for grades 3-8.

YWCA

259 East Putnam Avenue, Greenwich, 203.869.6501
Adrianne Singer, President and CEO
www.YWCAGreenwich.org

The Y provides supervised round robin youth badminton for all skill levels March through November and hosts tournaments sanctioned by the USA Badminton Association. The Y has a good indoor pool and many swimming programs, such as Aqua Babies for parents and babies 6 months to 3 years, Aqua Tots/Kids for ages 2 to 4 years who are ready to participate without the parent, Junior Aquatics K to 12 years and progressive learn to swim lessons. The YWCA is the home of the Dolphins swim team, a major competitor of the YMCA's swim team. In addition the Y hosts a great variety of programs, including bridge lessons from beginner to advanced, tournament bridge, zumba, youth & adult ballet, Boutelle Method fitness classes, belly dancing, mat pilates, spinning, climbing wall, basketball clinics, soccer, gymnastics, SCUBA certification, tennis, weight room, personal training, yoga and tai chi and many more classes. Experienced babysitters are available to watch children while you work out. Badminton is usually Monday, Thursday and Friday nights starting in March.

Hours: weekdays 6 am - 10 pm, Saturday 9 am - 5 pm.

YWCA Gymnastic Programs

259 East Putnam Avenue, 203.869.6501
www.YWCAGreenwich.org

Jelly Beans ages 16 - 36 months.
Tumble Tots ages 2 - 3 years.
Pre-Gymnastics ages 5 - 6 years.
Gymnastics ages 7 - 8 and 9 - 12.
Advanced Gymnastics instructor placement only.

Zombi Kite (kite boarding)

203.570.0582 www.zombikite.com

Joe Garan, a sailing instructor at the Old Greenwich Community Center, teaches Kite boarding in the Long Island Sound from Greenwich Point. You can get equipment from the e-store on his website.

STORES

Store Hours: Stores change their hours frequently, the hours given should only be used as a guide. Stores often move in and out of town, not surprising with rents running $85 to $150 a square foot. At these prices it's hard for local stores to survive unless it is supported by town residents. Shopping at these stores keeps our cherished stores in business.

Food Stores: Grocery stores, delicatessens, bakeries, ice cream, fruit & vegetables, butchers, seafood, spices, wine shops, chocolates, sweets and ethnic food markets are listed under FOOD & BEVERAGES.
Health Products: Pharmacies, vitamins, exercise equipment, health products and services are reviewed under the section HEALTH
Delicatessens are reviewed under FOOD.
Pet Services are reviewed under the section PETS
Video Rentals are Reviewed in the section CULTURE, under Movies: Video & DVD
Spas are reviewed in the section GROOMING
Accessories for Men & Women are listed under Shoes & Accessories.
Appliances are listed under Appliances and Cookware
Linens are listed under Bedding

TIP: BABY STORES ON CENTRAL PARK AVENUE

It's worth the drive to visit these baby stores which you will find along both sides of the street. Central Park Avenue is approximately 20 minutes away in Scarsdale, NY (Westchester County). You'll find everything you need for your children. Bring a lot of energy–it's going to be an exhausting day!
Directions: I-95 S to 287 W to exit 4 (RT-100A), L off Ramp towards Hartsdale. At 3rd main intersection R on Central Park Avenue.

STORE INDEX

by category

Antiques
A Woodhouse & Son
Antique Area of Stamford
   Antique and Artisan Center
   Connecticut Antiques Center
   Greenwich Living Antiques
   Hamptons Antique Galleries
   Harbor View Center for Antiques
   Hiden Galleries
   John Street Antiques
Braswell Galleries
   (antiques & auctions)
Greenwich Oriental Art
Hansen & Hansen
Mark's on Putnam
Rue Faubourg St. Honore
United House Wrecking
Vallin
Vintage Galleries
   (antiques & auctions)
Wyle Antiques

Aquariums
Aquariums are listed under Fish

Appliances, Cookware and Kitchen Equipment
Bath and Kitchen fixtures are listed under Fixtures
Aitorio Appliances
Bed Bath & Beyond
Cook and Craft
Crate & Barrel
Globe Kitchen Equipment
Harris Restaurant Supply
(Greenwich) Kitchen Works
P C Richards
Reo Appliances
Vinci's Home Products (Miele)
Williams-Sonoma

Art (Galleries, Supplies, Framing)
Aby M Taylor
Bendheim Gallery
Cavalier Galleries
Flinn Gallery
(A.I.) Friedman
J Pocker & Son
Michaels
Miranda Arts
Quester Gallery
Silvermine Guild Art Center
Weber Fine Art
Zorya

Auto Part Stores
Automobile and Motorcycle Dealers are listed under the section AUTOMOBILES
Advance Auto Parts
Auto Zone
Delta Auto Parts / Car Quest

Awnings
Modern Shade and Awning

STORE INDEX

by category

Babies/Toddlers (Clothing, Furniture, Equipment for Babies and Toddlers)
Maternity Clothing is listed under Clothing - Women
Anna Banana
Babies "R" Us
Baby CZ
Bellini Juvenile Designer Furniture
Buy Buy Baby
Carters
Gap Kids
Giggle
Jacadi
Janie and Jack
Maclaren Showroom

Bathroom
Tile is listed under Flooring
Bath and Kitchen fixtures are listed under Fixtures

Bedding (Mattresses and Linens)
Bed Bath & Beyond
Duxiana Beds
Home Boutique of Greenwich
Linen Press
Lynnens
Norwalk Mattress Company
Sleepy's

Bicycles
Cycle Dynamics & BikeEx
Dave's Cycle and Fitness
Greenwich Bicycles
Signature Cycles

Blinds
Draperies, Curtains, Blinds, Fabric are listed under Windows

Boating
See SPORTS for boating instruction and information
Beacon Point Marine
Landfall Navigation
Rex Marine Center
Small Boat Shop

Book Stores
See BOOKS and LIBRARIES for donations, stores and book sales.. These book stores are listed there:
> *Barnes & Noble*
> *Borders*
> *Diane's Books*
> *Gift Shop at Christ Church*
> *Just Books*

Cameras
See Photography

Carpets
See Flooring

Cell Phones
See Wireless

Children
Baby & Toddler Clothing, Furniture, Equipment are listed in this section under Babies
Children's furniture listed under Furniture
Toys and outdoor play items are listed under Toys
Clothing & Shoes for Children and Youth are listed under Clothing- Children
Children's Dancewear is listed under Dancewear

STORE INDEX
by category

Clothing - Men

Shoes & Accessories and Department Stores are listed separately
See SERVICES for tailors
Banana Republic
Brooks Brothers
Coppola Tailors
Darien Sport Shop
Gap
J Crew
JoS A Bank
Lacoste Boutique
Land's End
Lucky Jeans
Ralph Lauren
Richard's of Greenwich
Rugby by Ralph Lauren
Scoop
Syms
Vineyard Vines

Clothing - Women

Including maternity clothing
See SERVICES for tailors
Shoes & Accessories and Department Stores are listed separately
Lingerie is listed separately
Women's Sporting wear is listed under Sporting Goods
Women's Exercise wear is below
Albe Furs & Outerwear
Alice + Olivia
Ann Taylor
Ann Taylor LOFT
Anne Fontaine
Anthropologie
Banana Republic
BCBG Max Azria
Beach Box
Brooks Brothers
Carlisle / Per Se

Cashmere Inc
Christopher Fischer
Cochni
Courage.b
Darien Sport Shop
Dighton Rhode
Elsebe
Fred
Free People
Gabby
Gap
Great Stuff
Greenwich Furs
Helen Ainson
Irresistibles
J Crew
J McLaughlin
Kriti Collection
Lacoste Boutique
Land's End
LF
Lilly Pulitzer
Lucky Jeans
Madewell
Magashchoni
Michael Kors
Mommy Chic (maternity)
Mothers and Daughters
Olivine Gabbro
Out of the Box
Pastiche
Ralph Lauren
Reflection
Richard's of Greenwich
Rugby by Ralph Lauren
Scoop
(the) Side Door
Sophia's Great Dames
Sound Beach Sportswear
Steilmann
Syms

STORE INDEX
by category

Clothing - Women continued...

Tahiti Street (beach wear)
Talbots
theory
Tory Burch
Vineyard Vines
Zara

Clothing - Women's Exercise Clothing

bodd
Lucy
lululemon athletica

Clothing (Children and Youth)

Danceware is listed separately
Sportswear, including athletic shoes, is listed under Sporting Goods
Baby and Toddler Clothing are listed under Baby
Equestrian wear is listed under Riding
Scouting and Team Uniforms are listed separately

Anna Banana
Baby CZ
Candy Nichols
Carters
Children's Cottage
Claire's
Darien Sport Shop
Gap
Gap Kids
J Crew
Janie and Jack
Lacoste Boutique
Lilly Pulitzer
Sound Beach Sportswearh
Stuf
Syms
Vineyard Vines
Wishlist

Christmas Shops

Christmas Tree Shops
(the) Historical Christmas Barn

Cookware

Cookware is listed in this section under Appliances and Cookware

STORE INDEX

by category

Consignment/Resale (Furniture, Silver, Jewelry & Clothing)

Thrift Shops are listed separately under Thrift

Children's Cottage
Consign It
Consigned Couture
Consigned Design
Drapery Exchange
Estate Treasures of Greenwich
Mint
Roundabout
Second Time Around
Silk Purse
United House Wrecking

Construction
See Hardware

Cosmetics
L'Occitane
Sephora
Whole Body @ Whole Foods

Curtains
See Fabric

Dancewear
Beam & Barre

Department Stores

Discount stores and Outlets are listed under Outlets

Bloomingdale's
Burlington Coat Factory
Costco
Kmart
Kohl's
Lord and Taylor
Macy's
Marshalls
Neiman Marcus
Nordstrom
Old Navy
Saks Fifth Avenue
Sears
Target
T J Maxx
Wal-Mart

Discount and Off Price Stores

Discount, off price stores and Outlets are listed under Outlets

Doors (including Garage Doors)

See Hardware for Decorative Hardware

Ed's Garage Doors
Sliding Door Company
Interstate / Lakeland Lumber
Ring's End Lumber
Greenwich Lock and Door
(Charles) Stuttig Locksmith

Draperies

Draperies, Curtains, Fabric are listed under Fabric

472

STORE INDEX

by category

Electronics (Audio/Visual, Computer)

Cell Phones Stores are listed under Wireless, Land Phones are under Telephones

Apple Store
Audiocom
Bang & Olufsen
Best Buy
Computer Super Center
Cos Cob TV
Costco
P C Richards
Radio Shack
Wal-Mart

Eyeglasses

Doctors of Optometry (O.D.) hold a degree from a college of optometry. Optometrists are considered the general practitioners of eye healthcare who prescribe eyeglasses and contact lenses to correct nearsightedness, farsightedness and astigmatism. Opticians make the lenses. Ophthalmologists are medical doctors (M.D.) or Doctors of Ophthalmology (D.O.). who have completed medical school, and additional years of post-graduate training in ophthalmology.

20/20 Optical
20/20 Kids
Copeland Optometrists
LensCrafters
Optical Options
Optyx
Pearle Vision
Sunglass Hut
Trapp Optical
Vision Consultants

Fabric (Draperies, Curtains, Upholstery)

Blinds & shutters listed under Windows

(the) Barn
Curtain Works of Greenwich
Decorators Secret
Drapery Exchange
HB Home
Home Works
Weathervane Hill

Firearms

For instruction see SPORTS

Forest and Field Outdoor
Griffin & Howe
Hansen & Hansen

Fish & Aquariums

(Greenwich) Aquaria
House of Fins

Fixtures (Bathroom and Kitchen)

Best Plumbing
Klaff's
Mr. Shower Door
Porcelanosa
Waterworks

STORE INDEX

by category

Flooring (Carpets, Rugs, Tiles, Wood)

See installers listed in SERVICES
ABC Carpet Warehouse Outlet
Ann Sacks Tile and Stone
Apadana
AT Proudian
Ceramic Design
Exquisite Surfaces
Floor Covering Warehouse
Golden Horn
Greenwich Floor Covering
Klaff's
Riverside Floor Covering
Rye Ridge Tile
Safavieh
Stark Carpet Outlet

Florists (including Flower Shops, Nurseries & Garden Accessories)

Colony Florist
Cos Cob Farms
Flowers by George
Greenwich Hospital Gift Shop
Greenwich Orchids
Kenneth Lynch & Sons
Loretta Stagen Floral Designs
Mark Mariani's Garden Center
McArdle-MacMillen Florist &
    Garden Center
Sam Bridge Nursery & Greenhouses
Shanti Bithi Bonsai Nursery
Tulips Greenwich

Food

Food stores (such as bakeries, fish, vegetables, cheese, wine, grocery stores) are reviewed in - FOOD

Framing

Framing is listed under Art

Furniture (Indoor and outdoor)

See Office for Office Furniture
See Antiques for Antique Furniture
See Toys for Children's play sets
Baker Furniture
Bellini Juvenile Designer Furniture
Classic Sofa
Consign It
Crate & Barrel
Design Within Reach
Estate Treasures of Greenwich
Ethan Allen
Federalist
Go To Your Room
HB Home
Housewarmings
IKEA
Kids Home Furniture
Lillian August
Mis En Scene
Mitchell Gold + Bob Williams
Oriental Furniture Warehouse
Patio.com (outdoor)
Patti's Portico (outdoor)
Pierre Deux
Pottery Barn
Relax the Back
Restoration Hardware
Rinfret Home and Garden
Safavieh
Stickley
Trovare Home
Walpole Woodworkers (outdoor)

STORE INDEX

by category

Garden

Nurseries, plants and garden accessories are listed under Florists

Gift Shops
(Dishes & Crystal)

06830 Gifts
Baccarat
Bed Bath & Beyond
CM Almy (religious gifts)
(the) Connecticut Store
Gift Shop at Audubon Center
Gift Shop at Bruce Museum
Gift Shop at Christ Church
Gift Shop at Greenwich Hospital
Gift Shop at Hyatt Regency
Greenwich Exchange for Women's Work
Hoagland's of Greenwich
Juliska
Kate's Paperie
Michelangelo of Greenwich
Privet House
Quelques Choses
Splurge
Tiffany & Co
Toc Toc

Glasses

See Eyeglasses

Golf

Golf courses are listed under the section SPORTS - Golf
Golf equipment is listed under Sporting Goods

Guns

See Firearms

Hardware (decorative & fireplace hardware, contractor & construction supplies)

Ben Romeo
Do it Best Hardware
Feinsod
Grainger
Greenwich Hardware
Greenwich Lock and Door
Home Depot
Interstate Fire and Safety
    (fire extinguishers)
Interstate / Lakeland Lumber
Klaff's (decorative hardware)
Mr. Mail Box
(the) Nanz Company
    (decorative hardware)
Nordic Stove and Fireplace Center
    (fireplace hardware)
Post Road Iron Works
    (fireplace hardware)
Restoration Hardware
    (decorative hardware)
Ring's End Lumber
Rue Faubourg St. Honore
    (decorative hardware)
(Charles) Stuttig Locksmith
Super Handy Hardware

Health - (Equipment, Furniture & Products)

Pharmacies, vitamins, exercise equipment, glasses, hearing aids, physical therapy and medical equipment are reviewed in a the separate section - HEALTH
Spas are reviewed in the separate section - GROOMING

STORE INDEX

by category

Home Accessories

Accessory Store
Bed Bath & Beyond
Peacock & Beale
(the) Container Store
Crate & Barrel
Ethan Allen
Evelyn Artificial Flowers
Federalist
HB Home
Hoagland's of Greenwich
Home Goods
Housewarmings
Mill Street Home
Mis En Scene
Pier 1 Imports
Pierre Deux
Pottery Barn
Privet House
Restoration Hardware
Rinfret Home and Garden
Simon Pearce
United House Wrecking

Home Needs

See Lighting and Accessories
See Appliances and Cookware
See Paint and Wall Paper
Antique Furniture and accessories are listed separately under Antiques Furniture
Floor covering including wood, rugs, carpets and tile are listed under Flooring
Mattresses and Linens are listed under Bedding
Draperies, Curtains, Fabric are listed under Fabric
Blinds, Shades, Shutters, Replacement Windows are listed under Windows
Window and Door hardware are listed under Hardware
Door replacements are listed under Doors
Bathroom and Kitchen Fixtures are listed under Fixtures
Hardware is listed under Hardware
See Connecticut Closet in SERVICES

Horseback Riding

For attire and equipment see Riding
For instruction see SPORTS

Hunting

See Firearms

STORE INDEX

by category

Jewelry
A Woodhouse & Son
Alma Workshop
Beads in the Loft
Betteridge Jewelers
Consign It
Estate Treasures of Greenwich
Femmegems
Lux Bond & Green
Manfredi
Penny Weights
Peridot
Steven B. Fox
Tiffany & Co
Viggi

Kitchen
Appliances & Cookware are listed under Appliances
Kitchen and Bath tile are listed under Flooring
Kitchen & Bath Fixtures are listed under Fixtures

Lighting (Lighting, shades and accessories)
Accessory Store
Antan
Fashion Light Center
Klaff's
(the) Light Touch
Remains Lighting
Restoration Hardware
Rue Faubourg St. Honore

Linens
Linens are listed under Bedding

Lingerie
Patricia Gourlay
Petticoat Lane
Victoria's Secret

Luggage
Innovation Luggage
Tumi

Magazines & Newspapers
Avenue News
East Putnam Variety
Ronnie's News
Zyns News

Malls
See Shopping Center or Outlets

Music (instruments)
Atelier Constantin Popescu
Greenwich Music
(the) Music Source
Steinway Piano Gallery

Office (Furniture, Supplies, Service & Equipment)
Stamford Office Furniture
Staples
SWC Furniture Outlet

STORE INDEX
by category

Outlets, Discount, Off-Price Stores
ABC Carpet Warehouse Outlet
(the) Barn
Burlington Coat Factory
Carters
Clinton Crossing Outlet Mall
Costco
Decorators Secret
Direct Buy of Fairfield County
J McLaughlin Outlet Store
Jones New York discount store
Liberty Village Outlet Mall
Lillian August Outlet Store
Lynnens Too
Stark Carpet Outlet
Syms (off price)
Tanger Outlet Center
T J Maxx (off price)
Wal-Mart
Woodbury Commons Outlet Mall

Paint and Wallpaper
Farrow & Ball
McDermott Paint & Wallpaper

Party Goods
*See separate section on ENTERTAIN-
ING services including Caterers*
East Putnam Variety
Packages PlusNMore
Party City
Party Paper and Things
Strauss Warehouse Outlet

Pets
*Services and information are listed
in the separate section PETS*
(the) Canine Corner
Choice Pet Supply
Pet Pantry

Pharmacies
*Pharmacies are listed in the sepa-
rate section HEALTH*

Phones
See Telephones or Wireless

Picture Framing
*Picture Framing is listed in this sec-
tion under Art*

Photography
*PHOTOGRAPHERS are in a separate
section*
*Framing is listed in this section un-
der Art*
Camera Wholesalers
Images
Ritz Camera

Resale
*Resale shops are listed under Con-
signment*

Riding (Equestrian wear and equipment)
*For instruction see separate section
in SPORTS*
Beval Saddlery
Children's Cottage

Rugs
Rugs are listed under Flooring

STORE INDEX

by category

Scout Uniforms
Darien Sport Shop

Sewing
Including Knitting & Needlework
Nimble Thimble
Village Ewe

Shooting
See Firearms

Shopping Centers
Outlets are listed under Outlets and Discount Stores
Galleria
Ridgeway Shopping Center
Stamford Town Center
(the) Westchester Mall

Shoes, Handbags & Accessories - Men & Women & Children
Athletic Shoes are listed under Sporting Goods
Anne Klein
Coach
Cochni
DWS
Ella Vickers
French Sole
HH Brown
In Things
Kate Spade
Little Eric
Petticoat Lane
Plaza Too
Shoes N More

Skis and Skating
Skis and Skating are listed in this section under Sporting Goods

Sporting Goods (Equipment, Shoes & Clothing)
Boating is listed in this section under Boating
Bicycles are listed in this section under Bicycles
All Sports Apparel
Athlete's Foot
Bedford Sportsman
Bodd
Bruce Park Sports
Chilly Bear
Compleat Angler
Custom Golf of Connecticut
Darien Golf Center
De Mane's Golf
Eastern Mountain Sports
EuroChasse
Greenwich Golf Fitting Studio
Hickory & Tweed
Instant Replay
Lacrosse Unlimited
Lucy
lululemon athletica
Modell's
(Greenwich) Running Company
Orvis
Outdoor Traders
Recreation Equipment
Rex Dive Center
Rink and Racquet
Rudy's Tackle & Archery
Skaters Landing
(the) Ski & Scuba Connection
Soccer and Rugby
Sportman's Den
Tahiti Street
Treads and Threads
Utopia

STORE INDEX

by category

Stationery, Invitations & Greeting Cards
j papers
Kate's Paperie
Letter Perfect
Packages PlusNMore
Papyrus
Saint Clair

Team Uniforms
Bruce Park Sports
Lacrosse Unlimited
Rink and Racquet

Telephones (land lines)
See also Wireless
Radio Shack
Staples

Tennis
Tennis Equipment and Clothing is listed under Sporting Goods
Tennis Instruction is in the separate section SPORTS

Thrift
See the separate section THRIFT SHOPS

Tile
Kitchen and Bath tile are listed under Flooring
Tile masons are in SERVICES

Toys (including children's playhouses & outdoor play equipment)
Amish Land (playhouses)
Creative Playthings
Educational Warehouse
(the) Funhouse
Graham's Toys
(the) Great Outdoor Toy Company
Hobby Center
Smart Kids Company
Toys "R" Us
Wal-Mart
Walpole Woodworkers (outdoor)
Whimsies Doll House & Miniature Shop
Patio.com
(pool & ping pong tables)

Uniforms
Scout Uniforms are listed separately
Team Uniforms are listed separately

Wallpaper
See Paint and Wallpaper

STORE INDEX

by category

Windows (Blinds, Shades, Shutters, Replacement Windows)

See Fabric for upholstery & window draperies and curtains)
See Hardware for decorative hardware
Blinds To Go
Interstate / Lakeland Lumber
JSJ Window Treatments
Modern Shade and Awning
Ring's End Lumber

Wireless

A T & T Mobility
Paging Concepts
Radio Shack
Sprint Nextel
T-Mobile
Verizon Wireless
Wireless One Communications (Verizon)

TIP: LOCAL GOVERNMENT IN ACTION

The best way to understand how our town can be run so efficiently by the largest legislature in Connecticut (The RTM or Representative Town Meeting) is to attend some of their meetings. Meetings are open to the public and are held in the beginning of most months at the Central Middle School auditorium. Ask the Town Clerk (203.622.7700) for a schedule of their meetings and for an agenda, "The Call," or find it on the website at: www.greenwichct.org/rtm.
Guests always sit in the last rows.

STORE INDEX

by neighborhood

Armonk, NY
Hickory & Tweed

Bedford Hills, NY
Bedford Sportsman
Mark Mariani Garden Center

Bridgeport, CT
(The) Barn
Globe Kitchen Equipment

Bronx, NY
ABC Carpet Warehouse Outlet

Byram
De Mane's Golf Inc.
Go To Your Room
Greenwich Golf Fitting Studio
Mill Street Home
Mint
Rudy's Tackle & Archery
Side Door
Skaters Landing
Ski & Scuba Connection
Stuff

Clinton, CT
Clinton Crossing Premium Outlets
Tangier Outlet Center
   (Westbrook, CT)

Cos Cob
06830 Gifts
Apadana
Atelier Constantine
Beacon Point Marine
Cos Cob Farms
Cos Cob TV
Dave's Cycle and Fitness
Do it Best Hardware
Flowers By George
Hobby Center
Jos A Bank
JSJ Window Treatments
Packages PlusNMore
Party Paper & Things
Patio.com
Radio Shack
Sportsman's Den
Trouvare Home

Danbury
Amishland

Darien, CT
Compleat Angler
Drapery Exchange
Darien Golf Center
Darien Sport Shop
Helen Ainson
Orvis
Ring's End Lumber

Elizabeth, NJ
IKEA

Elmsford, NY
Oriental Furniture Warehouse
Syms

Flemington, NJ
Liberty Village

STORE INDEX

by neighborhood

STORE INDEX
by neighborhood

STORE INDEX
by neighborhood

STORE INDEX

by neighborhood

Norwalk, CT
Aitorio
Best Buy
Blinds To Go
Braswell Gallery
Direct Buy
Ed's Garage Doors
Educational Warehouse
Forest & Field Outdoor
Home Depot
J. McLaughlin Outlet
Jones NY Factory Store
Klaff's
Lillian August Flagship Store
Lillian August Home Outlet Store
Maclaren Showroom
Mr. Mail Box
Mr. Shower Door
Norwalk Mattress Company
Oriental Furniture Warehouse
PC Richards
Pier I Imports
Recreation Equipment
Reo Appliances
Rex Dive Center
Rex Marine Center
Small Boat Shop
Stark Carpet Outlet
TJ Maxx
Toys "R" Us
Utopia
WalMart
Weather Vane Fabrics

Old Greenwich
20/20 Optical & Kids
All Sports Apparel
Anna Banana
CM Almy
Canine Corner
Chili Bear
Cook & Craft
Fred
Feinsod Hardware
Fun House
Gift Shop at Hyatt Regency
House Warmings
Images
Linen Press
(the) Music Source
Pastiche
Quelques Chose
Sleepy's
Sound Beach Sportswear
Staples
Village Ewe

Orange, CT
Recreation Showroom

Oxford, CT
Kenneth Lynch & Sons

STORE INDEX
by neighborhood

STORE INDEX
by neighborhood

(Stamford, CT continued...)

Hiden Galleries
HomeGoods
Instant Replay
John Street Antiques
Juliska
Kids Home Furniture
Landfall Navigation
Lenscrafters
Lord & Taylor
Macy's
Marshall's
Michael's
Modell's
Nordic Stove & Fireplace Center
Old Navy
Party City
Pearle Vision
Pottery Barn
Ridgeway Shopping Center
Safavieh
Saks Fifth Avenue
Shanti Bithi
Stamford Office Furniture
Stamford Town Center
SWC Furniture Outlet
Target
United House Wrecking
Vintage Galleries
Williams-Sonoma

Waterbury, CT
(The) Connecticut Store

Westbrook, CT
Tangier Outlet Center

Westport, CT
Great Outdoor Toy Company
Steinway Piano Galleries
Walpole Woodworkers

White Plains, NY
Bloomingdale's
Coach
Container Store
Crate & Barrel
Galleria Mall
Kmart
Land's End
Neiman Marcus
Nordstrom
Old Navy
Sears
Stickley Company
Westchester Mall
Williams Sonoma

Wilton, CT
Historical Christmas Barn
Vallin Galleries

Yonkers, NY
Babies "R" Us

STORES

Grocery stores, bakeries, ice cream, fruit & vegetables, butchers, seafood, spices, wine shops, chocolates, sweets and ethnic food markets are listed under FOOD & BEVERAGES.

Pharmacies, vitamins, exercise equipment, health products and services are reviewed under the section HEALTH

Pet Services are listed under the section ANIMALS

Video Rentals are Reviewed in the section CULTURE, under Movies: Video & DVD

Spas are reviewed in the section GROOMING

Delicatessens are reviewed under RESTAURANTS.

THRIFT SHOPS are reviewed in their own section.

Store Hours: Stores change their hours frequently, the hours given should only be used as a guide.

06830 Gifts (Gift Shops)

522 East Putnam Avenue (Indian Field Plaza, Cos Cob)
203.340.2963
www.06830gifts.com
Charming baby gifts and housewarming gifts, many with a Greenwich theme. The shop promotes local products and artists.
Hours: Tuesday - Saturday 10 am - 6 pm.

20/20 Optical
20/20 Kids

15 Arcadia Road, Old Greenwich, 203.698.2255
www.20-20optical.com
The optician has a specialty working with children. Youngsters love to go there to pick out glasses.
Hours: weekdays 9:30 am - 5:30 pm, Saturday 9 am - 5 pm.

AT&T Mobility (Wireless)

42 Greenwich Avenue, 203.629.8008
www.wireless.att.com/cell-phone-service/welcome
The wireless subsidiary of AT&T Inc, with 80 million subscribers. It is the second-largest mobile phone company in the United States, behind Verizon Wireless. It provides GSM and UMTS voice communications.
Hours: weekdays 9am-7pm, Sat 10am-6pm, Sunday 11am-5pm.

STORES

A Woodhouse & Son   (Antiques-Silver & Jewelry)
7 West Putnam Avenue, 203.422.2500
www.AWoodhouse.com
Founded in 1690 in London. This shop specializes in antique jewelry and
sterling silver items such as: tea sets, candle sticks and serving pieces.
Hours: Tuesday - Saturday 10 am - 5 pm.

ABC Carpet Warehouse Outlet
(Home Decorating, Flooring)
1055 Bronx River Avenue (at Bruckner Boulevard), Bronx NY
 718.842.8770
www.ABCHome.com
A wonderland of rugs and carpets. ABC has been selling off-price rugs at
its huge Bronx warehouse for over five years. The company has expanded the space and filled it with bed linens, furniture and accessories.
Bargain hunters can buy ABC's merchandise for 20 to 70 percent off
downtown NYC prices. You can park in a secure parking lot attached to
the building.
Hours: weekdays 10 am - 5:30pm, Saturday 10 am - 7 pm,
Sunday 11 am - 6 pm.

Aby M Taylor (Art)
43 Greenwich Avenue, 203.622.0906
www.AMTFineArt.com
At the top of the Avenue, this gallery focuses on 19th and 20th century
American and European paintings and sculpture by known artists. Prices
range from $4,000 to $500,000.
Hours: weekdays 10 am - 5 pm, Saturday 11 am - 5 pm.

Accessory Store (Lamps & Accessories)
69 Jefferson Street, Stamford CT, 203.327.7128
www.StamfordShades.com
Dealers and decorators use this store and you should, too. They have a
large selection of lamp shades and chandelier parts. They also have
many lamps, display stands and more, all at great prices.
Hours: Monday - Saturday 10:30 am - 5:30 pm, Sunday noon - 5 pm.

Advance Auto Parts
305 West Avenue, Stamford CT, 203.406.0126
www.AdvanceAutoParts.com
With 3,300 stores, Advance is just smaller than AutoZone.
Hours: Monday - Saturday 8 am -9 pm, Sunday 9 am - 8 pm.

STORES

Aitorio Appliances

401 Westport Avenue, Norwalk, CT, 203.847.2471

For Service 203.846.1629.

www.Aitoro.com

Most top brands of kitchen, laundry appliances and BBQs, as well as televisions and home theater electronics. A good website to help you decide before you visit. Be sure to read the store policies on their website before you buy your flat screen TV here.

Hours: weekdays 9 am - 6 pm (Thursday to 8 pm), Saturday 9 am - 5 pm, Sunday 11 am - 5 pm.

Albe Furs & Outerwear (Furs - Women)

1212 E Putnam Avenue, Riverside, 203.637.3883

www.albefurs.com

They have stores in Westport and New Canaan as well as Greenwich. In addition to their attractive designs, they store, clean, restyle, repair and appraise furs.

Hours: Monday - Saturday 10 am - 6 pm, during the winter they may be open Sunday.

Alice + Olivia (Clothing - Women)

371 Greenwich Avenue, 203.826.8540

www.AliceAndOlivia.com

Contemporary women's clothing designed by founder Stacey Bendet. Her designs are worn by many celebrities and are sold in over 800 stores, such as Neiman Marcus. This is one of a few free standing stores.

Hours: Monday - Saturday 10 am - 7 pm, Sunday noon - 6 pm.

All Sports Apparel (Sporting Goods & Clothing)

146 Sound Beach Avenue, Old Greenwich, 203.698.3055

www.AllSportsApparel.com

Apparel for most sports, even yoga. Team licensed products including hats and jerseys. They carry field hockey and lacrosse equipment. Custom embroidery and screen printing.

Hours: weekdays 10 am - 5 pm, Saturday 10 am - 3 pm.

Alma Workshop (Jewelry)

4 Grigg Street, 203.869.0113

Just off Greenwich Avenue, this small workshop has jewelry designed for easy wear and compliments. They can repair silver jewelry.

Hours: Tuesday - Saturday 11 am - 6 pm.

STORES

Amishland (Playhouses)

66 sugar Hollow Road (Rout 7), Danbury CT 203.205.0204
www.AmishlandSheds.com, www.AmishlandofCT.com
Wonderfully detailed children's playhouses as well as attractive sheds.
Don't buy a playhouse until you have been here.
Hours: Open most days 9 am 5 pm.

Ann Sacks Tile & Stone (Bath & Kitchen Tile)

23 East Putnam Avenue, 203.622.8884
www.AnnSacks.com
A showroom filled with pretty tiles - many unique, such as pebble, wood
or concrete. Try the helpful website—they are owned by The Kohler Co.
Hours: weekdays 9 am - 5 pm.

Ann Taylor (Clothing - Women)

100 Greyrock, Stamford Town Center, 203.369.1616;
The Westchester, White Plains NY, 914.644.8380
www.AnnTaylor.com
High-end casual and classic professional clothing plus shoes. Their cloth-
ing is targeted at the more affluent career woman.
Hours: Monday - Saturday, 10 am - 9 pm; Sunday, 11 am - 6 pm.

Ann Taylor LOFT

Stamford Town Center, 203.406.9544
The Loft was established in 1996 as an extension of the original Ann
Taylor brand. It offers more relaxed fashions for work and home, in the
"upper moderate" price category. Although the selection is different from
Ann Taylor stores, the styles at the Loft stores are similar and the prices
lower.
Hours: Monday - Saturday, 10 am - 9 pm; Sunday, 11 am - 6 or 7 pm.

Anna Banana (Clothing-Children)

248 Sound Beach Avenue, Old Greenwich, 203.637.0128
Kathy O'Malley of Hoagland's, has gifted Greenwich with the most cheer-
ful, adorable clothing shop for babies and young children imaginable.
Fashions are by designers such as: Ralph Lauren, Lili Gaufrette, Charlie
Rocket, Hartstrings and E-Land.
Hours: Monday - Saturday 9:30 am - 5:30 pm.

STORES

Anne Fontaine (Clothing - Women)

234 Greenwich Avenue, 203.422.2433

www.AnneFontaine.com

Originally from Paris, with stores on Madison Avenue and in SoHo, this boutique specializes in black and white. You will find an assortment of sophisticated, trendy and top-of-the-line blouses for all occasions.

Hours: Monday - Saturday, 10 am - 6 pm; Sunday, noon - 5 pm.

Anne Klein (Shoes & Accessories-Women)

120 Greenwich Avenue, 203.622.4655

www.AnneKlein.com

Luxury accessories for the well dressed woman, such as handbags, shoes, scarves and glasses.

Hours: Monday - Saturday, 10 am - 6 pm; Sunday, 11 am - 5 pm.

Antan (Lamps & Shades, Gifts)

1075 East Putnam Avenue, Riverside (above Aux Delices) 203.698.3219

www.AntanAntiques.com, www.AntanGifts.com

If you see a lamp shade in a very pretty color, it may be from Monique Olmer's shop. For over 20 years, she has been providing Greenwich with unique lamps and shades. The shop has an interesting assortment of prints and other home accessories.

Hours: Tuesday - Saturday, 10:30 am - 5 pm.

Anthropologie (Home Decorating, Clothing - Women)

480 West Putnam Avenue, 203.422.5421

www.Anthropologie.com

A retailer of high-end casual clothing designed to appeal to the 30- to 40-something affluent professional woman. Though mainly clothing and accessories, the store also sells furniture and home furnishings. The company prides itself on its one-of-a-kind items. There are approximately 90 stores in the US.

Hours: Monday - Saturday 10 am - 7 pm (open to 8 pm on Thursday), Sunday noon - 6 pm.

Antique Area of Stamford (Antiques)

Tucked away in converted manufacturing buildings are collections of antique dealers with enough collectibles and antiques to suit just about anyone. With antiques from hundreds of dealers, it's hard to imagine anyone not finding something they want. A great outing for the antique enthusiast. When you are in the area, the Northern Italian Eclisse Restaurant is just around the corner. Don't forget to also look at Braswell Galleries in Norwalk.

Hours for Galleries in the Antique Area: Monday to Saturday 10:30 am - 5:30 or 6 pm, Sunday 12 pm - about 6 pm.

- **Antique and Artisan Center**, 69 Jefferson Street 203.327.6022
  www.antiqueandartisancenter.com www.StamfordAntiques.com
  55 dealers in 20,000 square fee.
- **Connecticut Antiques Center**, 850 Canal Street 203.355.9335
  www.connecticutStyle.com
  110 dealers in 13,500 square feet.
- **Greenwich Living Antiques**, 481 Canal Street, 203.274.5130
  www.GreenwichLivingAntiques.com
  63 dealers in 30,000 square feet.
- **Hamptons Antique Galleries**, 441 Canal Street, Stamford, 203.325.4019
  www.HamptonsAntiqueGalleries.com
  95 dealers in 26,000 square feet.
- **Harbor View Center for Antiques**, 101 Jefferson Street, 203.325.8070
  www.HarborViewAntiques.com
  70 dealers in 22,000 square feet.
- **Hiden Galleries**, 47 John Street, 203.363.0003
  www.HidenGalleries.net
  250 dealers in 47,000 square feet.
- **John Street Antiques**, 50 John Street, 203.324.4677
  www.JohnStreetAntiques.com
  20 dealers in about 15,000 square feet.

Apadana (Rugs)

539 East Putnam Avenue, Cos Cob, 203.422.0700

www.Apadanafinerugs.com

Apadana's presence in Greenwich is fairly new, but New Yorkers have known them for 20 years. They have antique and reproduction rugs in modern and traditional patterns.

Hours: Monday - Saturday, 10 am - 6 pm.

Apple Store

356 Greenwich Avenue, 203.302.6691

www.Apple.com/GreenwichAvenue

An attractive, large, sleek store with every conceivable Apple product, a Genius bar and lots of workshops.

Hours: Monday - Saturday, 10 am - 7 pm; Thursday until 8 pm; Sunday, 11 am - 6 pm.

(Greenwich) Aquaria (Fish)

1064 East Putnam Avenue, Riverside, 203.344.1572

www.GreenwichAquaria.com

The store is divided into fresh water and saltwater sections, they specialize in large tanks. The filtration systems can be run to the home's basement.

Hours: Closed Monday , Tuesday - Friday 11 am - 6 pm; Saturday 10 am - 6 pm; Sunday 10 am - 5 pm.

AT Proudian (Oriental Rugs)

120 East Putnam Avenue, 203.622.1200

www.ATProudian.com

A family-owned and operated Oriental rug business. They have been in Greenwich since 1974 and have a good reputation. A source for cleaning, repair and appraisal.

Hours: Monday - Saturday 10 am - 5 pm.

Atelier Constantin Popescu (String Instruments)

Cos Cob Plaza, 403 East Putnam Avenue, Cos Cob, 203.661.9500

www.atelierconstantinpopescu.com

Sells, repairs and rents string instruments. Professionals and amateurs alike count on his repair services. Constantin Popescu is a graduate of both the Bucharest Conservatory in Romania and of Juilliard School of Music. Constantin is the Principal Bassist of the Greenwich Symphony. The Riverside School of Music is located next to his store at 401 East Putnam Avenue. (203.661-9501).

Hours: weekdays 10 am - 6 pm, Saturday 10 am - 2 pm.

Athlete's Foot (Athletic Shoes)

73 Greenwich Avenue, 203.629.3338

www.theathletesfoot.com

A locally run franchise which is part of a large chain. Their goal is to be the definitive expert on athletic footwear. And, indeed, they have a very good selection of shoes.

Hours: weekdays 9:30 am - 7 pm, Saturday 9:30 am - 6 pm, Sunday, 11:30 am - 5 pm.

Audiocom (Audio/Visual)

321 Greenwich Avenue, 203.552.5272

www.audiocomhifi.com

They sell high quality audio, video and home automation equipment from their lower level 5,000 square foot space now on the Avenue. They have equipment you may not see anywhere else. They will design and install your home theater.

Hours: weekdays 9 am - 5 pm, weekends by appointment.

AutoZone (Auto Parts)

799 East Main Street, Stamford CT 203.406.1327

www.AutoZone.com

With over 4,000 stores, it is one of the largest auto stores in the world. Its major competitors are Advance, CarQuest and NAPA.

Hours: Monday - Saturday 7 am - 10 pm, Sunday 8 am - 8 pm.

Avenue News (Magazines & Newspapers)

375 Greenwich Avenue, 203.629.2429

A popular shop with friendly service and magazines on every topic. Stop in while you are on the Avenue or heading to the train station for a cold drink, snack or headache remedy.

Hours: Open every day 5 am - 9:30 pm.

Babies "R" Us

2700 Central Park Avenue, Yonkers NY, 914.722.4500

www.babiesrus.com

Mega baby store specializing in clothing, furniture, bedding, toys and other accessories for babies. This is just one of the baby stores on Central Park Avenue in Yonkers. Central Avenue is approximately 20 minutes away. It runs through Yonkers and Scarsdale.

Hours: Monday - Saturday 9:30 am - 9:30 pm, Sunday 11 am - 7 pm.

Baby CZ (Baby & young children's clothes)

360 Greenwich Avenue, 203.340.9932

www.BabyCZ.com

Designer Carolina Zapf, who grew up in Greenwich, makes exceptionally pretty clothing. Although some of the clothing is for children up to age 12, most is for infants and toddlers.

Hours: Monday - Saturday, 10 am - 6 pm.

Baccarat (Gifts - Crystal)

236 Greenwich Avenue, 203.618.0900

www.Baccarat-US.com

A table set with their French luxury crystal is very special. They also have a selection of pretty vases, giftware and jewelry.

Hours: Monday - Saturday, 10 am - 5:30 pm.

Baker Furniture

200 Greenwich Avenue, 203.862.0655

www.bakerfurniture.com

Now you can buy directly what once was the exclusive province of interior designers. Furniture, fabrics and accessories with a timeless elegance.

Hours: Monday - Saturday 10 am - 6 pm, Sunday noon - 5 pm.

Banana Republic (Clothing - Men & Women)

Stamford Town Center, 203.324.6323 and The Westchester
 914.644.8640

www.bananarepublic.com

They sell the Gap's higher end casual career clothing. Most of the clothes are rather trendy. In the US there are over 500 Banana Republic stores.

Stamford Hours: Monday - Saturday 10 am - 9 pm, Sunday 11 am - 6 pm.

Bang & Olufsen (Electronics - Audio/Visual)

365 Greenwich Avenue, 203.769.5500

www.bangolufsen.com

For over 75 years, this Danish Company has been creating exceptional video and audio systems, including loud speakers. Their cutting-edge designs are so attractive they have been on display at the Museum of Modern Art.

Hours: Monday - Saturday 10:30 am - 7 pm, Sunday noon - 6 pm.

STORES

(the) Barn (Fabrics, Home Decorating Accessories)
50 Hurd Avenue, Bridgeport, CT, 203.334.3396
www.thebarn-bridgeport.com
If you want to see a wide variety of fabrics, visit this old barn with 20,000 square feet of well priced bolts: silks, linens, velvets, cottons. You can also get upholstered headboards and throw pillows.
Hours: Monday - Saturday 10 am - 5 pm.

BCBG Max Azria (Clothing - Women)
200 Greenwich Avenue, 203.861.7303
www.bcbg.com
Bon Chic Bon Genre caters to modern women who want trendy, chic, unique fashions at mid-scale prices. The company's newest line of clothing is targeted at college students. Their upscale garments are in the Max Azria Collection. One feature of Max Azria's boutiques is a very restrictive return policy.
Hours: Monday - Saturday 10 am - 6 pm, Sunday noon- 6 pm.

Beach Box (Clothing - Women)
73 Greenwich Avenue (upstairs), 203.625.9696
www.outoftheboxclothes.com
During the summer, Out of The Box opens this shop selling swim skirts, tunics, sun dresses, cover-ups, pool party dresses and accessories.
Hours: summer: Monday - Saturday 10 am - 5 pm,
Sunday noon - 5 pm.

Beacon Point Marine (Boating)
49 River Road, Cos Cob, 203.661.4033
http://www.beaconpointmarine.com
New and used recreational and fishing boats, storage and service.
Hours: Monday - Saturday 10 am - 5 pm.

Beads in the Loft (Jewelry)
3 Lewis Street, 203.861.0086
www.BeadsInTheLoft.com
Beads in the Loft carries handmade custom jewelry. Unlike other jewelry stores, customers can also design their purchases themselves. They have beads and stones of every color and size, and everything in the store is made from semi-precious stones, precious stones and fresh water pearls, using 18 and 24 karat gold and sterling silver.
Hours: Tuesday - Saturday 10 am - 5 pm.

STORES

Beam & Barre (Children's Dance wear)
352 Greenwich Avenue, 203.622.0591
www.BeamAndBarre.com
Dance wear to suit even the most discriminating ballerina's tastes. Plus exercise wear, skating attire and costumes.
Hours: weekdays 10 am - 5:30 pm, Saturday 10 am - 5 pm.

Bed Bath & Beyond
(Home Decorating - Accessories, Appliances)
• 2275 Summer Street (Ridgeway Shopping Center), Stamford 203.323.7714
• 25 Waterfront Place, Port Chester, NY, 914.937.9098
www.BedBathandBeyond.com
A huge store with medium-to-high quality items for the bedroom, bathroom, breakfast room and kitchen. They operate 819 stores across the US. Their main competitor, Linens n' Things, has liquidated its 570 stores.
Stamford Hours: Monday-Saturday 9 am - 9 pm, Sunday 9:30 am - 6 pm.
Port Chester Hours: Monday - Saturday 9 am - 9:30 pm,
Sunday 10 am - 7 pm.

Bedford Sportsman (Fishing equipment & clothing)
25 Adams Street, Bedford Hills, NY, 914.666.8091
www.bedfordsportsman.com
Specializes in freshwater fly and spin fishing equipment. A good resource for New York watershed streams & guide services. They teach fly fishing during the summer.
Hours: Closed Monday, Tuesday - Friday 10 am - 6 pm,
Saturday 10 am - 5 pm, Sunday 11 am - 3 pm.

Bellini Juvenile Designer Furniture
(Children & Baby Furniture)
• 495 Central Park Avenue, Scarsdale, NY, 914.472.7336
• 984 High Ridge Road, Stamford CT, 203.703.2084
www.bellini.com
Well made baby and teen furniture.
Hours: Monday - Saturday 10 am - 5 pm (Saturday until 6 pm);
Sunday noon - 5 pm.

STORES

Ben Romeo (Contractor Supplies)
1 Edgewood Avenue (at West Putnam Avenue) 203.869.4108
The most needed items for contractors and landscapers. They have safety cones and Child Safety signs. They sharpen tools.
Hours: weekdays, 8 am - 4:30 pm.

Bendheim Gallery (Art)
299 Greenwich Avenue, 203.622.3998
www.GreenwichArts.org/currentshow.asp
Inside the Art Center, the Arts Council gallery has interesting exhibits you will not want to miss.
Hours: weekdays 10 am - 5 pm; Saturday noon - 5 pm, Sunday noon - 4 pm.

Best Buy (Electronics)
330 Connecticut Avenue, Norwalk CT, 203.857.4543
www.BestBuy.com
Best Buy is the biggest electronics retailer in the US, with 1,400 stores. The Norwalk store is 45,000 square feet. Their arch rival, Circuit City, has liquidated all 576 of its stores. Their new rival is Walmart, who saw the opportunity and is working hard to fill the gap.
Hours: Monday - Saturday, 10 am - 9 pm, Sunday, 11 am - 7 pm.

Best Plumbing (Tile, Bath & Kitchen Fixtures)
1989 W Main Street, Stamford CT, 203.975.9448
www.bestplg.com www.bestplg.com/Blog
Just across the Greenwich border on US 1, they represent a myriad of manufactures including Kohler. A nice showroom, worth the visit.
Hours: Monday - Saturday 9 am - 5 pm.

Betteridge Jewelers (Jewelry)
117 Greenwich Avenue, 203.869.0124
www.Betteridge.com
A third-generation family-owned business; buying, selling and collecting some of the finest jewelry. The shop specializes in fine timepieces, rare and exceptional stones, estate jewelry and pearls, plus a broad collection of classic and contemporary jewelry and silver to suit a diverse clientele. They carry many renowned brands, such as Cartier and Van Cleef & Arpel. Totally trustworthy with excellent service and repair, as well as appraisal services.
Hours: Closed Monday, Tuesday - Saturday, 9 am - 5 pm
(Call for holiday hours).

STORES

Beval Saddlery (Riding Attire and saddles)
50 Pine Street, New Canaan CT, 203.966.7828
www.Beval.com
A small chain with English saddlery and clothing. They do a good job fitting a saddle to you and your horse.
Hours: Monday - Saturday, 9 am - 5 pm (Thursday until 8 pm).

Blinds To Go (Windows)
411 Westport Avenue, Norwalk, 203.840.1357
www.BlindsToGo.com
One of a 120 superstores providing blinds and shades of all descriptions. They claim to be the largest retailer of these items in the world.
Hours: Monday - Saturday 10 am - 7 pm; Sunday noon - 5 pm.

Bloomingdale's (Department Store)
175 Bloomingdale Road, White Plains, NY, 914.684.6300
www.Bloomingdales.com
A large stand-alone store, with lots of parking. Bloomingdale's is a chain of upscale American department stores owned by Federated Department Stores, which is also the parent company of Macy's. Bloomingdale's has 36 stores nationwide. It competes on an average price level with Nordstrom and slightly below that of Saks Fifth Avenue and Neiman Marcus.
Hours: Monday - Saturday 10 am - 9 pm (Friday & Saturday until 10 pm), Sunday noon - 7 pm.

bodd (Exercise Clothing - Women)
181 Greenwich Avenue (second floor), 203.983.5470
www.BoddFitness.com
Boutique with stylish exercise wear for women. They also have a variety of exercise classes including pre & post-natal yoga as well as therapeutic yoga .
Hours: weekdays 8 am - 11 am; Saturday 9 am - 11 am.

STORES

Braswell Galleries (Antiques & Auctions)

1 Muller Avenue (entrance on Sniffin Street), Norwalk CT
 203.847.1234

www.braswellgalleries.com   www.antiquesofgreenwich.com
Occupying an old lace factory, this 40,000 sq. ft. place is crammed with
furniture, paintings and just about everything else. The Gallery typically
has mid-level antiques. The Estate center specializes in higher level antiques. Buyers can have fun taking part in their auctions, which are held
once or twice a month. Leave a silent bid or attend the auction and you
may be able to purchase the item you want at a very competitive price.
Remember all prices in the Gallery are negotiable, so don't just buy at
the listed price. For auctions the buyers premium varies from 17.5% (if
you pay in cash) to 20% for credit card purchases. The on-line services
charge an extra 3%. *See Antiques Area of Stamford for more antique galleries.*
Norwalk Gallery Hours: Open every day 10 am - 5 pm
(Sunday opens at 11)
Norwalk Auction Hours: Viewings normally are Thursdays 5 pm - 8 pm,
Friday and Saturday 10 am - 8 pm. Auctions are held at different times
and on different days, see their website.

Brooks Brothers (Clothing - Men & Women)

181 Greenwich Avenue, 203.863.9288
www.BrooksBrothers.com
This 12,000 sq. ft. store carries classic men's, women's and boy's cloth-
ing. Brooks has 240 stores and is the oldest men's clothier in the US.
Hours: weekdays 10 am - 7 pm, Saturday 9 am - 6 pm,
Sunday 11 am - 6 pm.

Bruce Park Sports (Sporting Goods , Team Uniforms)

104 Mason Street, 203.869.1382
www.BruceParkSports.com
A family owned sports store carrying team uniforms and equipment for
most sports. When I am not sure where to get something, they are always a good bet and they have excellent customer service.
Hours: Monday - Saturday 9 am - 5:30 pm.

STORES

Burlington Coat Factory (Department Store)

74 Broad Street, Stamford CT, 203.363.0450

www.Coat.com

An off-price store with a traditional department store layout, this national chain has 360 stores. They have branched out since their founding in 1924 and now sell women's apparel, including suits, shoes and accessories. They even have a baby department and sell linens. Its principle competitor is TJ Maxx.

Hours: Monday - Saturday 10 am - 9 pm, Sunday 11 am - 6 pm.

Buy Buy Baby (Babies)

1019 Central Park Avenue, Scarsdale NY, 914.725.9220

www.BuyBuyBaby.com

One of many baby stores about 20 minutes away on Central Avenue (see Babies R Us). Here, everything is for children ages 0-3. It's a large store, so wear comfortable shoes!

Hours: Monday - Saturday 9:30 am - 9:30 pm, Sunday 11 am - 7 pm.

Camera Wholesalers (Photography)

1034 High Ridge Road, Stamford CT, 203.357.0467

www.CameraWholesalers.com

A family-owned store that has been in business since 1978. They are authorized dealers for almost all makes of cameras and many are in stock. They have a knowledgeable staff to help you make selections.

Hours: weekdays 10 am to 6 pm (Thursday to 9 pm),

Saturday 10 am - 6 pm.

Candy Nichols (Clothing - Children & Youth)

67 Elm Street, New Canaan CT, 203.972.8600

www.candyNichols.com

This children's store is run by local moms, for moms who don't want to pay high prices. They know what kids think is "cool", and they select their merchandise to suit them. For years Candy Nichols had a shop in Greenwich. Devotees have followed them to New Canaan. They have children's clothing, toys and accessories from infants to girls' sizes 7 - 14 and boys' sizes 8 - 20.

Hours: Monday - Saturday 9:30 am - 5:30 pm.

(The) Canine Corner (Pets)

177 Sound Beach Avenue, Old Greenwich, 203.637.8819

For your dog or your dog-loving friends, this is THE gift shop.

Hours: Monday - Saturday 10 am - 5 pm.

Carlisle / Per Se (Women's Clothing)

283 Greenwich Avenue (Second Floor), 203.422.2464

www.CarlisleCollection.com

Traditionally doing trunk shows, the Connaught Group has opened a showroom showing their fashionable lines. Lots of custom possibilities. Hours: Monday - Saturday, 10 am - 5 pm (by appointment).

Carters (Clothing - Babies, Toddlers, Children)

2329 Summer Street (Ridgeway Shopping Center), Stamford CT
 203.975.9725

www.Carters.com

Mothers love this store for good buys for newborns, toddlers and kids (through size 7). This is where you will find all of the basics. Hours: Monday - Saturday, 9 am - 9 pm; Sunday, 10 am - 6 pm.

Cashmere Inc (Clothing - Women)

55 E. Putnam Avenue, 203.552.1059

www.Cashmereincct.com

Holly Adam has created a unique store with friendly help and a wide selection of high quality and very pretty sweaters, dresses, scarves and gloves. Hours: Monday - Saturday 10 am - 5:30 pm.

Cavalier Galleries (Art)

405 Greenwich Avenue, 203.869.3664

www.cavaliergalleries.com

Ronald Cavalier specializes in painting and sculpture by contemporary artists working in a representational style. You may already have smiled at one of the gallery's lifelike sculptures on a sidewalk in Greenwich or Stamford. Prices range from $100 to $100,000. Hours: Monday - Saturday 10:30 am - 6 pm; in the winter, Sunday noon - 5 pm.

Ceramic Design (Tile)

26 Bruce Park Avenue, 203.869.8800

www.ceramicdesignltd.com

The store is larger than it appears. They have a good selection of tiles and knowledgeable help. They will do a complete design for your kitchen or bath. They are an authorized Rutt Cabinetry Dealer. Hours: weekdays 9 am - 5 pm, Saturday 10 am - 4 pm.

STORES

Choice Pet Supply
44 Amogerone Xway, 203.869.4999
www.ChoicePet.com
One of nine Connecticut locations, they specialize in natural, organic and holistic foods for pets (dogs, cats, companion birds, small animals, fish and reptiles).
Hours: Monday - Saturday 8 am - 8 pm, Sunday 9 am - 6 pm.

Children's Cottage (consignment- Children)
23 Catoonah Street, Ridgefield CT, 203.438.3933
www.Childrenscottageonline.com
Children's designer clothing, infant to size 16. They usually have equestrian wear.
Hours: Monday - Saturday 9:30 am - 4:30 pm.

Chilly Bear (Clothing & Sports Equipment- Youth)
180 Sound Beach Avenue, Old Greenwich
203.622.7115 or 888.463.2707
www.chillybear.com
Richard Fulton's shop is a great resource for customized shirts and hats, as well a store for the hip young adolescent. It is filled with the latest teenage garb as well as skateboards, inline skates, paint ball guns and accessories. Very nice customer service.
Hours: Monday - Saturday 10 am - 6 pm, Sunday noon - 5 pm.

Christmas Tree Shops
393 North Central Avenue, Hartsdale NY, 914.948.3721
www.christmastreeshops.com
Christmas Tree Shops are bargain stores, selling everything from food to toys to household furnishings to, of course, Christmas decorations and wrapping paper. The chain is owned by Bed, Bath and Beyond.
Christmas Hours: November 1 - December 30, open 7 Days: 8 am - 10 pm; Closed November 26 and December 25; December 31, 8 am - 6 pm, January 1, 9 am - 9 pm.

Christopher Fischer (Clothing - Women)
103 Greenwich Avenue, 203.861.7400
www.christopherfischer.com
Stylish Cashmere clothing which they design and manufacture.
Hours: Monday - Saturday 10 am - 6 pm.

Claire's (Clothing - Children)

344 Greenwich Avenue, 203.618.4461

www.claires.com

Greenwich once had the title "Preppie Capital of The World". If Claire's is successful, does this mean Greenwich will lose this title? Claire's has 3,000 locations worldwide. It caters to girls, pre-teen through teenager. Claire's sells perfumes, as well as accessory products such as jewelry, make-up, hair and belt accessories. The store offers a wide variety of styles from punk, gothic, emo, and rock chick to pink, glittery, girly and flowery items. Claire's offers free ear piercing with the purchase of piercing studs and ear care antiseptic. Claire's owns "Icing by Claire's", which caters to gals 17-27.

Hours: Monday - Saturday 10 am - 8 pm, Sunday 11 am - 6 pm.

Classic Sofa (Furniture)

79 East Putnam Avenue, 203.863.0005

www.classicSofa.com

This is a custom sofa store; any size, any shape, any fabric. Select a model from the many samples in the showroom or show them a picture. Then choose your fabric and size. Within two weeks after the fabric arrives, the sofa will be in your home.

Hours: Monday - Saturday 10 am - 6 pm.

Clinton Crossing (Outlet Mall)

Route 81, Clinton CT, 860.664.0700

www.premiumoutlets.com

The largest outlet center in Connecticut (see also Tanger Outlet), they have seventy upscale stores. If you have time, have dinner at the nearby Inn at Chester, 318 West Main Street (Rts 145 & 81), Chester, CT, 860.526.9541 www.innatchester.com. Of course you could always go to exit 92 and visit Foxwoods Casino.

Regular Hours: Monday - Saturday 10 am - 9 pm, Sunday 10 am - 6 pm.

Directions: I-95 N exit 63.

CM Almy (Religious Gifts & Books)

228 Sound Beach Avenue, 203.637.2739

www.Almy.com

A supplier of clerical attire. The front of this shop is filled with Christian books and gifts. Devotional gifts, keepsakes and first communion gifts.

Hours: weekdays 10 am - 5 pm, Saturday 10 am - 2 pm.

STORES

Coach (Accessories- Women)
- Stamford Town Center, 203.965-0666,
- White Plains Westchester Mall, 914.644-8244

www.coach.com

For 65 years, this company has been a leading handbag designer. One of the hallmarks of the Coach company is their policy which states that any Coach product may be repaired for the life of the product by simply shipping it back to the home office, with a note or letter stating the problem. Its main competitors are Louis Vuitton (Westchester Mall) and Kate Spade (Greenwich Avenue).

Hours: Monday - Saturday 10 am - 9 pm, Sunday 11 am - 6 pm.

Cochni (Clothing, Shoes & Accessories -Women)
50 Greenwich Avenue, 203.422.0970

www.cochni.com

A boutique with fun items such as unbelievable belt buckles, jeweled slippers, cashmere sweaters with embroidery & trim, and a selection of silk scarves. All at reasonable prices.

Hours: Monday - Saturday 10 am - 6 pm, Sunday noon - 5 pm.

Colony Florist
315 Greenwich Avenue, 203.869.6400

www.colonyflorist.org

A family-owned shop giving Greenwich residents personal service for 50 years. If you grew up in Greenwich, it is likely your first corsage came from Colony. They do a lot of custom work. They will even decorate your Christmas tree as well as your mantel and banister.

Hours: Monday - Friday 8 am - 5:30 pm, Saturday 8 am- 4 pm.

Computer Super Center (Electronics - Computer & AV)
103 Mason Street, 203.661.1700

www.computersupercenter.com

For friendly help and expert advice on PCs and Apples try the Super Center. A good selection of hardware and software and a very active repair business. They also sell and service Sony LCD home theater equipment. We highly recommend this store. They will have what you need and they care.

Hours: weekdays 9 am - 6 pm, Saturday 10 am - 5 pm.

Compleat Angler (Fishing Equipment & Clothing)

555 Post Road, Darien CT, 203.655.9400
www.Compleat-Angler.com
A large selection of fly fishing and light tackle spin fishing equipment as well as outdoor clothing. Ask about their lessons and guide service.
Hours: Monday - Saturday 9:30 am - 6 pm (Thursday until 8 pm), Sunday 11 am - 4 pm.

(The) Connecticut Store (Gift Shops, Clothing)

116 Bank Street, Waterbury CT, 800.474.6728
www.TheConnecticutStore.com
This store specializes in items made in Connecticut. This is a great resource if you are looking for a unique gift. Best of all, you can buy almost everything from their website without making a trip. We especially like the blazer buttons from the Waterbury Button Company. Their selection is amazing.
Hours: Tuesday - Saturday 9:30 am - 5 pm.
Directions: I-84 East to exit 22.

Consign It (Consigned Furniture and Accessories)

115 Mason Street (Village Square) 203.869-9836
www.ConsignItInc.com
This shop is a good place to consign and a good place to buy pre-owned furniture, jewelry, silver and china. They do high-level tag sales.
Hours: Monday-Saturday 10 am - 5 pm.

Consigned Couture (Consignment Clothing)

134 East Putnam Avenue (Entrance from Milbank) 203.869.7795
Lots of slightly disorganized and slightly expensive designer clothing.
Hours: Monday - Saturday 10 am - 5 pm.

Consigned Designs by Ellen (Consignment Clothing)

115 Mason Street (Village Square) 203.869.2165
Consigned designer clothing such as: Hermes, Pucci, Prada, Armani.
Hours: Monday - Saturday 10 am - 5 pm.

(The) Container Store (Home Decorating)

145 Westchester Avenue (next to the Westchester Mall),
White Plains, NY 914.946.4767 www.containerStore.com
A 25,000 square foot store designed to help you organize your life and hopefully the life of your college student.
Hours: Monday - Saturday 9 am - 9 pm, Sunday 10 am - 6 pm.

STORES

Cook and Craft (Cookware)

27 Arcadia Road, Old Greenwich, 203.637.2755

www.CookAndCraft.com

This shop has a whole range of high quality essentials. The cookware, knives, utensils, gadgets, cookbooks and gourmet pantry items are selected by the owner, an ex-chef. They have a bridal registry.

Hours: Monday - Saturday 10 am - 5 pm. (Seasonal, hours vary).

Copeland Optometrists

203 South Ridge Street, Rye Brook NY, 914.939.0830

www.copelandoptometrists.com

For years, they were just over the border in Port Chester, but now they are 5 minutes away in Rye Brook. We followed them because of their reliable, caring service. Owned and operated by the Copeland Family, you can count on a good eye examination, the correct prescription and a set of fashionable glasses or contact lens at a reasonable price.

Hours: weekdays, 9 am - 6 pm (closed Wednesday, open Thursday until 8 pm); Saturday 9 am - 5 pm.

Cos Cob Farms (Flowers)

61 East Putnam Avenue, Cos Cob, 203.629.2267

A local store with fresh fruit, vegetables and flowers at reasonable prices.

Hours: Monday - Saturday 8 am - 7 pm, Sunday 9 am - 6 pm.

Cos Cob TV

5 Strickland Road, Cos Cob, 203.869.2277

www.CosCobTV.com

Looking for a small TV or large flat screen or an Apple iPod or iMac? This store, run by second generation owner Sean Mecsery, has been offering good prices and good service for more than 60 years.

Hours: Monday - Saturday 9:30 am -6 pm (Friday to 7 pm).

Costco (Grocery & Department Store)

1 Westchester Avenue, Port Chester, NY, 914.935.3103

www.CostCo.com

You have to buy a membership to shop at this international chain, but that hasn't kept this megastore, a.k.a. warehouse, from being a Greenwich hit. From pesto in their grocery section to a DVD player to a refrigerator, this huge store tries to give good value. If you want an expensive electronic item or a large quantity of a staple, this could be your best bet. If you want to run in quickly to get something, forget it.

Hours: weekdays, 10 am - 8:30 pm, Saturday, 9:30 am - 6 pm, Sunday, 10 am - 6 pm.

STORES

Coppola Tailors (Men's Formal Clothing)
347 Greenwich Avenue, 203.869.2883
A long time Greenwich store specializing in tuxedo sales and rental. They also do alterations.
Hours: weekdays 9:30 am - 5:30 pm, Saturday 9:30 am - 5 pm.

Courage.b (Clothing - Women)
53 Greenwich Avenue, 203.422.5660
www.CourageB.com
One of 4 locations, the other 3 stores are located in Scarsdale, Englewood and New York City. Pretty scarves and colorful clothing, some reminiscent of the popular fashions in the 60s. The name comes from the courage it takes to open a store.
Hours: Monday - Saturday 10 am - 6 pm,
Open Sundays noon -5 pm in the winter.

Crate & Barrel
(Home Decorating, Furniture & Cookware)
125 Westchester Avenue (Westchester Mall) White Plains, NY
914.682.0900
www.CrateAndBarrel.com
A chain specializing in housewares, indoor and outdoor furniture and home accessories. Much of the merchandise is direct from Europe. Their major competitors are IKEA, Pottery Barn and Williams-Sonoma.
Hours: Monday - Saturday, 10 am - 9 pm; Sunday, noon - 6 pm.

Creative Playthings (children's play equipment)
65 Harvard Avenue, Stamford CT, 203.359.9702
www.creativeplaythings.com
Co-located with The Fitness Store, www.TheFitnessStoreUSA.com. *(Reviewed in Health.)* They sell wooden play sets for homes and playgrounds.
Hours: Monday - Saturday 10 am -6 pm, Sunday noon - 5 pm.

Curtain Works of Greenwich (Windows - Curtains)
34 East Putnam Avenue, 203.622.2354
www.CurtainWorksofGreenwich.com
The perfect place to find ready-made curtains that have the designer look at reasonable prices. There are over 100 fabrics to choose from. Many of the silks are from India. They provide measuring services and hardware.
Hours: Monday - Saturday 9:30 - 5:30.

Custom Golf of Connecticut (Golf Equipment)

2770 Summer Street, Stamford, 203.323.7888, or 800.804.5754
www.GolfPsychos.com
Wide variety of golf clubs for sale or rent and some clothing. They do repairs and re-gripping as well as completely custom clubs. A good place for golf instruction during the winter.
Hours: weekdays 10 am - 6 pm (Thursday until 7 pm in summer), Saturday 9 am - 5 pm.

Cycle Dynamics & BikeEx (Bicycles)

12 Riversville Road, Glenville, 203.532.1718
Ken Adler used to work at Buzz's Cycle Shop before he started Cycle Dynamics, a full service sales and service store. Ken also operates BikeEx, a mobile repair shop that will come to your home to tune-up or repair your bicycles.
Hours: weekdays 10 am - 6 pm, Saturday 10am - 5 pm.

Darien Golf Center (Golf - Equipment & Clothing)

233 Post Road, Darien CT, 203.655.2788
www.DarienGolfCenter.com
Excellent selection of golf equipment and men's clothing. Very helpful service.
Hours: Monday - Saturday 9 am - 5:30 pm, Sunday 10 am - 3:30 pm.

Darien Sport Shop (Clothing - Men, Women, Children)

1127 Post Road, Darien CT, 203.655.2575
www.DarienSport.com
Good-looking casual and sports attire as well a ski and skateboard shop. They carry Boy and Girl Scout uniforms.
Hours: Monday - Saturday 9 am - 5:30 pm(Thursday until 7 pm).

Dave's Cycle and Fitness (Bicycles)

78 Valley Road, Cos Cob, 203.661.7736, 7803
www.gdaves.com
Slightly off the beaten path, this shop provides friendly, knowledgeable help for cyclists at all levels. A good place to select a bicycle or clothing. They can repair just about any type of bike.
Hours: Monday - Wednesday 10 am - 6pm, Thursday 10 am - 8 pm, Friday 10 am - 6 pm, Saturday 11 am - 4 pm, Sunday 11 am - 4 pm.

STORES

De Mane's Golf

35 Chapel Street, Byram, 203.531.9126

www.DeManeGolf.com

Golfers in the know visit Rick's shop for custom clubs and repairs. Their state of the art demo room allows you to compare clubs from different manufactures and determine which would be best for you. The demo room costs $150 hr.

Hours: Tuesday -Saturday, 10 am - 5 pm.

Decorators Secret (Fabrics)

441 Canal Street, Stamford, 203.323.5093

www.TheDecoratorsSecret.com

A warehouse filled with discounted bolts of fabric from overstocks at New York trade showrooms. A good place to buy your fabric. We recommend you use your own upholsterer.

Hours: Monday -Saturday, 10 am - 5:30 pm, Sunday noon - 5 pm.

Delta Auto Parts /Car Quest

315 West Putnam Avenue, 203.869.6550

www.CarQuest.com

Carquest has 3,400 stores throughout the US. It competes with Advance Auto Parts and Autozone.

Hours: weekdays, 8 am - 5:30 pm, Saturday 8 am - 2 pm.

Design Within Reach (Furniture)

86 Greenwich Avenue, 203.422.2013

www.DWR.com

A small chain dedicated to classic, modern furniture, most from known designers. Their goal is to provide furniture traditionally found only in design showrooms.

Hours: Monday - Saturday 10 am - 6 pm (Thursday to 7 pm), Sunday noon - 5 pm.

Dighton Rhode (Clothing-Women)

5 Lewis Street, 203.622.4600

www.DightonRhode.com

Beautiful designer clothing, in an elegant small shop just off the Avenue.

Hours: Monday - Saturday 10 am - 6 pm.

STORES

DirectBuy of Fairfield County (Furniture, Discount Store)

20 Glover Avenue, Norwalk CT, 203.845.9500

www.DirectBuy.com and www.directbuycares.com

www.DirectBuyNewYork.com/Fairfield.php

With 160 showrooms across the United States and Canada, they are one of the largest members-only buying stores. They provide manufacturer-direct wholesale prices on practically everything for the home, both inside and out. Consumer Reports reported that memberships at some Direct Buy locations in the New York area ranged from $4,600 to $4,990 for a three-year membership and then $190 a year for the next seven years. Consumer Reports estimated you'd need to spend about $20,000 to recoup your membership fee. But, if you are furnishing a home, this could be the place to go.

Hours: Tuesday - Friday 11 am - 9 pm; Saturday & Sunday 10 am - 5 pm.

Do it Best Hardware

136 East Putnam Avenue, Cos Cob, 203.869.9254

www.CosCob.DoItBest.com

This convenient, small hardware store has been helping residents for over 70 years. As you can imagine, after this length of time, they have what you need.

Hours: Monday - Saturday, 8 am - 6:30 pm; Sunday, 9 am - 4 pm.

Drapery Exchange (Window Drapery)

14 Center Street, Darien CT, 203.655.3844

www.DrapeXDarien.com

What a great idea! A consignment shop for beautiful draperies. Some almost new. None over 3 years old.

Hours: weekdays 10 am - 5 pm, Saturday 10 am - 1 pm.

DSW (Shoes-Men & Women)

5 Westchester Avenue (The Waterfront), Port Chester, NY

914.690.2841 www.DSWshoes.com

The Designer Shoe Warehouse has 300 stores in 37 states. This location carries more than 30,000 pairs of adult men's and women's shoes in an amazing variety of styles.

Hours: Monday - Saturday 10 am - 9:30 pm, Sunday 11 am - 6 pm.

STORES

Duxiana Beds (Bedding)
15 West Putnam Avenue, 203.661.7162
www.DuxBed.com
Made in Sweden with several layers of springs, Dux beds are guaranteed for 20 years and cost between $5,350 and $9,100 for a king-size bed and between $2,500 and $3,000 for a single. Owners of these beds tell us they are worth the price.
Hours: Monday - Saturday 10 am - 6 pm, Sunday noon - 5 pm.

East Putnam Variety (Magazines & Newspapers)
Whole Foods shopping Center, 88 East Putnam Avenue
203.869.8789
This conveniently located shop has magazines, cards, newspapers, and a myriad of party goods, including a fabulous balloon selection. Great customer service.
Hours: Monday - Saturday, 7 am to 9 pm; Sunday, 7 am - 3 pm.

Eastern Mountain Sports (Sporting Goods & Clothing)
952 High Ridge Road, Stamford CT, 203.461.9865
www.EMS.com
A general purpose chain sports store with an emphasis on camping, climbing and kayaking. A good place to find out about climbing and kayaking instruction.
Hours: weekdays 9 am - 8 pm, Saturday 9 am to 7 pm,
Sunday 11 am - 5 pm.

Ed's Garage Doors
136 Water Street, Norwalk CT, 203.847.1284
www.EdsGaragedoors.com
If you are looking for a new overhead door their large store makes selecting easy. They will repair or provide garage door openers for any door. They are a very reliable resource.
Hours: weekdays 8 am - 5 pm, Saturday 9 am - 3 pm.

Educational Warehouse
509 Westport Avenue, Norwalk CT, 203.846.2220
www.EducationalWarehouse.com
When you are looking for educational games, teaching supplies for the home classroom or developmental toys, they are a great resource. They have a huge selection of educational workbooks for children of all ages.
Hours: Monday - Saturday 9:30 am - 8 pm, Sunday 11 am - 6 pm.

STORES

Ella Vickers (bags)
85 Greenwich Avenue, 910.686.4932, 262.0216
www.EllaVickers.com
Ella Vicker's flagship store. She sells attractive, handcrafted bags made of tough, recycled sailcloth. We find these charming bags irresistible. Buy one before your next vacation. Ella shares her space with Karen Reyes, a photographer specializing in pregnant women.
Hours: Sunday - Monday noon - 5 pm, Tuesday - Saturday 11 am - 6 pm.

Elsebe (Clothing - Women)
51 East Putnam Avenue, 203.869.4760
Elegant casual and business attire from well known designers. Elsebe, the owner, is very good at helping you find just the outfit you need.
Hours: Monday - Saturday, 10 am - 5:30 pm.

Estate Treasures of Greenwich
(Consignment - Furniture, Jewelry, Silver)
1162 East Putnam Avenue, Riverside, 203.637.4200
www.EstateTreasures.com
An antique consignment shop which has a wide selection of jewelry and china. A good source for silver services and serving pieces. A large number of tables and desks, although some are high quality reproductions (always marked as reproductions).
Hours: Monday - Saturday, 10 am - 5:30 pm; Sunday, noon - 5:30 pm.

Ethan Allen (Furniture, Home Decorating, Flooring)
2046 West Main, Stamford, 203.352.2888
www.EthanAllen.com
This 30,000 square-foot store just on the border of Greenwich is the company's largest store. Its collections are divided between informal and classic— just about everything for a home, including a large selection of furniture, window treatments, area rugs and accessories.
Hours: Monday - Saturday 10 am - 6 pm (Thursday until 8 pm), Sunday noon - 5 pm.

EuroChasse (Fishing & Hunting)
398 Greenwich Avenue, 203.625.9501 www.EuroChasse.com
Two floors of fascinating gifts and fashionable men's and women's sporting apparel. If you plan to hunt in Europe, this is a must. They also have serious fly fishing equipment and gifts just right for your sporting friends. A good place to get your hunting license.
Hours: weekdays, 10 am - 6 pm, Saturday 10 am - 5:30 pm.

STORES

Evelyn (Artificial Flowers)
14 West Putnam Avenue, 203.661.6743
An abundance of silk flowers so real you will almost smell the fragrance.
Hours: Monday - Saturday 10 am - 5:30 pm.

Exquisite Surfaces (Flooring, Home Decorating)
11 East Putnam Avenue, Greenwich, 203.422.2005
www.xsurfaces.com
A unique and fun shop, featuring: elegant antique & reproduction Limestone fireplaces, new & antique French Oak flooring, terra cotta floor tiles & a variety of European hand crafted tiles. They have 5 locations, three west coast and two east coast.
Hours: Monday - Friday, 9 am - 5 pm.

Farrow & Ball (Wallpaper & Paint)
32 East Putnam Avenue, 203.422.0990
www.Farrow-Ball.com
A favorite of designers, this shop is open to everyone. The soft and classic patterns of the wallpaper are color coordinated with their paints. Paints are available in many colors and finishes. This British paint manufacturer can match just about any historic color pallet.
Hours: weekdays 9 am - 5:30 pm; Saturday 10 am - 3 pm.

Fashion Light Center (Lighting)
168 West Putnam Avenue, 203.869.3098
www.LightTrends.com
A handy, helpful local resource for bulbs, lampshades, lamps, chandeliers and repairs. This 3,500 square-foot showroom has more that 23,000 indoor and outdoor light fixtures and carries all of the top brands. The owner, Archie Russell, can help you with just about any lighting project. They have a good website.
Hours: Monday - Saturday, 9 am - 5:30 pm.

Federalist (Home Decorating, Furniture)
95 East Putnam Avenue, 203.625.4727
www.TheFederalistOnline.com
Not antiques, but only experts would know it. The shop is filled with fine reproductions of 18th century American furniture and accessories.
Hours: Monday - Saturday 10 am - 6 pm.

Feinsod True Value Hardware
- 268 Sound Beach Avenue, Old Greenwich, 203.637.3641
- 43 N Main Street, Port Chester NY 914.939.3872

www.feinsodhardware.com

Friendly, well-stocked hardware store run by people who take customer service that extra step. They even repair storm windows and screens.

Hours: Monday - Saturday 8 am - 5:30 pm, Sunday 9 am - 2 pm.

Femmegems (Jewelry)
89 Greenwich Avenue, 203.861.2531

www.femmegems.com

A pleasant place to try out your own skills at jewelry designing. You can start fresh or re-design something you already own. They also have pretty, pre-made baubles for gifts, just right for bridesmaids.

Hours: Monday - Friday, 10 am - 6 pm; Saturday, 10:30 am - 6 pm; Sunday noon - 5 pm.

Flinn Gallery (Art)
At Greenwich Library, 101 West Putnam Avenue, 203.622.7900

www.flinngallery.com

This attractive gallery on the second floor is sponsored by the Friends of Greenwich Library. It has rotating exhibits selected by a jury. The Gallery also hosts the annual juried exhibition of the Greenwich Art Society.

Hours: Monday - Saturday, 10 am - 5 pm (Thursday open until 8 pm); Sunday 1 pm - 5 pm. Closed on Sundays in July and August.

Floor Covering Warehouse
112 Orchard Street, Stamford, 203.323.3113

www.floorcoveringwarehouse.org

Tucked away, yet close to Greenwich, this family-owned rug and carpet store has good prices and good service.

Hours: Tuesday - Friday 8:30 am - 5 pm, Saturday 8:30 am - 3:30 pm.

Flowers By George
7 Strickland Road, Cos Cob, 203.661.0850

www.flowersbygeorge.net

Volunteers in the Hospital rave about their pretty arrangements. They also supply flowers for large events such as parties and weddings.

Hours: Tuesday - Saturday, 10 am - 5 pm.

STORES

Forest and Field Outdoor (Firearms)

4 New Canaan Ave, Norwalk CT, 203.847.4008

www.ForestAndField.com

A 12,000 square foot firearm store representing a variety of manufacturers of guns, clothing and equipment. They have a 14-point shooting range and offer pistol certification courses.

Hours: Tuesday - Friday 10 am - 7:30 pm, Saturday, 9 am - 5 pm.

Fred (clothing-women)

212 Sound Beach Avenue, Old Greenwich, 203.344.9533

www.OGFred.com

Owner Kelly Frey named the shop after her young daughter's nickname. Stylish clothing for young adults.

Hours: Monday - Friday, 10 am - 6 pm; Saturday 10 am - 5 pm.

Free People (Clothing- Women)

351 Greenwich Avenue, 203.622.0127 www.freepeople.com

Free People is a women's clothing store operated by Urban Outfitters, which also operates Anthropologie. This small chain has colorful, creative and somewhat quirky designs. They also carry women's accessories and lingerie.

Hours: Monday - Saturday 10 am - 6 pm (Saturday 7 pm), Sunday noon - 6 pm.

French Sole (Shoes - Women)

160 Greenwich Avenue, 203.354.9161

www.FrenchSoleGreenwich.com

Ballet flats to 3 inch heels, they feature comfort as well as style. Their flats are sure to be noticed.

Hours: Monday - Saturday 10 am - 6 pm, Sunday 11 am - 5 pm.

(A.I) Friedman(Art Supplies and Framing)

495 Boston Post Road, Port Chester NY, 914.937.7351

www.AIFriedman.com

Discount art and craft supply store frequented by many local artists. Large selection of quality pre-made frames and mats.

Hours: weekdays 9 am - 8:30 pm; Saturday 9 am - 6 pm; Sunday 10 am - 6 pm.

(The) Funhouse (Toys)
236 Sound Beach Avenue, Old Greenwich, 203.698.2402
www.funhouseofgreenwich.com
This is a store where you may happily take your children. They have a great variety of small, inexpensive items. Parents fill their party bags here. Good place to find a unique or hard-to-find gift. The staff couldn't be friendlier. They will suggest age-appropriate gifts, sure to please.
Hours: weekdays 10:30 am - 6 pm, Saturday 10 am - 5 pm.

Gabby (Clothing - Women)
70 Greenwich Avenue, 203.661.5044
This woman's boutique carries good quality and stylish sweaters, jackets, blouses and pants. The service is friendly and the atmosphere is appealing. If you quickly need to find something to wear for dinner on Friday night, you should give this place a try.
Hours: every day 10 am - 5:30 pm.

Galleria (Shopping Center)
100 Main Street, White Plains NY, 914.682.0111
www.GalleriaATwhiteplains.com/static/node1792.jsp
www.Simon.com
The anchor stores are Sears (914.644.1400), Macys (914.946.5015), Old Navy (914.682.0482) and H&M (914.422.3777). Sears bought Lands End in 2002 and has a Lands End store at this location.
Hours: Monday - Saturday 10 am - 9:30 pm, Sunday 11 am - 7 pm.

Gap (Clothing - Adult, Youth, Baby)
Stamford Town Center (100 Greyrock Place),
Stamford CT, 203.327.3448   www.Gap.com
The Gap targets teenagers - 40s. Its merchandise is divided between career clothing and trendy attire and includes maternity. Its lower price line is sold at Old Navy (an anchor store in the Ridgeway Shopping Center and in the Galleria). Banana Republic carries their higher end casual career clothing.
Hours: Monday- Saturday 10 am -9 pm, Sunday 11 am - 6 pm.

Gap Kids (Clothing- Youth, Adult)
264 Greenwich Avenue, 203.625.0662
www.GapKids.com
Casual clothes for babies to age 8.
Hours: Monday - Saturday 9 am - 7 pm, Sunday noon - 6 pm.

STORES

Globe Kitchen Equipment

300 Dewey Street, Bridgeport CT, 203.367.6611, 866.604.5623
www.GlobeEquipment.com
Just about everything for the commercial kitchen or a special home kitchen.
Hours: weekdays 8:30 am - 5 pm, Saturday 9 am - 2 pm.

Gift Shop at Audubon Center

613 Riversville Rd, 203.869.5272
The perfect place to find nature objects, field guides and books. Many unique gifts for children and adults.
Hours: Tuesday - Sunday, 9 am - 5 pm.

Gift Shop at Bruce Museum

1 Museum Drive, 203.869.0376
www.BruceMuseum.org
This attractive, high-quality store is filled with unique gifts from around the world, including many with educational value and an excellent selection of books. Merchandise complements the Museum's current exhibits. Be sure to attend their holiday gift bazaar.
Hours: Tuesday - Saturday 10 am - 5 pm, Sunday 1 pm - 5 pm.

Gift Shop & Book Store at Christ Church

254 East Putnam Avenue, 203.869.9030
www.ChristChurchGreenwich.org/Store
This is the "in" place to go when you need a special gift with meaning. Marijane Marks and her helpful staff have a fine selection of books, gifts, jewelry and greeting cards. During holidays, gifts cascade out of the shop, making the store a joy to visit.
Hours: Tuesday - Saturday 10 am - 5 pm, Sunday 10 am - 1 pm.

Gift Shop at Greenwich Hospital

5 Perryridge Road, 203.863.3371
www.GreenHosp.org
They have a wide array of gifts for patients, including pretty planters and beautiful nightgowns. The items selected by the volunteer staff have made this shop a place to go whether or not you are visiting in the hospital. Selections are well-priced and tax free.
All profits go the hospital.
Hours: weekdays 9:30 am - 8 pm, Saturday 10 am - 5 pm,
Sunday noon - 6 pm.

STORES

Gift Shop at Hyatt Regency
1800 East Putnam Avenue, Old Greenwich, 203.637.1234
Hotel guests love this shop, but we also dash there when we need a gift with "Greenwich" on it. Best buy: their silk ties!
Hours: Monday - Saturday 7 am - 11 pm, Sunday 8 am - 8 pm.

Giggle (Baby, Clothing & Furniture)
102 Greenwich Avenue, 203.622.6775
www.Giggle.com
A store for new parents, ready to help you stock your nursery with the best of everything. Their collection includes baby items, selected to be healthy, stylish and fun, from strollers, car seats, bedding and furniture to toys, baby care and cleaning products. Giggle is a small chain with 5 stores.
Hours: Monday - Saturday 10 am to 6 pm (Wednesday & Thursday until 7 pm); Sunday 12 pm - 5 pm.

Go To Your Room (Children's Furniture)
255 Mill Street, Byram, 914.419.1741
www.Go2URoom.com
Children's rooms do not have to be boring. Fernando Martinez, an Argentine furniture designer, creates colorful, whimsical furniture which will make any child smile.
Hours: Monday - Saturday, 10:30 am - 5 pm.

Golden Horn (Oriental Rugs)
464 N Main Street, Port Chester NY, 914.670.6666
www.RugRestoration.com
They specialize in restoration, cleaning and sale of fine oriental and European carpets. They can repair most woven art including tapestries. In addition to repairs, they have more than 2,000 new and antique rugs for sale in their 5,000 square foot space.
Hours: Monday - Saturday, 8:30 am - 6 pm.

Graham's Toys
60 Greenwich Avenue, 203.983.6800
www.LandBridgeToys.com www.GrahamsToys.com
A unique toy store, with toys you won't find anywhere else. We love their interesting children's books. They have a children's barber shop in the back, call for appointments.
Hours: Monday & Saturday, 10 am - 5 pm,
Tuesday - Friday 10 am - 6 pm.

STORES

Grainger (Industrial Supplies)
339 West Avenue, Stamford CT, 203.323.0005
www.Grainger.com
350,000 items including supplies, such as material handling, safety and security, cleaning and maintenance, pumps and plumbing, electrical, lighting, ventilation, tools, metal working, fluid power, heating and air-conditioning products, motors, and power transmissions. A paradise for the do-it-yourselfer.
Hours: weekdays, 7 am 5 pm.

Great Stuff (Clothing-Women)
321 Greenwich Avenue, 203.861.6872
www.greatstuff-online.com
Eclectic selections with a flair - informal and formal, with lots of possibilities for evening wear.
Hours: Monday - Saturday 10 am - 6 pm; Sunday, noon - 5 pm.

(The) Great Outdoor Toy Company (Children's play Equipment)
9 Kings Highway, Westport CT, 203.222.3818
www.TheGreatOutdoorToyCompany.com
Playhouses, hoops, trampolines, redwood swing sets with interchangeable parts, allowing you to make your own fun designs.
Hours: Monday - Saturday, 9:30 am - 5 pm; Sunday, noon - 5pm.

Greenwich Bicycles
35 Amogerone Crossway, 203.869.4141
www.GreenwichBikes.com
Road bikes, mountain bikes—this large store has all the right equipment and a very helpful website to review before you shop for a bike.
Hours: weekdays 10 am - 6 pm (8 pm Thursday), Saturday 9:30 am - 5:30 pm; April-September, open Sunday noon - 4 or 5 pm.

Greenwich Exchange for Women's Work (Gifts)
28 Sherwood Place, 203.869.0229
This small shop's mission is to help others help themselves. It has reasonably priced, handmade items. If you want to give a gift to a newborn or young child, you will adore their hand-knit sweaters and smocked dresses.
Hours: weekdays, 10 am - 4 pm; Saturday 10 am - 1 pm.

STORES

Greenwich Floor Covering
173 Davis Avenue, Greenwich, 203.661-2323
A family-owned flooring and carpet business, with an excellent reputation for service. Helpful on-site consultation is provided by owners Mark and Tina Grabowski. Their customers include local businesses, homeowners and schools.
Hours: weekdays 8:30 am - 4:30 pm.

Greenwich Furs (Fur clothing-Women)
5 West Putnam Avenue, 203.869.1421
Since 1948 this furrier has been helping Greenwich residents select, repair, remodel and store their furs.
Hours: weekdays 10 am - 5 pm, Saturday 10 am - 5 pm.

Greenwich Golf Fitting Studio
222 Mill Street, Byram, 203.532.4810
www.GreenwichGolf.com
Jacques Intriere repairs your clubs or analyzes your swing to fit custom golf clubs to make you a better golfer.
Hours: Tuesday, Wednesday, Thursday, 11 am - 6 pm; Friday, 1 pm - 6 pm; Saturday, 8:30 am - 4:30 pm. Hours may vary, call store for appointment.

Greenwich Hardware
www.GreenwichHardwareAndHome.com,
www.TaylorRental.com/GreenwichTR
- 195 Greenwich Avenue & Liberty Way Parking Area
  203.869.6750
- 300 West Putnam Avenue, 203.622.2350
Anyone moving into town will find this a valuable resource. A helpful place to call when you have forgotten something: they will deliver it to you. If you want to rent tools or power equipment, go to their Putnam Avenue store.
Hours: Monday - Saturday 8 am - 5 pm; Sunday 9:30 am - 4 pm.

Greenwich Hospital Gift Shop Flowers (Florist)
5 Perryridge Road, 203.863.3371
www.GreenHosp.org
The gift shop keeps a selection of fresh flowers in vases, get well balloons and a number of Baby and Mom items for the new moms. Call or buy on-line and they will deliver to your favorite patient.
Delivery Hours: weekdays 10 am - 4 pm, Saturday 10:30 am -4 pm.
No Sunday delivery.

STORES

Greenwich Lock and Door (Locksmith, hardware)
280 Railroad Avenue, 203.622.1095
www.GreenwichLockandDoor.com
A reliable local source for architectural hardware, doors, security products and lock-smithing. Good customer service.
Hours: Monday & Wednesday 7 am - 4 pm; Tuesday,
Thursday & Friday 8 am - 4 pm.

Greenwich Music
1200 East Putnam Avenue, Riverside, 203.869.3615
www.greenwichmusic.com
Their store is filled with sheet music and instruments. They have a large selection of guitars & drums and a helpful staff. A full line of instruments are available for rent; a great way to discover if that instrument is right for you or your child. They have a music school (Fraioli School of Music) next door where they give lessons for the instruments they carry. See their website for details.
Hours: Monday - Saturday 10 am - 6 pm.

Greenwich Orchids (Florist)
106 Mason Street, 203.661.5544
www.GreenwichOrchids.com
Grown in their 56,000 square foot greenhouse, the orchids are exquisite. They have many varieties, some with unusual colors. They also make lovely flower arrangements.
Hours: Monday - Saturday 9 am - 6 pm.

Greenwich Oriental Art (Antiques)
7 East Putnam Avenue, 203.629.0500
www.GreenwichOrientalArt.com
A mixture of old and modern oriental art. Their website gives a good sampling of what they carry.
Hours: Monday - Saturday, 10 am - 5:30 pm.

Griffin & Howe (Firearms, clothing, accessories)
340 West Putnam Avenue, 203.618.0270
www.griffinhowe.com
Excellent sporting firearms, clothing and accessories. This is the place where serious skeet and trap shooters buy their shotguns. They also have shooting schools and an excellent selection of rifles.
Hours: Monday - Wednesday 10 am - 6 pm, Thursday 11 am - 8 pm, Friday 10 am - 6 pm, Saturday 10 am - 5 pm.

Hansen & Hansen (Antique Guns)
244 Old Post Road, Southport CT, 203.259.7337
www.HansenGuns.com
They buy, sell and appraise antique firearms, swords, knives and related collectibles.
Hours: Tuesday- Friday 12 pm - 5 pm, Saturday 10 am - 4 pm.

Harbor View Antiques Center (Antiques)
101 Jefferson Street, Stamford, 203.325.8070
www.HarborViewAntiques.com
See Antiques Area of Stamford for a description.
Hours: Monday - Saturday 10:30 am - 5:30 pm, Sunday noon - 5 pm.

Harris Restaurant Supply (Cookware)
25 Abendroth Avenue, Port Chester NY, 914.937.0404
www.hrs-foodservice.com
Commercial restaurant supplier which also allows the general public to buy. Cooks go crazy here.
Hours: weekdays, 9 am - 4 pm.

HB Home (Home Decorating fabrics and Furniture)
28 East Putnam Avenue, 203.629.4999
www.hbhomedesign.com
HB stands for the name of the designers Patricia Healing and Dan Barsanti. Their furniture is a mix of stylish period and country designs.
Hours: weekdays, 10 am - 6 pm, Saturday 11 - 5.

Helen Ainson (Clothing - Women)
1078 Post Road, Darien CT, 203.655.9841
www.HelenAinson.com
For over 25 years Helen Ainson has helped ladies in our area look their best at special occasions. When you discover you are soon to be "mother of the bride," you will like their friendly, knowledgeable advice and fashions from over 150 manufacturers.
Hours: Monday - Saturday, 9:30 am - 5:30 pm
(Tuesday & Thursday until 7 pm).

HH Brown (Men's and women's shoes)
171 Greenwich Avenue, 203.809.1381
www.HHBrown.com
HH Brown is owned by Berkshire Hathaway and has its headquarters in Greenwich at 124 West Putnam Avenue. With 53 stores, it seems only natural to open a store in Greenwich to show off its 19 brands of shoes including vintage styles—saddle & suede shoes. The store also serves as a test site for new products.
Hours: Monday - Saturday 10 am - 6 pm; Sunday 11 am - 5 pm.

Hickory & Tweed (Skiing Equipment & Clothing)
410 Main Street, Armonk NY, 914.273.3397
www.HickoryAndTweed.com
A wide selection of skis, boots and clothing. Good technical help. When you are planning to buy equipment, this store is definitely worth the trip. It was voted the number one ski shop in America by Ski Magazine.
Hours: weekdays 10 am - 5:30 pm (Thursdays until 8 pm);
Saturday 9:30 am - 5:30 pm; Sunday (except July & August) noon - 4 pm.

(The) Historical Christmas Barn
146 Danbury Road, Wilton CT, 203.761.8777
www.HistoricalChristmasBarn.com
Yes, this Christmas store closes at 5 pm. They are in a residential zone and this seems to be a town rule. But what wonderful ornaments and figurines. This is like no other Christmas store you are likely to find.
Hours: Open every day, Monday - Saturday 10 am - 5 pm, Sunday 11 am - 5 pm. January - August closed Mondays.

Hoagland's of Greenwich (Home Accessories & Gifts)
175 Greenwich Avenue, 203.869.2127
www.Hoaglands.com
A first-class gift shop owned for years by a Greenwich resident with exquisite taste. This is THE place for brides and grooms to register. In addition to their crystal, china and silver, they have charming baby gifts.
Hours: Monday - Saturday, 9 am - 5:30 pm.

Hobby Center (Toys)
405 East Putnam Avenue (Cos Cob Plaza), Cos Cob, 203.869.0969
For years, kids in Greenwich have been rewarded for cleaning their room or finishing their homework with a trip to Ann's Hobby Center. Rockets and radio-controlled boats are favorites. No matter what your hobby, they are likely to have what you need.
Hours: Monday - Saturday, 9:30 am - 5:30 pm.

STORES

Home Boutique of Greenwich (Linens)
14 Lewis Street, 203.869.2550
www.HomeBoutique.com
When you feel like treating yourself or want to create a picture-perfect bedroom, visit this shop filled with pretty bed, bath & table linens.
Hours: Monday - Saturday 10 am - 5:30 pm.

Home Depot (Hardware)
www.HomeDepot.com
They have 40,000 brand names to choose from. Alas, the Home Depot Expo stores are closed.
* 600 Connecticut Avenue, Norwalk CT, 203.854.9111
Hours: Monday - Saturday 6 am - 10 pm, Sunday 8 am - 8 pm.
* 150 Midland Avenue, Port Chester, NY, 914.690.9755
Hours: Monday - Saturday, 7 am - 10 pm, Sunday 9 am - 6 pm.

Home Goods (Home Decorating- Accessories)
High Ridge & Cold Spring Road, Stamford, 203.964.9416
www.HomeGoods.com
When you are ready to accessorize a room, this store is a must. Casual, fun items at great prices.
Hours: Monday - Saturday, 9:30 am - 9:30 pm; Sunday, 11 am - 6 pm.

Home Works (Windows & Fabric)
509 North Main Street, Port Chester NY, 914.934.0907
www.HomeWorksNY.com
When you want to redo your window draperies or upholster a chair, they are a good resource for your fabric.
Hours: Weekdays 10 am - 5 pm (Thursday until 7 pm).

House of Fins (Fish)
99 Bruce Park Avenue, 203.661.8131
www.HouseOfFins.com
Owned by Greenwich resident Robert Bray, House of Fins has a huge inventory of everything you need to make a successful aquarium or stock a pond and good advice as well. Complete service and many exotic fish to choose from.
Hours: Monday - Saturday, 10 am - 7 pm; Sunday, noon - 5 pm.

STORES

Housewarmings (Home Decorating -Furniture & Gifts)
235 Sound Beach Avenue, Old Greenwich, 203.637.5106
Unique home furnishings and decorative accessories. Comfortable furniture with a choice of fabrics.
Hours: Monday - Saturday 10 am - 5:30 pm.

IKEA (Furniture)
www.Ikea.com
A huge store and a huge chain (296 stores), with moderate prices and several grades of Scandinavian designed furniture and housewares. Popular with Europeans. There is a supervised children's play area. A good place to go when you are on a limited budget and need to furnish a home or dorm room quickly.
• 1000 Center Drive, Elizabeth, NJ, 908.289.4488 (44 miles)
Hours: Monday - Saturday 10 am - 9 pm, Sunday 10 am - 8 pm.
Directions: I-95 S across the George Washington Bridge to the New Jersey Turnpike, exit 13A then follow signs.
• 450 Sargent Drive, New Haven CT, 203.865.4532 (51 miles)
Hours: Monday-Thursday 10 am - 8 pm, Friday & Saturday 10 am - 9 pm, Sunday 11 am - 7 pm.

Images (Photography)
202 Sound Beach Avenue, Old Greenwich, 203.637.4193
www.ImagesCenter.com
In addition to framing your photographs, they restore damaged photographs by removing scratches, tears and stains, enhance photographs to reduce red-eye or correct color and brightness, and, of course, enlarge, crop or add a border. No negative is required.
Hours: Monday - Saturday 10 am - 5 pm.

In Things (Shoes & Accessories-Women)
354 North Main Street (Steilmann Building), Port Chester NY
 914.934.9006
www.InThingsCorp.com
Unique shawls, footwear, purses and jewelry from India.
Hours: Monday - Saturday 11 am - 5:30 pm.

STORES

Innovation Luggage (Luggage)
17 East Putnam Avenue, 203.869.5322
www.InnovationLuggage.com
A national chain carrying less expensive luggage, casual bags, business cases and travel accessories. Nice selection, helpful service and good prices.
Hours: Monday - Saturday, 10 am - 6 pm, Sunday, noon - 5 pm.

Instant Replay (Sporting Goods - Hockey)
1074 Hope Street, Stamford CT, 203.322.7502
Located across from the Stamford Twin Rinks, is a shop where parents in the know can save money outfitting their family with every thing they will need for playing hockey or baseball. They have a wide selection of new and used equipment.
Hours: weekdays, 10 am - 6 pm (Thursday until 7 pm), Saturday ,9 am - 5 pm, Sunday 11 am - 4 pm.

Interstate Fire and Safety (Fire Extinguishers)
404 Willett Avenue, Port Chester NY, 914.937.6100
www.InterstateFireAndSfty.net
Fire extinguishers for home or business.
Hours: weekdays 8 am - 5 pm.

Interstate / Lakeland Lumber
(Hardware -Building Materials)
184 South Water Street, Greenwich, 203.531.8050
www.InterstateLumber.com
A good place for doors, windows and trim, especially windows.
Hours: weekdays, 7:30 am - 5 pm, Saturday, 8 am - Noon.

Irresistibles (Clothing-Women)
104 Main Street, New Canaan CT, 203.966.0608
www.Irresistibles.com
A small 13 store chain with contemporary sportswear for women. At a holiday luncheon, many of the ladies had purchased their pretty decorated sweaters at this shop.
Hours: Monday - Saturday, 9:30 am - 6 pm, Sunday noon - 5 pm.

STORES

J Crew (Clothing, Men & Women, Youth)
126 Greenwich Avenue, 203.661.5181
www.JCrew.com
A large store with classic, preppy-casual men and women's clothing.
Check out "Crew Cuts" for children ages 2 - 12. The high end adult clothes
are in the J Crew Collection. Michelle Obama wears J Crew clothes.
Hours: Monday - Saturday, 10 am - 6 pm; Sunday, noon - 5 pm.

J McLaughlin (Clothing - Women)
45 East Putnam Avenue, 203.862.9777
www.JMcLaughlin.com
Primarily women's informal preppy clothing - "stylish, but not stuffy"
Hours: Monday - Saturday 10 am - 5:30 pm.

J McLaughlin Outlet Store (Outlet)
68 Water Street, South Norwalk CT, 203.838.8427
Hours: Monday - Saturday 10 am - 6 pm, Sunday noon - 5 pm.

j papers (Stationery)
100 Bruce Park Avenue, 203.769.5104
Do you remember "The Papery" on Greenwich Avenue? It was a wonderful
shop for finding out-of-the-ordinary invitations and greeting cards. Jill,
who was the manager there has opened a shop on Bruce Park Avenue
carrying the same great selection and parking is easy. During the fall
and winter they carry Godiva Chocolates.
Hours: Every day 9 am - 5 pm (during the summer, closed Sunday &
Monday).

J Pocker & Son (Framing)
175 West Putnam Avenue, 203.629.0811
www.JPocker.com
A family business since 1926. Good suggestions for appropriate frames
and mats. They have a large portfolio of limited edition prints.
Hours: Tuesday - Saturday 10 am - 5:30 pm.

jacadi (Baby & Toddler Clothing)
22 Greenwich Avenue, Greenwich 203.422.2202
www.jacadiusa.com
This Paris based company has 400 boutiques worldwide and 27 US locations. Although the company has a wide selection of nursery furniture
and accessories, the Greenwich shop features their very fashionable, ultra simple, newborn through toddler clothing.
Hours: Monday - Saturday 10 am - 6 pm, Sunday noon - 5 pm.

STORES

Janie and Jack (Baby to Children's Clothing)
107 Greenwich Avenue, 203.422.5080

www.Janieandjack.com

Owned by the Gymboree company, there are over 100 Janie and Jack stores. They carry adorable clothing for children - babies to age 6.

Hours: Monday-Saturday 10 am - 6 pm, Sunday noon-5 pm.

Jones New York (Discount Women's Clothing)
517 Westport Avenue, Norwalk CT, 203.847.3794

www.JNY.com

A company owned store, co-located with Nine West shoe outlet, some merchandise is slightly discounted some is dramatically discounted. A good resource.

Hours: Monday-Saturday 10 am - 9 pm, Sunday 11 am - 6 pm.

JoS A Bank (men's clothing)
Cos Cob Plaza (409 East Putnam Avenue), Cos Cob, 203.869.6087

www.josbank.com

With over 400 retail stores, its clothing is targeted at male professionals. They have several different lines: the basic business express, executive collections, the midrange signature collection and the high quality signature gold collection. The Greenwich store is 4,000 square feet.

Hours: Monday - Saturday 10 am - 9 pm, Sunday noon - 6 pm.

JSJ Window Treatments (Windows)
3 Strickland Road, Cos Cob, 203.661.5123

www.JSJwindowtreatments.com

A reliable source for blinds, shades and shutters. They carry Hunter Douglas. Shades can be cut on the premises.

Hours: weekdays, 9 am - 5 pm; Saturday, 10 am - 2 pm.

Juliska (Glassware)
465 Canal Street, Stamford CT, 203.316.9118

www.Juliska.com

Stores all over the USA, like Saks, Neiman Marcus and Michael C Fina, carry this distinctive glassware. This flagship store has scrumptious table settings and dramatic pieces. Juliska's outlet store is located in Lillian August's outlet store at 85 Water Street in Norwalk.

Hours: Monday - Saturday 9 am - 5 pm, Sunday noon - 5 pm.

STORES

Kate's Paperie (Stationery, gifts)

125 Greenwich Avenue, 203.861.0025

www.KatesPaperie.com

Whether you're looking to design an invitation for a baby shower, birthday party or wedding, you will be impressed with the variety of creative and custom options gathered by Angelica Berrie the fashionable owner of this 5-store chain. Kate's carries an assortment of lovely calendars, stationery, paper, photo albums, arts and crafts supplies and much, much more. Remember to stop here when you need a gift.

Hours: Monday - Saturday 10 am - 6 pm; closed Sunday.

Kate Spade (Accessories- Women and Home)

271 Greenwich Avenue, 203.622.4260

www.KateSpade.com

Chic women's specialty shop: handbags, shoes, and home accessories.

Hours: Monday - Saturday 10 am - 6 pm, Sunday noon - 5 pm.

Kenneth Lynch & Sons (Garden Accessories)

114 Willenbrook road, Oxford CT, 203.264.2831

www.KLynchAndSons.com

If you are looking for an elaborate fountain, pretty garden bench, statuary, topiary, weathervane or sundial, this will be paradise for you. The Lynch family has been crafting garden ornaments for over sixty years. Ornaments are made to order. Their extensive catalog is available for $15 softcover.

Hours: weekdays, 8:30 am - 5 pm.

Kids Home Furniture (Children's Furniture)

11 Forest Street, Stamford, 203.327.1333

Baby and teen furniture and accessories at reasonable prices.

Hours: weekdays 9:30 am - 5 pm, Saturday 10 am - 3 pm.

(Greenwich) Kitchen Works (Cookware)

118 Greenwich Avenue, 203.983.3165

When you need a gift for someone who enjoys cooking, this shop has a wide selection of upscale kitchen-related products and specialty food items. A good place to buy an expresso coffee maker.

Hours: Monday - Saturday 9:30 am - 5:30 pm, Sunday 11 am - 4 pm (closed Sundays in August).

STORES

Klaff's (Lighting, Hardware, Fixtures)
28 Washington Street, South Norwalk
800.552.3371 or 203.866.1603
www.Klaffs.com
A tremendous selection of indoor and outdoor lighting fixtures, door hardware, bathroom fixtures. They even have kitchen cabinets, tile and mirrors.
Hours: Monday - Saturday 9 am - 5:30 pm (Thursday until 8 pm).

Kmart (Department Store)
399 Tarrytown Rd, White Plains NY, 914.684.1184
www.Kmart.com
Discount store, owned by Sears, which competes with Wal-Mart and Target: Clothing, footwear, bedding, furniture, jewelry, electronics and housewares. They are a primary source for Martha Stewart & Jaclyn Smith brands.
Hours: Monday - Saturday 8 am - 10 pm, Sunday 8 am - 9 pm.

Kohl's (Department Store)
431 Post Road (Shopping Center), Port Chester NY, 914.690.0107
www.Kohls.com
Similar to a JC Penney, they sell men's and women's clothing and accessories as well as some household items at discounted prices.
Hours: Monday - Saturday, 8 am - 10 pm; Sunday, 9 am - 9 pm.

Kriti Collection (Clothing- Women)
39 Lewis Street, Greenwich CT, 203.531.5722
www.KritiCollection.com
A SoHo boutique transplanted to Greenwich. This awesome shop has stylish, very wearable and attractively displayed clothing. The work of local artists is featured on their walls.
Hours: Tuesday - Saturday 11 am - 6 pm, Sunday noon - 5 pm.

Lacoste Boutique (Clothing, Men, Women & Youth)
98 Greenwich Avenue, 203.422.0180   www.Lacoste.com
A French apparel company founded in 1933 that sells preppie, high-end clothing. It is famous for its tennis shirts and the company's logo, a green crocodile. The founder, Ren Lacoste, was a famous French tennis player who achieved fame at tennis as well as in fashion. The family still owns control of the company.
Hours: Monday - Saturday 10 am - 6 pm (Thursday until 7 pm), Sunday 12 pm - 5 pm.

Lacrosse Unlimited (Sporting Goods)

1239 East Putnam Avenue, Riverside CT, 203.344.9402

www.LacrosseUnlimited.com or www.lulax.com

One of 19 stores, they sell equipment, clothes and team uniforms. Their custom apparel site is www.teamlu.com .They are a good source for sports camps, see www.millionlacrosse.com or www.fluxlacrosse.com.

Hours: Monday - Saturday 10 am - 9 pm, Sunday 11 am - 6 pm.

Landfall Navigation (Boating)

151 Harvard Ave, Stamford CT, 203.487.0775, 800.941.2219

www.LandfallNavigation.com

Captain Henry Marx, the owner, is very knowledgeable and helpful. If you have a boat, he has what you need: charts, supplies or just information. Be sure to get a copy of his catalog. They have excellent nautical gifts.

Hours: weekdays 9 am - 5 pm, Saturday 9 am - noon.

Lands' End @ Sears (Clothing - Men & Women)

100 Main Street (Galleria Shopping Center), White Plains NY
914.644.1400   www.LandsEnd.com

Attractive casual clothing for women, men and youth. Lands' End, an internet retailer, was purchased by Sears and has opened shops in a number of Sears stores.

Hours: weekdays 10 am - 9 pm, Saturday 9 am - 9:30 pm
Sunday 11 am - 6 pm.

LensCrafters

100 Greyrock Place, Stamford CT, 203.348.2080

www.LensCrafters.com

LensCrafters started in 1983 and has expanded to over 850 stores. They sell prescription eye wear and non-prescription sunglasses. They have the same parent as Pearle Vision. You can usually get a prescription before 6 pm and glasses within one hour.

Hours: Monday - Saturday 10 am - 9 pm, Sunday 11 am - 6 pm.

Letter Perfect

231 East Putnam Avenue, 203.869.1979

www.jlgreenwich.org

A stationery shop sponsored by and helping to support the Junior League of Greenwich. Be sure to stop in this nicely displayed shop when you need customized stationary, stylish invitations or a gift for your hostess.

Hours: weekdays, 10 am - noon.

STORES

LF (Clothing-Women)

319 Greenwich Avenue, 203.629-6193

www.LFStores.com

LF wants to be an alternative to mainstream brands. With their California ultra-hip merchandise, we think they have met their goal. We recently overheard a customer in Pucci boots, exclaim "That's cool" when examining a $180 pair of jeans.

Hours: Monday - Saturday 10 am - 6 pm, Sunday, noon - 5 pm.

Liberty Village (Outlet Mall)

1 Church Street, Flemington, NJ, 908.782.8550

www.PremiumOutlets.com

Shop until you drop. About 2 hours away, there are more than 120 outlet stores in a number of outlet centers in Flemington. Sixty of the shops are in Liberty Village.

Hours: Sunday - Wednesday 10 am - 6 pm,

Thursday - Saturday 10 am - 9 pm.

L'Occitane (Cosmetics)

236 Greenwich Avenue, 203.422.0234

www.LOccitane.com

Fragrances, candles and body care products with the soft scents of southern France. L'Occitane has more than 700 stores worldwide. The company does no animal testing and no animal product or by-product is used, except for beehive products.

Hours: Monday - Saturday 10 am - 6 pm, Sunday noon - 6 pm.

(The) Light Touch (Lamps)

12 Lewis Street, 203.629.2255

When you are looking for a lamp or lamp shade with character, be sure to stop in here.

Hours: Monday - Saturday, 10 am - 5:30 pm.

Lillian August (Furniture)

* 19 West Elm Street, Greenwich, 203.629.1539
* 32 Knight Street, Norwalk CT, 203.847.3314

www.LillianAugust.com

Sofas, chairs and desks designed by Lillian August. The Norwalk store, their Flagship Store, is housed in a converted factory. It has 60,000 square feet of selling space, double the size of the next largest store.

Greenwich hours: Monday - Saturday 10 am - 6 pm.

Norwalk hours: Monday - Saturday 10 am - 7 pm, Sunday 11 am - 6 pm.

Lillian August Outlet Store (Furniture)

85 Water Street (SoNo Square), South Norwalk CT, 203.838.0153
www.lillianaugust.com
Sofas, chairs and desks designed by Lillian August.
Hours: Monday - Saturday 10 am - 6 pm (Thursday until 7 pm),
Sunday noon - 6 pm.

Lilly Pulitzer (Clothing - Women, Children)

92 Greenwich Avenue, 203.661.3136
www.LillyPulitzer.com
Popular since the 1960's. Lots of pink and green and pretty colors for
upscale casual women and children. Totally charming mother - daughter
dress alikes.
Hours: Monday - Saturday 10 am - 6 pm, Sunday noon - 5 pm.

Linen Press (Linen)

16 Arcadia Road, Old Greenwich, 203.637.0200
Unique luxury items for bed, bath and table. Much of the inventory is
imported from France, Italy and Switzerland.
Hours: Monday - Saturday 10 am - 5 pm.

Little Eric (Children - Shoes)

15 East Elm Street, 203.622.1600
www.LittleEricGreenwich.com
A children's shoe store with high quality dress and play wear. A helpful
sales staff eliminates the usual shoe-shopping hassles.
Hours: Monday - Saturday 10 am - 6 pm, Sunday 11 am - 5 pm.

Lord and Taylor (Department Store)

110 High Ridge Road, Stamford, 203.327.6600
www.LordAndTaylor.com
A large full-service, stand-alone store, with easy parking and attractive,
up-scale fashions for men and women 35 and up. Father and son, Robert
and Richard Baker of Greenwich, purchased the chain in 2006. Lord &
Taylor's merchandise is on a par with Barneys New York, Saks Fifth
Avenue, Neiman Marcus and Bergdorf Goodman and slightly above
Bloomingdale's and Nordstrom.
Hours: weekdays 10 am - 9:30 pm, Saturday 10 am - 9 pm,
Sunday 11 am - 7 pm.

STORES

Loretta Stagen Floral Designs (florist)
Stamford CT, 203.323.3544
www.LorettaStagen.com
Innovative flower arrangements and party decorations for corporate events and weddings. She created a glorious party for us. She also offers classes and workshops in flower arranging. For five or more students, she will create a special class in their area of interest.

Lucky Jeans (Clothing-Men, Women)
244 Greenwich Avenue, 203.861.4039
www.LuckyBrandJeans.com
This large retro-shop is filled with garments reminiscent of the Jack Kerouac era. Everything from the shop's decor to the music is designed to make the 50's and 60's ooze from the clothing. Denim makes up most of their business. Lucky Brand Jeans first became popular due to the words, "LUCKY YOU" being stitched into the fly of every pair. They try to have the right pair of jeans for every body type. From their start in 1990 they have expanded to 110 stores.
Hours: Monday - Saturday, 11 am - 7 pm; Sunday 11 am - 6 pm.

Lucy (Exercise Clothing - women)
72-74 Greenwich Avenue, 203.661.1098
www.Lucy.com
Fashionable, comfortable athletic clothing for active women of all ages. Lucy specializes in apparel for Pilates, yoga, running and the gym with a variety of fits from sleek to relaxed. This Portland Oregon chain, with 90 stores across the US, is owned by VF Corporation owner of many sports brands such as North Face, Wrangler and Nautica.
Hours: Monday - Saturday 10 am - 6 pm, Sunday noon - 5 pm.

lululemon athletica (Exercise Clothing - men and women)
151 Greenwich Avenue, 203.622.5046
www.Lululemon.com
Often referred to as "lulu", this yoga-inspired athletic apparel company has 100 stores which not only sell athletic attire but encourage a healthy lifestyle. On Sunday they convert their store into a yoga studio. Join them for a free yoga class.
Hours: Monday - Saturday 10 am - 6 pm, Sunday noon - 5 pm.

STORES

Lux Bond & Green (Jewelry)
169 Greenwich Avenue, 203.629.0900
www.LBGreen.com
They carry David Yurman jewelry and Steuben gifts.
Hours: Tuesday - Saturday, 9:30 am - 5 pm.

Lynnens (Linen)
278 Greenwich Avenue, 203.629.3659
www.Lynnens.com
Since 1980 this high-end bed, bath, linen and nightwear store has been a real favorite of Greenwich residents. Lynne Jenkins has stocked her store with luxury products from around the world. Their specialties are service and customizing linens.
Hours: Monday - Saturday, 9:30 am - 5:30 pm.

Lynnens Too (Linen)
1 Bruce Place (in the basement), 203.629.3659
An outlet for discontinued items from Lynnens on Greenwich Avenue. Cash and checks only. No returns.
Hours: Thursday, Friday & Saturday, 9:30 am - 5:30 pm.

McDermott Paint & Wallpaper
35 Spring Street, 203.622.0699
www.McDermottPaintWallpaper.com
If you are planning to do any of your own home painting, you can count on good advice and Benjamin Moore paints from this longtime Greenwich shop. If you are trying to match a color, take a sample and they can duplicate it with their computer. A good selection of wallpaper as well as painting supplies.
Hours: Monday - Saturday, 7:30 am - 5 pm.

McArdle-MacMillen Florist & Garden Center
48 Arch Street, 203.661.5600, 800.581.5558
www.McArdles.com
Many pretty dinner tables are adorned with their arrangements. A good place to buy flowers (they have a large selection), corsages and plants. Come early on weekends during the garden season, as it is always busy or place an order on their website. They have a newsletter filled with helpful gardening tips. Be sure to get on their mailing list.
Hours: Monday - Saturday 8 am - 5:30 pm.

STORES

Maclaren Showroom (Baby Buggies)

10 Marshall Street, Norwalk CT, 203.354.4437

www.MaclarenBaby.com

This is a US factory store for the British company's fashionable, light-weight buggies (a.k.a. strollers), baby carriers and rockers. Maclaren products are sold in over 50 countries. The Techno XLR and the Techno MX3 models can be fitted with a car seat to become travel systems. Their repair center is also located in Norwalk at 25 Van Zant Street, 203.354.4439.

Hours: Tuesday - Saturday, 10 am - 5 pm, Sunday, noon - 5 pm.

Macy's (Department Store)

Stamford Town Center, 203.964.1500

www.Macys.com

Macy's holds a special place in many people's hearts. Macy's opened in 1858. The company competes on an average price level above Kohl's, J.C. Penney, and Sears, and below Nordstrom and sister chain Bloomingdale's.

Hours: weekdays, 10 am - 9 pm, Saturday ,9 am - 10 pm,

Sunday, 11 am - 8 pm.

Madewell (Women's Jeans & T-shirts)

256 Greenwich, Avenue, 203.661.1591

www.Madewell.com

Launched in 2006 by J. Crew, this 14-store chain's name was taken from a former Massachusetts workwear company. The workers in that 1937 company would be amazed at the edgy, ripped-up, ex-boyfriend jeans sold here for about $100 a pair.

Hours: Monday - Saturday, 10 am - 6 pm, Sunday noon - 5 pm.

Magaschoni by Ellen (Clothing Women)

115 Mason Street (Village Square), 203.869.2119

www.Magaschoni.com

Stylish designs for jackets, sweaters and blouses that can be worn together or as separates. Magaschoni has 4 free standing boutiques and 800 stores carry their designs.

Hours: Monday - Saturday, 10 am - 5 pm.

STORES

Manfredi (Jewelry)

121 Greenwich Avenue, 203.622.1414

www.manfredijewels.com

Roberto Chiappeloni's store focuses on current fashion and cutting-edge pieces. A good place to have your watch repaired.

Hours: Tuesday - Friday 10 am - 5 pm, Saturday 10 am - 5:30 pm

Mark's On Putnam (Antiques)

1142 East Putnam Avenue, Riverside, 203.990.0004

www.MarksOnPutnam.com

Attractively displayed mid-level antiques.

Hours: Monday - Saturday, 10 am - 5 pm, Sunday Noon - 5 pm.

Mark Mariani's Garden Center (Plants and Shrubs)

45 Bedford Road, Armonk NY, 914.273.3083

www.MarianiGardens.com

This stylish, unusual greenhouse and garden center is filled with shrubs, rare trees and decorative pottery. They also have a terrific café which is reviewed in the RESTAURANT section.

Hours: Monday - Friday 8:30 am - 5 pm, Saturday 8 am - 4 pm, Sunday 9 am - 4 pm.

Marshalls (Department Store)

- 2235 Summer Street (Ridgeway Shopping Center), Stamford CT, 203.356.9667
- 20 Waterfront Place, Port Chester NY, 914.690.9380

www.MarshallsOnline.com

Marshalls and T J Maxx have the same parent company and have similar product assortments. Marshalls sells brand name and designer clothing at off-prices. They carry clothing for men, women, kids, and teens. They also carry footwear, bedding, furniture, jewelry and housewares.

Hours: Monday - Saturday 9:30 am - 9:30 pm, Sunday, 11 am - 8 pm.

Michael Kors (Clothing - Women)

279 Greenwich Avenue, 203.618.1200

www.MichaelKors.com

Michael Kors is renowned for his classic, chic but sensible American sportswear and other clothing styles. His designs are worn by many celebrities. This store is one of about 20 USA Lifestyle Stores.

Hours: Monday - Saturday, 10 am - 7 pm; Sunday, 11 am - 5 pm.

STORES

Michaels (Craft Supplies)

- Ridgeway Shopping Center, 2233 Summer Street, Stamford 203.978.0026
- 27 Waterfront Place, Port Chester NY, 914.937.3060

www.Michaels.com

Michaels has over 1,000 stores. A favorite source for scrapbook makers. The average store contains over 40,000 different products for crafts, framing, beading, knitting, floral, and wall decor, as well as seasonal merchandise. Michaels provides custom framing and custom floral service, as well as classes and demonstrations—featuring skills such as cake decorating, beading and knitting. Michaels has children's birthday parties, where a craft is made.

Hours: Monday - Saturday, 9 am - 9 pm; Sunday, 10 am - 7 pm.

Michelangelo of Greenwich (Gifts)

353 Greenwich Avenue, 661.8540, 800.677.4490

www.MikeGifts.com

Wide selection of clocks, crystal, pewter, brass and silver which they will engrave for personal or corporate gifts. They have produced awards for the Super Bowl and the Pebble Beach Golf Tournament.

Hours: Tuesday - Saturday, 10 am - 5 pm; Sunday ,11 am - 5 pm.

Mill Street Home (Home Accessories)

227 Mill Street, Byram, 203.813.3600

www.millstreethome.net

Delightful selection of gifts and decorative items for your home.

Hours: Tuesday - Friday, 10 am - 5:30 pm; Saturday, 10 am - 4 pm.

Mint (Consignment)

253 Mill Street, Byram, 203.532.0200

www.MintVintage.biz

A real find. Who would believe this trendy shop is a consignment shop. Their title mint condition describes their selections. Catering to Children and young adults, this is a great place to find a brand name sweater, boys jacket or a party dress. The preppie little dress I bought for 4-year old Morgan, was a sample and had never been worn.

Hours: Tuesday - Friday, 10:30 am - 5:30 pm; Saturday, 10 am - 5 pm.

STORES

Miranda Arts (Art)

6 North Pearl Street, Suite 404E, Port Chester NY
914.935.9362, 318.7178
www.MirandaFineArts.com
Art Gallery featuring local artists. Patricia Miranda teaches painting and
gilding techniques to adults and youth. She does museum quality framing and frame repair.
Hours: Call for exhibition hours.

Mis En Scene by Claire Maestroni
(Furniture & Home Accessories)

34 East Putnam Avenue, 203.422.0567   (Indoor Furniture)
www.MisEnSceneGreenwich.com
Mix of contemporary and unusual home furniture and accessories. Good
place for unique lighting fixtures or hardware.
Hours: Monday - Saturday 10 am - 6 pm.

Mitchell Gold + Bob Williams (Furniture)

45 East Putnam Avenue, 203.661.4480
Www.MGandBW.com
A residential furniture manufacturer founded in 1989 by Gold and Williams. Mitchell Gold + Bob Williams products are sold through furniture
stores such as, Crate & Barrel, Restoration Hardware, Pottery Barn, ABC
Carpet & Home and Lillian August. The Greenwich location is their 18th
store. Their product line offers relaxed design slip covered and tailored
upholstery (including down-blend cushions, premium goose-down-blend
and comfortable sleepers), leather, sectionals, beds, ottomans, reclin-
ers, and dining chairs.
Hours: Monday - Saturday 9:30 am - 5:30 pm, Sunday noon - 5 pm.

Modell's (Sporting Goods)

• 2175 Summer Street (Ridgeway Shopping Center)
   Stamford CT 203.353.0700
• 421 Boston Post Road, Port Chester NY 914.934.1500
www.modells.com
They have over 140 locations in the Northeast carrying sporting goods
and related apparel. They have a wide selection of licensed professional
sports team items.
Hours: Monday - Saturday 10am - 9pm, Sunday to 7 pm.

STORES

Modern Shade and Awning
29 Willett Avenue, Port Chester NY, 914.939.4722
They manufacture canvas awnings and canopies to order. They will install and store for the winter. They also sell vertical blinds and wood shades.
Hours: weekdays, 8:30 am - 4:30 pm.

Mommy Chic (maternity clothing)
38 West Putnam Avenue, 203.422.5505
www.MommyChicMaternity.com
Just as the name indicates, this is a maternity store with stylish, chic clothing. Fashions, for work, casual and yes, dressy affairs. Gina Picon has stores in Westport and Newton MA.
Hours: Monday - Saturday, 10 am - 6 pm; Sunday, noon to 5 pm.

Mothers and Daughters /Comptoir des Cotonniers (women's clothing)
271 Greenwich Avenue, 203.869.0640
www.Mothers-and-Daughters.com
Paris on the Avenue. Lots of grey, comfortable and youthful styles.
Hours: Monday - Saturday, 10 - 6 pm; Sunday, noon- 6 pm.

Mr. Mail Box
7 Cross Street, Norwalk CT, 203.849.1144
www.MrMailBox.com
It would be hard to find a better mail box. They have lots of options, their prices are reasonable and they will install.
Hours: weekdays, 8 am - 5 pm; Saturday, 9 am to 3 pm.

Mr. Shower Door
651 Connecticut Avenue, Norwalk CT, 800.633.3667
www.MrShowerDoor.com
A large number of choices, they will help you design exactly what you need. A good website and store. They will come out to measure and install.
Hours: weekdays, 8 am - 5 pm; Saturday, 9 am - 4 pm.

(The) Music Source (Music)
1345 East Putnam Avenue, Old Greenwich, 698.0444
www.theMusicSource.org
They carry a wide selection of sheet music as well as strings and other small items. They also give lessons.
Hours: Weekdays noon - 5 pm, Saturday 10 am - 2 pm.

STORES

(The) Nanz Company (Decorative Hardware)
44 West Putnam Avenue, 203.629.1000
www.Nanz.com
Nanz has their own plant in Brooklyn, where they turn out beautiful,
high end hardware as well as custom designs.
Hours: weekdays 9 am - 6 pm.

Neiman Marcus (Department Store)
Westchester Mall (125 Westchester Ave) White Plains NY,
914.428.2000
www.NeimanMarcus.com
An upscale, specialty, retail department store which competes with
Bloomingdale's, Nordstrom, and Saks Fifth Avenue.
Hours: weekdays 10 am - 8 pm, Saturday 10 am - 7 pm,
Sunday noon - 6 pm.

Nimble Thimble (Sewing & Quilting)
21 Putnam Avenue, Port Chester NY, 914.934.2934
The resource for home sewing needs. Lots of fabrics, notions, quilting
supplies and sewing machines. This is the place to have your sewing
machine repaired.
Hours: Tuesday - Friday 10 am - 5 pm, Saturday 10 am - 1 pm.

Nordic Stove & Fireplace Center
220 Harvard Avenue, Stamford, 203.406.9881
www.nordicstoveandfireplace.com
Everything you might want for your fireplace. Good customer service.
Hours: Tuesday - Friday 10 am - 5 pm, Saturday 9 am - 4 pm.

Nordstrom (Department Store)
Westchester Mall (125 Westchester Ave) White Plains NY
 914.946.1122
www.Nordstrom.com
An upscale department store with clothing, footwear, accessories, handbags, jewelry, cosmetics and home furnishings. The company competes
at an average price level above J. C. Penney, Macy's, and Sears, on par
with Bloomingdale's, but below that of Neiman Marcus and Saks Fifth
Avenue.
Hours: Monday - Saturday, 10 am - 9 pm, Sunday 11 am - 6 pm.

Norwalk Mattress Company

145 West Cedar Street, Norwalk CT, 203.866.6913

www.NorwalkMattress.com

Near Greenwich is a mattress company that will custom make any size and any level of comfort or type of mattress, including space-age memory foam. Within 10 days you will have the mattress on your bed, all at very competitive prices.

Hours: Monday - Saturday, 9 am - 5 pm.

Old Navy (Clothing)

- 2175 Summer Street (Ridgeway Shopping Center) Stamford CT, 203.325.4088
- 100 Main Street (Galleria Shopping Center), White Plains NY 914.682.0469

www.OldNavy.com

Owned by the Gap which also owns Banana Republic. Their clothing is trendy and more affordable than the Gap or Banana Republic or competitors such as American Eagle (Stamford Center). They have specialized sections for infants, boys, girls, men and women, including a collection of business clothes for women.

Stamford Store Hours: Monday - Saturday, 9 am - 9 pm
Sunday, 10 am - 6 pm.

Olivine Gabbro

19 East Elm Street, 203.493.3526

www.OlivineGabbro.com

Grace Kang designs lovely, sophisticated women's wear and evening dresses. You will like this shop.

Hours: Monday - Saturday, 10 am - 6 pm.

Optical Options (Eyeglasses)

18 Greenwich Avenue, 203.661.2020

Call in advance to schedule an eye exam. They sell contact lenses and high fashion eyeware.

Hours: weekdays, 10 am - 5:30 pm, Saturday 10 am - 5 pm.

Optyx (by Gruen)

229 Greenwich Avenue, 203.862.9441

www.Optyx.com

High fashion eyeware, call ahead to schedule an eye exam.

Hours: Monday - Saturday, 9:30 am - 5:30 pm

STORES

Oriental Furniture Warehouse
(Furniture & Home Accessories)
- 602 West Avenue, Norwalk CT, 203.853.7553
- 609 Saw Mill River Road, Elmsford NY, 203.592.6320

www.OrientalFurnishings.com

A large selection of oriental furniture and accessories from Japan, Korea, China and Tibet.

Hours: weekdays, 10 am - 6 pm (Thursday to 8 pm),
Saturday 10 am - 7 pm, Sunday 10 am - 6 pm.

Orvis Company Store (Fishing Equipment & Clothing)
432 Boston Post Road, Darien CT, 203.662.0844

www.Orvis.com

Orvis is the world's largest manufacturer of high-quality fly rods and reels. They carry high-end fishing equipment, as well as clothes and luggage for the well-attired fisherman. They also have a large book and video selection. Ask them about their guide service.

Hours: Monday - Saturday, 10 am - 6 pm; Sunday 11 am - 5 pm.

Outdoor Traders (Sporting Goods & Clothing)
55 Arch Street, 203.862.9696

www.OutdoorTraders.com

Outfitters for just about any outdoor sport, trip or trek. Easy to park.

Hours: Monday - Saturday 10 am - 6 pm, Sunday 11 am - 5 pm.

Out of the Box (Clothing- Women)
73 Greenwich Avenue, 203.625.9696

www.OutOfTheBoxClothes.com

You will be happy you stopped by this out-of-the-ordinary clothing store. Jill duPont's name for the store is just right. You will love the jackets and the gorgeous fabrics. You will also love the prices. She has a workshop for alterations and custom work. If she doesn't have your size, she can usually get it. Upstairs Jill has shows, special events and seasonal offerings such as Beach Box.

Hours: Monday - Saturday 10 am - 6 pm, Sunday noon - 5 pm.

TIP: ART FOR LOAN
Located on the second floor of the Greenwich Library and sponsored by the Friends of the Library, you will discover 250 prints you can borrow to decorate your walls.

STORES

P C Richard (Electronics & Appliances)

444 Connecticut Avenue, Norwalk CT, 203.604.1104
www.PCRichard.com
PC Richard is a 100-year-old privately owned electronics store. The Chain has 52 stores in the NY area. They compete by providing better service and more knowledgeable staff than giants like Best Buy. This 33,000 square-foot store sells appliances as well as TVs and other electronics. Delivery, installation and service are all done by PC Richard employees. If you need something in a hurry, they can usually accomodate.
Hours: Monday-Saturday 9 am - 9 pm, Sunday 10 am - 7 pm.

Packages PlusNMore (Office Services & Cards)

215 East Putnam Ave (Mill Pond Shopping Center), Cos Cob
 203.625.8130
www.PackagesPlusNMore.com
Pretty wrapping paper and supplies. One of the few places that carries Greenwich gift items including postcards with local scenes. A dependable up-scale packing and shipping company, that will not only ship packages for you, but will pickup a package from your home or office upon request.
Hours: weekdays 7 am - 7 pm, Saturday 9 am - 4 pm;
Open Sunday during Christmas season.

Paging Concepts (Wireless)

26 Greenwich Avenue, 203.863.9200
www.PagingConcepts.com
One of two authorized Verizon Wireless dealers in town.
Hours: weekdays 10 am - 6 pm, Saturday 10 am - 5 pm.

Papyrus (Stationery)

268 Greenwich Avenue, 203.869.1888
www.PapyrusOnline.com
Papyrus has more than 170 stores nationwide selling fine custom social stationery and invitations. If you want a traditional or an out-of-the ordinary invitation, you will have fun here. The staff is talented at helping you choose and design invitations. You will be sending more greetings to your friends when you see their large selection of high-end greeting cards.
Hours: weekdays, 9:30 am - 6 pm (Thursday until 7 pm),
Saturday, 10 am - 6 pm, Sunday, noon - 5 pm.

STORES

Party City
- 2255 Summer Street (Ridgeway Shopping Center), Stamford CT 203.964.4961
- 435 Boston Post Road, Port Chester NY, 914.939.6900

www.PartyCity.com

If you can't find it at the Strauss Warehouse Outlet, try here. Party City is the largest retailer of party supplies. They operate 249 company-owned stores and 258 franchised stores, that often have different merchandise. You will find a giant, slightly disorganized store selling decorations, wrapping paper, helium balloons and custom made balloon bouquets, plastic eating utensils, tableware, paper plates, party music CDs, small toys, candy, and other items of a similar nature themed for birthday parties, weddings, baby showers, graduation, communion, confirmation, christenings and holidays. They print invitations and party banners right on site. They have a large assortment of Halloween costumes during the season.

Stamford hours: Monday - Saturday; 9:30 am - 8 pm ,(9 pm Thursday & Friday); Sunday, 10 am - 6 pm.

Port Chester hours: weekdays, 9:30 am - 8:30 pm; (Thursday and Friday to 9 pm); Saturday, 8:30 am - 8:30 pm; Sunday, 10 am - 6 pm.

Party Paper and Things (Party Supplies)
403 East Putnam Avenue , Cos Cob, 203.661.1355

An excellent selection of high quality party paper goods, wrapping paper, disposable serving dishes and lots of balloons. They will deliver for a very modest fee.

Hours: weekdays, 10 am - 5:30 pm; Saturday, 8:30 am - 4:30 pm.

Patio.Com (Home - Furniture)
600 East Putnam Avenue, Cos Cob

203.869.3084 (Office 800-340-4710)

www.Patio.com

One of 11 stores, this, independently owned, CT based, store sells a wide variety of outdoor furniture, as well as indoor sports equipment such as pool tables and ping pong tables. They are a major retailer of Brunswick Pool tables.

Hours: Monday - Saturday, 10 am - 7 pm; Sunday, 10 am - 6 pm.

STORES

Patti's Portico (Outdoor Furniture)
140 Highland Street, Port Chester NY, 203.869-6227
Is it possible Patti's Portico has been there over 12 years and we are just now discovering it? Our garden chair needed re-strapping and Patti DeFelice did a great job. Her showroom is filled with refurbished outdoor furniture to buy. This shop is easy to find, it is just off Main Street in Port Chester.
Hours: weekdays, 8 am - 3 pm.

Pastiche (Clothing-Women)
250 Sound Beach Avenue, Old Greenwich, 203.637.4444
Designer casual clothing with a fashionable dressy flair.
Hours: Monday - Saturday, 10 am - 5 pm.

Patricia Gourlay (Clothing - Women)
45 East Putnam Avenue, 203.869.0977
Brides-to-be love this fine lingerie shop. This is also a good place to find the right bra and very pretty items. Wonderful customer service! They are more conservative than their advertisements would indicate. You will enjoy shopping here!
Hours: Monday - Saturday, 9:30 am - 5:30 pm.

Peacock & Beale (Home Decorating - Accessories)
125 East Putnam Avenue, 203.6613540
www.PeacockAndBeale.com
As its website says, "interesting things for interesting homes." You'll find everything from an assortment of candles and drawer liners, to pillows, home design books, colorful place settings and even a few pieces of furniture.
Hours: weekdays, 10 am - 5:30 pm, Saturday, 11 am - 5 pm.

Pearle Vision
111 Broad Street, Stamford CT, 203.348.3200
www.PearleVision.com
With more than 1,000 stores, Pearle is one of the largest retailers of eyeware. They have the same parent as LensCrafters. Call for an eye exam appointment. Most glasses can be made within one hour.
Hours: weekdays, 9 am -6 pm (Thursday to 7 pm);
Saturday, 9 am - 5 pm.

Penny Weights (Jewelry)

124 Elm Street, New Canaan CT, 203.966.7739

This is a great place to find an inexpensive piece of jewelry for a teenager. Most of the jewelry is silver. The sales staff is friendly and helpful. The prices are terrific.

Hours: Tuesday - Saturday 10 am - 6 pm (Thursday until 8 pm), Sunday noon - 5 pm.

Peridot (Jewelry)

112 Mason Street, Greenwich, 203.629.3900

www.PeridotFineJewelry.com

One-of-a-kind artisan jewelry from leading US designers. Check their web site for dates of trunk shows where you can meet the designer.

Hours: Tuesday - Saturday 10 am - 5:30 pm.

Pet Pantry (Pets)

290 Railroad Avenue, 203.869.6444

www.PetPantryCT.com

Large store with a gigantic inventory. Friendly, helpful service. Our Jack Russell, Daisy, loves going here to pick her own dog food and meet new friends.

Hours: weekdays 8 am - 8 pm, Saturday 8 am - 6 pm, Sunday 9 am - 6 pm.

Petticoat Lane (Handbags and Lingerie)

347 Greenwich Avenue, 203.863.0045

www.BagShop.com

One of our familiar shops that has been on the Avenue a long time. This 6-store chain has a large selection of quality handbags and lingerie.

Hours: Monday - Saturday, 10 am - 6 pm; Sunday, noon - 5 pm.

Pier 1 Imports (Home Accessories)

777 Connecticut Avenue, Norwalk CT, 203.852.1718

www.Pier1.com

Affordable, 1,000 store chain carrying everything for the home, from table linens to wicker furniture and throw pillows.

Hours: Monday - Saturday 10 am - 9 pm, Sunday 11 am - 7 pm.

Pierre Deux (Home Decorating)

40 East Elm Street, Greenwich, 203.618-1825

www.PierreDeux.com

No longer do we have to drive to Westport or go to New York City to find these charming French-country themed fabrics, hand-crafted furniture, and gifts. You'll enjoy the room displays in this building located on the corner of Elm and Mason. This shop first opened in New York City in 1967 and now has 23 US locations.

Hours: Monday - Saturday 10 am - 5 pm, Sunday noon - 4 pm.

Porcelanosa (Tile & Bath Fixtures)

1063 East Putnam Avenue, Riverside, 203.698.7618

www.Porcelanosa-USA.com

A Spanish factory store. The company has over 8,000 stores world wide. All the tile and fixtures are their own design and are available only in their stores. A must see for anyone interested in modern designs.

Hours: Monday - Saturday 10 am - 6 pm.

Pottery Barn (Home Accessories & Furniture)

Stamford Town Center, Stamford, 203.324.2035

www.PotteryBarn.com   www.PotteryBarnKids.com

This fresh, appealing furniture is very popular in Greenwich. They have a strong emphasis on bed, bath, dining as well as adorable furniture for children. The Pottery Barn is a subsidiary of Williams-Sonoma and operates 200 US stores.

Hours: Monday - Saturday 10 am - 9 pm, Sunday 11 am - 6 pm.

Post Road Iron Works (Fireplace accessories)

345 West Putnam Avenue, 203.869.6322

www.PRIW.com

Serving Greenwich since 1927, although they do a lot of ordinary iron work, they are the local resource for ornamental welding. They also sell a good selection of fireplace accessories and can order weathervanes.

Hours: weekdays 8 am - 5:30 pm, Saturday 8 am - noon.

STORES

Privet House (gift shop)

18 Grigg Street, 203.340.9544

www.PrivetHouse.com

A store full of beautifully displayed home goods, art objects and curiosities you are not likely to see anywhere else. Try one of their unusually scented candles.

Hours: Tuesday - Saturday 11 am - 5 pm.

Quelques Choses (Home Accessories & Gifts)

259 Sound Beach Avenue, Old Greenwich, 203.637.5655

Hidden in an alleyway is this tiny shop brimming with charming home accessories and delightful gifts. They have unique cards and papers.

Hours: Tuesday - Saturday, 10ish - about 5 pm.

Quester Gallery (Art)

119 Rowayton Avenue, Rowayton CT, 203.629.8022, 523.0250

www.QuesterGallery.com

They specialize in fine 19th and 20th century marine art. This gallery is full of beautiful paintings. Prices range from $2,500 to $100,000, though most of the paintings seem to be in the higher range. They have an exceptionally informative website, with pictures of many of their paintings.

Hours: Monday - Saturday, 9 am - 6 pm.

Radio Shack (Electronics)

- 1265 East Putnam Avenue (Thruway Shop Center) Riverside 203.637.5608
- 160 East Putnam Avenue, Cos Cob 203.661.2212

www.RadioShack.com

Radio Shack operates over 3,000 stores. If you need a telephone, Cell phone or telephone supplies, a strange battery, or a piece of electronic equipment, they will probably have it.

Riverside Hours: Monday - Saturday 9 am - 9 pm, Sunday 11 am - 6 pm.

Cos Cob Hours: Monday - Saturday 9 am - 8 pm, Sunday 10 am - 6 pm.

Ralph Lauren

265 Greenwich Avenue, 203.869.2054

www.RalphLauren.com

Ralph Lauren has over 35 boutiques in the United States. Whether or not you are interested in buying something from Ralph Lauren, you have to tour this extraordinary shop. The store is breathtaking—so are the prices.

Hours: Monday - Saturday, 10 am - 6 pm, Sunday, noon - 6 pm.

STORES

Recreation Equipment (Sporting Equipment)

189 Connecticut Avenue, Norwalk CT, 860.233.2211
71 Raymond Road, West Hartford CT
www.REI.com
Founded in Seattle and with 110 stores, REI sells a great variety of outdoor equipment for sports such as camping, climbing, cycling, fitness, hiking, paddling, and snow sports. REI operates as a cooperative with a life time fee of $20 to join. REI Adventures offers vacations for active travelers all over the world. Offerings range from a 2 day weekend getaway in Yosemite to a 14 day trek to Everest Base Camp. In 2006 REI started the Outdoor School which has a series of one day outings in the local area and in store classes. Offerings include mountain biking, road biking, kayaking, backpacking, rock climbing, outdoor photography, family hiking, snowshoeing and others. Currently the nearest schools are in Boston or Philadelphia.
Check for Norwalk store opening date.
Hours: Monday - Saturday, 10 am - 9 pm; Sunday, 11 am - 6 pm.

Reflection (Clothing-Youth)

116 Greenwich Avenue, 203.629.2010
Attractive, fashionable clothes for young people at college tuition prices.
Hours: Monday - Saturday 9:30 am - 6 pm (Thursday till 7 pm),
Sunday 11:30 am - 6 pm.

Relax the Back (Health, Furniture)

367 Greenwich Avenue, 203.629.2225
www.RelaxTheBack.com
For people seeking relief and prevention of back and neck pain, they offer attractive posture and back support products and self-care solutions. Many products are exclusive to the store. Started in 1984 by an osteopath, there are now 121 stores.
Hours: Monday - Wednesday 10 am - 5:30 pm,
Thursday - Saturday 10 am - 6 pm.

Remains Lighting (Lighting Fixtures)

44 West Putnam Avenue, 203.629.1000
www.Remains.com
Located next to some of our favorite stores: Rue Faubourg St. Honore, which sells antique home accessories, and Nanz, which makes high end hardware. Remains sells antique lighting but also has its own factory, where they produce high quality lighting fixtures both original and based on classic designs.
Hours: weekdays 9 am - 6 pm.

STORES

Reo Appliances

233 East Avenue, East Norwalk CT, 203.838.7925
www.ReoAppliances.com
Large selection of major appliances at competitive prices. They service what they sell.
Hours: weekdays 9 am - 5 pm (Thursday to 7:30), Saturday 9 am - 5 pm.

Restoration Hardware (Home Accessories & Furniture)

239 Greenwich Avenue, 203.552.1040
www.RestorationHardware.com
An American chain with 133 stores. A very upscale, trendy store with a combination of decorative hardware and furniture based on period designs. It is fun to stroll through. The merchandise changes frequently.
Hours: Monday - Saturday 9 am - 7 pm, Sunday 11 am - 6 pm.

Rex Dive Center (Diving Equipment)

144 Water Street, South Norwalk CT, 203.853.4148
www.RexDiveCenter.com
A good place to go for your scuba equipment. You will be greeted by a friendly, knowledgeable staff. They provide lessons for beginners.
Hours: Tuesday - Friday 11 am - 7 pm, Saturday 9 am - 5 pm, Sunday noon - 5 pm.

Rex Marine Center (Boating)

144 Water Street, South Norwalk CT, 203.831.5236
50 Calf Pasture Beach Road, East Norwalk, CT 203.604.1295
www.RexMarine.com
If you are looking for a yacht or a small boat or boating paraphernalia, they are worth a visit. You can even charter a boat with captain. The Rex Boating Club provides training and rental boats.
Hours The hours vary, call ahead.

Riverside Floor Covering

5 Riverside Lane, Riverside, 203.637.3777
www.RiversideFloorCovering.com
A small showroom brimming with carpet choices from many manufacturers. They have been helping Greenwich residents for years.
Hours: weekdays 9:30 am - 5 pm, Saturday 9 am - noon.

STORES

Richard's of Greenwich (Clothing, Men & Women)
359 Greenwich Avenue, 203.622.0551
www.MitchellsOnline.com
A Greenwich classic carrying fine quality men's and women's clothing from the world's leading designers. Nowhere will you find better customer service.
Hours: weekdays 9:30 am - 6 pm(Thursday until 8 pm),
Saturday 8:30 am - 6 pm.

Ridgeway Shopping Center (Mall)
2235 Summer Street, Stamford CT
www.ubproperties.com/properties.php?propertyID=16
The anchor stores in this updated 400,000 square foot center are Marshall's, Old Navy and Michael's. It has a very large Bed, Bath and Beyond as well as a huge Super Stop & Shop.
Hours: Monday - Saturday 9:30 am - 9 pm
(Bed, Bath and Beyond is open Sunday 9:30 am - 6 pm).

Rinfret Home and Garden (Furniture & Accessories)
354 Greenwich Avenue, 203.622.0000, 0204
www.RinfretLtd.com
Classic English antique and reproduction furniture and accessories. If you are wondering what is "Classic Greenwich Style", you will want to visit this store and buy a copy of Cindy Rinfret's book.
Hours: weekdays 10 am - 6 pm, Saturday 10 am - 5 pm,
Sunday 12 pm - 5 pm.

Rink and Racquet (Sporting Equipment, Team Uniforms)
24 Railroad Avenue, 203.622.9180
www.RinkAndRacquet.com
Hockey (field & ice), figure skating, baseball, softball, lacrosse, roller blades, team uniforms. If they don't have what you need for ice hockey, it is probably not made.
Hours: weekdays 9 am - 5:30 pm, Saturday 9 am - 5 pm.

Ring's End Lumber (Hardware -Building Materials)
181 West Avenue, Darien, 203.655.2525
www.RingsEnd.com
A large supplier of lumber, hardware and building materials. Good displays of kitchens and windows. If possible, shop on weekdays; they can be very busy on weekends.
Hours: Monday - Saturday 7 am - 5 pm.

Ritz Camera (Photography)
82 Greenwich Avenue, Greenwich, 203.869.0673
www.RitzCamera.com
The largest retailer of cameras, even after reducing its size from 800 to 400 stores because of their 2009 bankruptcy. They have an extensive selection of cameras and batteries for watches and cameras. They do one-hour photo developing. You can e-mail your pics to www.RitzPix.com for prints in one hour or you can pick up at the store. If you buy a camera, they will give you free class lessons. A good place to get your passport photos or convert a video to DVD.
Hours: weekdays 8:30 am - 6:30 pm (Friday until 8 pm), Saturday 10 am - 6 pm, Sunday 11 am - 5 pm.

Ronnie's News (Magazines & Newspapers)
26 West Putnam Avenue, 203.661.5464
A convenient place to find your favorite magazines and newspapers. Get a gelato or smoothie while you are there.
Hours: weekdays 5 am - 6 pm, Saturday 6 am - noon.

Roundabout (Consignment/resale Clothing-Women)
48 West Putnam Avenue, 203.552.0787
Clothes must be from a well-known designer, in perfect condition, and less than 2 years old to be consigned. The store also buys show and end-of-season stock from designers.
Hours: Monday- Saturday 10 am - 5 pm, Sunday noon - 5 pm.

Rudy's Tackle & Archery (fishing & archery)
242 South Water Street, Byram, 203.531.3168
All your archery, freshwater and saltwater supplies.
Summer Hours: weekdays 7 am - 7 pm, Saturday 6 am - 6 pm, Sunday 6 am - 3 pm.

Rue Faubourg St. Honore (Home Accessories & Antiques)
44 West Putnam Avenue, 203.869.7139
For over 30 years this small shop has supplied antique lighting fixtures and fireplace accessories to Greenwich estates and vintage homes.
Hours: weekdays 9 am - 5 pm (closed 1 pm - 2 pm).

Rugby by Ralph Lauren (Clothing-Men & Women)

195 Greenwich Avenue, 203.861.7053

www.Rugby.com

Polo shirts, sweaters, denim wear with sporty prep-school look, targeted for men and women ages 18 - 25. Rugby was launched in 2004. The line's post-prep look has edgier styling and slightly lower price points than the signature Polo Ralph Lauren brand. Their shopping bags can be seen all over town.

Hours: weekdays 11 am - 6 pm, Saturday 10 am - 6 pm, Sunday noon - 5 pm.

(Greenwich) Running Company
(Running shoes, clothing & accessories)

2 Greenwich Avenue, 203.861.7800

www.TheRunningCompany.net

One of 12 stores devoted to running and looking good while doing it. They started in Princeton, New Jersey in 1998 and carry most major brands of running, walking and cross training shoes, as well as spikes, classy apparel and accessories.

Hours: Monday - Saturday, 10 am - 7 pm; Sunday, noon - 5 pm.

Rye Ridge Tile (Bath & Kitchen Tile)

520 North Main Street, Port Chester, 914.939.1100

www.RyeRidgeTile.com

The 6,000 sq. foot showroom is covered with a great variety of tile patterns from 75 different manufactures, making it easy to visualize choices. They also have the Villeroy & Boch line of very modern plumbing fixtures.

Hours: weekdays 9 am - 5 pm (Wednesday to 7 pm), Saturday 9 am - 4 pm.

Saint Clair (Stationery)

23 Lewis Street, 203.661.2927

www.ThereseSaintClair.com

Going to Cartier's for fine stationery is not necessary if you live in Greenwich. For many years Greenwich residents have shopped here for their invitations and elegant stationery. Stop in and see the range of things they can do.

Hours: Monday - Saturday 9:30 am - 5:30 pm.

STORES

Saks Fifth Avenue (Department Store)
- 205 Greenwich Avenue, 203.862.5300
- Stamford Town Center, 203.323.3100

www.Saks.com

An upscale clothing store that competes on a price level with Neiman Marcus, Bergdorf Goodman and Lord and Taylor and above Bloomingdale's and Nordstrom.

Greenwich hours: Monday - Saturday, 10 am - 6 pm,
Sunday, noon - 5 pm.

Stamford hours Monday - Saturday 10 am - 6 pm
(Thursday & Saturday to 7 pm),   Sunday, noon - 6 pm.

Sam Bridge Nursery & Greenhouses (Gardening)
437 North Street, 203.869.3418

www.sambridge.com

A family-run operation that has been welcoming Greenwich residents to their greenhouses since 1930. Many of the more than 100,000 plants available are grown in their own greenhouses. They offer classes on topics such as perennial gardening and pruning. You can select live or cut Christmas trees, which they will deliver to you when you are ready.

Hours: Monday - Saturday 8:30 am - 5 pm.

Safavieh (Furniture & Rugs)
248 Atlantic Street, Stamford, 203.327.4800

www.safaviehhome.com

This small 6-store chain has oriental rugs galore and lots of quality English, French and American reproduction furniture from firms such as Kindel, Baker, Widdicomb, Henredon and others. They have parking behind the store.

Hours: Monday - Wednesday 10 am - 7 pm, Thursday 10 am - 8:30 pm, Friday & Saturday 10 am - 6 pm, Sunday 11 am - 6 pm.

Scoop (Clothing, Men & Women)
283 Greenwich Avenue, 203.422.2251

www.ScoopNYC.com

One of 12 stores, from Manhattan to Greenwich Avenue, this clothing store has trendy and fun pieces designed to attract men and women of all ages, but perhaps the 12 to 25 year-olds are happiest here. You'll find everything from shirts, shoes, jewelry, hats, t-shirts and handbags.

Hours: Monday - Saturday 10 am - 6 pm, Sunday noon - 5 pm.

STORES

Sears (Department Store)
100 Main Street (Galleria Shopping Center), White Plains NY
 914.644.1400
www.Sears.com
Home furnishings, home improvement, appliances, electronics, cloth-ing, including a Land's End Store. They own the brands: Kenmore, Crafts-man & DieHard. Sears is famous for quality tools. In clothing, Sears competes with Macy's, pricing below Bloomingdale's, Nordstrom and Saks and above JC Penney and Kohls.
Hours: Monday - Saturday, 10 am - 9 pm; Sunday, 11 am - 6 pm.

Second Time Around (Consignment Clothing)
6 Greenwich Avenue, 203.422.2808
www.SecondTimeAround.net
At the top of the Avenue, almost on sidewalk level, is a large boutique with clothing so nicely displayed you might not realize it is all resale and designer over-runs. The Greenwich store is one of about 20 and anything consigned must be less than 2 years old. Items are priced at a third to a quarter of their original retail price.
Hours: Monday - Saturday 10 am - 6 pm, Sunday noon - 5 pm.

Sephora (Cosmetics)
75 Greenwich Avenue, 203.422.2191
www.Sephora.com
This French 750 store chain has a vast selection of men's and women's beauty products including makeup, skin care, fragrance, bath, hair prod-ucts, hair tools, and beauty accessories. There are eight make-up sta-tions, with consultants to help you bring out your inner self.
Hours: Monday - Saturday 10 am - 6 pm, Sunday noon - 5 pm.

Shanti Bithi Nursery (Bonsai Greenhouse)
3047 High Ridge Road, Stamford, 203.329.0768
www.shantibithi.com
Wonderful greenhouse of bonsai trees as well as supplies and lessons to create your own bonsai. They also have a nice selection of Asian garden ornaments. The classes (at all levels) are mostly on the weekend.
Hours: Monday - Saturday 9 am - 5 pm.

STORES

Shoes N More
251 Greenwich Avenue, 203.629.2323
www.ShoesNMore.com
A fun assortment of boy's and girl's clothing, sizes 2T - 16. They have an excellent shoe selection including Astor, Elefanter, Nike and Merrill. They carry some western boots and accessories. Twice a year they have a very good shoe sale (summer & after Christmas). They have six more locations in the NYC metropolitan area.
Hours: Monday - Saturday 9 am - 7 pm, Sunday 11 am - 6 pm.

(The) Side Door (Clothing-Women)
248 Mill Street, Byram, 203.532.5606
Casual wear for teens and the busy moms, at reasonable prices. Lots of samples and manufacturer's closeouts.
Hours: Monday - Saturday, 10:30 am - 5 pm,
Sunday, noon - 5 pm (closed Sundays in July and August).

Signature Cycles (Bicycles)
28 Bruce Park Avenue, 203.485.0500
www.SignatureCycles.com   http://Blog.SignatureCycles.com
Not your ordinary bicycle shop. Besides excellent customer service, all bikes are customized to meet your needs by one of five US manufacturers. They record your measurements and uses, so that you get the bike that would be best for you. All this comes at a slight premium over an equal, un-customized, bike. Check with them about weekly bike rides.
Hours: Tuesday - Friday, 10 am - 6 pm, Saturday, 11 am - 4 pm.

(the) Silk Purse (Consignment Furniture)
118 Main Street, New Canaan CT 203.972.0898
www.TheSilkPurse.com
For 35 years this shop which features formal polished furniture, has been a good resource for Greenwich residents. They also have paintings, decorative items and jewelry. This shop is well worth the visit.
Hours: Monday - Saturday, 10 am - 5 pm, Sunday, 12 am - 5 pm.

Simon Pearce (Home - Accessories)
325 Greenwich Avenue, 203.861.0780
www.SimonPearce.com
Beautiful handblown glass, pottery, lamps and furniture.
Hours: Monday - Saturday, 10 am - 6 pm, Sunday, noon - 5 pm.

STORES

Silvermine Guild Arts Center (Art)

1037 Silvermine Road, New Canaan CT, 203.966.9700

www.SilvermineArt.org

The Silvermine Arts Center has been a gathering place for artists and art lovers for almost 100 years. The Silvermine galleries have 20 shows each year in addition to the juried annual Art of The Northeast, held late in April. Silvermine offers many lectures, workshops and art classes. During the summer they run Art Day Camps for children ages: 5- , 8- 2 and 14-17.

Hours: Administration & School, weekdays 9 am - 5 pm;

gallery, Wednesday - Saturday noon - 5 pm, Sunday 1 am - 5 pm.

Skaters Landing (Skating Equipment and Clothing)

242 Mill Street, Byram, 203.542.0555

www.SkatersLanding.com

Buy your skating equipment from a skating instructor like Mark Magliola, and you know you are getting expert advice. This shop has everything you need for figure skating; skates, costumes, blades and sharpening. Make appointments for fittings and while-u-wait sharpening.

Hours: Tuesday 10 am - 5 pm, Wednesday 10 am - 2 pm,

Thursday 10 am - 6 pm, Friday 10 am - 2 pm, Saturday, 10 am - 3 pm.

(The) Ski & Scuba Connection

26 Saint Roch Avenue, Byram; 203.629.4766

Scuba lessons and equipment for scuba or snorkeling. Friendly, knowledgeable service. Sign on for one of their scuba trips with Don Brown, Master Instructor.

Hours: weekdays, 11 an - 6 pm, Saturday 10 am - 6 pm.

Sleepy's (Bedding)

- 159 West Putnam Avenue, Greenwich, 203.869.5255
- 1340 East Putnam Avenue, Old Greenwich, 203.637.8571

www.Sleepys.com

A chain of over 700 mattress and bedding shops, carrying most major brands as well as some exclusive to them. It is the largest specialty mattress retailer and the largest bedding retailer in the United States.

Hours: Weekdays 10 am - 9 pm, Saturday 10 am - 8 pm,

Sunday 11 am - 7 pm.

STORES

Sliding Door Company (Doors)
20 Jones Street, New Rochelle NY, 914.235. 3235
www.NYSlidingDoor.com
Sliding doors for just about any inside need.
Hours: weekdays 10 am - 5 pm.

Small Boat Shop (Boating)
144 Water Street (in Rex Marine), Norwalk CT 203.854.5223
www.TheSmallBoatShop.com
They carry sea and recreational kayaks, canoes, dinghies, row boats, rowing shells, small sail boats and paddle boats. Their services include tours, instruction, rentals, small boat storage and repair.
Hours: Monday - Saturday 10 am - 5 pm, Sunday 10 am - 3 pm.

Smart Kids Company (Toys)
17 East Elm Street, Greenwich, 203.869.0022
www.SKToys.com
The toys in Mary De Silva's shop may look like a lot of fun, but most have been selected to help in your child's growth and educational development through play. This local shop has a global clientele from the website and is very popular for party presents. If your child receives two of the same gift, they are very gracious with returns.
Hours: Monday - Saturday 9 am - 6 pm, Sunday 11 am - 5 pm.

Sound Beach Sportswear (clothing women & children)
239 Sound Beach Avenue, Old Greenwich, 203.637.5557
The sportswear is an interesting mix. Expect a friendly reception in this family owned business.
Hours: Monday - Saturday 10 am - 5:30 pm

Soccer and Rugby (Sporting goods)
42 West Putnam Avenue, 203.661.7622
www.SoccerAndRugby.com
Everything you need for soccer and rugby, attractively displayed.
Hours: weekdays 10 am - 6 pm, Saturday 10 am - 5 pm,
Sunday 11 am - 4 pm (in season).

STORES

Sophia's Great Dames
(Clothing - Costumes women and children)

1 Liberty Way, Greenwich, 203.869.5990

www.SophiasCostumes.com

Wonderful shop for vintage clothing, antiques, collectibles, gifts and costumes. A large selection of costumes (for all occasions) for sale or rent. Fun to visit.

Hours: Tuesday - Saturday 10 am - 5:30 pm.

Splurge (Gift Shop)

19A East Putnam Avenue, Greenwich, 203.869-7600

www.SplurgeGifts.com

We are delighted to discover this gift shop filled with artisan crafts: jewelry, glassware, clocks and a great variety of one of a kind gifts. Sonia Malloy has exquisite taste. The prices which range from $15 to $350 make it easy for you to splurge, so go ahead.

Hours: Monday - Saturday 10 am - 6 pm.

Sportsman's Den (Fishing)

33 River Road, Cos Cob, 203.869.3234

Supplies and classes on angling and fly fishing. One visit and you will be hooked. Get your fishing license here. They also carry heritage kayaks and kayaking accessories.

Hours: weekdays 9 am - 5 pm (Monday until 2 pm),
Saturday 9 am - 5 pm, Sunday 9 am - 2 pm.

Sprint Nextel (wireless)

1212 East Putnam Avenue, Riverside, 203.698.4900

www.Sprint.com

The third-largest wireless telecommunications network in United States, with 48.8 million customers, behind Verizon Wireless and AT&T Mobility. Sprint operates DCSNet, the U.S. Federal Government's private surveillance network. In 2009, Sprint turned over operations management to the Sweden-based Ericsson. Sprint operates a combination 3G & 4G wireless network.

Hours: weekdays 9 am - 7 pm, Saturday 9 am 5 pm.

Stamford Office Furniture

328 Selleck Street, Stamford, 203.348.2657

www.StamfordOfficeFurniture.com

New (& some used) furniture. They represent over 200 manufacturers. They sell and rent.

Hours: weekdays, 9 am - 5 pm.

STORES

Stamford Town Center (Shopping Center)

100 Greyrock Place & Tresser Blvd, Stamford CT, 203.324.0935

www.ShopStamfordTownCenter.com

A large attractive mall with 130 stores, including shops such as: Ann Taylor, Pottery Barn, Banana Republic, Limited, Brookstone, Mikasa, Sharper Image and Williams-Sonoma. Macy's (203.964.1500) and Saks Fifth Avenue (203.323.3100) are the anchor stores. There is a 40,000 sq. ft. Barnes and Noble and more than 5 stand-alone restaurants.

Hours: Monday - Saturday, 10 am - 9 pm; Sunday, 11 am - 6 pm.

Staples (Office Furniture and Supplies)

1297 East Putnam Avenue, Old Greenwich, 203.698.9011

www.Staples.com

Office supplies of every sort. This store also carries electronics and office furniture. They are the world's largest office supply retail store chain, with over 2,000 stores. Their major competitors are Office Max and Office Depot.

Hours: weekdays, 8 am - 9 pm; Saturday, 9 am - 9 pm,
Sunday 10 am - 6 pm.

Stark Carpet (Carpet Outlet)

17 Butler Street, (Loehmann's Plaza), Norwalk CT, 203.899.1771

www.Starksale.com

Good selection of carpets from the famous New York Designer source. Some wallpaper, fabric & furniture. Check their website for clearance sales.

Hours: weekdays, 9 am - 6 pm, Saturday, 10 am - 6 pm,
Sunday 11 am - 5 pm.

Steilmann (Clothing - Women)

354 North Main Street, Port Chester NY, 914.939.1500

www.Steilmann.de

This is a huge warehouse of classic European-style clothing. Steilmann is a German company.

Hours: everyday, 11 am - 5:30 or 6 pm (Thursday usually until 7 pm).

Steinway Piano Gallery

501 Post Road East, Westport CT 203.227.8222

www.Steinway.com   www.SPGWestport.com

The Steinway Piano Gallery, owned by the Steinway & Sons company sells and rents and finances their pianos. They have floor patterns to help you position a piano in your home.

Hours: weekdays 10 am - 6 pm, Saturday 10 am - 5 pm.

STORES

Steven B. Fox (Jewelry)
8 Lewis Street, 203.629.3303
A full service family-owned jewelry store specializing in precious jewels, pearls, watches, estate jewelry and objets d'art. Repairs done on the premises. They make estate purchases.
Hours: Monday - Saturday 9:30 am - 5 pm
Sunday noon - 5 pm, from Thanksgiving to Christmas

Stickley (Home-Furniture)
50 Tarrytown Road, White Plains NY, 914.948.6333
www.Stickley.com
Stickley mission furniture and fine English reproduction furniture.
Hours: Monday - Saturday 10 am - 6 pm (Monday & Thursday until 9 pm), Sunday noon - 5 pm.

Strauss Warehouse Outlet (Party Supplies)
140 Horton Avenue, Port Chester NY, 914.939.3544
www.StraussOutlet.com
Gift wrapping, party favors, balloons, paper goods, just about anything you might want for a party at great prices. They carry a huge selection of Halloween costumes during October.
Hours: weekdays, 9 am - 7 pm; Saturday, 9 am - 5 pm, Sunday, 10 am - 3 pm.

Stuf (Kids accessories & apparel)
1 North Water Street, Byram, 203.813.3639
www.StufGreenwich.com
A fun, popular store for teens and tweens. Stuf has accessories, toys and clothing for kids ages 7-16. Stephanie loves to shop here.
Hours: , Closed Monday; Tuesday - Saturday, 10:30 am - 5 pm; Sunday, 11 am - 4 pm

(Charles) Stuttig Locksmith
158 Greenwich Avenue, 203.869.6260
www.StuttigLocksmith.com
A fixture in Greenwich for many years, they provide a wide variety of locks and safes. Whether you have an emergency or just need a key copied, they can be counted on and trusted.
Hours: weekdays, 7:30 am - 5:30 pm.

STORES

Sunglass Hut

260 Greenwich Avenue, 203.629.7907

www.SunglassHut.com

Sunglass Hut International is North America's largest retailer of sunglasses. The company operates over 1,800 stores. They sell non-prescription, high fashion sunglasses.

Hours: Monday - Saturday 10 am - 7 pm, Sunday 11 am - 5 pm.

Super Handy Hardware

1 Riversville Road, Glenville Center, 203.531.5599

www.SuperHandy.com

A good old-fashioned hardware store with most everything you would need for light and heavy-duty home projects, barbecue grills and more. It's wonderful, you can stop in, tell one of the sales people what you want and they will find it for you immediately. From firewood to screen repair, they do it all.

Hours: Monday - Saturday 8 am - 5 pm, Sunday 9 am - 1 pm.

SWC Furniture Outlet (Office Furniture)

375 Fairfield Ave, Stamford CT, 203.967.8367

www.SWCOffice.com

A great resource for new and used office furniture at good prices in their 50,000 sq. ft. showroom. To sell furniture, call 888-404-3375 (it must be less than 10 years old and in good shape)

Hours: Monday - Friday 8:30 am - 5:30 pm, Saturday 10 am - 4:30 pm.

Syms (Clothing - Youth, Men, Women)

295 Tarrytown Road, Elmsford NY, 914.592.2447

www.Syms.com

Off-price children's, men's and women's designer and brand name clothing, in a warehouse setting. Syms has 33 stores in 13 states, their online store is www.ShopSyms.com.

Hours: Monday - Saturday, 10 am - 9 pm (Saturday to 8:30 pm), Sunday 11 am - 5:30 pm.

STORES

T-Mobile (Wireless)
10 Greenwich Avenue, 203.625.8100
www.T-Mobile.com
This is store 3,789. With 33 million customers, T-Mobile USA is the fourth largest wireless network in the U.S. after Verizon, AT&T and Sprint Nextel. In Germany, its home market, T-Mobile is the largest mobile phone operator with 36 million subscribers. The T-Mobile network predominately uses the GSM/GPRS/EDGE 1900 MHz frequency-band, making it the largest 1900 MHz network in the United States. 3G is offered in major cities.
Hours: Monday - Saturday, 10 am - 7 pm; Sunday, 11 am - 4 pm.

Tahiti Street (Women's beach & swimwear)
84 Greenwich Avenue, 203.622.1878
www.TahitiStreet.com
Perfect for a trip to the Caribbean or to look elegant on the beach. You can purchase bathing separates in different sizes.
Hours: Monday - Saturday, 10 am - 6 pm.

Talbots (Clothing - Women)
151 Greenwich Avenue, 203.869.7177
www.Talbots.com
Talbots has classic clothes for business women of all ages as well as a good sportswear line. They have an extensive women's petite department. Talbots is working hard to make their clothing more colorful, more playful and less dowdy.
Hours: Monday - Saturday, 10 am - 6 pm.

Tanger Outlet Center (Mall -Outlet)
Westbrook CT, 866.665.8685
www.TangerOutlet.com
With 65 stores, it is just barely smaller than Clinton Crossing and only one exit away. If you are in the area, you should stop by. See area description under Clinton Crossing.
Hours: Monday - Saturday, 10 am - 9 pm; Sunday, 10 am - 6 pm.
Directions: I-95 N to exit 65.

STORES

Target (Department Stores)
21 Broad Street, Stamford CT, 203.388.0006
www.Target.com
This discount department store is the 6th largest retailer in the US with 1,494 stores. They are the 3rd largest seller of music in the US. Target competes with Wal-Mart and Kmart. Since its founding in 1962, it has differentiated its stores from its competitors by offering what it believes is more upscale, trend-forward merchandise at low cost.
Hours: Monday - Saturday, 8 am - 10 pm; Sunday, 8 am - 9 pm.

theory (Clothing- Women)
396 Greenwich Avenue, 203.422.0020
www.Theory.com
You can't go wrong with the high-quality clothes from Theory, known for their contemporary fashions. The simple, quiet, "uncomplicated and un-assuming" (almost nondescript) fashions are perfect for business and social attire, as well sports wear. This store has wonderful suits and blouses for women, as well as dresses, sweaters, slacks, shoes and bags. There is also a small men's section. The Greenwich store is one of 16 signature US stores.
Hours: Monday - Saturday 10 am - 8 pm; Sunday noon - 5 pm.

Threads and Treads (Sporting Equipment and Clothing)
17 East Putnam Avenue, 203.661.0142
www.ThreadsAndTreads.com
A Greenwich fixture since 1979, this locally owned store is our favorite source for biking, swimming and running attire. They have entry forms for the latest races. They sponsor the Road Hogs which conducts classes for runners, cyclers and swimmers, of all ages and abilities.
Hours: Monday - Saturday 9:30 am - 6 pm, Sunday noon - 3 pm.

Tiffany & Co
140 Greenwich Avenue, 203.661.7847
www.Tiffany.com
This famous store has a nice collection of jewelry, silverware and giftware, as well as helpful sales people. It is one of 64 US stores.
Hours: Monday - Saturday 10 am - 6 pm, Sunday noon - 5 pm.

TJ Maxx (Department Store)
330 Connecticut Avenue, Norwalk CT, 203.854.9890
www.TJMaxx.com
The largest off-price apparel retailer in the US with over 700 stores. Merchandise is normally 20-50% below regular department store prices. In this 25,000 square foot store, they sell just about everything, from clothing and footwear to bedding, furniture, jewelry and housewares.
Hours: Monday - Saturday 9:30 am - 9:30 pm, Sunday 11 am - 8 pm.

Toc Toc
378 Greenwich Avenue, 203.422.6500
Who knows what this melange is about. Toc Toc has a touch of everything, from clothes to gifts. It is a fun collection. You never know what you will find.
Hours: Monday - Saturday, 10 am - 6 pm; Sunday, 11 am - 5 pm.

Tory Burch (Clothing-Women)
255 Greenwich Avenue, 203.622.5023
www.ToryBurch.com
Sportswear, swim wear, shoes, bags and jewelry by a New York designer. This store is one of 15 in the US. Her style has been described as Preppy-boho and is popular with the fans of Gossip Girl. Tory Burch has won many fashion awards.
Hours: Monday - Saturday 10 am - 6 pm, Sunday noon - 5 pm.

Toys "R" Us
59 Connecticut Avenue, Norwalk CT, 203.852.6988
www.ToysrUS.com
A mega toy store. The company currently operates 585 stores in the United States and 716 stores in 34 other countries. Its main competitors are Wal-Mart and Target.
Hours: Monday - Saturday 10 am - 9 pm, Sunday 10 am - 7 pm.

Trapp Optical
87 Greenwich Avenue, 203.552.1072
www.TrappOptical.com
High Fashion eyewear with a myriad of brands.
Hours: Monday - Friday 9:30 am - 5:30 pm, Saturday 9:30 am - 5 pm; Doctor on Wednesday 10 am - 4 pm & Saturday 10 am - 4 pm.

Trovare Home (Vintage Furniture)
245 East Putnam Avenue, Cos Cob, 203.869.5512
www.TrovareAtHome.com
Pamela Frisoll specializes in vintage furniture. Some of the vintage furniture is left untouched and some is modernized.
Hours: Monday - Saturday 10 am - 5 pm.

Tulips Greenwich (Florist)
91 Lake Avenue (at the Lake Avenue Circle), 203.661.3154
www.TulipsOfGreenwich.com
European floral design shop known for its creative and innovative bouquets of Dutch and French flowers.
Hours: weekdays 9 am - 5:30 pm, Saturday 10 am - 4 pm.

Tumi (luggage)
289 Greenwich Avenue, Greenwich, 203.861.2920
www.Tumi.com
Traveling is a hassle. Why not, at least, go in style. Attractive and distinctive luggage, wallets, business cases, even some sportswear. The company is named for a Peruvian ceremonial knife used for sacrifices.
Hours: Monday - Saturday 10 am - 6 pm, Sunday noon - 5 pm.

United House Wrecking (Home Accessories & Furniture)
535 Hope Street, Stamford, 203.348.5371
www.UnitedHouseWrecking.com
An unusual source for the unusual. Thirty-thousand square feet of inventory with everything from collectibles to antiques to architectural items to junk. Don't miss it.
Hours: Monday - Saturday 9:30 am - 5:30 pm, Sunday noon - 5 pm.

UPS Store
• Greenwich: 15 East Putnam Avenue, 203.622.1114
• Stamford: 65 High Ridge Road, Stamford, 203.356.0022
www.ups.com/tracking/tracking.html
Self-serve Drop Boxes
•   100 Field Point Rd, Greenwich
•   100 Mason Street, Greenwich

STORES

Utopia (skateboards)

150 Connecticut Avenue, Norwalk CT, 203.838.8782
www.UtopiaCT.com
One of the largest skateboard shops in the area.
Hours: Monday - Saturday, 9 am -9 pm, Sunday, 11 am - 8 pm.

Vallin Galleries (Antiques)

516 Danbury Road (Route 7), Wilton CT, 203.762.7441
www.vallinGalleries.com
Located far from the source of these antiques is a quaint saltbox filled
with a collection of Asian art, some rare, all beautifully displayed.
Hours: Call to make an appointment.

Verizon Wireless (Wireless)

www.verizonwireless.com
Verizon has 88 million subscribers and is the largest US network. The
company is a joint venture of Verizon Communications and Vodafone
Group. They can provide GSM/CDMA dual-mode phones. Verizon has been
criticized for making transfers of MP3s and ring tones difficult and re-
stricting EV-DO use. Wireless One Communications, Wireless Zone and
Paging Concepts are the authorized dealers in town. Verizon has no direct store in Greenwich.

Victoria's Secret (Lingerie)

200 Greenwich Avenue, 203.661.0158
www.VictoriasSecret.com
A popular shop with lingerie, beauty products and fashionable pajamas.
The stores were started to create a comfortable environment for men as
well as women to shop. There are over 1,000 US stores.
Hours: weekdays 10 am -7 pm; Saturday 10 am - 6 pm;
Sunday noon - 5 pm.

Viggi (Jewelry)

40 Greenwich Avenue, 203.622.2900
www.JewelsByViggi.com
Named for Danny Arbusman's wife, Viggi, this store specializes in dia-
monds from 3 to 20 carats.
Hours: Monday - Saturday 10 am - 5 pm.

STORES

Village Ewe (Sewing)
244 Sound Beach Avenue, Old Greenwich, 203.637.3953
www.TheVillageEwe.com
Beware of stopping here unless you are ready to get hooked on needle-point. Individual lessons for beginners can be arranged. Group classes are offered in the fall and spring. They are a full service needlepoint studio with over 1,500 hand painted canvases.
Hours: Tuesday - Saturday 10 am - 5:30 pm.

Vinci's Home Products (Miele Showroom)
37 Elm Street, Greenwich, 203.869.1114
www.VincisHomeProducts.com
An exclusive dealer of Miele products including vacuum cleaners, dish-washers, laundry systems, ovens, cook tops and wine coolers.
Hours: Monday - Wednesday, 10 am - 7 pm, Thursday, 10 am-8 pm, Friday, 10 am-6 pm, Saturday, 10 am- 5 pm, Sunday, Noon -5 pm.

Vineyard Vines (Clothing-Men, Women, Children)
145 Greenwich Avenue, 203.661.1803
www.VineyardVinesByRichards.com   www.VineyardVines.com
Greenwich residents are proud of this 5,000 square foot shop filled with colorful, informal, delightful clothing. Shep and Ian Murray of Green-wich began their company a few years ago by creating unique ties - worn by presidents, celebrities and many Greenwichites. You will love this shop.
Hours: Monday - Saturday 10 am - 6 pm (Thursday & Friday to 7 pm), Sunday noon - 5 pm.

Vintage Galleries (Antiques, Auctions)
528 Canal Street, Stamford CT 203.504.8485
www.VintageGalleriesAuction.com
They hold auctions ever 6 to 8 weeks. A buyer's premium of 20% is added to the final hammer price of each lot. In addition the on-line services usually charge an extra 3%.
Hours: Open every day, 10:30 am - 6 pm.

Vision Consultants (Eyeglasses)
45 East Putnam Avenue, 203.661-7711
Stylish frames in a convenient location. A nice choice of prescription ski and diving goggles.
Store Hours: Tuesday - Friday 10 am - 6 pm, Saturday 10 am - 4 pm.
Optometrist Hours: Thursday 2 pm -6 pm, Friday 10 am - 1 pm, Saturday 2 - 3:30 PM

STORES

Wal-Mart

680 Connecticut Avenue, Norwalk CT, 203.854.5236

www.Walmart.com

Founded in 1962, it is the largest retailer in the world. They are also the largest grocery retailer and the largest toy retailer in the US with an estimated 22% of the toy business. With the demise of Circuit City, they are hoping to also become the largest retailer of electronics. Walmart has been attempting to upgrade its merchandise to compete with Target.

Hours: every day 8 am - 10 pm.

Walpole Woodworkers (outdoor furniture)

1835 Post Road East, Westport CT, 203.255.9010

www.WalpoleWoodworkers.com

Outdoor furniture, some play sets, bridges, gazebos and more.

Hours: weekdays 9 am 6 pm, Saturday & Sunday 10 am - 5 pm.

Waterworks (Bath and Kitchen fixtures)

23 West Putnam Avenue, 203.869.7766

www.Waterworks.com

High-end bathroom and kitchen fixtures as well as a very nice selection of tiles. Excellent customer service.

Hours: weekdays 9 am - 5 pm, Saturday 10 am - 4 pm.

Weathervane Hill (Fabrics)

Loehmann's Plaza (467 West Avenue), Norwalk CT 203.838.2999

www.WeathervaneHill.com

A great many bolts of fabric and trim for windows, upholstery and bedding. They have their own workshop and will measure for you.

Hours: Monday - Saturday 10 am - 5:30 pm, Sunday noon - 5 pm.

Weber Fine Art (Art)

24 West Putnam Avenue, 203.422.5375

www.WeberFineArt.com

Modern post-war and contemporary art. Prices range from about $15,000 to $50,000

Hours: Tuesday - Saturday 11 am - 5 pm.

STORES

(The) Westchester Mall

125 Westchester White Plains NY, 914.683.8600

www.simon.com or www.simon.com/mall/directory.aspx?ID=105

An even larger mall than the Stamford Town Center boasting over 150 fine upscale stores including: Crate & Barrel, Pottery Barn Kids, Louis Vuitton, Gucci, Apple, Brooks Brothers, Tumi, Sony Style and P.F. Chang's China Bistro. Neiman Marcus (914.428.2000) and Nordstrom (914.946.1122) are the anchor stores.

Hours: Monday - Saturday 10 am - 9 pm, Sunday 11 am - 6 pm. Store hours may vary.

Whole Body @ Whole Foods (cosmetics and more)

90 East Putnam Avenue, 203.661.0631

www.wholefoodsmarket.com/stores/greenwich

Products to promote health and wellness, such as: vitamins, herbal teas, cosmetics, hair care and homeopathic remedies.

Hours: Open daily 8 am - 10 pm.

Whimsies Doll House & Miniature Shop

18 Lewis Street, 203.629.8024 www.whimsiesdollhouseshop.com

The ultimate dollhouse store.

Hours: Tuesday - Saturday 10 am - 5 pm.

Williams-Sonoma (Cookware)

- 100 Greyrock Place (Town Center), Stamford CT, 203.961.0977
- 125 Westchester Avenue (Westchester Mall), White Plains NY 644.8360

www.Williams-Sonoma.com

Speciality cookware and housewares as well as a variety of gourmet foods that are difficult to find elsewhere. Also look for cooking classes.

Hours: Monday - Saturday 10 am - 9 pm, Sunday 11 am - 6 pm.

Wireless One Communications (Wireless)

1269 Boston Post Road, Riverside, 203.637.5441

An authorized Verizon wireless dealer.

Hours: weekdays 9 am - 6 pm, Saturday & Sunday 10 am - 5 pm.

STORES

Wishlist (Clothing-Youth)
350 Greenwich Avenue, 203.629.4600
www.ShopWishList.com
Stylish clothing, nicely displayed, for sophisticated teens and pre-teens.
Hours: Monday - Saturday, 10 am - 6 pm; Sunday, noon - 5 pm.

Woodbury Commons (Mall, Outlet)
Harriman NY, 845.928.4000
www.PremiumOutlets.com
A huge outlet location with over 220 stores, including Burberrys and
Brooks Brothers. Definitely worth the 60-minute drive. If you go to the
website first and sign up for a coupon book, it can really pay off.
Hours: everyday, 10 am - 9 pm.
Directions: Take I-95 to I-287 W across the Tappan Zee Bridge and follow
I-87 N (New York State Thruway) to exit 16. Right at the exit.

Wyler (Antiques)
40 West Putnam Avenue, 203.622.2390
This jewel of a shop has 19th and 20th century English silver and fine
porcelain.
Hours: Tuesday - Saturday, 10 am to 5:30 pm.

ZARA (Clothing - Women, Children to size 13)
225 Greenwich Avenue, 203.861.7411
www.Zara.com
Zara, the flagship chain store of Inditex Group owned by Spanish tycoon
Amancio Ortega, launches around 10,000 new designs each year. The
company has 200 designers and can turn out a new design and have it in
the stores within 5 weeks, from start to finish. If a design doesn't sell
well within a week, it is withdrawn from shops. They have a zero adver-
tising policy, a very liberal return policy and over 1,500 stores worldwide. New designs usually arrive Monday and Thursday.
Hours: Monday - Saturday, 11 am - 6 pm; Sunday, 10 am - 7 pm.

Zorya (Art)
38 East Putnam Avenue, 203.869.9898
www.ZoryaFineArt.com
Emerging and established Ukrainian artists. Price range $3,000 -
$100,000.
Hours: Tuesday - Saturday, 11 am - 6 pm.

TEENS/YOUNG ADULTS

See also the sections CHILDREN and CHILD ENRICHMENT
See also FITNESS & SPORTS for year-around activities

United Way Resource Directory for Teenagers

The United Way has developed a 36-page resource directory for teenagers in the Greenwich community. It contains information and contact numbers of teen services offered in the area.
www.unitedway-greenwich.com/teen-connections

Arch Street Teen Center

100 Arch Street, 203.629.5744
www.ArchStreet.org
Founded in 1993, Arch Street (also known as the Greenwich Teen Center, Inc.) is a refurbished warehouse right on the harbor. Whether at the dance floor and bandstand or the upstairs snack shop with booths, Arch Street provides teens with the opportunity to be together in a healthy environment. Arch Street is more than just a place to hang out, the Center provides everything from college application advice and counseling help, to opportunities for teens to participate in community service projects or to learn leadership skills. Although there is an adult board, the teens run Arch Street through the teen board. This board has sixty members, from 9th to 12th grades, and has representatives from both private and public schools. Arch Street is open to Greenwich students from 7th through 12th grade.

Baby Sitter Training

Red Cross, Greenwich Chapter, 99 Indian Field Road, 203.869 8445
www.GreenwichRedCross.org
Boys and girls ages 11-15 learn the responsibilities of a babysitter, child developmental stages and basic childcare.

Boys and Girls Club

4 Horseneck Lane, 869 3224
www.bgcg.org
This club is awesome. The totally renovated facility has a gymnasium, game room, library, swimming pool, and the skating rink used for ice skating in winter, and roller skating/street hockey or basketball during other seasons. Members must be Greenwich residents or have a parent working in town. Transportation by bus or van is provided to and from several areas around town including Central and Western Middle Schools. The membership fee for ages 6-18 is $20 per year for residents or $120 for nonresidents. The Club also has a 77-acre preserve, Camp Simmons, for summer teen activities.

TEENS/YOUNG ADULTS

Boy Scouts

63 Mason Street, Greenwich CT 203.869.8424

www.greenwichbsa.com

www.GreenwichScouting.org

Boy Scouts, for boys in 6th grade until their 18th birthday; Venturing and Exploring, co-ed programs for high school students, ages 14 - 20.

Department of Parks and Recreation

www.greenwichct.org/ParksAndRec/ParksandRec.asp

The Department has a great many athletic programs for teens. For instance, the Skate Park described in PARKS is a good place for teens to meet. Also see all of the sports activities in FITNESS AND SPORTS.

Girl Scouts

(203) 762-5557 (800) 882-5561

www.GreenwichGirlScouts.com

They offer a broad range of activities for girls. Greenwich is part of the Girl Scouts of Connecticut www.gsofct.org. Greenwich has 60 troops with some 750 girls and 500 plus registered, trained adults. Cadettes, grades 7 - 9 (ages 11 - 14); Seniors, grades 9 - 12 (ages 14 - 17).

Greenwich Cotillion

www.JLGreenwich.org

Greenwich has a Cotillion every year at the beginning of summer for young ladies who wish to debut. The Cotillion, sponsored by the Junior League of Greenwich, is often described as a "fun party with dignity," but perhaps is more accurately described as a series of dignified fun parties. Attendance is by open invitation on a first-come, first-serve basis. Some years you need to send in your check and application the moment it is received; other years there is less demand and the event fills up more slowly. Young women in their senior year in high school and who reside in Greenwich or attend a Greenwich school, are invited to consider participating. To be included on the mailing list, contact the Junior League at 203.869.1979.

Greenwich Student Employment Service

203.625.8008

www.GHS-SES.org

GHS Student Employment Service helps employers who want to fill jobs find students looking for work. Jobs are not restricted to high school students. Graduates are also using the service.

Hours: Office is open school days 11:45 pm -2:00 pm

TEENS/YOUNG ADULTS

Junior Educator Program

Bruce Museum, 1 Museum Drive, 203.869.0376

www.BruceMuseum.org

High school students are trained to teach young children in the Museum's Neighborhood Collaborative program. Topics covered relate to the Museum's exhibits, such as turn of the century American art, costal ecology and Native American baskets techniques.

Safe Rides

Red Cross, Greenwich Chapter, 99 Indian Field Road, 203.869 8445

www.GreenwichRedCross.org

A service run by young people to keep other young people safe. Staffed Friday and Saturday nights from 10 pm 2 am.

Voices

www.voicesoftomorrow.org

This internet newspaper by and for tomorrow's leaders was founded by Greenwich resident Debra Mamorsky. It is a international publication written solely by 17-25 year olds for their peers around the world. The publication tackles important domestic, international and youth related issues.

YMCA Teen Programs

YMCA, 50 East Putnam Avenue, 869.1630

www.gwYMCA.org

In addition to the Y's traditional programs they offer a number of programs for teens. *See FITNESS & SPORTS for more information on the Y.*

Youth Council

American Red Cross, Greenwich Chapter, 869.8444 x 119

www.GreenwichRedCross.org

A great way to meet other teens from both public and private schools who are interested the Greenwich Community. They provide tutoring at elementary schools and provide disaster education to Seniors and help out with the Chapter's fund-raising events. The Greenwich Chapter has 900 volunteers, 400 of whom are youth. To be a youth council member, you must be in grades 9 to 12. There is a Junior Youth Council for 7th and 8th graders.

YWCA Teen Programs

203.869.6501 x 225   www.YWCAGreenwich.org

In addition to the Y's traditional programs they offer a number of programs for teens. *See FITNESS & SPORTS for more information on the Y.*

THRIFT SHOPS

Proceeds from these shops, which are often run by volunteers, go to helping others. Thrift Shops are "win-win" for everyone! Donating your unwanted possessions to thrift shops is a practical way to help our neighbors in need. Consigning is a good way to dispose of items without holding a tag sale or selling on e-bay. Without doubt, your unwanted item is bound to be another person's treasure. With our wish to help others and recycling our mission, donate, consign and explore the shops for fabulous buys!

See SHOPPING for Consignment Shops
See BOOKS for Book donations
See SERVICES for Computer and Cell Phone donations and eBay sales.

Act II Consignment Shop (Clothing)

48 Maple Avenue, 203.869.6359
In a lovely old stone house behind the Second Congregational Church there are five rooms of gently worn women's, men's and children's clothing. Also bric-a-brac and small household items.
Store Hours: Wednesday, 10 am - 5 pm; Thursday and
Saturday 10 am - 1:30 pm.
Consignment Hours: Wednesday noon - 3 pm; Thursday, 10 am - 1 pm.
Closed June through September.

Goodwill Industries of Western CT (Clothing, Home)

Greenwich Recycling Center, Holly Hill Lane
203.576.0000, 800.423.9787
www.goodwillwct.com
A large trailer with a friendly person ready to receive your donations is conveniently parked just inside our town "dump." Goodwill needs clothing, shoes, toys, tools, kitchenware, linens and small appliances in "saleable" condition. This is recycling in the true sense of the word.
Hours: weekdays, 7 am - 3 pm; Saturday, 7 am - noon.

Green Demolitions (Kitchens)

19 Willard Road, Norwalk CT, 203.354.7355
www.GreenDemolitions.com
Green Demolitions is a non-profit organization that recycles kitchen appliances, lighting and other home decorating items. They also sell floor models from retailers and trade shows. Prices are usually 50-75% off retail. Their store is 11,000 square feet.
Hours: Monday - Saturday 10 am - 6 pm (Thursday to 8 pm),
Sunday noon - 5 pm.

THRIFT SHOPS

Greenwich Hospital Auxiliary Thrift Shop (Clothing, Furniture)

199 Hamilton Avenue, 203.869.6124

This thrift shop is an experience in itself. You are unlikely to find a nicer thrift shop anywhere. Large furniture items plus clothing and books are welcome here. Our finds: an old steamer trunk and a lovely white Laura Ashley graduation dress for $45! One of our friends found a chesterfield coat! A holiday sale had so many people, the customers were waiting in line to get inside for embroidered sweaters and evening gowns.

Shopping Hours: Monday - Thursday 9 am - 4:30 pm,
Friday and Saturday 9 am-3 pm
Donation Hours: weekdays 8 am- 3 pm, Saturday 8 am- 2 pm.

Merry Go Round (Clothing)

38 Arch Street, 203.869.3155

Clothing and small objects are all neatly displayed.
Our finds: two pretty framed watercolors and a tennis skirt for $3.
Hours: Tuesday - Saturday, 10 am - 3 pm; Closed July and August.

Laurel House Thrift Shop (Clothing, Furniture)

501 Summer Street, Stamford CT, 203.327.7334
www.LaurelHouse.net
They will pick up items or you can drop them off.
Proceeds from their sales help educate, house and clothe people with mental illness.
Hours: weekdays, 9 am - 4 pm, Saturday 9 am - 3 pm.

TIP: FINDING TAG SALES

Tag sales a.k.a. estate sales or garage sales are a popular Greenwich weekend pastime. The Friday and weekend Greenwich Time newspaper lists tag sale locations.

THRIFT SHOPS

Rummage Room (Clothing)

191 Sound Beach Avenue, Old Greenwich, 203.637.1875

Notice the artistic window displays of this gem of a shop manned by cheerful volunteers. The shop is filled with clothing for young and old and interesting bric-a-brac.

Shop Hours: weekdays 10 am - 5 pm; Saturdays, 10 am - 1 pm.
Donation Hours: Monday - Thursday, 9 am - 5 pm;
Fridays, until 1 pm; Saturdays, 10 am - 1 pm. Closed in August.

Salvation Army (Clothing, Furniture)

Stamford Thrift Shop, 896 Washington Blvd, 203.975.7630
Truck pickup: 800.958.7825
www.SalvationArmy.com

A marvelous service is available for picking up furniture for donation. Every time we have called, a courteous, strong man has arrived promptly to take items destined to help people serviced by this most worthy organization. 2 to 4 days' notice is appreciated for pickups. A bin for donations (clothing only) is located inside our Recycling Center on Holly Hill Lane.Dispatcher Hours: Monday - Saturday, 7 am - 3 pm.

Neighbor to Neighbor (Clothing, Food)

Christ Church Annex, 248 East Putnam Avenue, 203.622.9208
www.N-to-N.org

This volunteer organization is greatly respected and appreciated in our Greenwich community. They have helped many people in a sensitive way. Donations of food, warm coats and clothing (in good condition) are always needed. The shop is restricted to people identified by our social service agencies as "in need" and the selections made in the nicely organized shop are free.

Hours: weekdays, 8:30 am - noon. Open two Saturdays every month.

TRAVEL

For Car and Truck Rentals see AUTOMOBILES
For Hotels and Inns worth a trip see HOTELS AND INNS
For an International Drivers License see AUTOMOBILES
For Commuting information see AUTOMOBILES
For Parking Permits at the Greenwich Station go to
  www.GreenwichCT.org/Parking/psParkingPermits.asp

TIP: PAMPER YOURSELF WITH PREMIER SERVICES WHILE AT THE HOSPITAL

Greenwich Hospital has been equated with staying in a Hyatt Hotel. All patients have their meals served on china and have access to the Get Well Network, an interactive system that allows them to watch television, check e-mail and order movies from their beds. Now patients can be pampered even more if they wish to spend an extra $125 per night. Premier Services include secretarial services as well as many other amenities and perks. See
www.greenhosp.org/patientservices.asp or
Premier Tender Beginnings:
www.greenhosp.org/medicalservices_maternal_tbp.asp

TRAVEL

The Verizon yellow pages has handy airport maps of La Guardia (LGA), Kennedy (JFK) and Newark (EWR).

Kennedy Airport (JFK)
Queens, NY, 718.244.4444
www.panynj.gov/airports/jfk.html

La Guardia Airport (LGA)
Queens, NY, 718.533.3400
www.panynj.gov/airports/laguardia.html

Newark Airport (EWR)
Newark, NJ, 973.961.6000
www.panynj.gov/airports/newark-liberty.html
Of the major New York City airports, Newark in New Jersey takes the longest to get to (80 minutes). Newark Airport is somewhat less congested than the other two. In addition, flights out of Newark are sometimes less expensive, especially for Continental Airlines, who uses it as a hub.

Westchester County Airport (HPN)
White Plains, NY,
General Information: 914.995.4860, 4856
www.co.westchester.ny.us/airport
This airport is located on upper King Street. It is newly renovated and has good parking facilities. Commercial flights are limited and somewhat more expensive than those from the major NYC airports, but nothing could be easier or more convenient. Some of the airlines that fly out of Westchester are: Air Canada, AirTran, American Airlines, Cape Air, Delta, Jet Blue, Northwest, United (Chicago), & US Airways.
Directions: Glenville Road to King Street; R on King; L at light to Rye Lake Rd.

TRAVEL

airport flight delay information

FAA Flight Delay Information

www.fly.faa.gov/flyfaa/usmap.jsp

A good source of independent information for airports around the country. Even if NY airports are clear, if the hub of the airline you are using is experiencing delays, your flight is likely to be delayed.

USA Today

www.usatoday.com/travel/flights/front.htm

This site provides real time flight information.

airport parking

Parking long term or overnight at short term airport parking lots is not recommended for new or late model cars. To be sure, use one of these private lots. The cost seems to be about the same, the service better and your car is safer.

Avistar Airport Valet Parking

aka: Parking Company of America

800.621.7275, 866.727.5728

www.AvistarParking.com

Avistar operates out of Kennedy, La Guardia and Newark. If you fly out of one airport, but return to another, they will transfer your car and have it waiting for you. Their website has good instructions to each of their airport locations. You must make a reservation in advance.

Skypark

Newark Airport, 973.624.9000, 800.PICK U UP

www.parkrideflyusa.com/ewr-newark-liberty-airport-parking/sky-park

SkyPark is self-parking with frequent shuttle service to the airport. SkyPark has a frequent user reward program. A reservation is usually not required.

Directions: Follows signs from I-95 (the New Jersey Turnpike) to Newark Airport, exit at Hayes Street onto Route 1 S. Skypark is on the R.

Avanti Limousine
15 Putnam Avenue Suite 271, 203.542.0739, 866.829.8735
www.AvantiLimousines.net
A limo service with offices in Greenwich and Stamford.

CT Limousine Service
800.472.5466 www.CTlimo.com
If you are traveling alone, this may be your least expensive way to get to La Guardia, Kennedy or Newark airports. Pick up at the Greenwich Hyatt.

Greenwich Police
203.622.8006, 203.622.8015, 203.622.8016 Karen LaBellu
A Greenwich off-duty policeman will drive you to any of the NY area airports and pick you up in your own car. This is often less expensive than limousine service.

Greenwich Taxi
At Greenwich RR Station, 203.869.6000
An old stand-by for getting around town or to the train station - call ahead and make a reservation to be picked up. This is a good way to get to the New York airports. Greenwich Taxi is open until 1:30 am.

Leros Point to Point Connecticut (Limo Service)
32 Pocconock Trail, New Canaan, CT 203.329.1301, 800.365.3767
www.LerosLimo.com
One of 5 tri-state locations, they provide travel to and from airports, and even set-up international ground travel.

Red Dot Airport Shuttle
800.673.3368
www.RideTheDot.com
Transportation to and from Kennedy and La Guardia airports from the Hyatt Regency in Greenwich.

Rudy's Limousine Service
203.609.8000, 203.869.0014, 800.243.7839,
Curbside Pickup 866.678.3700
www.RudyLimo.com   www.RudysLimousine.com
A comfortable, reliable service. When several people travel together, this is a wise choice. Their drivers are very professional and pleasant. Hours: 24 hours a day every day.

TRAVEL

Required for a Passport:
1. Completed and unsigned DS-11 application. You can download it from http://travel.state.gov/passport/forms/ds11/ds11_842.html
2. Proof of Citizenship (previous US Passport or certified birth certificate)
3. Two color photographs (2x2 inches, not from a vending machine)
4. Social Security number
   (not technically required, but you need it anyway)

Connecticut Passport Agency
50 Washington Street, Norwalk CT, 06854
Automated Appointment Number: 1.877.487.2778
www.Travel.state.gov
The Connecticut Passport Agency serves only customers who are traveling within 2 weeks (14 days), or who need foreign visas for travel. An appointment is required.
Hours: weekdays 9 am - 4 pm, excluding Federal holidays

Ferguson Library
One Public Library Plaza, Bedford & Broad, Stamford CT
203.964.1000
www.FergusOnLibrary.org/Content/Passport
You may be able expedite it by paying an additional fee, but the normal wait time can be as long as 6 weeks.
Hours: Monday - Thursday 9 am - 2 pm & 5 pm - 8 pm,
Friday & Saturday 9 am - 2 pm.

Greenwich Post Offices
You can apply weekdays from 9 am - 4 pm, through the Greenwich Avenue Post Office; the wait time may be as long as 6 weeks.

travel immunizations

Travel Immunizations
The Department of Infectious Diseases at Greenwich Hospital offers many types of immunizations required for foreign travel to less developed countries. Call 203.863.3270 for an appointment between 8 am & 4 pm. It is best to schedule one at least 6-weeks before your departure.

TRAVEL

passport photos

Ritz Camera Center
82 Greenwich Avenue, Greenwich, 203.869.0673

Action Arts Photography
242 Sound Beach Ave, Old Greenwich, 203.637.2685

travel agencies

Liberty Travel
2367 Summer Street, Stamford CT, 203.357.1300
ww2.libertytravel.com
Liberty is a large operation with over 189 stores, they have big buying power for packages in the Caribbean and Florida. They are a good place to go to get a cruise or packaged tour.
Hours: Monday - Thursday 9 am - 7:30 pm, Friday 9 am - 7 pm, Saturday 10 am - 5 pm, Sunday, noon - 4 pm.

Valerie Wilson Travel
1455 East Putnam Avenue, Old Greenwich, 203.637.5436, 3171
www.VWTI.com
With 14 locations, Valerie Wilson Travel is large enough to get you good rates and small enough to give you good service.
Hours: weekdays 9 am - 5 pm.

TRAVEL

public transportation (bus & rail)

See SENIORS for free Transportation Sources.
For more Commuting information see AUTOMOBILES

Connecticut Transit (CTtransit)

203.327.7433

www.CTTransit.com

CT Transit provides bus service from Greenwich and Old Greenwich to Port Chester, Stamford and Norwalk. They also operate one route in Greenwich.

• K-Bus starts at the Stamford RR station and goes through Greenwich to Port Chester.

• L-Bus goes from Sound Beach Avenue & East Putnam Avenue to the Stamford RR station and to North Stamford.

• I-Bus is an express connecting Greenwich and White Plains RR stations.

Greenwich Commuter Connection

800.982.8420

www.NorwalkTransit.com/GCC.htm

Norwalk Transit provides commuter bus routes linking the Greenwich RR station and the central business district. Service is during the morning and late afternoon rush hours.

Amtrak

800.872.7245

www.Amtrak.com

Operates from Stamford Station and connects to cities throughout the US and Canada.

Metro-North Commuter Railroad

800.638.7646

www.MNR.org

Offers frequent service to Grand Central Station, New York City, weekdays. Check the schedule for weekend and holiday times. Greenwich has four stations.

• Cos Cob Station, Sound Shore Drive, off Exit 4 of I-95
• Greenwich Station, Railroad Ave, off Exit 3 of I-95
• Old Greenwich Station, Sound Beach Ave, off Exit 5 of I-95
• Riverside Station, Between exits 4 & 5 off I-95

For Parking Permits at the Greenwich Station go to
www.GreenwichCT.org/Parking/psParkingPermits.asp

Citation Air

Five American Lane, Greenwich, 877.692.4828
www.CitationAir.com
A Greenwich-based company owned by Cessna. Individuals and businesses can buy an aircraft and defray costs by letting Citation Air charter it to other users, or you can buy a fractional ownership in a jet or just rent one of their 80 aircrafts.

TIP: GREENWICH LIBRARY DATABASES

The Greenwich Library subscribes to over 60 databases which can be accessed free of charge to Library card holders. Almost all of these databases can be accessed from your computer. To find a database of interest, like the Antiques Reference Database, call the Greenwich Library Reference Desk at 203.622.7910 or go to www.GreenwichLibrary.org/ResearchandResources

VOLUNTEERING

Greenwich has a wealth of volunteers committed to helping our town. Volunteering in Greenwich is not new. Our Town was originally governed by a town meeting. All interested citizens gathered to make the decisions. Now we have a Representative Town Meeting and many boards and commissions, yet they are all made up of volunteers. Read the history of many of the organizations serving our Town and discover that they have been helping for 20, 30, 50 or more than 100 years. Caring about our neighbors, sharing our time and our talents is our Town's strength and bond.

Local Papers such as the Greenwich Time periodically run columns listing the volunteer needs of various organizations in town.

Check the section on GREENWICH for a list of some of the Charitable and Service Organizations.

The Anderson Guide to Volunteers
www.GreenwichVolunteerGuide.com
When asked, "What makes Greenwich special?" the answer: Volunteers! Greenwich has a wealth of volunteers committed to making life in our Town the best it can be. Volunteers are the heart and soul of Greenwich. We wrote a special booklet, The Anderson Guide to Volunteers, listing over 120 Greenwich volunteer organizations, is designed around interest groups. Joining one of these organizations is a wonderful way to contribute to the Town and to make friends. If you would like a copy please call our main office at 203.629.4519 or e-mail Carolyn@GreenwichLiving.net. This guide is our gift to Greenwich.

The Volunteer Center of Southwestern Fairfield County
62 Palmer's Hill Road, Stamford, 203.348.7714
www.UCanHelp.org
Many, many volunteer opportunities are available in our surrounding areas. Check with The Volunteer Center for a comprehensive list of volunteer needs. They include Greenwich organizations as well as many other organizations in neighboring towns.

INDEX

INDEX

INDEX

INDEX

INDEX

INDEX

INDEX

INDEX

INDEX

INDEX

INDEX

INDEX

INDEX

INDEX

INDEX

INDEX

INDEX

INDEX

INDEX

INDEX

INDEX

INDEX

INDEX

INDEX

INDEX

INDEX

INDEX

INDEX

INDEX

Q

Q (Barbeque) 329
Quaker Religious Society of Friends
246
Quelques Choses 552
Quester Gallery 552

R

Racquet Club 441
Radio & television 209
Radio Shack 552
Rafting 422
Rail transportation 588
Ralph Lauren 552
Rand Insurance (insurance) 411
Raphael's Furniture Restoration
(furniture repair) 412
Rasa (Indian) 329
Ray's Lawn Service 400
Reading, Children 62
REAL ESTATE 242 - 243
Rebecca's (New American) 329
Recreation Equipment 553
Recycling 384
Cell Phones 412
Christmas Trees 412
Red Barn Stables (riding) 455
Red Cross 50, 188
Babysitting Training 65
Children's Safety Training 62
Greenwich Chapter 50
Transportation Services 374
Youth Council 577
Red Dot Airport Shuttle 585
Red Hat Society 374
Reflection 553
Refuse Collectors 384
Registration, Voter 240
Relax the Back 553
RELIGION 244 - 250
Remains Lighting 553
Renaissance Faire 79
Renaissance Festival 71
Rentals 383
Rentals, party 146
Renting a Bus 41

INDEX

INDEX

INDEX

INDEX

INDEX

INDEX

INDEX

U

V

INDEX

INDEX

INDEX

NOTES

NOTES

NOTES

NOTES

NOTES

ABOUT THE AUTHORS

Carolyn and Jerry Anderson

At what age does one discover that the ordinary is extraordinary? For Jerry and Carolyn Anderson, it was when they returned to Greenwich. Jerry had been away at Harvard as an undergraduate, and then as a graduate at Columbia where he received his Masters in Business and Doctorate in Law. Carolyn had been at Boston University as an undergraduate and then at Columbia where she received her Masters. Jerry and Carolyn were introduced by a Greenwich friend, married, and in 1968 they bought their home on Clapboard Ridge Road in Greenwich. No other town was ever considered.

Jerry grew up in Deer Park and went to Brunswick. His youth was filled with sailing on the sound, playing tennis in the Town tournaments and working on homework in the Greenwich Library. He learned to drive when Greenwich Avenue was a two-way street and dance lessons still required white gloves for boys as well as girls.

Carolyn is a Realtor and the President of Anderson Associates, a real estate firm specializing in Greenwich residential properties. Carolyn is also a former President of the Greenwich Association of Realtors and of the Greenwich Multiple Listing Service. She is an appraiser and a professional member of the American Society of Interior Designers. Prior to opening Anderson Associates, she designed and renovated many restaurants and residences in Greenwich. In her spare time she writes cookbooks and about art. Jerry and Carolyn rarely miss a new restaurant.

Their children, Clifford and Cheryl, were born in Greenwich Hospital. They thrived in the public school system, which launched them to successful academic careers at Harvard and Princeton. Cheryl and Clifford enjoyed the benefits of Greenwich's many resources: water babies at the Y, scouting, running in town races, camping on Great Captain's Island and visiting the wonderful exhibits at Bruce Museum.

However, this book is not just the work of Carolyn and Jerry. It is the product of all of the Anderson Associates. The Anderson Associates are a diverse group. They are all ages and lifestyles, with one interest in common—Greenwich. They live in, work in and love Greenwich. Most grew up and went to school in Greenwich. Each in their own way, has come to the realization that Greenwich is extraordinary.

ABOUT THE AUTHORS

Amy Zeeve

Amy is Vice President of Anderson Associates. Amy was the inspiration for and the original author of most of the first edition of the Anderson Guide. She is extremely well liked and admired in the real estate community. Because of the extraordinary real estate help she gives her clients, Amy is one of the few people we know whose clients regularly send her flowers.

Amy grew up in Colorado and graduated from the University of Colorado. She moved to Greenwich in 1993. Both Amy and her husband John live in and love Greenwich. They have two children, Charlie and Stephanie both students at Glenville School. Under the tutelage of Amy and John, both excellent golfers, Charlie already has a good golf swing and is #49 Maverick on the cover. Stephanie is creative and knows what's in fashion. This active youthful family has helped us keep the sections on children's activities and shops current.

ABOUT OUR ILLUSTRATOR

Vanessa Chow

Vanessa created the maps and drawings. She graduated from Greenwich High School, where she was one of their top art students and won awards at the Old Greenwich Art Society. Vanessa graduated magna cum laude from Connecticut College. She has studied art at Parsons School of Design, Silvermine, New York University, The Art Students League, The Chinese Academy of Fine Arts and Oxford University. She received her Masters Degree from the Rhode Island School of Design.

FEEDBACK FORM

We would appreciate your input.

IS THERE SOMETHING WE'VE MISSED?

_____

_____

_____

_____

HAVE YOU FOUND A MISTAKE?

_____

_____

_____

_____

HAVE YOU FOUND THIS BOOK USEFUL?
[ ] yes [ ] no
Comments: _____

_____

_____

_____

Please mail or fax this form to:
  Anderson Associates, Ltd.
  164 Mason Street
  Greenwich, CT 06830
  Fax: 203.629.4786

ORDER FORM

Please send me ____ copies of The Anderson Guide to Enjoying Greenwich Connecticut 8th Edition

Total number of copies _____ @ 25.00
    Price includes postage and sales tax.

Amount due $_____

I wish to pay by [ ] check or [ ] Credit Card

Name: _____

Address: _____

City: _____

State: _____ Zip: _____

Telephone: _____

Credit Card Number _____ _____ _____ _____

Expiration Date: ____/____ Security Code _____

Name on Card: _____

Signature: _____

You can fax, mail, email or phone your order to
        Anderson Associates
        164 Mason Street
        Greenwich, CT 06830
        tel: 203.629.4519
        fax: 203.629.4786
        carolyn@greenwichliving.net